Esther Urdang, PhD

Human Behavior in the Social Environment
Interweaving the Inner and Outer Worlds

Second Edition

Pre-publication
REVIEWS,
COMMENTARIES,
EVALUATIONS . . .

More pre-publication
REVIEWS, COMMENTARIES, EVALUATIONS . . .

"**S**ocial work students who have the good fortune to have this book as a text for their Human Behavior and the Social Environment class will actually enjoy this very readable overview of numerous theories and their application in case examples. Grounded in a bio-psychosocial perspective, this incredibly comprehensive book emphasizes the psychodynamic understanding of human behavior through examples from novels, biographies and autobiographies in addition to newspaper and magazine articles. . . . breathes life into the theories and manages to convey the vast complexity of life from birth to adulthood. Learning exercises at the end of each chapter help the student integrate the concepts into a social work practice framework. . . . A valuable contribution to social work education."

Nancy Boyd Webb, DSW,
Distinguished Professor of Social Work,
Fordham University

Online Resources from Routledge

Instructor's Manual

for

Human Behavior in the Social Environment
Interweaving the Inner and Outer Worlds
Second Edition

Esther Urdang

This Instructor's Manual accompanies the text *Human Behavior in the Social Environment: Interweaving the Inner and Outer Worlds* (*Second Edition*). Each chapter parallels the accompanying chapter in the text and includes materials from biographies, literature, and newspapers, as well as case illustrations to enrich students' understanding. Readers are encouraged to look beneath surface explanations and superficial solutions. This manual suggests ways to integrate these materials into the course: each chapter has its own recommended learning strategies, and expands on those referred to in the text.

In order to fully understand and help people, a broad psychodynamic perspective is essential, including content on psychopathology, relationship complexities, and differential diagnosis. Emphasis is therefore given in this manual, within a developmental framework, to the psychodynamic perspective, incorporating psychoanalysis, ego psychology, object relations, self psychology, constructivist, and narrative theories; this is interwoven with content on biological factors (including illness and disability), mental health problems, the social environment, systemic issues, and culture.

To download a PDF version/copy of the text please visit this website:
www.routledge.com/books/Human-Behavior-in-the-Social-Environment-isbn9780789034182

Human Behavior in the Social Environment

Interweaving the Inner and Outer Worlds

Second Edition

SOCIAL WORK PRACTICE IN ACTION

Edited by
Marvin D. Feit,
The University of Akron in Ohio, USA.

Human Behavior in the Social Environment
Interweaving the Inner and Outer Worlds

Second Edition

Esther Urdang, PhD

Routledge
Taylor & Francis Group

NEW YORK AND LONDON

First published 2002
by The Haworth Press, Inc.

This edition published 2008
by Routledge
270 Madison Ave, New York, NY 10016

Simultaneously published in the UK
by Routledge
2 Park Square, Milton Park, Abingdon, Oxon OX14 4RN

Routledge is an imprint of the Taylor & Francis Group, an informa business

Library of Congress Cataloging-in-Publication Data
Human behavior in the social environment: Interweaving the inner and outer worlds / Esther Urdang—2nd ed.
p. cm.
Includes bibliographical references.
ISBN 978-0-7890-3417-5 (hard 13 : alk. paper)
ISBN 978-0-7890-3418-2 (soft 13 : alk. paper)
1. Social psychology. 2. Developmental psychology. 3. Human behavior. I. Title.
HM1033.U73 2007
302-dc22

2007029882

ISBN 10: 0-7890-3417-4 (hbk)
ISBN 10: 0-7890-3418-2 (pbk)
ISBN 13: 978-0-7890-3417-5 (hbk)
ISBN 13: 978-0-7890-3418-2 (pbk)

To my husband
Elliott B. Urdang, MD, MA (In Russian)

ABOUT THE AUTHOR

Dr. Urdang has brought to the writing of this book a strong background as a clinician, supervisor, and social worker educator. She received her master's degree in social work at Adelphi University and her PhD in social work from Simmons College Graduate School of Social Work. She has practiced in a variety of settings including mental health clinics, family agencies, and hospitals. For twenty-seven years she was on the faculty as an adjunct associate professor of the Boston College Graduate School of Social Work where she taught human behavior, required clinical courses, and psychopathology. She was actively involved in the Field Education Department, where she served as assistant director of field education; she also did extensive faculty advising and developed and taught the Seminar for Field Instructors.

Dr. Urdang's published articles have centered on social work education, chiefly focusing on process recording, the process of student learning, and the development of the professional self. She has published in *The Clinical Supervisor, Smith College Studies in Social Work, Clinical Social Work Journal, Journal of Teaching in Social Work*, and *Social Casework.* One article, which discussed the use of a video lab, received the Simmons Alumni Special Recognition Award in 1999. The first edition of *Human Behavior in the Social Environment* (The Haworth Press) also received the Simmons Alumni award in 2003. Dr. Urdang also published *Becoming a Social Worker: The First Year.*

Currently, Dr. Urdang is involved in writing, providing supervision and consultation, and in private clinical practice. She is a licensed independent clinical social worker with over thirty-five years of experience in the field, and holds a Diplomate in Social Work from NASW. She is a research advisor, and adjunct associate professor at Smith College School for Social Work.

CONTENTS

Preface

This book is especially intended for graduate social work students, although all readers, beginning and advanced in the field of human services, such as nursing, medicine, education, counseling, and clinical psychology, may find this a helpful review or source of new knowledge. It has also been used at the undergraduate social work level.

This text is intended to accompany Human Behavior courses, focusing on maturation through the life cycle, psychological development, and family life. Physical illness and disability are also addressed, as our biological makeup and infirmities affect our well-being and social functioning. Many people today live long lives with major disabilities and illnesses; we must be sensitive to their needs and aspirations. Loss, which permeates the life cycle, is often a key dynamic in psychosocial problems and is stressed here, as this painful subject is frequently avoided by clients, students, and clinicians.

Many mental states, such as anxiety, depression, dissociative experiences, and psychosomatic involvement, are part of the human condition. When sufficiently intense they may impair functioning, in which case we regard them as pathological. Because we think of these states along a continuum, psychopathology is included here—rather than excluded as it often is from human behavior courses—as it is viewed as a content area separate from "normal" behavior. Furthermore, people with severe mental illness are encountered in social work practice in many different contexts; they face the same life cycle dilemmas as those judged to be "mentally healthy." Excluding them from a human behavior text would mirror the exclusion they often experience in society.

Although diversity, race, culture, and systemic issues, such as housing, social discrimination, violence, social policies, politics, and organizations, are included and integrated into the text, they are not addressed in depth; it is assumed these subjects will receive major attention in other courses.

Although this is not a book on clinical practice, special attention is given to problems students often encounter in practice, and many case illustrations are presented with relevant theory discussed. This is based on the conviction that a firm foundation in human behavior provides the underpinning for a sound perspective when contending with human problems.

In writing this book, I have drawn upon my vivid experiences as a social work educator for twenty-seven years, teaching human behavior and clinical social work, advising students, and serving as assistant director of field education at Boston College Graduate School of Social Work. I have also drawn upon my ongoing involvement in clinical practice.

These experiences have involved me in an active way with the puzzles, conundrums, and rewards of clinical work and have sensitized me to students' struggles in mastering the intellectual and emotional demands of social work training. In sharing my insights, I have highlighted problems that are particularly troublesome for students in the field, such as the feelings of incompetence often aroused by clients who have a history of rejected and distorted relationships.

Of course, some social work students do not plan to enter direct clinical practice but rather to become involved in administration, research, or social planning. Nevertheless, the emphasis on clinical work is intended to provide *all* future social workers with the core understanding of individual and family functioning, which is indispensable in both clinical and policy work.

For example, whether working with foster children directly, administering child-welfare agencies, or developing related policy at the governmental level, social workers who lack an in-depth understanding of the intense emotional impact of attachment, separation, loss, and maltreatment will be unable either to offer adequate clinical help or to design adequate social services and policies for this vulnerable population.

A biopsychosocial perspective is emphasized throughout this book. Although this has been the traditional foundation of social work, its psychodynamically based psychological component has gradually been depreciated. It has been displaced by an emphasis on cognitive-behavioral approaches, quantitative research-based outcome measures, and brief solution-focused treatments currently designed to meet the requirements of managed care.

In addition, the field has moved toward emphasizing the amelioration of social problems, with reliance on educational approaches for vulnerable populations and the promotion of social policy at the expense of the development of clinical social work. This book, while recognizing the importance of the outer social world, highlights the significance of the *inner world* of people, which shapes their sense of self-worth as well as their relationships and behaviors. Emphasis is therefore given to a psychodynamic perspective incorporating psychoanalytic, ego psychology, object relations, self psychology and constructivist theories within a developmental framework.

As the title of this book suggests, when viewed comprehensively life is characterized by a constant interweaving of inner and outer worlds; this is the perspective I wish to present. Accepting psychodynamic theory does not mean turning our backs on the "real" world with its troubling problems and inequities. Homelessness is a serious social problem requiring economic solutions and new housing policies. But we also need to understand and help homeless individuals, many of whom have deep underlying emotional problems, such as depression (leading to unemployment) and major mental illness (often untreated in today's climate of deinstitutionalization). We need to understand the homeless teenager, the "throwaway" child who has run away from abuse and neglect often as a result of and resulting in psychological traumatization and conflict that must be addressed.

Human behavior in the social environment is more than a subject for a textbook. It is the interwoven fabric of the world around us and the world within us. Although it is the subject matter of psychology and sociology, it has also been of profound concern to philosophers, historians, writers, and poets throughout the ages. To reflect this, I have incorporated materials from biographies, literature, and newspapers to enrich your understanding. As we begin this journey of learning together, I hope it will be with open eyes, inquisitive minds, and compassionate hearts that can see beneath surface explanations and superficial solutions.

Acknowledgments

This book is written for social work students and is based on my work with many students, over the years, who have been a constant source of stimulation and learning. I thank them for their contribution to my own development and for the inspiration working with them has given me in writing this book. My special thanks are also extended to those unnamed students who have given me their papers discussing their work with clients, which has added greatly to the depth of this presentation.

Warmest thanks are extended to my husband, Elliott B. Urdang, MD, MA (in Russian), who has been a constant source of support and encouragement as well as an active participant in this project in terms of vital editorial and technical assistance.

Carolyn Thomas, PhD, Professor Emeritus at Boston College Graduate School of Social Work, has provided editorial advice as well as great ongoing support.

The unending moral support of my children, Erik and Gwen, their respective spouses, Nan and Jerry, and my dear grandchildren, Sam Goodman Urdang, Zoe Brown, Jacqueline (Q) Urdang, and Haley Brown, is deeply appreciated.

I wish to express my eternal gratitude and love to my late parents, my mother, Rose Klepper, and my father, Mendel Klepper, MD.

Thanks to Cushing Memorial Library and Archives, Texas A & M University, for the use of items of Alice "Trix" MacDonald Fleming.

Thanks to Mr. John Walker, honorary librarian, The Kipling Society, London, for clarification of copyright.

My special thanks to the people of The Haworth Press for splendid editing, moral support, marketing efforts, and general encouragement.

Finally, to the memory of my dear colleague, Professor Robert Castagnola of Boston College, and of his wife Charlotte, for their spirit of caring and healing.

Human Behavior in the Social Environment, Second Edition

SECTION I:
THE BIOPSYCHOSOCIAL
PERSPECTIVE

Chapter 1

Overview

For every complex problem, there is a solution that is simple, neat, and wrong.

H. L. Mencken, *Aphorism*

INTRODUCTION

Human behavior is extraordinarily varied and complex. The unexpected behaviors of others often astound us, and, on occasion, we find ourselves bewildered by our own actions. We like to think of ourselves as logical and in control of our lives. However, the directions we sometimes take, the people we marry (and perhaps divorce), and the dreams we follow may be dictated by strong emotional forces that do not necessarily flow from logic and may not even be in our conscious awareness. As we pursue our dreams and desires, we do so within the social context of our lives, the constitutional makeup of our physical being, and the physical environment surrounding us, which may also decisively influence our destinies.

This book examines such complex questions as: Why do foster children placed in "good" homes run away and return to abusive parents? Why do people "who should know better" repeatedly reenter self-destructive relationships? Why does an intelligent, well-functioning person in a stable family situation plunge the family into serious debt through persistent and chronic gambling?

We observe the intensity of ethnic and political forces currently wreaking havoc in many countries, such as Iraq, and in the recent past in the former Yugoslavia, where reason has been swept away, and people who once lived peacefully as neighbors engage in ruthless massacres of each other. In

Human Behavior in the Social Environment, Second Edition

our own country, we struggle with violence, including domestic violence, and child physical and sexual abuse. "There were 903,000 substantiated cases of child maltreatment in 2001, most of which involved neglect" (U.S. Department of Health and Human Services, 2003) (Osofsky and Lederman, 2004, p. 221). The nation has recently been shocked by disclosures of sexual abuse of children committed by their clergy.

The biological world also affects and can determine our destinies. Throughout history, epidemics—such as the bubonic plague during the Middle Ages, the influenza epidemic after World War I, and now AIDS (acquired immunodeficiency syndrome)—have taken countless lives and wreaked havoc among the survivors. Anxiety increased worldwide in 2006, as a deadly bird flu virus spread to the human population. We feel helpless and frightened as powerful manifestations of the physical environment, such as hurricanes, tornadoes, and volcanic eruptions, assert destructive power over individual lives as well as the fabric of whole communities and sometimes entire countries. In 2004, we witnessed with anxiety and grief, the tsunami in Southeast Asia, and, in 2005, Hurricane Katrina in New Orleans, and a major earthquake in Pakistan.

For centuries, comets, a celestial manifestation of the physical environment, have had a disturbing influence on people. "Whenever the predictable clockwork of the heavens has been jarred by a comet hurtling unexpectedly through the sky, people throughout the ages have feared that unthinkable horrors would inevitably follow" (Johnson, 1997, p. A9). This country reacted with disbelief and puzzlement in 1997, when thirty-nine members of the Heaven's Gate cult in Southern California took their own lives as the Hale-Bopp comet crossed the sky. How did the convergence of the comet's flight, the members' life courses, adherence to a rigid cult culture, and the faith that an extraterrestrial spaceship awaited them lead to this organized and communal suicide?

When observing people over the trajectory of their lives, other paradoxes and puzzles emerge. Why do some people, with "average expectable environments" as children, seem unable to function as adults? On the other hand, how do others, wounded in childhood, evolve into creative and productive individuals? Let us consider the development of three young girls, who, having lost their mother at an early age, were raised by a rigid maiden aunt and an often-aloof father. As children they lost two older sisters and later saw their only brother become addicted to drugs and alcohol. They grew up socially alienated from others in their small village. It would not surprise us to learn that they struggled with depressive feelings during their lives, but how can we explain their creative genius and fame as the Brontë sisters?

Conundrum: acertijo, adivinanza

How did a slave, separated at an early age from his mother, who never knew who his father was, somehow martial his strengths and become a famous abolitionist and orator known to the world as Frederick Douglass?

Why do "ghosts" from the past haunt some parents, inhibiting them in their ability to love, whereas other parents are free from these "ghosts" (Fraiberg, Adelson, and Shapiro, 1975)? Ordinarily, we consider babies a source of great joy. The cooing baby with its foot in its mouth demonstrates a love of life and a pleasure of being in the world, which is infectious; emotionally tuned-in adults can feel this happiness radiating from a child. It is perhaps one of the life's greatest tragedies that some adults cannot feel this joy and are frozen in their response to their babies.

The actions and attitudes of human beings in their world are replete with conundrums and enigmas. Well-known female writer Jan Morris was born biologically a male and lived as a male for many years, married and had children. But since the age of four she felt that she was a female, rather than a male; this secret tormented her for many years. The only way to achieve inner peace, she concluded, was to realize her true identity: to transform "himself" into "herself," to physically change identity, which was accomplished through medical and surgical treatment. In her beautifully written and poignant book *Conundrum* (1997), she describes both her conflict and transformation, and ends on a note of uncertainty.

> My loves remain the same loves. . . . Have I discovered . . . the real purpose of my pilgrimage, the last solution to my Conundrum . . .? Sometimes down by the river I almost think I have: but then the light changes, the wind shifts . . . and the meaning of it all once again escapes me. (p. 160)

Such uncertainties often lead students to despair of ever grasping the complexities involved in case situations and to flee toward certainty, simplicity, and concrete "one-size-fits-all" solutions. After many years as both a practitioner and teacher of clinical social work, I remain a student of human behavior, still puzzling over the conundrums and enigmas of life. I invite you to share this search for understanding with me, as we contemplate the human condition, the social environments in which people live, and the dynamic interplay of psychological, physical, and social forces in life.

This book is written in the spirit of Winnicott, who values "ambiguity, openness, and creativity" in his search for understanding (Grolnick, 1990, p. 188).

GOALS OF THIS BOOK

This book is intended for the basic Human Behavior in the Social Environment course in graduate social work education, as the primary text for the semester that focuses on such micro topics as individual development and the life cycle. A supplementary text, focusing on systems, organizations, and culture more deeply is recommended for the semester concentrating on macro subjects. Though written for the master's-level social work student, undergraduate students have also utilized it successfully. Although the focus is on social work education, this book can benefit students of *teaching, nursing, medicine,* and *the human services fields,* who are also concerned with development over the life course, within a biopsychosocial perspective. It may also prove useful for practitioners wishing to review and resynthesize their knowledge about human behavior, and to those denied serious exposure to psychodynamic thinking in their training, but who realize the need to understand this perspective.

Students specializing in policy, administration, or community organization also need a firm foundation in human behavior in order to design policies and programs that meet human needs and analyze the consequences of policy decisions more thoroughly. If one understands, for example, the depth of attachment and loss issues, one is in a better position to understand not only the *need* for family preservation programs and sound adoptive programs, but also to understand the complexities in getting them to work. Understanding human motivations and biopsychosocial features in human existence requires considerable knowledge, sensitivity, and skill.

Clinical students, in turn, must acquire a systemic perspective so that they can appreciate how culture, political, and historical forces; race and ethnicity; social and physical environments; and organizations and policies affect their clients and their work with them. For example, vulnerable children in foster homes are affected not only by their feelings of loss and conflicts about attachment, but also may suffer maltreatment by their foster parents, in homes that are inadequately supervised by child welfare departments, within a system that is underfunded, understaffed, and buffeted by its own administrative power struggles.

In New Jersey in 2006, an adoptive mother was accused of seriously starving and maltreating her four adoptive children for years, until they were removed from the home. When the case was first reported to the Child Welfare Department two years earlier, it was found that "caseworkers were overburdened, with as many as eighty cases each, and often so poorly trained that they lacked a working knowledge of even the most fundamental departmental policies" ("Protecting New Jersey's," 2006, p. A22). Although almost

$350 million was then allocated to the agency, there has been minimal progress. This money "had apparently not been used to refine training or actually improve services, but to add to an already sprawling bureaucracy" (p. A22).

It is a daunting task to write a book about human nature and the social world, because no boundaries exist to this undertaking. Where does one begin, and what does one include? Endless theories and perspectives exist. Each person has his or her own story, each culture its own intricacies, and the interactions of people are expressed in myriad patterns. In attempting to resolve this conundrum, I have drawn from my experience as both a practitioner and a social work educator. Doing so has helped me form the book's goal: to impart to social work practitioners the basic knowledge to provide a firm beginning foundation for practice and for developing a professional self.

I have elected to emphasize a *psychodynamic* approach within a *biopsychosocial* perspective because I believe this provides the deepest understanding of the inner worlds of people as well as their interrelationships with the world around them. It is not possible within the scope of this book to give equal time to all theories or even to give total coverage to those theories that I am discussing. Two basic considerations have determined my choices: (1) presentation of ideas and theories that students can directly relate to practice issues, and (2) the need to present sufficient theoretical background so that students will be able to understand their conceptual context.

To bring human behavior theories to life, case vignettes taken from clinical practice are included. Occasionally constructed case examples will be presented, representing a composite mosaic of clients and problems. Excerpts from novels, biographies, and autobiographies have also been included. Readers may gain insights from the reflectiveness and sensitivities of writers to their own inner worlds as well as to their social and political worlds. Goldstein (1990) values the humanities through which "we discover that our own and our clients' triumphs and struggles have been played out in a multitude of ways in an effort to make sense of living and find meaning within it" (p. 41). Resonating with the spirit of this book, the humanities, he adds, "do not profess to offer answers; rather, they encourage the kind of disciplined questioning and reflection that are fundamental to what effective practice may be" (Goldstein, 1990, p. 41).

Newspaper and magazine articles are also cited, as they have much to say about human nature, social and political issues, systemic processes, and competing values and conflicts. Knowledge about human behavior and the social environment exists only in a limited form in textbooks. New knowledge, along with companion conundrums, come into being every day. Even old knowledge, looked at with fresh eyes, can offer new insights. Our clients, educated or uneducated, young or old, and well or disabled, have much to tell us about the riddle that we call life. A psychodynamic perspective instructs us how to ask them to become our teachers, to share with us their own discoveries, and their perplexities about the meanings of their lives.

This text aims to suggest ways of looking at the world around us, the world within us, and the world between us, and to suggest ways of listening, observing, understanding, and inquiring that will lead to an ongoing search for and discovery of meanings and answers.

STRUCTURE OF THE BOOK

This book is divided into four major sections. The first section discusses the major theoretical orientations; the second, human development and behavior over the life span; and the third, special issues. The final section integrates the major points in the book.

Each chapter includes suggested readings so that readers can expand their understanding of the materials presented and explore relevant new areas. Chapters also incorporate suggested learning exercises to enable students to become involved with the materials and to do their own research concerning people and the world around them.

Section I. The Biopsychosocial Perspective

This section includes eight chapters, the first six of which discuss the main perspectives as outlined in this chapter.

1. Overview
2. Psychoanalytic and Ego Psychology Theories
3. Object Relations, Self Psychology, and Cognitive-Behavioral Theories
4. Postmodern Theories: Constructivism, Relational Therapy, Narrative Theory, and Resilience
5. Social Systems and the Community
6. Culture and Diversity
7. The Family: Forms and Organization
8. The Family: Internal Structures and Special Family Problems

Section II. The Life Cycle

The second section of the book presents a picture of the life cycle from conception through old age. Biological, social, cultural, and familial factors are interwoven into this discussion. Emphasis is given to issues of attachment and loss, separation/individuation, violence, resilience, and creativity as they pertain to people at different life stages. This section includes the following three chapters:

9. Reproductive Issues, Infancy, and Early Childhood Development
10. Middle Childhood and Adolescence
11. Adult Development

Section III. Special Issues

In this section, special issues discussed in this overview chapter are presented. The three chapters under this section include the following:

12. Life Transitions, Turning Points, Crises, and Loss
13. Illness and Disability
14. Mental Health Problems

Section IV. Integration

In this final section, the perspectives discussed in this book are summarized and integrated.

15. Conclusion

THEORETICAL PERSPECTIVES

Psychodynamic Theory

While a psychodynamic stance within a biopsychosocial framework provides a sound and comprehensive *foundation* for exploring the human condition, critics of psychodynamic thinking often seem oblivious to the rich tapestry of thought this paradigm encompasses, criticizing this theoretical framework as though it were confined rigidly to early Freudian thinking centered on drive theory. Today, it in fact encompasses divergent and rich schools of thought, including ego psychology, object relations, and self psychology, and further modern additions include *constructivism* and narrative theory.

To emphasize psychodynamic understanding neither implies an exclusive reliance on psychodynamic treatment modalities or on long-term treatment models nor does it mean that other theoretical orientations, such as learning theory, family dynamics, or group approaches, should be ignored. These frameworks as well as systemic and ecological theories are incorporated in this book. Biological factors, including genetics, physical growth and maturation, sexuality, and psychosomatic issues, are also discussed. The cultural context of individual lives provides vital insights into human behavior, and this perspective will be interwoven throughout. This approach parallels that of Woods and Hollis (1990): *"In our psychosocial approach, ecological systems and psychodynamic perspectives have become inseparable"* (p. 9; italics in the original).

I would agree with Berzoff, Flanagan, and Hertz (1996) that insights afforded by a psychodynamic approach are not only valuable in psychotherapy, but also when "one is making a hospital discharge plan or completing a housing application. Clinical knowledge grounded in psychodynamic theory is one of the most powerful ways we have to look inside someone's heart and mind. Without it, we are almost blind, limited to the surface" (pp. 5-6).

Psychodynamic approaches also emphasize the clinical relationship that develops in each and every meeting with a client, whatever the goal. We learn to see past and beneath the angry acting out of the adolescent, whose behavior may be masking suicidal impulses, and by considering her underlying needs and motivations, not to alienate the foster mother whose controlling ways with her foster child frustrate us. Understanding the complexities of clinical relationships leads to the development of a more reflective practitioner and is a cornerstone in the development of the professional self.

Psychodynamically aware clinicians understand the importance of listening to themselves, in the service of awareness of their own feelings and attitudes, which may distort their perceptions of and responses to clients *(countertransference)*. This self-awareness can often be a difficult and disturbing process. More recently it has been discovered that "listening to ourselves" can be a useful guide for picking up clues regarding clients (a concept elaborated later on as *intersubjectivity*). In the midst of an interview, we may suddenly feel inadequate and guilty—feelings not belonging to our own basic psychological state at the moment, but which have been unconsciously transmitted to us by the client. This can contribute to our insight about the client's emotional turmoil. We can sensitize ourselves to recognize "alarm bells" from within, warning us of danger from a violent client, so that both of us can be protected.

Psychoanalytic Theory

Psychodynamic theory has evolved in different directions since Freud's original psychoanalytic work, but many of his basic insights remain valid today, and psychodynamic theories, even when diverging from his formulations, do rely on many of his basic premises. Freudian thinking has permeated modern thought, leaving its imprint on the arts, literature, philosophy, and history. In Edmundson's (1998) review of Jonathan Lear's book *Open Minded: Working Out the Logic of the Soul,* he reports Lear's assertion that "democracy needs Freud," because "without him . . . people will go around thinking they are acting rationally . . . all men and women should comprehend their proclivities for destructiveness and self-idealization in order to make the best-informed choices" (p. 10).

Learning how to listen to clients, to understand the world as they perceive and experience it, rather than assuming we know just what they mean is one of the contributions to our profession coming from psychoanalysis. Freud learned to listen intently to each patient. A lasting legacy has been the manner in which Freud "listened, heard, and understood his patients" (Edward, 1996, p. 23). His "respectful attitude . . . expressed through his communicative approach continue to influence analytically and many non-analytically oriented therapists today, irrespective of . . . their theoretical outlooks" (p. 23).

Freud also helped us to understand internalized psychological conflict, in which a person is "at war" with himself or herself. A struggle might ensue between the person's wishes and instinctual life (such as sexual feelings), as opposed to his or her conscience (or superego) with its self-prohibitions (e.g., against sexual activity). Even in our relatively sexually permissive society people often struggle with these conflicts, as we demonstrate in our case illustration at the end of the chapter. *Superego guilt,* a concept introduced by Freud, was much earlier described by Shakespeare, who created Hamlet, a character brooding with guilt.

Lewis Carroll, author of *Alice in Wonderland,* a man of imagination and wit, has puzzled his biographers as aspects of his psychological self remain hidden. Cohen (1996) discusses the continual *internal conflicts* (and superego guilt) he believed that Carroll experienced in relation to his attraction to prepubescent girls.

> Beneath the bubbles and the froth lived yet another force, however, a brooding guilt. . . . He was a good practicing Christian, but he nevertheless saw himself as a repeated sinner. Stern Victorian that he was, he could never give voice or employ pen and ink to record the nature of his sins, but the painful appeals to God for forgiveness that he confided to his diary reveal a man in spiritual pain for transgressions that surely go beyond ordinary failings like idleness or indolence. Lewis Carroll's strong and virile imagination must also have bred sexual fantasies. His dreams probably reached out beyond what he considered

accepted terrain and ventured into dangerous precincts. A severe disciplinarian, he never transgressed propriety or violated innocence. He was . . . superhuman, in today's terms, in controlling his impulses during waking hours. But the nights brought troubled thoughts for which he saw himself a miscreant. (p. xxi)

The development of *affect* and the transmission of affect to others are also of special interest in psychoanalytic thinking. Psychodynamic theorists recognize the power and significance of feelings in people: the *motivating force of affects*; the importance of recognizing and expressing feelings; the ability to modulate and keep feelings under control. "It is the nature and intensity of the affect generated by or in connection with a particular event that determines one's behavioral reaction: *affect is the gateway to action*" (Basch, 1988, p. 65; italics added).

The trauma of the destruction of the World Trade Center in New York on September 11, 2001, affected adults as well as children, and adults who are normally in a position to comfort their children were not always able to do so; thus, parental fear was transmitted to their children.

Many adults were experiencing a need to be protected themselves and were fearful about whether or not they or their children would ever be safe again. Further, young children depend on adults to help them make sense of their world. In this case, adults, the media, and even many national leaders were having difficulty making sense of the world. So young children and their parents were left with a mutual loss of trust as well as many new fears, outcomes we frequently see in traumatized young children. (Osofsky, 2004, p. 7)

Psychoanalytic theory enables us to understand how the past can still live in the present, providing another tool for further understanding. Some mental health professionals consider a person's past irrelevant and prefer to deal only with the here and now. Moultrup (1981) observes that inasmuch as "each moment passes into the past instantly, it would seem to be logically impossible to deal strictly with the 'present'" (p. 120). Although the objective past is significant, so also is "that which might have been, i.e., fantasy, hopes, etc., . . . they are a part of an individual's or family's experience" (p. 120). Some cultures place emphasis on the past. Believers in Confucianism, Buddhism, and Taoism have "reverence for the family's past and its ancestors . . . [which] provides a strong sense of continuity and obligation" (Germain, 1991, p. 111).

People experiencing trauma in their *adult past* may find that it affects the rest of their lives. In fact, trauma in the past life of parents can be *transmitted* to their children, who are growing up in an otherwise trauma-free environment. Anxiety experienced by Holocaust survivors, for example, can be experienced by their children who never experienced the Holocaust and who may not even understand the source of this feeling. There are "intergenerational patterns . . . *common everyday patterns* through which anxiety and silence are transmitted"; although the parents may be silent, this does not impede the transmission of anxiety. "Unexplained silences further intensify the affective, fearful power of children's fantasies" (Brown, 1998, p. 270).

The vitality of the past is evident in the *repetition* of significant distressing past experiences, which may not be in conscious awareness, but is an attempt at mastery. In applying Freud's concept of the *repetition compulsion* to victims of trauma, Glodich (1998) observes that a person "reproduces it [the trauma] not as a memory but as an action; he repeats it, without knowing, of course, that he is repeating, and in the end, we understand that this is his way of remembering" (p. 336).

The drivenness to repeat can also be seen in *transference* reactions, that is, a patient *displaces* feelings and attitudes from past significant relationships onto the therapist. Brooks (1984), discussing the working through of transference within the therapeutic process, notes that

> the transference . . . becomes the peculiar space of a deadly serious play, in which affect, repeated from the past, is acted out as if it were present, yet eventually in the knowledge that the persons and relations involved are surrogates and mummers. . . . Disciplined and "subjugated," the transference delivers one back to a changed reality. (p. 235)

Brooks (1984), who incidentally is a literary scholar, and not a psychoanalyst, observes that Freud has made important contributions to literary theory. He is particularly impressed with Freud's emphasis on the patient's "need to repeat, rather than simply remember, the past" (p. 98), and relates the relevance of repetition to literary texts:

> Repetition is so basic to our experience of literary texts . . . rhyme, alliteration, assonance, meter, refrain, all the mnemonic elements of literature and indeed most of its tropes are in some manner repetitions that take us back in the text, that allow the ear, the eye, the mind to make connections, conscious or unconscious, between different textual moments. . . . An event gains meaning by its repetition, which is both the recall of an earlier moment and a variation of it. (pp. 99-100)

Freud's important legacies have naturally been both developed further and criticized by later theorists. Many reject his emphasis on the primacy of the drives, or instinctual life, without giving due weight to issues of attachment, relationship, and the impact of the external world on human development. Others partially or fully accept Freud's emphasis, but at the same time re-dress it by giving much greater theoretical weight to issues on which he did not focus. Psychoanalytic theory is explored in Chapter 2, which also in-cludes a discussion of ego psychology, one of its major advances.

Ego Psychology

An important component of personality is the ego, that portion of per-sonality structure which, in Freud's basic conceptualization, mediates be-tween the id (the unconscious contents of the mind, especially those linked with instinctual forces or drives) and the superego (the conscience). (These terms are used in full recognition that they are not concrete actualities but useful constructs.)

Heinz Hartmann (1958), the "father of ego psychology," developed and expanded the Freudian concept of the ego to focus on its interaction with and adaptation to the external world. He spoke of autonomous ego func-tions (such as the development of language and memory) that develop in the conflict-free sphere of the ego (that part of the ego that is not involved with "settling conflicts" between the id and the superego). "As a result, ego psy-chology encourages practitioners to think about developmental processes across the life cycle, about the unfolding of human capacities in response to the interaction between environmental influences and inborn developmental potentials" (Schamess, 1996, p. 68).

Ego psychology also offers a window of insight into psychological de-fenses and ego functions. The clinician's assessment of the ego functions can contribute greatly to understanding people and their adaptation to life. Does a person have good reality testing? What can be seen about the indi-vidual's ability to function on a daily basis? Is he or she capable of good judgment? Is there cohesiveness of personality, or is there a tendency to slip into psychosis under stress?

Major ego defenses are examined so that we can understand what they mean and how they could be used. Defenses are chiefly unconscious mental mechanisms that help an individual ward off anxiety, affording protection from unwanted thoughts and feelings. Defenses can be both adaptive and maladaptive, depending on the context and how they relate to a person's functioning and accurate perception of the world. People with problems of alcoholism, for example, frequently use the defense of denial (and often their family members do the same) to avoid confronting the problem and the consequences of the drinking behavior. In this context, the defense is maladaptive, as denial facilitates continued drinking, which can have serious detrimental effects on the person's health, job functioning, and social relationships. The utilization of this defense, however, does enable the drinker to continue to fulfill whatever emotional needs are met (or felt to be met) by drinking.)

Ego defenses were first discussed by Freud, elaborated on by Anna Freud, and expanded by object relations theorists. Freud introduced the defense of repression, which is receiving a great deal of attention recently in regard to the major controversy related to recovering repressed memories of childhood abuse.

Object Relations Theory

Object relations theory, focusing on identity development, emphasizes the importance of good nurturing, and early secure attachment experiences, which lead to the capacity to form relationships throughout life. Through these early nurturing relationships, children develop *internalized images* of others *(object representations),* as well as internalized images of themselves *(self-representations).* If children have "good enough" nurturing, they will develop love and trust in their caretakers, which in turn leads to the development of good feelings about themselves. Although these initial feelings about self and others can be modified through later experiences, patterns of relating often persist. One of the debates in the field concerns the extent to which the effects of early influences determine later relationships, and the degree to which they may be dramatically altered by later experiences.

In the following example, we can see the client, Meg, struggling with her feelings of discomfort in a social situation, which can be best understood from an object relations perspective.

> Meg discussed her experience when she was invited to a dinner party. She was introduced to a man who was friendly and who expressed an interest in her work. She was relaxed and animated as she talked to him. Later in the conversation, when she learned that he was a judge, she immediately felt anxious and frozen. She felt intimidated by his "authority," although, she admitted, he was not "acting like an authority." She could feel herself starting to respond in an inhibited manner.

Meg was not reacting to this man's genuine acceptance and warmth objectively. She perceived him internally as a critical judge of her; she *projected*

outward : exterior

her internalized negative feelings about herself onto him and reacted to him as though he was indeed critical.

In object relations theory, *objects* refer to people. (The rather unusual meaning of the term in this context is derived from early Freudian usage, when the mother was seen as the object of the infant's needs and drives.) Object relations is concerned not only with the real-world relationships people have with one another, but also their internal reactions to and conceptions of other people as well as their inner feelings about themselves.

> In addition to our loves, friendships, and rivalries, we have intricate relationships within us. They are not static images, but rather, powerful influences on how we feel about ourselves and relate to others. The people around us also affect us within ourselves. The exploration of these internal and external relationships has led to a growing body of knowledge called object relations theory. (Hamilton, 1990, p. 3)

People may present an outward appearance, which can be dramatically at odds with their inner self-image (or self-representation). The novelist Franz Kafka, when a child, was positively regarded by his teachers, but this picture was not congruous with his negative self-image, nor with his subjective reaction to his teachers (object representations).

> Whatever misgivings Kafka may have had about his scholastic abilities, the evidence of his grades suggests both ample talent and application. He was, in fact, a star pupil throughout the first four years, popular among his classmates and exceedingly well liked by his teachers. But the constant struggle to conform and perform left him drained to the point where, in his memory, the whole experience boiled down to a viscous mixture of boredom and fear, in which the teachers floated as so many faceless figures, *Respektspersonen* [persons held in respect] indistinguishable from one another as, day in and day out, they sat in judgment over him. (Pawel, 1984, p. 33)

Winnicott, an object relations theorist, has made many contributions to both psychiatry and social work; his ideas "lend depth and precision to social work's person-in-environment perspective" (Applegate and Bonovitz, 1995, p. 8). Winnicott's concepts include the good-enough mother, transitional objects, play, the false self, the capacity to be alone, and the development of creativity.

One of Winnicott's major concepts is the *holding environment*—referring to the nurturing and a sense of security mothers provide to their children.

(Although Winnicott includes the father as an important figure, he stresses the relationship to the mother as the primary caregiver, which in the context of his times was usually the case. Today we recognize the significance of the father, even during the very early days of the child's life, and generally refer to "parenting" rather than "mothering.") Winnicott applied this concept to case management services to disturbed children and adults, which is potentially ego supportive when accompanied by a social worker's caring and empathy. This holding environment also includes the provision of supportive services and environments that are sensitively matched to the needs of the client (Kanter, 1990).

The *bonding* and *attachment* behaviors of parents and children are of great interest to psychodynamic theorists; good bonding leads to good ego development, whereas poor bonding can have an adverse effect on all areas of physical, social, and emotional development (Bowlby, 1988; Goldberg, 1995; Holmes, 1995; Talbot, 1998). Attachment theories are relevant to many child welfare issues: to family reunification programs (Maluccio, Pine, and Warsh, 1996); to child maltreatment (Morton and Browne, 1998); and to early intervention programs (Shapiro and Gisynski, 1989). Attachment theory also can shed light on issues of intimacy and commitment with which adults struggle; in late adulthood the loss of attachments, forming new attachments, and renegotiating attachments to adult children are of major importance.

While attachment is critical to human development, so is the reciprocal ability to separate and become an autonomous individual, while still maintaining connections with others. Mahler, Pine, and Bergman (1975) explore the separation/individuation experience, focusing on the processes by which infants move away from their close maternal orbit, explore the world, develop a sense of individuality apart from mother, and finally negotiate the right "space" between themselves and mother to maintain closeness without losing autonomy. Although Mahler, Pine, and Bergman (1975) assert that these developments occur primarily within the first three years of life, they do note that separation/individuation issues reverberate throughout the life cycle. Adolescents go through a "second step in individuation" (Blos, 1962, p. 12), and their normal storms and rebellions can be viewed as part of this struggle.

Object relations theory, elaborated in Chapter 3, also helps us to understand the formation of identity, our sense not only of "who we are, but that we are" (Mahler, Pine, and Bergman, 1975, p. 8). Self psychology stresses the deep-lying structure of self-identity, the vicissitudes of its development, and the attainment of self-cohesion.

[handwritten margin note: Attachment theory]

Self Psychology

Self psychology, formulated by Heinz Kohut, focuses on the development of the self, and asserts that children depend on affection and empathy from selfobjects, who are their parents, or parent substitutes. Selfobjects essentially refer to people who meet a person's needs for developing and sustaining a secure view of self and self-esteem. Individuals from infancy onward thrive within warm, safe relationships, which foster a sense of well-being and self-worth. "Indeed, the need for selfobject responses is always present, waxing and waning with the ups and downs of the strength and vulnerability of the self" (Wolf, 1994, p. 81).

The key to self psychology therapy is the therapist's development of empathetic understanding of the patient. Internalizing this empathetic therapeutic relationship, patients develop a firmer, more stable sense of self and self-esteem. The mutual examination of the therapeutic relationship (or selfobject transference) by the patient and the therapist becomes the major aim of treatment (Donner, 1991).

An illustration of the utilization of *selfobjects* is seen in *Vivienne: The Life and Suicide of an Adolescent Girl* (Mack and Hickler, 1981). Vivienne, fourteen, took her own life by hanging herself (after several previous suicide attempts). Struggling for a long time with feelings of low self-esteem and depression she felt uplifted when a new teacher provided her with a warm and supportive relationship; he was a critical figure to her (i.e., selfobject) in her life in terms of her self-esteem. The loss she felt when he left the school and moved across the country appears to have been devastating. "Well over a year before he left, Vivienne anticipated that she would feel deeply bereaved, and wrote that her 'joy will be gone in a year'" (p. 101). The departure of the teacher had "a greater significance than his loss as a person. It struck at the core of Vivienne's psychological vulnerability" (p. 101). The good feelings about herself which Vivienne felt in his supportive presence could not be sustained in his absence.

> Kohut postulates that if there had been a significant disturbance in the parent-child relationship . . . the child will be left especially vulnerable to later injuries to self-esteem . . . [and] will then seek idealized parent figures in adolescence or adult life . . . to replace something missing in the self . . . losses of these objects at critical times will bring about not merely a loss of self-esteem but terrible emotional pain, a sense of nothingness, and, potentially, a dissolution in the structure of the self. (Mack and Hickler, 1981, p. 107)

Self psychology, with its emphasis on self-structure, empathy, and self-objects is discussed further in Chapter 3.

Postmodern Theories: Constructivist and Narrative Approaches

Constructivism is concerned with how individuals construct their perceptions of self and others, of the world around them, and the meanings and values they choose. We are actively involved in the creation of our world; "the analysand is not just the fly caught in the web, but is the spider, the designer of the web as well" (Mitchell, 1988, p. 257). *Meaning-making* is a central concept in constructivism: "Without a fundamental core of meaning about which we can have conviction, life becomes problematic" (Saleebey, 2001, p. 34). This theory asserts that "there is no ultimate objective truth, that each person interprets experience in terms of his/her background, cultural and personal" (Turrini, 1996, p. 447). Some writers see this theory as a movement away from the "positivistic assertions of the scientific basis of psychoanalysis . . . to increasingly subjective and relativistic theoretical developments" (Coleman, 1996, p. 47). Positivism or scientific empiricism generally holds to the verification principle, according to which a proposition is meaningful only if "some *sense* experience would suffice to determine its truth" ("Infoplease," 2006; italics added).

Kegan (1982) credits Jean Piaget (discussed in Chapter 9) as being the central figure in the development of developmental-constructivist thought, in his studies of how children make sense of the world, and begin to reason. Children are not born with innate knowledge of the world but figure out how "people work," and how "things work"; this process of mental construction evolves through maturity and experience. A young baby, for example, will not look for an object that has disappeared (to the baby it no longer exists), but an older baby (who has developed a sense of *object permanence* [note: here "object" refers to a physical object], will search for it.) Throughout life, people continue to work at understanding their physical and social environments and attribute meaning to their experiences.

Saari (2005) observes that a constructivist orientation can "link the inner and the external worlds" (p. 4), including the influence of culture on the individual.

> I want to propose the simple idea that human beings need to create a picture of the environment in which they function in order to be able to create a sense of who they are in that environment; that is, their identity. Understanding that our personal identity is dependent upon

the way in which we understand our environment can explain many things. (Saari, 2005, p. 4)

Constructivism asserts that observers are always involved in their observations; the "act of observing" inevitably affects what is being observed (Lee and Greene, 1999, p. 24). In the treatment situation, this means that the therapist is not a passive recipient of the patient's transference feelings, but is a "real" participant in the therapeutic dialogue. Harry Stack Sullivan, a pioneer of *interpersonal theory,* stressed that psychotherapy is a two-person system; borrowing the term *participant observer* from anthropology, he emphasized the importance of examining the duality of the therapeutic relationship, in which the therapist is a participant observer (DeLaCour, 1996). The object relations concept of intersubjectivity is related to constuctivist theory; however, not all constructivists accept the tenets of object relations theory, adhering primarily to its social, interactional aspects, rather than to the concepts of internalization of self and object representations.

Dean (2002) discusses the important ramifications constructivism has for clinical work.

> No longer was the therapist able to stand outside of the therapeutic process and render objective judgments about it. Constructionism taught that the clinician does not have privileged access to an unambiguous reality that is inaccessible to the client (Hoffman, 1983; Slavin, 2001). Post-modern social constructionists saw therapy as an interactive process in which meaning is continuously co-constructed by the participants. (Dean, 2002, p. 15)

Cultural perspectives are important in social constructivist theory, which explores the effect of culture on individuals, and the interpretations individuals make of their cultures. This perspective prevents us from assuming that we know just what it must be like for a person to be a member of a given culture. We need to understand each person's cultural background, values, and possible cultural conflicts; a person might belong to several cultures, some with competing values, such as being a Latina immigrant as well as a lesbian.

In addition, people often have strong religious, political, or social beliefs that can take dominant roles in their lives. The deep convictions of dedicated missionaries are no less compelling to them than are the deep passions of the suicide bomber. Competing values between people can produce serious conflict: marital disagreement about parenting and the ongoing, pro-choice/ pro-life battles. Constructivism is discussed further in Chapters 4 and 6. An important offshoot of this perspective is narrative theory.

(i.e., a gradual exposure to frightening objects or situations) has been help-ful in decreasing anxiety, and behavior modification has been very success-ful in work with autistic children.

Cognitive therapy, developed by Beck (1976), focuses on changing faulty thinking that can be the basis of problematic feelings and behavior. If peo-ple, for example, think poorly of themselves, are convinced they will al-ways fail, and tend to catastrophize (that is believe everything they do or plan will not work), therapy focuses on helping them understand their ha-bitual manner of thinking and replace these thought patterns with more pos-itive ones.

Cognitive-behavioral theories make important clinical contributions, however they have serious limitations when they are used exclusively, and dismiss the insights of the psychodynamic orientation. Attempts have been made to integrate cognitive-behavioral techniques with psychodynamic treat-ments; this is discussed further in Chapter 3.

THE EMBATTLED PLACE OF PSYCHODYNAMIC THEORY

In recent years, psychodynamic theory has in large measure been driven out of social work education, replaced by cognitive-behavioral, solution-ori-ented, problem solving, and ecological approaches (Berzoff, Flanagan, and Hertz, 1996; Goldstein, 2002; Mishne, 1982; Sanville, 1994; Urdang, 1999), with an emphasis on "evidence-based" theory and "empirically based" in-terventions (Howard et al., 2003; Thyer, 2003). The scope and nature of the "evidence" and the "empirical basis" have been restricted in such a way as to exclude any clinical data that is either not readily quantifiable or thus far impossible to quantify. This excludes a wide range of data recorded or per-ceived on a more subjective level—thus nearly eliminating the entire uni-verse of the hard-to-define and/or subjective. How does one evidence past experience, or disguised attitudes, or "empirically observe" what is within the inner thoughts of ourselves and our clients? As Hamlet says to his friend: "There are more things in heaven and earth, Horatio, Than are dreamt of in your philosophy."

A strengths-based perspective has become another dominating force in social work practice and education (Saleebey, 2001, 2003), and, while in-trinsically compatible with a psychodynamic perspective, it is generally presented as replacing this theory. Practitioners of postmodern approaches often disregard psychodynamic theory, although others do integrate these viewpoints into psychodynamic practice.

Many factors militate against psychodynamic teaching, including the long-standing schism in social work between advocates of clinical work and advocates of social policy and social change; a major emphasis on quantitative research and outcome measures; and divergences in theoretical perspectives.

Conflicts Between Clinical Work and Advocates of Social Change

Psychodynamic clinical social work is dismissed by some social workers and educators as irrelevant, as a means to "blame the victim" rather than eliminate social oppression and injustices. This schism is not new and has been with social work throughout its history. Austin (1997) notes that

> in the widely read *Unfaithful Angels: How Social Work Has Abandoned Its Mission,* Specht and Courtney (1994) cited Jane Addams as the prophet of social work's true vision and called on the profession to reject an individual psychotherapy model in favor of a practice model based on the community as the unit of intervention and on group work and adult education as the primary interventive approach. (p. 608); (Urdang, 1999, p. 12)

It is regrettable that divisiveness exists between proponents of work with the community as opposed to individual intervention, as the uniqueness of social work is the melding of these approaches. The *psychosocial* perspective, which deals concurrently with the individual (psyche) and the social, now augmented by a biological perspective (the biopsychosocial), has been the unshakable focus of the field in modern times. Furthermore, social action and advocacy are important tools of the clinical social worker. If people are starving, food is a priority. If children live in crime-ridden neighborhoods where they see their friends murdered, safety is a priority. If gays and lesbians are harassed and beaten, protection is a priority. If adolescents are becoming infected with HIV and develop AIDS, treatment and prevention are priorities.

However, the community is not a corporate mass; it is composed of individuals, each unique. One of social work's highest values has been to recognize and respect the uniqueness of the individual—to appreciate the humanity, the suffering, the human dignity, and the spirit of every person (Chenot, 1998). Chenot cites Pray (1991), who has said that "'honoring the uniqueness of the individual is central to social work practice,' and is 'the core social work value'" (p. 80) (Chenot, 1998, p. 302).

It is indeed paradoxical that the time-honored social work values of caring for and individualizing the person are placed in opposition to the equally time-honored values of social policy and change, often to the disadvantage of the former in social work education. Yet nothing in principle dictates that one cannot be oppressed and suffer from inner emotional conflict at the same time. If children see their friends murdered, they often suffer emotionally, have nightmares, and experience other trauma-related symptoms. Gays and lesbians need protection from harassment, but they also may need help with the same myriad life issues that heterosexual people do. If adolescents are becoming infected with HIV and develop AIDS, they need individualized support as they face this life-threatening illness. Poor people are no less entitled to skilled professional help simply because they are poor; they also struggle with the purportedly "middle-class" problems of depression, marital conflict, and substance abuse.

From a *systemic perspective,* a powerful controlling force today in the mental health field is *managed care;* keeping costs down is the primary goal. Brief treatment and supposedly efficient case management are given emphasis: "The spectre of managed care was propelling clinical social workers, responsible for the majority of therapy in the nation, to find short and simple solutions to long and complex problems" (Rose, 1996, p. xix). Coupled with this emphasis on short-term models has been the preference accorded to cognitive-behavioral constructs, with outcomes that can be measured. Quantitative outcome measures are emphasized, and statistical verification, rather than psychodynamic understanding, becomes the "royal road" to insight into the human condition.

Conflicts Between the Psychodynamic Orientation and Quantitative Research

Strong emphasis in social work practice and education is placed on empirically based interventions, which lend themselves to quantitative measures. This has been accompanied by utilization of practice guidelines (PGs), "which set down the 'best' methods of helping clients with particular problems" (Thyer, 2003, p. 22).

> A related development has been the appearance of practice textbooks that take a "problem-focused" organization (usually arranged by mental disorder) and then describe the appropriate (that is, empirically supported) assessment methods and interventions. (Thyer, 2003, p. 23)

While Thyer (2003) argues that any theoretical approach can be utilized in empirically based interventions, as long as they are "scientifically judged as effective" (p. 23), this approach fosters cognitive-behavioral methodologies, because they are easy to quantify. Psychodynamic issues are often dismissed as irrelevant if they are not quantifiable, rather than being examined as a source for further inquiry. In a human behavior textbook, Zastrow and Kirst-Ashman (2004) state:

> ⌐Research does not support either the existence of his [Freud's] theoretical constructs or the effectiveness of his therapeutic method. Part of this lack may be due to the abstract nature of his concepts. It is very difficult, if not impossible, to pinpoint the location and exact nature of the superego. (Zastrow and Kirst-Ashman, 2004, p. 91)⌐

Given the fact that psychodynamic treatments are concerned with such complexities as strong affects, unconscious processes, defenses, and transference phenomena, quantification becomes problematic. Research is difficult "because of the complex interaction of variables, the subtle intrapsychic and intersubjective factors, and the contextual issues associated with the study of humans in general, and complex mental states in particular" (Hanna, 1992, p. 155).

While we cannot "locate" the superego (nor the id for that matter), they nevertheless exert powerful emotional influences on our lives. Celestial black holes, intriguing to astronomers, are also invisible, but nevertheless exert enormous power on the bodies that enter their fields. We can't see the unconscious, we can't touch our memories, or know fully the sources of our emotions, but these forces are at work in our lives, in our views of ourselves and our relationships with others.

Although difficult, research in psychoanalytic treatment "is far from bleak" (Brandell, 2004, p. 14), and many studies have been undertaken, including those by the Anna Freud Centre, the Columbia Psychoanalytic Center, and the Menninger Foundation Psychotherapy Research Project. Fonagy and Target (2002), at the Anna Freud Centre in London have been doing multifaceted research of child psychoanalytic treatment for the past fifteen years, including follow-up outcome studies, using techniques as varied as applying standardized assessment scales, process evaluations of individual sessions, and combining quantitative as well as qualitative methodologies.

In one recent meta-analysis, extending over thirty-five years, seventeen studies in which patients were treated with short-term psychodynamic therapy were examined; it was found to be "an effective treatment for a variety of psychiatric disorders" ("Psychodynamic," 2006, p. 5). Interest has been

developing in qualitative research and its concern with subjective worlds and experiential narratives.

A further complexity in studying the effectiveness of psychodynamic therapy is the absence of a unified psychodynamic therapy; there are diverse theories, competing opinions, and individual styles within this framework.

Conflicts Between Theoretical Approaches

Not only are there disagreements among divergent schools of thought, such as psychoanalysis and behavioral approaches, but psychodynamic theorists also do not always agree with each other; theoretical conflicts have existed since the beginning of psychoanalysis. Postmodern theories suggest that there are many ways of knowing, that many narratives of a life can be constructed, that clinicians are active participants who affect the therapy, and that knowledge is relativistic and time- and culture-bound. The postmodern viewpoint conflicts with "positivist" empirical outlooks, including cognitive behavioral approaches, as well as with "positivist" psychodynamic approaches that adhere to strict principles of interpretation.

In a review of Judith Mishne's book *Multiculturalism and the Therapeutic Process,* Ringel (2003) praises Mishne's self-psychological approach to working with culturally diverse clients, noting that her utilization of empathy is particularly effective. However, when Mishne speaks positively of drive theory and ego psychology, Ringel is highly critical.

> Mishne's attempt . . . to illustrate concepts from Drive and Ego psychology (such as fixation, regression, and defenses) as diagnostic tools, however, seems less successful. These theories, which are based on a one-person rather than a two-person psychology (in which relational dynamics are more central to treatment), have been associated in the recent past with gender inequality, heterosexism, and exclusion of ethnic and cultural considerations. Dr. Mishne's use of these theories seems to impose a rigid and archaic framework on clients who come from ethnically diverse communities. . . . Drive and Ego psychology seem to promote a more *pathologizing and hierarchical perspective.* (p. 212; italics added)

Ringel (2003) refers to "pathologizing and hierarchical perspectives" in strongly negative terms, as though finding "pathological" processes at work within people is to dehumanize them, and that assuming a role of authority in therapy is to become authoritarian. Should clinical work consist of egalitarian encounters between two people sharing their stories and perspectives?

Pathologizing

Strengths
Perspective

One person (the client) is hurting and/or not functioning as well as might be and seeks professional help. The professional brings his/her expertise to bear on listening to, understanding, and assessing what is wrong (and what is right) and what needs remediation. The client's story, motivation, goals, and thoughts about the treatment process are important parts of the intervention. If the client is experiencing a troubling *psychopathological* state such as anxiety, depression, or extreme confusion, the clinician needs to understand this, without marginalizing the person.

The strengths perspective, increasingly a major force in social work practice and education today, also speaks out against pathologizing people, and emphasizes promoting their strengths. Saleebey (2001) observes that the emergence of this school of thought is a reaction to "society's obsession and fascination with pathology, problems, moral and interpersonal aberrations, violence, and victimization" (p. 78). While he acknowledges the reality of abuse, violence, cancer, schizophrenia, and racism, he stresses that growth and "regeneration" can develop when people face these crises. "From the vantage point of a strengths perspective, *it is as wrong to deny the possible as it is to deny the problem* . . . adherents of the strengths perspective *do not believe,* with good reason, that most people who are the victims of abuse or their own rampant appetites or that all people who have been traumatized inevitably become damaged goods" (Saleebey, p. 79).

> The strengths approach requires that we understand that everyone (no exceptions here) has strengths and resources, external and internal. These assets may be realized and a part of a person's life or they may be inchoate—unrealized and unused. But the understanding and work of people who employ a strengths perspective is driven by the search for, definition of, and employment of people's assets and resources in helping them walk, however hesitatingly, toward their hopes and dreams. We are called on here to venerate the remarkable richness of human experience, to acknowledge that every individual, family, and community has an array of capacities and skills, talents and gifts, wiles and wisdom that, in the end, are the bricks and mortar of change. (Saleebey, 2001, p. 76)

Disparaging both the psychopathological perspective and psychoanalytic theory (although crediting defenses as being helpful tools), Saleebey (2001) cites "empowerment approaches . . . the resilience literature . . . solution-focused orientations as well as narrative approaches" as being compatible with the strengths perspective. Noting that although "social workers for

years have insisted that they build on the strengths of clients," he implies a skepticism that they have indeed done so (p. 77).

The strengths perspective contributes to both clinical work and community interventions, and illustrations of this are given throughout this book; one example: teenagers who have had past difficulty with the law are now serving as teen judges and lawyers in juvenile courts (Chapter 9). However, when the strengths perspective becomes an exclusive interventive approach, with its focus on "transformation and redemption" (Saleebey, 2003, p. 152), the important aspects of personal history and working through psychological pain become lost. For as Saleebey observes, "A positive orientation to the future is far more important . . . for healing and helping than an obsession with a dark and disappointing past" (Saleebey, 2001, p. 78). If we ignore the "obsession with a dark and disappointing past," and disregard the intensity of certain mental states, we cannot free the client's strengths from the forces that enslave them.

While the curative value of therapeutic relationships is emphasized in the strengths perspective, there is no discussion of the complexities of developing one with people who have difficulty relating, who are defended against closeness and see supportive relationships as threatening. Saleebey (2001) dismisses psychodynamic theory, with no reference to object relations theory or self psychology, and the depth of insights they offer in building clinical relationships.

Students today are responsible for dealing directly with increasingly complex problems within complex fieldwork systems. "Multiproblem clients, over-burdened supervisors, fewer agency resources, and increases in home-based services result in some students handling more difficult cases with reduced or inadequate supervision, and working in riskier environments" (Jarmon-Rohde et al., 1997, p. 33). It becomes more critical than ever before that students enter the field with a strong foundation in human behavior, based on a sound knowledge of psychodynamic concepts to help them maintain a firm footing as they are buffeted by multiple pressures. At the same time, this psychodynamic understanding must be embedded in a systems perspective.

Systems Theory

As the poet Donne reminds us: "No man is an island, entire of itself." We are all part of multiple systems. In talking directly to you, if you are a student, I note that you are currently part of the system of a social work school, where the rules, expectations, work demands, relationships with peers and faculty, and tuition you pay all have an impact on you. Socially, you have friends, family, perhaps belong to organizations, have a religious affiliation, or a political orientation. Your current student status (with its accompanying time constraints) may affect all of your social involvements. You may be a long-standing member of your community; you may be a newcomer, perhaps just moving here to go to school. You live in housing that may be comfortable, or you may be sharing an apartment with six people, which may be stressful (or stimulating) for you. You may or may not have a system of social supports.

You have ethnic, racial, cultural, religious (or nonreligious) backgrounds and a sexual orientation, all of which affect your identity, your values, and your current perspectives on life and social work training. You come from a family with whom you may or may not be currently involved in complex ways. You may be in good health, or you may be having health problems (or concerned about someone else's health). It would not be unusual if you were feeling some degree of anxiety and self-doubt as you begin your new career. You know you will probably change through your graduate training, but you do not know how this will happen, or the nature of that eventual change.

Thinking in these terms exemplifies a systemic approach, a perspective to be applied to all client work and agency activity. *Macrolevel* systems include society, community, and organizations; *microlevel* systems include individuals, families, and groups. As a student, your school, placement agency, and organizations would be examples of *macrosystems.* Your friends, colleagues, and family are part of your *microsystem.* Micro- and macrolevel systems often interconnect and interact.

Macrosystem issues, such as managed care, may affect your agency's funding, resulting in insufficient cases assigned to you (because you won't be covered by insurance payments), which means you may not be able to write the necessary school papers which may in turn worry you about passing. This anxiety may be transmitted to your family, which may increase the stress they feel about your education in the first place.

I will address systemic thinking from two perspectives: the first involves the *processes* of systemic interactions (as we noted above when we discussed the chain of events that could affect you as students). The second aspect of a systems perspective involves looking at major systemic *issues* such as poverty, homelessness, divorce, violence, physical and sexual abuse, and addictions, and how they affect people. Discrimination against various groups in our society, including racial minorities, women, homosexuals, the elderly, and the disabled, is also addressed, and women's rights and the men's movement are discussed. Presently, many advances are taking place in civil rights, progress is being made by racial and ethnic minorities, and there is growing acceptance of gays and lesbians; we also see serious regressions and backlashes, and an intense, well-publicized debate involves same-sex marriages.

Hurricane Katrina's devastation of New Orleans in the summer of 2005 is a microcosm of systemic problems and processes. The power of nature overwhelmed the city as a Category 4 hurricane destroyed levees and flood waters inundated the city. There was a tragic loss of life, and survivors had harrowing experiences of survival, in some cases experiencing post–traumatic stress disorder or other severe emotional reactions. Many physically and psychiatrically ill patients did not receive needed care; some in nursing homes drowned. Families were broken apart, temporarily or sometimes permanently through dislocation or death. Homelessness and joblessness became rampant problems overnight. Close-knit communities disappeared as people dispersed across the country. Lawlessness prevailed and there were reports of looting. Massive organizational breakdown occurred, as governmental agencies were not able to meet basic needs. Racism was often cited as the reason for the neglect of the large, poor black population of the city. Political upheaval was inevitable as blame was passed from one agency to another and from one level of government to another. Although parts of the city have been restored (enough to hold a Mardi Gras in 2006), many sections remain uninhabitable, and conflicts continue around rebuilding, corruption, and political power. The ultimate fate of New Orleans remains unsettled.

Ecological theory, which "studies the relations between organisms and their environments . . . [which are] characterized by continuous reciprocal exchanges or transactions, in which people and environments influence, shape, and sometimes change each other" (Germain, 1991, pp. 15-16), which is vividly illustrated by events in New Orleans, is an important contribution to systemic thinking. Ecological theory leans heavily on the concepts of *adaptation* and *coping* (Fraser, 1997; Germain, 1991). It contributes important concepts to social work, such as the varied *nature of communities* and the utilization of *social networks* and *social supports* to enable people to lead more productive lives (Germain, 1991).

The ecological concept of *goodness-of-fit* describes the matching of a person with specific needs (such as an employment problem), with someone or some place (such as an employment service) where the best chance for meeting these needs could exist. For example, a man with creative abilities was placed in a job requiring rote mechanical skills and did poorly. When alternatively transferred to a position where his creative abilities were used, he flourished. "An individual's temperament, needs, and preferences and the available opportunities can be evaluated and, whenever possible, matched to better suit both sides. This perspective contributes to a 'no-fault' approach to reducing person-situation disequilibrium" (Woods and Hollis, 1990, p. 29).

Ecological and systems theories are discussed in Chapter 5, race, ethnicity, and social class in Chapter 6, and gay and lesbian issues in Chapters 7 and 11.

Culture

Culture plays an important role in the development of a person's values, relationships, worldview, and identity. "Culture refers to the traditions, values, customs of child-care and socialization practices and includes rituals and artifacts that symbolize the group's belief systems" (Lewis and Ipen, 2004, p. 13). Cultures can be based on race and/or ethnicity, and even within these categories, subcultures frequently exist. Though definitions of culture generally assume involvement over the life span, with "child-care customs" and the presence of "artifacts," there are cultural groups that people join (or form) later in life, based on other common characteristics, such as sexual orientation. Many deaf people belong to the deaf community with its own values and rituals.

Individuals may have mixed cultural backgrounds such as a multiethnic heritage, or be a part of several cultures whose values may conflict, such as black and gay cultures. Cultures are not static; cultural values may undergo changes as we have seen in this country in recent years, with the many transformations in the roles of women and men, and greater acceptance of gays and lesbians. Conflicts about values and lifestyles can occur *within* cultures as well as *between* cultures. It is therefore important to individualize the meaning of culture in individual lives, as a *constructivist* approach encourages us to do.

Cultural factors can affect people psychologically in dramatic ways. Ved Mehta, the writer, for example, was born into a Hindu family in India, where his father, a physician, was strongly influenced by English education and culture. Ved, who became blind at three, grew up within India's strict caste system. Although this disability per se does not define a caste, he himself was a potential "outcast" due to his blindness, which was highly stigmatized. His education in the United States exposed him to cultural values different from his own, as well as to the cultural values of the world of the blind, against which he rebelled. His autobiography "explore[s] the boundaries of time and memory, the clash of culture and self, and the meaning of place and exile—as I have experienced them" (Mehta, 2001, p. 345).

Immigration is a major experience in which issues of acculturation and marginality impact on the evolving self-identity of the immigrant.

> Immigration from one country to another is a complex and multifaceted psychosocial process with significant and lasting effects on an individual's identity. Leaving one's country involves profound losses . . . [and] a renewed opportunity for psychic growth and alteration. (Akhtar, 1995, p. 1052)

Immigration itself can also become a politically charged issue, as in the spring of 2006, when national attention was focused on the approximately 11 million illegal immigrants living in the United States. Conflicts have erupted in relation to the security of U.S. borders, the drain on local communities in providing medical, educational, and social services for these individuals, and whether (and how) their presence should become legalized. Major protests ignited when national legislation was introduced to criminalize illegal immigrants.

> Protesters began pouring into the streets of cities from Los Angeles to Philadelphia to vent their outrage. They were illegal immigrants, and their American-citizen children emerging from behind their shield of invisibility, plus legions of voters who count the newcomers as family, friends and neighbors, in numbers "bigger than the Vietnam War demonstrations," [Senator] McCain says. "I never could have predicted that we would have 20,000 people in Arizona or half to three-quarters of a million in Los Angeles." (Tumulty, 2006, p. 30)

Cultural influences impact clinical work, affecting the attitudes people of various cultures have toward emotional and relationship difficulties, trauma and abuse, as well as toward receiving clinical help. "Each culture has specific social and religious rituals for its members' experience of loss, tragedy, and disaster" (Lewis and Ippen, 2004, p. 11). Suicidal behavior in black and Hispanic adolescents, for example, is found to be influenced by strong cultural condemnation of self-destructive behaviors (Wyche and Rotheram-Borus, 1990), and may therefore take the form of provoking a homicide against the self. Suicide is dishonorable and "dying is . . . more honorable if it occurs in rage and aggression rather than in passive solitude. Provoking a fight and being killed as a result may be culturally more appropriate as an expression of suicidal intent" (Wyche and Rotheram-Borus, p. 327).

Finally, cultural differences (as well as similarities), including issues of race, ethnicity, social class, and gender (as well as gender-identity) between

(Marans and Adelman, 1997, p. 202), which must be considered in a developmental framework. Within this presentation, family, culture, and life course perspectives are interwoven with developmental issues, including resilience, adaptation, reorganization, creativity, attachment, loss, and separation-individuation.

Chapter 9 focuses on reproductive issues, infancy, and early childhood development, and Chapter 10 discusses middle childhood and adolescence. Adult development, discussed in Chapter 11, has been a neglected subject until recent years, as an earlier belief existed, influenced by psychoanalytic thinking, that major developmental and maturational landmarks were achieved by the end of adolescence. It is recognized today that many developmental and psychological changes continue in the adult personality (Levinson and Levinson, 1996; Levinson et al., 1978; Nemiroff and Colarusso, 1990).

Chapter 11 is in part devoted to late adulthood, in recognition of the dramatic increase in longevity, the large numbers of aging Baby Boomers, and the varied needs in this group, which ranges from the healthy and vibrant "young-old" to the frail elderly. The lives of adult children are often deeply affected in many ways by the caretaking responsibilities they assume for their elderly parents.

SPECIAL ISSUES

Three topics of special significance merit separate chapters: life changes, transitions, crises, loss, and death (Chapter 12); the mind-body interaction, illness and disability (Chapter 13); and mental health problems (Chapter 14).

Life Transitions, Turning Points, Crises, and Loss

As we evolve through the life cycle, and experience many physical, psychological, and social changes, we make new adaptations to these transitions. Achievements such as walking, entering nursery school, graduating from college, and marrying can be accompanied by losses such as separating from parents. Loss may also be experienced in more traumatic ways, including divorce, deterioration of physical abilities, or the death of loved ones. Life crises can also present opportunities for growth.

Grieving for major losses in life or the lack of grieving, can have important emotional consequences for us; *unresolved grief* often results in psychosomatic disorders, depression, or disturbed relationships. William Styron (1990), the novelist, wrote an autobiographical account of his bout of serious depression, describing his despair and preoccupation with suicide. During the height of his despair, he suddenly became aware of his unresolved grief for his mother as the root of his depression.

> I'm persuaded that an even more significant factor was the death of my mother when I was thirteen . . . the death or disappearance of a parent, especially a mother, before or during puberty—appears repeatedly in the literature on depression as a trauma sometimes likely to create nearly irreparable emotional havoc . . . especially . . . if the young person is affected by . . . "incomplete mourning" has . . . been unable to achieve the catharsis of grief, and so carries within himself through later years an insufferable burden of which rage and guilt, and not only dammed-up sorrow . . . become the potential seeds of self-destruction. (pp. 79-80)

Other factors such as the relationship of the bereaved to the deceased, and supportive and reparative experiences after the loss, including "replacement" figures, are also considered as are cultural contexts, including mourning rituals. There has been little attention to working with grief in social work courses (Kramer, 1998), and only recently has social work practice and education begun to emphasize end-of-life issues (Berzoff and Silverman, 2004). These topics are discussed in Chapter 12.

The Mind-Body Interaction, Illness, and Disability

The biological is a critical aspect of human behavior and human development, starting with the commencement of our physical existence, the role of our genetic make-up, our growth and development, and culminating in death. While mind-body dualism—that is, that mind and body are separate entities and operate independently of each other—remains a subject of controversy, the point of view taken in this book is that there is a close, dynamic interaction between both, that in reality they are inseparable. These issues are discussed in Chapter 13.

Illness and disability, when they occur, have profound and widespread biopsychosocial effects on patients, their families, and social networks. *Psychological* sequelae can include feelings of loss, changes in self-image and self-esteem, shame, depression, and sometimes suicidality. Barbara Ceconi, an MSW in social work, lost her eyesight suddenly while in college due to juvenile diabetes (Ceconi and Urdang, 1994).

> Her initial feelings and experiences in relation to her blindness were "akin to those of grieving the loss of a significant friend or family

member. I was mourning the loss of my eyesight." She experienced rapid mood changes, feeling "anger, depression, fear, and isolation. . . . Being helpless, not able to function independently, not having a career were the thoughts running through my head." Barbara's statement resonates with one made by Reverend Thomas Carroll who said, "It is superficial, if not naive, to think of blindness as a blow to the eyes only, to sight only. It is a destructive blow to the self-image which man has carefully, though unconsciously constructed throughout his lifetime, a blow almost to his being itself." (Ceconi and Urdang, 1994, p. 181)

Family members who have sick or disabled relatives may experience feelings of loss, anger, and depression and may also assume caretaking functions (which can prove stressful). They may need to make adjustments (which they may be unable to make) in their family structure. Systemic issues, such as societal attitudes toward the disabled, the limited availability of medical and support services, and the impact of managed care on patient treatment are also important variables.

Today, in our country, obesity is increasing in all age groups, giving rise to many medical problems; a major concern is the dramatic resultant increase in childhood diabetes. AIDS continues to be a major health problem both in this country and around the world. Anxiety is rising about a possible worldwide epidemic of bird flu. These subjects are included in the discussion in Chapter 13.

Psychopathology

Psychopathology (disturbances of thinking and feeling) is not exclusively the province of the so-called mentally ill, but is experienced by all human beings in varying degrees. Feelings of depression and anxiety, for instance, fade in and out of our state of mind, and are included in our consideration of human behavior. However, the line between normal emotional states and pathological conditions is not always easy to draw. Many people in this country are affected directly (as patients) or indirectly (as families or friends of patients) by various types of mental illness, including *schizophrenia, mood disorders, anxiety disorders,* and *characterological or personality problems.* Children of depressed mothers, for example, are at serious developmental risk (Brody, 1998).

Some social work educators resist teaching the psychopathology knowledge base because of concerns regarding "pathologizing" the client; the supposed imposition of a "hierarchical" relationship by the clinician and its alleged violation of the strengths perspective. As a result of the "specialization" approach in social work education, mental health problems have become the exclusive purview of the psychiatric social worker, but this overlooks the fact that an intimate relationship exists between serious psychological problems (forms of psychopathology) and many social problems such as violence, sexual abuse, suicide, the breakdown of the family, and homelessness. It also ignores the fact that many forms of psychopathology of a very wide spectrum of kind and severity may be present in the background functioning of clients in any social service sphere. These are not typically announced by the client, and workers must therefore be able to discern their presence themselves, and have appropriate understanding of how to manage their effect on the situation they are dealing with. For example, obsessive-compulsive features may interfere with carrying out behavioral assignments, or paranoid suspiciousness may impair the establishment of basic trust between client and worker. Understanding this dimension of human behavior is simply facing reality, and in no way needs to dehumanize the client. Ackerson (2003) expressed concern that mentally ill parents have often been stigmatized by the child welfare system and may, as a result, unnecessarily lose their children; in addition, many child welfare workers have inadequate preparation to assess mental health issues or to provide help to mentally ill parents.

Mental health problems can also coexist in people with physical illness and disability. Assessment of mental status and psychopathological functioning is of critical importance in working with end-of-life care patients as well (Walsh-Burke, 2004).

In the assessment process, it is important for social workers to ascertain whether clients have been diagnosed with, or experienced the symptoms of *any* mental disorders prior to a life-limiting illness because these symptoms are usually exacerbated by medical illness, treatments, or bereavement. Without accurate history and a complete assessment of factors contributing to symptoms of anxiety and mood disturbance, inappropriate or ineffective treatment can aggravate distress rather than alleviate it. (Walsh-Burke, 2004, p. 377)

Patients themselves can resist getting better; they sometimes prefer aspects of remaining ill to regaining their psychological strengths. Kay Redfield Jamison, a professor of psychiatry at Johns Hopkins School of Medicine and a prolific author on manic-depressive illness (bipolar disorder), is herself afflicted (or blessed, as she sometimes feels) with manic-depressive illness. In her impressive autobiography, *An Unquiet Mind* (1996), she discusses her struggles with this illness. Although she is a person of unquestionable strengths, who vigilantly struggled to overcome the tenacity and chronicity of this illness, her resistance to treatment had been strong. She felt a sense of loss in giving up her symptoms, particularly "the high flights of mind and mood" that she experienced.

> Even though I was a clinician and a scientist, and even though I could read the research literature and see the inevitable, bleak consequences of not taking lithium, I for many years after my initial diagnosis was reluctant to take my medication as prescribed. . . . Why did it take having to go through more episodes of mania, followed by long suicidal depressions, before I would take lithium in a medically sensible way?

> Some of my reluctance, no doubt, stemmed from a fundamental denial that what I had was a real disease. . . . Moods are such an essential part of the substance of life, of one's notions of oneself, that even psychotic extremes in mood and behavior somehow can be seen as temporary, even understandable, reactions to what life has dealt. In my case, I had a horrible sense of loss for who I had been and where I had been. *It was difficult to give up the high flights of mind and mood, even though the depressions that inevitably followed nearly cost me my life.* (Jamison, 1996, p. 91; italics added)

Chapter 14 provides an overview of schizophrenia, mood disorders, anxiety disorders, and characterological or personality problems. Attention is also given to depression, the addictions (including gambling), borderline pathology, and post–traumatic stress disorder, which is often a consequence of abuse and violence. Developmental disabilities, including retardation, autism, and Asperger's syndrome are also discussed.

ILLUSTRATION OF THE BIOPSYCHOSOCIAL APPROACH TO A CASE

In concluding this overview, the case of Mrs. Billings is presented, illustrating the application of the biopsychosocial approach to a clinical social work case.

Mrs. Billings, a thirty-two-year-old Caucasian woman, was admitted to an inpatient psychiatric facility for treatment of depression, complaining of fatigue, feeling tearful, and concerned that her symptoms were intensifying. She reported one previous psychiatric hospitalization for a suicide attempt and depression. She has very low self-esteem, strong feelings of guilt, and is very self-consciousness. "It is hard for me to make friends. . . . I am uncomfortable with people." She is married, to Mr. Billings, thirty-six, who runs a store in their small rural town; they have two children, Susan, ten, and Todd, eight. The family lives on a 100-acre farm with cows and horses.

As we think about Mrs. Billings, several questions suggest themselves for further exploration. First, let us consider her relationship with her husband. Is he a potential source of support? Might conflict in their relationship be contributing to her depression? Mr. Billings drove some distance to the hospital to visit with his wife, and he readily accepted the recommendation for a social work interview. Both Mr. and Mrs. Billings were seen individually for one session and then had a joint interview.

Mr. B., thirty-six, relates well and seemed insecure, passive, and eager to please. He is concerned about his wife but feels helpless in terms of knowing what to do for her. He tries to help her at home . . . "maybe she feels guilty about that . . . I wash dishes for her . . . she fusses at me for this . . . tells me to do my farm work." Both Mr. and Mrs. B. feel that something is missing in their relationship; they each see their own involvement in their marital problems. Mr. B. stated: "We don't sit down and talk to each other . . . that is one of our problems . . . I can't stand to have her mad at me." He added that his wife "just holds her feelings inside . . . things keep building up in her." Mrs. B. commented that she likes her husband. "I feel as comfortable with him as I ever did . . . can be myself with him."

Mrs. B. talked openly about her sexual problems. There is a "coolness between my husband and myself. . . . I won't let him kiss me or hold my hand. . . . I don't want him to touch me . . . can't tolerate the idea of sex." When first married, "I enjoyed sex," but since the birth of her two children she has had a fear of getting pregnant. "Why I'm that way, I don't know." Concerning their present sexual life, Mr. B. stated: "We don't talk about it."

The Billings are aware of their impaired communication patterns but seem unable to move ahead on their own to correct the problem. They both express caring feelings for each other, relate well to the interviewer, evidencing a basic capacity to relate, but at present this capacity is *inhibited*. Sexual problems are serious, although the baseline of their sexual functioning was at a higher level in the past. Mrs. B. reports sexual fears and relates this to a horror of becoming pregnant. Her general sense of superego guilt is pervasive (she may have an excessively punitive, critical superego); problems and conflicts about "mothering" also seem key issues in her fear of becoming pregnant. The transactional nature of the marital problems become obvious; the inner conflicts of Mrs. B. affect her response to Mr. B., which in turn affect his response to her, so the spiral escalates. As we examine the interaction of this couple, Mrs. B's inner state, poor self-image, conflicts, and anxieties come into focus.

Mrs. B. has fears of pregnancy, which we hypothesized are related to her anxieties about mothering. What characterizes her relationship to her two children? To what extent are they a source of pleasure to her; to what degree a source of conflict?

Mr. B. states that the children are doing well and get along in school. He feels that they (especially his daughter) "get on his wife's nerves." Mrs. B. expressed concern that her behavior affects both children. Her son is "bordering on an ulcer." She finds that she "fusses at them for small things. . . . I'm afraid I'm making them high strung." Recently her daughter came home from school with school pictures of herself and started crying while showing them to her mother. Mrs. B. said that she used to be the same way: ". . . I was ashamed of my looks . . . did not want to show my pictures."

We can observe the effects of the mother's temperament and depression on the children. The interactional nature of the family system becomes apparent. We see the expression of ambivalence, as she shows some concern and empathy as well as irritation toward her children. We see the possible beginnings of a psychosomatic condition, as their son may be developing an ulcer. The object relations perspective helps us to understand how her daughter has internalized some of her mother's attitudes and feelings.

It will be instructive to look at the family in the larger system of work, extended family, friends, and community. As we proceed with this exploration, we can see that the family, especially Mrs. B., while having some social contacts, has relatively closed boundaries with the outside world; socially they are relatively isolated.

Mr. Billings works in a store, which he now owns after making a financial arrangement with Mrs. B.'s father who had owned it previously. Mr. B. works his farm by himself "every spare minute I have." He enjoys living in this small town, has friends, and meets many people in the store. But he finds that it is a "relief to get out on the farm . . . you can fed up with the public . . . they are hard to please." Mrs. B. works as a salaried bookkeeper for her father. Although she likes office work because "it is methodical," she is under some pressure working for her father "who leaves too much to her."

The Billings have no outside interests, except camping, which they do once a year. Mr. B. reports that his wife "doesn't enjoy this, does it mostly for the kids . . . would really rather go to a motel." He feels he should take his wife out more. "It's a help for her to eat out . . . but I would just as soon eat home." Mr. B. would like to go to church (which Mrs. B. refuses to attend because of her weight) and to lodge meetings, "but I don't want to leave her and the kids alone." Mrs. B. has no "real close friends." They don't visit or have others come to the house. "She worries because the house is not polished." Mrs. B.'s mother comes over once a week to help her clean the house. Mrs. B. has complained to her husband about her mother "being a problem to her . . . mother cries on her shoulder."

We find an *enmeshed family system* in which the Billings' economic and employment situations are intertwined with those of Mrs. B.'s parents. There is not a goodness-of-fit between Mrs. B. and her social environment. Working for her father and having her mother help at home weekly adds to Mrs. B.'s distress, rather than her pleasure. Her resentment is internalized, increasing her depression. Although she would most likely benefit from having friends, her poor self-image makes having friends a difficult chore for her, and her isolated lifestyle adds to her depressed feelings. Also, we can see her depressed moods controlling the family's activities to some extent. Mrs. B. has little pleasure in her life. *Anhedonia,* the inability to experience pleasure, is one of the symptoms of depression; for Mrs. B., it also seems characterological, that is, part of her personality, in that it has been an entrenched feature since her early life. In terms of the ego function of management of needs and feelings, there is great inhibition of both aggressive and pleasurable feelings, and an abundance of superego guilt.

Turning to biological factors, we see that Mrs. B. complains of fatigue, which is a symptom of depression; but could be related to other illnesses, such as anemia. She complains of dizziness and shortness of breath. She had gained forty pounds in the last three years, adding greatly to her self-consciousness. Mr. B. noted: "When she is nervous, she tends to eat more." Her physical problems were evaluated; nothing significant was found. She was then referred to the psychiatric service.

Researchers have found evidence for a biological basis for depression; Mrs. B. may be constitutionally prone to this disorder. However, to see her depression exclusively in biological terms would blind us to the complex psychosocial factors in her life. Medication was helpful to her, but individual and marital therapy might help her live a more satisfying life. We saw earlier that her son might be developing an ulcer, a condition with psychosomatic implications. When Mrs. B. came to the hospital to be evaluated, her mother also came for an evaluation for stomach problems.

In an effort to understand how her past might live in the present, Mrs. Billings was asked about her early family life. She described a number of family problems and she, on her own, related them to her present sense of self. From a self-psychological perspective, we can see that she experienced serious empathic failures on the part of her parents and did not receive adequate mirroring or admiration from them. She did not receive sufficient acceptance from her family to build healthy self-esteem.

Mrs. B. was the second of three children and "got along well with her parents," but "blamed them for many of my problems . . . never felt I could talk to them." With some guilt she added, "They never had a chance themselves." Mrs. B.'s mother was six months old when her own mother died, and she was then raised by an aunt in a large family, not receiving much attention. Mrs. B.'s parents were "never free in their praise of me . . . maybe they did praise me when I got good grades . . . but never for anything else." If something "bothered me, I would bottle it up and brood over it . . . I imagine that's what I've been doing now."

Sex was never discussed at home; she never saw her parents kiss or hold hands. Her own femininity was never encouraged. "I never learned to wear make-up . . . still can't fix my hair . . . was never told I was pretty." In growing up, she usually had a few "fairly close friends . . . was never very comfortable with people at large." Mrs. B. graduated from high school, then went to business school, worked successfully, and had ambitions to be a doctor, which she never pursued.

Looking at Mrs. B.'s background from an object relations perspective, we see, from an intergenerational perspective, that the early loss of her mother's mother was a significant factor, probably affecting her mother's ability to mother, and then, subsequently, Mrs. B.'s capacity to mother. Some role reversal is also occurring, at least presently, as Mrs. B. complains that her mother tends to lean on her emotionally. She has internalized many of the interactions with her family, which has affected her psychological development, including her self-image as well as present relationships with others. It was recommended that upon discharge Mrs. B. receive both individual psychotherapy and marital therapy, rather than exclusive medication management.

CONCLUSION

A biopsychosocial perspective with an emphasis on psychodynamic understanding is the foundation of this book. As we confront the multitude of psychological and psychosocial theories today, the array of perspectives and choices can be overwhelming; constructivists advocate the deconstruction of theory, implying that our own subjectivities leave us incompetent to "render objective judgments" regarding the therapeutic process (Dean, 2002, p. 15). Admonishments to avoid hierarchical relationships with clients can cause us to flee from making diagnostic assessments and by advocating a kind of therapeutic nihilism, deter us from asserting reasonable and appropriate direction in treatment or service interactions with clients.

The importance of assessing ego functioning, defenses, psychopathological states, and psychodynamic factors within a biopsychosocial perspective is strongly urged in this book. Although some theorists advocate their theory for all treatments and all occasions, we should be free to choose which theory or theories seem most appropriate for a given client. Storytelling for children is cited as being a useful technique in child therapy (Brandell, 2004). But is it useful for all children at all times?

> Storytelling isn't for everyone; nor is it invariably effective even for the same client at different points in the treatment process. Certain children with developmental disabilities may be incapable of the minimal cognitive organization required for even the most elementary story. Others whose expressive language is compromised by developmental or organic factors may prefer play activities that do not highlight spoken language. Still others may enjoy the reciprocal storytelling process early in the treatment relationship but later express a preference for alternative play activities. . . . Indeed, like any other technique in the child therapist's repertoire, storytelling should be deployed with sensitivity and in accord with a particular child's preferences. (Brandell, 2004, p. 269)

Psychodynamic theory helps us develop the sensitivity, empathy, and listening skills to individualize clients, to understand their experiential worlds, and together to build a working alliance. Having a psychodynamic perspective does not imply that all treatment necessitates long-term in-depth psychotherapy, but it enables us to offer skilled help to the widest range of clients, from those seeking help with disabled relatives, to adolescents running away from home. *[handwritten: Psychodynamic theories]*

This perspective does not suggest that other approaches, such as cognitive-behavioral interventions, group therapy, or environmental interventions are excluded, but rather does suggest that they be applied with an in-depth understanding. This orientation helps clinicians to become self-aware and reflective, and to use their insights (some evoked by intersubjective clinical encounters) in the service of work with clients. The psychodynamically oriented and knowledgeable clinician can tolerate and accept clients' strong affects, without retreating into concrete solutions when these are not called for. A psychodynamically aware clinician understands that clients sharing pain, expressing feelings they are fearful or ashamed of, and thus freeing themselves from past shackles can enhance and mobilize their strengths.

We will explore the integration of biological, social, environmental, and cultural factors into the psychodynamic perspective, as we observe the interweaving of the inner and outer worlds throughout this book.

This chapter has presented an overview of the philosophy and format of this book. I incorporate a biopsychosocial perspective with an emphasis on psychodynamic understanding.

LEARNING EXERCISES

In addition to professional books and articles (newspaper and magazine articles), life stories contribute to our understanding of human behavior and the social environment.

1. *Newspaper Assignment.* Select 2 newspaper articles of human interest, and analyze them from a biopsychosocial perspective, looking at the interactions of psychological, social, and systemic processes. It is recommended that you do this throughout the course, searching for material relevant to class content.
2. *Biographical Analysis.* Biographical materials provide excellent insights into the interactions of psychological development, social relationships, and social and cultural contexts over the life span of an individual. Select a well-written biography or autobiography and read it along with the course, observing how the person whose life is depicted evolves, and critically applying what you are learning in class to your analysis of the book.

SUGGESTED READING

Articles

Ceconi, B., and E. Urdang. 1994. Sight or insight? Child therapy with a blind clinician. *Clinical Social Work Journal* 22: 179-192.
Glodich, A. 1998. Traumatic exposure to violence: A comprehensive review of the child and adolescent literature. *Smith College Studies in Social Work* 68: 321-345.

Books

Frank, M. G. 1996. A clinical view of the use of psychoanalytic theory in front-line practice. In *Fostering healing and growth: A psychoanalytic social work approach,* ed. J. Edward and J. Sanville, pp. 59-76. Northvale: Jason Aronson.

Germain, C. 1991. The ecological perspective. In *Human behavior in the social environment,* pp. 9-37. New York: Columbia University Press.

Kirby, L. D., and M. W. Fraser. 1997. Risk and resilience in childhood. In *Risk and resilience in childhood: An ecological perspective,* ed. M. W. Fraser, pp. 10-33. Washington, DC: NASW Press.

McFeely, W. S. 1991. *Frederick Douglass.* New York: W. W. Norton and Co.

McGoldrick, M., J. Giordano, and N. Garcia-Preto. (eds.) 2005. *Ethnicity and family therapy,* Third edition. New York: The Guilford Press.

Saleebey, D. 2001. *Human Behavior and Social Environments: A biopsychosocial approach.* New York: Columbia University Press.

Chapter 2

Psychoanalytic
and Ego Psychology Theories

Tell me where is fancy bred,
Or in the heart or in the head?
How begot, how nourished?

Shakespeare, *Merchant of Venice*

INTRODUCTION

This chapter encompasses psychoanalytic and ego psychology theories, particularly the ego functions and defense mechanisms. Psychodynamic understanding is relevant to clinical interventions in any social work setting; all clients have an inner mental/emotional life, although they may not be asking for help in exploring or altering it. People dealing with medical problems, aging parents, or child welfare issues are coping with critical life situations to which they bring their unique personalities, vulnerabilities, and ways of relating. The deeper our understanding and sensitivity to their underlying needs, feelings, ego functioning, and defensive operations, the better able we are to anticipate and deal with the complexities of working with them, their relationship demands on others and ourselves, and the resulting dilemmas in which we can become entangled. Learning to appreciate the complexities of human behavior will enable students to analyze their participation in the casework encounter with greater objectivity.

PSYCHOANALYTIC THEORY

Freud felt that it was his fate to "agitate the sleep of mankind" (Gay, 1988, p. xvii). This agitation was pronounced in his day and persists to the

Human Behavior in the Social Environment, Second Edition

present. "Freud has been called genius, founder, master, a giant among the makers of the modern mind, and no less emphatically, autocrat, plagiarist, fabulist, the most consummate of charlatans" (p. xvi). The goal of psycho-analysis, he asserted, was to "struggle with the 'demon'—the demon of irrationality—in a 'sober way'" (p. xvii). However, bringing irrationality under scientific scrutiny "only made his ideas about the nature of human nature seem all the more dismaying, all the more unacceptable. No wonder that mankind has for the most part defended itself against Freud's message with angry denials" (p. xvii).

Freud was born in 1856, began his medical practice in Vienna as a neu-rologist, and, in 1885, studied with Charcot, who was treating patients with hysterical symptoms, such as paralysis or blindness, for which no physical basis existed. From Charcot, Freud learned how to remove these symptoms through hypnotic suggestion and used this method "with varying degrees of success" (Brenner, 1974, p. 6). Freud became frustrated with hypnosis, finding that it was often difficult to induce, that the cures were often transi-tory, and that during the course of this treatment some women patients be-came "sexually attracted to him . . . something which was most unwelcome to him" (p. 7).

Freud's early collaborator, Breuer, told him about a patient he had previ-ously treated; Freud wrote about this as the famous case of Anna O. Breuer's work, and Freud's understanding of the implications of this work led to a major breakthrough for the development of psychoanalysis. For Breuer, however, this case led to flight from the fledgling psychoanalysis. Anna O. was later identified as Bertha Pappenheim, who became famous as a femi-nist reformer and social worker (Swenson, 1994).

Joseph Breuer, a general physician, had been asked to treat Bertha for a number of medical problems, including coughing that her mother was con-cerned could be tuberculosis. Bertha's father was at that time terminally ill with this disease, and Bertha and her mother were caring for him at home (Rosenbaum and Muroff, 1984).

> When Breuer came to attend Bertha Pappenheim, he found more than the cough. She had paralysis of the right arm, both legs were para-lyzed, and she could move only the fingers of her left hand. She was unable to feed herself, and she was barely able to turn her head because of what appeared to be a paralyzed neck muscle. She complained of vi-sual difficulty, so that she could neither write nor read. Other special-ists had been consulted before Joseph Breuer, and they could find no physical basis for Bertha's complaints. Breuer recognized at once the

mental and emotional problems that were involved. (Rosenbaum and Muroff, 1984, p. 2)

During the course of therapy, when she was under hypnosis (or put herself into a hypnotic trance), Bertha was able to talk about her symptoms, adding information related to her background. As she did so, her symptoms began disappearing. Bertha referred to this talking as "'chimney sweeping' (Rosenbaum and Muroff, 1984, p. 4) and to the treatment as 'the talking cure'" (p. 5). Talking included the recollection of a significant dream involving a snake about to attack her father; when she tried to prevent this, her arm became paralyzed. Apparently, after recounting this dream and her anxiety surrounding it, "her right arm was no longer paralyzed" (p. 5). Breuer, satisfied with the results, then terminated treatment, not anticipating what followed.

> That very evening Breuer was called to the Pappenheim home, and there he found Bertha in a hysterical state imagining that she was giving birth to a child, which she told Breuer was his. Although he was in a state of shock, he managed to hypnotize her and calm her. He left the Pappenheim apartment in what he later described as a "cold sweat." He never returned to the Pappenheim family. . . . (Rosenbaum and Muroff, 1984, p. 5)

The case of Anna O. led Freud to the exploration of the vital role of unconscious processes and to an understanding of how "neurotic symptoms will disappear when the unconscious cause or causes are permitted to come to awareness" (Rosenbaum and Muroff, 1984, p. 11). Anna O.'s discovery of the "talking cure" led to Freud's development of the use of free association in treatment. Freud did not "discover" the unconscious; earlier philosophers and writers, including Descartes, Goethe, Schiller, Coleridge, Wordsworth, Leibnitz, and Schopenhauer, had described aspects of the unconscious (Rosenbaum and Muroff, 1984). Shakespeare also wrote of deep inner forces and understood that dreams had power and meaning. However, Breuer and Freud "originated . . . the first systematic study of the unconscious. Freud applied his scientific training so that he could study the irrational and unconscious and make it rational and conscious" (p. 11).

The Anna O. case highlights some of the enduring contributions of psychoanalysis, including the power of the unconscious, the appearance of repressed conflicts in neurotic symptom formation, and the therapeutic utilization of dreams. It also highlights the importance of *transference* and *countertransference* issues, although, at that time, these were not well understood. Breuer did not see Anna O. in his office; he came to her home for treatment, at times twice daily. Bertha indicated that he was the "only one who could feed, understand, console, or help her. There was a considerable amount of touching—she recognized him at times by touching him; he gave her massages" (Swenson, 1994, p. 157). Breuer "abandoned" Anna O. abruptly, as her father, by dying, had abandoned her. Both Anna O. and Breuer were young, attractive people. The feelings that were stirred toward each other (and by each other) were never addressed, and the fact that Anna O. had transferred some of her love and sexualized feelings for her father onto Breuer were not understood by him, although later, when hearing about the case, Freud did understand this.

Drive Theory

Anna O. affords us a glimpse into the "subterranean" world of feelings so deep and intense that they can overpower the intellect and the body as well as alter behavior. Freud stressed the importance of instinctual forces in the development of the personality, emphasizing the role of the drives of sexuality (libido) and aggression. "The psychological theories which Freud developed were always physiologically oriented as far as it was possible for them to be so" (Brenner, 1974, p. 15). Although some psychodynamic theorists today dismiss Freud's emphasis on the primacy of sexuality and/or aggression in psychological development, the concept of the intensity of drives and feelings has been expanded and transposed to other areas of development, such as the innate drive for attachment. If looked at in this broader perspective, we can observe intense feelings become driving forces that fuel (with psychic energy) human motivation and behavior. Basch (1988) has referred to affect as *"the gateway to action"* (p. 65; italics added).

If a drive or need, such as sexuality or attachment, is not met by an external agency, for example, nurturance, love, or by the executor actions of the individual independently, the energies of drives or needs and their associated affects (feelings) seek gratification or satisfaction through substitute means.

A social work student was assigned the case of Joan, a young, unmarried, overwhelmed, and neglectful mother who took little interest in her child. The student built a positive relationship with Joan, connected her with appropriate community resources, enabled her to return to school, and helped her feel more competent. Joan continued to show no interest in her child and could not bond with her. She cognitively reexamined her life goals and felt it was in the baby's best interest as well as her own to give this child up for adoption. Shortly after the adoption was finalized, the woman became pregnant again.

We can hypothesize that Joan, deprived of adequate maternal nurturing herself, had a deep unmet need to be nurtured, to feel "full" and "not empty," and was seeking a special connectedness that she never experienced and did not know how to recreate. Her strong affective or drive-directed need to become pregnant again was stronger than her cognitive understanding of the present inappropriateness of motherhood for her. Joan's behaviors are familiar to child welfare workers who see mothers with similar attachment conflicts.

Freud analyzed childhood development in terms of age-related drives and the means of their gratification as playing a dominant role in the psychological development of the child. Every child, for example, passes through the *oral stage,* in which the needs for eating and sucking predominate and if these needs are not met, problems, such as thumb sucking or overeating, needing immediate gratification and becoming chronically dependent may develop and continue throughout life. Freud's "psychosexual drive theory synthesized the concept of children's erogenous zones as being associated with the kinds of relationships, attachments, symptoms, character traits, and psychological preoccupations they face at each stage of development" (Berzoff, 1996b, p. 29). The five developmental stages Freud discussed are the *oral phase* of infancy, the *anal phase* of toddlers, the *oedipal phase* of the preschool child, the *latency phase* of the school-age child, and the *genital phase* of adolescence, which are discussed in Chapters 9 and 10. The *id,* the repository of instinctual feelings, drives, and needs, is a dynamic force that presses to be discharged. The id does not concern itself with reality; timelessness, rulelessness, and a peremptory quality exists in the id. The id, however, does not exist in isolation but is part of a larger psychological system including the *ego* and the *superego,* postulated by *structural theory.*

Structural Theory

Structural theory explains how drives are expressed and mediated and how conflict between drives and expectations of the external world are resolved. Examining the Latin meanings of the three key mental structures we find the following: the id means "it," suggesting the primal, given engine of behavior; the ego means "I," suggesting the notion of the executive self; and the superego means "the higher ego." The id "comprises the psychic representatives of the drives, the ego consists of those functions which have to do with the individual's relation to his environment, and the superego comprises the moral precepts of our minds as well as our ideal aspirations" (Brenner, 1974, p. 35).

The ego and the id can have a cooperative relationship, as the ego deals with the environment "for the purpose of achieving a maximum of gratification or discharge for the id . . . the ego is the *executant* for the drives" (p. 37; italics in the original). However, the id, ego, and superego may come into conflict as a normal, manageable phenomenon or as a disruptive one.

If we reexamine the Anna O. case from this perspective, we can see that Anna's deep feelings related to her attachment to her father as well as conflict about nursing him might not have been acceptable to her superego (or conscience). The "war" between these segments of her psychic apparatus was too strong for the ego to mediate; the result was *symptom formation,* in which the conflict and the underlying wishes are expressed in a substitute (albeit uncomfortable and dysfunctional) manner. When some of her conflict is resolved through the "talking cure," the symptoms abate. In everyday life, we continually deal with conflicts between our wishes, our reality, and the "rules" we must live by; we usually handle these conflicts with the help of our *defense mechanisms,* which operate predominantly on an unconscious level. These are discussed later in this chapter.

Distinctive types of thought processes are associated with the id and the ego. *Primary process* thinking is associated with the id; *secondary process* thinking refers to the ego. In reading this book, you are engaging in structured secondary process thinking as you attempt to comprehend the ideas and to integrate your understanding with other learning and life experiences. Secondary process thinking is "ordinary, conscious thinking as we know it from introspection, that is, primarily verbal and following the usual laws of syntax and logic" (Brenner, 1974, p. 48). Primary process thinking relates to the id, and its representations are those of the instinctual life. Logic, the constraints of time, and the need for consistency are not relevant in primary process thought. Artists may gain inspiration for their painting through primary process mechanisms, but in order to execute the painting they must purposefully and coherently apply secondary thought processes to obtain the needed materials, decide on colors, brushes, composition, subject matter, and so on.

Primary thought processes are often manifested in serious mental illness in which a breakdown in formal thought processes and content and a serious break with reality take place. However, primary process thinking is not per se pathological. Developmentally it tends to color the thinking of young children. A schizophrenic patient may have no sense of time in a realistic sense, but this is also true of the young child. "It is several years before a child develops a sense of time, before there is anything comprehensible to him but the 'here and now'" (Brenner, 1974, p. 49). The presence of primary process thinking does not in itself indicate mental illness; "it is the dominance or exclusive operation of the primary process that constitutes an abnormality when it occurs in adult life" (p. 49). An excellent example of the pairing of both types of thinking is found in dreams, with daydreams as an intermediate form.

Dreams

The interpretation of dreams was and remains an essential part of the psychoanalytic process. Freud (1959) wrote that "psychoanalysis is founded upon the analysis of dreams; the interpretation of dreams is the most complete piece of work the young science has done up to the present" (p. 28). Dreams allow repressed thoughts and affects (in disguised form) into consciousness while in the dream state, as sleep tends to "produce a relative weakening of the defenses" (Brenner, 1974, p. 166) as well as a paralysis of action. Freud (1959) has described the state of sleep.

> We are not accustomed to expend much thought on the fact that every night human beings lay aside the garments they pull over their skin, and even also other objects which they use to supplement their bodily organs . . . for instance their spectacles, false hair or teeth, and so on. In addition to this, when they go to sleep they perform a perfectly analogous dismantling of their minds—they lay aside most of their mental acquisitions. . . . The feature characterizing the mind of a sleeping person is an almost complete withdrawal from the surrounding world and the cessation of all interest in it. (p. 28)

Dreams have both *latent* and *manifest* content. The manifest content is the story of the dream, those aspects that the dreamer may be able to recall. The latent content is the "unconscious thoughts and wishes which threaten to waken the dreamer" (Brenner, 1974, p. 150). The unconscious mental processes "by which the latent dream content is transformed into the manifest dream we call the *dream work*" (p. 150; italics in the original).

The following dream was related to me in a personal communication:

A young woman reported a dream in which she was putting her bicycle inside her coat (the manifest content). Upon awakening, she was quite puzzled by her actions in the dream. "But why my bicycle?" Suddenly, in a flash memory, she recalled that she used to refer to her bicycle as her "baby" (latent content). She realized that a meaning of the dream was that she was wishing for a baby *(dream work),* which she could acknowledge as a true desire.

In the following case, where play therapy was utilized with Brian, an eight-year-old boy, *dreams* and *fantasy* were significantly pertinent to the treatment (Barton and Marshall, 1986). The case, recorded by two social workers, emphasizes the impact of termination, which led to Bryan's revealing new material about past trauma, which he shared before "it was too late" to deal with it.

Brian's parents divorced when he was three; he remained with his mother under very chaotic and neglectful circumstances. His father, now remarried, was seeking legal custody of Brian. Brian was initially seen with "disturbances in sleeping, eating and toileting, excessive clinging, and distractibility at school" (Barton and Marshall, 1986, p. 141). Play therapy with Brian and family work with his father and stepmother were undertaken. A number of themes appeared in the early phase of Brian's treatment. These "involved fears of annihilation, abandonment, and the fusion of generational boundaries" (p. 142). Brian "was also concerned with issues of self esteem, his worth and integrity as an autonomous individual, and his believability" (p. 142).

> One extended fantasy involved Brian being pursued by a faceless man who pushed him off the Washington Monument into a pond of hungry sharks. When the President and a policeman appeared, they were more concerned with locating the culprit than with rescuing Brian. Brian was disinclined to draw their attention to him since "their backs are turned, they can't see me and they don't care anyway." (Barton and Marshall, 1986, p. 142)

Brian made very good progress during his eight months of treatment, and two months were used in preparation for termination. During the termination phase, Brian reported a bad dream that involved "a glove reaching up from the bed and pulling him into a black, bottomless hole. . . . Brian associated to times in his biological mother's household when he had experienced the same nightmare" (Barton and Marshall, 1986, p. 144). Brian's play enactments and discussion of more fantasy material led to the revelation of his sexual abuse by his mother, her boyfriend, and "all former household members" (p. 145). In the following passage, veiled hints of abuse are symbolically represented in the fantasy material.

> Utilizing anatomically correct dolls . . . the boyfriend was described [by Brian] as "gay" and was manipulated to make seductive-assaultive gestures in attempts to quiet the frightened boy doll. . . . The adult male doll, dressed in women's underwear, chased the boy doll out the window into a tree, from which the adult fell into a pond of hungry

dolphins, and was jailed. . . . With a pair of scissors [Brian] made stabbing motions at the genitalia of the adult male doll, then at his own genitals. Finally, he cut a lock of his own hair, then the corners of a calendar on which [his therapist] had marked the date of their last session.

Th[is] fantasy . . . was a symbolic reformulation of Brian's fantasy with the Washington monument and the sharks. This time, however, anger was directed not toward the self, but more appropriately toward the object of his anxiety: the boyfriend was victimized and punished. . . . In addition, Brian's subliminal manipulation of the scissors was interpreted . . . as the signs and symptoms of the type of unresolved intrapsychic conflict which is typical of sexual abuse. (Barton and Marshall, 1986, pp. 144-145)

The clinician's knowledge of Freud's contributions led to the understanding of the anxiety, unconscious fantasy, symbolic content of dreams, and internalization of guilt (blaming the self), which were all present in this case. The utilization of these fantasies within the context of Brian's life led the clinician to help Brian disclose the abuse and helped him and his father to cope with the trauma.

The interpretation of dreams remains an important component of psychoanalysis and psychodynamically oriented work today, even though various theoretical schools emphasize different meanings and interpretations; object relations therapists emphasize the dreamer's interpersonal world, and self psychologists focus on the patient's struggle to attain a cohesive self (Alperin, 2004). Constructivists are interested in the dream narratives, the meanings attributed to them by the dreamers, and the means by which dreams facilitate patients' "attunement to their inner experience[s]" (Mahoney, 2003, p. 138). Alperin (2004) suggests that all schools of thought have something to contribute to dream analysis, and there should be an "integrated" approach, which would be "consistent with the sciences emphasizing many layers and complex causes and with what we know about the psyche— that it is multisided, multilayered, and multidetermined" (Lippman, 2000) (p. 467).

In the following illustration, a young man's attempt to reconstruct his past history and identity was aided through his recurrent childhood dreams. John was one of a group of six orphaned children from the Terezin, Czechoslovakia, concentration camp in World War II, who were brought to England and received special group care at Bulldogs Bank, under the auspices of Anna Freud and the Dann sisters. These (unrelated) children, about three years of age when they arrived, had lived for approximately two years "as a peer group in an atmosphere of ongoing terror and loss at Terezin, where they were cared for at starvation-level circumstances" (Downey, 2001, p. 42).

John stayed for a year at Bulldog Banks and was then adopted by an English family; this family was nurturing, but adamantly refused to tell him anything of his adoption or his past life. He "was amnesic for Terezin," could remember little of events before his adoption, but had "vague memories of living with a group of children" (Downey, 2001, p. 58).

John had two recurrent dreams after his adoption. "In one repeated dream he is in a big house near a racetrack. The house is surrounded by tall trees. In the second dream he is looking down on the hills and 'pretty lights'" (Downey, 2001, p. 58). His adoptive mother was not interested in his dreams, "telling him to forget about them, that everyone had such meaningless dreams!" (p. 58). However, as he grew older, he became active in learning his history, discovered his former name, his mother's name, where she was buried, learned about Terezin, and that he had lived in Lingfield, from where he was adopted.

> He traveled to Lingfield, which is the site of a racetrack, and found the house in his first dream. . . . He soon confirmed that the beautiful dream of looking down at the lights captured quite specifically the evening view from Bulldogs Bank, where he had spent such a momentous year. (Downey, 2001, p. 59)

Today, some clinicians work actively with dreams; others dismiss them as irrelevant and/or unscientific (they are not "observable" behaviors). Some practitioners with a strong biological orientation assert that dreams are only a manifestation of REM brain activity found in sleep and have no other meaning. Some psychodynamically trained clinicians use the method of *free association* to understand the unconscious meaning of dreams; other clinicians may use dream interpretation in a modified form.

Sackheim (1974), a social worker, advocates the use of dreams in casework treatment, noting that "like any other life experience, they admit of interpretation on varying levels" (p. 29). Catalano (1990) incorporates children's dreams in his clinical social work practice. Research has provided "insight into the dreams of children and adolescents with emotional disturbances and how they differ from those without such disturbances. . . . Dreams provide a wealth of useful material about the issues, feelings, and memories most important to the child" (p. 139). Goelitz (2001), a social worker, found that cancer patients, through discussion of their dreams, became more attuned to their feelings and could discuss their anxieties and fears of death more openly; dream work has value for patients with other life-threatening illnesses such as AIDS, in trauma work, as well as in other clinical situations.

Dreams, myths, spirituality, and storytelling are intertwined and play a significant role in many cultures. In the Native American Blackfeet tribe in Montana, the very first of the highly significant mythical Napi stories is about "the power of dreams" with which Napi (also called Old Man) endowed the Blackfeet. These dreams were revered and the people "would follow the advice they saw in their dreams" (Carbaugh, 2001, p. 117); dreams and sleep can "empower one with new insight and energy" (p. 118).

There is a Native American practice involving the "'dreamcatcher' [which] is hung above the bed of a sleeping child (Osofsky, 1992)" (Borenstein, 2003, p. 250).

> This small hoop is woven through the center in the manner of a spiderweb and then decorated. According to Native American legends, the dreamcatcher keeps the child safe. It acts as a filter, diverting the bad dreams while allowing only the good dreams to enter the child's world. (Borenstein, 2003, p. 250)

Dreams have been a source of wonder, enlightenment, and mystery over the ages; but it was Freud who developed the psychodynamic and symbolic understanding of dreams, and applied this to psychoanalysis.

While Freud continued to focus on unconscious libidinous processes, he also became interested in the functions of the ego, and discussed the significance of "object relations in *The Ego and the Id* (Freud, 1923)" (Brandell, 2004, p. 22). This turning point in psychoanalysis "paved the way for the gradual emergence and more systematic development of a general psychology of the ego," with a widening interest in the "sociocultural context" (p. 44). Two major contributors to this new development were Anna Freud and Heinz Hartmann.

EGO PSYCHOLOGY

Anna Freud

Anna Freud, the daughter of Sigmund Freud, was one of his closest collaborators; remaining faithful to the basic tenets of psychoanalytic thought, she also evolved along her own path, and was a major figure in developing child psychoanalysis. Two of her major works are *The Ego and Mechanisms of Defense* (1936), and *Normality and Pathology in Childhood* (1965). She was one of the three founding editors of *The Psychoanalytic Study of the Child.*

Anna Freud, who trained initially as a teacher, had a comprehensive view of the child's involvement with school, with parents, and significant others in their lives. She was involved with the Edith Jackson nursery, working with "Vienna's poorest (often homeless) families and young children. . . . She always gave great weight to the capacity of the child's ego to benefit from caregivers, teachers, and peers and never recommended child analysis as appropriate for everybody" (Colonna, 2001, p. 10).

Anna Freud and her father fled from Vienna to England as the Nazis came to power, and during World War II, Anna and her colleague, Dorothy Burlingame, directed nurseries for children who were evacuated from their London homes and separated from their parents. Their developing insights about attachment and loss led to revisions in then-current theory, as well as modifications in the care of these children (Young-Bruehl, 1988).

The concept of *developmental lines* in children is considered one of Anna Freud's finest contributions; she asserted that the goals of child analysis was "the return [of the child] to normal development" (Colonna, 2001, p. 11), rather than the removal of symptoms. She also asserted that severe disturbances in children did not necessarily result from very early mother-child relationships.

> She offered a great number of "developmental lines"—lines of *normal* development—along which and between which disturbances can occur. She argued that pathology is multiple, multilateral, taking forms in childhood and adulthood which are not necessarily directly or simply causally related or even similar. (Young-Bruehl, 1988, pp. 461-462)

Anna Freud's insights about developmental understanding have been debated within the field of psychoanalysis: Is not the goal of psychoanalysis (with both children and adults) the resolution of psychological conflicts, rather than promoting the resumption of psychological growth? Can these two aims be easily differentiated? Does psychotherapy incorporate both aims, and if so, to what extent is a "real," reparative relationship with the therapist an essential ingredient? Should the mother-infant interaction become the therapeutic model? The field of psychoanalysis is currently debating these vital and complex issues (Abrams, 2001), which are further addressed in the discussion of relational psychotherapy in Chapter 4.

Anna Freud worked with six children from the Terezin concentration camp at Bulldogs Bank, and although it incorporated psychoanalytic theory, milieu treatment, rather than psychoanalysis, was utilized primarily. The Freud-Dann (1951) paper describing this is titled: "An Experiment in

Group Upbringing" (Downey, 2001, p. 39). It "emphasizes the possibilities for the resumption of psychological growth through the provision of *a proper holding environment* rather than through the usual analytic mode of verbalization and interpretation" (p. 40; italics added). John (discussed above in terms of his dreams) and his peers depended on the group's identity and cohesion for their emotional survival. The group seemed to function in a "protean maternal fashion" (p. 44).

In fact, psychoanalysis or any form of individual psychotherapy would not have been possible when the Terezin children first came to Bulldog Banks, as they could not tolerate individual one-to-one intimacy with any adult. A major aim was to help the children reach the point where they could accept an individual relationship with an adult: "what could be done to reverse group process in a group that had ostensibly brought itself up" (Downey, 2001, p. 43)? Anna Freud's work with milieu treatment was a forerunner of later advances, such as residential treatment schools for children and therapeutic foster homes (Dowling, 2001).

In some ways, Anna Freud was an early object relations theorist, stressing the importance of children's relationships to their caregivers, teachers, or therapists, emphasizing the value of the child's "identification with a trusted adult . . . and . . . alliance with him . . ." (Neubauer, 2001, p. 24). However, Anna Freud also remained committed to the more orthodox analytic approach "in order to arrive at a more honest view of the *inner life*" (p. 24; italics added).

One of Anna Freud's lasting contributions to mental health training was her utilization of direct observations of children in a variety of settings, to enable trainees to

> develop a sense of the strength of . . . [children's] egos and their capacity to progress toward normality. She stressed that the observer needed time to learn to look and listen in a new way, regardless of any experience he or she might bring . . . she expanded her interests and activities into community outreaches that combined to form a picture of many aspects of development. These included observations in the baby clinic, toddler group, nursery school, and a school for blind and outreaches in the in-home care of families of the blind. These were important for the child analyst in learning to put himself into the skin of the child. (Colonna, 2001, p. 12)

Observations of children are discussed further, including the research of Margaret Mahler (Chapters 3 and 9) and of Daniel Stern (Chapter 9).

Observations and interviews with "normal" children and adults are recommended as learning exercises for readers of this text.

Anna Freud, during her long professional lifetime, contributed significantly to psychoanalysis and to the training of psychotherapists. She started and directed the Hampstead Clinic [now the Anna Freud Clinic] in London, which is a leading training and research center for child treatment, incorporating parent guidance and nursery school education. Her contributions, highly relevant to social work education and practice, include the development of play therapy, elaboration of the defense mechanisms, advocating therapeutic involvement with families, and offering insights into the impact of loss and separation. She strongly stressed the significance of the social milieu in work with children. One famous frequently told anecdote was her response to learning that a "harassed, frenetic mother" was applying for clinic service: "It is not quite clear yet whether the child needs analysis or the mother needs a housekeeper" (Young-Bruehl, 1988, p. 409).

Heinz Hartmann

Heinz Hartmann (1958), who was himself analyzed by Sigmund Freud, is considered the "father of ego psychology," developing and expanding the Freudian concept of the ego to focus on its nonpathological interaction with and adaptation to the external world as well as the internal realm. He defined adaptation as "primarily a reciprocal relationship between the organism and its environment" (p. 24).

Hartmann (1958) did not dispute the notion of the ego as a mediator of conflicts; however, his interest in development was broader than the study of intrapsychic conflict. He asserted that "not every adaptation to the environment, or every learning and maturation process, is a conflict" (p. 8). It was his proposal that "we adopt the provisional term *conflict-free ego sphere* for that ensemble of functions which at any given time exert their effects outside the region of mental conflicts" (pp. 8-9). Hartmann describes these maturational processes:

> I refer to the development *outside of conflict* of perception, intention, object comprehension, thinking, language, recall-phenomena, productivity, to the well-known phases of motor development, grasping, crawling, walking, and to the maturation and learning processes implicit in all these and many others. (Hartmann, 1958, p. 8)

These [autonomous] ego functions develop as they meet the "average expectable environmental conditions" (Hartmann, 1958, p. 46) and require such an environment to thrive. This is analogous to the development of a flower. Assuming that the seeds are "good" and not "damaged," a plant will grow, develop roots, buds, flower, and so on, but only if the environmental conditions of soil, sunshine, and water are propitious. However, when "the average expectable environment" is not present, as when an infant raised in an orphanage does not receive adequate nurturing, the ego apparatuses will not mature; developmental landmarks of walking, language, logical thought, and so on might be extremely delayed and distorted.

The notion of the ego embodies the capacity to integrate and synthesize external and internal reality, "past and present," and ideas and feelings (Vaillant, 1993, p. 7). The ego encompasses adaptation, mental synthesis, defensive operations, and "adult development and creativity" (p. 8). Erik Erikson (1963) stressed the importance of mastery of developmental stages in both childhood and adulthood to produce ongoing ego growth, and also emphasized the development of identity; his theories are discussed in Chapters 9, 10, and 11.

The primary ego functions are discussed in detail now, followed by a section on ego defenses.

Ego Functions

Classifications of ego functions vary from author to author; Upham's (1973) classification of seven ego functions is used in this discussion:

1. Perception
2. The cognitive functions
3. The management of needs and feelings
4. The management of object relationships
5. The executive function
6. The integrative function
7. Ego identity

In practice, it is important to assess the *baseline* of a given ego function, which means looking at the person's past attainment of a specific function before the present evaluation.

The ego is more than the summation of these seven functions; it has "successfully accomplished its organizing and synthesizing functions when individuals experience themselves as coherent, functional human beings with an enduring sense of personal identity" (Schamess, 1996, p. 70). Individuals can have uneven patterns of ego functioning, in which one ego function—for instance, perception—may be well developed, whereas identity formation might be shaky. "A working understanding of ego functions is enormously helpful both in evaluating client's strengths and weaknesses, and in predicting how they are likely to respond to different therapeutic interventions" (p. 71).

Perception

Outer perception is concerned with the ability to perceive the world in a realistic manner; *inner perception* refers to the capacity to turn attention inward and to observe one's feelings and motivations (Upham, 1973).

Outer perception. People have attained good outer perception when they are able to orient themselves to "reality," to the "social world" surrounding them, especially to "human relationships," and can view their concerns, circumstances, and the people they relate to "in a reasonably realistic way without significant distortion" (Upham, 1973, p. 123). *Reality testing* "differentiates cues coming from within from those which come from external reality. It prevents assigning [one's] own ideas and feelings to sources outside of [one's] self" (p. 122). If a man will not enter a store because he is convinced everyone inside is spying on him, we might speculate that he has a serious problem with reality testing (unless he is indeed under surveillance).

A client, Ms. O'Toole, had difficulty distinguishing between her internal feelings and wishes, on one hand, and reality, on the other.

Ms. O'Toole told her therapist that she had killed her neighbor. She hated this man who was very mean and wished he would die. Shortly afterward, he died; she was convinced she had murdered him because of her strong wishes. Her therapist, Mrs. Wendover said, "Suppose I did not feel like coming to work today and wished it would snow. If it started to snow, did I do that?" Ms. O'Toole looked at her therapist, smiled, and said: "Oh, you are funny, Mrs. Wendover." The therapist was explicitly using the function of reality testing to help Ms. O'Toole realize that she was not omnipotent enough to cause her neighbor's death through her thoughts.

It is not uncommon for people to feel guilty about bad wishes toward others that later actually happen in some independent way, but it is less common for individuals to be convinced that they were perpetrators of this reality. This is an example of *magical thinking,* which Piaget (Elkind, 1981) finds universally present in early childhood, but which is largely modified in essentially normal individuals by continual retesting of reality. Persistence of fixed magical thinking along especially absurd lines is characteristic of abnormal mental states.

Although perhaps not manifesting serious difficulties with reality testing, people can have problems with outer perception, sometimes *chronic,* sometimes *situational.* Witnesses to a car accident might report differing perceptions of what happened, distorted by their anxiety. Family members involved in conflict might misperceive each other's intentions or messages.

Sarah was expressing anger with her husband because of his inattentiveness. She thought that he was being particularly unfair because he would not let her buy a new pair of shoes. Her therapist asked if she had told him she wanted new shoes. Oh, no, she replied, he should have known—he should have asked!

Sarah expected her husband to be able to read her mind—another form of primitive or magical thinking.

Connoisseurs of detective literature realize the importance of gathering the "facts"—the relevant descriptive details of interactions and time sequences—rather than suppositions that are then regarded as facts. Helping clients observe more objectively and analyze their own interactions can facilitate their capacity for outer perception.

Clinicians must distinguish their own perceptions, prejudices, and biases, which may color their assessment of the client's perceptions, from ascertainable facts. Cultural contexts should likewise be considered, as clients may perceive certain events and relationships in ways shaped by their culture and that may not be readily understood by a clinician from another culture.

Inner perception. Inner perception enables people to observe and reflect on themselves and their feelings, as well as on "the related awareness of the effect of their own urges, feelings, and activities on other persons" (Upham, 1973, p. 122). Clients may develop increased self-awareness or inner perception through the therapeutic process.

The attainment of self-awareness is a highly valued goal for social work students. Jane, an MSW student, for example, realized through supervisory discussion that she tended to "push" her client away because she felt threatened by the hostile feelings the client expressed toward her. With this insight Jane revealed a good capacity for inner perception (and, correspondingly, an ability to utilize social work training).

Jessica told her therapist that a friend who had moved to Europe visited her after many years of absence. After several happy days together, the friend returned to Europe, and Jessica felt sad and cried, not knowing when she would see her friend again. At the same time, Jessica was joyful as she told of her sadness, because she had experienced her sadness; in the past, she would not have known she was sad—a black wave of depression would have descended upon her instead.

The Cognitive Functions

Cognitive functions encompass capacities such as thinking, remembering, using language, planning, problem solving, and making judgments.

A person's baseline of good cognitive functioning may be temporarily diminished due to extreme stress, serious physical illness, or emotional turmoil. "Clinicians base their assessment of cognitive capacity: (1) on the client's ability to present a clear and coherent picture of his difficulty and to respond appropriately to the practitioner's verbal communication, and (2) on evidences of previous levels of development" (Upham, 1973, p. 128).

Alzheimer's disease, affecting older adults, seriously impairs memory and leads to a general decline of cognitive functions. Strokes can have a major impact on cognitive functioning, destroying centers of the brain involved with thinking, information processing, and communicating. Severe alcoholism can permanently damage brain tissue.

People with mental retardation may have cognitive deficits, but, on the other hand, their severely "limited understanding and ability to communicate" may be further aggravated "by the widespread under-estimation by others of their capacity to learn and to make choices and participate in decision making" (Mittler, 1992, p. 163).

People with various problems, including attention deficit disorder, learning disabilities, or chronic dependent characerological issues may have difficulty thinking through situations and understanding both causes and effects of behavior and may not have acquired successful problem solving techniques. They may need help thinking through problems and solutions to them.

Some people persistently use poor judgment in situations, as we can observe in the following account of Mr. Morgan.

Mr. Morgan had not been employed for a year and was eager to obtain a job offered to him. He arrived half an hour late for his interview because he stopped to buy some lottery tickets and, although there was a line, he thought that if he could win the lottery, a lot of his problems would be solved. When he was questioned about being late, he insulted the interviewer because he felt the man had no right to question him about his use of time. He launched into a tirade about the importance of lottery tickets and how winning one was a much better way of living than sweating over a bum forty-hour-a-week job with lousy pay. Mr. Morgan did not receive this position and complained to his friends about the injustices of the world. Mr. Morgan has an impaired capacity to assess cause and effect and to use sound judgment. He has limited capacity for inner perception in terms of self-reflection and seeing his effect on others.

Cognitive functions are typically impaired and distorted in psychotic states. A major diagnostic sign of schizophrenia is a thought disorder, a gross impairment in thinking capacity. Patients may exhibit problems in their *content of thought* (their thoughts and ideas) and in their thought process (or forms and coherence of thought). A man with a delusion that he is Napoleon is having a problem in his content of thought; if challenged he may also demonstrate illogic in arguing the basis for this belief. If he has racing thoughts or thought blocking, he would be having difficulty with the process of thought (Sadock and Sadock, 2003).

Basic logic is regularly impaired by the schizophrenic process; the individual suffering from schizophrenia tends to regress to a lower level of logicality. "Schizophrenic cognition in some aspects corresponds to the primary process of the Freudian school" (Arieti, 1974, p. 571). The logic often used is "paleologic, based on a principle enunciated by von Domarus" (p. 574). For instance, a patient might argue thus: "All deer are swift. All marathon runners are swift. Therefore, all deer are marathon runners." This is termed identification through the predicate (which refers to finding similarities in the characteristics of the subject). *"Whereas the normal person accepts identity only upon the basis of identical subjects, the paleologician accepts identity based upon identical predicates"* (Arieti, 1974, p. 574; italics in the original). By applying von Domarus's principle, "even bizarre and complex schizophrenic delusions can be interpreted" (p. 575). In other words, meaning and "logic" exist beneath thought processes that, on the surface, appear totally meaningless and illogical.

People may have a basic capacity for cognitive functioning but show faulty reasoning, such as having a self-defeating way of thinking of themselves or reasoning about certain emotionally charged situations in nonproductive ways. Cognitive therapy (discussed in Chapter 3) was developed as a method for correcting the faulty thinking that may be the basis for dysfunctional attitudes, feeling states, and behavior (Beck, 1976).

In summation, assessment of cognitive functioning can guide a therapist in deciding what level of treatment might be appropriate and which limitations in thinking, appraising, and judging must be taken into account, or which can possibly be strengthened. Clinicians should consider differences in education, culture, and language in appraising a person's cognitive functioning.

Management of Needs and Feelings

Managing one's needs and feelings involves the capacity to recognize what one is feeling and to recognize and accept one's emotional needs while meeting these needs in a realistic and socially appropriate way. It "include[s] the capacity to tolerate frustration, to postpone gratification, to find substitute gratifications, to find detour routes to satisfaction when a given route is blocked, to reconcile and synthesize conflicting needs, feelings, or aims, and to handle related feelings" (Upham, 1973, p. 131). In discussing Mrs. Billings in Chapter 1, we noted that anhedonia, the inability to experience pleasure, was one of her depressive symptoms, as well as an entrenched personality feature. Mrs. Billings had a severe inhibition of both aggressive and pleasurable feelings, and an abundance of superego guilt. This suggests major disturbances in the management of needs and feelings.

In discussing the related concept of *autonomous gratification,* Arieti and Bemporad (1978) refer to people's ability to obtain "self-esteem or pleasure through their own efforts" (p. 166). For example, when a client spoke of her delight in drinking a cup of coffee each morning at the window while she watched the boats glide past on the water, she demonstrated her love of life and her capacity for *autonomous gratification.* Arieti and Bemporad assert that the inability to experience this gratification as well as the driven need to gain self-esteem through the approval of others (the dominant other) is related to the development of the depressive state, as seen in their case illustration in the following:

> Nancy, a highly successful executive who began psychotherapy after years of visiting internists with vague pains and insomnia, exemplified this fear of autonomous gratification. Although she . . . made an attractive salary, she could not bring herself to furnish her apartment comfortably or live in a manner commensurate with her income. She considered anything spent on herself to be a shameful extravagance, but would buy inordinately expensive gifts for her parents. Nancy was equally self-sacrificing with her free time and canceled social engagements if her boss asked her to work late or if her father asked to see her. In actuality Nancy was unable to enjoy a social evening unless she could somehow relate it to her work. . . . She found it difficult to date and dreaded sexual confrontation. . . . Eventually Nancy confessed that even her work, which seemed to be her major concern in life, brought her no pleasure in itself but only served as a means of pleasing her boss. Whenever she gained recognition from him or when she was praised by her father, Nancy become ecstatic with a great sense of well-being and felt vibrant and alive. (Arieti and Bemporad, 1978, p. 166)

Related to autonomous gratification is the capacity to *self-soothe:* to be able to console or comfort oneself not only when life is comfortable, but during times of stress as well, such as being good to oneself or permitting oneself to feel better. Listening to music, painting, gardening, and taking a warm bath are examples of what some people do to soothe themselves when they are under stress.

Some choose maladaptive methods of self-soothing, such as excessive drinking. Others, including people with borderline personalities who may not have the capacity to self-soothe, need selfobjects (dependence on others to meet unmet emotional needs) to provide this relief (Adler, 1985). When this is not available, they are "faced with the ultimate threat of disintegrative annihilation of the self" (p. 34).

Many people, including those with borderline personalities, may have difficulty controlling and directing their feelings in adaptive ways. They may have poor impulse control, express anger explosively, or act-out sexually. Freud commented that "the postponement of gratification is the hallmark of maturity" (Vaillant, 1993, p. 70).

In assessing the baseline of impulse control, we explore whether chronic problems have been present (such as a pattern of violence or perpetrating sexual abuse) or a new behavior, perhaps reactive to situational stress, has appeared. People may lose control when intoxicated; sometimes loss of control may be related to a neurological disorder. The assessment of impulse control is part of the mental status exam determining the client's sense of social appropriateness and possible dangerousness (including suicidal impulses) (Sadock and Sadock, 2003). Cognitive disturbances, psychoses, and chronic characterological defects may impair impulse control, which may be assessed in the interview from current history and observed behavior.

People can become flooded with feelings of anxiety that they are unable to control—sometimes in response to a crisis, sometimes as part of an ongoing anxiety state, such as panic disorders, in which they can temporarily be so overcome with anxiety that they may feel unable to function.

The Management of Object Relationships

The individual's capacity to relate to others and the quality and patterns of these relationships are important aspects of ego functioning. "It is the single most important function of the ego because it enables the child to become human" (Upham, 1973, p. 139). Noam and Fischer (1996) comment that "people are fundamentally social, and relationships . . . especially close ones, form an essential foundation for the development of human beings, molding each person's mind and behavior" (p. ix). The importance of early relationships for attachment and trust has been widely recognized (Bowlby, 1988; Kohut, 1971; Mahler, Pine, and Bergman, 1975; Mitchell, 1988;

Winnicott, 1965), although some disagreement exists about how permanent the effects of these early interactions are, and how later events and relationships may modify early patterns. Mitchell (1988) argues for the importance of understanding past experiences not because "the past lies concealed within or beneath the present, but because understanding *the past provides clues to deciphering how and why the present is being approached and shaped the way it is*" (p. 149; italics added).

Many writers, particularly those with a psychodynamic orientation, stress the importance of parental nurturance, warmth, acceptance, the development of secure attachment, and the provision of a "holding environment" (Winnicott, 1965) for the development of good adaptation and mental health. The ego functions will flourish in the "average expectable environment" (Hartmann, 1958). However, growth and development are not without conflict even under optimal conditions. Normal conflict is inherent in separation and individuation (Mahler, Pine, and Bergman, 1975), since, as Mitchell (1988) asserts, "being a self with others entails a constant dialectic between attachment and self-definition, between connection and differentiation, a continual negotiation between one's wishes and will and the wishes and will of others" (Mitchell, 1988, p. 149).

Relationships within the family and with others can be a source of great distress (Noam and Fischer, 1996). "The most extreme example . . . is maltreatment, including the injuries of physical abuse and the boundary transgressions of sexual abuse. . . . Developmental consequences can be devastating" (p. xii). Daily events much less conspicuously severe than these can also produce serious consequences. "It is the day-to-day conflicts and small abandonments, the chronic sense of not being listened to that often create long-lasting effects" (p. xii).

Object relations theory, to which we shall return in the next chapter, offers many insights into the development and complexity of human relationships. Cultural factors can also affect patterns of relationships.

Executive Functioning

The executive function of the ego involves the ability to carry out everyday goal-directed activities. "This function makes it possible to decide and to act effectively and in ways which demonstrate social competence" (Upham, 1973, p. 142). Social workers may assess the executive functioning of clients to determine whether they can care for themselves or their families. For example, an elderly woman, living alone, may at times appear confused but upon assessment is found to be capable of shopping, cooking, and caring for herself and her apartment. Her executive functioning appears adequate to warrant her living independently without the need for protective services, although at a later date she may consider assisted living arrangements.

A person with a baseline of excellent executive functioning may be temporarily incapacitated owing to illness or extreme stress. "Anxiety caused by stress, trauma, or hopelessness and discouragement may interfere with the client's use of previously adequate patterning of executant ability. He may seem immobilized" (Upham, 1973, p. 144). On the other hand, some clients may have a history of poor executive functioning, such as the schizophrenic patient who may need long-term external supports, including a day program and job training, to support executive functioning. A person with temporarily impaired executive functioning due to anxiety or stress may also need some type of external supports, although probably only on a short-term basis.

Overwhelmed parents, unable to cope adequately with the needs of their children, may be responsive to supportive services offered (which may be thought of acting as auxiliary executive ego functions).

Mrs. Kramer, an African-American woman, lived on the fifteenth floor of a housing project with her husband and ten children. Overwhelmed by life and her large family, she rarely went outside as she had no carriage for the baby, and taking her family downstairs in the elevator was too stressful. Children ran pell-mell over the small apartment; little goal-directed activity or play material existed. The children were all well fed, adequately clothed, and attended school, and no evidence existed of either physical abuse or serious neglect.

Mrs. Kramer was very responsive to the supportive services offered by a social worker and a homemaker. The homemaker did not "take over" and do things for her, but involved her in working out a realistic schedule and engaging in household activities together. The older children were enrolled in after-school activities, the younger ones in preschool programs. Mrs. Kramer began to go outside. When Mrs. Kramer gave birth to her eleventh child, she decided to have a tubal ligation. When the case was terminated, Mrs. Kramer and her family had achieved an overall higher level of executive functioning.

The Integrative Function

The active but often unnoticed process of integration occurs when social work students apply classroom learning when working with clients. Integration is the "act of bringing together the parts into an integral whole. . . . The singleness of individual parts remains a characteristic of the mind during the greater part of the infantile period. . . . Gradually . . . the individual parts begin to act in cooperation with one another. It is the harmonizing of separate parts that is called integration" (Campbell, 1989, p. 377). The ability to "learn and to integrate new patterns into ego functioning exemplifies the integrative or synthetic function" (Upham, 1973, p. 146). The capacity to *integrate* implies that a person can "flexibly learn and adaptively change his behavior patterns to fit reality. He can then integrate these patterns into his total functioning" (p. 147).

Each social work student usually finds that his or her ways of intervening with people are modified gradually, and a professional self evolves, without the individual necessarily realizing that his or her integrative capacity has been developing. A student, for example, may initially react to a client's acting-out behavior with anger, but gradually develops a deeper understanding of the sources of the client's anger as well as a greater responsiveness to the client's feelings.

The capacity for integration underlies a person's ability to utilize therapy for gaining insight and learning new coping skills. Some clients may show good intellectual understanding of their issues but lack the integrative capacity to translate their understanding into change. Others may appear to be making no changes but, through a slow process, often imperceptible, suddenly feel "everything is coming together." Integration is an elusive process.

Ann, a first year MSW student, was the volunteer subject of a study in which her learning and professional development were examined over the course of her first year of graduate social work school. One of the goals of the study was to gain a deeper understanding of the factors that contributed to her learning.

> One day in February, Ann came into my office with a good deal of animation and buoyancy. All seemed to be gong well: "Things are looking up . . . I received my grades and I have three A's . . . I feel better about myself . . . about school . . . about my placement. . . . Education can be fun!" Leaning forward expectantly, I asked: "What is making it work? What is happening?" And Ann answered: "I don't know!" . . . And yet, perhaps this very lack of clarity was indeed quite profound! Because what Ann was reporting was the experience of *integration,* and indeed, true integration is often so profound that it leaves the person with a sense of the "inexplicable." (Urdang, 1974, p. 94; italics in the original)

Ego Identity

Ego identity encompasses the development of a sense of self, self-esteem, sexual identity, and physical identity (including such attributes as "beauty" or "disability") and may also contain elements of religious, cultural, racial, professional, and social group identities. The development of identity gives us our sense of not only "who we are, but *that* we are" (Mahler, Pine, and Bergman, 1975, p. 8; italics added).

Object relations theory and self psychology stress the deeper-lying structure of self-identity, the vicissitudes of its development, and the attainment of self-cohesion. Upham (1973) asserts that "through the sense of identity, the individual integrates all of his ego functioning and achieves a feeling of wholeness and relatedness, both within himself and in respect to his place in society" (p. 148).

By examining the baseline of a person's sense of identity, we can begin to determine whether we are looking at a person with a long-standing stable pattern of self-identity who has currently regressed, or whether a chronically unstable pattern is the case. Many types of traumatic experiences "may disturb a previously well-formed identity" (Upham, 1973, p. 150). Certain losses, such as going through an unwanted divorce or living in a dysfunctional relationship, can affect one's sense of identity. "Loss of a sexual organ or bodily part changes body and self-image from intact and reliable to damaged and unreliable" (p. 150).

Members of minorities may continually experience discrimination and rejection to the degree that "their sense of self worth is more or less constantly assaulted . . . there is . . . cumulative impact of chronic narcissistic injury caused by poverty, emotional neglect, environmental violence, and inferior status in society" (Pérez Foster, Moskowitz, and Javier, 1996, p. xv).

A strong relationship exists between ego identity and the development of object relationships, as the sense of self develops in relation to the nurturing received and "messages" conveyed about self that come from the family and other significant others. Children must separate from but concurrently remain attached to the family and distinguish themselves as separate from others. Some may never fully develop a sense of an autonomous self but remain perpetually dependent on another (sometimes termed the dominant other or selfobject) for self-esteem needs.

People with a strong sense of ego identity can differentiate themselves from others, and therefore are said to have good ego boundaries. They can feel they are separate from another in the sense of being a distinct personality as opposed to merging with another—that is, being lost as a separate individual or, to use earlier terminology, be "swallowed up" by the other. People with distinct and stable ego boundaries can tell the difference between what is "inside" and what is "outside" themselves and can differentiate what they feel from what others are feeling.

Mark Vonnegut (1975) experienced a severe schizophrenic episode after his graduation from Swarthmore College and his move to a commune in British Columbia. After his recovery, he wrote an insightful autobiography describing his experiences with this illness. Slipping into a psychotic world was very frightening; his sense of reality as well as his sense of self became very confused, diffuse, and unreliable. He wondered whether a part of him was attempting to hypnotize himself day and night by repeating the idiosyncratic phrase: "Is the tea in the tongue or in the leaves?" The boundaries between his self and others were so porous that he feared that others would go down into his psychosis with him. Speaking to his friend Simon, he said: "Sometimes I think I'm being hypnotized by compost. . . . I guess I'm afraid of losing control somehow and running amuck and so *if you could hypnotize me then you could control me and everything would be all right*" (Vonnegut, 1975, p. 80; italics added).

Fluidity of identity boundaries can be a normal developmental phenomenon and challenge as well. Social work students may themselves face many professional boundary issues in their work with clients. Foster children may wish the clinician to become a replacement for their parents; but clinicians cannot simply adopt them or take them home. The professional-client boundary must be clear.

In an assessment of ego boundaries, a cultural perspective must be taken, as the processes and parameters of the delineation of appropriate boundaries and parental management of separation-individuation issues may vary among cultural groups.

Before leaving the subject of ego functioning, I will add two related concepts to the discussion: (1) strengths and competence and (2) the superego and moral development.

Competence

Competence and mastery refer to a person's capacity to deal effectively with life and to experience a sense of accomplishment. White and Allport (Maluccio, 1980) stress the motivational importance of competence that "is an important force in human behavior" (p. 285). In White's formulation, the major ingredients of competence are "self-confidence, ability to make decisions, and trusting one's judgment. The ego is strengthened through the cumulative experience of producing desired effects upon one's surroundings" (p. 284). Saleebey's (2001) strengths perspective emphasizes supporting clients' strengths to promote their feelings of competence.

A child gains satisfaction from building a structure of blocks; a student is pleased with himself for passing a difficult examination; a woman is proud that she now has mastered the skills of driving—all are examples of the achievement of competence.

Clinical social workers aim to help clients gain greater competence in social functioning as well as to help them enjoy their achievements with enhanced perceptions of themselves as competent, adequate, and effective. A variety of therapeutic interventions, including environmental modifications, are used to achieve this; adjusting the environment can help people gain a sense of competence. For instance, providing wheelchair access can increase social participation; special education provides children with education appropriate to their needs. The ecological perspective stresses competence and goodness-of-fit between the person and the environment.

Linda Valli attended weekly psychotherapy sessions for anxiety and low self-esteem. In this encounter, her determination, recognized by the clinician, led Linda to discuss her competency further.

Linda commented that she was feeling better and making an effort to face herself more. She drove to the clinic (driving was initially anxiety provoking), deciding that "the dependency would make it worse." She also went to a large party on Saturday and stayed after experiencing some initial anxiety, which disappeared in half an hour. When the therapist commented that Linda's actions demonstrated a lot of determination, she agreed and said that she had been determined to put herself through culinary school and had accomplished this. She worked nights to support herself through school.

Agency

Linda, although shy and fearful, was determined, had strong motivation to get better, and was actively involved in treatment. She had a good sense of *agency,* which refers to *self-direction and will,* an important concept that has been a source of controversy in the psychotherapy field (Mitchell, 1988). To what extent do people have the ability to take control of their lives, or are they dominated by unconscious drives and feelings? How do we understand the development of characteristics such as persistence, courage, motivation, the assumption of responsibility for one's actions, and the assumption of active involvement in life? Mitchell (1988) has suggested that we are actively involved in the creation of our world; "the analysand is not just the fly caught in the web, but is the spider, the designer of the web as well" (p. 257).

Agency and meaning-making are important aspects of constructivism (Mahoney, 2003), and the life course perspective (Hutchison, 2005). The children of Terezin "possessed the ego resiliency and behavioral determination of survivors. . . . In contemporary terms they may be viewed, yet again, as agent vis-à-vis mother or world rather than as merely passive recipients or victims of fate" (Downey, 2001, p. 47). Agency and its role in the development of resilience are discussed further in Chapter 4.

Developing ego strengths is one aspect of a general process that includes moral development as a component task (Vaillant, 1993, p. 116).

Moral Development

Superego and moral development refer to the formation of a conscience, that is, the inner voice that reflects a sense of what is right and what is wrong and the development of values; the "core of moral character lies in the capacity to identify with another human being . . . to become able to empathize with other persons, and to feel remorse for transgressions against others" (Upham, 1973, p. 152). Freud introduced the concept of the ego ideal, which represents "those standards of behavior toward which we aspire" (Nemiah, 1961, p. 37) and reflects positive, approving aspects of the superego, while the conscience reflects more the prohibitions of the superego, its negative or critical aspects.

An important distinction exists between guilt and shame. Guilt is concerned with internal psychological conflict and is thus an attitude of the self toward the self. For example, Lewis Carroll was evidently tormented with brooding guilt as he struggled with his sexual attraction to prepubescent girls (Cohen, 1996).

Shame, on the other hand, is concerned more with how we feel others are perceiving us—whether we will lose face because of our actions. "Shame implies the failure of the ego to live up to an ego ideal and can result in the loss of self-esteem and depression . . . [it] contrasts with guilt, which is a transgression of the ego that conflicts with the superego" (Tang, 1997, p. 335). In Western or American culture, people might feel shame when being fired (or even "downsized") from a job, not graduating on time, or having a physically handicapped or mentally ill relative. In China, which "values relationships above all else, it is not surprising that shame plays a more important role in shaping a child than guilt" (p. 335). People often try to defend themselves from the painful feelings of guilt and shame.

Vaillant (1993) observed that the ego's "wisdom also encompasses defense" (p. 8).

Ego Defenses

Defenses are normal, healthy, and necessary for everyday functioning, protecting the self (ego) from experiencing anxiety and other forms of inner tension. The "defenses—like . . . immune mechanisms—protect us by providing a variety of illusions to filter pain and to allow self-soothing" (Vaillant, 1993, p. 1).

Ego defenses were first discussed by Freud, then elaborated by Anna Freud, and later expanded by object relations theorists. Freud's model of defenses stressed internal drives and feelings, seeking outlets in action, which the ego had to regulate and control. However, this model has subsequently been expanded to include the impact of outside forces and relationships that a person may need to defend against. The external as well as the internal may be perceived as threatening. "Thus the ego must control . . . desire, conscience, people, and reality" (Vaillant, 1993, p. 7).

Individuals utilize most defenses over the course of a lifetime. A key issue in clinical assessment is the extent to which the defenses control or dominate a person's ego functioning, producing serious distortions in reality testing and judgment, problematic relationships, and destructive or self-destructive behaviors.

Vaillant (1993) has classified the defenses into four categories: (1) psychotic defenses; (2) immature defenses; (3) neurotic (intermediate) defenses; and (4) mature defenses. Schamess (1996), while adapting Vaillant's classification, nevertheless has reservations about this classification, since well-functioning individuals "actually employ a wide range of defenses, including some that are categorized as developmentally early or immature. It seems likely that the ability to call on, as needed, a wide range of different defenses is an indication of mental health" (p. 85). Following is a list of fifteen defenses (another defense, *splitting,* is discussed in Chapter 3) that are generally recognized by social workers. I will amalgamate the classifications of Vaillant (1993) and Sadock and Sadock (2003). Sadock and Sadock (2003) refer to the psychotic defenses as "narcissistic defenses" (p. 206).

Developmentally Early/Psychotic Defenses

<u>Denial</u>. This defense fends off awareness of some aspect of external reality that is painful or threatening; people with substance abuse problems and their families tend to deny that a problem exists. A mother might deny signs that her boyfriend is making sexual overtures to her daughter. A man with a tumor growing on his neck may deny its existence to avoid facing his fears of cancer. A close friend may plan to move far away, but we may remain "oblivious" to this event, denying the situation by not facing or talking about it.

In psychotic denial, external reality may be severely distorted. While it is normal to employ "denial in fantasy; our deceased loved ones come alive in our daydreams . . . psychotic denial leads us to set a place for them at the . . . table" (Vaillant, 1993, p. 43). Denial can serve adaptive uses in everyday life. We know that we will die someday; but we usually deny this as we go about our daily business.

Projection. Projection is related to blame. A man might be described as projecting the blame for a divorce onto his wife. However, technically, when used as a defense, projection refers to the attribution of a wish or impulse (which is disavowed) onto some other person or some nonpersonal object in the outside world. In other words, I don't feel angry at you—you are angry at me. "It is the act of giving objective or seeming reality to what is subjective. The expression implies that what is cast upon another is considered undesirable to the one who projects" (Campbell, 1989, p. 563).

As with the other defenses, projection has a spectrum of use: from the "normal," in which reality testing is still reasonably intact (e.g., Susan believes that Jim is attracted to her, when the reverse—that is, she is attracted to him—is the case) to its manifestation in mental illness, in which the capacity to test reality has been lost. William, who is mentally ill, first disavowed his angry feelings and then projected them onto the FBI and the communists; he felt he was in danger from both groups and led his life so as to prevent detection. Projection is one of the major defenses in *paranoid schizophrenia* and other paranoid conditions.

An extension of this defense is *projective identification,* a concept attributed to Melanie Klein, one of the early object relations theorists. Projective identification is a complex defense and has been "defined differently by almost every chronicler of defenses . . ." (Vaillant, 1993, p. 58). In this process an individual avoids recognizing and taking responsibility for or ownership of traits that are threatening to him or her, and in a complex way, ascribing these attitudes to (or projecting them onto) another person. This is done in such a way that the other person reacts with the same kind of behavior or attitudes being disavowed by the person utilizing this defensive maneuver.

If Bill, the client, feels disorganized and is afraid to own these feelings, he projects them onto or ascribes them to Sally, the therapist, interacting with her in such a manner that she may actually conform to these projected feelings and act as though she feels disorganized. In this scenario, Bill might behave in such a confused manner (attempting, for example, to subtly demand that Sally understand and comment on his incoherent story) that Sally (making an earnest attempt to follow this illogical account) may likewise become confused and disorganized. Bill might take this one step further and criticize Sally for being too incompetent to follow a simple story.

This entire process may be further reflected subsequently in supervision, where the therapist (although unaware of this at the time) continues to respond to the client's feeling state and reenacts these feelings while in session with her supervisor (Kahn, 1979). This behavior has been referred to as *parallel process.* In the following illustration, the supervisee has absorbed the helplessness and disorganization of her client, and in contrast to her prior well-defined presentations, comes across as disorganized and diffuse: "The supervisor . . . suggested that there might be a similarity between her feelings and those of the client. The worker . . . said that this client had aroused so much disorganized feeling . . . that she felt almost helpless and in despair" (p. 525).

Bowen (1985) discusses the *family projection process,* a specific variation of projective identification that takes place within a family. A mother may feel helpless, but, rather than owning the feeling, projects it onto the child, so that not only does she perceive this child to be helpless but may be so overprotective and infantilizing that the child may feel helpless, and act helpless; therefore, the mother can be the strong one, caring for the needy, weak child. "With her adequate self she mothers her weak self which is perceived to be in the child" (p. 8). In this process, "the mother's attention was determined from inside herself rather than the reality of the situation" (p. 8). This process occurs in all families to some degree; however, it becomes a more serious problem when it is a chronic pattern of interaction, and the child becomes "fused" (i.e., does not develop adequate ego boundaries and does not feel a sense of autonomy and differentiation in relation to the mother).

Projective identification is a major defense in *borderline personality disorder.* The clinician is often the unwitting actor in the scenario created by the patient's projecting disavowed feelings onto the therapist.

Ms. Schmidt, a child welfare worker, was asked by her client, Mrs. Bosworth, to place her son, whose oppositional behavior she could not handle. When Ms. Schmidt attempted to carry out the plan, the mother became very angry, verbally attacking the social worker. She concluded her tirade by stating: "There are plenty of children out there that you can help. Why don't you go and help them?" Mrs. Bosworth subsequently called up Ms. Schmidt's supervisor to complain about Ms. Schmidt's incompetence. In these instances, Mrs. Bosworth was disavowing her own angry feelings toward her son and her wish to "be rid of him." She involved Ms. Schmidt in acting out this wish for her, then attacked her for this "hostile" act, while she could remain the innocent victim of this "outrage."

Projective identification, when understood and processed by the clinician, can be used to encourage the psychological growth of the patient. If therapists can feel the clients' projected feelings arising within themselves, such as suddenly feeling incompetent or helpless when with their clients, they can utilize this insight therapeutically rather than act out the feeling by becoming helpless (or defend against it by proving the opposite, that they are not incompetent or helpless). "It may be that the essence of what is therapeutic" resides in a "therapist's ability to receive the patient's projections, utilize facets of his own mature personality system to process the projection, and then make the digested projection available . . . [to the patient] through the therapeutic interaction" (Ogden, 1982, p. 20). However, there are clients, such as Mrs. Bosworth, who may not have the capacity for this insight; but if Ms. Schmidt becomes aware of this process, she can handle it in an effective manner, rather than feeling personally threatened. Understanding projective identification is critical in clinical work utilizing intersubjectivity, the reciprocal subjective reactions and interactions of the client and clinician (Stolorow, Atwood, and Brandchaft, 1994).

Immature Defenses

Vaillant (1993) states that he does not use the term "immature defenses" in a judgmental manner but to stress that the "ego develops into adult life" (p. 45).

Acting out. Acting out is defined as "the direct expression of an unconscious wish or impulse . . . to avoid being conscious of the affect" and the associated ideation (Vaillant, 1993, pp. 52-53). In acting out, the person, through action, experiences relief from psychological tensions and conflicts. In utilizing this defense, some individuals engage in many "impulsive delinquent acts and temper tantrums" that explode so violently "as to allow the user to be unaware of their passion" (p. 53). The risk-taking behaviors of some teenagers may be a form of acting out. As a rule, "adolescent streetwalkers are running from the risk of incestuous molestations or other abuse at home" (p. 52).

While generally discussed in negative terms, acting out can have an adaptive value, as a struggle against despair and passivity, and a cornerstone of resilience (Dugan, 1989). The positive aspects of adolescent acting out are discussed in Chapter 10.

Passive aggression. In passive aggression, the individual defends against the awareness of the aggressive nature of his or her behavior by concealing the aggression in the disguise of apparent passivity. For example, rebelliousness and resistance are cloaked in procrastination. We have all encountered the adolescent who seems outwardly to comply ("Oh yes, I will definitely get my paper in on time"), but then procrastinates or makes excuses ("I finished typing it, but the wind blew it away").

Vaillant (1993) views the so-called defense mechanisms referred to as *turning against the self* as a form of passive aggression. In serious situations of turning against the self, adolescents might burn themselves, deliberately cut themselves, or attempt suicide. This mechanism may represent aggression expressed in an extremely disguised form, turning it as far away as possible from its real object and putting oneself in its place; ordinary passive aggression, however, in which little harm is inflicted on the individual except in the sense that the behavior may be socially self-defeating, should not be conceived of as turning against the self.

The unconscious object of suicidal behavior may also be the internal image of another person (such as a rejecting spouse) who is the target of the suicidal individual's rage. This rage is in profound conflict with the same individual's love for that object.

Identification with the aggressor. When utilizing the defense of identification with the aggressor, an individual identifies with certain characteristics of a person by whom he or she is threatened rather than reject the aggressor outright, when the aggressor is more powerful and at some level needed by the less powerful individual. This process also allows the individual to feel some measure of control. In a famous kidnapping case, the victim appeared to have taken on similar characteristics as her captors, participating with them in a bank robbery.

The first description of this defense has been attributed to Anna Freud, but Meyer (2005) observed that in fact Ferenczi described it at an earlier time.

> I had a patient who . . . was rather bad, and was beaten every week, sometimes in advance. When he was beaten he suddenly began to think consciously, "How nice it will be when I am a father and can beat my child!" . . . An identification of this kind leads to a change in a part of the mind. . . . First we are afraid of punishment, then we identify ourselves with the punishing authority. Then father and mother lose their importance; the child has built up a sort of internal father and mother. (Ferenczi, 1928, 1955a, p. 73) (Meyer, 2005, p. 21)

In discussing the children from Terezin, Downey (2001) observed their use of identification with the aggressor, which pitted "passivity versus activity, vulnerability versus power" (p. 51).

> It is hardly a stretch to think of the children's constant hostile litany of "blodder," "aunt," or "fool" directed toward themselves at times and rather constantly toward their adult servants as having arisen from

identification with the insults of the guards at Terezin. . . . So, on the one hand the children, who had been exposed to the brutality of the guards and their dogs, were frantically fearful of any dog. On the other hand, as a group they were capable of themselves becoming a growling, biting, warring watchdog! (Downey, 2001, p. 51)

Identification with the aggressor is common in psychological life and is prominent in cases involving physical and sexual abuse. An abused child may attack another child, attempting to master the trauma by acting out the role of the aggressor. This mechanism is often found, less harshly, in childhood games in which children's anxiety is "converted into pleasurable security" (Freud, 1946, p. 119) by pretending to become the very things they dread. A boy who is to undergo a difficult medical procedure might imitate this procedure in his play, where he (as doctor) performs the procedure on a teddy bear.

Anna Freud (1946) cites a case of a boy in an elementary school involving identification with the aggressor, in which the psychologist, August Aichorn, consulted.

The boy was brought to him because of a habit of making faces. The master complained that the boy's behavior, when he was blamed or reproved, was quite abnormal. On such occasions he made faces which caused the whole class to burst out laughing. . . . When master, pupil and psychologist were together, the situation was explained. Observing the two attentively, Aichorn saw that the boy's grimaces were simply a caricature of the angry expression of the teacher and that, when he had to face a scolding by the latter, he tried to master his anxiety by involuntarily imitating him. The boy identified himself with the teacher's anger and copied his expression as he spoke, though the imitation was not recognized. Through his grimaces he was assimilating himself to or identifying himself with the dreaded external object. (Freud, 1946, p. 118)

Somatization. In somatization, a conversion of psychological tensions and conflict into somatic (physical) problems and complaints occurs. A person might experience headaches, or stomach distress, for example, when in conflict, but the nature of the conflict causing the tension might not be apparent; people often present in a general practitioner's office with physical complaints that may be masking psychological problems. Somatization can be found in a number of psychological disturbances, including somatization, conversion, and post–traumatic stress disorders; it is a common defense in victims of child abuse (Kilgore, 1988). Somatization is discussed further in Chapters 13 and 14.

Some cultural groups may present more readily with somatic rather than psychological problems. In China, for example, "because individual feelings are considered unimportant but close attention is paid to physical needs," many patients with underlying depressive symptoms "often presented with somatic complaints. In a world view that makes no distinction between the mind and the body, it is the body that carries the 'illness' in a socially acceptable way and without the shame that goes along with mental weakness" (Tang, 1997, pp. 335-336).

Regression. Regression behaviorally and/or attitudinally to a more immature, earlier level of development operates as a defense by allowing the individual to play out the role of the more dependent, less socially accountable child as well as permitting more direct forms of instinctual gratification and aggression. This may occur at any age.

A universal manifestation of regression is seen in young children experiencing the arrival of a new sibling, who, although having achieved good developmental levels, may regress to using immature language, demanding to be fed, and wetting or soiling themselves. To determine whether (and to what extent) regression has taken place, it is important to obtain a baseline of previous functioning. Was the child ever proficient in self-care skills, language, and toilet training? The same principle applies in the assessment of older individuals.

Regression also plays an important role in creativity and is essential to healthy development, as the ability to regress permits people to play, relax, enjoy vacations, gain pleasure from sexual activity, and, periodically, withdraw from the demands of the world.

Regression *in the service of the ego* is also an important phenomenon. A child may regress before a new developmental landmark is achieved; a patient in therapy may regress prior to an advance in growth; in both instances, the ego is in the process of synthesizing and consolidating old patterns to prepare for the integration of new development. Regression in the service of the ego can also be observed during times of illness: a man having a heart attack who allows himself to be treated in a dependent or more regressed manner will do better medically than one who denies his illness and resists "being taken care of."

Regression as a permanent state can present serious problems in functioning, depending on how chronic and pervasive it is. In schizophrenia, a marked regression occurs in various areas of functioning and cognitive processes. However, *schizophrenic regression* is different from other forms of regression "because it usually fails in its purpose and still further regression is necessary until, finally, the process may lead to complete dilapidation" (Campbell, 1989, p. 626).

Neurotic Defenses

According to Vaillant (1993), neurotic defenses are "closer to reality [than psychotic and immature defenses]. . . . The user feels responsible for his or her conflicts, and neurotic defenses often reflect compromise" (p. 60).

Displacement. A boss yells at his employee, who yells at his wife, who yells at her son, who kicks the dog are examples of displacement. The affect, anger, is experienced and owned (not disavowed as in projection), but displaced onto what is perceived to be a safer object, psychologically, than the one toward whom it is really directed. To feel and express anger directly can be threatening to the psychological integrity of the person, as anger may produce anxiety related to superego guilt, fear of rejection or abandonment by the object of the anger, psychological retaliation, and so on. Thus, the employee felt safer being angry at his wife than the boss. Although a reality element may have been present, that is, the possibility of loss of job, he may have felt a psychological prohibition against expressing anger toward a person in authority.

Displacement is the primary defense in *phobias*. On the surface, the patient is fearful of something in the external world (such as elevators or dogs), which is seen (by psychodynamic therapists) as a displacement from a feeling (or a person) causing anxiety. The anxieties underlying phobias can result from many sources. In agoraphobia (the fear of open spaces and traveling away from home) "separation anxiety clearly plays a leading role" (Sadock and Sadock, 2003, p. 611). Therefore, one is not likely to get to the bottom of "phobics" anxiety by questioning . . . [them] about the exact object of their fears. . . . We must look everywhere else for the source of their "distress" (Vaillant, 1993, p. 24).

Displacement is seen in play therapy. "Parent dolls are murdered and put in garbage cans. The result is relief, not guilt" (Vaillant, 1993, p. 60). The child is relieved because not only has he preserved his real parents, but he has also gained emotional release by expressing or displacing his anger onto a safe object: the dolls. A foster child who correctly sensed that he was about to be removed from his foster home was playing a telephone game with his therapist. He said to her: "Tell Harold [his foster-home caseworker] that the bank is on the phone—he owes them a lot of money, and they are going to take away his house!" (The caseworker becomes "dispossessed" rather than the child.)

Displacement is also observed in transference, when the patient displaces feelings from a past significant person (often the parents) onto the therapist.

A client said to her therapist: "I feel you are sitting there judging me." The therapist asked whether she were doing or saying anything to give her client this impression. "No," the patient replied. "I guess I feel that way about everyone." "It is not surprising," the therapist replied. "You have told me how judgmental your mother has always been toward you."

As the therapist was not in fact being judgmental, we can say that displacement was occurring.

Isolation. Isolation or *isolation of affect,* as it is sometimes called, refers to the disowning of feelings associated with a given idea or event even though the actual idea or event might be recalled. Citing Freud, Campbell (1989) noted that when using this defense "what remains in consciousness is nothing but an ideational content which is perfectly colorless and is judged to be unimportant" (p. 386).

Why do "ghosts" from the past haunt some parents, inhibiting them in their ability to love their children, whereas other parents are free from these "ghosts" (Fraiberg, Adelson, and Shapiro, 1975)? The authors focus on parents who have been abused and make a distinction between those who subsequently abuse their own children and those who do not. Those formerly abused parents who do *not* become abusers can remember not only the event, but their feelings associated with this event. "These are the parents who say: I remember what it was like. . . . I would never let my child go through what I went through" (Fraiberg, Adelson, and Shapiro, 1975, p. 419). According to this formulation, when parents become abusers, two defenses have been at work. In the first, identification with the aggressor, the parents have formed a pathological identification with their own abusing parents. In the second, although they could vividly recall the abuse, they could not recall the associated feelings; isolation of affect was at work. The dissociated/isolated affect, presumably rage and the associated tension, cannot remain totally hemmed in; it was discharged at least in part through reenactment of the abuse.

Although the concept of social isolation, in which a person remains removed from other people, is an important object relations concept, it should not be confused with isolation of affect, which is a unique defense mechanism.

Dissociation. Dissociation is a complex mental process, one of the first major psychopathological phenomena to receive scientific attention in the

Sometimes the suppressed impulse breaks through, and the person acts out the feelings and wishes that had been under control. Vaillant (1993) discusses a well-publicized situation of a crusading religious leader who had regularly denounced the "decline of morals and decency in our country," yet who subsequently was discovered to have had sexual relations with both a male and female student where he taught and then went on to officiate at their wedding (p. 78).

In the Chinese culture, where there are strong prohibitions against anger, reaction formation is a major defense (Tang, 1997). This is often "manifested in an oscillation between a ready compliance to authority and murderous, antiauthority rampages such as occurred during the Cultural Revolution from 1966-1976" (p. 336). The occurrence of the "rampages" would be an example of acting out the suppressed side of angry feelings formerly held in control by the reaction formation.

Repression. In repression, thoughts and feelings perceived to be dangerous by the ego are rendered unconscious; a person may have no recollection of an emotionally painful experience. It is "the active process of keeping out and ejecting, banishing from consciousness, ideas or impulses that are unacceptable to it" (Campbell, 1989, p. 631). There is a distinction between primary and secondary repression. When individuals use primary repression, they are not admitting mental/affective activity into consciousness in the first place. It is "the curbing of ideas and feelings before they have attained consciousness; secondary repression excludes from awareness what was once experienced at a conscious level" (Sadock and Sadock, 2003, p. 208). Freud's (Brenner, 1974) discussion of the mechanisms of dreaming is based on the concept of repression, which banishes from waking thought forbidden ideas and impulses, which then may return in disguised form at night in dreams; Freud referred to the analysis of dreams as the "royal road to the unconscious" (Brenner, 1974, p. 150).

Repression plays an important role in psychological functioning. We repress aspects of our instinctual life (and primary process thinking) to some extent and develop secondary process thinking to adapt to external reality.

It might be helpful to view repression on a continuum; a sufficient amount of repression enables us to function without being continually diverted by pressing internal preoccupations, while permitting us to be attuned to our feelings and wishes. Insufficient repression, appearing in psychotic states, may result in such primitive and inappropriate ways of thinking, and relating, that the individual's ability to function adequately in the real world may be severely impaired. Severe repression, on the other hand, can require the expenditure of so much psychic energy that the ego may become constricted, resulting in, among other problems, a rigidity of personality, lack of spontaneity and imagination, and an inability to play. Severe repression can produce somatic symptoms, such as migraine headaches and conversion phenomena, depression, anxiety states, and so on.

Although on the surface dissociation and repression may seem to be similar, the psychological processes involved in each are different. Repression appears to achieve its defensive aim by impeding the access of troubling mental contents as a whole to consciousness, whereas dissociation appears to achieve its defensive aim by breaking connections between components of troubling mental contents, thus submerging the essential significance of the underlying whole.

A current controversy exists over the issue of the accuracy of repressed memories of sexual abuse. Alpert (1995) summarizes this conflict.

> The controversy over the validity and impact of adult memories of childhood abuse has been oversimplified by the media and has resulted in a division. One side of the controversy acknowledges that memories for childhood abuse may be delayed and recalled decades after the abuse. The other side believes that recovered memories of childhood trauma are more likely the result of suggestion from misinformed therapists, self-help books, or other forms of influence. This dialogue . . . has been harmful to the mental health professions, practitioners, and the people served by them. (p. xix)

There is probably truth in both arguments; many people have been abused and may not recover memories until later in life. There are also indications that some people may be suggestible and "fantasize" about events that may not have occurred. Furthermore, evidence of manipulative behaviors exists in this arena; it is not unknown for parents in custody disputes to prompt their children to accuse a parent of abuse that may never have occurred; strong suspicion exists that similar manipulations may occur in some instances on the part of police, prosecutors, and mental health professionals. In this emotional sphere, the importance of maintenance of objectivity is a critical factor, as this uncharted realm continues to be explored.

Mature Defenses

The mature defenses enable people to integrate conflicts, to "balance and attenuate the four lodestars of reality, people, conscience, and desire" (Vaillant, 1993, p. 67).

Sublimation. Sublimation is the conversion of feelings and impulses into socially acceptable and constructive behavior. In this formulation, the child, rebelling against toilet training, sublimates the wish to control his or her feces into playing with mud or clay. Many adult activities, including various forms of artistic expression, are examples of successful sublimation. "Sublimation allows instincts to be channeled, rather than blocked or diverted" (Sadock and Sadock, 2003, p. 208).

Humor. Humor, as a defense, can help people handle stress or conflict by draining the seriousness from situations. "Freud suggested [humor] 'can be regarded as the highest of these defensive processes'" (Vaillant, 1993, p. 72). We can recall times when people have described a distressing event that they have mastered to a sufficient degree so that it becomes a funny story in the telling, further enhancing mastery.

Characterological Mechanisms of Defense

Defensive operations can become incorporated into character, as adaptational behavior. Heinz Hartmann (Vaillant, 1993) stated that "defensive processes may simultaneously serve both control of the instinctual drive and adaptation to the external world" (p. 116). The development of creativity, for example, is a "striking example of adaptation to instinctual conflict evolving into sustained behavior" (p. 116). These defensive operations can be adaptive or maladaptive or both; what may be adaptive in one sphere of life (a high degree of organization at work) might be maladaptive in another sphere (a spouse might complain of a partner's "overorganization" and "control" at home).

Young-Bruehl (2006), in her therapy with two homeless, gay young men, named Transformation and Ricardo, focused on the character traits that were presenting the most difficulty in their lives: With Transformation, the "character trait that gave him the most trouble . . . was his passivity, his willingness to accommodate to others who exploited him." Ricardo's "key trait was aggressivity, a tendency to explode at 'the authorities'" (p. 327).

Characterological mechanisms of defense can develop in relation to traumatic experiences. In one study, adults were interviewed twenty years after they had survived the disastrous Buffalo Creek flood as children (Honig et al., 1993). The researchers were struck by the fact that while few symptoms of post–traumatic stress disorder remained, these former survivors had developed "'patterns of adaptation' which may have originated as coping responses to the trauma" (p. 334). These patterns, which could develop into "characterological mechanisms of defense, appeared to be more or less adaptational from the perspective of the individual's subsequent emotional development and from the perspective of the individual's capacity to confront other stressful events" (p. 334). In one case study, Henry, who assumed a great deal of responsibility for others during the flood crisis, was found twenty years later to have incorporated "this strong sense of responsibility" (p. 340) as a fixed, predominant aspect of his personality and functioning.

Discussion. We all need and utilize defenses; they protect the ego from perceived internal and external dangers. Key considerations in examining defenses include assessing the strength, flexibility, or rigidity of the defenses; their utilization for adaptation and coping; whether they help the person deal with reality or provide a false sense of the world; and the extent to which defenses constrict or promote a person's emotional and cognitive life.

A clinician may immediately wish to confront a client's unhealthy defenses and replace them with healthy ones; however, one should interpret defenses cautiously and supportively, exploring underlying conflicts and offering "an alternative mode of coping" (Vaillant, 1993, p. 111). It can be reassuring to students who are afraid of harming clients through their interventions to learn of Vaillant's observation that the "ego is wily, resilient, and wise." People will not "give up defenses they need just because we point them out" (p. 111).

CONCLUSION

Psychoanalytic and ego psychology theories help us appreciate that clients have a life history, with established patterns of relating to people, varying levels of trust, and an ego organization that may be solid or unstable. We can get caught up in a whirlwind of relationship tangles and "crunches" (emotionally charged impasses) with clients; we may feel overidentified or repulsed, or confused and helpless. Learning how to analyze ego functions, defense mechanisms, and other psychological processes enables us to reach the pain and suffering of the client more deeply without losing ourselves in the process. Although some social workers will argue that we are medicalizing and pathologizing the client, we would argue that we are aiming for as much objectivity as it is possible to muster in intense clinical situations. If we learn how to listen and what to listen for, we will be able to go beneath the surface communications of people to ascertain what underlying thoughts and feelings are present. Scuba-diving instructors might suggest to students, preparing how to go beneath the surface of the water, what types of undersea life to look for, and where they can be found. Then the learners are ready to observe the wonders of the undersea world for themselves and continue their own explorations. These students, however, first must accept that there could be a world under the sea; if they believe that all that exists are the waves, seaweed, and shells and crustaceans that are washed ashore, that is all they will ever know. So I ask the reader to look at what is not visible—the unconscious, internal representations, defenses, and internal conflict—rather than remain with superficial knowledge.

Freud's agitation of the "sleep of mankind" (Gay, 1988, p. xvii) is one of the most insurmountable sources of resistance to Freudian thought. Further intensifying resistance to Freud was resistance *by* Freud and his inner circle to deviations from orthodox theory, a kind of fortress mentality. Although Freud revised his theory as he deemed necessary based on *his* new insights, he did not welcome serious disagreement from his followers. Many bitter and acrimonious intellectual and personal disputes followed and led to the establishment of divergent schools of thought by such disciples as Jung, Adler, Ferenczi, and Rank. Tensions have existed among theoreticians of human behavior since the time of Freud, including both external battles between those of competing theories, such as, between behaviorists and psychodynamic practitioners, as well as internal battles among adherents of the same school.

The intensity of the theoretical wars tended to keep adherents of the various psychoanalytic approaches from seeing the commonalities of their ideas (Mitchell, 1988), and from seeing how their differences might complement each other.

Psychoanalysis seems to have lost much of its influence today (Brandell, 2004), while pharmacotherapy and "short-term talking therapies predominate" (Goode, 1999b, p. D1). However, the profession has responded with a renewed vitality and a willingness to deal with change (Goode, 1999b), which includes admitting people without medical degrees to the profession; social workers are among the nonmedical applicants "flocking" to analytic institutes (Sanville, 1994, p. 131).

Psychoanalysis, while maintaining emphasis on traditional analysis (with its current variations) has expanded to include various forms of psychotherapy, milieu treatment, interdisciplinary collaboration, and involvement with patients who might not be candidates for analysis, such as Young-Bruehl's (2006) treatment of two homeless young men (this chapter) and Seligman's (1994) work with at-risk infants, involving home visiting with their multiproblem families (Chapter 9). Freud himself also had a broader view of the potential contributions of psychoanalysis. Speaking at the

International Psychoanalytic Congress in Budapest in 1918, Freud expressed his vision that

> the conscience of society will awake and remind it that the poor man should have just as much right to assistance for his mind as he now has to the life-saving help offered by surgery; and that the neuroses threaten public health no less than tuberculosis, and can be left as little as the latter to the impotent care of individual members of the community. (Young-Bruehl, 1988, p. 81)

During Freud's lifetime, psychoanalysis did expand its focus, including work with psychotic patients, with people suffering from trauma (such as the war neuroses), and the development of analysis with children and adolescents. "But the analyst for whom Freud's social vision became a credo most deeply and lastingly was his daughter [Anna]" (Young-Bruehl, 1988, p. 81). As segments of the social work profession today devalue psychological help for the poor and minorities and focus instead on social change and empowerment, Freud's message that "the poor man" also has the "right to assistance for his mind" demands serious attention.

Psychoanalytic knowledge and practice continue to evolve, contributing to comprehensive approaches to healing in our increasingly complex world (Dowling, 2001).

> In our present extremity of social upheaval, poverty, disease, and the seemingly unending trauma of war and genocide, it is relevant to devote renewed energies to a better understanding of how *psychoanalytically informed care,* both in foster or adoptive families and in group settings, can undo repressions, heal traumatically frozen personalities, and help set children on the path of progressive development. (Dowling, 2001, p. 75; italics added)

Dowling's advocacy of "psychoanalytically informed care" underscores a central theme of this book; not every case situation is amenable to (nor needs) psychotherapy, but as clinical social workers utilize the depth of understanding that psychoanalytic theories provide, the more multidimensional, insightful, self-aware, and skilled are their contributions to clients. Discussion of psychodynamic theory continues in Chapter 3, focusing on object relations theory and self psychology, and adding the perspectives offered by cognitive and behavioral theories. Chapter 4 on postmodern theories includes constructivism, relational psychotherapy, and narrative theory. The puzzling question of how some children and adults who have had difficult life experiences appear to adapt well is discussed in Chapter 4's final section on resilience.

LEARNING EXERCISES

1. Encourage students to examine the section on psychodynamic theory in several human behavior texts, and critically analyze the way in which psychoanalytic theory is presented.
2. Utilizing small group exercises, assign each group several ego functions and defense mechanisms and request them to discuss and illustrate them in preparation for class presentation.

SUGGESTED READING

Article

Swenson, C. J. 1994. Freud's "Anna O.": Social work's Bertha Pappenheim. *Clinical Social Work Journal* 22: 149-163.

Books

Brandell, J. R. 2004. *Psychodynamic social work.* New York: Columbia University Press.
Berzoff, J., L. M. Flanagan, and P. Hertz. (eds.) 1996. *Inside out and outside in: Psychodynamic clinical theory and practice in contemporary multicultural contexts.* Northvale, NJ: Jason Aronson.
Putnam, F. W. 1997. *Dissociation in children and adolescents: A developmental perspective.* New York: The Guilford Press.
Vonnegut, M. 1975. *The Eden Express: A personal account of schizophrenia.* New York: Praeger Publishers.
Young-Bruehl, E. 1988. *Anna Freud: A biography.* New York: Summit Books.

Chapter 3

Object Relations, Self Psychology, and Cognitive-Behavioral Theories

We are at times as different from our real selves as from other people.

La Rochefoucauld, *Maximes,* No. 135, 1665

INTRODUCTION

In Chapter 2, the development of psychoanalysis and the influence of ego psychology on psychodynamic thought was presented. We now turn our attention to advances in psychodynamic theory, including: object relations theory, highlighting attachment, internalization of representations of self and other, and separation-individuation; and self psychology, stressing the central roles in psychological development played by identity, self-cohesion, and empathy. Following this, cognitive and behavioral theories are presented; their divergence from psychodynamic theory is noted, and how they can be used in complementary ways with psychodynamic approaches is suggested.

OBJECT RELATIONS THEORY

In the context of this theory, objects refer to people toward whom the self (the subject) is drawn; presumably it refers back to the general notion of the "love object" in Freud's works. Object relations theory emphasizes internal reactions to and conceptions of others, as well as inner feelings about oneself.

Human Behavior in the Social Environment, Second Edition

The projection of feelings onto others, activated by internalized objects, is illustrated in the following case:

A very engaging client, positively involved in her clinical treatment, was very anxious before she came to the office, fearful that the therapist would be judgmental and critical. When asked by the clinician if she had done or said anything to give this impression, the client remarked: "Not yet!" The discussion turned to the client's mother, who could be supportive and sympathetic, but who overall tended to be critical of the client; her surprise "attacks" could not be anticipated by the client. It became clear that the client was expecting and attempting to "defend" herself against similar behavior from the clinician.

In this example, the client's internalized view of her mother (an internal object) was coloring her feelings about her present relationship with the clinician and, correspondingly, her behavior in this relationship. This root of her anxious, self-critical attitude was also adversely affecting her self-image (her self-representation). Mother's estimation of her must be the correct one.

Melanie Klein was the first psychoanalyst to revise Freud's theory (while retaining the concepts of the instinctual drives) by adding the perspective of interpersonal relationships (St. Clair, 1986). Fairbairn (St. Clair, 1986), utilizing Klein's theory, departed completely from Freudian drive theory by proposing a "'pure' object relations position, which asserts that the main drive that a person has is *a drive for a relationship,* not the satisfaction of biological instinct" (p. 13; italics added). Fairbairn asserted that "the seeking out and maintaining of an intense emotional bond with another person" is the fundamental motivation in life (Mitchell, 1988, p. 27).

Children's emotional connection to their parents is of utmost importance to them, to be maintained at all costs. Understanding this, Fairbairn gained insight into the paradoxical situation of the "loyalty of abused children to their abusing parents" (Mitchell, 1988, p. 26). Foster children need to blame someone for being removed from their homes; often they blame themselves, enabling them to retain the belief that their parents will come back for them, while denying that the parents are at fault. "No matter how weak or abusive are the parents, the child needs to believe that they are the best of all possible parents" (Levine, 1990, p. 58).

Foster children may have difficulty in attaching to their foster families because of a pattern of insecure attachments; they may also feel that loving their foster parents is a betrayal of their biological parents. The often "punishing" rejection of foster parents by the child and overt aggression directed toward them can be a painful burden for foster parents (Levine, 1990).

People who have had secure attachments to a nurturing figure generally have a solid sense of self and tend to have positive and pleasurable interpersonal relationships. Those who have received inadequate nurturance and support, developing a "shaky" sense of self, may avoid intimate relationships with others, fearing closeness. For example, Jonathan Swift, born in seventeenth-century Ireland, whose father died before his birth, was abandoned by his mother when he was very young. He grew up under the tutelage of emotionally unsupportive paternal uncles (Glendinning, 1999). Although he achieved great fame as a political satirist, a bishop, and a writer, he remained wary of committed relationships. "His prescribed strategy for emotional survival is flight from all risk of grief, pain or disappointment—at the price of fleeing also from the pleasure and sweetness which make life worth living for most people" (p. 223).

Some people, also deprived of adequate nurturing may, unlike Swift, constantly seek relationships in which they demand total attention and nurturing. Sometimes this works; the person who finds another with a need to nurture develops a complementary relationship. However, people in need of nurturing often are attracted to those with similar needs, leading to disappointment and conflict, as neither person can meet the deep needs of the other.

Some emotionally needy people become engaged in enmeshed relationships in which the individuality of each is lost, as they fuse into a unit, always together (but frequently not "tuned in" to each other). Some enmeshed couples follow this pattern into the divorce process, when they find that they cannot get along with each other but are not able to let go (Kressel, 1997). Enmeshed families are discussed further in Chapter 8.

Social workers encounter people who have entered into self-destructive relationships, which serve "as vehicles for *the perpetuation of early ties to significant others.* The child learns a mode of connection . . . and these learned modes are desperately maintained throughout life" (Mitchell, 1988, p. 27; italics added). Viewed from this vantage point, the perplexing picture of a woman growing up with an abusive father and then marrying a man who is abusive to her becomes more understandable. It is not uncommon to see children born to teenage unmarried mothers becoming teenage unmarried parents themselves.

The intergenerational transmission of child maltreatment has been observed when an object relations perspective is applied to the study of child abuse (Hughes, 1998; Morton and Browne, 1998; Zeanah and Scheeringa, 1997). If children receive "insensitive parenting" (Morton and Browne, 1998, p. 1098), they will introject an image of themselves as unlovable and deficient; subsequently, they are unable to develop caring, consistent relationships with their own children. "This may be the primary process by which child maltreatment continues from one generation to the next. Thus, it is the caregiving relationship that is transmitted across the generations rather than violence per se" (p. 1098). Mitigating circumstances (or protective factors enhancing resilience) can prevent this transmission; these include supportive substitute care when growing up, involved and supportive spouses, and the development of self-awareness about their abusive experiences (often with the assistance of therapy) (Morton and Browne, 1998).

Object relations theory has contributed to a deeper understanding of the use of self by the clinician; its concepts promote the clinician's attunement to feelings evoked in them by their clients; these feelings are then explored in a therapeutic manner.

Dan, who had a history of disturbed attachments, presented many anxieties and deep insecurities about himself in therapy. On several occasions, when the clinician made a sensitive and attuned comment to Dan, he would laugh in what felt to the clinician to be a disparaging manner. Instinctively, the clinician felt defensive, wondering whether she was off the mark, and changed the subject. During one session, when Dan again laughed "at her," she realized that she was feeling put down. This time, she brought this behavior to his attention. She asked him if he realized that when she said something of a sensitive nature, he would laugh at it. He was able to discuss his discomfort with the feelings she evoked in him, which led to a meaningful interchange. The clinician speculated that perhaps his put-down of her was the way he was made to feel when he had tried to express painful feelings to others in his past.

In this illustration, the clinician, although initially thrown off balance by the client's disparagement of her insights, was able to use her defensive emotional reaction by processing it within her self, and then sharing this with her client. She was utilizing the concept of *intersubjectivity,* which refers to the reciprocal subjective reactions and interactions between the client and clinician. This concept has been receiving increasing attention (Mattei, 1999; Schamess, 1999; Stolorow, Atwood, and Brandchaft, 1994).

An important feature of intersubjectivity is the defense known as projective identification (discussed in Chapter 2), whereby clients project their own disavowed feelings onto others, including their therapists. This process may evoke irrational feelings in clinicians, who may unwittingly react to those feelings; Ogden (1982) recommended that clinicians should become aware of these projections, and share them therapeutically with the patient. Object relations family therapists also actively utilize projective identification in their treatment of families (Scharff and Scharff, 1987).

A family therapist, in talking with a couple, found that the wife was often sarcastic to both her husband and to himself. The therapist found himself getting angry at the wife and was inclined to make "hostile" interpretations to her, under the guise of increasing her insight. He subsequently realized that her interactional style must also be affecting her husband, who had a need to deny the force of his wife's anger, and that the wife's hostility had origins in her embattled childhood family. The therapist's intervention involved dealing with the wife's hostility in a direct but empathic manner and relating this both to her present interactions and past history.

Object relations family therapy is discussed further in Chapter 8. *Attachment theory,* a major component of object relations theory, sheds light on the importance of relationships throughout the life cycle.

Attachment Theory

"Human development begins with people in relationships" (Noam and Fischer, 1996, p. xvii). Although some debate exists as to whether (and to what extent) later reparations can make up for early deprivations in nurturing relationships, it is generally accepted that babies need to be held, hugged, smiled at, and talked to. "Attachment behaviors have as their objective the promotion of proximity and contact. The loss of the mother, whether she is absent or unable to provide adequate nurturing, has major consequences that lead to a specific sequence of reactions which Bowlby called protest, despair, and detachment" (Frankel, 1994, pp. 87-88).

Bowlby and Spitz observed, many years ago, the effects of institutionalization on children, such as failure to thrive (sometimes culminating in death), anaclitic depression, and failures in attachment (Karen, 1990). Worldwide attention, in the past decade, focused on the serious physical and psychological damage to institutionalized children who were exposed to severe deprivation of basic caretaking and nurturing. Talbot (1998) described the horrendous experiences (and subsequent developmental impairments) of infants in Romanian and Soviet orphanages who were confined "to cribs in . . . gloomy, ill-heated orphanage[s] with a small, rotating staff of caretakers who might spend an average of 10 minutes a day talking to them or holding them" (p. 26).

Many of these children developed severe attachment disorders, but attachment disorders have also been observed in our country in children whose caretakers are unable to nurture them adequately; many of these children are served by child welfare agencies. *Reactive attachment disorders* have been diagnosed in children under five years of age; one early manifestation is a failure to thrive syndrome, in which the infant may appear seriously malnourished, apathetic, and display a sad affect (Sadock and Sadock, 2003). This particular syndrome does not result from physical illness (such as a gastrointestinal malabsorption disorder) but is related to inadequate nurturing.

With time, other symptoms of a reactive attachment disorder may develop. According to the American Psychiatric Association's *Diagnostic and Statistical Manual of Mental Disorders,* Fourth Edition (DSM-IV) (1994), an attachment disorder is marked by "disturbed and developmentally inappropriate social relatedness in most contexts . . . and is associated with grossly pathological care" (p. 116). This disorder is distinguished from *pervasive developmental disorders* (such as *autism,* an extreme lack of social relatedness, with a presumed biological basis), whereas attachment disorders are reactive to poor caretaking.

> In the *Inhibited Type,* the child persistently fails to initiate and to respond to most social interactions in a developmentally appropriate way. The child shows a pattern of excessively inhibited, hypervigilant, or highly ambivalent responses. In the *Disinhibited Type,* there is a pattern of diffuse attachments. The child exhibits indiscriminate sociability or a lack of selectivity in the choice of attachment figures. (DSM-IV, 1994, p. 116; italics added)

Hughes (1998) describes Katie who was subjected to "physical abuse, verbal and emotional abuse, and long periods of emotional neglect" during her first five years (p. 19). Emotional neglect has its own toxic effects.

> The endless acts of emotional violation to Katie's heart and soul through [maternal] looks of disgust, screams of rejection, and the deadly silence of indifference were what led to her losing her desire to form an attachment with her parents. The trauma of sexual and physical violence is well documented. The "trauma of absence," which characterizes neglect, is less obvious to many. The cycle of abuse that leads inexorably from one generation to the next is powered most forcefully by the inability to enter and maintain meaningful attachments. (Hughes, 1998, pp. 19-20)

Sometimes children have specific characteristics that may contribute to the parent's difficulties in nurturing, such as disabilities or temperamental incompatibilities with the parent. Children may also have attachment problems due to circumstances involving separations from parents and/or multiple placements out of the home (Sadock and Sadock, 2003).

Bowlby (1988) postulates deep instinctual needs for attachment and asserts that "emotionally significant bonds between individuals have basic survival functions," that is, humans require each other for basic biological survival. Bowlby's findings have been supported by Main (1995) along with Ainsworth, who have done extensive research into the formation of childhood attachments, observing the importance of children bonding with their caretakers, leading to their development of a "secure base." Main (1995) classifies attachment behaviors into four categories: the *secure* attachment, *insecure-avoidant* attachment, *insecure-resistant/ambivalent* attachment, and *disorganized/disoriented* attachment. These patterns are discussed in Chapter 9.

Bowlby (1988) asserts that a biological basis exists for attachment behaviors in humans, as in many animals, as the "cybernetic systems situated within the CNS [central nervous system] of each partner . . . have the effect of maintaining proximity to each other" (p. 29). In keeping with Bowlby's use of *ethology* (the study of the behavior of animals and human beings, especially in their natural environments) the following narrative by an American in Britain conveys the intensity of attachment behavior in sheep.

Ingrid loved sheep, and she loved the Yorkshire Dales. Wandering the footpaths, she passed mother ewes with their lambs, noticing their continual awareness of each other; if the distance between them became too great, they would search until they found each other.

Ingrid and her husband enjoyed listening to the evening song of the sheep, in a wide range of melodies and pitches, answered by equally varied calls in other tones. A farmer's wife told them that the music of the sheep was their calling to one another; lamb and mother recognize each other's unique calls. These calls became intense at shearing time, as mothers are temporarily separated from their lambs. High pitched and intense bleating would occur as they sought reunion. Ingrid could not forget the image or sound of this frantic, searching. This is akin, she thought, to what human babies and mothers experience at the preverbal level.

Bowlby (1988) refers to the importance of internalizations and object representations during the attachment process. "Each partner builds in his or her mind working models of self and of other and of the patterns of interaction that have developed between them" (p. 29). Bowlby hypothesizes that the way in which attachment bonds "develop and become organized during . . . infancy and childhood . . . are major determinants of whether a person grows up to be mentally healthy" (p. 29). Relationships between parents and children that are "characterized by emotionally open and sensitive communications are the royal road to the development of adequate and flex-ible internal working models of self and other" (Bretheron, 1996, p. 16).

Three major objections leveled against attachment theory, with its em-phasis on the bonding of the child and mother, especially during the first three years of life, include (1) insufficient acknowledgment that children usually form multiple attachments; (2) minimization of the child's capacity for adaptation; and (3) inattention to positive changes in later stages of a child's life (such as good parenting through adoption) that can help repair earlier deprivations. Later negative events, such as the death or mental ill-ness of a parent of a secure child, can also "increase the child's vulnerabil-ity" (Frankel, 1994, p. 86). Schaffer (1994) claims that "a child's future is not shaped by events in the early, so-called formative years; development is rather a matter of a slow process of genetic and environmental interactions that continue throughout the time of psychological growth" (p. 39). The child's adaptation to early deprivations and the development of resilience is discussed in Chapter 4.

Research provides evidence that children develop multiple attachments in addition to mother-child bonds, which include bonds to their fathers, their extended family, and their siblings (Frankel, 1994; Lieberman, 1984). Relationships to siblings can "ease adjustment to conflicts and stresses by providing a positive source of reference and sense of support through sib-ling bonds" (Thomlison, 1997, p. 58). Today's increased utilization of day care for infants as well as older children has demonstrated the child's capac-ity to adapt to multiple caretakers, but questions have also been raised about whether subtle negative developmental effects may show up later; this is discussed further in Chapters 7 and 9.

While attachment and bonding are vital to children's physical and emo-tional well-being, they also need to move away from the intensity of the ma-ternal orbit, to walk, to develop autonomy, and to tolerate solitude, while still maintaining an emotional connection with mother and others. Mahler, Pine, and Bergman (1975) have done extensive research on this complex process of separation-individuation in the human infant.

Mahler: Separation and Individuation

Mahler's work "has been of central importance to virtually all American object relations theories" (Hamilton, 1990, p. 56) and provides many con-cepts useful in the understanding of diverse situations encountered in social work practice such as child welfare services, placement of the elderly, and parent-child therapy.

Mahler, Pine, and Bergman's (1975) longitudinal study of normal children utilized observations in a nursery school setting and in the home. They explored "the psychological birth of the human infant," the establishment of a sense of identity, and psychological separation from as well as the maintenance of connection with the mother. In this context, separation refers to the feeling of being a separate individual—"the intrapsychic achievement of a sense of separateness from mother" (p. 8).

Four major subphases have been identified in the separation-individuation process: (1) differentiation; (2) practicing; (3) rapprochement; and (4) the beginnings of emotional object constancy.

Forerunners of Separation-Individuation

There are two phases the child must pass through before reaching the four major subphases of the separation-individuation process. These are the normal *autistic* (nonpathological) and *symbiotic* phases.

Autistic phase. During the first few weeks of life the child is in an autistic (auto: by one's own agency) stage of total absorption, has an "inborn unresponsiveness to outside stimuli" (Mahler, Pine, and Bergman, 1975, p. 41), and lacks awareness of a mothering person. Current early infant research indicating that children have greater perceptual awareness and more interaction with the mother and the environment than previously recognized has led to criticism of Mahler's characterization of this phase. Disagreement has also arisen because the term autistic has been applied to the pathological states of *infantile autism* and the autistic thinking characteristic of schizophrenia; nevertheless, Mahler did not imply a pathological state, but stressed its general meaning of inwardly focused self-absorption.

Acknowledging the new infant research, Mahler sought a more normalizing and less pathological term for this stage (Edward, Ruskin, and Turrini, 1992). However, she remained committed to the idea that there is an "early period in human existence when the infant's focus is directed inward and during which awareness of the outside is relatively minimal" (p. 13).

Symbiotic phase. From the second month onward, the child enters the symbiotic phase, becoming aware of its mother, and forming a "dual unity" with her, an "omnipotent system" (Mahler, Pine, and Bergman, 1975, p. 44). There is a sense of "oneness," of sharing a common boundary, which "forms the primal soil from which all subsequent human relations form" (p. 48). The mother's holding, cuddling, having eye contact, and talking to the child are important in this stage. Modifying this concept later, Mahler (Edward, Ruskin, and Turrini, 1992) "described symbiosis as referring to two organisms, intimately tied to each other, developing along in parallel" (p. 14).

This interaction *"shapes not only the personality of the child, but also that of the mother"* (p. 14; italics added). Parents may also develop psychologically as they enter the developmental stage of parenting.

The concept of symbiosis, with its emphasis on merging, has also been criticized by some as being too extreme or pathologically focused. Stern has asserted that symbiosis does not square with present research regarding the infant's capabilities (Edward, Ruskin, and Turrini, 1992). However, recent neurobiological research supports this concept, and Schore has proposed that symbiosis be returned to psychoanalytic theory (Montgomery, 2002).

> During the mutual gaze of the mother-infant dyad, the mother's face triggers high levels of endogenous opiates in the child's growing brain (Hofer, 1984; Panksepp, Siviy and Normansell, 1985). This pleasurable state promotes psychological drawing together (entrainment) between mothers and infants. Research on the psychobiology of attachment provides further evidence for matching between a caregiver and a child's endocrine and central nervous systems. (Montgomery, 2002, p. 183)

The concept of symbiosis enables us to understand a number of both normal and pathological phenomena in life. "The wish to merge and the fantasy of merging with another are commonplace in the language of love and in love itself" (Edward, Ruskin, and Turrini, 1992, p. 31). The research of Silverman, Lachmann, and Milich (Edward, Ruskin, and Turrini, 1992) suggests that symbiotic wishes are part of "everyday experiences and activities such as love, religion, meditation, and even jogging" (p. 31).

Symbiosis may be at work when a psychotic person is unable to distinguish "between self and object," and may also be involved in the "profound feelings of panic or dissolution of the self under the impact of separation or loss" (Edward, Ruskin, and Turrini, 1992, p. 31). Ms. O'Toole (discussed in Chapter 2), who believed she had murdered her neighbor because she had wished him dead, later suffered a psychotic break. Her clinician, Mrs. Wendover, visited her in the hospital.

When Mrs. Wendover entered the visiting room, Ms. O'Toole greeted her, saying: *"I am Mrs. Wendover."* Mrs. Wendover replied: "No, I am Mrs. Wendover." Ms. O'Toole found chairs for them and brought over two glasses of water. When it was time to leave, Mrs. Wendover said good-bye and walked toward the elevator. When she looked back, she noticed that Ms. O'Toole had picked up Mrs. Wendover's glass and was holding it in a secretive manner, trying to hide her action as she drank from it.

Ms. O'Toole is suffering from a major disruption in her ego boundaries. She is not indicating that she wants to be like Mrs. Wendover, which would be an identification. She thinks she *is* Mrs. Wendover, which illustrates a psychotic merger. Drinking from her therapist's glass is probably indicative of her wish to incorporate her therapist as part of herself. If this bizarre behavior is examined in the light of Mahler's theory of the symbiotic phase, we can view it as a regression to the symbiotic state; from that perspective, it is not outside of the normal human condition.

Ego functioning will thrive in the close human attachment of the symbiotic stage (Mahler, Pine, and Bergman, 1975), if this stage is progressive and nurturing. "In the context of the symbiotic exchange . . . ego functions such as anticipation, frustration tolerance, delay of drive discharge are developed and the ego as a whole becomes increasingly organized and structured" (Edward, Ruskin, and Turrini, 1992, p. 32). This conceptualization is similar to Hartmann's (1958) observation that the "autonomous ego functions" will grow in the "average expectable environment." If the child does not receive adequate nurturing, not only will relationship capacities become potentially impaired, but in addition the other ego functions will not adequately develop.

The First Subphase: Differentiation and the Development of the Body Image   Hatching

At about four to five months old, infants move out of the symbiotic orbit, beginning the process of *differentiation* from mother, marked by *hatching:* the infant's facial expressions begin to change, and a "certain new look of alertness, persistence, and goal-directedness" [emerges]. . . . An infant with this look has "hatched" (Mahler, Pine, and Bergman, 1975, p. 54). Infants about six months old reach to touch their mother and pull at her nose, her hair, or her necklace. The child begins "straining his body away from mother in order to have a better look at her . . . in contrast to simple molding when held" (p. 54). This arching away from mother has a serious developmental purpose, as the child begins to move toward individuation.

The child develops an interest in transitional objects during this phase, a concept Mahler, Pine, and Bergman (1975) attribute to Winnicott. The child is beginning to self-soothe, with an object that is like its mother but is not, and one that the child can control. Linus's blanket (from Charles Schulz's "Peanuts" comic strip) is a well-recognized transitional object. Citing Greenacre, Mahler, Pine, and Bergman (1975) note that the child's needs for physical contact with the mother are "touchingly expressed in the infant's insistent preference for an object which is lasting, soft, pliable . . . and

rapprochment = acercamiento.

remain[s] saturated with body odors" (p. 54). In addition, "the mother's preferred soothing or stimulating pattern is taken over . . . and so becomes a *transitional pattern*" (p. 55; italics added).

Transitional objects are in evidence throughout life, and at the end of life are often part of mourning rituals, linking the mourner with the person who has died. Objects such as photographs and special possessions are often treasured by the bereaved, and should "be recognized as ways of providing a soothing function for the mourner" (Berzoff, 2004, p. 251). After the destruction of the World Trade Center in New York, and the bombing in Oklahoma City, "mourners could be seen holding teddy bears, or posters, or photographs of the dead" (p. 251).

The Second Subphase: Practicing

The practicing subphase (starting from ten to twelve months and continuing to sixteen to eighteen months) is accompanied by an increase in physical mobility; crawling and walking enable infants to greatly increase their exploratory forays into the world. This (in the "average expectable environment") fills children with joy; at times they appear more interested in their explorations than in their mothers. Borrowing Greenacre's term, Mahler, Pine, and Bergman (1975) speak of the child's "love affair with the world" (p. 70), adding that the child "seems intoxicated with its own faculties and with the greatness of his own world" (p. 71).

During the practicing subphase, as children become more autonomous and delighted with new discoveries—including discoveries of their own new-found abilities—they seem to lose interest in mother. Perhaps, these feelings are also related to "the elated escape from fusion with, from engulfment by mother" (Mahler, Pine, and Bergman, 1975, p. 71). However, the child needs mother and will periodically return to her for comfort. This *emotional refueling* "perks him up and restores his previous momentum to practice and explore" (p. 290). The child also maintains a connection with mother through seeing and hearing her.

The Third Subphase: Rapprochement

Although exciting, the practicing stage has its psychological dangers; becoming aware of their separateness from their mothers, children often develop *separation anxiety.* Yet, they do not want to regress to the symbiotic orbit; they are having too much fun! But how to create the right distance between closeness and independence, between autonomy and connection?

This is the dilemma of *rapprochement* (occurring between eighteen and twenty-four months) as described by Mahler, Pine, and Bergman (1975).

> Around 18 months our toddlers seemed quite eager to exercise their rapidly growing autonomy to the hilt. Increasingly, they chose not to be reminded that at times they could not manage on their own. Conflicts ensued that seemed to hinge upon the desire to be separate, grand, and omnipotent, on the one hand, and to have mother magically fulfill their wishes. . . . The prevalent mood changed to that of general dissatisfaction, insatiability, a proneness to rapid swings of mood and to temper tantrums. The period was thus characterized by the rapidly alternating desire to push mother away and to cling to her—a behavioral sequence that the word "ambitendency" describes most accurately. (Mahler, Pine, and Bergman, 1975, p. 95)

Intense rapprochement struggles also characterize adolescence, and present dilemmas throughout the life cycle, as we negotiate distance-closeness issues in relationships with others. The philosopher Arthur Schopenhauer was reported to have observed that porcupines struggle to find the right distance between each other. They move closer together for warmth on a cold night; finding that their quills hurt each other, they move apart, only to be too cold again. Finding the right distance is not only a problem for porcupines but for people as well. It is a crucial problem for people with borderline personalities, as they continually struggle to maintain the right distance in all their relationships. One client stated: "I don't want to be submerged and yet I'm scared of being too much of an individual."

In the Japanese culture, the emphasis is on integration within one's family and social networks rather than on differentiation and autonomy, as stressed on the whole in contemporary American culture (Tamura and Lau, 1992). Yet, newly married Japanese couples also need to work out closeness and separation issues in their relationships with each other and with their new extended families.

> Major tasks of a marriage in any culture are the formation of a secure marital relationship and the realignment of relationships with the members of the extended families of both spouses. It is complicated and difficult for Japanese couples to achieve both because relationship with the extended family is more emphasized. In Japan there is a popular phrase: *A distance where soup does not get cold;* that is, the ideal distance between the parents' and children's households would be a few blocks away where they can easily deliver foods without the

soup getting cold. The soup would be too hot if the two generations live together, but too cold if they live far apart. (Tamura and Lau, p. 327; italics in the original)

The Beginnings of Emotional Object Constancy

In this final phase (occurring between twenty and twenty-two months until thirty and thirty-six months), complex developmental phenomena occur. First, children internalize an image of their mother, which can comfort them in her absence (termed *object constancy*). This leads to internalization of a positive image of themselves.

Object
Constancy

With the development of object constancy, the child's negative and positive images of the mother become fused into one consistent image (representation) of her. This enables children to modify their angry feelings toward mother and to experience anger while still having loving feelings toward her. If all goes well, children will normally develop feelings of ambivalence, wherein both good and bad feelings toward a loved person can coexist. A mother, for example, might resent her child's demands at times, but her overwhelmingly positive feelings for the child predominate and thus help her temper or modulate her angry feelings. It is, therefore, conversely important for the child to develop object constancy as this "fosters the fusion of the aggressive and libidinal drives and tempers the hatred for the object [mother] when aggression is intense" (Mahler, Pine, and Bergman, 1975, p. 110).

When object constancy does not develop, and the child experiences a conflictual relationship with its mother, if the mother goes away, however temporarily, it "stirs up considerable expressed or unexpressed anger and longing; under such conditions, the positive image of the mother cannot be sustained" (Mahler, Pine, and Bergman, 1975, p. 114).

The defense that develops in response to inadequate development of object constancy is *splitting,* wherein the good and bad feelings (about the self or another or a situation) are handled in an all-or-none fashion at any given time. Ambivalence per se is unstable and not sustainable, and the psychological dilemma is "solved" allowing either the positive or the negative, but not both simultaneously, into consciousness, with dissociation of the other (Shapiro, 1978). "In splitting, the positive and negative fantasized relationships remain alternatively in consciousness with the complementary side dissociated" (p. 1307). Splitting occurs in everyone to some degree; however, many object relations theorists see splitting in the borderline personality as a predominating and immature defense (Shapiro, 1978).

Kernberg suggested that borderline patients' core difficulty lies in their inability to bring together and integrate loving and hating aspects of both their self-image and their image of another person. [They] cannot sustain a sense that they care for the person who frustrates them. Kernberg saw this characteristic failure in the achievement and tolerance of ambivalence . . . as diagnostic. He suggested that loving fantasized relationships and hating ones are internally "split" for the borderline patient to prevent the anxiety that would result if they were experienced simultaneously. (Shapiro, 1978, p. 1307)

The splitting of staff by borderline patients is often observed on inpatient psychiatric units. Patients will, often successfully, manage to pit the "good" staff (those who appear to favor them) against the "bad" staff (those who appear to disfavor them) (Tashjian, 1979); the following example, illustrates such splitting by K, a young adult man in a psychiatric hospital.

Indeed, he devalued the whole hospital experience as he mythologized his high school years, endowing them with success and freedom from conflict. He attempted to split the staff by identifying the "good" and the "bad" and, in doing so, alienated most of them. For instance, he had a special fixation about a black psychiatric technician on the basis of his color. He saw himself as better than blacks, yet feared them because of a projected retaliatory rage. He repeatedly called this man a "jungle bunny," yet could not see why the man would be sensitive to such an epithet. K tried to get me to fire the technician (who was remarkably patient with K's abuse) and, when I would not entertain such thoughts, saw us as aligned against him. He was relentless in his attack as, at the same time, he pleaded for help. He wore the staff out, driving them beyond their capacity to understand him or to listen to my explanations of his patterns of maladaptive object relations; by the end, the staff's countertransference reactions were negative and apparent. Thus the milieu, which ideally should have aided him in working through his conflicts and strengthening his ego, became an arena for continued destructive behavior and sterile repetition compulsion. (Tashjian, 1979, pp. 44-45)

Internalization is "the key concept in modern psychoanalytic developmentalism" (Grolnick, 1990, p. 28). The development of object constancy and its reliance on the process of internalization, as described in Mahler's work, sheds light on the process of identity formation. Identity formation (successful or failed) and struggles in its formation are universal. Although

"lacks . . . the essential element of creative originality." (Applegate and Bonovitz, 1995, p. 72)

Seneca, a young woman in Toni Morrison's (1999) novel *Paradise,* reflects on her past experience as a foster child; although not uncared for or even unloved, she clearly doubted that she was approved of for herself, sensing that she had gained approval through conformity, as "she took reprimand quietly, ate what was given, shared what she had and never ever cried" (Morrison, 1999, p. 135). As Seneca adapted to her foster homes by external compliance to her perceptions of expected behaviors, her false self evolved.

"Parentified" children of alcoholic parents often sacrifice their true selves while assuming caretaking functions and effecting parental wishes. The depressive person's reliance on the dominant other (Arieti and Bemporad, 1978) bears a resemblance to the false self. Winnicott (Giovacchini, 1993) discusses a "continuum of the false self 'ranging from the healthy, polite aspect of the self to the truly split-off, compliant, false self that is mistaken for the whole person'" (p. 254).

The Capacity to be Alone

The capacity to be alone "is one of the most important signs of maturity in emotional development" (Winnicott, 1965, p. 29). The experience of a close nurturing relationship fosters tolerance for and even pleasure in aloneness. "The basis of the capacity to be alone is the experience of being alone in the presence of someone" (p. 36). With good enough mothering, the child is not alone when left alone, as the image of the mother has become internalized and is available through a "self-evocative function" (Grolnick, 1990); this is similar to the development of object constancy (Mahler, Pine, and Bergman, 1975). The capacity to be alone can encourage the "imagination to flourish" (Storr, 1988, p. 106).

Self psychology was developed by Kohut in the 1970s and 1980s and has similarities to object relations theory, as both study the development of the self; but each theory has a different perspective, and each offers unique insights.

SELF PSYCHOLOGY

Kohut's theory of self psychology discusses the development of the self, emphasizing the development of cohesion of the self; when the self does not cohere, "fragmentation and emptiness of the self" occur (Wolf, 1988, p. 11). Understanding the subjective world of the individual is a cornerstone of Kohut's theory; empathic responsiveness of the therapist becomes the key to effective treatment. Kohut has broken with Freud's drive and conflict theories, as have other object relations theorists, such as Fairbairn and Winnicott. Kohut observed that a major difference between self psychology and psychoanalytic theory is the latter's emphasis on drives, which eventuate in "Guilty Man," whereas he focused on the "Tragic Man," who personified "the essence of fractured, enfeebled, discontinuous human existence (Kohut, 1997:238)" (Brandell, 2004, p. 63).

Through the utilization of a healing therapeutic relationship, which becomes the focus of treatment, the patient is enabled to achieve a firmer, more stable sense of self and self-esteem. The examination of the therapeutic relationship (or selfobject transference) becomes the major goal of treatment; when interpretations are made, they encompass *"reactivated selfobject needs"* of the patient, which have been evoked by the treatment (Donner, 1991, p. 57; italics added).

Selfobjects

Selfobjects essentially refer to people who meet a person's needs for developing and sustaining a sense of self and self-esteem. The presence of positive selfobjects (nurturing parents or parent-substitutes) during childhood is critical for the development of a cohesive sense of self; however, selfobject experiences are needed throughout adulthood (both through close relationships with others and through evoked memories of past selfobjects). "Along with food and oxygen, every human being requires age-appropriate selfobject experiences from infancy to the end of life" (Wolf, 1988, p. 11).

In Chapter 1, we discussed Vivienne, who committed suicide when she was fourteen. Her initial depression and shaky self-esteem had improved during the period when she received support from a warm and empathic teacher. However, when he left to move across the country, Vivienne could not replace this loss and was overcome with depression. The teacher was not merely an idealized older person to her; he was needed to "replace something missing in the self" (Mack and Hickler, 1981, p. 107). Therefore, his leaving was more than a sad loss; it produced a "terrible emotional pain, a sense of nothingness, and, potentially, a dissolution in the structure of the self" (p. 107). From the self psychology perspective, Vivienne appears to have related to the teacher as a selfobject.

If Vivienne had received therapy with a self psychology orientation, the emotions and wishes for need fulfillment that she had directed toward this teacher might have been transferred to her therapist, and if this selfobject transference had been brought out into the open in an empathic manner and worked through, then Vivienne might have developed a firmer sense of self, without needing others so desperately to give her permission to feel good about herself.)

In her novel, *Villette,* Charlotte Brontë (Bell/Brontë, 1853) describes Paulina, six, who comes to live with Mrs. Bretton for several months. Paulina's mother has recently died, and her father, brooding and overcome by guilt, is prescribed travel as a remedy by his doctors. So he temporarily leaves Paulina with Mrs. Bretton, an old family friend. Paulina is grief stricken when he leaves, but "repressed it. That day she would accept solace from none; nor the next day: she grew more passive afterwards" (p. 18). Paulina then develops a relationship with Graham, Mrs. Bretton's sixteen-year-old son. Her world centers on Graham, who becomes her selfobject (this was Brontë's artistic and human insight in 1853, more than a century before Kohut developed his concept). In the mornings, Paulina would persuade Mrs. Bretton to include a sweet cake for Graham to take to school, insisting that "he would like it" (p. 21).

> Graham did like it very well, and almost always got it. To do him justice, he would have shared his prize with her [Paulina] to whom he owed it; but that was never allowed: to insist, was to ruffle her for the evening. To stand by his knee, and monopolize his talk and notice, was the reward she wanted—not a share of the cake.

> With curious readiness did she adapt herself to such themes as interested him. One would have thought the child had no mind or life of her own, but must necessarily live, move, and have her being in another: now that her father was taken from her, she nestled to Graham, and seemed to feel by his feelings: to exist in his existence. (Bell/Brontë, 1853, pp. 21-22)

An interesting note is that Charlotte Brontë wrote this (and her earlier novels) under the name Currer Bell. She and her two sisters (Anne and Emily), who were also important writers, wrote under pseudonyms, and each chose a man's first name. This was done to help ensure publication, as there was a good deal of discrimination against women writers at that time.

Empathy

A major tenet of self psychology is the understanding and use of empathy, the ability to "participate in another's feelings and experiences and to understand them" (Sutherland, 1989, p. 137). The appropriate application of empathy is the affective cornerstone of self psychology therapy. When the client feels understood, "new 'compensatory structures' are built" and a "stronger, more cohesive self structure" can gradually emerge (Lynch, 1991, p. 16). Empathy is vital in any form of clinical work; it allows the client "to feel understood in a way that connects the person to others" (Donner, 1991, p. 54).

> Empathy is a message . . . coming from a selfobject, that one is a human among humans. The most disavowed thoughts and affects . . . held by a client to be out of the realm of "normal" . . . can, in the context of empathy, be brought into the thinkable sphere of self experience. . . . Immersion in a therapeutic relationship characterized by sustained empathy can increase ownership of self. . . . This . . . inevitably expands one's ability to view others through a more empathetic lens. (Donner, 1991, pp. 54-55)

The development of empathy is one of the major skills for clinical social work students to acquire in developing a professional self (Urdang, 1999). However, the therapeutic use of empathy can create complexities; receiving an empathic response from the therapist can create anxiety in some patients (Kohut, 1971). The "immediate pleasure" of feeling understood can be followed by the fear of "a regressive merger experience" with the therapist in certain kinds of clients (p. 306). Patients can fear giving up the security of their "narcissistic isolation" as they face the risks of getting close to others. Kohut (1971) describes a patient whose fears of "empathic contact with another person and of participation in the world, were movingly portrayed . . . in [the following] dream" (p. 306).

> This man had lost his mother in very early childhood and had lost a number of other mother figures subsequent to the first loss. He dreamed that he was alone in his house, his fishing equipment by his side, looking out the window. Through the window he saw numbers of fishes swimming by, big and little, and attractive, and he was yearning to go fishing. He realized, however, that his house was at the bottom of the lake and that as soon as he opened the window to fish the whole lake would flood the house and drown him. (Kohut, 1971, pp. 306-307)

Case Illustration

Kohut (1971) developed self psychology through his work with patients with narcissistic personality disorders, a group of self-centered and self-absorbed patients who had been difficult to treat with standard psycho-analytic techniques. Self psychology has subsequently been extended to the treatment of many "disorders of the self" (Wolf, 1988, p. 24), including treatment of addictions and alcoholism, in which alcoholism is considered "a disorder of the self" (Levin, 1991, p. 3); treatment of eating disorders, which involve many "'self' issues" ("self-esteem and self-cohesion") (Barth, 1991, p. 223); and in the treatment of depression, in which the therapist's "empathic attunement to the emergence of the selfobject transferences . . . [can lead to] the restoration of the patient's . . . sense of cohesion" (Deitz, 1991, p. 201).

Wagner (1991) applies self psychology concepts to treating abusing parents who were often abused themselves as children. "Bereft of empathic selfobjects [i.e., nurturing caretakers] . . . [and] subject to multiple traumatic empathic failures, they were unable to develop a cohesive sense of self" (p. 249). Unable to meet their children's needs, the parents turned to their children (as selfobjects) to meet *their* needs; when the children are unable to nurture their parents and appear "unresponsive, the parent feels injured and may respond with infantile rage" (Wagner, 1991, p. 249).

Allyson, twenty-five, is a white mother of two children, whose seven-year-old son was removed from the home because of abuse (Wagner, 1991). She lives with her daughter Jenni, three, and has a history of alcoholism and multiple hospitalizations for depression.

> Consistently deprived of the mirroring and confirming experiences that would allow for an internalized cohesive sense of self, Allyson faces mothering with a split-off and painfully needy self. She looks to her daughter . . . to gratify her needs. When Jenni is unable to gratify those needs, Allyson regresses to narcissistic rage. . . . Allyson is unable to be empathically connected to either of her children. Out of her own inability to find inner soothing and self-love, Allyson is unable to provide these to her children. (Wagner, 1991, p. 251)

Allyson made progress during her therapy, using the supportive therapist "as a selfobject" (Wagner, 1991, p. 258). In this approach, the primary emphasis was directed toward repairing and rebuilding her own sense of self and learning ways to soothe herself and regulate her emotions (developing the ego function of management of needs and feelings). The underlying assumption in this approach is that when this is accomplished, the mother will internalize the good selfobject (the therapist) and incorporate the therapist's positive regard for her into her own personality. Only then will she be able to serve as a good enough selfobject for her children, because the clinician "provides mirroring and soothing functions, and helps the abusive parent-patient anticipate and regulate her needs, she is able to internalize, or *transmute,* the therapist's selfobject functions into self-functions" (p. 258; italics added).

Self psychology has evolved and has developed divergent approaches, although empathy, selfobjects, and selfobject transferences remain key concepts (Brandell, 2004). Infant research has supported and expanded many of its major formulations, such as Lachmann and Beebee's focus on "self-regulation and transmuting internalization" (p. 66). Self psychology is one of the theoretical underpinnings of the new paradigm, *relational psychoanalysis,* which is discussed further in Chapter 4.

We now turn to the cognitive and behavioral theories which, in contrast to psychodynamic theories, focus primarily on intellectual thought processes and observed behaviors, generally dismissing unconscious conflicts, motivations, and affects from their approaches, although there is increasing movement toward integration with psychodynamic concepts.

BEHAVIORAL AND COGNITIVE THEORIES

Cognitive and behavioral therapies have been developing at a rapid pace. For some clinicians, they are the mainstay of their practice; others may use them within a psychodynamic context. Cognitive and behavioral approaches are often combined into cognitive-behavioral treatment (CBT).

Behavior Theory

John B. Watson introduced behaviorism into psychology in 1913, stressing that "psychology must abandon its focus on subjective 'mentalistic' concepts and instead focus exclusively on behavior" (Ashford, Lecroy, and Lortie, 1997, p. 65). Watson developed the concept of learning theory, which emphasizes that development proceeds from learning experiences and focuses on "studying *observable stimuli* and *observable responses* to the stimuli" (p. 66; italics added). From this perspective, concepts such as the unconscious and mental representations of self and other would not only be irrelevant but also devoid of meaning. A further addition to learning theory, by B. F. Skinner, was the concept of *operant conditioning,* "a form of learning that occurs when responses are controlled by their consequences" (p. 66).

Operant conditioning, which utilizes *positive reinforcement,* encourages desired behaviors by providing positive responses or rewards, such as giving movie privileges for completing homework. As no simple one-to-one correspondence exists between a consequence and its effect, an individualized study of a person's motivational system is necessary, as a reward for one child (a movie) might not be a reward for another, who might dislike or be fearful of movies or prefer some other type of reward. Furthermore, consequences "aversive to some may be reinforcing for others"; scolding is usually viewed as a negative (or aversive) experience by children, but may be a positive (positive in the sense that it conditions increased frequency of the reprimanded behavior) reinforcer as it is "a form of attention" (Sadock and Sadock, 2003, p. 145).

Behavior Therapy

Positive reinforcement can be used purposefully or inadvertently by clinicians. A clinician may intentionally praise a client who progressively takes steps to improve a work situation. A clinician may inadvertently use negative reinforcement by appearing uninterested when a client talks about childhood conflict, but inadvertently use positive reinforcement by listening with avid attention when sexual issues are discussed. Social work students have been shown to respond positively to praise (a reinforcer) from their supervisors (Nelson, 1974). Paradoxically, some clients with depressive traits and severe superegos might find praise uncomfortable and react negatively to this reinforcer.

Mrs. Billings (discussed in Chapter 1), hospitalized for depression, was visited by her husband, who asked if he could take his wife out of the hospital for lunch. The interviewer encouraged this, recalling Mr. Billings saying that he should take his wife out more—"it's a help for her to eat out." From a behavioral perspective, this intervention was aimed at behavioral change; the positive reinforcing aspects of this experience might encourage continuing this behavior at home. In this instance, a behavioral approach was incorporated into a predominantly psychodynamic orientation, without the interviewer being explicitly aware that she was utilizing a behavioral intervention; this happens many times.

Joseph Wolpe (1976) developed *systematic desensitization,* which is the *"overcoming of unadaptive anxiety response habits"* (p. 61; italics in the original). Desensitization involves application of relaxation techniques combined with gradually leading the client to the feared object (sometimes in imagery, sometimes in reality), whether it be airplanes, snakes, or other phobic situations. Bandura (1976) discusses a treatment model for agoraphobic patients (those phobic about the world outside of their homes) in which the therapist participates in activities with the patient. "Clients accompany the therapist into the avoided situation over a period of several days. The longer they are exposed to the aversive events, the more dramatic is the experience that what they dread does not happen" (pp. 44-45). Gradually the therapist's participation diminishes and the patient's solo exposure is increased.

In a *modeling* procedure, the client learns from the therapist's purposefully modeled behavior, such as when the therapist demonstrates various ways of being assertive (assertiveness training) (Bandura, 1976). Modeling may also be more subtle, on the basis of the assumption that the client may learn to handle situations more calmly and logically by observing the way the therapist calmly and logically approaches problem-solving with the client.

In Chapter 2, while discussing the ego's executive functioning, a homemaker assigned to a woman overwhelmed with the care of her ten children was described. The homemaker did not take over and do things for her, but through modeling involved the client by engaging in household activities with her. Social work students may refer to a particular professor as a role model for them, indicating that his or her ways of responding, with empathy and caring, enabled them to further develop these characteristics in themselves. *Social skills training,* utilized with many populations, involves procedures such as "instructions, prompts, modeling, behavioral rehearsal, feedback, and homework assignments" (Curran and Monti, 1986, p. 2). One program with schizophrenic patients focuses on enhancing their abilities with "interpersonal skills, nutrition and meal planning, health and hygiene, money management, prevocational [guidance], [learning how to access] community resources and social networks" (Brown, 1986, pp. 97-100). Some programs involving patients' relatives aim to "reduce family patterns that have been implicated as factors contributing to schizophrenic relapse" (Curran and Monti, 1986, p. 3).

Social skills training has been applied in other contexts, including communication skills training for married couples (Jacobson, 1986), the treatment of children with peer-relationship difficulties (French and Tyne, 1986), and is one aspect of a behavioral approach in the treatment of autistic children (Groden and Baron, 1988).

Treatment approaches vary among behaviorists, and a range of opinion exists on "theoretical orthodoxy" as opposed to "theoretical integration." Thyer (1988) observes that "behavioral approaches have had a major influence on clinical social work education and practice" (p. 127) and, cites Rubin's review of research, affirming the effectiveness of "problem-solving and task-centered methods" that have often been combined with behavioral work (p. 128). Helen Singer Kaplan (1974) developed a form of sex therapy that incorporates behavioral approaches to sexual dysfunction as well as psychodynamic interventions. She recommends the "combined and integrated use of prescribed, systematically structured sexual experiences and psychotherapeutic intervention within a basic psychodynamic context" (p. 220). Wachtel (1977) advocates an approach combining psychoanalytic understanding with behavioral techniques that promote active intervention on the therapist's part. Marmor (1971) suggests that "all psychotherapy, regardless of the techniques used, is a learning process" (p. 26).

Although behavior therapy and cognitive therapy are different approaches, with different underlying assumptions, they have often been combined into cognitive-behavioral therapy.

Cognitive Theory

In Chapter 2, we examined the ego function of cognition and the importance of intellectual functioning, judgment, appraising, and reasoning in coping with daily problem solving in life. People with serious deficits in cognitive functioning, such as those impaired by schizophrenia, or mental retardation, brain tumors, or Alzheimer's disease, often have serious problems in their psychosocial functioning. Other problems with cognitive functioning can develop; people in emotional crisis may suddenly be unable to apply their usual sequential, logical thinking to the crisis, and those with chronic characterological problems may have ongoing deficits in judgment and logical thinking. Cognitive approaches such as enhancing reasoning and judgment as well as reflective techniques (Woods and Hollis, 1990) are a traditional part of the psychodynamic, ego psychological framework utilized by clinical social workers for many years, although they are regularly overlooked in many discussions of cognitive therapy.

Cognitive therapy, generally presented as standing in marked contrast to psychodynamic theory, developed during the 1950s and 1960s; it emphasizes the way people think about themselves and their lives. It is important to the cognitive theorist to examine the "beliefs, expectations, thoughts, opinions, evaluative standards, attributions and images" which may "operate to promote an individual's well being or . . . function as determinants of disturbance and dysfunction; 'the pathway' to change is through cognitive change" (Granvold, 1999, p. 63). In other words, it is thoughts (ideas or attitudes embodied in ideas) (such as "I always fail") that produce affective distress; therefore, if the person's thinking changes (to "I can be successful") and he or she realizes that thoughts of inevitable failure are a "bad habit" of thinking, then self-esteem will improve, and will be accompanied by positive affect.

While cognitivists generally adhere to the primacy of cognitive factors in therapy, they have incorporated behavioral techniques, and the literature frequently refers to cognitive-behavioral therapy (CBT). As generally practiced,

CBT is time-limited, with specific treatment goals that have been mutually agreed upon; "out-of-session" time is utilized by clients' active participation in tasks such as journaling; behavioral outcomes that can be measured are part of the treatment planning; "certainly these features are appreciated, and now required by third-party payers and others" (Northcut, 1999, p. 38). A proliferation of studies on CBT affirms the efficacy of this approach (Northcut, 1999), and CBT is often acclaimed as the treatment of choice for many psychiatric, emotional, and interpersonal problems. Endorsements, such as the assertion that Beck's (1976) model of cognitive therapy "is one of the most useful psychotherapeutic interventions currently available for depressive disorders" (Sadock and Sadock, 2003, p. 959), are common.

Some cognitive therapists adhere to an "orthodox" approach, while others integrate diverse theories and methodologies; currently "more than twenty distinct varieties of cognitive therapy have been identified" (Granvold, 1999, pp. 55-56). Constructivist theory, influential in social work, is also applied by some cognitive theorists; "the essence of cognitive theory is that human existence is about meaning making" (p. 60), which is the basic premise of constructivist theory.

Cognitive Theory and the Unconscious

While cognitive theory does not utilize the concept of the Freudian unconscious, the concept of the cognitive unconscious, which "includes beliefs, rules, and cognitive-affective schemata" (Eagle, 1987, p. 166) introduced into cognitive theory, is similar to the constructivist view of "tacit knowing," which acknowledges that the mind actively organizes experiences (Northcut, 1999, p. 43). "Constructivist perspectives emphasize the operation of tacit (unconscious) ordering processes, the complexity of human experience, and the merits of a developmental, process-focused approach to knowing (Mahoney, 1995, p. 7)" (Northcut, 1999, p. 43). This is similar to Arieti and Bemporad's (1978) formulation that "motivation is not necessarily instinctual but is very often the result of complicated cognitive constructs which have become unconscious" (p. 362).

The *schema* (plural *schemata*) is a concept appearing in psychodynamic and cognitive approaches; it is concerned with the organization of thought and experiences. Beck (1976) describes schemata as organized patterns of thinking and ordering of ideas, such as the depressive triad. Piaget (Elkind, 1981) refers to schemata in describing the development and organization of thought in the child. His schemata are "tied to mental operations and cognitive structures" (p. 8). Bowlby's (1988) attachment theory implies the development of schemata by describing how "each partner builds in his or her mind working models of self and of other and of the patterns of interaction that have developed between them" (p. 29). Bowlby's approach involves intellectual processing or cognition (working models) as well as developmental concepts of self and other.

Eagle (1987) describes a commonality present in the idea of schemata, noting that "the concept of self- and object representations is intended to refer to the implicit schemata, images, and working models—whatever language one chooses to use—one implicitly has of oneself and others. Related concepts include self-image, body-image, identity, and object constancy" (pp. 170-171). The cognitivists are interested in these self-schematas, which are "relatively inflexible, general rules or silent assumptions (beliefs, attitudes, concepts) about self and one's relationship with others and the world" (Granvold, 1999, p. 59). When these schemata are negative and dysfunctional, they are responsible for emotional problems, and "effective psychotherapy is highly contingent upon accessing and modifying them" (p. 59).

Beck (1976), the originator of cognitive therapy, has categorized schemata and flawed thought processes that lead to emotional difficulties. The tendency to overgeneralize refers to "unjustified generalization on the basis of a specific incident. For example, a child makes a single mistake and thinks, 'I never do anything right'" (pp. 94-95). It is not unusual to find students thinking this way: "I failed this test—I don't know anything—I shouldn't be in graduate school!" In cognitive therapy, the clinician brings these habitual thought patterns to a person's attention, attempting to replace them with more positive and adaptive attitudes.

Cognitive Theory and the Therapeutic Relationship

The therapeutic relationship, of central importance in psychodynamic work, has not been emphasized in cognitive theory, but this has been changing, and leading cognitivists, such as Beck, have stated that the therapeutic relationship should not be ignored; therapy with people with personality disorders has also highlighted the need to work on the relationship (Northcut, 1999). Countertransference issues of cognitive therapists are receiving more attention, as therapists attend to their own "feelings, attitudes and cognitions toward their clients" (p. 43).

When studying the reduction of symptoms in depressed clients who were treated with CBT, Castonguay and colleagues (Drisko, 1999) observed that there was progress

> only where there was a strong therapeutic alliance and strong emotional involvement by the client. Improvement was not necessarily

associated with the therapist's focus on the interpersonal consequences of cognitions and behaviors; indeed, such a focus was found counterproductive without a solid working alliance. (p. 160)

Cognitive Theory and Emotion

Cognitivists have generally under- or devalued emotion as having a central role in human behavior; patients' emotions were "intrusive, maladaptive, debilitating, generally unpleasant to experience, and negative in effect" (Granvold, 1999, p. 76). Emphasis was placed on helping clients manage and control their needs and feelings (such as anger and depression). Although helping clients cope with their emotions is also an activity of the psychodynamic clinician, psychodynamic treatment generally aims to help clients *experience* their emotions in their relevant contexts, leading to insight, which in turn can normalize dysfunctional behaviors and relationships. However, in recent developments, constructivist cognitivists (in contrast to traditionalist cognitivists) have come to value working with affects as "powerful ways of knowing," and they encourage affective expression rather than "its control" (p. 76).

High levels of anxiety and depression can influence specific cognitions (such as "I am no good"), but can also impact *overall* cognitive functioning. A person with normally good cognitive functioning can become temporarily cognitively impaired by an emotional crisis. Reducing levels of anxiety and depression through therapy and/or psychosocial intervention with the family and school can improve school functioning.

In an article titled, "Psychoanalysis as Cognitive Remediation," Weinstein and Saul (2005) discuss analytic treatment of Natalie, a young adolescent girl with dyslexia, who had been receiving "intensive cognitive remediation" without much improvement in her academic functioning. During psychoanalytic play therapy, Natalie was able to get in touch with her fears about her father and conflictual feelings for him (of which she had been unaware). As she improved emotionally, there was a dramatic increase in her reading and spelling skills.

> It is our argument that the analysis allowed Natalie to access skills that had been acquired during previous remediation efforts, but had remained dormant or *blocked by conflict* . . . her inability to learn, or to retrieve what she knew, was also a way of warding off an affective awareness of the traumatic overstimulation of events with her father. (Weinstein and Saul, 2005, p. 253; italics added)

Natalie's enthusiasm and interest in learning and reading also increased; she was now more amenable to the incorporation of cognitive approaches: "The child can begin to think about learning, to think about thinking" (Weinstein and Saul, 2005, p. 260). Cognition and affect are interactive, both on a conscious and unconscious level; emotions are generally connected to thoughts, and thoughts often evoke emotions; "the brain cannot be separated from the heart" (Vaillant, 1993, p. 4). Noam (1996) describes the integration of thought, feeling, and experience. "The powerful abilities to make *cognition emotional* and *feelings reflective* has profound implications for the inner experience and the pursuit of a vital, true self" (p. 144; italics added).

Examples of Cognitive Therapy

A key concept in cognitive therapy is that of *attributions,* which is emphasized in social cognition theory (Heller and Northcut, 1999). "Attributional style refers to 'people's views about the cause of life events, including their own behavior and that of others . . . implied causality' (Granvold, 1994a, p. 15)" (Heller and Northcut, 1999, p. 113). When peoples' attributions are brought to their attention, they can be examined, and possibly modified; this has applications in work with individuals, couples, and families. In the following marital therapy case, Yolanda and Rod were helped to look at their rigid attributions regarding one another.

> This couple regularly presented fixed polarities in their attributions toward the other. For example, Yolanda and Rod were viewed as overresponsible versus underresponsible, uptight versus carefree . . . and productive versus lazy. To address these fixed polarizations the couple was taught to identify uncomfortable disturbing emotions by acknowledging their feelings as well as the automatic thoughts that entered their minds. . . . Rod and Yolanda discussed the possibilities for cognitive distortions, including polarized thinking, over-generalizations, and mind reading. Again, they were introduced to tools that helped them to challenge their own thinking. To slow down the escalating process of debate, each partner had to ask: What information supports or challenges my interpretation? Is there logic that supports my perception of what I've assigned to him or her? Could there be any other explanation for this behavior? (Basham, 1999, p. 150)

Catastrophizing, another faulty thought process emphasized by Beck (1976), is often found in anxious people; it is characterized as "anticipation of extreme adverse outcomes. The thinking of the anxious patient is grooved toward considering the most unfavorable of all possible outcomes of a situation" (Beck, 1976, p. 93). In the following example, Carol is catastrophizing.

Carol is a bright woman who functioned well in an administrative position but sought therapy because of symptoms of anxiety. She brought up her interest in a man who seemed attracted to her. They had brief (but intense) conversations in the office but never saw each other outside of work. Carol said she was afraid of getting married to him—what if they had nothing to talk about? What if he lost interest in her? What would it be like for her to live with him? Her therapist asked: "Maybe you should date first?" Carol looked at her therapist and burst into laughter—she could see that she was catastrophizing—that is, building up a negative scenario that is doomed to failure without going through appropriate, reality-based steps in building a relationship.

Beck (1976) utilizes cognitive therapy for depressive disorders, and bases treatment on the identification of a "depressive triad" of thoughts: "a negative conception of the self, a negative interpretation of life experiences, and a nihilistic view of the future" (p. 84). Patients are helped to reconceptualize their basic life assumptions. Beck has incorporated behavioral approaches into his therapy, such as "mobilizing the patient into more activity and positively reinforcing certain types of activity," but asserts that the ultimate "goal is cognitive modification" (pp. 267-268).

Discussion

Cognitive therapy, often combined with behavioral therapy (CBT), has become one of the most widely used forms of treatment today. Its challenging ideas contribute to diverse models of intervention; Northcut and Heller (1999) stress ways in which it can enhance psychodynamic social work. Cognitive approaches, however, are not new to social work and have been incorporated into its psychodynamic, psychosocial framework for years. As noted above, clinical social workers have utilized reality testing and psychoeducational appproaches, problem-solving and decision-making techniques, and encouraged thinking about consequences of behaviors. Woods and Hollis (1990) describe one level of social work treatment as "reflective discussion of the person-situation configuration" (p. 127), and note that

clients sometimes need help in understanding financial matters, a work situation, medical recommendations, or the implications of their own or someone else's physical condition. . . . Over and over again, workers strive to help clients *think* about the effects of their own actions on others, or about their consequences for themselves . . . the best procedure for the worker is not to "explain" the relationship between behavior and consequences, *but to lead the client to see the sequence themselves.* (Woods and Hollis, 1990, pp. 126-127; italics added)

In insight-oriented therapies, cognitive insights accompany the expression of feelings; patients gain both emotional and intellectual understanding of their conflicts, and its impact on them. Acknowledging that clinical work involves an integrative approach, Basch (1988) comments that "by the time treatment has been completed the therapist has probably made use of a combination of dynamic, behavioral, and cognitive techniques" (p. 55).

While cognitive theory and CBT offer insights, suggest new approaches, have had successful outcomes, and support aspects of existing social work practice, serious reservations exist about its *exclusive* use for all clients and all problems. One limitation of CBT is that cultural and social factors have "been largely neglected in the vast cognitive literature" (Heller and Northcut, 1999, p. 116). CBT has also not given sufficient study to trauma and its psychological sequelae "in the formation of schemas, core beliefs, and the like" (Northcut, 1999, pp. 41-42).

Although cognitive therapy has moved to include the impact of the therapeutic relationship, it is not universally applied, and concepts such as intersubjectivity may be minimized or absent in practice. Some clients have difficulty in forming relationships, and may need considerable time and greater awareness of the inner and outer wellsprings of their distress and maladaptive behaviors before they are able to work in a collaborative way with their CBT therapists. One client, when told by her therapist that their clinic was moving to brief six-week treatments, commented: "Six weeks! Do you know how long it took me to trust you?" Clients may need ongoing supportive grief work or long-term treatment to enable them to function, and/or to repair psychological damage which is chronic and pervasive; as another client commented: "Even a broken bone takes a long time to heal." Springer (1999) discusses limitations of CBT for adolescents needing long-term support and therapeutic help, and her observations have applicability to many adult clients.

For adolescents who have suffered multiple losses, physical or sexual trauma, and social or cultural alienation, a sole focus on cognitive or behavioral reformulations is likely to be inadequate. Psychic representations of the self as unworthy, unlovable, and expendable are not easily relinquished . . . clinicians need adequate time with their adolescent clients in order to help them access, bear, and place in perspective the nature and consequences of exceptionally difficult childhood and adolescent experiences. (Springer, 1999, p. 198)

CONCLUSION

As psychodynamic theory has evolved, the centrality of human relationships (i.e., the interpersonal social environment) and their contribution to the development of self-esteem and identity formation have been increasingly highlighted; attachment and loss experiences become major events to analyze in the study of lives. Object relations theory postulates that early human relationships determine how children see themselves, internalizing the responses from nurturing figures into their self-concepts. Mahler's concept of separation-individuation focuses on the inherent struggle that children experience in separating from their parents and becoming more autonomous, while still maintaining this important bond. The dialectical tension between separation-individuation is present throughout the life cycle, and has its parallel in community life as individuals experience ongoing conflict between social conformity and personal freedom.

The contribution of self psychology, as formulated by Kohut, emphasizes the development of the self, the formation of identity and self-cohesion, and stresses the importance of relationships (selfobjects) in the formation of identity and throughout life. Self psychology's utilization of empathy in treatment has been adopted by diverse schools, and its concepts have been incorporated into relational psychoanalysis, discussed in Chapter 4.

Cognitive behavioral therapy (CBT), with its goals of cognitive and behavioral change is in the forefront of psychotherapeutic treatment today; some cognitive therapists are now moving in the direction of adding psychodynamic concepts to their work, such as the role of the treatment relationship and the utilization of affects. The current predominance of CBT and the empirical research findings reporting its success play into the demands of insurance companies for short-term, "evidence based" treatment. This can create serious consequences for all those in need of longer-term care; again, Springer's (1999) comments in reference to troubled adolescents can be universally applied.

The contemporary U.S. mental health care system, by virtue of its emphasis on short-term treatment, is leaving in its wake an entire cohort of adolescents whose clinicians are not allowed the time and resources we know it takes to help them establish or reestablish a normative developmental trajectory. A high emotional as well as social and financial price is paid and will continue to be paid by current and future citizens. (Springer, 1999, p. 198)

Finally, there are serious consequences for social work training in which CBT and a "prevailing generalist approach . . . over the last several decades" has been in effect (Applegate, 2004, p. 33).

Knowledge for practice increasingly has become skill-based and performance-oriented, to the relative neglect of issues of meaning, emotion, and the dynamics of inner life. . . . So-called competency-based training, focused on behavior rather than the person behaving, does little to equip social work students with the critical analytic skills they need to address the multilayered complexity of their clients' problems. (Applegate, 2004, pp. 33-34)

As social work and the mental health field, in general, have been moving toward short-term evidence-based practice, there are pulls in the opposite direction, toward relational psychotherapy, constructivism, and narrative theory. These subjects are discussed in Chapter 4, along with the concept of resiliency.

LEARNING EXERCISE

Discuss one case in class in terms of how it might be handled by clinicians using the different theoretical perspectives of object relations theory, self psychology, and cognitive behavioral theories. Highlight some similarities as well as divergences in theory and technique.

SUGGESTED READING

Articles

Bowlby, J. 1988. Developmental psychiatry comes of age. *American Journal of Psychiatry* 145: 28-37.
Jones, K. 2005. The role of father in psychoanalytic theory: Historical and contemporary trends. *Smith College Studies in Social Work* 75: 7-28.

Books

Applegate, J. S., and J. M. Bonovitz. 1995. *The facilitating partnership: A Winnicottian approach for social workers and other helping professionals.* Northvale, NJ: Jason Aronson.

Jackson, H. (ed.). 1991. *Using self psychology in psychotherapy.* Northvale, NJ: Jason Aronson.

Mack, J. E., and H. Hickler. 1981. *Vivienne: The life and suicide of an adolescent girl.* New York: A Mentor Book, New American Library.

Mahler, M., F. Pine, and A. Bergman. 1975. *The psychological birth of the human infant.* New York: Basic Books.

Mitchell, S. 1988. *Relational concepts in psychoanalysis.* Cambridge, MA: Harvard University Press.

Northcut, T. B., and N. R. Heller. (eds.) 1999. *Enhancing psychodynamic therapy with cognitive-behavioral techniques.* Northvale, NJ: Jason Aronson.

Chapter 4

Postmodern Theories:
Constructivism, Relational Therapy,
Narrative Theory, and Resilience

Carriages rolled alien round us, stout
houses stood about us, solid but unreal—and none
ever knew us. *What* was real in that All?

Rainer Maria Rilke, *The Sonnets to Orpheus*

POSTMODERN THEORIES

Postmodern thought, currently permeating many disciplines, argues for the subjective nature of knowing and rejects the modernist "search for scientific truths, the quests for certainty, objectivity and rationality" (Ornstein and Ganzer, 2005, p. 566). Postmodernism encompasses diverse points of view, but its underlying constructivist premise posits "that there is no fixed reality, only constructed versions of reality determined by the perspective of the one doing the describing" (DeLaCour, 1996, p. 214). So, while people are affected by their social and cultural contexts, they are nevertheless active agents in their own lives, have the capacity to change and to create meaning. Constructivist thinking has contributed to relational therapy (and relational psychoanalysis) and to narrative theory, the subjects of this chapter. Resilience, discussed in the final section of this chapter, is a corollary issue.

CONSTRUCTIVISM

In a *New Yorker* cartoon titled "Theories of Everything," a father, a mother, and their teenage son and daughter are sitting on a couch; they are not talking

Human Behavior in the Social Environment, Second Edition

to each other, but their thoughts are revealed (Chast, 1998, p. 42). The father is thinking: "Everything's gone downhill since 1964." The mother thinks: "Everything is *my fault*." The daughter, glaring at her mother, thinks "Everything *is* your fault." And the young teenage boy thinks: "Everything would be perfect if I had a dirt bike." This scene portrays four individuals living within the same family context, but their preoccupations, interpretations, and the meanings (or theories) they have constructed are different.

Individuals are not passive recipients of fate, but actors in their own worlds, as they traverse "streams of life that relentlessly require new directions and connections" (Mahoney, 2003, p. xii). Although constructivism is ascribed to postmodern thinking, its philosophical underpinnings have a long history, starting with the philosophies of Lao Tzu and Buddha in the fifth and sixth centuries BC. "The Tao (literally, the 'path' or 'way')" describes "the fluidity of life and its essential embrace of seemingly opposite elements (the 'yin' and 'yang')"; change is always with us, especially in "our inner lives" (p. 3). Buddha observed that we fully participate "in the construction of our worlds by means of our thoughts, fantasies, and all manner of imaginings" (p. 3).

In ancient Rome, Heraclitus emphasized the evolving nature of existence: "Everything that is must also be becoming" (Mahoney, 2003, p. 4).

> It was Heraclitus who immortalized the statement that one cannot step into the same river twice. It is not just the water that is moving or the river that is changing. The person is also changed by the experience. We are neither spectators nor pawns in our lives. As Cris Williamson has put it in musical verse, we are both the changer and the changed. (Mahoney, 2003, p. 4)

Later European philosophers including Vico, Kant, Vaihinger, and Schopenhauer made important contributions to constructivist thought. Kant "portrayed the mind as an active organ of self-organization," and Schopenhauer stressed the importance of will (Mahoney, 2003, p. 4). In recent decades prominent proponents of constructivist theory include Albert Bandura, Gregory Bateson, Jerome Bruner, Viktor Frankl, Kenneth Gergen, Paul Watzlawick, and Jean Piaget (Mahoney, 2003). Watzlawick's focus on interpersonal and behavioral aspects of communication is relevant to constructivism's emphasis on intersubjectivity (presented in Chapter 8); Piaget's psychological theories of cognitive development, related to the child's construction of reality, meaning, and morality, are discussed in Chapters 9 and 10.

The constructivist perspective stresses *"meaningful action by a developing self in relationship"* (Mahoney, 2003, p. 5; italics in the original). Lifespan development is viewed as an ongoing, complex, and dynamic process, with periods of organization and disorganization. "Human development rarely follows a simple, linear path. It is more often a zigzag course, with frequent sticking points, repetitive circles, occasional regressions, and a few startling leaps and falls. The particulars may seem dizzying in their diversity, yet there are patterns" (p. 9).

While patterns imply "principles," and therefore a theory of human behavior is important, Mahoney (2003) asserts that it is more important to understand phenomenology (an existentialist term for the subjective experience of reality) than it is to develop "categories" (p. 10). Self psychology also emphasizes "the therapist's sustained, empathic immersion in the subjective experience of the client" (Brandell, 2004, p. 66).

Understanding the experiential world of others was also stressed by August Aichorn, an early psychoanalyst, who applied this concept in his pioneer work with juvenile delinquents. Anna Freud (Young-Bruehl, 1988), his close friend and colleague, highlighted this in her obituary for him in *The International Journal of Psychoanalysis*.

> "Whoever wants to work successfully with young delinquents has to be capable of stepping out of his own secure position in the social community, to identify himself with the offender, and thereby to become receptive to and understanding of the intricacies of the delinquent's character structure". . . . Unsuitability for the work he characterized as follows: "People who cannot escape from their own superego demands and invariably remain identified with society fail to win the confidence of the delinquent or to understand the workings of his mind." (Young-Bruehl, 1988, pp. 301-302)

It was important to Aichorn that the juvenile develop a relationship with him:

> The stronger his attachment to me and his identification with me . . . the more he loosens his hold on "delinquency" and incidentally becomes social. . . . This strikes me as an excellent method for building up a criminal gang for myself—if my inclinations went that way. (Young-Bruehl, 1988, p. 302)

RELATIONAL THERAPY

In relational therapy, the therapist is not considered an expert, but a participant observer in the therapy, which is "an interactive process in which meaning is continuously co-constructed by the participants" (Dean, 2002, p. 15). Central to this idea is the move away from the

> "one-person" psychology of traditional psychoanalysis (where the focus is on the patient), to a "two-person" perspective of the clinical process (where the focus is on the interactions of the two participants)—a fundamental change in perspective that many believe has transformed the theory and practice of psychoanalysis. (Brandell, 2004, p. 68)

Social work practitioners have traditionally valued the working relationship as critical to the practice of clinical work (Applegate, 2004). In psychoanalysis, the transference relationship (or "transference neurosis") is a central focus of treatment, and in self psychology therapy, the resolution of the selfobject transference is the major goal. Interest in the clinical relationship has increasingly developed in other disciplines, such as cognitive therapy, discussed in Chapter 3. This burgeoning interest in the therapeutic relationship tends to focus on postmodern relational theories, which is in sync with modifications in many psychodynamic treatments.

As relational therapists have moved away from a "one-person" psychology to the new "two-person" psychology, the focus has emphasized *interpsychic* interactions (Applegate, 2004), although Ghent (Brandell, 2004), for example, states that "the intrapsychic as well as the interpersonal" is important (p. 67). However, within a relational model, intrapsychic conflicts are viewed more as interpsychic conflicts, thought to develop in relation to internalized significant others. When a patient's internalized conflict is addressed in relational therapy, it "is usually seen as *taking place between opposing relational configurations rather than drive and defense* (Ghent, 1992:xviii)" (Brandell, 2004, p. 67; italics added).

Underlying relational therapy is the assumption that human relationships and the drive for attachment are fundamental in psychological life, and so the transactions between the clinician and the client become the major focus of treatment. Therapists are seen as active participants, rather than "detached observers," and therefore their feelings, reactions, and thoughts in each session are subject to ongoing self-scrutiny. Insight is no longer the primary aim of treatment; experiencing the authenticity of the therapeutic relationship is vital to the patient's development of an authentic sense of self.

Therapists strive to be "aware of their affective states, internal processes, and visceral bodily experiences" (Ornstein and Ganzer, 2005, p. 568). Stolorow's theory of intersubjectivity is widely used within this framework, and emphasis is placed on the defense of projective identification, "the only defense mechanism that has an interpersonal component" (p. 569). Attention is also given to clients' temperaments, biological make-up, as well as their social and cultural contexts.

Relational psychoanalysis has developed from theoretical contributions that include object relations theory, self psychology, current research on infant development, and Harry Stack Sullivan's theory of interpersonal psychoanalysis (developed in the 1930s and 1940s). Sullivan rejected Freudian emphasis on the primacy of the drives, stressing the critical role of relationships in human development; his major concepts were "forerunners to many current theoretical trends . . . [which] include self psychology, narrative, constructivist and intersubjective approaches, and the school of interpersonal psychoanalysis" (DeLaCour, 1996, p. 199). Sullivan was insightful about the key role anxiety (which is "interpersonal in nature") plays in psychological life; and he "attributed" this "noxious affect to . . . all of the 'difficulties of living'" (p. 211).

Sullivan stressed the curative role of the therapeutic relationship, and introduced his famous concept of the therapist as a "participant observer," borrowing this term from anthropology. Anthropologists become participants in the cultures they observe, which, in turn, affects the behaviors of their subjects, the subjects' interactions with the anthropologists, and anthropologists' own subjectivity; in a similar manner, the therapist and patient are involved in ongoing interactional processes.

The therapist's countertransference, per se, is considered too narrow, too one-sided, from a relational perspective, and the concept of *enactments* is preferred, which involves the client's habitual patterns of response and relationship, but which is colored by the therapist's responses and interactions; attention to enactments is a vital part of the therapeutic process. "The therapist's personal vulnerabilities and issues are always implicated to some extent in an enactment and similarly are examined in terms of how they are being stimulated by the client's recreation of her or his preexisting relational patterns" (Ornstein and Ganzer, 2005, p. 570).

There are diverse, and conflicting, viewpoints about relational psychoanalysis. While some theorists see this as a future direction for psychoanalysis, others express concern that following this theory would lead to a disastrous abandoning of the basics of psychoanalysis. Balter (1999) emphasizes the necessity for patients to become aware of their unconscious processes, and for this to happen, attention must be centered on their *intrapsychic* world, accessed by their free associations. Focus on interpersonal interactions with active participation by the therapist, by contrast, will destroy this process, as well as the analyst's essential *neutrality*.

Neutrality and detachment are not synonymous, although these terms are often used interchangeably; citing Renik's concept of the analyst's "behavioral minimalism," Balter (1999) comments that neutrality is "an oft-criticized, much satirized, but enduring aspect of the analytic situation" (p. 121). The *New Yorker,* for example, often satirizes psychoanalysts' detachment (as well as other absurdities), such as doing crossword puzzles while the patient is lying on the couch, unaware of the analysts' lack of involvement. In Philip Roth's *Portnoy's Complaint,* Portnoy's girlfriend disparages her analyst's detachment, wondering if he is actually alive, but resolves this question one day when she phones him and hears his voice on the answering machine. Of course he's alive, she says. Whoever heard of a dead man with an answering machine!

Balter (1999) does not see neutrality as detachment, but as an ongoing, *active involvement* in helping patients explore their psychic life. He quotes Arlow's description of the mutuality of the analytic process.

> The joint search by patient and analyst for the picture of the patient's past is a *reciprocal process.* In a sense, we dream along with our patients, supplying at first data from our own store of images in order to objectify the patient's memory into some sort of picture. We then furnish this picture to the analysand, who responds with further memories, associations, and fantasies; that is, *we stimulate him to respond with a picture of his own.* In this way the analyst's reconstruction comes to be composed more and more out of the materials presented by the patient until we finally get a picture that is trustworthy and in all essentials complete. (Arlow, 1969) (Balter, 1999, p. 109; italics added)

Balter (1999) observes that relational analysts rely on "their own subjectivity and intuition," and although this is "highly developed," he is concerned that "they do not wait for many of the patient's free associations and do not suspend their own attention very much." Although they "interpret quickly and accurately," their interventions exclude "extensive observations by analyst or patient" (p. 112). Leary (Balter, 1999) has expressed concern that in postmodern analysis the focus is on the "constantly unfolding present," and therefore the "social constructivist accounts of psychoanalysis are ahistorical: without memory, there is no history" (p. 119).

> "Narrative reconceptualizations nod to historical reasons but these are then reinterpreted as present-day tellings. In key respects, postmodernism purges the analytic situation of the need to grapple with history, with things that once were and had an effect. . . .
>
> . . . The emphasis on the present and the unfolding moment diverts attention from that which *endures* in persons, in social transactions, and

in the world in which they occur. (Leary, 1994, p. 457)" (Balter, 1999, p. 119; italics in the original)

Couch (1999) addresses the dilemma of maintaining neutrality without being detached, emphasizing the "real relationship (the reality oriented contact between patient and analyst)," outside of the formal aspects of therapy (p. 131), such as the analyst's informal interchanges with patients that do not have a specific therapeutic focus; responding with "genuine reactions to important aspects of the patient's life as a fellow human being" (p. 151).

> The absence of these natural responses by the analyst, especially when called for by actual tragedies, losses, failures, successes, disappointments, and other significant events in the patient's life, can be the cause of the most serious errors in an analysis—namely, the professionalized creation of an inhuman analytic situation, divorced from real life. (Couch, 1999, p. 151)

Couch (1999) points to the dilemma for the psychoanalyst—how to preserve the social detachment and neutrality essential for the psychoanalytic process while maintaining a genuine relationship with the patient. Although the concept of analytic detachment is attributed to Freud, Couch points out that Freud himself established authentic relationships with his patients, citing accounts written by some of Freud's patients of their analyses with him. The following excerpt was taken from a diary, "published posthumously" (Blanton, 1971), of one of his patients, an American doctor, Smiley Blanton, discussing his first session with Freud (Couch, 1999, p. 143).

> "At all times he seemed in close touch with what I was giving him. There was none of that cold detachment which I had imagined was the attitude an analyst is supposed to take. As we went along, Freud's simple manner made me feel secure and easy. At the same time, there was a detachment which was not repelling but pleasant. I talked until I heard a clock strike four. I rose at once, stopping in the middle of my sentence. 'I am sorry the hour was so short,' said Freud as he accompanied me into the hall. He asked if I knew my way to the station, and I assured him that I did." (Blanton, 1971) (Couch, 1999, pp. 143-144)

Couch (1999) maintains that Freud "created a human and realistic atmosphere in which he subtly blended interpretive work with building a therapeutic alliance (and a personal) and real relationship with his patients" (p. 146); many later analysts have interpreted Freud's written works as prescribing more rigid attitudes toward patients than the ones Freud himself held. "I contend that Freud's clinical style is analytically sounder and more effective than the more rigid and impersonal technique of 'modern' analysis" (p. 146).

Anna Freud (Couch, 1999) spoke about the importance of recognizing and responding to the real relationship between the patient and the analyst.

> With due respect for the necessary strictest handling and interpretation of the transference, I feel still that we should leave room somewhere for the realization that analysts and patient are also two real people, of equal adult status, in a real personal relationship to each other. I wonder whether our—at times complete—neglect of this side of the matter is not responsible for some of the hostile reactions which we get from patients and which we are apt to ascribe to "true transference" only. But these are technically subversive thoughts and ought to be handled with care. (Anna Freud, 1954) (Couch, 1999, p. 138)

It is not easy to find "the appropriate balance" between detachment and personal responsiveness, while also avoiding the pitfalls of overinvolvement with its "excessive impingement of the analyst's real personality and realistic gratifications or interventions" (Couch, 1999, p. 147). Relational psychoanalysis and relational psychotherapy, involved with an ongoing direct interaction with clients, and with the "constantly unfolding present," may have an even greater struggle to find "the appropriate balance" between a warm, genuine, and authentic clinical relationship and one that turns into a personal, social relationship.

Although we have been exploring these issues in relation to psychoanalysis per se, for the social worker they are entirely germane to the ongoing balances that must be maintained in any helping relationship, in whatever service context. One such issue is self-disclosure.

Self-disclosure by the therapist is regularly utilized in relational therapy (Ornstein and Ganzer, 2005), although the question of how much should be "disclosed" to a patient remains a subject of ongoing debate (Sweezy, 2005). Considerations in deciding to disclose personal information include the context, the nature of the client's request, the therapist's motivation, and how this disclosure will be utilized in treatment. The therapist's message: "I was there—I know what you mean," can derail entering into the client's own experiencing (and meaning-making) of a particular event.

Sweezy (2005) expresses concern about the risk to the therapist by self-disclosure; whereas the client has the right to confidentiality, the therapist does not have this protection, and the client can use this new information inappropriately. "Once the therapist has made a disclosure, it is no longer her/his choice to hold that information private" (p. 82).

Relational therapy is heralded by some clinical social workers as "the model for the future" (Ornstein and Ganzer, 2005); the value of the therapeutic relationship, the utilization of intersubjectivity and enactments, and the need for the clinician's self-awareness are highlighted in this model. Opinions differ as to the extent that relational therapy, with its focus on enactments, should be the *primary* focus of treatment, and to what extent it might *accompany* other approaches. Not every client will be amenable to this level of insight treatment; some may be more responsive to alternative approaches, such as cognitive techniques, or to group rather than individual treatment. Clients may have presenting problems such as end-of-life issues, or be seeking to adopt a child, in which case a primary focus on therapeutic enactments would likely be inappropriate unless there are special indications discovered in the course of assessment. Finally, focusing too exclusively on transactional aspects of therapy can serve *defensive* purposes, enabling clients to avoid uncomfortable and painful aspects of their "real" lives outside of therapy; the "other 23 hours."

The *principles* of relational therapy, however, can be applied in all casework encounters. A relationship is essential to any type of intervention, as is the clinician's self-awareness and sensitivity to intersubjective interactions, even if this awareness is never shared with the client. Sometimes intersubjective reactions can be *translated* less explicitly into appropriate words or actions by the clinician, or serve tacitly as clues as to how to proceed.

A relative of a psychiatric patient who is about to be discharged from the hospital was being interviewed by the social work intern to determine whether he could provide supportive help to the patient. The intern was frustrated in the interview, as the man was uncomfortable and could not answer her questions. When asked in supervision if she had thought about bringing his discomfort out into the open, she was surprised—"But I'm not doing therapy with him." She learned that discussing his discomfort could be helpful to both of them, that this interview was a *clinical encounter,* that there are *different levels* of clinical intervention, and that while such an encounter may not be therapy in the strict sense, this does not negate the usefulness of reflecting on the client's feelings within the relationship.

In the practice of relational therapy, clients co-create stories of themselves, based on early interpersonal experiences; later, in the course of therapy, new stories are co-created with new meanings. Storytelling is a vital component of narrative theory: "A large part of our meaning making is experienced and expressed as narrative (story): our stories, our selves" (Mahoney, 70).

NARRATIVE THEORY

Storytelling was the lifeblood of Arthur Conan Doyle; early memories of his mother's stories "stand out so clearly that they obscure the real facts of my life" (Stashower, 1999, p. 22). Conan Doyle devoured books and at his boarding school, Hodder, experienced his "debut as a story-teller. . . . On a wet half-holiday . . . with an audience of little boys all squatting on the floor, with their chins upon their hands, I have talked myself husky over the misfortunes of my heroes" (p. 23).

Conan Doyle became a consummate storyteller, his Sherlock Holmes tales mesmerizing worldwide audiences, as hungry for them as were the little boys in Hodder, listening "with their chins upon their hands." Telling stories and listening to stories are part of human nature, even if most of us lack Conan Doyle's artistry. Stern (1985) speculates that developing narratives "may prove to be a universal human phenomenon reflecting the design of the human mind" (p. 174). Brockmeier and Harré (2001) observe that "every culture of which we know has been a story-telling culture" (p. 42).

Storytellers and audiences need each other, and their interaction, the development of their *intersubjectivity,* is the essential core of narrative theory. The principles of narrative theory are visible in everyday discourse, in the stories we tell about ourselves, how we wish specific listeners to respond to us, and how we may alter these stories in response to our listeners. In the 1920s, the Russian literary theorist Mikhail Bakhtin introduced the term *dialogic,* emphasizing the speaker-listener connection; this "has captured the imagination of scholars in a multitude of disciplines" (Josselson, 1995, p. 332), and is highly relevant to the patient-clinician encounter as well. Bakhtin proposed that the novel illustrated the dialogic concept, as it portrayed "multiple voices, multiple standpoints, and multiple experiences of reality" (p. 332).

> As readers of novels, we enter into a dialogic relation with the author and with the characters, all of whom are in dialogic relation to each other, exchanging and apprehending each other's meanings, all from a particular position in time, space and culture. (Josselson, 1995, p. 333)

Clinicians are in a "dialogic relation" to clients, responding to their life stories as both examine clients' relationships to present and past "characters" in their lives. Clinicians process the stories they hear from their own psychological, relational, cultural, and theoretical "positions." What clients reveal to clinicians, how they tell their stories, are influenced by their perceptions of how clinicians listen and understand; clinicians, at the same time, are influenced by their own subjective reactions to clients and their stories. A goal of relational therapy is to help the client develop an "authentic" self; the notion of identity, given prominence in narrative theory, is differentiated from its use in traditional psychology with its focus on the "internal workings of the mind." Relational therapy investigates the interpersonal world in the "discursive arena" of the dialogic process (Brockmeier and Carbaugh, 2001, p. 12).

Identity

Identity encompasses a person's sense of self while experienced in a deeply subjective manner, it develops, according to object relations and self psychology theory, through intersubjective encounters. "Self-making is powerfully affected not only by your own interpretations of yourself but by the interpretations others offer of your version" (Bruner, 2001, p. 34).

> It becomes plain, as one observes this process of self-formation, that it is probably a mistake to conceive of Self as solo, as locked up inside one person's subjectivity, as hermetically sealed off. Rather, Self seems also to be intersubjective . . . to include [one's] friends and colleagues . . . the notes one has filed, the books one has on one's shelves. (Bruner, 2001, pp. 34-35)

The development of a sense of self begins in infancy, and is closely related to the development of language, to stories one hears about oneself, and to stories one begins to tell about oneself. People are interested in exploring their personal histories, in the process developing a sense of "autobiographical consciousness" that contributes to their development of a sense of identity (Freeman, 2001, p. 287). The concept of self includes more than self-identity; Harré (2001) describes the "multiplicities of the self," meaning that people often represent themselves to others in multiple ways. In addition, how one thinks about oneself often changes overtime (p. 60). Frederick Douglass (McFeely, 1991) and Jean Piaget (Vonèche, 2001), for example, have both written several versions of their autobiographies, presenting themselves differently to the changing audiences they wanted to reach. The "multiplicities of the self" are influenced by cultural factors, and the various social roles a given person plays, such as the self as doctor, husband, father, son, basketball player, and scout leader.

Saari's (2005) concept of *identity complexity* illuminates how identity "is constantly being modified, being created, and recreated, in negotiations with our interactive partners throughout our entire lives." The social environment is also influential; when clinicians help clients "construct or reconstruct an identity . . . this construction must also include that of a world within which the client lives" (p. 9). Saari (2005) contrasts her view that identity is always evolving with Erikson's stance that identity "is consolidated in adolescence and remains relatively stable and monolithic thereafter" (p. 10). The question of whether identity is continuous or discontinuous and whether there is a plasticity of human identity, as opposed to a stability and coherence throughout life, is an ongoing controversy relevant to the development of resilience.

An ethical stance (Freeman and Brockmeier, 2001) is an important dimension of identity, as are conscience and moral judgment: "As the act and process of self-assessment, conscience is inextricably bound up with many other moral concepts, such as ideals of character or virtue, feelings of guilt and shame, and the religious loyalties or ultimate concerns which shape a person's identity" (Barbour, 1992, p. 1). Although clients may suffer from shame and superego guilt, these characteristics can coexist with self and interpersonal deception. Clients may deliberately distort their present and past stories in order to "deceive" the therapist, because of "instrumental" concerns, such as having their child returned to them by the child welfare agency, or due to "psychological" concerns, such as a need to manipulate and control, a wish to be admired, or a fear of censure. This is a commonly neglected phenomenon. Gediman and Lieberman (1996) observe that when deception occurs in therapy, the therapeutic interaction is affected.

> Central and crucial to our position is the belief that deception manifests itself not just individually, but *as a dyadic, interactive, relational process,* involving not just the false communication of a deceiver but also a receptive Other who responds to that communication and person. This Other's reactions—belief or disbelief—are partly induced by the deceiver and partly by the personal storehouse of unconscious identifications and fantasies that touch on particular deceptions to which he or she is vulnerable. (Gediman and Lieberman, 1996, p. 40; italics added)

If relational therapists operate on the premise that there are no objective realities, but only subjective versions of the truth, assessing deception can be problematic. A particularly complicated problem is assessing accuracy and distortions in the recall of past events.

Memory and the development of identity are inextricably interwoven. As St. Augustine commented, the capacity for memory is one of the conditions for creating continuity of the self throughout life (Olney, 1998).

Memory

In his *Confessions,* St. Augustine discusses the phenomena of memory, observing that there is a "present of the past, in the form of memory, and a present of the future, in the form of anticipation or awaiting" (Brooks, 1984, pp. 328-329). Utilizing the metaphor of weaving, Augustine describes this integration of memories.

> "There are all the things I remember to have experienced myself or to have heard from others. From the same store too I can take out pictures of things which have either happened to me or are believed on the basis of experience; *I can myself weave them* into the context of the past, and from them I can infer future actions, events, hopes, and then I can contemplate all these as though they were in the present. (Conf. 10.8, 218-19)" (Olney, 1998, p. 20; italics added)

Augustine's utilization of "weaving, as a characteristic metaphor for the operation of memory," is a core concept of life writings (Olney, 1998, p. 20). Neither memory nor weaving are static but in motion, and just as weaving will produce changing forms, the process of active recall will "bring forth ever different memorial configurations and an ever newly shaped self" (p. 20). Telling a story of one's life, then, becomes a dynamic process; this would be different from utilizing rote memory, such as the repeating of a memorized psalm. Yet, reciting a psalm perhaps may not be as rote as it initially appears, as when Hegel noted "that the old man repeats the same prayers he learned as a child but now altered, weighted, given entirely new coloring by the experience of a lifetime" (p. 21).

The dynamic process of the narrator recalling the past, while developing a new understanding or perspective, has been termed *retrospective teleology* (Brockmeier, 2001).

The narrative therapist observes that "new meanings may be attributed to past happenings that were not attributed to them at the time of their occurrence" (Freeman and Brockmeier, 2001, p. 82). Proust's *A la recherche du temps perdu [Remembrance of Things Past]* (1919) illustrates vividly how recalling and reliving the past can produce remembrances of "a richness and depth that was impossible to grasp and to evaluate when they were experienced originally" (p. 80).

Evaluating the accuracy of a primary memory is a complex task—to know whether other memories may have been "fused" onto this first memory, reinforcing or perhaps distorting the original memory. Augustine does not insist on the primacy of his own memories, but includes experiences that he may "have heard from others," or "believed on the basis of experience" (Olney, 1998, p. 20).

In his autobiography, Nuland (2003) discusses his perplexity in judging the accuracy of an early traumatic memory related to his conflictual relationship with his father. He remembers how his father exploded with rage at him when, as a toddler, Nuland stuffed his father's watch and chain into a wall socket and experienced an electric shock.

> How can I be so sure about my father's rage on that day? Is it really possible that at two and a half I could already have learned to anticipate such an excessive response, or am I looking back on the entire episode reflected in the mirror of so many subsequent paroxysms of self-righteous outrage? (Nuland, 2003, pp. 14-15)

Nuland (2003), struggling to understand if his memory is accurate, shares his uncertainties with the reader; he is processing his experience of remembering. Mary McCarthy also processes her uncertainty about the "facts" in her past life, a trait in McCarthy which Barbour (1992) applauds: "I submit that a form of this dialogue is intrinsic to the writing of every autobiography, although it is rarely formulated theoretically or rendered so vividly" (p. 30). McCarthy (1957) remembers her father as

> a romancer, and most of my memories of him are colored, I fear, by an untruthfulness that I must have caught from him, like one of the colds that ran around the family. . . . Many of my most cherished ideas about my father have turned out to be false. (p. 11)

McCarthy (1957) was six when her father died suddenly (as did her mother) in the influenza epidemic of 1918; she poignantly recalls memories of a loving man, attentive and indulgent to her. She recollects that once she and her father "heard a nightingale together, on the boulevard, near the Sacred Heart convent," and then adds: "But there are no nightingales in North America" (McCarthy, 1957, p. 11). McCarthy, describing the magic of the nightingales' song, creates an authentic experience of sharing a special relationship and a "fairy story" with her father; she also cautions the reader about the veracity of this account. "McCarthy provides a scrupulous account of how memory and imagination and historical guesswork were woven together and, guided by conscience, formed into an account of the essential truth of the past" (Barbour, 1992, p. 29).

Clinicians, too, are concerned with clients' memories, in helping clients retrieve them, analyze them, and perhaps see them with a new perspective. However, clients' memories can be incomplete or inaccurate, inaccessible, or too painful to share with a therapist, and so they work together to get to "the essential truth of the past." It is striking how many similarities exist in clinical work and biographical analysis. Looking at both enterprises through the lens of narrative theory (Urdang, work in progress) can be illuminating.

BIOGRAPHICAL WRITINGS AND CLINICAL WORK

Biographers (as do clinicians) have responsibility for entering into the life of another, and conveying an experiential as well as a factual understanding of that life, both knowing that their own attitudes and emotional responses to the subject may be influencing their work (Urdang, work in progress). Autobiographies are considered more "reliable" than biographies by some who believe autobiographies provide an authentic, first-hand portrayal of the subject's life and experiences. Spengemann (1980), however, notes that St. Augustine "set the problem for all subsequent autobiographies: How can the self know itself?" (p. 32). Some writers, like Gandhi, emphasized the importance of telling the truth, and "his autobiography is a self-conscious endeavor to test his capacity for the truth" (Barbour, 1992, p. 12). However, not all writers can reasonably assert this moral claim, as some take great pains to conceal the truth.

Conan Doyle (1924), in his autobiography, omitted "shameful" details (such as his father's alcoholism and mental illness), while placing emphasis on his own achievements and bravery. Piaget's (Vonèche, 2001) autobiographies focused on the development of his psychological theories, omitting details of his personal life. By contrast, Ved Mehta (1979, 1984, 1987a, b, 1988, 2001, 2003), an Indian writer, in his series of autobiographies, chose to share his inner life with the reader, his achievement of mastery over his blindness, and his painful interpersonal and psychological struggles.

Autobiographies are written from various motivations, and with various goals, such as describing an adventure, bearing witness to political and historical events, discussing experiences with (and sometimes triumphs over) physical and/or mental illness (the "quest" narrative), or conveying spiritual or political messages. Nuland's (2003) autobiography focused on his father and their relationship. "I am writing this book to help me come to terms with my father. I am writing this book to finally make peace with him, and perhaps with myself" (Introduction [unpaged]).

Some autobiographies are written as confessions, which may include apologies; "as its origin in the Greek *apologia* ('defense') indicates, in an apology the author defends his past conduct against moral criticisms" (Barbour, 1992, p. 11). The confession of wrongdoing is generally seen as a highly desirable and meritorious act; the apostle Paul was thought to have "required a broken conscience as the only gateway to salvation" (p. 20). The fictional autobiographies of Kierkegaard, Dostoevsky, and Camus "have been first-person confessions, public articulations of a guilty conscience" (p. 21). For some writers "introspection and self-accusation" is the highest good, and can eclipse "kindness, justice, or loyalty to any conviction or person" (p. 21).

A scandal erupted in 2006, surrounding the memoir *A Million Little Pieces,* written by James Frey and publicized on the *Oprah Winfrey* TV show (Grossman, 2006; Wyatt, 2006). Frey wrote of his addiction to drugs and alcohol and subsequent rehabilitation. Oprah Winfrey's enthusiastic endorsement helped the book achieve best seller status overnight. When "untruths" were found in his book, she confronted him, and in a second appearance, they both confessed and *"apologized,"* conceding that he had "made a mistake" (Wyatt, 2006, p. A1). Frey explained that

> he had developed a tough-guy image of himself as a "coping mechanism" to help address his alcohol and drug addiction. "And when I was writing this book," he said, "instead of being as introspective as I should have been, I clung to that image." (Wyatt, 2006, p. A1)

In an earlier defense *("apologia")* of his book, on the *Larry King Live* TV show, Frey stressed "the fundamentally subjective nature of his memoir. 'It's an individual's perception . . . my recollection,'" and stressed that "the emotional truth is there" (Grossman, 2006, p. 62). From a constructivist standpoint, he is presenting his *experience;* from a moral perspective, his audience is being deceived. By contrast, Mary McCarthy's sharing with the reader her problems exploring her early life has produced "the essential truth of the past" (Barbour, 1992, p. 29). Olney (1998) comments that *"True Confessions*—which are neither true nor confessions—set the tone for our time and they come more or less directly out of Rousseau" (p. 147; italics in the original).

Jean Jacques Rousseau felt he was a special person with a special message; he is considered by some biographers to be a master in "self deception" (Barbour, 1992; Olney, 1998). In the *Confessions,* written in 1770,

Rousseau presents himself as having a special aptitude for knowing his feelings; his "Confessions" are offered as a gift to mankind, in which he portrays himself as a model for self-knowledge: "to offer himself as an other so that readers may have a 'pièce de comparison' by means of which they might know themselves" (Olney, 1998, p. 413). However, as Barbour (1992) observes, "rationalization and exculpation of his behavior always characterize his discussion" (p. 19). A consequence of Rousseau's "self-deception" is his "aversion to considering either the consequences of his actions or the perspectives of other persons" (Barbour, 1992, p. 34), and when he actually confesses to doing something wrong, "he presents himself as an innocent victim of a corrupting environment" (p. 15).

Rousseau rationalizes the placement of all five of his children in an orphanage (notorious then for poor conditions and a high rate of mortality) (Olney, 1998).

> I will be content with a general statement that in handing my children over for the State to educate, for lack of means to bring them up by myself, by destining them to become workers and peasants instead of adventurers and fortune-hunters, I thought I was acting as a citizen and a father, and looked upon myself as a member of Plato's Republic. (Rousseau as cited in Olney, 1998, p. 144)

People are often concerned with how they represent themselves to others, so it is not surprising to see this characteristic present in self-writings. Ottilie Assing (Diedrich, 1999), an intimate companion of Fredrick Douglass, was not only concerned with how she represented herself to others, but also needed to "invent" a self-portrait that was acceptable to herself.

> The narrative Ottilie Assing constructed was more than a chronology of events; she was restructuring, rearranging, rereading experience; she was molding, selecting, and deleting memory, until the story of her life became compatible with the persona she invented. Like Douglass, she masked interpretation as representation. . . . In approaching her texts we must try to wrestle with both, her representations of herself and Douglass as historical presence and as individual human being. (Diedrich, 1999, p. xx)

While it is not uncommon to stress one's self-importance, some writers choose to appear self-effacing. Conway (1998) made the astute observation that women reformers of the nineteenth century often chose to play down their will power, determination, and agency in effecting changes in their social worlds, referring to their interventions as something that "just happened" (p. 48). In writing about Jane Addams, a major figure in the development of social work and the Settlement House Movement, Conway (1998) comments,

> Through her extensive use of conditional tenses and the passive voice, Addams is able to conceal her own role in making the events of her life happen and to conform herself to the romantic image of the female, seeming to be all emotion and spontaneity, and to be shaped by circumstances beyond her control. Once we grasp her skill in doing this we have learned an important point about later-nineteenth- and early-twentieth-century women's autobiography. We can be sure that whenever women autobiographers are hiding behind the passive voice and the conditional tense, they are depicting events in which they acted forthrightly upon a preconceived, rational plan. (Conway, 1998, pp. 49-50)

Clients also present and represent themselves in unique ways, which can present challenges for clinicians, and while the relational therapist envisions therapy as an authentic experience for the client, this is not always possible. There are factors within the patient-therapist relationship itself that may also impede authentic discovery, such as "making, pretending, and denying so that the [patient's] self-estrangement in the end cannot be fully overcome" (Wyatt, 1986, p. 207).

Like autobiographers, biographers also have varied motivations for writing about lives, for choosing particular subjects, and for deciding which themes to focus on. Robert Caro, the biographer of Robert Moses (former Park Commissioner in New York City) and Lyndon Johnson, chose these men because both were powerful, and the subject of the acquisition of power was of interest to him. Rodin and Key (1984) focused on Conan Doyle's medical career, with the intention of dispelling the many supposed "myths" characterizing him as an incompetent physician who made no contributions to medicine.

The relationship of biographers to their subjects is fraught with meaning and emotion (as is the relationship between the clinician and patient) (Urdang, work in progress). Biographers have subjective reactions to their subjects even if they have never met, and even if the subjects have been long dead. Maria Diedrich (1999), for example, wrote the biography of Ottilie Assing (who died sixty-six years before Diedrich was born), focusing on Assing's relationship to Frederic Douglass. Diedrich observed that her own family "were served Assing-Douglass fare for breakfast, lunch, and dinner, and for years" (p. viii).

The biographer-subject relationship can initially be positive or negative, can deepen in either direction, be ambivalent, and may evolve along different pathways over time. Covert identification, for example, with subjects or clients is a professional hazard for both biographers and clinicians. Holroyd (2002) cites "a somber warning" by Robert Graves, who "suggests that the art of biography is shaped and distorted by the biographer's need to identify with his subject," and he quotes Graves' poem (p. 28).

Subdue your pen to his handwriting
Until it prove as natural
To sign his name as yours.

Limp as he limped,
Swear by the oaths he swore;
If he wore black, affect the same;
If he had gouty fingers,
Be ours gouty too.

(Graves as cited in Holroyd, 1993, p. 28; italics in the original)

The biographer (and clinician) have responsibility for the accurate communication and interpretation of the subject's life story, which is filtered through the biographer's (and clinician's) observations, affected by intellectual, cultural, emotional, and relational factors in their lives. The biographer sifts through bits and pieces of the puzzles that make up a life, to assess what is there and what is not there. "In fact, these gaps and fissures are as important as the pieces we were able to recover" (Diedrich, 1999, p. xxi); this is also a truism for clinical assessment. In assembling the pieces of a subject's life, biographers (and clinicians) make decisions on what to include or exclude, and explore themes and meanings that *they* deem significant. Interpretations of events and motivations can vary among biographers and clinicians in relation to the same person; the same event can elicit multiple interpretations.

Rudyard Kipling, for example, spent almost six years (from ages six to twelve) in a foster home in England, while his parents, who never visited, remained in India. He was left there by his parents (without explanation) along with his sister Trix, then three. From a cultural perspective, it was not unusual for Anglo-Indians (English people living in India) to send their children to England for their education and health.

From Kipling's (1937) perspective, this was a nightmarish existence. Although there is no dispute about the actuality of this placement, Kipling biographers have disagreed about the impact of this experience on him. Shengold (1981) asserted that the foster mother's attempts at his "soul murder" left deep scars on Kipling's personality; "the atmosphere was full of sadism, disguised as religious righteousness" (p. 215). Carrington (1956) and Seymour-Smith (1989) cast doubt on the veracity of Kipling's description of his experience, with Seymour-Smith suggesting that "Kipling's abandonment has now gained the status of a myth" (Seymour-Smith, 1989, p. 19). Kipling's sister Trix, who wrote two brief accounts of this early experience they shared, "came to believe in this myth, perhaps in part because of her own resentment of her parents and of Rudyard, and even herself embroidered it" (p. 19).

Hermione Lee (2005) has explored ways in which biographers handle uncertainties and missing data about their subjects, and asserts that the biographer's ultimate concern should be "How a life can be brought home to us" (p. 4). She describes complex problems facing the biographer.

> How do biographers deal with moments of physical shock, with the subject's secret bodily life, with the mystery of death, and with the aftermath of rumour and reputation? How do they nose out the personality and the life of the writer through the often ambiguous or deceptive evidence of their work? What part do blame, resentment, personal affection, idealisation, judgment, and defensiveness have to play in the courtroom drama of life-writing? Where do biographers start from, and how do they know when to stop? (Lee, 2005, p. 4)

Clinicians confront dilemmas similar to those faced by biographers as they search for themes and meaning, weaving a life history from the client's fragmentary memories, and speculating on the potential significance of "missing pieces," probing for feelings that may be hidden safely from awareness ("or defended against"). Clinicians, as do biographers, collect data from records and secondary sources (such as relatives, schools) and evaluate the possible bias and/or reliability of these sources.

Biographers of Charlotte Bronte, for example, have relied heavily, in their interpretations of Charlotte's life, on the many letters she wrote to her friend, Ellen Nussey, who was devoted and loyal, but also "respectable, unintellectual [and] ladylike" (Miller, 2001, p. 66). However, Ellen's personality and Charlotte's relationship to her may have affected what (and how) Charlotte chose to write to her, such as denying in a letter to Ellen that she was the author of *Jane Eyre,* but sharing this information in a letter to her good friend Mary Taylor, a "strong-willed feminist" who was then living in New Zealand (p. 20). It is very possible that "Charlotte would have been more open in her letters to the independent feminist Mary Taylor . . . but unfortunately for posterity Mary destroyed them [the letters] in a bid to save them from prying eyes" (p. 66).

As a phenomenon, the destruction of Charlotte Bronte's letters by Mary Taylor is not uncommon. Families and friends of potential biographical subjects, as well as subjects themselves, can be defensive and protective about privacy. Dickens was not alone among writers when he burned his personal papers and letters toward the end of his life; others, aware that "they could not destroy the letters they had sent to other people, drafted warnings to their executors against biographers"; this did little good, "for literary biographers have no conscience about such matters" (Holroyd, 2002, p. 7).

> Thackeray told his daughters: "When I drop there is to be no life written of me, mind this." And J. M. Barrie set his curse on any would-be biographer by praying: "May God blast anyone who writes a biography of me." George Eliot, too, declared that "biographers are generally a disease of English literature"—and this despite the fact that she lived happily with Goethe's biographer, G. H. Lewes. (Holroyd, 2002, p. 4)

Clinicians can also be constrained by issues of privacy and confidentiality. Obtaining past records of patients and their families or interviewing teachers or doctors might be enlightening, but clients may not grant permission. Some clients (and their relatives) do not even wish to be seen, but when social services and/or psychotherapy are legally mandated (perhaps for child custody disputes, substance abuse, or domestic violence) clinicians can face the prospect of reluctant and resistant subjects.

However objective a biographer strives to be, whatever primary and academic sources are utilized, subjectivity is always present, influencing what materials to include (and exclude), and how to interpret data.

> In the end we have to acknowledge that much of the person into whose life we delve must necessarily elude us, and perhaps even more significant, that much of the life we reimagine and reconstruct is about our own life, our own prejudices, dreams, agonies, and joys. We are made aware of our own potentials and limitations as we try to come to terms with another human being's potentials and limitations. This is the humbling aspect of writing biography. It is also what makes biography "the most seductive and the most untrustworthy of literary genres." (Mehegan, 1997) (Diedrich, 1999, p. xxi)

In writing reports and evaluating evidence, clinicians also make subjectively colored interpretations. Spence (1986) refers to "narrative smoothing," in which therapists may add and/or omit details that support their suppositions, "which allows interpretation to masquerade as explanation, and which effectively prevents the reader from making contact with the complete account . . . [or] coming up with alternative explanations" (pp. 212-213). Diedrich (1999) observes the biographer's subjective involvement in biographical writing, and emphasizes the importance of acknowledging this. Competent clinicians do not deny their subjectivity, but utilize their insights on behalf of their clients.

APPLICATIONS TO CLINICAL PRACTICE

Although Freud has been criticized by many, including present-day constructivists, as a "positivist," with a drive-dominated, mechanistic framework, others see him as an excellent narrative therapist. Brooks (1984) refers to psychoanalysis as a "primarily narrative art, concerned with the recovery of the past through the dynamics of memory and desire" (p. xiv). Freud saw an analogy between detective work and psychoanalysis, as both look for "explanations" (p. 270); Freud's famous patient, the Wolf Man, in his memoirs, commented on Freud's interest in Sherlock Holmes.

> Once we happened to speak of Conan Doyle and his creation, Sherlock Holmes. I had thought that Freud would have no use for this type of light reading matter, and was surprised to find that this was not at all the case. . . . The fact that circumstantial evidence is useful in psychoanalysis when reconstructing a childhood history may explain Freud's interest in this type of literature. (Brooks, 1984, pp. 269-270)

Psychoanalysts, as well as clinicians of other theoretical orientations, incorporate basic narrative precepts in different ways; "it is part of the appeal of the narrative metaphor that it does not prescribe procedure . . . but this new language does provide us with new ways to think about old problems" (Josselson, 1995, p. 337). Sometimes specific procedures such as keeping journals, or forming reminiscence groups for the elderly, are recommended. In reciprocal storytelling "in the context of psychoanalytic child psychotherapy," children tell their own stories to the clinician, who talks to them in terms of the feelings and content present in these stories (Brandell, 2004, p. 268). Drisko (1999) described his therapy with Jerry, nine, a Latino boy in foster placement, to whom he read the story of *Rapunzel*.

Two parts of the story held him in rapt attention: First was how the parents' own neediness led them to take cabbage from the witch's garden, and how the witch required their child as punishment. I wondered aloud how weak these parents must be to give up their child, but Jerry noted they had no choice and the witch's powers were incredible. The second part Jerry adored was how the prince found Rapunzel, was blinded by the witch, and finally was reunited with Rapunzel, whose tears brought him sight and her perfect love. He identified with the Prince who was so strong and tried so hard but suffered so much. While he listened repeatedly and with great interest to the ending, he never responded to any of my queries about how much the prince gained from the care of others. Clearly, both the story and the opportunity to displace his situation into a fantasy with a happy ending was meaningful and inspiring. (Drisko, 1999, p. 175)

In this excerpt Drisko (1999) focused on Jerry's core issues in a non-threatening way, within the metaphor of the story. When Drisko commented that Rapunzel's parents were weak, he was giving Jerry an opportunity to criticize his own parents for giving him away, but Jerry was not ready for this, and continued to "blame" the witch. Drisko accepted his point of view, and was cautious not to have Jerry feel "coerced, controlled, or manipulated" (p. 176); the use of storytelling enabled Jerry to safely disagree with him.

McLuckie (2005) utilized narrative family therapy with a nine-year-old girl with an obsessive compulsive disorder, helping her and the family to increase a sense of potential for mastery by *"externalizing"* the problem, such as by giving it a different name, one that permits of the possibility of change and evolving a narrative which envisages that potential:

> children often rename OCD in such terms as "fear" or "worry," referring to the anxiety that stems from the obsessive thought patterns; names such as "worry washing" are often used by the child to refer to excessive ritualistic hand washing. (p. 91)

Emphasizing the importance of not "pathologizing" the child, McLuckie recommends play, puppets, and drawings, which help in the externalizing process.

Edelson (1993), finds narrative and psychoanalytic theory compatible; the core themes in psychoanalysis and psychotherapy can be presented "in language about telling and enacting stories" (p. 294), which is "an extension of commonsense or folk psychology" (p. 310). He focuses on the experiential and feeling states of patients, which should not be submerged by an overuse of theory; patients should not be placed on a "procrustean theoretical bed" (p. 320). Trainees are taught to *"eschew the vague and general, and instead to pursue the particular"* (p. 316; italics in the original), that is, the details of their patients' narratives, which should not be interrupted by therapists supplying labels or interpretations; Edelson quotes himself:

> Out with conceptual labels summarizing or classifying experiences! Out with vagueness! . . . Ask yourself as you listen to the patient: Can you see a scene in your mind, a particular time and place, particular characters? Can you see what they are doing? Hear what they are saying? (pp. 316-317)

Coleman (1999) also incorporates narrative theory into his analytic work; he transposes a narrative orientation into psychodynamic terms.

> We order and reorder our life experiences through stories. We give disconnected moments of experience an ongoing form and meaning. Using stories, we begin to distinguish self and nonself, leave the frame of magical merger, and create an autonomous storyteller. The ego is an organ of recognition and an organizer of time. (Coleman, 1999, p. 238)

Reminiscence is used in clinical work with the elderly; telling their life stories enhances self-esteem, memory, and coping, and improves social relationships. Spira (2006), reviewing Gibson's (2004) book, *The Past in the Present: Using Reminiscence in Health and Social Care,* observes that Gibson "carefully chooses the term reminiscence work rather than reminiscence therapy to convey the strengths perspective and a person-centered approach rather than one based on dysfunction" (p. 125). Gibson applies this approach both in individual work and in mutual aid groups.

Composing life books for foster children, to help them put together the chaotic story of their lives, is a frequent practice of child welfare workers. Writing, as homework, in the form of keeping journals in which clients record their thoughts and feelings, is popular with cognitive-behavioral and constructivist therapists. Working with addicted clients, Diamond (2000) suggests that they keep journals as well as write letters to significant others, and a good-bye letter to alcohol. Writing about oneself can be therapeutic; sometimes it becomes "the defining moment and healing encounter in a person's life" (p. 337); autobiographical writing can lead to ongoing personal growth (Barbour, 1992).

Autobiography . . . requires that one take stock of one's past, seizing it as something to be weighed, assessed, and evaluated in the light of a normative model of life. Autobiographical self-construction thus requires *self-distancing;* it is a "second-reading" of experience . . . guided by the demand that one confront oneself "honestly" and own up to the trouble spots of one's history. As such, it is the way we make sense of our lived lives in order to face the possible lives we envision. (Freeman and Brockmeier, 2001, p. 80; italics added)

Examining the intersubjective encounter of the narrator and listener, Edelson (1993) recommends observing the "microprocess" of the therapy; "*the immediacy of the therapeutic moment*' (Shapiro, 1989)" (Edelson, 1993, p. 317; italics in the original). Microprocessing focuses on the verbal and affective interactions of the clinician and patient; it examines their effects on the therapeutic hour; it provides a means to study the intersubjective, dialogic relation. It highlights the "moment-by-moment dynamic . . . the blips and perturbations, the minute changes of affect and emphasis" (p. 317). Microprocessing has achieved prominence through the work of Daniel Stern (1985), who has studied the intimate verbal and nonverbal interactions of mothers and infants through videotaping.

Interviews are sometimes recorded by video- or audiotaping. Process recording, a detailed account of what transpired in the interaction and within the interviewer, is generated after the interview. Spence (1986) emphasizes clinician's processing of the interview, including their feelings and interactions; he notes resistance by some analysts to "unpack[ing] the session more fully . . . [because they] often choose to protect themselves from too detailed an awareness of how they function—in part for narcissistic reasons" (p. 230). The development of self-awareness and the ability to analyze the interactional aspects of the interview are educational goals for social work students; process recording aids in this endeavor. Although process recording has a long history in social work, a history of resistance to this procedure also exists (Urdang, 1979).

Narrative theory has contributed to the development of qualitative research utilized across disciplines; historians use oral histories to gain insight into the experiences of people living through major social/historical events; anthropologists inquire into cultural patterns and beliefs; and clinical studies include experiential aspects of life's vicissitudes and the impact of therapy on clients.

Harrison (2006) has reviewed Fessler's edition of oral histories that captured the powerlessness and pain of women who felt they had no choice but to surrender their children to adoption; this is related to their pre–*Roe v. Wade* social context. In a study of American Indian women who have survived domestic violence, Murphy, Risley-Curtiss, and Gerdes (2003) analyzed each subject's story "in terms of her own conscience, context, and use of language . . . the interview itself empowered each woman" (p. 177). Midgley and Target (2005) conducted a follow-up study of adults who had been in child analysis at the Anna Freud Centre in London, focusing on their "attitudes toward being in therapy" and their "memories of therapy and the therapist." This methodology provided valuable data; it is an "under-used source of knowledge for an understanding of the psychoanalytic process" (p. 157).

Postmodern theories highlight the plasticity of human development and adaptation, and argue that identity remains fluid and open to change through interpersonal encounters throughout life. This perspective relates to recent interest in resilience—how children and adults experiencing adverse and traumatic circumstances adapt to life in constructive ways.

RESILIENCE

It is not unexpected that children, exposed to parental loss or other trauma, become depressed, or that adults living through such crises as environmental disasters, war, the death of a child, or marital desertion, might suffer a psychological collapse. What is unexpected, and more difficult to explain, is why some children and adults do not inevitably break down, slowly or rapidly, but are resilient as they forge ahead with their lives. Even more profound is the observation that some individuals gain strength from their adversity, adapting and coping successfully. Writers such as Charles Dickens, Charlotte Brontë, Edgar Allan Poe, and Rudyard Kipling have not only survived adverse circumstances, but their adaptation and creativity have been fueled by these conditions; in turn, the development of "creative imagination . . . can exercise a healing function" (Storr, 1988, p. 123).

The complex phenomenon of resilience has been viewed through different theoretical lenses and evaluated with different measures. Vaillant (1993) observes that "we all know perfectly well what resilience means until we listen to someone else trying to define it" (p. 285). To Vaillant (1993), "resilience conveys both the capacity to be bent without breaking and the capacity, once bent, to spring back. Thus, I like the definition that Emmy Werner and Ruth Smith give for resilience: 'The self-righting tendencies within the human organism'" (pp. 284-285). Stella Chess (1989) asserts that it is important, for preventive purposes, to understand its development, how "such individuals defy the voice of doom" (p. 180).

Cohler (1987) uses the terms "invulnerable or resilient" to describe those children who are "able to cope with the effects of misfortune and adversity" (p. 363). Ingram and Price (2001) prefer the term resilience to invulnerability because "invulnerability suggests an absolute level of protection from psychopathology," whereas resilience "implies a diminished, but not zero, possibility of psychopathology" (p. 14). This suggests the coexistence of resilience and vulnerability, a concept emphasized by Noam (1996): "We need to end idealizing the self's complexity, the linear movement from limited ability to great capacity, and instead focus on the continued struggles between strengths and weaknesses to the end of life" (p. 138). The coexistence of resilience and vulnerability is illustrated in the life of Rudyard Kipling.

> His years in the House of Desolation [his English foster home] left effects that continued to inhibit Kipling's ability to feel joy and to love, and that sometimes flawed his art. Yet, the soul murder was far from completely effected: Kipling's identity was preserved, and he became a great artist. The struggle to fight off the soul murder and its effects strengthened him, and gave him motive and subject matter for his writing. I have connected those terrible years of his childhood to his flaws and to his greatness. Kipling's story touches on the mysteries of the origin of mental sickness and of creativity. The explorer must be prepared for contradiction and complexity. (Shengold, 1981, p. 251)

We will return to Rudyard Kipling after a review of the literature related to resilience. When discussed from an ecological framework, resiliency encompasses interacting factors in the environment and in the individual that impose risk and/or provide protection for the child (Begun, 1993; Kirby and Fraser, 1997); it incorporates a developmental framework to "allow for changes in resilience in individuals at different points in time and to explain the cumulative effects of risk" (Kirby and Fraser, 1997, p. 19).

Environmental risk factors include limited opportunities for education or employment, racial discrimination and injustice, poverty, child maltreatment, interparental conflict, parental psychopathology, and poor parenting. Individual psychosocial and biological risk factors include biomedical problems and gender (Kirby and Fraser, 1997). Environmental protective factors take include opportunities for education; employment; growth and achievement; social support; presence of a caring, supportive adult (not necessarily the parent); positive parent-child relationships; and effective parenting. The role of school in a child's life has received increasing attention, and positive school experiences (including relationships with teachers and peers) can be instrumental in promoting resilience; this is discussed further in Chapter 5.

Individual psychosocial and constitutional protective factors include easy temperament, competence in normative roles, self-efficacy, self-esteem, and intelligence (Kirby and Fraser, 1997). Other authors have utilized these or similar factors in discussing resiliency; some have added additional points, such as the importance of attributional style (discussed in Chapter 3), which is "how we regard our responsibility for the good and bad events that befall us" (Vaillant, 1993, p. 305), a point emphasized by Saleebey (2001). If, for example, a child believes his mother's depression is due to his being "bad," he might respond differently from a child who understands that mother is sick (i.e., not his fault), and that while she loves him very much, she cannot show it now.

Attachment is a major contributor to resiliency: "The pathway followed by each developing individual and the extent to which he or she becomes resilient to stressful life events is determined to a very significant degree by the pattern of attachment he or she develops during the early years" (Bowlby, 1988, p. 34). Thomlison (1997) comments: "Compared with children who have no bonds of attachment, children who have a deep sense of belonging and security are widely known to function more adaptively across settings. Such attachments occur, first and foremost, because of a positive, caring caretaker from birth—a caretaker who is available in times of stress for support" (p. 57).

When caring relationships and social supports are in scarce supply, the child's ability to "recruit the invested attention of others" (Kegan, 1982, pp. 26-27) can be critical; Vaillant (1993) and Saleebey (2001) refer to social attractiveness in this context. It is unfortunate that many children deprived of early positive attachment experiences, who desperately need close, caring relationships, *also* desperately need to reject this closeness, sometimes out of fear of attachments and, in addition, if in placement, to avoid the betrayal of their birth parents. Vaillant (1993) observes that it is not sufficient for social supports to be present: "They must be *recognized and then internalized.* Social experience is not what happens to you, it is what you do with what happens to you" (p. 311; italics added). The roles others play in our lives can be transforming, but "only if we can metabolize influential other people" (p. 180).

Temperament has been recognized as a factor in promoting resilience (Chess, 1989; Kirby and Fraser, 1997; Saleebey, 2001; Vaillant, 1993). Chess (1989) observed that temperaments "had been insufficiently studied with respect to their influence upon developmental outcomes" (p. 182). She evaluated nine temperamental characteristics in children: "activity level;

rhythmicity; approach or withdrawal; adaptability; intensity of response; threshold of responsiveness; quality of mood; distractibility; and attention span and persistence" (pp. 184-185). Not only is temperament relevant to the way children are affected by events, but conversely their "temperamental qualities influenced their caretakers"; therefore, child-caretaker goodness-of-fit can "influence the quality of adaptation of children" (p. 183).

Paradoxically, although children need parental closeness, under some conditions there is "a high virtue in distancing from noxious family onslaughts and underminings, in leaving behind irreconcilable conflicts" (Chess, 1989, p. 198). For example, the capacity for adaptive "defensive distancing" from their families, developed by some children of alcoholics, can be differentiated from unconstructive

> reactive distancing. . . . The adaptive distancer . . . tends to use some form of flight away from the pull of parental alcoholism but, unlike the reactive child, the adaptive one is more likely *to flee toward activities and relationships* that allow some breathing room for reparative work. (Berlin and Davis, 1989, p. 97; italics added)

Felsman (1989) cites this "flight toward relationships" as a key factor in the resiliency he found in the "gamins," the street children [boys] of Colombia who are potentially

> at high risk for psychopathology. . . . Darting in and out of traffic, begging in open-air restaurants, singing for change on city buses, bathing in public fountains, or sleeping together curled up among stray dogs, these young ragamuffins manage the often-tangled course of human growth and development with little or no support from the traditional institutions of family, school, church, or state. (p. 56)

In describing their substitute social support system, the special place of peer relationships in their lives is emphasized. Other researchers who have studied disadvantaged children have also observed a similar tendency to rely on peers.

Defense mechanisms are critical to the way resilience develops: "I shall continue to point to maturity of defenses as the 'god in the machine' that seems to account for otherwise inexplicable resilience" (Vaillant, 1993, p. 297). Other characteristics involved in the development of resilience include hope and faith (Saleebey, 2001; Vaillant, 1993); "hope and belief in a better or positive future sustain many children and adults as they confront harsh circumstances" (Saleebey, 2001, p. 71). Vaillant (1993) adds the category of "luck" (p. 305), which implies circumstances over which we have no actual control. The commonly heard, "I was in the right place at the right time" reflects the perceived role of luck.

Imagination and creativity can promote psychological growth in adverse circumstances. Saleebey (2001), citing Wolin and Wolin, notes that "children can be 'challenged by trouble to experiment and respond actively and creatively. Their preemptive responses, repeated over time, become incorporated into the self as lasting resiliencies'" (p. 180). Reading can foster the imagination, connecting readers to others, exposing them to other worldviews, teaching ways of coping, and enabling them to gain hope from seeing others overcoming difficult life situations. Conway (1998) suggests that we have a strong interest in autobiography because "we want to know how the world looks from inside another person's experience, and when that craving is met by a convincing narrative, we find it deeply satisfying" (p. 6). For some, it may also be deeply healing.

Writing, too, can have a healing function. It was reparative in the lives of Charlotte Brontë, her sisters Emily and Ann, and her brother Branwell, who lost their mother when they were very young. As children they were immersed in the literary worlds they created themselves, in which they participated and shared with each other. For them, writing was not merely a solitary activity, but an interactive process. Anne and Emily created the imaginary kingdom of Gondal, "as important in the scheme of their lives as what was on the kitchen table" (Fraser, 1988, p. 95).

Rudyard Kipling

Rudyard Kipling, after a secure first six years of life in India, spent the next six years separated from parents. They remained in India, while he lived, along with his three-year-old sister Trix, in a foster home in England, which he called "The House of Desolation." This incredibly devastating experience did not result in "soul murder" (Shengold, 1981, p. 251). Although the experience left emotional scars, his resilience as well as his creativity evolved. We will look at the risk factors he encountered, and the protective factors that fostered this favorable outcome.

Kipling's development of strong emotional attachments during the first six years of life were major contributing factors in his successful survival. Kipling's father was the director of an art school in India; the family lived on its grounds, and he was raised primarily by his beloved ayah (a Portuguese Roman Catholic nursemaid), and Meeta, his Hindu bearer. In his autobiography (1937), he wrote

> My first impression is of daybreak, light and colour and golden and
> purple fruits at the level of my shoulder. This would be the memory of
> early morning walks to the Bombay fruit market with my *ayah* and
> later with my sister in her perambulator. . . . Meeta, my Hindu bearer,
> would sometimes go into little Hindu temples where . . . I held his
> hand and looked at the dimly seen, friendly Gods. . . . In the afternoon
> heats before we took our sleep, she [Ayah] or Meeta would tell us
> stories. . . . (Kipling, 1937, pp. 3-4; italics in the original)

It was not uncommon for children raised in Victorian Britain and India
during this period to be raised by servants, "on the principle that parents
should be rather remote figures" (Mason, 1975, p. 30). In India, as opposed
to England, however, "the servants were much more indulgent" (p. 30).
Kipling recalls that, in the early evening, he and Trix were dressed up, and
went to the dining room

> with the caution "Speak English now to Papa and Mamma." So one
> spoke "English," haltingly translated out of the vernacular idiom that
> one thought and dreamed in. The Mother sang wonderful songs at a
> black piano and would go out to Big Dinners. (Kipling, 1937, pp. 4-5)

The only major deviation from this routine occurred in 1868, when Kipling
was two years and three months old, and his mother, pregnant with Trix, returned to her relatives in England with him for this birth. Father, Meeta, and
Ayah remained in India. Mother, Kipling, and the newborn Trix returned to
Bombay, and life resumed its normal course. "But the boy remembered
these first six years of indulgence and magic as overwhelmingly wonderful" (Shengold, 1981, p. 212).

When Rudyard was six, and Trix was three, their parents took them to
England, left them in the Holloway's foster home, returned to India, and did
not see their children for five years and three months. Although the Kiplings
had family in England, it is thought that the parents did not wish to involve
relatives in caring for the children. The Kiplings did not know the Holloways;
they chose this family from a newspaper advertisement. Although it was a
common practice for Anglo-Indians to educate their children in England,
the children were usually older. Prior to the children's leaving, Kipling's
mother gave birth to a third child who died, and it's possible troubled feelings about this event precipitated an early departure.

Mrs. Holloway has been described as an angry, rejecting, and rigid
woman, sadistic toward Rudyard and encouraged her son Harry's sadistic

behavior to Rudyard, six years his junior. Kipling always referred to Mrs. Holloway as "the Woman" and wrote

> It was an establishment run with the full vigour of the Evangelical as revealed to the Woman. I had never heard of Hell, so I was introduced to it in all its terrors. . . . Myself I was regularly beaten. The Woman had an only son of twelve or thirteen as religious as she. I was a real joy to him, for when his mother had finished with me for the day he (we slept in the same room) took me on and roasted the other side. (Kipling, 1937, p. 8)

Rudyard, deprived of his sun-filled, love-filled home, suffered in this dark, rejecting, and punishing environment. The Kiplings also never told the children about this placement; they never said good-bye. When their parents left, Rudyard and Trix thought they were briefly visiting the Holloways. Trix retrospectively expresses their despair at this abandonment:

> I think the real tragedy of our early days, apart from Aunty's [Mrs. Holloway's] bad temper and unkindness to my brother, sprang from our inability to understand why our parents had deserted us. We had no preparation or explanation; it was like a double death, or rather, like an avalanche that had swept away everything happy and familiar. . . . They doubtless wanted to save us, and themselves, suffering by not telling us . . . but by so doing they left us, as it were, in the dark, and with nothing to look forward to. . . . As it was, we felt we had been deserted, "almost as much as on a doorstep," and what was the reason? [Debating and dismissing various possible excuses, Trix then concludes:] But there was no excuse; they had gone happily back to our own lovely home, and had not taken us with them. There was no getting out of that, as we often said. (Fleming, 1939, p. 171)

Rudyard's first three years in this home were not quite as dismal as the later years, as Captain Holloway, Mrs. Holloway's husband, a retired sea captain, was protective toward Rudyard, taking him for long walks and regaling him with stories of the sea and his adventures; tragically, he died of liver cancer in 1874. Rudyard had fond memories of him; not only did he lose another kindly father figure, but he lost his protection against Mrs. Holloway and her son. "Then the old Captain died, and I was sorry, for he was the only person in that house as far as I can remember who ever threw me a kind word" (Kipling, 1937, p. 8).

Details of the "quality" of his early parental relationships are not known, but his parents seemed to have been benign, although somewhat removed figures, and no suggestions of malevolence exist; when reunited, strong family bonds did develop. Although "abandoned" at the Holloways, there was a flow of letters between the children and their parents (although none remain), and Rudyard received books from them. Trix and Rudyard were social supports and allies to each other, and Rudyard told Trix stories of their past. While

> remembering the past was a torment to the children . . . it also restored the promise of bliss. . . . Rudyard's imagination also helped—in his stories to Trix he conjured up an idealized world and wonderful parents. All this kept the children together so that the desertion didn't mean complete isolation. (Shengold, 1981, p. 220)

His relationship to Trix "helped strengthen Kipling's masculinity and also his identity. Toward her he was able to feel and act like the protective parent that both so needed" (Shengold, 1981, p. 247).

Finally, during his stay at The House of Desolation, Rudyard, for a month each year, would visit his mother's sister, Aunt Georgy (Georgiana), a "life-saving" highlight of his life.

> But, for a month each year I possessed a paradise which I verily believe saved me. Each December I stayed with my Aunt Georgy, my mother's sister, wife of Sir Edward Burne-Jones [a famous artist], at the grange, North End Road. At first I must have been escorted there, but later I went alone, and arriving at the house would reach up to the open-work iron bell-pull on the wonderful gate that let me into all felicity. When I had a house of my own, and The Grange was emptied of meaning, I begged for and was given that bell-pull for my entrance, in the hope that other children might also feel happy when they rang it. (Kipling, 1937, p. 14)

The Grange was full of love, fun, friendly cousins, creativity, and intellectual stimulation.

> At The Grange I had love and affection as much as the greediest, and I was not very greedy, could desire. There were most wonderful smells of paints and turpentine whiffing down from the big studio on the first floor where my Uncle worked. (Kipling, 1937, p. 14)

Perhaps this evoked memories of his father's art school, while Aunt Georgy may have stirred memories of his mother. Kipling remained involved with this family throughout his life; he felt especially close to Aunt Georgy, in whom he could always confide. Returning to the Holloways was painful, "and for the next two or three mornings there [I would] cry on waking up. Hence more punishments and cross-examinations" (Kipling, 1937, p. 17).

Reading was both an intellectual achievement and a major psychological breakthrough for Rudyard; he found this to be a special experience.

> I was made to read without explanation, under the usual fear of punishment. And on a day that I remember it came to me that "reading" was not "the Cat on the Mat," but a means to everything that would make me happy. So I read all that came within my reach. As soon as my pleasure in this was known, deprivation from reading was added to my punishments. *I then read by stealth and the more earnestly.* (Kipling, 1937, p. 9; italics added)

Reading became "a means to everything"; the books from home may have helped him retain a connection to his parents. "There were not many books in that [the Holloway's] house, but Father and Mother as soon as they heard I could read sent me priceless volumes" (Kipling, 1937, p. 9). Reading may also have stirred memories of Ayah and Meeta who "would tell us stories and Indian nursery songs *all unforgotten*" (pp. 3-4; italics added), and of Captain Holloway, who told him tales of his sea adventures; reading became a "transitional object" experience, memory, and gift.

Rudyard also shared imaginative play with Trix, who wrote "We had a sort of play that ran on and on for months, in which we played all the parts. I'm afraid there was generally a murder in it; or we ran away to sea and had the most wonderful adventures" (Fleming, 1947, p. 1). Rudyard and Trix had a very deep bond with each other, and the fact that Mrs. Holloway doted on Trix, as she continued her hostile behavior to Rudyard, was discussed by the children, with Rudyard assuring Trix that he understood this, and that Trix should not feel as though she were betraying him. The children would often communicate in secret codes and shared secret knowledge. *Robinson Crusoe,* a gift from his father, evoked images of trading with natives, and he set up his own trading post

> in a mildewy basement room where I stood my solitary confinements. My apparatus was a cocoanut shell strung on a red cord, a tin trunk, and a piece of packing-case which kept off any other world. Thus fenced about, everything inside the fence was quite real. . . . I have learned since from children who play much alone that this rule of "be-

ginning again in a pretend game" is not uncommon. *The magic, you see, lies in the ring or fence that you take refuge in.* (Kipling, 1937, pp. 11-12; italics added).

Kipling was a hypervigilant child, "watchful and wary; alert to the changing moods of adults which might presage anger. This prescient awareness of what others were feeling and how they displayed their emotions probably stood him in good stead when he came to write" (Storr, 1988, pp. 114-115). Trix commented: "He loved going about and seeing things; he was always observing; he had a camera in his brain . . . he had the golden gift of making everybody talk to him" (Fleming, 1947, p. 3).

The defense of acting out can "be an indicator of hope and potential for success in the face of adversity" that may lead to the development of "resiliency" (Dugan, 1989, p. 157). Rudyard rebelled against Mrs. Holloway, defying her restrictions whenever he could; when she prohibited his reading, "I then read by stealth and the more earnestly" (Kipling, 1937, p. 9). Rudyard's ability to distance himself emotionally from Mrs. Holloway and her son Harry and his ability to defy the "voice of doom" (Chess, 1989, p. 180) contributed to his resilience.

Rudyard developed severe vision problems after almost six years with the Holloways, and Aunt Georgy sent for his mother, who returned from India and removed the children from the Holloways, taking them to Epping Forest where they had an idyllic time. After this, Rudyard attended Westward Ho!, a boarding school in England; after a rocky start he did well, made friends, continued his voracious reading, and developed his writing skills through working on the school paper. Graduating when sixteen, he returned to India, lived with his family, worked successfully on a newspaper, and began writing short stories about life in India, which became popular. After seven years in India, he moved to London and started his renowned literary career.

Kipling had a stable, secure marriage and a happy family life, but was devastated by the sudden illness and tragic death of Josephine, his beautiful six-year-old daughter, and later by the death of his son, John, twenty-one, killed in World War I. He had friendships with famous and influential people, and was a popular figure with the public, but toward the later part of his life, became such a staunch defender of the Empire and vocal ultraimperialist that he became a subject for ridicule.

Kipling had depressive episodes and sleep problems, waking up in the middle of the night and walking around the house; "I did not know then that such night-wakings would be laid upon me through life; or that my fortunate hour would be on the turn of sunrise, with a sou'-west breeze afoot"

(Kipling, 1937, p. 21). He described several "breakdowns" he experienced, but details are vague. He wrote to his friend Mrs. Hill in 1890:

> You do well to say that the half year has begun. It has and I have broken up. My head has given out and I am forbidden to work and I am to go away somewhere. This is the third time it has happened. . . . I can do nothing to save myself from breaking up now and again. (Ricketts, 1999, p. 158)

Kipling had fears of darkness, which was reflected in his writings, with his frequent contrasts between darkness and light; although highly sociable and productive, ghosts from the past would sometimes torment him, as we can see from his speech to students at McGill in 1907:

> Some of you here know—*and I remember*—that youth can be a reason of great depression, despondencies, doubts, waverings. The worse because they seem to be peculiar to ourselves and incommunicable to our fellows. . . . There is a *certain darkness into which the soul* of the young man sometimes descends—*a horror of desolation, abandonment and realized worthlessness,* which is one of the most real of hells in which we are compelled to walk [1907, p. 21]. (Shengold, 1981, p. 235; italics added)

Kipling's wry sense of humor is present in his stories, and his playfulness (an important factor in developing and maintaining resilience) is especially prominent in his *"Just So Stories,"* addressed to "My Best Beloved" (his daughter Josephine). In this passage, we can see the powerful whale devouring all in front of him, while the small "stute" fish tries to protect himself by outwitting the whale.

> In The Sea, once upon a time, O my best Beloved, there was a whale, and he ate fishes. He ate the starfish and the garfish, and the crab and the dab, and the plaice and the dace, and the skate and his mate, and the mackereel and the pickereel, and the really truly twirly-whirly eel. All the fishes he could find in all the sea he ate with his mouth-so! Till at last there was only one small fish left in all the sea, and he was a small 'Stute fish, and he swam a little behind the Whale's right ear, so as to be out of harm's way. Then the Whale stood up on his tail and said, "I'm hungry." And the small 'Stute fish said in a small 'stute voice, "Noble and generous Cetacean, have you ever tasted man?" (Kipling, 1982, p. 209)

Trix did not fare as well as her brother; she was to succumb to serious and recurrent mental illness (including a severe breakdown when her mother died), beginning when she was thirty. Her diagnosis remains uncertain; she may have developed schizophrenia or a bipolar disorder (Flanders, 2001). Her symptoms "ranged from mutism to hypermanic states in which she did not stop talking, mostly nonsense. She refused all food, and at one point appears to have been nearly catatonic" (p. 289). She was hospitalized, and then, although married, her mother insisted on caring for her, which she did for several years. Trix regained stability when middle-aged (Flanders, 2001; Ricketts, 1999).

While Trix may or may not have been biologically disposed to mental illness, it is probable that the many "at risk" circumstances of her life served at least as triggers. When they moved to the House of Desolation, Trix was three and did not have the more solid sense of self, identity, and object constancy that Rudyard had developed. Trix was loved by Mrs. Holloway, but was also frightened by her, and terrified of Harry who tormented both children. She rebelled in some ways against Mrs. Holloway, but was more dependent on her for affection than Rudyard was. That Trix became a devout evangelical is not surprising, while Rudyard became devoutly antireligious. Inexplicably, Trix was not invited to Aunt Georgy's home and Rudyard went alone for his yearly visits. Trix had no social supports in her early life, other than her brother and an affectionate relationship with Jane, a maid in the home.

> I was heavily handicapped by having no teacher but Mrs. . . . . [Holloway], except for dancing, for six long years, and I never saw girls of my own age save once a week at Sunday School, where talking was forbidden, or in the winter at Dancing Class, where it was discouraged. Small wonder that my first school report described me as being "absolutely ungrounded, curiously ignorant, but singularly well-read." (Fleming, 1939, p. 170)

After Mrs. Kipling took the children from the Holloways' home, she inexplicably replaced Trix there when Rudyard went to Westward Ho! and she returned to India. Trix wrote sad letters home as a teenager, and Mrs. Kipling expressed concern that Trix was developing "some morbid religious notions and is tormenting herself with the fear that we shall be disappointed in her in some way" (Ricketts, 1999, pp. 52-53). At fifteen Trix rejoined the family, including Rudyard, in India. This was a warm, creative, and happy period for the family, and they enjoyed their literary collaborations. Trix was a talented writer, and popular in India's social life; she married

Captain Jack Fleming, after a difficult engagement. Her father expressed concern about the match, noting that Fleming had "many virtues," but he was also "somewhat austere; not caring for books nor for many things for which our Trix cares intensely" (p. 112). After her many breakdowns, he commented that Fleming was a man "who would give a brass monkey depression" (p. 303).

The details of Trix's life are not as well known as that of Rudyard; her more fragile ego could not sustain the emotional demands of her later life. We don't know how her separations from Rudyard in adult life (they often lived in different parts of the world), or later relationship with her parents (and separation from them), and her relationship with her husband affected her emotionally, nor do we know how she experienced the clashes of the different cultures in which she lived. Trix's brief memories of her life with her brother are charming, perceptive, and endearing; it is tragic but also perhaps noteworthy that she did not develop the resilience to prevent her suffering.

Finally, from the perspective of resiliency, in looking at Kipling's cousin Phil, the son of Burne-Jones and Aunt Georgy, who grew up in the "paradise" which had "saved" Kipling, we see a man who could not find himself, and who drifted through life as a playboy. Under the surface of the gaiety of the Grange, as perceived by Kipling, were serious problems that must have affected Phil, such as his father's depressive episodes, and marital discord centering, in large measure, on his father's liaisons with other women. Phil and his parents had difficulties separating from each other; his father had high expectations of himself and transferred these to his son, who did not meet them. In his early years, Phil was raised by nursemaids, and it is doubtful that they displayed the warmth and affection of Ayah and Meeta. "Phil was a small nervous child and had great difficulty mixing with other children. Everything worried and frightened him" (Flanders, 2001, p. 135). Rudyard developed a closer relationship to his Aunt Georgy than Phil did; "it was a relationship that mothers and sons rarely have in reality—certainly not the kind Rudyard had with his own mother, or Georgy with her son" (p. 299).

As Phil grew up he "came to be no more comfortable in his skin" (Flanders, 2001, p. 161), and lived in the shadow of his father's artistry and fame. His own "attachment to painting was rather half-hearted"; his talent at "comic drawing" was disparaged by his father, who requested Phil "solemnly to swear never to use his comic abilities commercially" (p. 202). Phil's mother once said, "His very love and reverence for his father has in a way crippled him" (p. 277). Rudyard knew success as a young writer; Phil never experienced any substantial success. Although often criticized by his parents, he was also indulged by them; when in later life Bourne-Jones was offered a baronetcy, he accepted this largely because of Phil, who "mixed with the Prince of Wales's set" and, Flanders (2001) suggests, Bourne-Jones thought a "baronetcy would make all the difference to the smart set's view of him" (p. 258).

When Rudyard returned from India to London as a young writer, he took Phil, four years his senior, under his wing "feeling he was in need of care" (Flanders, 2001, p. 226). Rudyard's confidence, sense of agency, hard work, and a life fueled by his creative imagination and writing were characteristics missing in Phil. Rudyard's "recruitment" capacities led to building relationships; Phil had many social contacts, but never married and had few close friends. Both Rudyard and Phil, as children, had difficulties to overcome; Rudyard struggled to survive and became resilient; Phil succumbed. In Phil's obituary the *Times* wrote "He inherited . . . the artistic temperament at its full tension: But with him it was perhaps less a gift than a burden" (p. 326).

Discussion of Resilience

Resilience lacks uniformity in definition; external characteristics such as competency or vocational success are highlighted, but internal, experiential factors can be overlooked: "personal success may be attained at the cost of spontaneous enjoyment of life" (Cohler, 1987, p. 406). Some children may seem resilient, but develop problems later; children of mentally ill parents may "feel pressured to maintain maturity and responsibility for themselves and others, which may have later costs in terms of continuing adjustment" (p. 406). In the aftermath of Hurricane Katrina of 2005, many distraught parents had difficulty in providing emotional support to their children. "Every teacher in town knows a child hiding his emotions to protect a troubled parent; psychologists call it 'parentification'. It's hard to avoid the impression that there's a lot of parentification going on" (DeParle, 2006, p. 27).

A seemingly resilient person may be "propped up" by relationships to others who are selfobjects, with a relatively fragile resilience "disappearing" when the selfobject disappears, as we saw with Vivienne, when her supportive teacher left. Nurturing relationships, however, can be reparative for some, leading to further psychological growth.

Becoming parents can be rewarding, enhancing maturity, but may also stir up latent conflicts, producing dysfunction (such as anxiety and/or depression), in a previously well adapted person; some act out unmet needs or conflicts with their children, unconsciously attempting to maintain their own emotional equilibrium in the process.

Saleebey (2001) observes that we all have "possibilities within us and around us" for both vulnerabilities and resilience, but prefers to address strengths and hope rather than "pathologizing" people, or encouraging "victimhood" (p. 78). Healing vulnerabilities, however, can lead to greater resiliency; Ingram and Price (2001) state that, whether genetic or psychological, "the locus of vulnerability processes is within the person" (p. 10). Supportive relationships do aid in strengthening resilience; however some people, fearing closeness and dependency, reject supportive outreach.

The onset of mental illness itself can create vulnerability for further episodes. Ingram and Price (2001) discuss Post's (1992) concept of *"kindling,"* which he has applied to affective disorders:

> Each episode of an affective disorder leaves a residual neurobiological trace that leads to the development of pathways by which increasingly minimal stress becomes sufficient to activate the mechanisms that result in a disorder. Such a process thus leads to increased vulnerability. (p. 9)

Treatment focused only on symptom reduction or removal is inadequate, but should be focused on "the mechanisms that helped to bring it about" (Ingram and Price, 2001, p. 13).

Vulnerability developed in childhood can persist over a lifetime, although in some people latent vulnerability surfaces later in life. In studying vulnerability, it is important "to adopt a lifespan perspective . . . understanding the long-term trajectory of these vulnerability factors and their consequences is thus an extremely important quest" (Ingram and Fortier, 2001, p. 52). This should go hand-in-hand with studying resiliency factors, their counterbalancing effects and concordant or discordant pulls. Reading biographies, autobiographies, and other biographical materials is an excellent way to study the trajectory of lives in a multidimensional manner, with its reverberations of resilience and vulnerability (Urdang, work in progress).

Finally, to the perplexing question of what is resiliency, Vaillant (1993) asks more questions:

> Does this merely mean survival in the face of vulnerability and multiple risk factors, or should we think of resilience only when it also permits happiness? Is it enough that the vulnerable patient survives the operation and that the orphan survives the concentration camp, or, to be called resilient, must they be able to run and laugh and feel joy as well? The reader must choose. (p. 285)

CONCLUSION

Postmodern theories invite us to be skeptical of "given" knowledge and preexisting theories, and warn us against relating to clients within a rigid, mechanistic framework. At the same time they encourage us to explore the subjective, experiential aspects of their lives, and understand their meaning-making. Accordingly, the therapeutic relationship, with its "two-person" psychology, is co-constructed by clinician and client, with emphasis on its mutuality, immediacy, and authenticity. Narrative theory, based on the need for storytelling in peoples' lives, highlights the ongoing interactions of the narrator and the audience (and of the client and therapist)—the "dialogic" encounter. Narrative theory, with its interdisciplinary approach, offers insights into memory and the intersubjective development of identity.

Constructivists argue that psychological theories have no special objectivity or validity, and warn of dangers in placing clients on the "procrustean bed" of favored theories. Ironically, they fail to subject their own perspective to self-criticism regarding the danger of placing clients on the "procrustean bed" of constructivist theory. Constructivists criticize other theories as being products of their times and culture, and offer instead a theoretical orientation that is a product of their own "postmodern" time and culture. Unfortunately this stance, rather than incorporating the rich history of psychodynamic insight, tends to consign it to a relativistic insignificance.

Reliance only on the validity of subjective experiences can thwart the provision of appropriate clinical treatment based on sufficient biopsychosocial assessment; it presents serious challenges in terms of exercising our role, undermines our expertise, and vitiates our acquired expert knowledge. We have a professional responsibility to make judgments about treatment interventions and to protect our clients from harm (in the broadest sense) to themselves and others. Northcut and Heller (2002) warn us of the dangers of "sliding down the slippery slope of constructivism" (p. 217).

It should be obvious that clients cannot be the only experts on treatment goals, given the possibility of harm to self or others. There are times when action is needed to protect clients, family members, and ourselves, as well. We may make mistakes because of our biases, but conservative action is infinitely preferred over too little, too late. Given also that we are designated by society (despite whatever flaws society has) to be responsible for providing responsible treatment, we cannot abdicate our roles as authorities about the theory and practice of psychotherapy. (Nichols, 1993) (Northcutt and Heller, 2002, p. 220)

In their discussion of relational therapy, Ornstein and Ganzer (2005) present a case in which a woman announces to her clinician that she has a gun in her pocketbook and plans to kill herself during the session. The therapist sees this as an *enactment,* and interprets this to the client as mirroring the way her "mother teased and tormented her" (p. 570). The discussion of this insight helped the client "to feel contained," and when she left was "no longer threatening suicide" (p. 570). Vital questions were never raised in the article relating to the client's suicide potential, her safety during the week, and the disposition of the gun.

Relational psychotherapists emphasize a two-person psychology, with an interpersonal focus, although some clinicians add an intrapsychic perspective. However clients can be locked in struggles within themselves, with their *internal* needs and *intrapersonal* conflicts.

> . . . psychotherapists and patients who favor interpersonal themes tend *to neglect intrapersonal scenarios*—for example, those that are about the patient's relation to his body and his attitudes toward and feelings about the wishes he has in that relation. Similarly, it is my impression that a patient's own responses to his wishes, feelings, and actions play a larger role in character and symptom pathology than might be guessed from the patient's (and sometimes the psychotherapist's) preference for telling stories in which the responses of other persons to him as well his response to them are emphasized. (Edelson, 1993, p. 297; italics added)

Theoretical schools of psychotherapy proliferate (including those which claim to be atheoretical), with subdivisions within these schools; they tend to promote and defend themselves, disavowing other theories. Progress, however, is being made in integrating concepts from diverse schools, such as incorporation of both psychodynamic and cognitive-behavioral concepts into therapy. "Integration has gradually emerged, and the ideological cold war has slowly abated" (Norcross and Knight, 2000, p. 273). In 1983, a group called Society for the Exploration of Psychotherapy Integration was formed, and in 1991, a new publication appeared: *Journal of Psychotherapy Integration* (Granvold, 1999, p. 71).

Granvold (1999) notes that Luborsky and colleagues found in their research that treatment outcomes were "approximately the same" for therapists from diverse theoretical schools; this eventuated in the "Dodo bird hypothesis," that is, all treatment approaches are equally effective; in *Alice's Adventure in Wonderland,* the Dodo bird concluded after a race: "Everyone has won and all must have prizes" (p. 72). Even though the Dodo bird's egalitarian approach is praiseworthy, I reassert the premise of this book: Psychodynamic understanding within a developmental biopsychosocial framework is the foundation for sound clinical assessment and intervention, as it offers the deepest understanding of both inner and outer worlds, and their interactions. The assessment of ego functions, defenses, and psychopathology is essential to this approach, which is not a "one style fits all" model, but is highly individualized, incorporating diverse approaches as needed.

Constructivist concepts, such as understanding the client's values, attributions, and experiential world, and working together toward the creation of new meanings, contribute to this undertaking: ". . . psychotherapy is an emotional and interpersonal process involving unique people, not simply an impersonal EVT [empirically validated treatment] of disembodied disorders (Norcross, 1977)" (Norcross and Knight, 2000, p. 277).

Relational psychotherapy's model of a "two-person" therapy contributes the concept of the therapist being a participant-observer in treatment. I would argue, however, that *competent* "one-person" psychotherapy *is* a "two-person" model. The therapist's direction of treatment does not equate with authoritarian treatment (even in the case of mandated treatment)—the therapeutic relationship, intersubjective enactments, the process of therapy and the therapeutic alliance should be subjects for ongoing therapeutic dialogue.

The insights offered by narrative therapy suggest that an interdisciplinary approach be incorporated into social work training, as history, literature, and anthropology share similar quests for knowledge about the shaping and development of lives. Tomalin (2002), in her biography of Samuel Pepys, a famous seventeenth-century diarist, comments that Pepys observed "the complex relations between the inner and outer worlds of a man" (p. 378).

The social context of lives is important to social work clinicians with a biopsychosocial orientation, just as it is to constructivists, and is explored in Chapter 5, followed by Chapter 6 on culture.

LEARNING EXERCISE

Storytellers and audiences need each other; the development of their intersubjectivity or their dialogic relationship is the core of narrative theory; this theory also has its parallel in clinical work, in the relationship between the client and clinician. Illustrate this concept by applying it to your biographical (or autobiographical) reading. If a biography, how does the writer relate to the subject; does this change over time? If an autobiography, how would you describe the narrative voice of the author, and how do you react to this?

SUGGESTED READING

Articles

Floersch, J. 2000. Reading the case record: The oral and written narratives of social workers. *Social Service Review* 74: 169-192.

Josselson, R. 1995. Narrative and psychological understanding. *Psychiatry* 58: 330-343.

Tosone, C. 2004. Relational social work: Honoring the tradition. *Smith College Studies in Social Work* 74: 475-485.

Books

Brockmeier, J., and D. Carbaugh. (eds.) 2001. *Narrative and identity: Studies in autobiography, self and culture.* Amsterdam/Philadelphia: John Benjamins Publishing Company.

Couch, A. S. 1999. Therapeutic functions of the real relationship in psychoanalysis. In *The psychoanalytic study of the child,* ed. A. J. Solnit, P. B. Neubauer, S. Abrams, and A. S. Dowling, Vol. 54, pp. 130-168. New Haven, CT: Yale University Press.

Diamond, J. 2002. *Narrative means to sober ends: Treating addiction and its aftermath.* New York: The Guilford Press.

Diedrich, M. 1999. *Love across color lines: Ottilie Assing and Frederick Douglass.* New York: Hill and Wang.

Lee, H. 2005. *Virginia Woolf's nose: Essays on biography.* Princeton: Princeton University Press.

Mahoney, M. J. 2003. *Constructive psychotherapy: A practical guide.* New York: The Guilford Press.

Chapter 5

Social Systems and the Community

A thousand fibers connect us with our fellow men; and among those fibers, as sympathetic threads, our actions run as causes, and they come back to us as effects.

Henry Melvill, *Golden Lectures for 1855*

INTRODUCTION

Physical, economic, social, cultural, technological, political, and ideological influences are constantly impinging on us, as we absorb and filter the impact of the world around us. Our values and conflicts, as well as the innermost sense of our identities, are intertwined with our experiences in and relationships to our human and nonhuman environments. People react emotionally when they get a good job, when they are "downsized," when they become homeless due to natural disasters or to lack of affordable housing, when their marriages are not sanctioned because they are gay, and when violence permeates neighborhoods, schools, and families.

People are active participants in their social worlds; they are the "spiders weaving their webs"; they join communities, churches, vote, and develop ideologies. An *ideology* can be a *driving force* in the lives of people: Strong emotional energies are invested in issues such as antigun control (or gun control) and involvement in religious groups, cults, or political movements. The "religious right," a strong force in our present culture, and its positions on subjects such as separation of church and state, and abortion influence political and legal processes.

Events in this country sometimes reach crisis proportions, as when Hurricane Katrina devastated New Orleans in 2005, a crisis that remains ongoing as the city attempts to reconstruct itself, amidst economic, political,

Human Behavior in the Social Environment, Second Edition

racial, and psychological turmoil. The destruction of the World Trade Towers in New York City on September 11, 2001, caused immediate shock, trauma, and grief, and was followed by the United States. "War on Terrorism," with its many repercussions. The United States invaded Afghanistan and Iraq, resulting thus far in the deaths of more than 3,600 service men and women, an expenditure of over $313 billion dollars from the federal budget, and the eruption of major political and legal controversies about privacy, human rights, torture of prisoners, and the Geneva Convention. Iraq itself has imploded into a violent confrontation between its Shiite and Sunni populations, fueled by Al-Qaeda and other militants, while the country's infrastructure and fabric of everyday functioning remains in disrepair.

In this chapter, we examine physical and social environments, their impact on people, and how people impact on them, concurrently with the ongoing interweaving of inner and outer worlds. People incorporate aspects of their community and cultural identifications into their own sense of self (Saari, 2005); this close interrelationship offers insights into why "we are so deeply affected, psychologically, by disruptions and transformations within our communities and societies" (Ainslie and Brabeck, 2003, p. 45). We begin this chapter by introducing the ecological perspective, with its focus on the interactions of people and their environments, incorporating physical environments (landscape and weather, urban and rural settings, and housing as well as homelessness), and social environments (communities, support networks, economic issues, employment, education, and organizations).

The final section introduces the social problems of discrimination, violence, the impact of the addictions on society, the increasing use of prisons for social control, and the "warehousing" of the mentally ill. We also examine loyalties, conflicts, competing interests, and ideologies in relation to individuals, families, communities, and organizations.

These subjects are not readily categorized, as systems often overlap in reality. Housing projects, for example, part of the physical environment, also constitute a social environment, with its frequent social problems of discrimination and violence. Social policy influences the lack of adequate funding for low-income housing and perpetuates the housing crisis and homelessness. Conflicting ideologies and values relating to segregation versus integration, and financial aid for poor people, affects social policies related to low-income housing.

Policies and social issues will change between the writing of this chapter and your reading of it; so, we need to understand the complex intertwining of people, environments, social issues, ideologies, and organizations, and how we are affected by both the stability and the precariousness of the world around us.

THE ECOLOGICAL PERSPECTIVE

The ecological approach to social work emphasizes that person-environmental relationships are "characterized by continuous reciprocal exchanges or transactions, in which people and environments influence, shape, and sometimes change each other" (Germain,1991, p. 16).

The complex and problematic interactions between the fragile ecosystem of the Galapagos archipelago and its residents illustrate this perspective.

Until recently, large parts of the Galapagos Islands, a major inspiration for Darwin's theory of evolution, remained protected as a national park, a Marine Resources Reserve, and a UNESCO World Heritage Site. Major changes now threaten to upset its "fragile environmental balance" (Lemonick, 1995, p. 80); many of the competing interests and ideologies affecting this microcosm are also reflected, in different ways, in our own society.

> The giant tortoises known as *galapagos,* which gave the islands their name, still amble across the scrubby landscape, sea-lion pups and Galapagos penguins gaze unafraid at scuba divers, marine iguanas crawl over volcanic rocks along the shore, and strolling tourists have to detour around blue-footed boobies (a type of seabird) busily performing courtship rituals. Puerto Ayora, the islands' largest town (pop. 8,000), comprises a tranquil collection of quaint hotels, craft shops and seafood restaurants. (Lemonick, 1995, p. 80; italics in the original)

Competing interest groups in the Galapagos include those concerned with preserving the archipelago's pristine environmental status and others who feel economically oppressed by environmental restrictions such as prohibitions against sea cucumber fishing. During a melee over this conflict, the entrance to the Charles Darwin Research Station was blockaded, some workers were held as hostages, scientists were "harassed," and the tortoises were threatened (Lemonick, 1995, p. 80).

In another protest, residents, seeking greater local control, seized both the research station and the airport for two weeks, complaining that their demands were being ignored (Lemonick, 1995). The large influx of tourists contributes to the systemic complexities. Although many tourists and tour operators respect the environment, some ships dump waste directly into the sea (Lemonick, 1995).

The increase in tourism has led to a dramatic increase in immigrants looking for tourism-related jobs, resulting in a strain on the waste management and water systems as well as on the fabric of society itself (Lemonick,

1995). Resenting the new immigrants, many residents have accused them of importing and establishing an illicit sex and drug culture (Lemonick, 1995). In addition, people have allegedly brought with them many off-islands species of plants and animals, endangering local life-forms. The now-huge goat population, for example, is consuming vegetation that form a vital part of the tortoises' food supply (Lemonick, 1995). Fishermen have been over-fishing illegally, posing a threat to the sea life.

Competing groups include the national government (wanting to control excessive exploitation of the Galapagos Islands, yet wanting to retain the tourist income); the local government (seeking greater autonomy); the conservationists (concerned about maintaining the ecological system while acknowledging the islanders' need to make a living); and the "natives," the flora and fauna, and the tourists themselves. The local governmental group has threatened violence. Resolution has been difficult, as issues of political control, political autonomy, economic gain, and ideologies about conservation are pitted against each other.

THE PHYSICAL ENVIRONMENT

Physical environments, including landscapes, natural resources, weather, the effects of global warming, the presence of active volcanoes, or proneness to earthquakes can affect human feelings and behavior.

Visitors to Iceland are often moved by its stark beauty, but may feel overwhelmed by the barrenness of much of the landscape, the absence of vegetation, and the paucity of animal life. Iceland became a training ground for the first moon astronauts to help them acclimate to living in a "moonscape." Presently, active volcanoes, geysers, hot springs, and a tendency toward earthquakes are part of the environs. One Icelandic native expressed her belief that the untamed nature of her country is what inspired its people to become interested in trolls, fairies, and the Icelandic sagas.

Physical environments can have special meaning and significance to people; to Native Americans, "working in harmony with natural forces is a way of life" (Attneave, 1982, p. 65). Animistic beliefs hold that the spirit or soul inhabits everything in nature. "Not only animals but plants, rocks, mountains and bodies of water exist as personalities or as vehicles of expression for the spiritual forces of the universe" (p. 65).

Nature can foster mental health, when people "remain in touch with its *restorative and healing forces* (Searles)" (Germain, 1991, p. 30; italics added). Germain (1991) describes "the sense of serenity and wonder felt by those fortunate enough to experience mountains, seashore, and countryside—and the powerful influence of wilderness therapy and organized camping for persons of all ages and varying states of physical and mental health" (p. 30).

Studying an individual's physical environment requires sensitivity to issues such as personal space, crowding, and privacy (Gutheil, 1992). Living in a house (or an institution) with no physical privacy or storage space of one's own can have negative psychological effects. "Some [physical] environments have a welcoming quality . . . and encourage the development of ongoing interpersonal relationships. . . . Other environments work against the formation of relationships . . . such [as] jails and hospitals" (p. 392). In some psychiatric facilities, the "spatial arrangements are so different from normal experiences that they induce stress and may elicit behavior that appears bizarre" (p. 392).

Robert Caro (1983), in his biography of Lyndon Johnson, depicts the Texas hill country of Johnson's childhood because he felt that to understand Johnson, one had to know his special environment. "The hill country was a trap—a trap baited with grass" (p. 8). Initially, new settlers to this area were impressed by the richness of the flourishing grass.

> The tall grass of the Hill Country stretched as far as the eye could see, covering valleys and hillsides alike. . . . To these men [the settlers] the grass was proof that their dreams would come true. In country where grass grew like that, cotton would surely grow tall, and cattle fat—and men rich. In country where grass grew like that, they thought, anything would grow. How could they know about the grass? (Caro, 1983, p. 11)

The soil was thin, the roots shallow, and brush, which had been thinned by fires, grew back, blocking out the grass. Grazing increased: "The cattle ate the grass—and then there was no longer anything holding . . . the soil" (Caro, 1983, p. 21). Floods complicated matters. Succeeding on such land "required . . . a pragmatism almost terrifying in its absolutely uncompromising starkness"; the Johnsons "were . . . particularly unsuited to such a land" (p. 26). Losing their agricultural investment they lived a life of genteel poverty; the family regarded the father as a failure, resulting in family interactions that played a large role in Lyndon Johnson's psychological development (Caro, 1983).

Climatic conditions can have serious physical and emotional consequences; in this country, the most dangerous kind of "extreme summer heat and humidity . . . [has] become more frequent . . . over the last half century . . . [this] has more impact on people's health than any other kind of severe weather, and . . . the elderly are most vulnerable" (Stevens, 1998, p. A1).

The absence of warmth and sunlight has received recent attention; some people develop depression reactive to seasons—a condition termed seasonal affective disorder (SAD) has been distinguished in recent years (Kaplan, Sadock, and Grebb, 1994); SAD "occurs repeatedly at the same time of year, usually starting in fall and ending in spring"; light therapy, antidepressants, and cognitive therapy were found to be effective treatments ("Winter Depression," 2004, p. 4).

Physical disasters, such as floods, tsunamis, tornadoes, hurricanes, and earthquakes, can affect people's lives and psychological states. In 2005, Hurricane Katrina, the worst physical disaster ever to strike this country, affected Alabama, Mississippi, and Louisiana. New Orleans was flooded as levees collapsed, destroying homes, and causing overwhelming losses due to death, illness, and injuries; it was estimated that 300,000 people became homeless, most of whom were black (Dao, 2006). Fear and chaos reigned, as systemic and political problems intermingled with the breakdown of communities, schools, medical services, and the processes of daily existence.

Bureaucratic entanglements proliferated at a great rate; the Federal Emergency Management Agency (FEMA), for example, provided trailers to house the homeless, but disputes arose about where they should be located, and the availability of necessary utilities. "The problems in administering the $4 billion trailer program mirror those of other major recovery efforts undertaken since the hurricanes crippled the region, and appear to be the result of failures at all levels of government" (Steinhauer and Lipton, 2006, p. A1).

Criminal activities have flourished; graft and corruption, rampant in Louisiana before the storm, increased in scope with millions of dollars of federal money at stake. "Growing numbers of subpoenas may soon be issued across Louisiana, where local politics remains a blood sport and corruption has been a bad habit" (Eaton, 2006, p. A1). Individuals were found to have defrauded the government of millions of dollars through false claims. Auditors involved in examining this problem have stated that FEMA "was to blame for much of the abuse because of a woefully inadequate accounting system" (Lipton, 2006, A11).

Racial tensions have escalated; almost 70 percent of New Orleans' population had been African American prior to the hurricane, and were the hardest hit by the storm, as their neighborhoods were closest to the levee breaks. "Indeed, race has become a subtext for just about every contentious decision the city faces: Where to put FEMA trailers; which neighborhoods to rebuild; how the troubled school system should be reorganized; when elections should be held" (Dao, 2006, p. WK1).

Mental health problems have dramatically increased especially post–traumatic stress disorder and depression; rates of suicide and substance abuse have accelerated. Many people suffering from emotional problems had no history of psychiatric problems, and people of all socioeconomic levels have been affected. At a time when more care was needed, less help was available. Louisiana "estimates that the city has lost more than half its psychiatrists, social workers, psychologists, and other mental health workers, many of whom relocated after the storm" (Saulny, 2006b, p. A15); insufficient numbers of beds have been available in psychiatric hospitals for the number of patients who needed them; the police department have become the major caretakers. Dr. Osofsky, chairman of the Department of Psychiatry at Louisiana State University, observing the conditions of ruin and destruction surrounding everyone, commented on the urgency of rehabilitating the city; "the mental health needs are related to this" (Saulny, 2006b, p. A15).

Environmental concerns are now subjects of major national and international debate; the battles between conservationists and sea cucumber fishermen on the Galapagos Islands exemplify this universal conflict. Should federal lands in Alaska be preserved, or drilled for oil; should the rain forests of Panama be conserved, or converted into farmland? Global warming is viewed as a serious threat by many countries, affecting weather (both droughts and floods), rising sea levels (with an imminent threat to people living in coastal areas), and diseases among animals, as well as the depletion of some species. One cause of alarm has been the rapid rate of glacial meltdown in Greenland (Lemonick, 2006).

> Glaciers that flow toward the ocean in the southern half of the enormous frozen island are among the world's fastest moving, and their massive outpouring of ice now contributes fully a sixth of the annual rise in sea level. According to a study in the current issue of *Science*, they have nearly doubled their rate of flow over the past five years, to about 8 miles a year, dumping icebergs and meltwater into the already rising ocean faster than anyone expected. (Lemonick, 2006, pp. 58-59; italics in the original)

Concerns have been raised about pollution, both in the oceans and in local water supplies, and about disposal of radioactive and other toxic waste material. "Abandoned, uncontrolled toxic dumps and poorly controlled landfills used for hazardous wastes are found in or near some rural and urban communities, especially poorer ones" (Germain, 1991, pp. 60-61).

Finally, on microscopic and submicroscopic levels, new viruses and drug-resistant bacteria have made an international appearance; severe acute respiratory syndrome (or SARS) and bird flu have left illness and death in their wake, with worldwide anxiety about its further transmission and the lack of an effective vaccine. Shortly after 9/11, the deliberate and sinister spread of anthrax by an unknown individual via the postal service in the United States developed into a national crisis, with increasing fears about terrorists using biological weapons.

The international AIDS epidemic has created innumerable systemic problems, including disability, death, a dramatic increase in the number of orphans (especially in Africa), and infections in children. Although advances have been made in treating this disease, it continues to increase on an international level; the Joint United Nations Program on HIV/AIDS reported, at the end of 2005, "an estimated 4.9 million people were infected with HIV during the year—up from 4.6 million in 2003" (Cohen, 2006, p. 30). In the United States, although there has been a decline, nevertheless 40,000 new cases are reported each year, mostly in black and Hispanic young people engaging in heterosexual sex, the majority of whom are unaware of their condition (McNeil Jr., 2006). There is also an increase of HIV and AIDS in older adults; "between ten to fifteen percent of . . . new cases occur in individuals fifty and older" (Levy-Dweck, 2005, p. 37).

Preventive measures, such as sex education in schools, sterilized needles for drug users, and outreach sexual educational measures for the elderly, can reduce the spread of this disease; however, these and other preventive measures are difficult to implement, because of cultural, religious, and political influences. Furthermore, AIDS carries a social stigma that few other diseases carry, and seeking help and confiding in others becomes more problematic. AIDS is further discussed in Chapter 13.

Computer Technology

Although not, strictly speaking, a feature of the physical environment, the advent of computer technology has had a profound impact in a multiplicity of ways on human existence and society; it is "a cultural crossroad of work, play and social interaction" (Marriott, 2006, p. A1). The employment market has been affected, contributing new jobs for some as well as leading to unemployment for others, who have not acquired the strong educational backgrounds necessary for "high tech" jobs. Internet communications have made the outsourcing of American jobs (to the detriment of some U.S. workers) more feasible. Education, at all levels has been affected, at the institutional level, as students can take courses, complete assignments, and communicate with their teachers on the Internet. On an informal level, this technology has created a knowledge explosion, where information ranging from maps and driving directions to scholarly books and reference materials are readily accessible. A wide range of Internet-based community-like arenas have also developed, from chat rooms to scholarly and professional forums, to the so-called blogs (short for weblogs, interactive sites for the expression of views on every subject imaginable).

There had been initial concern, in relation to the issue of equality of opportunity, that blacks and Hispanics might be left behind while whites and Asian Americans were making the most use of computer technology (Marriott, 2006). However, it turns out that African Americans and English-speaking Hispanics are increasingly "gaining access to and ease with the Internet, signaling a remarkable closing of the 'digital divide,'" although the economically based limitations of ownership at home of cutting-edge hard- and software create a situation in which "Internet access solely at institutions can put students at a disadvantage" (Marriott, 2006, p. A1).

Many support groups have proliferated on the Internet, allowing people suffering from illnesses or life crisis to share their stories and offer advice. In the present military conflict in Iraq, the U.S. government has spent millions of dollars for Internet equipment for military personnel, including Web cameras, which experts find have "helped ease the isolation of soldiers' lives, as well as the turbulence of coming home, the often-bumpy transition from combat to kiddie pool and from commanding to compromising" (Alvarez, 2006, p. A1).

The serious unavailability of mental health professionals in rural areas and prisons has been the impetus behind the growing use of computer technology involving distance contact, including on-screen visual imaging of the participants ("telepsychiatry" and/or "telemedicine") (Johnson, 2006). The possible subtle effects of "telepsychiatry" on the interpersonal essence of the therapist-client relationship remain to be seen.

An unanticipated offshoot of the Internet is various forms of online confession sites, within or outside of a religious context. The founder of one such site, mysecret.tv, noted that "after 16 years in the ministry he knew that the smiles and eager handshakes that greeted him each week often masked a lot of pain. . . . But the accounts of anguish and guilt that have poured into mysecret.tv have stunned him"; examples were of guilt over failure to protect sibs from a molesting parent and a concealed homosexual relationship (Banerjee, 2006, p. A11).

There have been serious downsides to the advent of computer technology, such as online gambling, scams, identity theft, fraudulent dating services, and the abuse and exploitation of children through "the spread of child pornography on the Internet" (Eichenwald, 2006a, p. A22). Pedophiles have easy access to children through online chat rooms, and by going "online to seek tips for getting near children—at camps, through foster care, at community gatherings and at countless other events" (Eichenwald, 2006b, p. A1).

Finally, computers have even found their way ever more deeply into our unconscious as objects of "anxiety-filled dreams" (Kelley, 1998). In 1909, the book *10,000 Dreams Interpreted* by Gustavus Hindman Miller "featured dream objects like absinthe, reapers and saltpeter," and now "dream lexicons are filled with cars and airplanes"; it would not be surprising if "control panels and File Not Found messages will be regularly showing up in the collective subconscious" (Kelley, 1998, p. E1).

Rural Social Work

The physical environment encompasses both urban and rural settings. Urban problems such as overcrowding, poor housing, and crime are frequently addressed in the social work literature; less attention has been paid to rural problems. What is rural America? Generally, it is assumed that most people in rural areas are farmers, work in forestry or are miners and fishermen, with the largest number of positions in service fields (Davenport and Davenport III, 1995). In fact, the decline of family farms has affected rural life and has many economic and social ramifications (Remnick, 1998).

Rural areas have been classified by "specialization of their economic function" by sociologists in the U.S. Department of Agriculture, and, although some overlap occurs, the populations of most rural counties belong primarily in one or two groups, which include farming-, manufacturing-, and mining-dependent counties; specialized government (with military bases or state universities); persistent poverty (especially in the Mississippi Delta, parts of Appalachia, and many Native American counties); federal lands; and destination retirement communities. This variety "dispel[s] the myth of one rural America" (Davenport and Davenport III, 1995, p. 2077).

The population in rural America is not homogenous; it includes such groups as the Missouri Amish, Louisiana Cajun, North Carolina Hmong, New Mexico Pueblo, Mississippi African American, and Southwestern Tex-Mex. In addition, many refugees are being placed in rural areas (Davenport and Davenport III, 1995).

Social workers in rural areas are usually employed by public agencies, such as child welfare, mental health, and corrections settings. Their employment generally lacks the professional supports and social resources found in larger metropolitan areas (Davenport and Davenport III, 1995). Germain (1991) observes that "the incidence and prevalence of malnutrition, substandard housing, maternal and infant mortality, unemployment and underemployment, poverty, water pollution, and increase in divorce are greater than in urban communities" (p. 60).

In many rural areas, residents develop a sense of community, leading to the development of mutual support systems. These include social networks and "natural helpers," the latter being relatives and friends, "first-line purveyors of informal mental health, social, and health services" (Patterson et al., 1988, p. 272), whom others seek out. These social supports can be of assistance to rural social workers, who often have minimal resources available.

Conversely, though some benefit from community solidarity and social supports, others who do not conform to community expectations may be excluded from these supports. Homosexuals, for example, can have a more difficult time coming out in rural areas than in larger cities.

Social workers in rural communities, especially those who are used to urban living, face special problems relating to privacy and confidentiality and to the maintenance of professional boundaries in the community in which they serve as well as reside. "Transplanted [social work] urbanites . . . refer to 'life in a goldfish' bowl. Everyone seems to know what everyone else is doing, and one's personal life affects one's professional life more than it does in urban settings" (Davenport and Davenport III, 1995, p. 2082). Attendance (or lack of attendance) at local church services might be noticed; not employing the only community plumber because he is a client and seeking such services out of town could cause hard feelings. Value conflicts may arise between rural residents "who tend to be more conservative and traditional, and social workers, who tend to be more liberal and nontraditional. . . . Social workers urging anti-gun legislation and anti-hunting rules may quickly lose community acceptance" (p. 2082).

In recent years, rural social work, which had been out of the mainstream of social work practice and education, has been developing its own voice and sphere of influence. The Rural Social Work Caucus has been influential, sponsoring conferences and institutes on rural social work; several graduate schools of social work as well as undergraduate social work programs have developed rural curricula (Davenport and Davenport III, 1995).

Housing

Where we live and how we feel about it are important aspects of all our lives. As students, you might be living in an apartment with five or six other students, and enjoy it, or feel stressed by "overcrowding," or you could be living with your parents (which you might or might not prefer). You may feel safe in your neighborhood or you might be afraid to walk alone in it.

Today, housing problems are widespread, related to both the spiraling costs of housing and the lack of moderately priced housing. An increase in the gap of income distribution resulted in an increase of families and children living at the poverty level, and a shortage of moderately priced housing had an impact on families with young children; this has resulted in seriously inadequate housing for many, and often led to homelessness (Giovannoni, 1995).

Urban renewal has led to relocations for many people, often with great emotional cost. "As Fried . . . pointed out in *'Grieving for a Lost Home,'* as many as one-third of the people who left their homes and communities because of urban renewal showed signs of clinical depression two years after relocation" (Cohen and Phillips, 1997, p. 480).

Various governmental programs over the years have assisted people with housing, including low-interest mortgage loans; subsidizing housing developments for those with middle and low incomes; the establishment of rent controls; and the establishment of the U.S. Department of Housing and Urban Development (HUD) in 1965. The decline in governmental financial aid for housing needs as well as a trend toward eliminating rent controls have contributed to the present housing crisis.

Public Housing Projects

Public housing projects have been a major source of controversy over the years. Public housing projects are often slums that the federal government helped to create in its effort to eradicate slums (Belluck, 1998b). Since the late 1990s, there has been a massive governmental effort to raze many projects that have been "crippled by flawed policies and mismanagement and overwhelmed by poverty and crime"; although the aim was to move people into better neighborhoods, they often found themselves in poor neighborhoods with as many problems as the projects (p. 1).

Programs have been developed to link social services with housing developments where tenants continue to live. One program, in an impoverished section of the South Bronx, offers programs to tenants that include on-site counseling and referral services related to economic (and rent payment) issues, employment and training, and mental health and family issues (Cohen and Phillips, 1997). The tenants were also aided in developing their own tenants' association and becoming involved with community organizations. Cohen and Phillips (1997) reported positive results and felt that this program had built a sense of community for the tenants; this is critical, as "a sense of community can be extremely fragile in low-income, urban neighborhoods where residents have experienced steep economic decline and abandonment" (p. 480).

Some communities in the South Bronx have acted on their own behalf, such as those in formerly devastated neighborhoods of the 1970s, full of empty buildings; "residents in the communities that urban experts had given up on took back the streets, scraped together grants from foundations and meagerly financed city programs, occupied and renovated abandoned buildings, and turned rubble-strewn lots into neighborhood gardens" (Gratz, 2006, p. A23). Over 67,000 new housing units were developed; once the residents made progress, the city and private developers responded with funding. "In these neighborhoods, the residents were catalysts for renewal" (p. A23). Housing projects have been built for the elderly and for the disabled with special features, such as handrails and access for wheelchairs. In 1998, a special housing complex, GrandFamilies House, was built in Dorchester, Boston, to house grandparents raising their grandchildren (Dowdy, 1998). "Nearly 4 million children live in households headed by grandparents, according to 2003 data released by the US Census Bureau" (Llana, 2006), and grandparents in poor neighborhoods had a special need for this housing, as many "found themselves falling through . . . the social-service safety net. . . . Some were prohibited from bringing grandchildren into elderly housing complexes, so they searched for affordable housing [which was] . . . in short supply" (Dowdy, 1998, B8).

Funded by both public and private sources, this project contains special facilities for both children and the elderly (Dowdy, 1998); this "social experiment," the first of its kind, has become a "national model," and funding for other complexes was approved by Congress in 2003 (Llana, 2006).

Homelessness

Homelessness is the catastrophic outcome of failed social policies relating to housing, including lack of rent controls, inadequate funding, and the deinstitutionalization of the mentally ill.

The scarcity of affordable housing is one of the major factors leading to the dramatic increase of homelessness in the United States. Although precise statistics are not available, there is nevertheless a dramatic increase of homelessness in the United States since 1980, due in large measure to the scarcity of affordable housing (First, Rife, and Toomey, 1995). Obtaining a precise number of homeless people is difficult because of the lack of clarity about the definitions of homelessness. Is a person homeless only if living on the street or in a shelter? The homeless may make other types of arrangements (by virtue of which they may or may not be considered homeless): They may move in with other people; reside in "welfare hotels," utilize "migrant farmworker housing," or live in "single-room occupancy hotels" (p. 1331).

Currently there are about "600,000 people [who] are homeless on any given night, and 2 million at some time in any given year"; the United States Department of Health and Human Services estimated that there are between 100,000 and 200,000 people who are "chronically homeless" ("The Homeless," 2005, p. 4). Many of the homeless population, "about a quarter to a third," have been diagnosed with a major mental illness, "usually schizophrenia, bipolar disorder, or severe depression—and the proportion is growing" (p. 4). Approximately "45 percent of homeless mentally ill persons are also dependent on alcohol or other substances" (Sadock and Sadock, 2003, p. 1377).

Homeless Mentally Ill

During the deinstitutionalization process of the late 1950s, state psychiatric hospitalizations declined "from nearly 600,000 beds" to "about 60,000 beds today" ("Prisoners of Mental," 2003, p. 5). Unfortunately, although many civil libertarians felt that returning mentally ill people to the community would be more humane than locking them away from society, the comprehensive services needed for maintaining them in the community have not been provided. People with mental illness are often incarcerated in prisons "for minor crimes that are survival strategies . . . or for behavior directly produced by psychosis" (Kaplan, Sadock, and Grebb, 1994, p. 204).

> Homeless mentally ill persons are not simply undomiciled. They are often totally disaffiliated, with few, if any, links to the community. They are unemployed, socially isolated, and out of contact with their families. Homeless women may be more likely than men to have intact social skills and social networks. In general, homeless mentally ill persons are difficult to treat because of their high levels of withdrawal and suspicion, psychopathology, homeless life-style, or negative past experiences with the mental health system. (Sadock and Sadock, 2003, p. 1377)

It is becoming increasingly evident that a close association exists between depression and homelessness (Holloway, 1999). Dr. Fieve, who pioneered the use of lithium, has asserted that intensive outreach work in finding people with depressive disorders could substantially cut down the number of homeless ending up in shelters (Holloway, 1999). As bipolar (formerly called manic-depressive) disorder may be difficult to diagnose, many patients remain untreated. During the depressive state, a patient may feel very tired and therefore often becomes dysfunctional. Dr. Fieve added that "you've probably lost your job because of excessive absenteeism and poor performance. . . . This is where homelessness sets in. Your family can't deal with you," and you are most likely to leave home (Holloway, 1999, p. 3).

Homeless Families

During the 1990s, families were observed to be the "fastest growing segment of the homeless population" (First, Rife, and Toomey, 1995, p. 1331), and the numbers are still increasing. A study, in 2005, of 24 U.S. cities, concluded that "families with children accounted for 33 percent of the homeless population" (U.S. Conference of Mayors, 2005); applications for emergency shelters "increased by an average of 5 percent" (U.S. Conference of Mayors, 2005) in 63 percent of these cities. Although shelters added approximately 8 percent of additional beds, nevertheless, "an average of 32 percent of requests for shelter by homeless families were denied in 2005 due to lack of resources" ("Homeless Families with," 2006).

Four major factors contribute to the rise of homeless families: substantial decreases in income for poor people; decreasing availability of low-cost housing; federal cutbacks in providing housing for people with low incomes and cutbacks in welfare benefits; and the need to move from housing that is unsafe as well as dealing with family conflict and abuse (First, Rife, and Toomey, 1995); homeless women often report physical and/or sexual abuse (Goldberg, 1999).

Homeless children who are with their parents "constitute from one-half to two-thirds of the homeless family population" (First, Rife, and Toomey, 1995, p. 1332). Typically, these families are headed by a single mother with one or two children; the average age of the children is six years. These families move often and frequently and "have lived marginal, low-income lifestyles before experiencing homelessness" (p. 1332).

Children in these families suffer the negative effects of homelessness (First, Rife, and Toomey, 1995). The numbers of children who are homeless has not been determined, but there is clear evidence as to the serious consequences to their health, and to their regularity in attending school. Research conduced by the Institute of Medicine (1988) reported that "43 percent of homeless preschoolers examined manifested serious developmental delays" (Giovannoni, 1995). In addition, they tend to have "high levels of anxiety and depression and . . . [other] emotional and behavioral problems" (First, Rife, and Toomey, 1995, p. 1332); this includes "feeling a decreased sense of support and an increased sense of isolation" (Schmitz, Wagner, and Menke, 2001, p. 69).

Runaways and Homeless Youths

It is not known how many youths run away and how many are homeless, as authorities are not always notified of runaways, and some runaways are difficult to find (Bass, 1995). However, in the United States "the homeless youth population is estimated to be between 500,000 and 1.3 million young people each year (Center for Law and Social Policy, 2003). According to the U.S. Conference of Mayors, unaccompanied youth account for 3 percent of the urban homeless population (U.S. Conference of Mayors, 2005)" ("Homeless Youth," 2006).

Many runaways and homeless youths come from dysfunctional families, where they have been physically and sexually abused, and where substance abuse, violence, psychiatric disorders are frequently encountered; there two times as many of these youngsters who have lived in child welfare facilities, than who had lived with family members (Bass, 1995).

The words "push out" and "throwaway" have been coined to refer to youths who leave home because their parents (or legal guardians) have encouraged them to leave, have abandoned them, or have abused and neglected them. Nearly 25 percent of the youth who are considered runaways are, in fact, "throwaways" (Loppnow, 1985, p. 516). Adolescent runaways are discussed at greater length in Chapter 10.

Homelessness is a serious problem affecting diverse populations and having multiple root causes. Progress is being made with the "chronically homeless" (approximately 10 percent of the total homeless group), who have been differentiated from those homeless people who use shelters only on a temporary basis. A national program, which places the chronically homeless in their own apartments, has been established and implemented by 219 cities (Eckholm, 2006a). Philip F. Mangano, Executive Director of the United States Interagency Council on Homelessness, asserted that "it is cheaper to put the chronically homeless right into apartments, and provide medical and addiction treatments there, than to watch them cycle endlessly through shelters, soup kitchens, emergency rooms, detoxification centers and jails" (Eckholm, 2006a, p. A19). This "housing first" approach began in New York, in 1990, by encouraging this group to move into their own apartments, and then providing them with social work and psychiatric services. This approach has decreased the number of homeless in many cities, and federal funding for this program has increased (up to $4 billion) (Eckholm, 2006a). Bob Erlenbusch, chairman of the National Coalition for the Homeless, expressed reservations about this program, in terms of insufficient attention being paid to underlying problems such as "federal programs for low-income housing, which can prevent homelessness, [which] have languished in the Bush years or been cut" (p. A19).

THE SOCIAL ENVIRONMENT

Economic

Economic factors are one of the most compelling aspects of life affecting (and being affected by) human behavior. Survival itself depends on having sufficient economic resources so that one does not starve or become homeless. Severe forces of nature, such as floods and drought, can lead to crop failures and ensuing famine, destroying the economic base of communities or entire countries. Political turmoil can trigger economic chaos, and economic crisis can produce political turmoil. The Great Depression of the 1930s in this country caused untold hardship for millions and ultimately resulted in the New Deal programs (such as Social Security) of the Roosevelt administration. In contrast, the serious economic problems in Germany fueled the rise of Nazism, leading to the massive destruction of Europe and its peoples in World War II.

According to the Census Bureau, the "median household income rose slightly faster than inflation last year [2005] for the first time in six years" (Lyman, 2006b, p. A1). However, this finding is somewhat illusory, as people did not earn more money; their real earnings actually decreased from what they had been in 2004. What accounts for this increase is that more family members were working to balance the budget; in addition, some people had income outside of wages. It was also reported that more Americans, now about 46.6 million, have no medical insurance (Lyman, 2006b).

Although the number of those living at the poverty level remained steady, and did not increase as they had for four previous years, "there has been a sharp increase in those living in extreme poverty"; greater numbers of poor people live in rural areas, and their children are particularly affected (Lyman, 2006b, p. A12).

> The infant mortality rate of the poor is almost double the rate of the affluent (Kornblum & Julian, 2001). The poor have less access to medical services and receive lower quality care from health care professionals. The poor are exposed to higher levels of air pollution, water pollution, and unsanitary conditions. They have higher rates of malnutrition and disease. Schools in poor areas are of lower quality and have fewer resources. As a result the poor achieve less academically and are more

apt to drop out of school. They are more apt to be arrested, indicted, imprisoned, and given longer sentences for the same offense. They are less likely to receive probation, parole, or suspended sentences. (Kornblum & Julian, 2001, cited in Zastrow and Kirst-Ashman, 2004, p. 435)

At the microlevel, each social worker's ability to provide services to a client, such as a foster home, or therapy, are related to available financial support. Managed care, with its major influence on health care and mental health services—usually of a restrictive nature—is based on the economic profit motive. In families, tensions can escalate about both the availability of money and its distribution. "In order to truly comprehend the frustrations and anger experienced by many clients, the economic realities they confront must be appreciated and shared on an emotional level" (Longres, 1995b, p. 291).

Subjective feelings about finances exist such as money enhancing psychological security, status, and self-esteem, and representing love. In therapy, clients often have more difficulty talking about money than about sex; therapists may experience discomfort "intruding" into the private world of a person's finances, especially about paying (or not paying) fees. In therapy (as in life), feelings about paying, receiving, and "not having enough" money can be tied to emotional issues about being nurtured and loved.

Addictions, such as to drugs or gambling, can wreak havoc with a family's finances. People in the manic phase of bipolar affective disorder often overspend, sometimes in inappropriate ways (such as Dr. Jamison's 1996 account of buying all the snakebite kits in a drugstore during one of her manic phases). These buying sprees often bankrupt a person and/or family, and add a heavy burden of guilt to the depression following this phase.

Employment

Employment not only generates income but often contributes to self-esteem and personal satisfaction; for many, it serves as an "organizing principle" in life. A positive work experience can provide "an outlet for creativity, satisfactory relationships with colleagues, pride in accomplishment, and increased self-esteem. Job satisfaction is not wholly dependent on money" (Kaplan, Sadock, and Grebb, 1994, p. 58). Lack of employment can produce serious psychological stress.

The effects of unemployment transcend those of loss of income; the psychological and physical tolls are enormous. The incidence of alcohol dependence, homicide, violence, suicide, and mental illness rises with unemployment. The person's core identity, which is often tied to occupation and work, is seriously damaged when a job is lost, whether it is through firing, attrition, or early or regular retirement. (Kaplan, Sadock, and Grebb, 1994, p. 58)

Employment issues involve people at all levels of society; job availability, satisfaction, downsizing, layoffs, and retirement affect both executives and factory workers. An entire community that is economically based on one industry, as is common in rural areas, can prosper or be devastated by the success or failure of that industry (Davenport and Davenport III, 1995). A close relationship exists between economic factors, employment, and population changes in a community. Upstate New York is being seriously affected by the departure of many of its young, often well-educated people, along with their families. "The migration is turning many communities grayer, threatening the long-term viability of ailing cities and raising concerns about the state's future tax base" (Roberts, 2006b, p. A20). Lack of employment opportunities, including slow job growth, seem to be underlying factors in this exodus.

Women, the elderly, those with disabilities, and minorities (including people of color, immigrants, and homosexuals) often face job discrimination, which calls for remediation by legal action, advocacy, and/or legislation. People with developmental and physical disabilities and/or with mental illness may benefit from specialized training, job placement, and social supports.

In today's economy, lack of education can produce unemployment (or underemployment) because of the "high tech" nature of many jobs for which people with inadequate educational backgrounds cannot compete. Members of minorities, especially those with low socioeconomic status and those living in impoverished inner-city communities, face serious unemployment problems; "the most overwhelmed persons were minority males who were often jobless, homeless, moving from mother to girlfriend to girlfriend, back to mother. . . . How to help them conquer 'uselessness' is a tall order but one that is a pressing national poverty question" (Hopps, Pinderhughes, and Shankar, 1995, p. 6). In the past, black males found work, but now "economic restructuring has broken the figurative back of the black working population" ([citing Wilson], p. 7).

Some community revitalization programs have focused primarily on creating jobs and/or businesses, building toward comprehensive services later; others have included employment objectives as part of a basic comprehensive plan. Delgado (1997) has argued that some programs see communities from a "deficit perspective" and in doing so have "ignored community assets in the search for revitalization strategies" (p. 445). He refers to the significance of "the presence and role of small businesses in the life of communities of color" (p. 447). Focusing his discussion on the establishment of beauty parlors "as economic settings and sources of support for Latinos and other women of color" (p. 448), Delgado asserts that small businesses in the Latino community can have multiple advantages.

> Latino small businesses can provide access to services for disempowered groups in their role as urban sanctuaries (residents can patronize a business without fear of being rejected because of their ethnic or racial background), as providers of culture-specific items and services, and as providers of information related to the homeland. Their accessibility to the community (geographical, psychological, cultural, and logistical) makes these institutions excellent settings for collaborative activities. (Delgado, 1997, p. 450)

Public School Education

Public school education is a matter of national concern and debate, including quality of education, adequacy of teachers, funding responsibilities, vouchers, school integration, violence, dropout rates, and the serious lack of teachers and equipment in inner-city schools. "Too often these schools have become as impoverished as their surrounding communities" (Dupper and Poertner, 1997, p. 415).

Dropout rates are very high; "nearly 1 out of 3 public high school students won't graduate. . . . For Latinos and African Americans, the rate approaches an alarming 50 percent. Virtually no community, small or large, rural or urban, has escaped the problem" (Thornburgh, 2006, p. 32). The National Center for Education Statistics reports that children "from the lowest income quarter are more than six times as likely to drop out of high school as kids from the highest" (p. 32). President Bush's "No Child Left Behind" policy, signed into law on January 8, 2002, is controversial, with opponents arguing that there is insufficient funding, and that the emphasis on passing standardized testing places undue pressure on teachers to the neglect of other important aspects of the curriculum.

> Dropping out of high school today is to your societal health what smoking is to your physical health, an indicator of a host of poor outcomes to follow, from low lifetime earnings to high incarceration

rates to a high likelihood that your children will drop out of high school and start the cycle anew. (Thornburgh, 2006, p. 32)

Academic failure has been associated with "higher mortality rates, higher incidence of suicide, and more frequent admissions to state mental hospitals" (Richman and Bowen, 1997, p. 95). Approximately 67 percent of prisoners, across the country, had left school, and Northeastern University, in 2002, reported that almost 50 percent of dropouts between sixteen and twenty-four years old, were not employed (Thornburgh, 2006, p. 40).

Positive school experiences, by contrast, can enhance self-esteem and mastery, increase skills and the potential for employment opportunities. Given the importance of supportive relationships to children's development, a positive school experience can act as a "protective function" by providing a setting "for supportive relationships" (Kirby and Fraser, 1997, p. 25).

Education develops the capacity to read—a necessity for the acquisition of knowledge, and from a *developmental perspective* reading opens the door to ideas, feelings, experiences, sources of inspiration, and aids in the development of fantasy; for Rudyard Kipling (discussed in Chapter 4), reading helped "save" his psychological life. Frederick Douglass, a former slave and prominent abolitionist was enabled, largely through his self-taught reading skills, to develop his ideology and oratory (McFeely, 1991). Maya Angelou (1997), a black writer and poet, spoke of the value of reading in her life, as a source of comfort, companionship, and fantasy. Vaillant (1993) suggests that reading may be an important source of resilience worthy of further study.

Schools are discussed further in Chapter 10.

Communities

A source of strength in Maya Angelou's childhood in Stamps, Arkansas, was the solidity of the black community to which she and her grandmother belonged; being part of a community, with its social networks, support systems, and organizations, affects a person's psychological well-being and family life. Communities can be physical entities, in terms of geography and location, such as a small town or a neighborhood, or they can be communities of interest, not necessarily in physical proximity, such as a religious community, an artistic community, or the gay and lesbian community; individuals often belong to multiple communities, such as employment and cultural communities (Germain, 1991). People incorporate aspects of their community and cultural identifications into their own sense of self, and "through processes of internalization, environments and culture become 'part' of the person's self-concept" (Germain, 1991, p. 37). The community groups to which clients belong can have differing (or opposing) goals and value systems that may cause conflict for them.

An example of a community that would represent both a geographical location and a group of "like" people was reported recently (Davey, 2005) as being planned in South Dakota for deaf persons, "a place built around American Sign Language, where teachers in the new school will sign, the town council will hold its debates in sign language and restaurant workers will be required to know how to sign orders" (p. A1). Others, "however, particularly advocates of technologies that help deaf people use spoken language, wonder whether such a town would merely isolate and exclude the deaf more than ever" (Davey, 2005, pp. A1, A12). These complexities are discussed further in Chapter 6 on culture.

Belonging to a community of "like" people does not guarantee homogeneity, or a lack of conflict about "rules" and "standards." In the lesbian "culture," women "fall along a continuum from conservative to liberal in their philosophical approaches to life," and differences exist in the degree of integration with mainstream "culture" that lesbian women seek (Tully, 1995, p. 1591). Issues relating to separation and integration also confront other minority groups, such as the controversy over interracial adoption.

Community affiliations can impact a client's emotional state; being part of a community can be a source of strength and joy, but may prove distressing at times. Some clients may belong to groups that are very controlling of all aspects of their lives, such as some religions or cults; others may drift, belonging to no group, experiencing aloneness or disconnection. The Mahlerian concept of separation-individuation has its parallel in community life, as the individual experiences an ongoing tension between social conformity and personal freedom.

Informal Support Systems

Informal support systems of various kinds exist in communities and organizations, including self-help groups and social networks, in which natural helpers may participate (Germain, 1991).

Self-Help Groups

Self-help groups—people with common problems who meet to provide mutual support and informal education—have proliferated in recent years, and many can now be found on the Internet; one of the oldest and best-known groups is Alcoholics Anonymous (AA). Many groups focus on patients and their families with medical problems, such as The National Association for People with AIDS, Mended Hearts (for heart-attack victims), and stroke clubs. The National Association for the Mentally Ill (NAMI), composed of mentally ill people and their families, has a large membership. Some groups maintain "lifestyles," or have special interests that may be "different" from those of "dominant groups"; examples are "Widow-to-Widow Programs; Parents Without Partners; ALMA (Adoptees' Liberty Movement Association)" (Zastrow and Kirst-Ashman, 2004, p. 316).

The multiplicity of self-help groups has been thought by some to be a "modern search for community . . . a new way of establishing a common life—a type of affiliation that is especially useful in crisis" ("Self-Help Groups—Part I," 1993, p. 2). These groups can be a "preventive force and a stabilizing influence [which] can complement formal services" (Germain, 1991, p. 74). These groups often meet without professional people, although professionals may initiate them or serve as consultants.

Some self-help groups focus on social change, and may have an educational agenda, raise funds, or become politically active (Germain, 1991). Groups, such as the National Gay and Lesbian Task Force, and AIDS Action, have multiple goals, providing supportive services for members as well as being politically active. Groups such as "food co-ops, day care co-ops, [and] neighborhood improvement associations" may affiliate with one another and become *resource-exchange networks,* which "are a significant force for the empowerment of impoverished or devalued communities" (Germain, 1991, p. 75).

Conflict can occur between mental health professionals and self-help groups; in one instance, former psychiatric patients established "radical self-help groups originally designed to assert their rights and challenge the established system" ("Self-Help Groups—Part II," 1993, pp. 1-2). However, generally an increase in cooperation and mutuality between professionals and self-help groups has taken place. "The absorption of AA techniques into alcoholism treatment is one example of a trend toward the adoption of self-help practices by professionals" (p. 2).

Although a lack of systematic research into the effectiveness of self-help groups exists, informal evidence suggests satisfaction and improvement on the part of many participants. However, certain "limitations and dangers" of these groups have also been noted ("Self-Help Groups—Part II," 1993, p. 3).

> Groups will not work for people who are paranoid or who believe themselves to be unique. Leaders may be well-meaning but incompetent. Perhaps the greatest danger is that a self-help group will perversely undermine its members' confidence by insisting that they define their lives solely in terms of the issues discussed by the group, excluding other forms of community and disabling themselves for life outside

its confines. In that situation the group works mainly to preserve itself (or the power of a leader) at the expense of the self-respect and freedom of its members. ("Self-Help Groups—Part II," 1993, p. 3)

A variety of *mutual aid groups* are facilitated by social workers, who may provide direction and a "mediating" function for the group, but "the source of the helping [shifts] from the group leader to the members themselves" (Shulman and Gitterman, 1986, p. 3). This approach has included work with bereaved children (Vastola, Nierenberg, and Graham, 1986); parents of sexually victimized children (Jones, 1986); and institutionalized schizophrenic women (Poynter-Berg, 1986).

Group members receiving help may also gain through the process of helping others. "Skovholt explained that helping enhances the helper's sense of effectance and competence, and maturity is enhanced by being able to give as well as receive" (Lee and Swenson, 1986, pp. 368-369); mutual aid groups present "a needed balance in an 'age of narcissism'" (p. 374). One study of 400 elderly couples reported that giving to others actually enhanced life; "if giving is what matters, people need opportunities to help others more than they need reasons to feel that others are helping them" ("Life-Giving Support," 2004, p. 7).

Social Networks

Social networks are informal interpersonal connections that serve as a source of support and aid, and include any combination of family, friends, neighbors, co-workers, coreligionists, natural helpers, and so on.

> Social networks serve as coping resources for dealing with life stressors. They facilitate mastery of the twin tasks of problem solving and management of feelings by providing emotional support, information and advice, and tangible aids, and by undertaking action. They may also serve a primary preventive function in effectively staving off an imminent stressor. In carrying out these functions effectively, informal systems also contribute to the member's self-esteem and relatedness and may enhance the sense of competence and self-direction. (Germain, 1991, p. 76)

Studies have pointed to an important link between social support and a person's overall health in the physical, social, and psychological spheres (Germain, 1991; Richman, Rosenfeld, and Bowen, 1998), and may be a factor promoting resilience (Kirby and Fraser, 1997). In one study of women with metastatic breast cancer, those receiving weekly supportive group therapy (in addition to chemotherapy) lived twice as long as a control group receiving only chemotherapy (Spiegel, 1990); some people have been enabled to cope with internment in a concentration camp through group support (Schlossberg, 1981). During World War II, "the degree of relatedness between the soldier, his immediate fighting unit, and their leader" afforded soldiers "the strongest protection against overwhelming terror" (Herman, 1997, p. 25).

Currently, 115,000 American children have been directly affected by having parents serving in the military in Iraq or Afghanistan. Operation Purple has established privately endowed (free) summer camps for these children in twenty-two states, to enable them to share their experiences and anxieties with each other (Lee-St. John, 2006).

> A lasting benefit—especially for those who don't live on a military base—is *the support network* built during their week at camp. "Nonmilitary people don't know what it's like to have someone you love in an uncivilized, faraway place tell you on the phone, 'oh, that's a car bomb going off, but I'm kind of used to it,'" says Courtney Rinnert, 11, whose Army Reservist stepdad spent 15 months in Iraq. "These people share the same experience as you" (Lee-St. John, 2006, p. 15; italics added)

Natural Helpers

Natural helpers are people in a community who are not professionally qualified or assigned to perform a service (such as a doctor or a social worker) but are informally recognized and accepted for their ability and interest in helping others; they are persons in the social milieu who have "unique wisdom, resourcefulness, and caring qualities" (Germain, 1991, p. 81). Helpers can assist neighbors with chores such as babysitting and medical care, by their involvement as mediators in problem solving, or as advocates. Natural helpers are an asset in rural communities (Germain, 1991; Patterson et al., 1988); in the Hispanic community, folk healers often play key roles (Germain, 1991); "the Puerto Rican *espiritista* is likely to make use of séances and role-playing to rid the ailing individual of evil sprits as well as to call on the person's protective spirits for help in the cure" (Ramirez, 1998, p. 174; italics in the original).

Pets can be important natural helpers, as companions to people, especially to those who live alone, including the elderly and/or disabled. Pets may assist in minimizing loneliness, and "as nonjudgmental companions pets can provide informal emotional support" (Netting, Wilson, and New, 1987, p. 61). It has been suggested that psychosocial assessments incorporate evaluations of the "individuals' relationships with their companion animals," and that peoples' concerns about their animals should be recognized; helping to arrange care for pets, for example, might be particularly important when people are hospitalized (Risley-Curtis, Holley, and Wolf, 2006, p. 267).

Seeing Eye dogs have assisted visually handicapped people for many years, and animals have been trained to assist people with other handicaps. Recently, a dog named Rainbow was trained to aid a veteran who needed both a wheelchair and prosthetics for mobility, an innovative combination requiring special training (Strom, 2006, p. A16). Rainbow now works with Roland Paquette, a veteran, and former medical sergeant, whose legs were severely damaged in Afghanistan. Rainbow was trained by the newly founded Canines for Combat veterans, part of the New England Assistant Dog Service, which has been in business since 1976, training dogs to help people with physical handicaps.

Rainbow's trainer was Thomas Davison, a prison inmate; in an interesting offshoot of this program, several inmates have been trainers. Training Rainbow for Paquette was meaningful to Davison: "It's great to do something that really helps someone else, especially a guy like him. . . . I've never had a chance to do that, and wasn't sure I could handle the responsibility" (Strom, 2006, p. A16). The State Corrections Commissioner, Kathleen Dennehy, was impressed with the positive impact this program had on the prison atmosphere. "'Officers stop by to pet the dogs, they smile, maybe they strike up a conversation with the inmate training the dog,' Ms Dennehy said" (p. A16).

A variety of pet-facilitated therapies are being utilized in psychotherapy with children and adults (Brickel, 1986; Germain, 1991). Dolly, a Seeing Eye dog, acted as a pet therapist, aiding her owner, a blind clinician, in her play therapy with children (Ceconi and Urdang, 1994). The "human-animal bond" has been receiving increasing recognition in social work practice (Netting, Wilson, and New, 1987; Risley-Curtis, Holley, and Wolf, 2006).

ORGANIZATIONS

Organizations permeate our life on both formal and informal levels. In this section, employment organizations and their impact on the psychosocial well-being of their employees are highlighted, with emphasis given to the impact social work agencies as organizations have upon clients and social workers. "Irrational interactions [within organizations] are expected rather than ignored. Systems theories emphasize constant assessment and adjustment" (Zastrow and Kirst-Ashman, 1997, p. 31).

Current social issues are often reflected in places of employment: affirmative action; decisions affecting "spousal" benefits to partners of homosexual employees; time granted (or not granted) for family care; the provision of day care (sometimes for both children and elderly parents) in workplaces; and deciding whether to tolerate office romances, and how to differentiate this from sexual harassment.

Clients may discuss employment problems related to interpersonal relationships at work (with administrators and/or peers); feeling their work is not recognized and appreciated; feeling inadequate (and perhaps like an "imposter") in fulfilling their positions; wishing for and/or fearing promotions; and feeling dissatisfied with present job and/or confused about vocational goals. Problems at work can stem from psychodynamic conflicts, from organizational stress, or a combination of both. Kaplan, Sadock, and Grebb (1994) discuss some of the psychodynamic conflicts found in work settings.

> People with unresolved conflicts about their competitive and aggressive impulses may experience great difficulties in the work area. They may suffer from a pathological envy of the success of others or fear success for themselves because of their inability to tolerate envy from others. (Kaplan, Sadock, and Grebb, 1994, p. 797)

Some employees (including social workers) may feel stressed about job demands and be "burned out" by "physical, psychological, and emotional exhaustion"; this type of stress can result in "job dissatisfaction, tension, anxiety, irritability, procrastination, frequent absences from work, and a decision to leave the job" (Queralt, 1996, p. 289).

In Japan, serious economic declines in the 1980s led to cutbacks in the workforce, with many Japanese workers being required to work long hours. "Experts estimate that approximately one million workers in Japan are putting their lives at risk from overwork and almost 10,000 workers die of it per year" ("Karoshi and Karojisatsu in Japan," 2004). The term *"karoshi,"* which means "death from overwork," is now used worldwide; Japanese workers have been committing suicide because of overwork in increasing numbers, and *"karojisatsu* (suicide from overwork) has also become a big social issue in Japan" ("Karoshi and Karojisatsu in Japan," 2004). In an earlier legal decision, the family of a man who committed suicide was deemed entitled to compensation and the judge "blamed [the] man's suicide on . . . working

80-hour weeks and ordered the government to compensate his family" ("Japan Ordered," 1999, p. A5).

Interpersonal tensions in organizations related to issues such as competition, status, the acquisition of power, and interpersonal conflict can affect both individuals and the collective functioning of the organization. (Although we are stressing work organizations here, power struggles as well as other interpersonal conflicts can occur in churches, social clubs, schools, and any organization of any size.) For example, major difficulties were reported to have erupted in the English department at Duke University (Scott, 1998).

> The upheaval at Duke offers a glimpse into the arcane world of an academic department, one in which a complex mixture of ideological, generational and personality differences among its 40 members led to explosive skirmishes over hiring and tenure, graduate-student admissions and the distribution of departmental tasks and perks. . . .
>
> But Duke's difficulties also reflect tensions in English departments nationwide at a time when many have been struggling to redefine their mission [a conflict between the use of classic literature and literature being used to highlight political issues and promote social change]. (Scott, 1998, pp. A1, A17)

Social Work Organizations

Social work organizations (from state bureaucracies to group private practices) are "embedded in social and physical environments. They affect and are affected by political, economic, and cultural forces" which have considerable impact on the services offered to clients, as well as the well-being of social workers (Germain and Gitterman, 1980, p. 138). Today, managed care is a major issue affecting medical, psychiatric, and social work practice (Geller, 1996; Strom-Gottfried, 1997; Urdang, 1999). Many social agencies now place emphasis on short-term services and quantitative outcome studies. "Social workers are confronted by an increasing emphasis on accountability, more for quantity, than for quality of service" (Gitterman and Miller, 1989, p. 152); agencies "have been forced to reinvent themselves and operate more like businesses" (Jarmon-Rohde et al., 1997, p. 31).

Competing interests of staff and administration often exist within organizations (Gitterman and Miller, 1989).

Different positions in the hierarchy develop different priorities and publics to please. Executives are concerned about funding, organizational stability, regulatory issues, and external politics. Clinicians are concerned about client problems and available services and all are concerned about their respective prerogatives and personal interests. These interests are often in conflict, competing with other priorities and creating tension inherent in organizational life. (Gitterman and Miller, 1989, p. 154)

The interpersonal climate of the agency also affects clients, clinical staff, and social work students placed there; analytic work of psychoanalytic candidates undergoing their training can also be affected by administrative requirements and constraints of their analytic institutes (Kernberg, 1965).

Alfred Staunton described a psychiatric hospital as a "small society with established hierarchical categories"; he observed that conflict or lack of clarity about staff responsibilities can be *"transmitted to patients, whose symptoms may be exacerbated as a result"* (Kaplan, Sadock, and Grebb, 1994, p. 189; italics added). In an agency "where staff morale is low . . . the informal system may support scornful, punitive or uncaring attitudes toward clients" (Germain and Gitterman, 1980, p. 143); negative attitudes can also be directed at social work interns.

The impact of the emotional climate of agencies on the supervision of social work interns was explored in a study of the self-perceptions of beginning field instructors (Urdang, 1994). Most instructors reported external and internal stresses affecting them; however, it was the interpersonal climate of the agency that was decisive on how this was experienced; a negative interpersonal climate was reported by Brett.

Brett, whose agency had been in a struggle for "survival," felt tension due to the push for "productivity." He feels his clinic "is one of the hardest places I've been at. There is a certain competitiveness here. . . . You get blamed for stuff." Brett also complained about the agency's rigidity and authority. "The agency is like fiefdoms—the directors like shoving their responsibility and power—The director of X has to give his approval for pictures to be hung, so it is very rigid and compartmentalized." (Urdang, 1994, pp. 95-96)

Many [of these systemic problems] impacted on his student, such as removing cases [from her] for financial reasons. He felt he "tried to keep her away from office politics, but I couldn't." Her anxiety level around these issues "was tremendous," although this diminished.

Brett was also open with his student about the tensions, intervened actively on her behalf in several situations, and encouraged her to talk with him about what was happening. (Urdang, 1994, pp. 98-99)

Rose, another beginning instructor, reported that external and internal stresses in her agency were alleviated by a supportive interpersonal climate.

After discussing a number of serious systemic issues, Rose concluded that her unit was "a very unique bunch of individuals, and it is one of the reasons that I am still here . . . we do an amazing job of trying to take care of each other ourselves." She also felt that the group has the ability to "process the dynamics" of how systemic issues impact on their own work. (Urdang, 1994, pp. 97-98)

SOCIAL ISSUES

Four major social problems are discussed in this section: *discrimination, violence, substance abuse,* and *imprisonment.* Immigration, another critical social issue, is discussed in Chapter 6.

Discrimination and Prejudice

Prejudice is distinguished from discrimination, although a close relationship exists between the two processes. "Prejudice is a positive or negative attitude, opinion, or prejudgment concerning a person or group usually formulated on the basis of selective perception and held without sufficient evidence or justification" (Queralt, 1996, p. 170). Although a person may be prejudiced positively toward another, the term usually has negative connotations, such as having negative, stereotyped attitudes about all black people or all old people.

Discrimination, however, while often stemming from prejudice, involves "an unjustified negative or hostile *action* toward a certain group or individual" (Queralt, 1996, p. 170; italics in the original); one is acting to exclude or deprive or harm a person in some way. Some places of employment or housing developments, for example, exclude ethnic minorities; gay men in small towns have often felt both prejudice and discrimination against them (Firestone, 1999).

Hate crimes are forms of violence that target individuals or organizations "because of their racial, ethnic, religious, or sexual identities or their sexual orientation or condition of disability" (Barnes and Ephross, 1994, p. 247).

This type of crime includes "arson of homes and businesses, harassment, destruction of religious property, cross burnings, personal assaults, and homicides" (p. 247). The United States has made many legal and social advances (such as major civil rights legislation passed during the Johnson presidency) in combating discrimination and ensuring equal rights. Although evidence exists of greater acceptance of diversity among Americans (including a high degree of intermarriage and the election of minorities to high positions of political power), some groups are dedicated to promoting discrimination and hate crimes. Mark Potok, of the Southern Poverty Law Center reported that there are "some 800 racist groups operating in the U. S. today, a 5 percent spurt in the past year and a 33 percent jump from 2000"; many of these groups are fueled by anti-immigration causes (Ressner, 2006, p. 36).

> With immigration perhaps America's most volatile issue, a troubling backlash has erupted among its most fervent foes. There are, of course, the Minutemen, the self-appointed border vigilantes who operate in several states. And now groups of militiamen, white supremacists and neo-Nazis are using resentment over the estimated 11 million illegal immigrants in the U.S. as a potent rallying cry. "The immigration furor has been critical to the growth we've seen in hate groups, says Mark Potok . . . [this] debate seems to have reinvigorated members of the antigovernment militias of the 1990s. Those groups largely disbanded after the Oklahoma City bombing." (Ressner, 2006, p. 36)

The frequent "negative stereotyping" of Arab Americans before 9/11, "has now become significantly more pronounced, and hate crimes against them has increased 500 percent" (Abudabbeh, 2005, p. 430).

Advances have been made in hate crime legislation, both on state and national levels. One important piece of legislation, the James Byrd Jr. Hate Crimes bill was signed into law by Texas Governor Rick Perry in May 2001 (Shannon, 2001). James Byrd Jr., a black man, was killed in Jasper, Texas, in 1998, by being dragged along a road chained to a pickup truck driven by white men, two of whom belonged to a white supremacist group; the murder that "shocked the country" also "traumatized Jasper and created immense tensions that threatened to fragment the community" (Ainslie and Brabeck, 2003, p. 43); but the community did not fragment. Ainslie and Brabeck (2003) studied the community for two-and-a-half years, to learn how the community was affected by this murder.

Jasper, a small community has a population of 8,000, comprised of 44 percent African American and 48 percent white residents; unemployment is high, poverty is prevalent, and there is a history of racial tensions. However, Jasper is a "Center Holds Model," which includes both white and black people in its major social, economic, and political spheres, that enabled it to "absorb potentially divisive (and regressive) conflicts, impulses and anxieties" (Ainslie and Brabeck, 2003, p. 49). African Americans form a large middle class and hold important positions, including the mayor, the hospital CEO, a school principal, teachers, and many police officers.

No time was lost in looking for the three criminals, who were apprehended the night of the crime; the next day the sheriff reported the case to the FBI as a hate crime. Several days later, the police chief and FBI agents attended a meeting of the Jasper Ministerial Alliance, whose ministers represented both black and white churches (the existence of such an integrated group of ministers being unusual for Texas), and their help was sought to reduce the community's fears, and to reassure them that these men would be brought to trial. When John William King, one of the murderers, was later sentenced to death, he was the first white person in Texas to receive this punishment for killing a black person. Finally, important to this peaceful resolution was the support of James Byrd's family, "who were part of the 'center', and they were invested in maintaining the cohesion of the community" (Ainslie and Brabeck, 2003, p. 49).

The peaceful settlement of the Byrd case in Jasper was preceded by many legal and legislative civil rights battles; during the days of Jim Crow, lynching of black men in the south was a common occurrence for which there was no censure and no punishment. Impediments that prevented black people from voting have largely been eliminated by civil rights legislation.

Legislation has dramatically enhanced the rights of minorities, including women, gays and lesbians, the elderly, immigrants, the mentally ill, and the physically disabled; utilizing the political process has been important in advancing these rights and liberties, the disadvantaged groups often leading the way themselves. Women's advocacy for equal rights to education and employment has been an active social issue. NOW (the National Organization for Women) has had a serious impact on legislation, the political process, and other social changes that have advanced the interests of women. Lesbian and gay organizations "have gone from being outcasts of the left to being an expected presence in politics" (Lacayo, 1998, p. 35). Hispanic voters are being taken seriously as a voting bloc (Beinert, 1998); the disabled have more political clout now than they have ever had (Rosenbaum, 1999).

People who are different or behave differently from others in their minority group may face special problems; deaf people who refuse to use sign language may not be accepted in the deaf culture; black people can have conflict with other black people based on the lightness or darkness of their skin color; and tensions can exist between people of different social classes who belong to the same racial or ethnic group. Members of more than one minority group may experience conflict existing between these groups, in terms of competing value systems, and actual prejudicial and discriminatory behaviors. "Black and Chicano gays may fail to find acceptance either among white gays or in their own communities" (Berger and Kelly, 1995, pp. 1072-1073).

People who do not have "minority" status may also have experienced social prejudice because they were "different"; they may not have gone to church when others did, or may *not* have discriminated against minorities when that was the norm. Students may feel out of the mainstream of the social life of their schools.

Discrimination is discussed throughout the book, involving race, culture, ethnicity, immigration, and social class in Chapter 6; women's issues, men's issues, and gay and lesbian lifestyles in Chapters 7 and 11; the elderly in Chapter 11; the physically ill and disabled in Chapter 13; and the mentally ill in Chapter 14.

Violence

Violence affects people of all ages and socioeconomic levels, although "research points to poverty as a major risk factor for violence" (Stainbrook and Hornik, 2006, p. 54). Many women (and sometimes men, especially in prison) are victims of rape; partner violence is found in both heterosexual and homosexual couples. Children (and infants) can be victims of parental murder and physical and/or sexual abuse and may witness partner violence; they may live in fear of school violence and of neighborhoods plagued by murder and gunfire. Immigrants frequently have a history of trauma (such as torture, political imprisonment, and massacres), and the elderly, often suffer physical and sexual abuse (committed by family members or staff of custodial facilities).

A National Center for PTSD Fact Sheet (Goguen, 2006) noted that in "a national survey of girls and boys 10 to 16 years old, over one-third reported being the direct victim of different forms of violence including aggravated assault, attempted kidnapping, and sexual assault. Researchers have found that an even higher number of urban children have been exposed to indirect community violence (e.g., they have witnessed violence or know a victim)."

The current knowledge and openness about domestic violence has resulted in more people turning for help to social agencies, shelters, EAP programs at work, and the police (Groves and Augustyn, 2004); many police departments now offer special training to enable officers to handle domestic violence situations (Zastrow and Kirst-Ashman, 2004). Schools and medical and social services are also more aware of child physical and sexual abuse, and offer early protective and intervention services. Nevertheless, physical and sexual abuse continue to affect many adults and children, with serious biopsychosocial consequences. According to the Centers for Disease Control and Prevention (CDC) "about 1.5 million women and 834,700 men are physically and/or sexually assaulted by an intimate partner each year" (Tracy and Johnson, 2006, p. 115); physical abuse has also been found in gay and lesbian couple relationships (Carlson and Maciol, 1997).

Physical and sexual abuse can dramatically affect a child's ongoing development and leave significant psychological scars on adults who have been abused as children (including their ability to parent) (Glodich, 1998; Kilgore, 1988; Osofsky, 1997; Tracy and Johnson, 2006). Experiencing violence as a child leads to "psychological, interpersonal, and sexual difficulties that persist into adulthood . . . and . . . significant neurocognitive deficits that undermine information-processing and problem-solving capabilities throughout the life course" (Tracy and Johnson, 2006. p. 116). Furthermore, unless positive experiences intervene *"traumatized children are likely to be drawn to groups and ideologies that legitimize and reward their rage, their fear, and their hateful cynicism"* (Garbarino and Kostelny, 1997, p. 40; italics in the original).

Although most sexual abuse of children occurs within the family and extended family, many children have been victimized by other adults, some strangers, and many times, by adults whom they trust, such as teachers and priests. In the past few years, a scandal has rocked the Catholic Church, as the extent of sexual abuse of children by priests has been brought into the open and prosecuted. One response to the problem of cover-up has been a growing movement to make clergy mandated reporters of abuse by law. "Approximately 21 states require clergy to report child abuse" (by 2006, the number has increased to at least twenty-five); in addition, "North Carolina, Rhode Island and Texas require any person to report and [also] deny clergy-penitent privilege in child abuse cases" (Williams-Mbengue, 2004).

Children have also been affected by violence in schools, often inner-city schools. The massacre at the Columbine High School in Littleton, Colorado, however, took place in a suburban setting; most school shootings have taken place in either suburban or rural areas. Many commentators feel these violent acts by youths were caused by multiple interacting factors, including the psychological difficulties of the youths, family relationships, socialization problems, the availability of guns, and the prevalence of violence in the media. "The message from studies of adolescents who kill others or themselves is that no single factor can explain their actions" (Goode, 1999a, p. A24).

On the other hand, adults are also not infrequently involved. A particularly egregious "massacre of the innocents" took place recently when an adult neighbor lined up six Amish schoolgirls at school and shot them to death; police "said investigators who reviewed notes left by the gunman for his wife and children indicated he was 'angry at life' and 'angry at God'" ("Killer Was," 2006).

Although guns are not generally considered the major *motivation* for murder, the fact that they are so accessible in our society is emphasized by many. Dr. Mann, a researcher at Columbia University, is cited as saying "When vulnerable kids crack, the weapons that are at hand make the consequences of that vulnerability more serious" (Goode, 1999a, p. A24). The two gunmen at Columbine High School had four guns with them during their attack (in addition to planting many explosives) (Brooke, 1999). In the Jonesboro, Arkansas, school murder of four girls and one teacher in 1998, the two boys (eleven and twelve years old) were armed with three rifles and seven other guns, which they took from their families' homes (Labi, 1998).

Intense public debate continues regarding gun control, both at the national and state level, where many laws have been enacted (Verhovek, 1999). The National Rifle Association (NRA), a powerful lobbying group, has been active in opposing this legislation, citing a constitutional right to bear arms. Many Republicans and some Democrats in Congress are very reluctant to promote gun control (Seelye, 1999).

In the meantime, according to the Children's Defense Fund's "new report on the toll gun violence is taking on America's children: More 10- to 19-year-olds die from gunshot wounds than from any other cause except motor vehicle accidents"; in addition, "children who die every year from gunshot wounds come from all racial groups and are all ages. Some of them are too young to start kindergarten: in 2003, 56 preschoolers were killed by firearms" (Wright Edelman, 2006).

We also cannot ignore the alarming incidence of client violence (including homicide) toward mental health and child welfare workers. The National Association of Social Workers reported in March, 2006 that "55 percent of 5,000 licensed social workers surveyed said that they faced safety issues on the job. . . . A survey in 2002 of 800 workers found 19 percent had been victims of violence and 63 percent had been threatened" ("Killing in," 2006).

Violence is a major problem in the United States, with multiple causations, consequences, and suggested solutions; a close association has been found between domestic violence and substance abuse (Tracy and

Johnson, 2006). We return to this subject throughout the book, discussing violence and sexual abuse in the context of the family (Chapter 8) as well as its effects on the development of children and adults throughout the life cycle (Chapters 9, 10, 11).

Substance Abuse

Substance abuse affects many in this country, including young adolescents (and sometimes even younger children), leading to serious psychological, physical, and social consequences as it wends its way through the life cycle, culminating in such abuse by the elderly. It is not uncommon for substance abuse to coexist with mental illness (dual diagnosis), complicating both the symptomatology and treatment of each; approximately 45 percent of the homeless mentally ill have a dual diagnosis (Sadock and Sadock, 2003). Substance abuse is interactive with both psychological and social forces; a depressed person, for example, may drink to self-medicate; social and interpersonal problems, such as unemployment, violence, and trauma can increase substance use, as was seen in the aftermath of Hurricane Katrina in New Orleans; and abusing substances impairs employment performance, leads to increases in crime, violence, and child maltreatment, and places greater demands on the child welfare system (Liederman, 1995).

Curbing substance abuse has been debated in terms of the effectiveness of our country's "War against Drugs"; the question of whether drugs should be legalized raises intense controversy. The United States has intervened internationally against drug smuggling, including assisting Columbia and other Latin American countries in campaigns to eradicate marijuana crops through the use of herbicides such as paraquat. In Afghanistan, "squabbles between Western military commanders and the Karzai government over antidrug policies have allowed poppy growth to reach an all-time peak" (Ratnesar with Baker, 2006, pp. 39-40).

Although social unrest contributes to substance abuse, social and community approval (explicit and implicit) of substances can contribute to its use. It has been observed, for example, that excessive binge drinking (higher than national rates) by young people, from twelve years of age and on, occurs in Wyoming (the highest rate), Montana, and North and South Dakota; addiction to drugs such as amphetamines is also prevalent. One rationale given for this excess is "the boredom of the big empty" (Egan, 2006, p. A10). However, drinking is also intrinsic to the region's culture; parents drink, children's drinking is accepted, a plethora of bars exist in town, and there is strong resistance to passing alcohol-related bills, such as prohibitions against drinking and driving. Again exemplifying the interweaving of the past and the present, the personal and the communal, early social trauma has been cited as being responsible for substance dependence: The deportation from eastern cities of approximately 200,000 children, who were adopted by Western families starting in 1854, and lasting about seventy-five years. "The orphan trains, as they were called, left a psychic print, some counselors and historians say" (Egan, 2006, p. A10).

Substance abuse is associated with domestic violence directed toward partners and children (Tracy and Johnson, 2006).

> Rates of co-occurring domestic violence perpetration and substance abuse are thought to range from 23 percent to as high as 100 percent (Corvo & Carpenter, 2000). According to the CWLA [Child Welfare League of America] (2003), 70 percent of child maltreatment cases involve substance abuse, and a child whose parents have problems with alcohol or other drugs are three to four times more likely to be abused and/or neglected than those children whose parents do not. Cash and Wilke (2003) found that having been sexually abused prior to the age of 15, having an alcoholic parent, and having an extended family history of substance abuse significantly predicted the odds of a mother's neglecting her children later in life. (Tracy and Johnson, 2006, p. 116)

Substance Abuse and Imprisonment

The United States has the "dubious distinction of having the highest incarceration rate in the world" (Arditti, 2005, p. 251), including many men (mostly African American) and women (primarily African American and Hispanic) imprisoned for drug offenses. In June 2005, there were 2,186,230 prisoners held in Federal or State prisons or in local jails, including 106,174 women (O'Brien and Young, 2006, p. 359). Drug offenses account for the dramatic increase in women prisoners; "many women who previously would have remained in their communities under supervision are now being incarcerated." Although abusing substances is a major problem, "it is estimated that only 25 percent of state and federal prisoners participate in either drug treatment or other drug abuse programs" (O'Brien and Young, 2006, p. 362).

Arizona, with votes of large majorities of its citizens, was the first state to require treatment rather than imprisonment for people convicted of drug offenses. In more than forty states, judges and prosecutors are being given the authority to decide when offenders can be referred to treatment rather than to prison (Egan, 1999). Arizona has reported good results: 77.5 percent of offenders tested drug free after the treatment program. This program "saved Arizona $5,053,014 in prison costs in the 1998 fiscal year" (Wren, 1999, p. A16). After deducting program costs, the net savings was $2.5 million.

The recent death of the Nobel Prize laureate, Milton Friedman, has recalled his antidrug war views that "drug prohibition was unsound public policy, economic insanity and inherently immoral"; he strongly opposed criminalizing people who used substances (Blumner, 2006). "He understood that as long as there was demand there would be supply, and by making drugs illegal, those enriched by the drug trade would be a violent, corrupting element of society" (Blumner, 2006).

Incarceration of the Mentally Ill

Jails have replaced mental institutions as repositories for many mentally ill people since the 1960s (Butterfield, 1999b). Approximately 15 percent of prisoners are seriously mentally ill, and "more than half abuse alcohol or drugs" ("Prisoners of Mental," 2003, p. 5); dual diagnosis (of major mental disorder and substance abuse) is found in both women's and men's prisons (Butterfield, 1998). Women prisoners are reported to have a particularly high rate of mental illness (about 24 percent), including major depression, and bipolar disorders (O'Brien and Young, 2006). The term *transinstitutionalization* describes "the movement of people from state hospitals to nursing homes and also to jails" (Solomon and Draine, 1995, p. 25); the homeless mentally ill, as noted earlier, are frequently incarcerated. "Few of the mentally ill inmates have committed serious crimes or are dangerously violent" ("Prisoners of Mental," 2003, p. 5).

Many mentally ill prisoners receive no mental health services ("Prisoners of Mental," 2003, p. 5).

> Correctional authorities may not recognize or acknowledge mental illness. But even if they know that an inmate needs help, they usually have no way to provide it. Prison staff are not trained for the extra care and supervision required. The mentally ill may be assaulted physically or sexually by fellow inmates who sense their vulnerability or are annoyed by their behavior. Some become discipline problems and are relegated to punitive segregation (solitary confinement) which can only aggravate their symptoms. They may get some medication but rarely receive any other treatment. It is no surprise that suicide is the leading cause of death among prison and jail inmates. ("Prisoners of Mental," 2003, p. 5)

Professor Kay Redfield Jamison has asserted that even if psychological services are provided to mentally ill prisoners, the prison setting hinders treatment. "'Inmates get deprived of sleep,' she said, 'and isolation can exacerbate their hallucinations or delusions'" (Butterfield, 1999b, p. A10).

An increase has also occurred in the incarceration of teenagers with severe mental illness as a result of the relatively greater cuts in available psychiatric inpatient facilities for them (Butterfield, 1998). The National Center for Mental Health and Juvenile Justice has reported that "20 percent of the more than 100,000 adolescents in juvenile detention facilities have a serious mental illness" ("Prisoners of Mental," 2003, p. 5).

The present inadequate treatment of the mentally ill is accompanied by a knowledge explosion regarding progressive treatment methodologies and medication research; model programs offering comprehensive services to patients and families have been demonstrated. And yet in reality, for large numbers of patients, we have retrogressed rather than progressed in our humane treatment of their persons and their illness. The use of jails as repositories for the mentally ill goes back to the nineteenth century, when the dehumanizing treatment of patients as no better than recalcitrant animals was decried by Dorothea Dix (Butterfield, 1998).

Families of Prisoners

The fact that many children have a parent in prison or on probation has been recognized only recently (Butterfield, 1999a); in 1999, there were approximately 1.5 million children who had parents in prison (O'Brien and Young, 2006). Children of prisoners tend to be poor, and their families are often beset with abuse, neglect, and drug abuse; separation from the imprisoned parent creates additional stress (Butterfield, 1999a). "Women are more likely to have had dependent children living with them prior to incarceration (64 percent of women vs. 44 percent of men)"; and their "separation from children, particularly when the prison is located far [away] . . . takes an enormous psychological toll on women, including grief, emptiness, anger, guilt, and fear of loss of their children" (O'Brien and Young, 2006, p. 363).

Children (as well as partners, spouses, and other relatives) having a parent in prison are not only affected by feelings of loss, but can be deeply affected by the stigma of incarceration, which can increase their feelings of isolation and shame, resulting in *disenfranchised grief* (difficulty expressing grief related to situations which do not receive social approval) (Arditti, 2005, p. 253). Interest has been growing in working with children of prisoners, in setting aside hospitable family visiting space within prisons, as well as offering parenting classes and other programs to both incarcerated mothers and fathers. Research suggests that supporting family relationships reduces recidivism and has a positive effect on children (Butterfield, 1999a).

When released from prison, people face multiple problems, including mental and physical health problems, substance abuse, financial need, employment, housing, and reestablishing relationships with family and friends, comprehensive services are needed. (O'Brien and Young, 2006; Stoesen, 2006). There has been increasing interest in aiding prisoner reentry on a federal level and within the social work profession (Stoesen, 2006).

CONCLUSION

In this chapter, attention has been focused on the physical and social environments in which we and our clients live; we need to appreciate that social and political processes are constantly at work in our lives, even if we are unaware of them, as we might be unaware of the intricacy of our body's chemistry.

Social justice and social action are within the tradition of the social work profession, and we need to address these pressing issues. However, "correct" social policies will not end all personal pain and dysfunction. As we look at people with an array of social problems, including homeless mentally ill individuals, runaway (or "throwaway") teenagers (often from failed foster home experiences), people with violent impulses they cannot control, their traumatized victims, and the great reliance people place on illegal and prescribed drugs to cope with stress and inner distress, we become aware of serious underlying psychological problems requiring skilled clinical work.

Perhaps we need more skills than in the past, because we see people with complex disturbances, many of whom flee from the help they need (often with attachment disorders so severe that they may not know how to relate to genuine human support). We must learn how to reach behind the "rejecting" facade and not feel rejected, to care about others without complying with wishes for inappropriate physical or social contact or for "merger." We must exercise caution so that we do not automatically or blindly follow an empowerment agenda with individual clients before determining what it is they are seeking and are capable of coping with, and is consistent with meeting what may be more fundamental needs.

LEARNING EXERCISE

Interview a person (who is not a client or a family member) with the purpose of understanding that person's perceptions of his or her involvement in groups, organizations, and the community, on both formal and informal levels. How does this individual describe himself or herself racially, ethnically, and culturally, and how does he or she feel that these affiliations affect his or her life? Is this person involved in the political process on any level, and what are his or her thoughts about this?

SUGGESTED READING

Articles

Delgado, M. 1997. Role of Latina-owned beauty parlors in a Latino community. *Social Work* 42: 445-453.

Dulmus, C. N., L. A. Rapp-Paglicci, D. J. Sarafin, J. S. Wodarski, and M. D. Feit. 2000. Workfare programs: Issues and recommendations for self-sufficiency. *Journal of Human Behavior in the Social Environment* 3(2): 1-12.

Dupper, D. R., and J. Poertner. 1997. Public schools and the revitalization of impoverished communities: School-linked, family resource centers. *Social Work* 42: 415-422.

Newhill, C. 1995. Client violence toward social workers: A practice and policy concern for the 1990's. *Social Work* 40: 631-636.

Park, J., and J. Miller. 2006. The social ecology of Hurricane Katrina: Rewriting the discourse of "natural" disasters (2006). *Smith College Studies in Social Work* 76: 9-24.

Weinreb, L., and P. H. Rossi. 1995. The American homeless family shelter system. *Social Service Review* 69: 86-107.

Books

Caro, R. 1983. *The years of Lyndon Johnson: The path to power.* New York: Vintage Books.

Lee, J. A. B., and C. R. Swenson. 1986. The concept of mutual aid. In *Mutual aid groups and the life cycle,* ed. A. Gitterman and L. Shulman, pp. 361-377. Itasca, IL: F. E. Peacock Publishers.

Webb, N. B. (ed.) 2006. *Working with traumatized youth in child welfare.* New York: The Guilford Press.

Chapter 6

Culture and Diversity

We are all much more simply human than otherwise.

Harry Stack Sullivan, *Aphorism*

INTRODUCTION

In the winter of 1999, three-day-old twins were brought to a public adoption center in Bogotá, Colombia, by their U'wa tribe parents because they wanted their children to live (Kotler, 1999). The alternative, decreed by their tribe, was to leave them in the woods (or throw them into a river) to die, because twins, according to tribal beliefs, are an evil omen. However, when the center attempted to place these children, a major custody battle ensued. The tribe fought to halt the adoption, stating that they wanted time to consider changing their customs and might accept the twins back, but social workers and child care advocates opposed this solution; they feared for these children to be returned to those people who might have "discarded them in the wild" (p. A11). Following extensive negotiations, the government agreed to give the twins back to the U'wa tribe after the tribe "agreed to place the rights of these two children above their cultural beliefs" ("Twin Babies Spared," 1999, A14).

This case raises a number of important issues: (1) How far can "culturally diverse Colombia . . . go in protecting minority practices" seen as unacceptable by the majority (Kotler, 1999, p. A11)? (2) To what extent do human rights take precedence over cultural values? (3) How did these parents make their decision (brave and humane by our standards, but rebellious and perhaps "dangerous" by the tribe's standards)? How did they come to deviate from such strong cultural constraints, asserting their autonomy in the process? Did they act solely on their own or did someone outside their tribe

Human Behavior in the Social Environment, Second Edition

offer guidance? However, they arrived at this solution for the survival of their children, their *will* prevailed (at least temporarily) over long-established custom. Yet their autonomy was not absolute; when they returned to their tribe, they were isolated from the community to be "cleansed of impurities linked to the birth. For four years, they cannot visit other houses or share food with neighbors" (p. A11).

In this chapter we shall look at the ways culture influences the individual and how individuals adapt to, conform to, rebel against, or sometimes reshape culture to their own ends. The concept of culture "incorporates all the symbolic meanings—the beliefs, values, norms, and traditions . . . shared in a community and [that] govern social interactions among community members or between members and outsiders" (Longres, 1995b, p. 74). Though cultures can be viewed at the macrolevel, such as the cultures of Japanese people or Native American people, they can also be observed at the microlevel, as developed by small groups, such as communes, cults, or fraternities and sororities; institutions and organizations are said to have their own internal culture.

People can belong to more than one culture and one race; many in the United States, for example, are multicultural. Tiger Woods, the famous golfer, explained that he did not think of himself as an African American. "I'm just who I am" (White, 1997, pp. 33-34). He was born to a black American father and a Thai mother and refers himself with a name that he made up. " 'I'm a Cablinasian,' which he explained is a self-crafted acronym that reflects his one-eighth Caucasian, one-fourth black, one-eighth American Indian, one-fourth Thai and one-fourth Chinese roots" (p. 33). A dramatic increase has occurred in the number of multiracial children in the United States since 1970; the U.S. Bureau of the Census in 1990 reported more than 2 million such children (White, 1997), and Kent et al. (2001) stated that in the 2000 Census "about 4 per cent of children were identified as multiracial" (p. 19), representing roughly a 25 percent increase over the 1990 census.

Issues of diversity emphasized in this chapter include ethnicity, race, social class, and culture; the clash of values between cultures as well as within cultures is also highlighted. Diversity related to gender and sexual orientation is discussed in Chapter 11, to disabilities in Chapter 13, and to mental illness in Chapter 14.

Immigration is addressed, highlighting both the sociopolitical issues and the psychological adaptations people make as they move from one culture to another. "Immigration from one country to another is a complex and multifaceted psychosocial process with significant and lasting effects on an individual's identity" (Akhtar, 1995, p. 1052). There are now more than 31 million people living in the United States, who were born in other countries; "twenty percent of the nation's children have at least one foreign-born parent!" (McGoldrick, Giordano, and, Garcia-Preto, 2005, p. 18). In 2006, many children of immigrants entered our public school system, making it "the most dazzlingly diverse since waves of European immigrants washed through the public schools a century ago" (Dillon, 2006a, p. 1).

Illegal immigration to this country, and the controversy over the 11 million undocumented immigrants, many from Mexico, were major sociopolitical issues in 2005-2006 (Swarns, 2006) and continuing into 2007.

Two recently created cultures playing a dominant role in their members' lives are discussed: one, the culture of the deaf, is an ongoing, supportive group, seeking to empower themselves and one another in their shared world of deafness. The other, the Heaven's Gate sect, had a tragic (according to my viewpoint) outcome, resulting in mass suicide (a triumphant new beginning, from their viewpoint). Diversity and culture affect social work practice in many ways, sometimes unrecognized: diagnostic assessments; the nature of treatment as well as the therapeutic relationship; and the need for resolution of complex value conflicts between clinicians and clients.

In discussing culture in this chapter, three major approaches are addressed: *cultural sensitivity, cultural competence,* and *constructivism.* Applying concepts of cultural sensitivity, the social worker emphasizes the common human needs of all clients, applies a basic casework approach, but at the same time recognizes that people may have different values and perspectives and is open to learning about the client's culture (Lee and Greene, 1999). The culturally competent clinician learns about the client's specific culture to develop "culture-specific concepts . . . and techniques from within the specific context" (p. 23).

However, although being culturally competent may help the clinician understand behaviors that may appear inexplicable without knowledge of the client's cultural background and values; the danger exists of "stereotyping" the client and assuming that culture is the explanation for every client's behavior. Cultural competence may also lead us to believe that clients accept all tenets of their culture and that, in fact, they participate in just one culture.

The constructivist sensitively explores culture, while at the same time individualizing clients, and learning the meaning of their culture to them. My perspective is that a combination of cultural sensitivity, cultural competence, and a constructivist framework is the most effective in working with people from cultures both diverse from and similar to our own. An awareness of one's own cultural background and biases becomes an important ingredient in preparing to understand and respect the culture of another.

CONSTRUCTIVISM AND CULTURE

Considering cultural understanding from a constructivist perspective affords one the opportunity to approach each client with an open spirit of inquiry; we must listen to the client's story (or narrative) and understand how clients perceive their problems and their ideas about solving them.

> The therapist's questions should bring the conversation to the *edge of what language experience reveals,* so that further questioning involves the formulation of what has not been said or thought before [by the client]. The therapist is a respectful listener who does not *know too soon* nor *understand too quickly.* (Goolishian and Winderman, 1988, pp. 140-141; italics in the original)

Lia Lee is a Hmong child who developed epilepsy when she was three months old and living in California with her immigrant family. Her family realized she had *quag dab peg,* which means "the spirit catches you and you fall down" (Fadiman, 1997, p. 20). The constructivist approach does not assume, but asks how the parents perceived this problem; for the most part, the family wanted the spirit to be cured. However, as they informed their social worker, they viewed the condition as an "honor" and considered their daughter to be "an anointed one . . . in their culture" who might become a "shaman" in the future because she had "these spirits in her." Among the many professionals who had dealt with the family, only the social worker had thought to elicit the family's notion of the *"cause of their daughter's illness"* (Fadiman, 1997, p. 22; italics added).

The judgment of normality, within a constructivist perspective, is culturally constructed—"normality is always in the eyes of the observer" (Berzoff, Flanagan, and Hertz, 1996, p. 11). What, for example, is "normal sexuality," and who defines this? Whether homosexual marriages should be legalized reflects the present debate on the subject of sexual normality. Sophie Freud (1999) points out that "different sexual practices have been viewed as perverse in different historical periods. Masturbation was held responsible for a wide range of mental illnesses in the eighteenth and nineteenth century" (p. 336).

Culture is not static. Becker views "culture as always a work in progress" (Saari, 1999, p. 223). He asserts,

> People create culture continuously. Since no two situations are alike, the cultural solutions available to them are only approximate. Even in

the simplest societies, no two people learn quite the same cultural material; the chance encounters of daily life provide sufficient variation to ensure that. No set of cultural understandings, then, provides a perfectly applicable solution to any problem . . . [so people] . . . must . . . adapt their understandings to the new situation. . . . Even the most . . . determined effort to keep things as they are would necessarily involve strenuous efforts to remake and reinforce understandings so as to keep them intact in the face of what was changing. (Becker, 1986, p. 19, cited in Saari, 1999, p. 223)

In a multicultural society people may develop more than one set of values and beliefs. This can be a source of stress, especially when the value systems of each conflict. This is illustrated by the problems faced by religious individuals who happen also to be homosexual; homosexuality is considered taboo in many religious systems.

Diversity exists in multiple forms. It can be invisible, in terms of a person's private thoughts, hidden physical symptoms, or "closeted" actions; at other times it is highly visible, apparent in distinctive gender and racial characteristics or physical disabilities. People "who are different" may find acceptance in some (or all) social groups, or their differences may create a real or a felt sense of alienation.

DIVERSITY

Diversity issues will be examined both from a social and a psychological perspective, and include ethnicity and race, social class, immigration, and culture.

Ethnicity and Race

Are white Anglo-Saxon Protestants members of an ethnic group (Sollors, 1986)? Is a majority group considered ethnic? Or are only minorities or subgroups to be considered ethnic? It is a "widespread practice to define ethnicity as otherness" (p. 25). The word ethnic has its roots in the Greek word *ethnikos,* which means "gentile" or "heathen" (p. 25). In the mid-1800s, the concept of "ethnic" evolved to mean "peculiar to a race or nation." Expressing reservations about this concept, Sollors cites Cohen's statement that to "many people, the term ethnicity connotes minority status, lower class, or migrancy. This is why sooner or later we shall have to drop it or to find a neutral word for it, though I can see that we shall probably have to live with it for quite a while" (p. 39).

According to McGoldrick, Giordano, and Garcia-Preto (2005) ethnicity is,

> the concept of a group's "peoplehood," refers to a group's commonal-
> ity of ancestry and history, through which people have evolved shared
> values and customs over the centuries. Based on a combination of
> race, religion, and cultural history, ethnicity is retained, whether or
> not members realize their commonalities with each other. (p. 2)

It is important to incorporate an understanding of a client's ethnicity and
culture into psychosocial assessments; "exploring cultural patterns and hy-
potheses is essential to all our clinical work" (McGoldrick, Giordano, and
Garcia-Preto, 2005, p. 5).

Race, considered one aspect of ethnicity, is a controversial concept that
can lead to stereotyping and prejudiced thoughts and actions. Objecting to a
rigid use of racial categories, Spickard, Fong, and Ewalt (1995) argue that
the increase of diversity of racial groupings "suggests a deconstruction of
the very notion of race"; in this country "there were 43 racial categories and
subcategories on the 1990 census form" (p. 581). In the 2000 Census, according to the Texas State Data Center, Department of Rural Sociology, at
Texas A&M University, "the combinations of the six racial groups used resulted in 63 separate racial categories and, if these are divided into those of
Hispanic and those not of Hispanic origin, there are 126 combinations of
race/ethnicity" ("Comparing Race/Ethnicity," 2001).

In a book on the impact of culture and class on psychotherapy, the authors
explain why they chose to leave the word "race" out of their title (Pérez
Foster, Moskowitz, and Javier, 1996).

> It is especially important that we confront the fact that the division of
> the world into black and white is a delusion of civilization. People are
> not black or white. Where the line is drawn is politically and psycho-
> logically motivated. The fact that "race" is the only ethnic grouping in
> this culture that does not allow for the possibility of dual identity be-
> lies its delusional rigidity. While "race" clearly has powerful psycho-
> logical meanings that are discussed in many of the chapters in this
> volume, we felt it was important not to lend it continuing scientific re-
> spectability by using it in our title. (Pérez Foster, Moskowitz, and
> Javier, 1996, xvi-xvii)

I chose to retain the words ethnicity and race in this book because of the
strong positive feelings many people have with these designations; acknowledging race and ethnicity can help people develop their sense of identity and involvement with their communities. I also did not want to bury the

strong negative emotions that can be evoked by these words; the intensity of ethnic loyalties and ethnic hatreds fuels (and has fueled) many wars and serious conflicts. The negative and positive usages of ethnicity are not mutually exclusive.

The constructivist perspective encourages understanding the meaning of ethnicity and race to each individual client and family; clinical social workers should also assess how clients relate to others outside their racial, ethnic, and cultural groups. Sollors (1986) cites Barth as stating that it is "the ethnic boundary that defines the group, not the cultural stuff that it encloses" (p. 27). How people relate to outsiders is particularly relevant when client and therapist are of different ethnicities and races.

America has come a long way in its development of human rights and improvement in race relations; children of mixed races attend school and play together; the rate of interracial marriages is increasing (Spickard, Fong, and Ewalt, 1995), as is the number of minority professionals and respected political figures. However tensions continue to exist, and at times explode; affirmative action issues fuel major political debates; and hate crimes continue to make the news.

In general, when racial issues are discussed, black Americans are the major focus; however, Native Americans, Asians, and Hispanics have their own unique issues, which are drawing increasing attention. This section will focus on these four groups.

African Americans and American Blacks

The use of the term African American is generally viewed as a "progressive" term signifying an acceptance and integration of this group. In the past, the term Negro (viewed by many as derogatory) was widely used; then the use of black (connotating racial pride) became customary. However, while generally accepted, the term African American is not universally agreed upon (Longres, 1995a); it is not all encompassing, in that not all black Americans have come from Africa; there are groups of Haitians, Jamaicans, and Azoreans, among others. The terms African Americans, American blacks, and blacks are used interchangeably in this book.

The black population in the United States encompasses persons belonging to different subcultures, different social classes, different political views, and vary in the ways that their self-identities and opportunities in life have been adversely affected by racial, prejudicial, and discriminatory experiences. Black persons may also belong to other cultural groups not related to race and differ to the degree that they feel a need to remain "separate" from the mainstream culture or to be integrated into it; to the degree they are comfortable with white friends (or spouses); and the degree to which they may be looked down upon or look down on others for "acting white."

Antiblack racism and slavery. Blackness does not provide a cloak of invisibility; skin color is readily apparent (unless the person has very light pigmentation) and often subjects the individual to overt or subtle rejection.

Ralph Ellison (1980) discusses invisibility from a different perspective; the individuality of the black person is often rendered invisible by the white observer who sees only a stereotype and not a person. The protagonist of his novel declares himself to be an invisible man:

> No . . . not a spook like those who haunted Edgar Allan Poe; nor am I one of your Hollywood-movie ectoplasms. I am a man of substance, of flesh and bone, fiber and liquids—and I might even be said to possess a mind. I am invisible, understand, simply because people refuse to see me. Like the bodiless heads you see sometimes in circus sideshows, it is as though I have been surrounded by mirrors of hard, distorting glass. When they approach me they see only my surroundings, themselves, or figments of their imagination—indeed, everything and anything except me. (Ellison, 1980, p. 3)

Antiblack racism, in this country, has its roots in the slave system that was maintained for 200 years, and was an oppressive, brutal, dehumanizing experience. Black people were stolen and kidnapped from their homelands, brought to this country on slave ships notorious for their inhumane conditions, and sold at auction to white Americans, who had no regard for the needs of these people or for keeping their family members together. This was justified in the minds of many as an economic necessity and on the premise that black Africans were an inferior race.

Recently there has been an increase in the publication of books describing the slave experience, which are "stripping away whatever is left of the velvety romance of benign slave holders presiding over docile slaves. And they are emphasizing efforts of the enslaved to escape or rebel and the punishments they faced that ranged from branding to amputation" (Carvajal, 1999, Section 4, p. 5).

A powerful book about slavery and its psychological impact is William Styron's (1993) *The Confessions of Nat Turner.* It is a fictionalized account of a true event: A major but unsuccessful slave rebellion that Nat Turner led in 1831, in southeastern Virginia. Although Styron received the Pulitzer Prize for this work, controversy nevertheless surrounded his novel, published at "one of the most explosive moments in the history of race relations in America" (Horwitz, 1999, p. 83). Black critics raised questions about

Styron's depiction of Nat Turner and asked whether a white author was capable of understanding the slave experience; historians disputed the facts of this case, the details of which still remain murky. Acknowledging that the details of these excerpts may be historically incorrect, I chose to include them here because the emotional impact of the slave experience appears to "ring true" to historic accounts from other sources.

Nat Turner was tried and hanged. In the following scene, Nat is talking to Gray, his white, court-appointed lawyer, whose self-righteous deprecatory attitude is apparent. Gray tells Nat about the fate of his co-conspirators: ". . . Out of this whole catastrophic ruction only round one-fourth gets the rope. . . . Mealy-mouthed abolitionists say we don't show justice. Well, we do. . . . That's how come nigger slavery's going to last a thousand years" (Styron, 1993, p. 25).

Slave experiences ranged from abject misery and brutality to some physical comfort and comparatively benign conditions; Nat and his mother were house slaves who lived comfortably with a humane master. Although lacking freedom and denied basic legal rights, Nat was not a field slave who toiled long hours at physical labor and lived in slave quarters; he understood this distinction (Styron, 1993). One evening he became aware of his own troubled feelings when, in the dwindling light, he saw

> a line of Negro men trooping up from the mill . . . wearily playful . . . as they move homeward with the languid, shuffling, shoulder-bent gait of a long day's toil. . . . I turn away (could there have been a whiff of something desperate and ugly in that long file of sweating, weary men which upsets my glowing childish house bound spirit?). (pp. 125-126)

Marse [Master] Samuel was kind to Nat and proud of his intelligence and ability to read. Marse Samuel explains his strongly held view that "the more . . . enlightened a Negro is made, the better for himself, his master, and the commonweal. But one must begin at a tender age, and thus . . . you see in Nat the promising beginnings of an experiment" (Styron, 1993, p. 124). Marse Samuel arranged for Nat to have special training in carpentry and promised him that, when he was older, he would have his freedom and would be apprenticed to a carpenter in Richmond.

However, the land of the plantation becomes infertile (common in the area due to overcultivation of cotton). Marse Samuel leaves for richer land, and Nat is left behind, with promises that his next owner will carry out the arrangements for his freedom. This is not to be. Suddenly Nat is a slave in the full sense of the word and lives with a series of masters, most of whom cruelly exploit him. It is not the exploitation that fuels his rage; it is the betrayal by Marse Samuel. In the following passage, Nat recalls being sold at a slave auction by his second master, Reverend Eppes.

> "But you can't do this! You and Marse Samuel had a written agreement. You was to take me to *Richmond!* He *told* me so!"

> But the Reverend Eppes said not a word, counting bills, each golden second climbing from penury to riches . . . as . . . he verified his booty. . . .

> "You *can't!*" I shouted. "I've got a *trade,* too! I'm a carpenter!" . . . I experienced a kind of disbelief . . . close upon madness, then a sense of betrayal . . . then . . . hatred so bitter that I . . . thought I might get sick on the floor . . . hatred for Marse Samuel, and the rage rose and rose in my breast until . . . in my mind's eye I saw him strangled by my own hands. (Styron, 1993, pp. 246-247)

In this passage, we see the impact of total abandonment on Nat and the failed promises of Marse Samuel; Nat becomes engulfed in a nightmare world. He screams and pleads for recognition of his rights; his pleas are not only unheard but silenced. He is helpless and powerless; his despair turns into the rage, which ultimately fuels his motivation for a slave rebellion. Perhaps more recent racial "insurrections" and riots are fueled by similar feelings of betrayal, despair, utter powerlessness, and "soul murder."

> The situation of Black slaves brought to this country was devastating not only because their immigration was forced . . . but also because they were psychophysically manhandled by the "host" population. They were used as targets of projection and, in an act of collective "soul murder" (Shengold, 1989), brainwashed to believe in their inherent racial inferiority. Effects of the intergenerational transmission of this trauma (Apprey, 1993) are still evident. (Akhtar, 1995, p. 1055)

The Civil War freed the slaves, but many white people, especially in the South, retained oppressive power and disdain for the personhood of the black person. Lynchings, for which there was no legal recourse, were common; Jim Crow laws were passed in the South: "The system prescribed how African Americans were supposed to act in the presence of whites, asserted white supremacy, embraced racial segregation, and denied political and legal rights to African Americans" (Zastrow and Kirst-Ashman, 1997, p. 216).

Maya Angelou (1997), who spent a large portion of her childhood in Stamps, Arkansas, in the 1930s, discussed random lynchings as well as the many ordinary humiliations experienced by black people in her community. In one degrading incident, Annie (her grandmother), whom she called Momma, brought Maya to a white dentist in town, knowing that he did not treat black patients but in hope that he will relent in her case for two reasons: Maya was in severe pain, and the dentist owed Annie a favor, as she had lent him money in the past when he was in difficulty.

> Momma said, "Dentist Lincoln. It's my grandbaby here. She got two rotten teeth that's giving her a fit." . . . "Annie?" . . . He was choosing words the way people hunt for shells. "Annie, you know I don't treat nigra, colored people." . . . "Seem like to me, Dentist Lincoln, you might look after her, she ain't nothing but a little mite. And seems like maybe you owe me a favor or two."

> . . . "It's been paid, and raising your voice won't make me change my mind. My policy". . . . He let go of the door and stepped nearer Momma. The three of us were crowded on the small landing. "Annie, my policy is I'd rather stick my hand in a dog's mouth than in a nigger's." (Angelou, 1997, pp. 188-189)

While Dentist Lincoln was insulting to Momma, she was not cowed. She realized that she could not win this battle, but assertively made her request. Momma is a very strong character; she runs a grocery store and is highly respected in her community. Momma does not seem to have experienced "soul murder." The main character in the *Invisible Man,* by contrast, has had his "soul murdered" by a web of events, all racially entwined, leading to a Kafkaesque world of betrayal, lack of opportunity, exploitation, and feelings of total powerlessness.

Debates continue today about the extent of the psychological consequences of racial prejudice and discrimination. Research on the effects of discrimination on the mental health and self-esteem of individuals has produced mixed findings. Self-esteem is not adversely affected by racism in all instances (Zastrow and Kirst-Ashman, 2004); "simple or clear conclusions remain elusive and contradictory" (Mattei, 1996, p. 237).

> There is no question that cultural discontinuity, ethnic or racial devaluing, and assaults present significant challenges for minority youth. At the same time we know that minority children are not *inevitably* less adjusted, nor do they invariably experience lower levels of self-esteem. (Mattei, 1996, p. 237)

Psychological consequences of racism. In assessing how the psychological consequences of prejudice and discrimination affect any given African-American individual, three major factors should be taken into account: systemic issues; resilience and other protective factors; and biopsychosocial assessment, including the person's self-perceptions about being black and the impact of minority status on their lives. These three criteria can be applied to understanding the impact of discrimination on a person of any minority.

Systemic issues. Major positive changes in political, legal (including the major civil rights legislation), educational, and employment opportunities for black Americans should be taken into account. Racial segregation in schools, for example, was declared unconstitutional by the *Brown v. Board of Education* Supreme Court decision in 1954 (Zastrow and Kirst-Ashman, 1997). The civil rights movement and subsequent legislation led to voting rights and greater protections for black citizens. Black people are prominently represented in professions, in business, in the news media, and in political office at most levels of government. Other positive developments fostered by the civil rights movement include the "'Black is beautiful' and similar esteem-building social voices, [and] the search for heritage and legacy (memorialized in Alex Haley's 1976 *Roots*)" (Akhtar, 1995, p. 1055). "Celebrations, such as Kwanza, are ways of promoting pride for African Americans" (Zastrow and Kirst-Ashman, 2004, p. 199).

Socioeconomic status is relevant; members of minority groups with low socioeconomic status, for example, who live in impoverished inner-city communities face serious economic, employment, and housing problems. Poor, undereducated, young black males "are becoming ever more disconnected from the mainstream society, and to a far greater degree than comparable white or Hispanic men. Especially in . . . inner cities . . . finishing high school is the exception, legal work is scarcer than ever and prison is almost routine, with incarceration rates climbing for blacks as urban crime rates have declined" (Eckholm, 2006b, p. A1).

However, many black families are part of a growing middle class, and some are represented in the upper class. "A middle class has emerged that is better educated, better paid, and better housed than any group of African Americans that has gone before it" (Zastrow and Kirst-Ashman, 2004, p. 198). There are several distinct African-American cultures, and as "one goes up the socioeconomic scale, the impact of institutional racism on ego development lessens" (Miles, 1998, p. 110). However, the impact of systemic issues on any given individual must be examined both in terms of objective experiences, and the subjective constructed meaning of these events to the person.

Psychological and cultural resiliency. Resiliency, both on psychological and cultural levels, can help develop a protective shield against prejudiced attitudes and treatment. Social organizations, such as African-American churches, have been a source of political action and personal support to many of their members (Zastrow and Kirst-Ashman, 2004). That a majority group may discriminate against a minority group does not necessarily mean that the latter is psychologically devastated; in fact, it can engender a sense of group cohesiveness and strength in the group subjected to such hostility.

> Afro-Americans have survived a harsh system of slavery, repression, and racism. Although there have been casualties, there have been many more survivors, achievers, and victors. The cultural heritage of coping with adversity and overcoming has been passed on from generation to generation, laced with stories of those with remarkable courage and fortitude. (Zastrow and Kirst-Ashman, 1997, citing Powell, p. 219)

Maya Angelou (1997) describes her all-black school graduation in Stamps, Arkansas. Her moving account captures the pride and involvement of the whole community in this event, including days of preparations and celebrations beforehand. The ceremony is spoiled for her by the white school superintendent's very condescending speech; his underlying message was that the black people in the audience were uneducated laborers and that "anything higher that we aspired to was farcical and presumptuous" (Angelou, 1997, p. 180). Then Henry Reed, the class valedictorian, gave his speech and led his class in singing the Negro national anthem. "The tears that slipped down many faces were not wiped away in shame" (p. 184).

> We were on top again. As always, again. We survived. The depths had been icy and dark, but now a bright sun spoke to our souls. I was no longer simply a member of the proud graduating class of 1940; I was a proud member of the wonderful, beautiful Negro race.

> Oh, Black known and unknown poets, how often have your auctioned pains sustained us? Who will compute the lonely nights made less lonely by your songs, or by the empty pots made less tragic by your tales? (Angelou, 1997, p. 184)

Biopsychosocial assessment. A biopsychosocial assessment sheds light on the psychological effects of discrimination within the context of a person's life, relationships, and opportunities. Clients' self-perceptions of their racial identity and racial conflicts vary; "some patients have only vague anxieties that are experienced as related to their ethnicity, while others are directly and deeply impacted by it" (Thompson, 1996, p. 123). The quality of family life and attachments of children are crucial factors in their adaptation and are important protective factors mediating against psychological harm from discrimination.

Thompson (1996), who is a black woman psychoanalyst, found that one of the most intricate therapy issues was separating out a patient's racial issues from his or her personality issues. "In treating many black patients, the initial clarification of their struggles requires what I call a type of 'racial surgery', which involves helping them discern the differences between those struggles that would be theirs regardless of ethnicity, and those that might be complicated specifically because of their race" (p. 125).

Skin color is involved in the development of racial identity and can produce discrimination not only from nonblack people but discrimination within the community of black people. "For many people of color, the factor of skin color itself is deeply intertwined with the sense of self-value" (Thompson, 1996, p. 125). In some black families preferences may exist for one child over another based on the lightness or darkness of skin, and differences of skin color can affect peer relationships and choice of marriage partners (Harvey, 1995; Williams, 1997). Williams warns against assuming that all black people place higher value on light skin than on dark skin; Harvey asserts that therapists should not make assumptions about clients' feelings about their skin color but rather should inquire. "Skin color can be perceived as a positive dynamic in the clients' lives as well as a negative factor. Some individuals and families view their blackness as a badge of honor" (Harvey, 1995, p. 8).

Therapists should address the complex issues of blackness, whiteness, integration, and separation directly with clients. Differences in race can complicate transference and countertransference issues between therapist and patient, and often issues of trust must be worked through; however, having a therapist of the same race "is not devoid of race-related impasses" (Thompson, 1996, p. 139). The discussion of racial and cultural similarities and differences affecting clinical work is elaborated in the final section of this chapter.

Native Americans

On September 28, 1999, groundbreaking ceremonies were held in Washington, DC, celebrating the opening of the National Museum of the American Indian (Clines, 1999). This event signified an important step both in recognizing the rights, history, and dignity of Native Americans and in acknowledging the history of oppression and exploitation perpetrated by the U.S. government. The museum opened on September 21, 2004.

A century after the tribal devastation of the Indian wars, a place of honor on the capital Mall was finally extended to the nation's Native Americans today as construction began on a museum that Indian leaders vowed would celebrate their history of indominability, "even if it tells a sad story, even if it's a hard story to look at."

With hundreds of tribal members and chiefs in attendance savoring ancient ritual and hopeful speeches, the museum . . . was hailed as a long overdue antidote to centuries of racist stereotyping, broken treaties and federal "civilization regulations" that failed to rein in rich tribal cultures with a policy of assimilation. (Clines, 1999, p. A18)

In another act of reconciliation, the Peabody Museum at Harvard University, on May 19, 1999, returned the remains of approximately 2,000 Pueblo Indians to their ancient site in Pecos Valley, New Mexico, from which they had been excavated by archaeologists (Goldberg, 1999a). In 1990, Congress passed the Graves Protection and Repatriation Act; since then, Indian remains and other sacred relics have been returned to the appropriate tribes. This act of repatriation has a twofold significance: the respect for ancestors is very strong in Native American cultures; in addition, the historic "grave robbing" by white Americans is now being rectified.

In a different realm, U.S. Congress passed the Indian Child Welfare Act in 1978, stressing restraint in the removal of Native American children from their families and tribes, to prevent their placement in non–Native American adoptive or foster care homes (Goldstein and Goldstein, 1996). "The rate of out-of-home placement for American Indian and Alaska Native children has been from 5 to 20 times greater than rates for comparable non-Indian populations" (Robin, Rasmussen, and Gonzalez-Santin, 1999, p. 70). This Indian Child Welfare Act sought to reverse the long-standing practice of removing children from their cultural heritage and imposing a variety of assimilation experiences on them, against the will of their people.

The term Native Americans, although recognizing the fact that these groups were both the original natives and current citizens of this country, is not universally accepted: Westerfelt and Yellow Bird (1999) note that they

use the term "indigenous peoples" . . . [as] a more appropriate descriptor for the aboriginal populations . . . [since] indigenous peoples . . . are not . . . from India. They are the descendants of the First

Nations . . . [The term] Native Americans . . . may refer to most native born Americans. (p. 146)

History of Native American exploitation. The history of the treatment of Native Americans is marked by acts of violence (including massacres), economic exploitation, and systematic attempts to destroy their culture; the massacre of men, women, and children at Wounded Knee is one frequently cited example (Brown, 1972). Black Elk, a Native American present at the massacre, has written

> I did not know then how much was ended. When I look back now from this high hill of my old age, I can still see the butchered women and children lying heaped and scattered all along the crooked gulch as plain as when I saw them with eyes still young. And I can see that something else died there in the bloody mud, and was buried in the blizzard. A people's dream died there. It was a beautiful dream . . . the nation's hoop is broken and scattered. There is no center any longer, and the sacred tree is dead. (Brown, 1972, p. 419)

The U.S. government removed Native Americans from lands that settlers wanted (Longres, 1995b), and advanced the doctrine of Manifest Destiny to justify their removal.

> To justify these breaches of the "permanent Indian frontier," the policymakers in Washington invented Manifest Destiny, a term that lifted land hunger to a lofty plane. The Europeans and their descendants were ordained by destiny to rule all of America. They were the dominant race and therefore responsible for the Indians—along with their lands, their forests, and their mineral wealth. Only the New Englanders, who had destroyed or driven out all their Indians, spoke against Manifest Destiny. (Brown, 1972, p. 8)

The Indian Removal Act of 1830 sanctioned the forced removal of tribes from their property.

> The 900-mile march from Georgia to what is now Oklahoma is often referred to as the "trail of tears." The U. S. Army forcibly removed some 100,000 native people from the southern states, costing the lives of thousands and shattering any trust they might have placed in their European dominators. (Longres, 1995b, p. 121)

As settlers moved further west and wanted more Indian land, new policies were made for this acquisition and Indian wars declared.

Many Native Americans were placed on reservations where the land was usually very poor. According to Edward Spicer (Longres, 1995b), the policy of coercive assimilation was developed, under which Indian cultural life (such as religious rituals) was often prohibited, and Christian missionaries prevailed; children were often sent to distant boarding schools "where they could be Americanized" (Longres, 1995b, p. 122).

Mean Spirit, a novel set in Oklahoma in the 1920s, depicts the exploitation and murder of Indians by white Americans and government officials, primarily to obtain the oil found on their lands (Hogan, 1990). The "forced" attendance of Indian children at boarding schools is also described. Nola, who has seen her mother murdered, experiences constant fear and anxiety. She lives with Mrs. Graycloud and does not want to go to the Indian boarding school; Mrs. Graycloud, knowing her anxieties, wants her to stay home. In this passage, the school nurse and the man from the Indian Affairs office confront Belle (Mrs. Graycloud) and Nola.

> The agent lays down the law; Nola must be enrolled: " 'I can't let you do that,' Belle said. . . . Nola . . . only recently had . . . begun to speak after the death of her mother." Obviously unwilling to be dissuaded, the protest was dismissed with: "We've heard what's been going on . . . but we want to examine her ourselves." . . . Belle . . . interrupted. "She's anemic." Her face was tense. . . . The nurse looked in one of Nola's ears. "She seems normal and even bright for an Indian girl," she said sweetly. . . . The Indian agent signed an order stating that Nola would have to appear at school . . . or . . . be picked up by the sheriff . . . his was an order by law. The old woman looked defiant but said nothing. . . . She was defeated. (Hogan, 1990, pp. 122-123)

Nola attended the Indian School, but was ultimately dismissed because the administration could not cope with her behavior. When she returned home, many of the Indian women came to visit her, but not because of the "shame" of expulsion; they wondered how she had outwitted the system, and whether their children might adopt some of her methods!

Current issues. In recent years, as the United States has begun to make amends to the Native American population, the outlook is brighter for this group. There has been an eightfold increase over the past century from a population of a quarter million, which itself had represented a profound decline from the height achieved before the colonial period (Clines, 1999, p. A18).

Native Americans have made progress in recent years "strengthening their sovereignty and culture, making their way into American politics and government and—for a small but rising number of tribes—growing rich with new casino revenue" (Kershaw, 2006, p. 20). Women have assumed important administrative, teaching, and leadership positions in their tribes; 133 were tribal leaders in 2006 (Davey, 2006). A new organization, Women Empowering Women for Indian Nations (WEWIN), had its first meeting in Minnesota in the summer of 2006, with a focus on political activism in their tribes, states, and the country. Increasing numbers of Indian women have attained college educations, now far surpassing the rate of Indian males. "The downside, some of the women said, is that the rise of women may also reflect the struggles some of the men are wrestling with on reservations—joblessness, alcoholism, poverty" (Davey, 2006, p. A9).

Health and social problems exist in many Native American communities where "people are experiencing increasing rates of mortality and morbidity due to such factors as alcohol and drug abuse, suicide, homicide, motor vehicle accidents, and child abuse and neglect" (Weaver, 1999, pp. 127-128); they are also "overrepresented in the homeless population" (Westerfelt and Yellow Bird, 1999, p. 145).

> Indigenous peoples experience disproportionately high levels of poverty and income deterioration . . . , work fewer annual hours and receive lower hourly earnings than whites . . . , and experience higher levels of unemployment . . . , residential mobility . . . , and alcoholism. . . . (Westerfelt and Yellow Bird, 1999, p. 147)

Illegal drug dealing has become a major problem on Indian reservations; there is a "violent but largely overlooked wave of trafficking and crime that has swept through the nation's Indian reservations in recent years, as large-scale criminal organizations have found havens and allies in the wide-open and isolated regions of Indian country"; drug activity includes smuggling across Mexican and Canadian borders (Kershaw, 2006, p. 1). This has given rise to Indian criminal rings, corruption among law enforcement officials, and fueled serious drug addiction and violence on some reservations; the drugs include marijuana, Ecstasy, Meth, and cocaine (Kershaw, 2006).

There have been many lawsuits fought out between Indians and the U.S. government over the years. One such suit was brought by Elouise Cobell, who is a banker and a member of the Blackfoot tribe in Montana "on behalf of nearly 500,000 Indians who say the government has squandered more than $100 billion in grazing, energy and mineral royalties from Indian lands" (Files, 2006, p. A16). Judge Lambert, who had ruled against the Interior

Department in 2005, was not thought to be impartial, and was removed from the case in 2006. He had strongly criticized the Interior Department, calling it " 'the morally and culturally oblivious hand-me-down of a disgracefully racist and imperialist government that should have been buried a century ago' " (Files, 2006, p. A16). With the consent of the plaintiffs, the case was referred for mediation by the Senate Indian Affairs Committee.

The Native American population is very diverse; many Indian tribes exist, and "tribal subcultures are many and varied" (Attneave, 1982, p. 56). It is a common error to assume that "all Indian populations in a region are alike, not recognizing that, even though a Navajo, a Hopi, an Apache, and someone from Laguna Pueblo may all live in the southwest desert, each has a different language and set of traditions" (Attneave, 1982, p. 56). Conflicts between tribes can exist as they have historically; for example, intense land disputes have arisen between the Navajo and Hopi tribes (Attneave, 1982).

Many Native Americans actually do not live on reservations (which are the focus of much of the mental health material written about this group) (Attneave, 1982; Gross, 1995); according to the Bureau of the Census in 1991, more than 70 percent of Native Americans live in urban settings (Walters, 1999). About 50 percent of American Indians have married outside their race during the past fifty years (Spickard, Fong, and Ewalt, 1995). Attneave (1982) notes that in an urban setting about 50 percent of American Indian families seeking family therapists will be "well-educated, typically middle-class people with similar problems and similar attitudes as the rest of [the] clientele" (p. 57). Problems relating to intermarriage are frequently discussed; "working out the details of everyday life can result in the collision of Indian and dissonant cultural values" (Sutton and Nose, 2005, p. 50).

The importance of utilizing and strengthening a Native American cultural identity, and offering culturally sensitive services, is emphasized by many writers (Angell, Kurz, and Gottfried, 1998; Weaver, 1999; Westerfelt and Yellow Bird, 1999). Brave Heart (1999) discusses the emotional sequelae of the "historical trauma" of the Lakota people, including the Wounded Knee Massacre, as well as the "forced removal of Lakota children from home and their abusive institutional treatment" (p. 112). She speaks of the intergenerational transmission of these traumas from parents to children, with serious psychological and social consequences, and emphasizes treatment focusing on "incorporating awareness of [this] trauma and the recathexis [reattachment] to traditional Lakota values" (Brave Heart, 1999, p. 111). Clinicians "should be aware of such phenomena as suicide, depression, and alcoholism within the context of ongoing oppression combined with a genocidal history" (Sutton and Nose, 2005, p. 47).

Although a strong case is made for incorporating and promoting Native American cultural values into social work interventions, objections to this dominant point of view have been made, which argue that some Native Americans may wish to choose different values and follow other paths. Gross (1995) strongly asserts that the "politically correct approach" has made "it difficult . . . to derive views of Indianness that were congruent with the diversity of American Indian life and views" (p. 208). She expresses concern that only the voices of Native American social workers are heard and that one's views are disqualified if one is not an American Indian; this can "inhibit the development of a contemporary discourse on the subject of 'Indianness'" (Gross, 1995, p. 211). She warns that the "traditionalist" views of Indian identity prevail, which leaves those Native Americans with a different viewpoint unheard.

> American Indians who choose to assimilate or . . . depart from tradtionalist values are left with no Indian identity references against which they might then positively regard themselves or be positively regarded by others. . . . American Indians who advocate for mineral resources development may be defined as "bad" Indians (meaning not in harmony with nature). (Gross, 1995, p. 211)

In working with indigenous people, culture and cultural identity are exquisitely sensitive areas of exploration; a clinician may struggle to find a balance between not imposing further coercive assimilation practices on people who have had their cultural beliefs and values degraded and prohibited, and not imposing an indigenous value system on people who may view themselves through a different lens.

Asian Americans

The term Asian Americans cover a wide spectrum of people with different ethnicities, races, and nationalities (Longres, 1995b; Segal, 1991). The earliest Asian immigrants were the Japanese and the Chinese, who initially experienced years of serious discrimination and exploitation in this country. After Pearl Harbor, "110,000 Japanese—mostly U.S.-born citizens of Japanese origin—were forced to sell their properties and were detained in relocation camps" (Queralt, 1996, p. 194). Ultimately the U.S. government acknowledged the injustice of its actions and provided financial compensation to these former detainees.

The three largest Asian groups in the United States have been the Chinese, the Filipinos, and the Japanese (Queralt, 1996). According to the

San Francisco Chronicle, "Americans of Chinese descent numbered 2.43 million in 2000, almost 600,000 more than Filipinos, the second-largest Asian group . . . Indo Americans . . . are now the third-largest Asian group, displacing Japanese Americans" (Kim, 2001). In more recent years, Asian immigrants have included people from Korea, India, Vietnam, Cambodia, and Thailand. People from Hawaii and Samoa compose the largest populations of Pacific Islanders in the United States (Ewalt and Mokuau, 1995).

Some groups, such as the Chinese, Japanese, Filipinos, and Asian Indians have been successful occupationally and economically in the United States. Asian Americans have made strong political gains, including increasing numbers of elected Asian or Pacific Americans at various levels (Ratnesar, 1998).

The diversity of Asian Americans is great, both in terms of culture, current socioeconomic status, adaptation, and psychological stress. In contrasting the Asian Indian population, for example, to Vietnamese and Cambodian people, major differences are immediately apparent. People coming from Cambodia and Vietnam have experienced many traumas and hardships in their homelands and in their attempts to reach the United States, increasing the problems involved in adapting. Indian immigrants, in contrast, tend to be highly educated and to speak English well (Segal, 1991). There are approximately 2 million Asian Indians in the United States, whose incomes exceed those of other immigrant groups (Perry, 2006).

Asian Indians generally have been exposed to "Western values and beliefs which facilitates their entry into American society . . . are . . . a very select group. . . . Most Indians come . . . to seek educational or professional opportunities" (Segal, 1991, p. 234). These factors have led to a higher degree of integration into American society and greater freedom to settle where they choose rather than in enclaves, with the development of very few ghettos. Their professional mobility has insulated them from the hostility endured by otherwise similar groups (Segal, 1991).

Diversity exists within this subgroup; there are "thirty-six linguistically and regionally diverse professional and cultural organizations of Indians" in the greater Detroit area alone (Mehta, 1998, p. 133). Indians, as other immigrant groups, can experience conflict in cultural values, such as parent-child conflict as children become more assimilated to American values and lifestyles. "Many of these children experience a turbulent adolescence as a result of these conflicts" (Segal, 1991, p. 236).

Cambodian and Vietnamese immigrants have experienced "multiple traumas, including living in war-torn areas . . . being forced to witness the . . . deaths of loved ones . . . the dangers of escape . . . cultural differences . . . the transition . . . from a rural agrarian . . . to a highly technological urban society . . . family fragmentation . . . and . . . unfamiliar climate" (Amodeo et al., 1996, p. 404). Many experience mental health problems, including "post–traumatic stress disorder," "survivor's guilt," and increasing alcoholism and drug abuse (p. 404). Anxieties of traumatized Cambodian women often appear in physical symptoms, and frequently these symptoms "did not appear until after initial resettlement tasks were accomplished"; there is a need for innovative, culture-specific services for these women (Nicholson and Kay, 1999, p. 470); one such program is described later in this chapter.

Hispanics

The Latino population in this country has been rapidly growing, and is increasing by approximately "400,000 new immigrants a year" (Garcia-Preto, 2005, p. 153). The U.S. Census Bureau reported that there were 39.9 million Hispanics in 2003, as they became this country's "largest race or ethnic minority" (p. 153). This figure does not include the large number of undocumented and illegal migrants residing here. The many Latino children under eighteen "have recently been compared to the baby boomer generation" (p. 153).

The terms Hispanics and Latinos are generally used to describe a group of people that is actually a group of very diverse peoples "who come from different countries with different cultures and sociopolitical histories" (Garcia-Preto, 2005, p. 154); they represent many racial groupings and racial mixtures (Longres, 1995a). Some people from Argentina and Uruguay are descended primarily from Europeans; the Caribbean Island countries and Panama are populated largely by mixed European and African races; Hispanics from Mexico and Central America are often of mixed European and indigenous Indian descent. Longres (1995a) has observed that "most Latinos are ambivalent about race: They are comfortable with mixed races, but they are inclined to celebrate European heritage over any other"; In the United States, there can be "interpersonal barriers among Latinos" based on race (p. 1217). Opinions differ about the names used to designate the Hispanic population. Those involved with political activism tend to use the name Latino, although Hispanic and Latino are often used interchangeably (Longres, 1995a). *Hispanic* has been a recent unifying name; many in this group, however, prefer to refer to their nationalities (Garcia-Preto, 2005; Longres, 1995a).

> Proclaiming their nationality is very important to Latinos; it provides a sense of pride and identity that is reflected in the stories they tell, their music and poetry. Longing for their homeland is more pronounced when they are unable to return to their homes either because they are

here as political exiles, or illegally, or because they are unable to afford the cost of travel. In therapy, asking the question, "What's your country of origin?" and listening to the client's stories of immigration help to engage the family and gives the therapist an opportunity to learn about the country the client left behind, the culture, and the reasons for leaving. (Garcia-Preto, 2005, p. 154)

Socioeconomic factors vary for groups within the Hispanic population (and some variability always exists within each group). Mexican immigrants are "the largest group of Latinos . . . (66.9 percent)" (Garcia-Preto, 2005, p. 158); many are from rural areas, are very poor, and have low levels of education (Garcia-Preto, 2005; Partida, 1996). Most Mexican Americans live in California and the Southwest. Although Mexican-American men have a high employment rate (80 percent), their (frequently) nonskilled jobs are often unsteady and the pay is low. Numbers of illegal immigrants have come to this country to seek work because of the desperate poverty they experienced in Mexico; illegal immigration has become the subject of intense national debate. Controversies, such as the issue of building a fence on our border with Mexico, enacting punitive restrictions (such as imprisonment or deportation) or more humane proposals, such as providing worker permits, and offering citizenship to those illegal immigrants currently here, are major political issues today.

Puerto Ricans, who number about 3.2 million, are the next largest group, living primarily in the Northeast, especially in New York City. They have automatic citizenship, due to Puerto Rico's political status within the United States (Garcia-Preto, 2005); they often move back and forth from the island to the United States.

Most are relegated to an existence of marginality and hold the status of being the poorest among the Latino groups . . . their unemployment rate is also the highest. . . . Drug addiction, alcoholism, and AIDS have also plagued Puerto Ricans both at home and on the mainland. (Garcia-Preto, 2005, p. 159)

Cubans, who represent the third largest Hispanic-American population, have done well economically (Jiménez-Vazques, 1995; Queralt, 1996); most live in Florida, New York, and New Jersey (Garcia-Preto, 2005). Many Cuban refugees arrived in 1959, following Castro's revolution, most of whom were "white, relatively well-educated, middle-class persons of Iberian Spanish extraction" (Queralt, 1996, p. 188); because they were refugees from communism, they received political asylum and aid from the U.S. government. The second group of immigrants, arriving in 1980, known by the "pejorative label" *Marielitos,* "came from a lower socioeconomic background and were more racially mixed." Then in the 1990s, after a serious decline in the Cuban economy, "thousands of Cubans took the risk of reaching this country via makeshift rafts. Many were captured by the United States before reaching land and [were] returned to Guantanamo Bay" (Garcia-Preto, 2005, p. 160).

People from the Dominican Republic, Central America and South America have been coming to the United States in increasing numbers. The Dominicans, who numbered about 1,000,000 in 2000, live mostly in New York City and New Jersey (Garcia-Preto, 2005), and "experience higher levels of poverty and unemployment than other Hispanic people" (Swarns, 1998, A1). A number of Dominicans, however, have done well in business, and of this group, 7 percent have established their own businesses (Williams, 1999). Dominicans have been developing very popular hair salons.

> Much like Koreans who have made nail salons their franchise and Indians, Afghans, and Pakistanis who have made cab driving theirs, Dominican immigrants have made beauty their business in New York, bringing with them their own hair-straightening techniques and home-brewed conditioners.
>
> That many of the Dominican salons' customers are African American has caused tension with African-American beauty salon operators, who resent the competition. Adriano Espaillat, the city's first Dominican assemblyman, commented that no shortage of hair existed: "There's plenty of hair around for everybody. . . . Unless you're like me—going a little bald." (Williams, 1999, A20)

Overall, many Latinos in the United States live in poverty; "jobs are scarce . . . housing is substandard and unaffordable; they have no health benefits; and difficulties with understanding and speaking English often keep them on the periphery . . . one quarter of their children under 18 live in poverty" (Garcia-Preto, 2005, p. 157). There has been an increase in the number of Latino children graduating from high school, but their graduation rate of "57 percent, as compared with 88 percent for non-Hispanic White and 80 percent for African-Americans is still a significant difference (U.S. Bureau of the Census, 2000)" (Garcia-Preto, 2005, p. 157).

The Latino population has made many political gains in this country over the years, which, in turn, have affected the garnering of support for their interests. "From 1976 to 1996, Latinos increased their voter registration by 164 percent, compared with 31 percent for the rest of the nation"

(Dedman, 1999, p. 22). Their vote in 1996 "astounded political experts with both its explosive growth and its unpredictability (Gonzalez, 2000)" (Garcia-Preto, 2005, p. 153). Many Hispanic elected officials now hold office, but, compared to the voter turnout, their number "has not risen so fast" (Dedman, 1999, p. 22).

In the 2006 mid-term elections, according to exit polls, "Hispanics accounted for 8 percent of the total vote. That is about equal to the Hispanic vote's record turnout in the 2004 presidential election, and much more than its turnout in previous mid-term elections" (Oppenheimer, 2006, p. 2). The majority of Hispanics (73 percent) voted for Democratic candidates, as opposed to 26 percent voting for Republicans. This was an increase in democratic support. Oppenheimer attributed these changes to "anti-immigration hysteria spearheaded by Republicans in the House" (p. 5).

Bilingual education, advocated by Hispanics, has been a subject of congressional debate and has been a major political issue in several states. Educational experts disagree about the efficacy of this approach; an underlying concern about reaching this population in an educationally sound manner is the very high school dropout rate across the country for Hispanic children.

In a trend in the opposite direction, many New Yorkers have been studying Spanish, as they feel they can no longer ignore the bilingual nature of New York (Ojito, 1999).

> And non-Hispanic New Yorkers by the thousands, from mothers with babies to office workers, doctors and priests, are responding to the trend in a practical way. They are signing up for Spanish lessons—in their own homes, at work and in night schools. (Ojito, 1999, pp. A1, B4)

Bilingual education remains a conflictual issue in 2007.

Hispanics face problems similar to those of other immigrant groups, including culture shock, assimilation difficulties, and conflicts with their children in terms of traditional (Hispanic) and new (American) cultural values, as well as a range of mental illnesses.

> Living in communities that are infested with crime, drugs, rape, and AIDS, most are frightened, especially for their children. Many are experiencing intense feelings of loss, missing the family they left behind. . . . For a significant number, as in the case of Salvadorans and other Central Americans, the effects of postwar trauma continue to be part of their experience. (Garcia-Preto, 2005, p. 163)

Latina teenage girls are especially "endangered"; they have the highest rates for attempted suicide (usually nonlethal) compared to non-Hispanic black and white teenage girls; the number is higher for "Latinas who are the first generation born in the United States" ("Protecting New Jersey's," 2006, p. A22). Latinas often leave school, become involved with drugs, and have more unmarried pregnancies at very young ages; "federal statistics show that about 24 percent of Latinas are mothers by the age of 20—three times the rate of non-Hispanic white teens" (p. A22). Suicide attempts of Latina teenage girls are discussed further in Chapter 10.

Although a need exists for counseling and mental health services, many Hispanics are reluctant to use these services—in part because they "do not see sharing personal problems with a stranger as being 'curative'" (Partida, 1996, p. 253). Many Hispanics rely on *curanderos* or *curanderas* (folk healers), believed to have supernatural powers, rather than physical or mental health practitioners (Garcia-Preto, 2005; Kilborn, 1999; Ramirez, 1998). On the other hand, Hispanic patients may be approached by clinicians who offer only concrete and limited services, overlooking the possibility that the patients may also be amenable to the insights of appropriately applied psychodynamic approaches.

There are two opposing viewpoints concerning psychotherapy for Latinos; one claiming that this population is not amenable to psychodynamic treatment; the other view asserts that psychodynamic treatment may be very relevant to their problems. Opponents of psychodynamic treatment emphasize Latinos' purported lack of psychological awareness and their propensity for responding to concrete measures (Gelman, 2003).

> The type of stereotypic characteristics ascribed to Latinos, such as concreteness and lack of psychological mindedness, although empirically unsubstantiated . . . have acquired "spurious validity" through constant repetition in the literature . . . several theoretical works report that Latino clients are passive, dependent, will focus on external problems, will establish the therapist as an authority figure, and, in deference be silent. . . . Such reified stereotypes of Latinos lead to views of them as "poor candidates for psychotherapy." (Gelman, 2003, p. 84)

Clinicians who have done psychodynamic therapy with the Latino population find that it can be beneficial "once it is adapted and refined to meet the sociocultural needs of this population, as social work teaches us to do with any framework and for any client" (Gelman, 2003, p. 84). Javier (1996) has observed that psychodynamic treatment that "emphasizes personal exploration gives this [the Hispanic] population a more powerful, respectful, lasting, and effective tool to deal with the vicissitudes of their lives" (p. 98). Mental health services sensitive to the needs of the Hispanic population warrant further development and study (Gelman, 2003).

Social Class

Social class, defined in terms of *social stratification,* ranks people in comparison to others using the following criteria: "the amount of money they earn, the level of education they have completed, the prestige of their occupation, or the prestige conferred on them by others in the community" (Longres, 1995b, p. 75). Social class membership can affect relationships; for example, a professional family might be upset if a daughter marries a factory worker with a high school education; a therapist with a lower-middle class upbringing might feel uncomfortable with an upper-class client.

Even if people belong to a common racial and/or ethnic group, they may react differently to others within their group, based on *class differential.* Brad, for example, was a college student from the African-American upper class whose parents "both held challenging high-profile positions in major corporations" (Miles, 1998, p. 104). When attending an Ivy League college, he encountered interpersonal problems with other African-American students related to class distinctions.

> For the first time in his life, Brad encountered black students from the ghetto. They instantly disliked him, accusing him of being "too white." Because they constituted the largest part of the black university community, Brad had little support. Every part of his character and his socialization were attacked by these students. . . . Soon, Brad wore dreadlocks and baggy clothes, and was dating an inner-city girl with multiple braids in her hair. Brad was seen as an embarrassment to his family. (Miles, 1998, pp. 104-105)

India has a strict caste system, with the lowest caste being the untouchables. Legal changes now protect their rights, better employment opportunities are available to them, and they have greater political power than in the past, although in the minds of many, nothing has changed. To complicate this picture, the untouchable caste is fragmented by constant jockeying for position. The *balmiki* subcaste is at the absolute bottom of the pecking order; they derive their living from cleaning and disposing of human waste. Srichand, a member of this caste, was doing this work when he was murdered on September 2, 1998 (Bearak, 1998).

> Srichand had been chosen for death by a gang of jatavs, another un-
> touchable subcaste that, in the ancient pecking order of India, is a few
> notches above the balmikis. Days before, a balmiki boy had left the
> city with a jatav girl, a departure the balmikis took to be teen-age love
> and the jatavs considered a spiteful kidnapping. (Bearak, 1998, p. A3)

A strike was staged over caste and affirmative action issues in India in
May 2006. Medical students, concerned about the reduction of the scarce
number of places available to them, objected to the government's decision
to increase the quotas for colleges and medical school admission for those
in "certain 'backward' castes . . . [who are] known in the bizarre parlance
of Indian bureaucracy as 'other backward classes', or O.B.C.'s." Although
"caste no longer necessarily determines a person's vocation, it does determine to a large extent whom one marries, dines with and, most important
for this debate, votes for"; these "other backward castes" have influential
voting power (Sengupta, 2006, p. A3).

Social class issues can affect treatment relationships as well as treatment
alternatives offered to clients. At times, the mental health field has discriminated against the poor, as against Hispanics, on the premise that they are not
amenable to psychotherapy; however, with appropriate approaches, they
can benefit from clinical treatment (Javier, 1996).

> I have witnessed the growth of many of my poor patients who were able
> to take advantage of psychoanalytic interventions in various degrees.
> Many required a period of didactic approach in which they learned a
> new "conceptual matrix," that is, a verbal reformulation of their symp-
> toms and the importance of their personal dynamic history. . . . They
> were, however, eventually able to appreciate the importance of insights
> for the modification of their conditions. Other poor patients came into
> the treatment situation with a great deal of curiosity about and desire
> for understanding their own internal world. (Javier, 1996, p. 99)

The social class of clients is often overlooked in undertaking a psychosocial assessment; however, the realities and the perceptions of their social
class membership may be a significant treatment issue.

IMMIGRATION

Akhtar (1995), an immigrant from India and a psychoanalyst, discusses
the experience of immigration, which entails many losses but also offers an

opportunity for psychological growth; *internal immigration,* in which a person moves to a culturally different region within the same country may pose similar stresses and opportunities.

> Leaving one's country involves profound losses. Often one has to give up familiar food, native music, unquestioned social customs, and even one's language. The new country offers strange-tasting food, new songs, different political concerns, unfamiliar language, pale festivals, unknown heroes, psychically unearned history, and a visually unfamiliar landscape. However, alongside the various losses is a renewed opportunity for psychic growth and alteration. New channels of self-expression become available. There are new identification models, different superego dictates, and different ideals. One thing is clear: immigration results in a sudden change from an "average expectable environment" (Hartmann) to a strange and unpredictable one. (Akhtar, 1995, p. 1052)

Giving up one's native language for English can be a painful experience. Freud, an immigrant escaping from Nazi Germany to England in late life, wrote in a letter:

> "Perhaps, you have omitted the one point that the emigrant feels so particularly painfully. It is—one can only say—the loss of the language in which one had lived and thought, and which one will never be able to replace with another for all one's efforts at empathy." (Akhtar, 1995, p. 1069)

Developing an ability to speak as well as to feel and think in another language is one aspect of identity change. An indicator that this is happening is the "increasing dominance of the acquired language, which begins to appear in spontaneous humor, dreams, and in talking in one's sleep" (Akhtar, 1995, p. 1070).

An immigrant's proficiency in using the English language needs to be assessed, as an insufficient command of English or preoccupation with correct usage can detract from the clinical encounter. Some clients may need bilingual therapists or benefit from an interpreter. Even for bilingual clients, different meanings may attach to words in their language that may have a different meaning for an English speaking therapist. Clinicians have often "assumed that verbal fluency in a second language represents lockstep translation of an experience (distant or recent) 'lived' in the native tongue . . . that languages function as interchangeable verbal modules for the expression of the same ideas" (Pérez Foster, 1998, p. 6). Pérez Foster (1998) recommends that the intricate and often subtle aspects of bilingual clinical work be given special attention and study.

The acculturation process is complex; people vary in the degree to which they remain embedded in their native cultures, become acclimated, or develop a new bicultural identity. Assimilation can produce stress in families, as members may be in different places along this spectrum. Partida (1996) describes family conflict in Mexican immigrants.

> Because children . . . are able to learn the new language much easier than the parents, they become the holders of power, knowledge and control, a fact that often leaves parents disempowered and feeling unable to follow through with limit setting. . . .
>
> The adults' incapability corrodes the child's ethnic pride and identification. (Partida, 1996, p. 246)

The host country's attitude strongly impacts the adaptation of immigrants (Akhtar, 1995): Are they welcomed or resented? Do they receive political asylum and resettlement programs, or are they rejected and "hunted down," as illegal immigrants? Do immigrants have support from family and others from their culture after arrival, or are they isolated?

In 2005-2006, immigration, specifically the presence of more than 11 million illegal immigrants in the United States, surfaced as a major social and political issue. Competing interests were involved; many businesses and farms wanted immigrant laborers to work at jobs that Americans were unwilling to take. There were national security concerns about controlling the borders; federal legislation to build a security fence between the United States and Mexico was signed into law in October 2006. Conservatives generally supported restrictive laws imposing penalties on both immigrations and employers who hired them (Hulse and Swarns, 2006). More liberal lawmakers favored granting temporary worker permits and giving citizenship to illegal immigrants already residing here (Swarns, 2006).

The country is divided on this issue; some support civil rights and the humane treatment of immigrants; others want them deported. Groups of citizens have acted as vigilantes, patrolling the border or employment agencies where immigrants gather, and harassing them, attempting to photograph them in order to send their pictures to governmental agencies (McCarthy, 2005).

Many immigrants, legal and illegal, live in fear. The cutbacks in medical care to immigrants is one example of the spreading negative attitudes toward this group. In 2005, approximately "80 bills in 20 states sought to cut non-citizens' access to health care or other services, or to require benefit agencies to tell the authorities about applicants with immigration violations"; as a result, "more and more immigrants are delaying care or retreating into a parallel universe of bootleg remedies and unlicensed practitioners" (Bernstein, 2006, p. A1).

Immigrants bring with them a past that may be traumatic and that might also include troubled relationships or psychological instability prior to specific war and immigration trauma. They may, in addition, encounter stressful psychosocial problems in adaptation to the United States. It is, therefore, not unusual to see immigrants manifest a variety of psychiatric problems, including post–traumatic stress disorder, substance abuse (Amodeo et al., 1996), and depression (Kinzie, Leung, and Boehnlein, 1996). In August 1999, for example, a forty-one-year-old man from Sri Lanka, who lived in Toronto for ten years, jumped to his death in the path of a subway train, holding his three-year-old son, who also died. He had a history of depression (Elliott and Bourette, 1999). A spokesman for a community organization who had counseled Sri Lankan refugees noted that:

> Immigrants are particularly vulnerable to depression and often do not seek help. . . . Depression . . . reaches a certain level and then it bursts . . . adapting to a new culture and often a new social status while trying to support a family can be overwhelming. (Elliott and Bourette, 1999, p. A5)

Domestic violence can also be seen in immigrant families; many women may choose to keep this "family secret," and some may be fearful of the repercussions of reporting it. A "pervasive myth," is that "domestic violence does not exist in the Asian community"; but it does indeed exist (Masaki and Wong, 1997, p. 439). This presents special complications for Asian female immigrants who may depend on sponsors who are their batterers. "The batterers use this as another means of control: 'If you leave me, I'll get you deported!'" (p. 444). The Marriage Fraud Amendment Act of 1990 offers special protections to women in this situation.

Immigrants, as other minority persons, may find that:

> Knowing and experiencing more than one world not only presents significant challenges, it also offers richer possibilities—more flexibility and a different set of alternatives and choices given a supportive family and community resources. In fact, Latino adolescents who

sustain an integrated bicultural identity show the best levels of psychosocial adjustment. (Mattei, 1996, p. 237)

Gains can be made through the acculturation process, as the person's
identity undergoes a metamorphosis and becomes a "hybrid" identity, with
a new richness and new possibilities (Akhtar, 1995). However, change does
not come easily, nor is it without pain and ambivalence. Akhtar describes
his own immigrant experiences in a poem, as seen in these excerpts.

> Like the fish who chose to live on a tree,
> We writhe in foolish agony.
> Our gods reduced to grotesque exhibits.
> Our poets mute, pace in the empty halls of our conversation.
> The silk of our mother tongue banned from the fabric
> Of our dreams,
>
> Forsaking the grey abodes and sunken graves of
> Our ancestors, we have come to live in
> A world without seasons.

(Akhtar, 1995, p. 1077)

Akhtar (1995) wrote this poem nine years after his immigration. Now,
twelve years later, he has written a more optimistic paper. He ponders the
meaning of this contrast, while acknowledging that this paper "reveals the
advance in my own mourning process" (p. 1078).

> What does including this poem in the paper indicate? Continued pain
> or its mastery or some combination of both? More important, why is it
> that I expressed my pain of loss in poetry and my pride over mastery
> of this loss in prose? (Akhtar, 1995, p. 1078)

This is reminiscent of the reflections of Jan Morris (1997) after her successful male-to-female sexual transformation. She wonders whether she has
found "the real purpose of my pilgrimage, the last solution to my Conundrum?" (Morris, 1997, p. 160). Both Jan Morris and Salman Akhtar have
made major pilgrimages; both are forever changed, and continue to wonder
about the impact of these changes as they contemplate the complexities of
their lives.

As clinical social workers, we have the opportunity to explore with others their nuanced responses to major transitions. People who have made

major journeys in life have much to teach us about change, identity, culture, loss, despair, resilience, and hope.

DEVELOPING NEW CULTURES

The concept of culture "incorporates all the symbolic meanings—the beliefs, values, norms, and traditions—that are shared in a community and govern social interactions among community members or between members and outsiders" (Longres, 1995b, p. 74). Cultures are usually discussed in ethnic, racial, and religious terms, with the recent addition of gay and lesbian cultures. New cultures, however, constantly emerge; some are relatively small but people's identifications and feelings of connectedness become intertwined.

One group that has come together and developed a distinctive culture is the deaf; they have developed their own language (American Sign Language or ASL) and in addition to this "a body of shared knowledge, shared beliefs, cherished narratives and images, which soon constituted a rich and distinctive culture" (Sacks, 1989, p. 136).

Other developing cultures include religious sects, cults, and gangs; one recent cult, the Heaven's Gate sect, ended with the mass suicide of its leader and members.

The Culture of the Deaf

Deafness has almost universally been seen as a major disability; to Helen Keller being deaf was more difficult than being blind: "'Blindness cuts people off from things, ... Deafness cuts people off from people'" (Dolnick, 1993, p. 37). Alexander Graham Bell, whose mother was deaf, saw deafness as a "swindle and a privation and a tragedy" and his technological advances to help the deaf as being in the service of "'correcting' God's blunders, and in general, 'improving on' nature" (Sacks, 1989, p. 149).

A major breakthrough in education for the deaf was associated with the founding of the American Asylum at Hartford by Laurent Clerc and Thomas Gallaudet in 1817. American Sign Language (ASL) was introduced and became the model for other schools for the deaf in the United States. These schools were mostly residential, and their students' involvement in these communities helped lessen their feelings of isolation, and aided the transmission of deaf culture. Many of the graduates would live near the schools or sometimes work there. Sacks (1989) refers to the 1840s as the "'golden age'" of the development of deaf culture and community (p. 139).

In 1857, Thomas Gallaudet's son, Edward (who, like Bell, had a deaf mother and who learned sign language as a child), was instrumental in founding the first college for the deaf (established in 1864), later called Gallaudet College. However, during the 1860s, a serious controversy developed about educating the deaf. Gallaudet, who strongly favored sign language, was opposed by Alexander Graham Bell, who believed signing should be prohibited. Although Gallaudet College was very successful in producing academically qualified graduates, the battle to use sign language was lost upon Gallaudet's death.

Sacks (1989) asserts that for the seventy-five years following the 1880s, the "suppression of sign . . . had a deleterious effect on the deaf . . . not only on their education . . . but on their image of themselves and on their entire community and culture" (p. 139). ASL has made a strong comeback, and Sacks credits the student strike at Gallaudet in 1988 as being a major factor in further increasing deaf pride and activism.

The issue at the heart of the strike was the students' request for a deaf president of Gallaudet. Although Gallaudet was "the only liberal arts college for the deaf in the world" it "in all its 124 years . . . has never had a deaf president" (Sacks, 1989, p. 125). The students' protest was successful: The hearing president resigned and was replaced by King Jordan, the Dean of the School of Arts and Sciences, who had been deaf since he was twenty-one. Although there was general jubilation at this event, some dissent occurred "since he was postlingually deaf" (i.e., he was not deaf prior to the onset of language, an important distinction in deaf culture) (p. 157).

Sacks (1989), a neurologist, first visited Gallaudet in 1986 and 1987 and found it "an astonishing and moving experience" (p. 127).

> I had never before seen an entire community of the deaf, nor had I quite realized . . . that Sign might indeed be a complete language—a language equally suitable for making love or speeches, for flirtation or mathematics. . . . I had to see the absolutely silent mathematics department at work; to see deaf bards, Sign poetry . . . and the range and depth of the Gallaudet theater; I had to see the wonderful social scene in the student bar, with hands flying in all directions as a hundred separate conversations proceeded—I had to see all this for myself before I could be moved from my previous "medical" view of deafness (as a "condition," a deficit, that had to be treated) to a "cultural" view of the deaf as forming a community with a complete language and culture of its own. I had felt there was something very joyful, even Arcadian about Gallaudet. (Sacks, 1989, p. 127)

For many deaf people, deafness is part of their identity, not something they wish to have fixed, and, however well intended, trying to fit the deaf into the world of the hearing can in fact "imprison them in a zone of silence" (Dolnick, 1993, p. 43). To some, for example, the idea of a cochlear implant to diminish deafness is anathema. The editors of *Deaf Life* have expressed their opposition to implants (Dolnick, 1993): "'An implant is the . . . ultimate denial of deafness, the ultimate refusal to let deaf children be Deaf'" (p. 43).

The issue of separation or integration of deaf people with hearing people is a major point of contention; groups for the disabled have long fought for mainstreaming and integration, whereas concern has been expressed by the deaf community about the disappearance of residential schools for the deaf and about the integration of deaf children into the public school system, where they may not have other deaf children with whom to associate.

The deaf culture does not represent all people who are deaf, although its influence predominates. People who have lost their hearing later in life "miss their earlier access to spoken communication, and they miss sound" (Luey, Glass, and Elliott, 1995, p. 179). For many of these people, "deafness is both a disability and a loss; it is something to be mourned" (p. 180). Not all deaf people (including those who are prelingually deaf) prefer sign language; some prefer other types of communication, including lip reading or cued speech, "which is phonetically based and uses hand-shapes to represent specific speech sounds" (p. 179). These preferential differences in communication can give rise to intense disputes between different factions of the deaf world.

Such a dispute arose at Gallaudet in 2006, surrounding the appointment of a new President, following the resignation of King Jordan, who, by then, had been President for eighteen years. Dr. Jane Fernandez, the president-designate, was ultimately denied this position by the Board of Trustees, following months of "widening and unrelenting protests by students, faculty, alumni and advocates" (Schemo, 2006, p. A1). She was in favor of technological advances for the deaf, as well as accepting spoken language at Gallaudet, a policy not acceptable to the protesters. Although Dr. Fernandez was born deaf, she spoke English, and did not learn sign language until she was twenty-three, which was "too late for some opponents" (Cloud, 2006, p. 64). This upset at Gallaudet

> erupted at a time of sweeping change in the deaf world, with technological advances like cochlear implants and more effective hearing aids being felt by those in the forefront of the deaf-rights movement as an assault on deaf culture and deaf identity. (Schemo, 2006, p. A1)

In clinical work with deaf people, comprehensive psychosocial assessments should include understanding the meaning of deafness in their lives, their degree and nature of involvement (or noninvolvement) with the deaf community, and their attitudes toward deafness as an identity issue.

The Heaven's Gate Sect

Cults stir as much controversy among people, as trying to define them does; they are typically viewed as "small, unorthodox, possibly dangerous fringe groups whose members are influenced by a charismatic leader" (Robbins, 1995, p. 667). The use of the term "'new religious movements' (NRMs) [attempts] to avoid the pejorative connotation of the term 'cult'. . . [but] there are no universally accepted distinctions between NRMs and other religious groups" (p. 667). Negative reactions to cults arose in the mid-1970s, and dramatically increased in 1978 after the Jonestown, Guyana, mass suicides and/or murders in which over 900 people died (Lacayo, 1997). An active anticult movement has developed that includes people whose children are cultists (Robbins, 1995); cults, however, continue to proliferate.

The Heaven's Gate sect received national attention in the spring of 1997, when its thirty-nine members committed suicide in Southern California. This sect, as other cultures, had mutually shared "symbolic meanings—the beliefs, values, norms, and traditions" (Longres, 1995b, p. 74), which coincided with the coming millennium and the appearance of the highly visible Hale-Bopp comet.

The "charismatic" leader of this cult, Marshall Applewhite, left a suicide note discussing the group's action ("Statements That Heaven's Gate," 1997). In one excerpt he wrote that:

> We came from the Level Above Human in distant space and we have now exited the bodies that we were wearing for our earthly task, to return to the world from whence we came—task completed. The distan[t] space we refer to is what you[r] literature would call the Kingdom of Heaven, or Kingdom of God. ("Statements That Heaven's Gate," 1997, p. A12)

Some members had been in the sect for twenty years; others had joined more recently. They were an integrated group in terms of race, ethnicity, gender, and social class; "they were rich and poor, black, white and Latino—people who shared little more than willingness, or a need, to suspend disbelief, and in the end to participate in a common death" (Gleick, 1997, p. 31).

The Heaven's Gate group, as most cults are, was tightly organized and all aspects of life were controlled by Applewhite and his doctrines. "They woke at predetermined intervals to pray. They ate the same food at the same hours. They wore short haircuts and shapeless clothing" (Bruni, 1997, p. 1). Applewhite and five of his male followers were castrated; "shedding any signs of sexuality was integral to the cult" (Gleick, 1997, p. 32). Group members renounced "sex, drugs, alcohol, their birth names, and all relationships with family and friends, [so that] disciples could become ready to ascend to space" (p. 34). Galanter (1982) asserts that religious sects typically have a "shared belief that members' work is devoted to some grand plan . . . the basis for the mystical manipulation of members' activities" (p. 1542).

Examining the nature of sects affords insight into the close interactions between individual and group psychology; it illuminates how cult members can accept a group belief system that supersedes their personal autonomy and takes precedence over family, friends, and life itself. From a psychodynamic perspective, it has been observed that people can be driven to join cults by their own inner needs, such as psychological turmoil and a paucity of social ties. "Their preoccupations with purpose and destiny are closely associated to a dissatisfaction with interpersonal relations, leading to loneliness and a sense of alienation" (Galanter, 1982, p. 1539).

For many, cults may provide multiple selfobjects (i.e., the reliance on others to meet unsatisfied inner needs, especially pertaining to attachment and self-esteem). Research findings suggest that charismatic cults may aid some members in dealing with psychological problems, leading to remission of substance abuse, improved self-esteem, and an enhanced capacity for social relationships (Galanter, 1982).

THE IMPACT OF CULTURAL ISSUES ON CLINICAL SOCIAL WORK

Not understanding diverse cultural attitudes and values can adversely affect clinical work, resulting in: inaccurate biopsychosocial assessments; failure to comprehend clients' motivation and perceptions of treatment; clashes between clinicians and clients over values and lifestyles; and complications in transference and countertransference issues (especially when cultural factors are not openly discussed).

Biopsychosocial Assessments

Behavior can be misinterpreted if it is viewed as pathological, when it may be simply culture-specific. A man could be thought to be delusional, for example, if he serves tea to his dead father and holds conversations with him. However, if this man is Japanese, he may be acting in accordance with his cultural belief that the dead are involved with the living and "the departed continue to be experienced as being alive" (Freeman, 1998, p. 53).

> A 39-year-old Haitian man is sent to the psychiatric emergency room by the police because "he was sitting in the park looking stoned and talking to himself." Upon assessment, the patient gave no evidence of substance abuse or psychosis. He stated that he had been in a healing trance brought on by the incantations of a *houngan* (voodoo priest). The man expressed the fear that another *houngan* wished to "put me in the coffin and make him his slave." (Pies and Keast, 1995, p. 14)

The cultural perspective informs us that "the basic Haitian mind-set is shaped within the voodoo . . . religious beliefs and practices that [remain] the central focus of Haitian life" (Bastien, 1995, p. 1149). In addition, hallucinations may be found in "normal, non-psychotic Hispanic individuals exposed to a variety of stressors" (Pies and Keast, 1995, p. 14); hallucinations are also accepted in other cultural groups, such as the Chinese, who view them as a normal event, and consider them to be "possession by ancestors speaking for the family" (Gee and Ishii, 1997, p. 232).

Nonverbal behaviors often provide diagnostic insight; however, these behaviors may be culturally determined rather than clinically significant. Haitians, for example, maintain eye contact with a person in conversation, but they "look away when they are listening. Prolonged eye contact is considered to be staring and, in the case of young children, disrespectful" (Bastien, 1995, p. 1152).

On the other hand, pathology can be overlooked in the effort to be bias free; behaviors and symptoms may be erroneously ascribed to cultural factors (Solomon, 1992). "Thus, a therapist facing an Asian American who is withdrawn may consider such behavior typical of Asian American peoples instead of recognizing it as a sign of possible depression" (p. 374). A complication in distinguishing what is cultural and what is pathological is the fact that cultures are not constant; "they can and sometimes do change rapidly"; assessing culture's role can cause "mischief for students of psychopathology across cultures" (Westermeyer, 1985, p. 803).

Having an open and inquiring mind about cultural influences, using supervision and consultation when needed, and learning from clients can enhance understanding of cultural complexities in clinical work. Furthermore, in formulating a tentative biopsychosocial assessment, one can outline questions about puzzling cultural and psychological dilemmas that need further exploration in ongoing active interactions with the client.

Culture-Bound Syndromes

Some psychiatric syndromes may be culture bound and found only in specific cultures or groups (Kaplan, Sadock, and Grebb, 1994). Windigo, for example, is a condition that can be found among Native American Indians. It is a "fear of being turned into a cannibal through possession by a supernatural monster, the windigo" (Kaplan, Sadock, and Grebb, 1994, p. 190). *Grisi siknis,* observed in the Miskito of Nicaragua, involves "headache, anxiety, irrational anger toward people nearby, aimless running and falling down" (Westermeyer, 1985, p. 799).

In Japan, during the past ten years, the phenomenon of *"hikikomori"* (translated as "withdrawal") has developed at an alarming rate; in this "culture-bound syndrome," young men withdraw into their rooms at home where they remain, with no outside social involvement, sometimes for years (Jones, 2006, p. 48). Although some females have this problem, approximately 80 percent of the estimated 100,000-320,000 people (perhaps up to one million) who suffer from it are male. The longer this persists, the more difficult it is to reverse. The etiology of this syndrome is not known. Dr. Tamaki Saito, an expert on this problem, has stated that it is "largely a family and social disease, caused in part by the interdependence of Japanese parents and children and the pressure on boys, eldest sons in particular, to excel in academics and the corporate world" (p. 49). In other cultures, young men might actively rebel from social constraints, "but in Japan, where uniformity is still prized and reputations and outward appearances are paramount, rebellion comes in muted forms, like hikikomori" (p. 49).

Treatment Issues

Cultural identifications and behaviors can influence willingness to accept help, and transference, countertransference, and intersubjectivity issues. The "cross-cultural clinical arena charged with its terrors, suspicions, and disavowed prejudices, provides some of the most fertile spaces for minds to collide and collude in their attempts to know each other" (Pérez Foster, 1999, p. 270).

Clients' Response to Clinical Services

Although the clinical services encountered in the United States are, generally speaking, a product of Western culture, people from many cultures can benefit from psychodynamically based therapeutic approaches, if the help offered is sensitive to each client's cultural issues. Parenthetically, it should be noted that many other cultures offer their own forms of psychotherapy and healing provided by healers, including shamans, "witch" doctors, medicine men, and *curanderos;* turning to a healer may not necessarily be a foreign experience. Common elements cut across the varieties of healing, including support, acceptance, receiving directives, abreaction, and gaining strength from belief in the power of the healing person. Native healers may use "techniques of confession, atonement, and absolution" (Ramirez, 1998, p. 174), which are akin in some ways to standard therapeutic practices in this country. The healer is often a religious figure in other cultures, but adding the dimension of spirituality to clinical encounters has recently been advocated by some clinicians in the United States.

The basic social work rule should apply to cross-cultural work: Start where clients are, and learn what receiving help means to them, as well as their conceptions of how this help works. It is often assumed that middle-class white Americans are sophisticated about clinical services, while those from minority cultures are not. The reverse may be the case; furthermore, people can be educated to engage in the role of the client in the therapy situation.

Cambodian immigrants, while often suffering from loss, grief, and post–traumatic stress disorder, may have difficulty asking for help to overcome these problems (Nicholson and Kay, 1999). "Because there is no comparable human services system in Cambodia, most Cambodians view requesting human services as an inappropriate and shameful solution" (p. 470). Nicholson and Kay (1999) found that some Cambodian women were responsive to a support group where cultural issues were recognized; group activities were used to engage them and help them feel "more cohesive and less isolated" (p. 474). Direct skills were taught (such as learning how to ride the subway, use the telephone, and shop); health needs were discussed, as well as their interest in learning English; they were enabled to reach out to support networks in their own communities. The women brought Cambodian food to each session; having lunch together became an important ritual. One of the therapists was an American social worker; the other was a Cambodian who translated Khmer into English during group sessions.

Ultimately, the women were able to talk about their painful grief and loss issues, expressing feelings that they had never shared before "without . . . the somatic symptoms that had previously caused them to flee the room" (Nicholson and Kay, 1999, p. 475).

Clash of Values

Some therapists have been successful in integrating folk practices with traditional therapy. In one project, physicians and medicine men collaborated to treat North American Indian patients; in another, efforts were made to incorporate methods used by Puerto Rican *espiritistas* into traditional health and mental health services (Ramirez, 1998). Buddhist monks have consulted and collaborated with mental health workers on behalf of Southeast Asians with substance abuse problems (Amodeo et al., 1996).

The clinician and client can find themselves in conflict over competing cultural values. Should a therapist advocate for greater freedom for Americanized teenagers while their Hispanic or Asian-Indian families value exerting greater control and protectiveness? A therapist's strong convictions that religious issues are private matters belonging outside therapy, might conflict with some Hispanic clients who want faith healers involved in their treatment.

One cultural dilemma arose in treating Mrs. P., a Jamaican woman with a panic disorder: The patient avoided discussion of her marital problems, which were at the core of her panic (Watts-Jones, 1992). Mrs. P.'s husband had strong patriarchal expectations, traditional in their culture, and placed a number of restrictions on his wife's activities outside the home; he also refused to talk to the therapist, who felt that the wife would not get well unless she asserted some autonomy. The therapist was torn between deferring to the client's cultural norms and confronting the way that might reinforce her dysfunctional patterns (Watts-Jones, 1992).

> Clearly, traditional Jamaican values were a central issue. . . . My own values about gender roles . . . were in marked conflict with the client system. . . . It was important to insure that my therapeutic approach was not simply clinical imperialism. (Watts-Jones, 1992, p. 109)

When the therapist decided to share this dilemma with Mrs. P., as a collaborator in the therapy, Mrs. P. chose to work toward developing a more egalitarian relationship with her husband and broadening her outside activities. Marital tensions continued. Although Mrs. P. wanted to have a good marriage, she did not want, at the same time, to jeopardize the possibility of her own improved functioning; the decision to tackle the client's cultural norms must be made carefully and collaboratively (Watts-Jones, 1992).

Conflicts Relating to Treatment Issues

An example of conflict in clinical practice between a "political agenda" and a psychodynamic orientation was observed in the case of Amanda, a fourteen-year-old African-American girl who saw both her mother and her brother murdered in a poverty-stricken neighborhood where murder was endemic (Frank, 1996). Amanda was an intelligent teenager with good ego functioning who was referred for counseling when her schoolwork began to deteriorate. She did not want to see the African-American social worker who was assigned to her because of her race; "her loathing of people of color was expressed in an unbridled way" (p. 69). She responded very positively to the "white, blond-haired" social worker, Adele, and "disclosed her own deep wish to be white" (p. 69). Amanda's wishes were in conflict with the agency's goals, which placed emphasis on children developing a positive racial identity.

> Adele [the clinician] . . . had to cope with veiled resentment and dis-approval from her African-American colleagues that she had been as-signed to work with Amanda after Amanda's refusal to work with the first therapist. . . . She was subtly admonished for not focusing on Amanda's hatred of her color. She was urged not to comply with her patient's wish to walk along Newbury Street . . . [Boston's chic shop-ping street], where she would admire the white mannequins and re-mark on the peaceful looks on their faces. (Frank, 1996, p. 70)

Adele did go to Newbury Street with Amanda, where the teen's story and her grief slowly unfolded. Amanda expressed her conviction that her mother was killed because she was black. "If we were rich and white and didn't live in Roxbury maybe none of this would have happened to my family" (Frank, 1996, p. 72). She also thought that her mother died because she (Amanda) was "bad and ugly," and later concluded that "the bad in her life was due to being black" (p. 72). She ultimately was able to integrate her losses into her life and her self-image; she wrote the following story about herself (Frank, 1996) in the guise of a little girl who had "shielded herself from . . . pain through hatred of herself, her neighborhood, and her race. . . . Eventually the little girl felt her pain and her friend [the therapist] could feel it too" (p. 73). By learning to "live with her loss and the fact that she would never really understand it," she could "live with these awarenesses [and] didn't have to keep her false explanations" (p. 73).

The agency was concerned about Amanda's rejection of her racial iden-tity; they did not understand that her "racial split . . . was a defense" (Frank,

1996, p. 74). Paradoxically, however, when her grief was resolved, her distorted perceptions of herself and her racial identity were also resolved. This case discussion points out the hazards of allowing the political to override clinical considerations. Frank (1996) wrote this chapter "with a sense of urgency" because "psychoanalytic concepts are no longer studied in depth" (p. 74). Amanda chose to accept her racial identification; but what if she had chosen not to do so? Should clients have the right to accept or not to accept fully (or in part) their ethnic identities? If Amanda chose never to accept her racial identity fully, should she be free to make this decision?

Cultural Aspects of Transference and Intersubjectivity

The self of the clinician is involved in the treatment relationship on multiple levels. Although it has long been acknowledged that therapists' reactions to their clients are colored by the personality characteristics of each, attention has been paid more recently to the way in which social characteristics, such as ethnic and cultural issues, may also affect the therapeutic relationship; complex issues can arise when working with people from different cultures as well as when working with people from within the same culture.

Working with people from different cultures. Working with people who are ethnoculturally different can set off strong emotional reactions in either partner of the therapeutic dyad and "frequently provides more opportunities for empathic and dynamic stumbling blocks, in what might be termed 'ethnocultural disorientation'" (Comas-Diaz and Jacobsen, 1991, p. 392). A tendency exists on the part of some therapists to attribute any of the patient's comments about differences to "defense and resistance. However, . . . we have found that this approach hinders the exploration of conflicts related to ethnicity and culture" (p. 392). This principle also applies to other types of differences between the clinician and client, including disability, gender, sexual orientation, and so on.

Working with people from the same culture. Members of minorities are often recruited to receive mental health training to enable them to help clients from their own cultures. In Israel, for example, ultra-Orthodox Jews enrolled in a three-year (nonreligious) social work program, which was very unusual, as secular education is not accepted by this group (Sontag, 1999). However, these ultra-Orthodox men *(haredim)* were responding to the need for professional help with serious social problems arising in their communities.

In addition to breaching the iron gate between the haredi world and the universities, the social work program will create a professional cadre of ultra-Orthodox social workers, who can better understand the cultural and religious norms of the haredi world. There are a few ultra-Orthodox women who are social workers, but in a society rigidly divided by sex, there was an especially great need for male professionals. (Sontag, 1999, p. A5)

Cofesí (2002), a Latina psychoanalyst, speaks of the advantages of working with Latina clients. Although noting that "there is the danger that analytic neutrality will be sacrificed to overidentification with the patient's social reality," she observes the advantages of matching Latina analyst and patient, as she describes her work with her Latina patient Delores.

The similarity in our shared bicultural experience elicits what could be called a fellow-immigrant countertransference; our shared bicultural experiences evoke a fantasy of we-ness, allaying feelings of self-other differences that may be more readily pronounced in cross-cultural interactions. The analysis takes place mostly in English. We shift to Spanish when an idea or feeling state cannot be as well represented in English. Our shared proficiency in two languages also contributes to the transference-countertransference experience of sameness. (Cofesí, 2002, p. 446)

Working with clients from within the same culture can raise special countertransference issues for therapists who might have unresolved problems about their own cultural identities. What Pérez Foster (1999) found "most disturbing" were "treatment failures" with individuals from her own Caribbean background, who "somehow detected in me the probable confusion I felt at the time about my own bicultural identity" (p. 273).

Mehta (1998), an Asian-Indian therapist, found problems in treating people from her own ethnicity, such as the patient's tendency to attempt to control the therapist, especially when she worked with parents who were having difficulties with their children.

A common rescue fantasy is elicited based on a pseudo-bond of one immigrant helping another in a foreign country. . . . However, there is also a rapid fantasy formation of parents having control over the Indian therapist. . . . Nina's parents' immediate overt comfort with me as a fantasy family member and physician for their daughter gave way later to subtle derogation of the psychoanalytic framework of time and money . . . a sense of disappointment in me for being too "Americanized" in order to defend against their own personal difficulties with limit setting. (Mehta, 1998, p. 150)

A Bedouin-Arab social worker in a Mideastern country faced a literally life and death situation when he started to work with a seventeen-year-old unmarried, pregnant Bedouin-Arab woman who was a member of his village (although he had not known her previously) (Al-Krenawi, 1999).

> In Bedouin-Arab society, it is common for women caught in pre- or extramarital affairs to be killed by an immediate family member in order to preserve *Ar*, or family honor, and to erase the shame that was perceived to have been brought to the family. (Al-Krenawi, 1999, p. 489)

When Al-Krenawi first met with this client, he found himself in great emotional turmoil.

> I had two years' practice experience and had never encountered a problem of such complexity. I was shocked by the story and had feelings of anger toward the man who had put this woman in such a situation; but I also found that I was angry too at the woman who had violated cultural values of premarital chastity. The client's story raised many questions. . . . I felt that this case "put me in the corner." I did not know what to do. During the meeting with the client, I asked her, "how come you did that? Were you blind?" I criticized what she had done. I forgot my role as a social worker and spoke to her from my membership in the Bedouin-Arab culture. (Al-Krenawi, 1999, p. 490)

Al-Krenawi (1999) realized that he was in conflict with his professional values, knowing that he was "trained to respect the client and treat her with empathy and support" (p. 490); he decided to place his professional values above his personal beliefs. He felt that he could not "stand aside while the girl was exposed to her family and murdered, as she surely would have been—[this would be] far worse than my own moral dilemma" (p. 491). Al-Krenawi's decision also posed a personal risk to him: "I would incur considerable damage to my personal and professional reputation" (p. 491).

His interventions were successful: the woman, removed to a shelter, had her baby (who died three days later, before adoption could be effected); she returned to her community and ultimately married and had children.

Al-Krenawi feels that although his dilemmas were unique to his culture, there is an applicability to other situations, as "practitioners in many other non-Western cultures or socially marginal groups must also face cases where they must weigh the health or life of a client against the traditional values and norms of their own and their clients' communities" (Al-Krenawi, 1999, p. 494).

CONCLUSION

In this chapter, we have examined the roles of diversity and its relationship to human behavior and clinical work, and that race, ethnicity, social class, and culture are important variables to understand when working with people. We have seen how strong ethnic identifications and cultural beliefs can be guiding principles in life and in the formation of social relationships, and how sometimes these beliefs can take precedence over life itself. We have observed that individuals grapple with cultural constraints and sometimes rebel and form new meanings for themselves. The constructivist framework illuminates how people uniquely create meaning in their lives and interpret their own cultures and ethnicities.

In keeping with the basic premise of this book, that life is complex and full of enigmas and conundrums, we have looked beneath the surface of some cultural customs and beliefs to see underlying conflicts, dilemmas, and uncertainties people face in accommodating to cultural demands and expectations. A psychodynamic approach remains important in understanding cultural phenomena, as inner worlds and affective lives of people are universally present, although myriad variations exist in the expression of feelings and in patterns of behavior.

Culture is transmitted first through family experiences, as psychologically unformed children are socialized to adapt to the world around them.

LEARNING EXERCISE

Discuss the advantages and drawbacks of assigning clients to clinicians who have similar cultural backgrounds. Role-playing exercises involving an aspect of culture that affects family relationships may be developed in small groups to present to the class. For example, a scenario can be included depicting cultural rituals and customs and/or a situation reflecting cultural conflict among family members. Similar scenarios involving client-clinician interactions can also be developed.

SUGGESTED READING

Articles

Dolnick, E. 1993. Deafness as culture. *The Atlantic Monthly* 272 (September/3): 37-53.
Drachman, D. 1995. Immigration statuses and their influence on service provision, access, and use. *Social Work* 40: 188-197.

Gelman, C. R. 2003. Psychodynamic treatment of Latinos: A critical review of the theoretical literature and practice outcome research. *Psychoanalytic Social Work* 10: 79-102.

Keefe, P. R. 2006. The snakehead. *The New Yorker* April 24: 68, 70, 73-74, 76, 78, 80-82, 84-85.

Books

Akhtar, S. 1999. *Immigration and identity: Turmoil, treatment, and transformation.* Northvale, NJ: Jason Aronson.

Hogan, L. 1990. *Mean spirit.* New York: Ivy Books.

Jackson, L. C., and B. Greene. 2000. *Psychotherapy with African American women: Innovations in psychodynamic perspectives and practice.* New York: The Guilford Press.

Lee, E. (ed.) 1997. *Working with Asian Americans: A guide for clinicians.* New York: The Guilford Press.

Pérez Foster, R. 1998. *The power of language in the clinical process: Assessing and treating the bilingual person.* Northvale, NJ: Jason Aronson.

Pérez Foster, R., M. Moskowitz, and R. A. Javier. (eds.) 1996. *Reaching across boundaries of culture and class: Widening the scope of psychotherapy.* Northvale, NJ: Jason Aronson.

Chapter 7

The Family: Forms and Organization

No matter how many communes anybody invents, the family always creeps back.

Margaret Mead, Encarta Book of Quotations, 2000

INTRODUCTION

In her novel, *Paradise,* Toni Morrison (1999) describes Seneca, a young woman who visits her boyfriend in prison; he asks her to request money he needs from his mother. After a long bus trip, Seneca arrives at his mother's home to find her angry at her son, refusing to give the money bequeathed to her by her husband to "somebody who drove a car over a child and left it there, even . . . her only son" (p. 133). Seneca defends her boyfriend; Mrs. Turtle (his mother) dismisses this with: "I've known him all his life" (p. 133). Seneca leaves but decides to return to the house to ask Mrs. Turtle if she might use the phone.

> At the door . . . she heard sobbing. A flat-out helpless mothercry— a sound like no other in the world. . . . Alone, without witness, Mrs. Turtle had let go her reason, her personality, and shrieked for all the world like the feathered, finned and hoofed whose flesh she never ate—the way a gull, a cow whale, a mother wolf might if her young had been snatched away. (Morrison, 1999, p. 134)

Mrs. Turtle has disowned her son; but she could not disown her strong attachment to him.

Ambivalent feelings toward one's family are universal, even when not inwardly recognized or outwardly acknowledged. If families break down, complex emotions often arise, including depression, rage, lowered self-esteem, feelings of betrayal, and fear of attachments, as unfulfilled needs remain, playing havoc with the emotional life of adults and children, and having serious consequences for a child's ego development.

Babies are totally helpless at birth, dependent on their families to meet their every emotional and physical need. As children grow, tensions relating to separation-individuation, limit setting, relationships with siblings, values, and so on are inevitable. However, bonds of attachment, acceptance, and support can withstand such tensions and sustain family ties, as negative and conflictual feelings are worked through and modulated. Ambivalent feelings become more difficult (or impossible) to work through when attachment and support are replaced by rejection, abuse, or abandonment.

Many forms and structures of family life exist today in addition to traditional two-parent heterosexual families; single parent, stepfamilies or blended families, families headed by gay parents, kinship foster families, and adoptive families continue to proliferate. Public opinion is strongly divided on what constitutes a family. Major debates, legal decisions, and political referendums question whether gay marriages should be legalized and whether gay couples can jointly adopt children.

Social workers today are confronted by a diversity that challenges conventional theories based on working with "traditional" families (Goldstein, 1999). However, every family, even the "traditional" family, is unique; a constructivist stance, emphasizing the perceptions, values, and goals of each family without prejudging it, can illuminate our understanding of a family's life.

There are also universal issues to assess in all families; a key construct is the presence (or absence) of secure attachments, which extend throughout the life cycle from childhood through old age. Secure attachments are important to children in any family structure (although they may be manifested in various forms in different cultures); they are the building blocks for developing a capacity to relate to others, as well as the development of healthy ego functioning. Attachment is determined less by the structure of the family per se and far more by the quality of relationships within the family.

A child might develop a greater basic sense of security through attachment to an adoptive gay couple who relate in a caring, warm manner to the child, than another child who might develop with two emotionally cold and distant heterosexual birth parents. Goldstein and Goldstein (1996) discuss the importance of *"continuity of care"* as being of vital importance to a child's successful development, stressing this as a guiding principle in working with children needing out-of-home placement (p. 50; italics added).

> We urge, therefore, that placements and the procedures for placement maximize a child's opportunity for being wanted and for maintaining on a continuous, unconditional, and permanent basis a relationship with at least one adult who is, or is capable of becoming, the child's psychological parent. By "psychological parent" we mean "one [or more] adults who, on a continuing, day-to-day basis, through interaction, companionship, interplay, and mutuality, fulfills the child's psychological . . . as well as physical needs. Psychological parents may be biological, adoptive, foster, or common-law parents, or any other [adults]." (Goldstein and Goldstein, 1996, p. 51)

Henry (1999), while emphasizing the importance of *parental permanency* for children, adds that the "experience of *psychological and physical safety* is a developmental imperative of childhood" (p. 561; italics added). Many children today are neglected and/or physically and/or sexually abused within their own families often with serious psychological and developmental consequences (Dore, 1999; Morton and Browne, 1998; Tracy and Johnson, 2006). To leave these children with their birth families "may be far more damaging than removal to a permanent, safer environment" (Adnopoz, 1996, p. 415).

If children are removed from the home to protect them, further psychological harm can result from lack of continuity or permanency. Furthermore, when children are removed, will they actually be moved to a "permanent, safer environment," or will they be moved through a system of revolving foster homes, where they may never know permanency? Deciding whether to remove children or have them remain with their families (or people they perceive to be their families) is one of the most complex and profound decisions social workers must make.

Serious disruptions in family life are common today, including alcoholism, domestic violence, homelessness, and problematic (and sometimes disrupted) adoptions. Divorce, often though not necessarily associated with disruption of family life, is endemic. "Annually, over 1 million children under the age of 18 experience a divorce in their families (U.S. Census Bureau, 2001)" (Zastrow and Kirst-Ashman, 2004, p. 448); children of unmarried parents are also affected when their parents separate. Approximately "10 million children live with a parent who is separated or divorced" (Lopez, 1998, p. 60).

Leaving a damaged marriage or relationship can be a strength, and many families successfully transition from the loss of their original family to other arrangements. Nevertheless, painful psychological and social consequences often follow divorce (and separations) for parents as well as their children, which include experiencing loss and grief; transitioning to new homes, lifestyles, and new stepfamilies; and adapting to decreased financial resources. The ideals of continuity of care and permanency become transformed for many children.

FORMS AND STRUCTURES OF FAMILY LIFE

This section discusses the traditional family, single parents, blended families, gay families, adoptive families, foster families, kinship foster families, and grandparents raising their grandchildren.

The Traditional Family

The traditional family is defined as consisting of a husband (male), wife (female), and their children, although this is no longer the predominant picture of family life in this country. According to the U.S. Census Bureau in 2001, approximately 35 percent of families are traditional (which includes people who have been previously married) (Zastrow and Kirst-Ashman, 2004).

Changing Roles of Fathers and Mothers

The women's movement is one influence that has produced major changes in traditional family life, with shifts in the power structure and in the roles of men and women, including the number of women in the workforce. In 1948, for example, "only 11 percent of all married women with children under age six were in the labor force," but by 2001 "this figure was over 60 percent (U.S. Census Bureau, 2001)" (Zastrow and Kirst-Ashman, 2004, p. 457). However, after the middle of the 1990s, the numbers leveled off, and the rate has been declining roughly since 2000 (Porter, 2006). Many mothers, according to research studies, were finding themselves stressed as they attempted to meet all their responsibilities; generally they devoted time to their children, but to the neglect of other activities; "employed mothers, on average, worked at home and on the job a total of 15 hours more a week and slept 3.8 fewer hours than those who were not employed" (p. C2). More women are also attaining higher education, and marry and have children later than they had in the past.

Fathers now generally have greater involvement in family life and child care than before (Crockenberg and Leerkes, 2000; Ross, 1984). Earlier writings on child development stressed the importance of the mother-child bond; current writings emphasize the significance of the father in his direct interactions with his child from infancy on (Crockenberg and Leerkes, 2000). Fatherhood also has significant ramifications for a man's psychological development; a child "affects a man's identity as a father as well as the self-identity and masculinity bound up with his paternity" (Ross, 1984, p. 382).

There has been an increase in the number of stay-at-home fathers; 2,216,000 preschoolers were cared for by fathers in 2002; the numbers of fathers providing care for children up to fifteen years of age with employed mothers rose from 3.15 million in 1988 to 3.42 million in 2002—an 8.5 percent rise (Overturf Johnson, 2005). Many employed men provide care for their children during the day while their wives work; the fathers then go to work on the night shift. Some families cannot make ends meet, even when both parents are working, and sometimes at least one parent is working more than one job. Some low-income families, owing to a combination of low wages and high rents, find themselves at the poverty level (Longres, 1995b); some find themselves homeless. Homelessness itself can cause separation in a traditional family. "Some family shelters may not admit all members of a family because they lack space, while others do not allow men (and adolescent boys) to stay with their female companions, relatives and children" (Choi and Snyder, 1999, p. 57).

For many fathers, however, there is no outside employment; their full employment is child care. Some stay-at-home fathers often find social isolation to be a problem (as many stay-at-home mothers have), and some have experienced social disapproval and/or condescension from others. Some dads found "'a glass wall' separating mothers from fathers in parks and school yards" (Marin, 2000, p. 18). Many fathers find support groups of other stay-at-home fathers, including Internet communications, to be helpful.

Use of child care as a substitute for parental care in the home has increased and includes "center-based care, child-care homes, care by relatives, and in-home care by nonrelatives" (Hungerford, Brownell, and Campbell, 2000, pp. 519-520). The effects of day care on developing children, especially for children under age three, are controversial; the quality of substitute child care is a critical factor in assessing its effects, as is the quality of the child's relationships in the home. Commenting on the lack of uniformly strong standards for child care in this country, Margaret Carlson (1997) observed,

"What an odd society it is that requires more training and licensing of the person who cuts your hair than the person to whom you entrust your most precious possession" (p. 30).

Although concluding that child care is a normative experience in this country, Hungerford, Brownell, and Campbell (2000) are cautious in generalizing about the effects of this experience on children; they prefer the questions: "Under what circumstances do children thrive or suffer in early child care, and how do different sources of influence mutually shape development?" (p. 519). They recommend further research to include study of long-term effects on children as they develop.

Intermarriages

The increase in racial and ethnic intermarriages across many groups and cultures is also changing the picture of traditional families (Spickard, Fong, and Ewalt, 1995).

> Intermarriage is occurring at triple the rate of the early 1970s. More than 50 percent of Americans are marrying out of their ethnic groups; 33 million American adults live in households where at least one other adult has a different religious identity. (McGoldrick, Giordano, and Garcia-Preto, 2005, p. 26)

Children born of intermarriages add to the number of Americans who are multiethnic; "the simple understanding of race and the easy targets of racism grow more complex" (Spickard, Fong, and Ewalt, 1995, p. 583). Multiethnicity increases opportunities for celebrating diversity and accepting others with greater comfort and even pleasure. At the same time, intermarriage can pose problems for families who may experience discrimination within their own extended families and their communities; personal problems of adaptation may also arise as couples face issues related to cultural differences (McGoldrick, Giordano, and Garcia-Preto, 2005). In the interracial marriage of an Asian American and a non-Asian, for example, partners "may not even be aware of the different cultural value systems that shape their perceptions of reality" (Crohn, 1997, p. 434). The impact of ethnicity and culture on individuals and families is discussed in Chapter 6.

Single Parents

The number of babies being born to unmarried mothers has been rising dramatically since the end of the 1990s; during 2005 approximately 4.1 million children were born, and of these over 1.5 million were born to unmarried mothers ("Babies Born," 2006). Most of these babies were not born to teen-age mothers, as in past years; in fact there was a decrease of adolescent pregnancies in girls between ages ten and seventeen; this "group's overall birthrate [declined] to the lowest level of record" (p. A19). The greatest increase occurred in women in the twenty- to thirty-year-old age range, and was thought to be related to the increase of women choosing to postpone marriage, and to those residing with their partners outside of marriage; "having a child out of wedlock, the experts noted, is no longer the source of shame it once was" (p. A19).

Unmarried women in their thirties and forties were having babies out of their concerns about getting older and becoming unable to have babies later; from 1999 through 2003, "there was an almost 17 percent jump in the number of babies born to unmarried women between ages 30 and 44, according to the National Center for Human Statistics" (Egan, 2006, p. 46). An increasing number of single women are also adopting children.

As the numbers of single mothers with children is growing, so is the group of unmarried men with children. According to the Census there were 2.2 million of these dads:

> A 62 percent increase over 1990 and a 171 percent increase in the past two decades. Some are divorced fathers with sole or joint custody; some are widowers or single men with adopted children. And as many as a third may be unmarried fathers living with the mothers of their children. (Roosevelt, 2001, p. F2)

More gay men are now able to gain legal custody of their own biological children and/or adopt children. This greater involvement in single fatherhood is also manifested in increased participation in fathers' rights groups, such as the American Coalition for Fathers and Children, seeking to achieve more liberal custody laws for divorced fathers (Dominus, 2005).

Single parenthood is found across all socioeconomic and racial groups, but there are approximately three times as many single custodial mothers as single custodial fathers (Roosevelt, 2001). A spectrum of psychosocial functioning is found in this group; many well-functioning single-parent families are raising well-functioning children, and the strengths and competencies of many of these families have been receiving greater recognition (Strand, 1995; Zastrow and Kirst-Ashman, 2004). However, a large segment of single mothers experience major stresses related to poverty and employment (Strand, 1995); many single mothers and their children are found in the homeless population (First et al., 1995; Longres, 1995b).

Poverty affects single-parent families significantly more than two-parent families. Differences in the average income levels of single-parent, female-headed families and two-parent families are striking and deplorable. Thirty-seven percent of female-headed families are in poverty, compared to 12 percent for two-parent families. (U. S. Census Bureau, 2001) (Zastrow and Kirst-Ashman, 2004, p. 453)

Serious problems raising children often develop in these families; many single mothers who are struggling with poverty, and living in inner-cities are overwhelmed with parenting demands, become involved with the child welfare system, often requiring foster care and residential treatment for their children, frequently with the goal of reunification (Strand, 1995).

In assessing the effects of single parenting on both parents and children, it is important to understand how the single parent experiences being a single parent and being without a partner, and to observe the basic quality of attachment the child has to the custodial parent and has (or had) to the missing parent (or fantasy of an unknown parent). It is understandable for social workers to "buy into" a negative picture of the missing parent painted by a primary client; it is extremely important to exercise professional objectivity in these situations. Other assessment considerations include available social supports; the physical and mental health of the parents and children; financial status; adequate housing; and employment opportunities (and job satisfaction).

Finally, we should bear in mind that not all missing parents in single-parent households are missing. Some fathers (or mothers), although not part of the household, may frequently visit and, in terms of relationships, be a part of the family. One study, for example, suggested that "young black children benefit from the presence of nonresident fathers, particularly when these fathers are an 'active' presence in their lives" (Jackson, 1999, p. 156).

Increasing numbers of heterosexual and lesbian women, many of whom are financially secure and employed, choose to be single parents, sometimes through adoption, and sometimes through artificial insemination, choosing either a known donor or applying to sperm banks. Some join special groups or seek help on the Internet. Some women, for example, joined "Single Mothers by Choice" in 2005, a support group in existence for 25 years, with a current membership of approximately 4,000 (including some in other countries); 75 percent of its members turn to sperm banks, following the long-standing practice of many lesbian couples (Egan, 2006), and of couples who have fertility problems (Grady, 2006a). It is estimated that about 30,000 children a year are fathered by donors, but numbers are uncertain as banks do not keep records of the resulting children who are born and the industry is generally not regulated (Egan, 2006); "demand for donor sperm is high and getting higher" (Grady, 2006a, p. D5).

The Internet has assisted women in the quest for anonymous donors; connections can easily be made to rosters of sperm banks and the names of reproductive endocrinologists; prospective mothers can scan information profiles (and sometimes pictures) of donors, and, after making a decision, can purchase semen from sperm banks through the Internet. The Internet also provides a frequent source of support to women, as they share information, experiences, and worries with one another. Although supplying actual biographical information (and submitting medical data and undergoing AIDS testing), sperm donors remain anonymous. Currently donors tend to be more open, some consenting to allow their biological child at age eighteen to get in touch with them; donors are often paid more for this additional service (Egan, 2006).

Although donors remain anonymous, their code numbers and biographical information do not. Many mothers who wish to have a second child can request the same father. A wish for connection and family ties is often present, motivating mothers to contact other mothers whose child was fathered by the same man, and for half-sibs to seek each other out; there have been family gatherings attended by both mothers and half-sibs, with frequent plans for continuity of these relationships. This stands in marked contrast to many divorced women, who often have negative feelings about the spouse's new partner and progeny (although positive relationships have also developed in this context).

One criticism of donor anonymity is that their offspring could unknowingly become involved in incest; "several documented cases of unwitting incest have been noted, including a son who unknowingly married his mother and a brother who married his half-sister. In 1960, Israel passed an open-records law primarily to avert such disasters" (McRoy, Grotevant, and White, 1988, p. 8). In addition, although sperm donors provide medical records, potential genetic problems in their extended families are often not known. This is particularly the case for "rare" genetic disorders. In 2006, a doctor in Michigan was suddenly consulted for five cases of severe congenital neutropenia, a very rare genetic blood disease, and learned, through inquiry, that all five of the afflicted children (from four families) were fathered by the same sperm donor (Grady, 2006a). The donor had been in good health, and his test results for infectious diseases were found to be negative. Generally sperm banks test for more common genetic disorders, such as cystic fibrosis, but not for rare disorders; in this case, the man in question probably did not even know that he was a carrier. Questions have been raised about the hazards of secrecy, and the lack of regulation of sperm banks, including no follow-up on the health of children produced; "a lot is not known, and many participants want it that way" (Grady, 2006a, p. D5).

There are some participants who do want to know more; the "Donor Sibling Registry," on the Internet for the past three years, with 5,000 members, is a site where mothers and their children can search for others who were fathered by the same sperm donor; "for children who often feel severed from half of their biological identity, finding a sibling—or in some cases, a dozen—can feel like coming home" (Harmon, 2005, p. 1). Many children (who often have difficulty understanding and explaining who their father is) hope that one day he will contact them himself; in the meantime, "they are building a new definition of family that both rests on biology and transcends it" (Harmon, 2005, p. 20).

Teenage Parents

The dramatic increase in single mothers is not found in the teenage population; to the contrary, there is a marked decrease in adolescent pregnancies ("Babies Born," 2006), though Latina teens have a high pregnancy rate ("Young Latinas," 2006). Some teen mothers and their children do well. However, many encounter economic and housing difficulties, have problems completing schooling and vocational plans; they often come from high-risk environments, and they may be involved in other risky behaviors (Wakschlag and Hans, 2000). They are usually unprepared for parenting, and their children tend to have developmental complications.

Teenage parents may be depressed or abuse substances; many adolescent mothers have been sexually abused, "which increases their risk for mental health problems" (Wakschlag and Hans, 2000, p. 135). Those who have been traumatized and have symptoms of "PTSD may experience a significant decrease in the emotional, physiological, and cognitive resources available to them, *just* as they are faced with the demands of motherhood" (DeRosa and Pelcovitz, 2006, p. 223; italics in the original).

> Compared to older mothers, younger mothers have been shown to be less responsive to their children, to engage in harsher discipline, and to be more depressed. . . . The children of adolescent mothers are more likely to have pre- and perinatal difficulties, to exhibit developmental and behavioral problems during early childhood and beyond, and to become teenage parents themselves. (Wakschlag and Hans, 2000, p. 129)

Teenage fathers have generally received little attention, although more recently research and services have been directed at this population (Kiselica, 1995); they are at "increased risk for educational problems, truancy, drug use, aggression, and delinquency" (Benson, 2004, p. 448). Many of these fathers "do not want to abandon their baby . . . [they] face the same emotional struggles and dilemmas that teenage mothers do, and many fathers want a baby for the same reasons that teenage mothers want one" (Ashford, Lecroy, and Lortie, 1997, p. 353).

The general assumption that most of the fathers of babies born to adolescent mothers are themselves adolescents is not based in fact. "Perhaps surprisingly, it appears that only 20-40 percent of the partners of adolescent mothers are themselves adolescents" (Wakschlag and Hans, 2000, p. 131); there are "large age discrepancies" between teen mothers and the fathers, which "sometimes indicate abuse of the young women" (p. 132).

Teenage mothers are going through the adolescent stage with its normative conflict with parents and tensions relating to separation-individuation. Some have serious preexisting problems with their mothers; becoming a mother (and often raising the child in the grandmother's household) can complicate these relationships; in some instances, the grandmother may be an important source of support; in others, she may increase the young mother's emotional as well as parenting conflicts (Woods and Hollis, 1990). "Because co-residence is required for teen mothers to receive public assistance in some US states, the issue of mandatory co-residence is important" (Benson, 2004, p. 447). It has been suggested that grandmothers be included in interventions in a "three generation approach to adolescent parents" (Wakschlag and Hans, 2000).

The complex problems of adolescent pregnancy require comprehensive planning of services for both mothers and fathers, including education, job training, birth control education, parenting education, support groups, building a network of social supports, couples counseling, and early childhood intervention programs for the children. The need for mental health intervention is an important consideration, "although mental health and family interactions have generally not been a direct focus of intervention" (Wakschlag and Hans, 2000, p. 140).

The Blended Family

People separated from partners or divorced (or widowed) often remarry, or develop new relationships, and may bring children with them into their new unions; the new family is now a *blended family,* which may also include children acquired by this new couple (through birth, adoption, or fostering). Other terms to describe this constellation are "stepfamilies . . . reconstituted families, and nontraditional families" (Zastrow and Kirst-Ashman, 1997, p. 496).

Although positive relationships between all members can develop, entering into a blended family presents partners and children with greater complexities than are likely to arise in a new traditional family; they must work out separation and/or divorce issues and mourn the loss of their earlier relationships, which may include loss of former extended families and social networks. One divorced woman commented that if you have children you are never totally divorced; you are usually involved for years with your former spouse in relation to child care, custody, and visitation issues; children may feel conflict when visitations are colored by parental acrimony.

Problems involving children also include adaptation of stepparents and stepchildren to one another; children's adaptations to (and jealousies about) stepsiblings; the accommodation of former family routines, rituals, myths, and so on to new family expectations; and possible changes in lifestyles (Germain, 1991).

Grieving is critical in accepting the losses inherent in the divorce or separation process; however, anger and denial may prevent this or "because mourning is perceived as a threat to the new family, it is often blocked" (Scharff and Scharff, 1987, p. 378). One teenage boy (Bruce) had difficulty mourning the loss of his birth mother, from whom he was separated following a divorce. He lived with his father, stepmother, and stepbrother, and visited his mother, who lived with a farming family, every other weekend. Scharff and Scharff (1987) describe a family therapy session dealing with a family dispute, which Bruce precipitated, following a visit with his mother.

> Marge [stepmother] was already mad at Bruce for coming home late from his mother's . . . and for dirtying the living room with straw and mud from his boots. She and Fred [Bruce's father] were both mad at Bruce's mother for failing to supervise him adequately, whereas Bruce was delighted with the visit to his mother, feeling that he had had a great time doing farm work with her . . . without worrying about being a mess. Marge was concerned that Bruce go to school with matching clothes and clean shoes, which was not the way his mother had raised him.

> Although it was quite reasonable for Marge to prefer Bruce to shed his gear in the basement and behave in ways appropriate to their townhouse life-style, Bruce could not keep separate the two kinds of existence when unconsciously he longed to merge them. At the moment of returning home, *he was still longing for his mother and holding on*

to her through bits of mud and hay. His "bad" behavior provoked Marge to be a "bad" mother, which emphasized the image of the "good" mother he was missing. The child was in the midst of two cultures in collision. (Scharff and Scharff, 1987, p. 379; italics added)

This excerpt poignantly reveals the depth of Bruce's attachment to his mother and his pain in losing her; "holding on to her through bits of mud and hay" illustrates his use of these materials as transitional objects.

Clinical social workers can offer individual, couples, and family therapy, to those having problems with blended family life.

Gay and Lesbian Families

It was announced on December 6, 2006, that Mary Cheney, age thirty-seven, Vice President Cheney's daughter, was expecting a baby in the spring; what made this item particularly newsworthy is that she is a lesbian, living with her partner, with whom she has lived for the past fifteen years; no information was given about the baby's father. This news reactivated the intense debate about same-sex marriages, strongly opposed by President Bush, who has been advocating for its ban through a constitutional amendment (Rutenberg, 2006, A30). All of this has confronted the participants in this situation with a multiplicity of dilemmas, at the intersection of the political and the personal.

Jennifer Chrisler, the executive director of Family Pride commented: "The news of Mary Cheney's pregnancy exemplifies, once again, how the best interests of children are denied when lesbian, gay, bisexual and transgender citizens are treated unfairly and accorded different and unequal rights and responsibilities than other parents" (Rutenberg, 2006, A30). Charles Dobson (2006), Chairman of Focus on the Family, was quick to respond with critical comments about gay marriage, citing religious principles.

> In raising these issues, Focus on the Family does not desire to harm or insult women such as Cheney and Poe [her partner]. Rather, our conviction is that birth and adoption are the purview of married heterosexual couples. Traditional marriage is God's design for the family and is rooted in biblical truth. When that divine plan is implemented, children have the best opportunity to thrive. That's why public policy as it relates to families must be based not solely on the desires of adults but rather on the needs of children and what is best for society at large. (Dobson, 2006, p. 123)

Gay marriage has been a particularly volatile national issue in the past few years. In 2005, Kansas was the eighteenth state to ban same-sex marriages (Shorto, 2005), and in the 2006 election, six additional states passed similar constitutional amendments, though it was defeated in Arizona ("Romney Pushes," 2006). Same-sex civil unions became legal in Vermont six years ago and in Connecticut last year. The Supreme Court of Massachusetts legalized same-sex marriage in 2003, enabling over 8,000 couples to marry there. Governor Romney of Massachusetts, opposed to this legalization, was attempting to have the state legislature review this issue in November 2006 (which it has avoided thus far), and failing to do this, is planning to ask the court to enable this question to be on the ballot.

In what came as a surprise to many, New York State's Court of Appeals, in July 2006, ruled against gay marriages and turned this question over to the legislature; many had thought it would pass as "New York is undoubtedly more liberal or more tolerant than many other places" (Roberts, 2006a, p. A17).

New Jersey's Supreme Court, in November, 2006, ruled that gay couples "are entitled to the same legal rights and financial benefits as heterosexual couples," but there was disagreement about whether "their unions must be called marriage or could be known by another name"; this conundrum was referred to the State Legislature. Writing the dissenting opinion for those in favor of using the term marriage, Chief Justice Deborah T. Poretz stated that the "semantic distinction of marriage versus civil unions was itself a meaningful one, arguing that the institution 'bestows enormous private and social advantages'" (Chen, 2006, p. A24).

The New Jersey State Legislature voted to sanction same-sex civil unions on December 14, 2006; "gay couples could now gain adoption privileges, inheritance rights and the ability to take a partner's surname without going to court" (Mansnerus, 2006, p. A1). However, there was also disappointment among gay advocates that marriage itself was not sanctioned, and they argued that "the separate institutions were inherently unequal and promised to keep pushing for nothing short of marriage itself" (Mansnerus, 2006, p. A1).

Although the prospect of legalization of gay marriage is presently in a precarious state, there are nevertheless many openly gay unions and gay families, and greater public acceptance of this lifestyle. Civil unions of gays have a higher level of acceptance among the public than gay marriages (as noted in New Jersey, Connecticut, and Vermont); the increasing extension of "specific rights and benefits to gay couples . . . suggests that many who object to gay marriage nevertheless see an underlying civil rights issue" (Shorto, 2005, p. 37).

Gays and lesbians form families varying in structure and composition; many are birth parents (and often their children have been born in a prior or current heterosexual relationship). Some divorced gays and lesbians live as single parents or with a partner, and may share custody of their children with a former spouse; blended families may develop, with each partner bringing children from former unions, and sometimes new children are added. Increasingly, lesbian women may decide to have children through adoption or through insemination of self and/or partner by a donor (Erera and Fredriksen, 1999). Some gay men choose a woman to act as a surrogate mother; parenthood may also be attained through adoption, foster care, or stepparenting.

Acceptance of homosexuality seems to be growing today in this country; yet homophobia as well as overt discrimination and acts of violence against this population remain. Children of gay and lesbian parents can encounter discrimination from other children and adults. Paradoxically, advances such as introducing educational programs on homosexual parenting into schools can lead to a backlash of gay bashing or various forms of rejection (Morales, 1995). Sometimes lesbian mothers are rejected by sectors of their lesbian communities that are opposed to motherhood (Lott-Whitehead and Tully, 1993; Parks, 1998).

Research on the development and adaptation of children brought up in gay households reveals that they are not more prone to mental health problems or to becoming homosexual than are children brought up in heterosexual families (Sadock and Sadock, 2003); similar findings were reported in relation to children adopted by gay families (Pace, 2006c); when children of lesbian mothers have developmental problems they are related not to "the mother's sexuality" but to other areas of "family functioning" (Parks, 1998, p. 383). Gay fathers may be more motivated than nongay fathers to provide their children with consistent and supportive care, and when not the custodial parent, will honor their visiting responsibilities; they also tend to have more confidence in themselves as good fathers (Morales, 1995). Many gay families develop informal social networks; in lesbian families, for example, a "major source of social support is their own lesbian community that tends to function as an extended family" (Erera and Fredriksen, 1999, p. 268).

Family law issues concerning custody, support, and visitation can cause special problems for gays and lesbians; laws as well as some individual judges may be biased against gay and lesbian parents.

Adoption

There are approximately 2.5 million children and youth (under eighteen) who are adopted each year in the United States (Sadock and Sadock, 2003). In most traditional legal adoptions, a child (often an infant) is placed, on a permanent basis, with a married couple (typically infertile) who assume full parenting rights and responsibilities for that child. Today, adoptions increasingly take place in nontraditional families by single persons or gay couples, by stepparents, when a birth parent remarries, or by foster parents or relatives who have acted as caretakers for a child.

Some children are adopted when they are older; those with special needs are difficult to place and may await adoption for years. International adoptions have been increasing, as have interracial adoptions, both of which remain controversial. Finally, the concept of the permanency of adoption has been eroded, as some birth parents challenge the legality of their child's adoption, and as a number of adoptive parents terminate the adoption, unable to cope with their adopted child.

The tradition of treating identifying information about birth parents as strictly confidential is breaking down, as more adoptees search for their birth parents, and as more adoptions become open; the latter approach permits birth parents and adoptive parents to have some knowledge of each other and allows for some type of ongoing contact between them (Cushman, Kalmuss, and Namerow, 1993).

In the 1970s, social changes—including the increase in abortions, the tendency for unmarried women to keep their own children (diminishing the supply of babies available for adoption), and the increase of infertile couples—affected the adoption scene: "The number of couples waiting to adopt had become significantly larger than the number of healthy infants available for adoption" (Caplan, 1990, pp. 40-41). Affected also by sociopolitical and biological trends, an increase in interracial and international adoptions has evolved, along with an increasing utilization of reproductive technologies, and a greater number of privately arranged adoptions (often through lawyers), accompanied by decreased utilization of adoptions facilitated by social agencies.

On one level, adoption is an excellent solution for all parties involved in the adoption triangle: the birth parents (although usually only the birth mother is discussed), who are unable (socially, financially, and/or emotionally) to raise their child, yet wish for a secure home for their offspring; the child, who otherwise faces the life of being a "psychological orphan" with no permanent family; and the adoptive parents who want a child to love and to raise. For gay and lesbian people or heterosexual single people who might otherwise be childless, it is a way to have a child to nurture. Some adoptive families have the motivation and capacity to work with children with special needs.

However, on psychological and social levels, adoption, even when highly successful, can be a very complex psychological and social process for all members of the adoption triangle as issues of loss and insecurity can plague each member in different ways. It should be added that not all adoptions are entered into voluntarily by the birthparents; sometimes their rights to be parents have been terminated by the courts due to neglect and/or abuse, and adoption is mandated.

Birth Parents

Birth mothers face emotional conflicts in relinquishing their babies for adoption, often experiencing feelings of loss, guilt, pain, and grief; they may or may not have gone through an appropriate mourning process. Even with the passage of time, these emotional issues do not necessarily disappear; "they had a need to know about the well being of their child over the years" (Chapman et al., 1986, p. 204). Silverman observed that birth mothers who were "told to 'forget' denied part of themselves by shutting off their feelings" (p. 205).

The profound nature of relinquishing a child for adoption requires exploration with those clients who have experienced this, even if this event was in the distant past. Some birthmothers retain memories of the birth, have fantasies about the child that they had given away, may wish for reunion, and observe silent rituals on the child's birthday or on other significant occasions.

Unresolved feelings about giving up her child may affect a woman's future relationships with men (or with the father of the baby) and can color attitudes toward later children. Many women have had their babies in secret and entered into an adoption process in which strict confidentiality was guaranteed; they may wish to retain this secret; however, other birth mothers no longer want secrecy and have banded together for mutual support and advocacy. Organizations such as Concerned United Birthparents, Inc. have been formed by birth parents; their goals are to make "adoption more client-centered, to permit adult adoptees access to original certificates and identifying information, to allow birthparents visitation rights when adoptees are of a certain age, and to help birthparents resolve guilt feelings" (McRoy, Grotevant, and White, 1988, p. 12).

Many children adopted today are older children who may know their birth parents; these parents may pursue legal actions to have the adoption overturned and/or may engage in behaviors that can be physically or psychologically damaging to the child, as they seek to continue their parenting role. It is not uncommon to find a birth mother replacing her lost child through another pregnancy.

Unmarried fathers generally seem to be forgotten in the adoption process, their "rights remain an unsettled area, a delicate balancing act between the importance of biological ties and the undisrupted placement of babies whose mothers relinquish them for adoption" (Lewin, 2006a, p. 1). The courts have been finding that when the birthmother has decided on the adoption process, the father's parental rights must also be considered, if they are asserted.

The Adopted Child

Adopted children are affected by many influences: preadoptive experiences; the quality of their relationship to the adoptive parents; relationships to the extended adoptive family; ongoing relationship (if any) with birth parents, siblings, or extended family; economic and employment status of adoptive family; cultural conflict; and the presence of physical and mental health problems in the adoptive parents and in the child. If an adopted child is having problems, there is a tendency to assume that this is because of adoption issues, when adoption itself may play only a peripheral role.

It is common, however, for adopted children to wonder about their birth parents, and why they were given up for adoption. Therapists who work with adopted clients should be alert to their fantasies about their birth mothers; sometimes adoptees have kept their thoughts about birth mothers from adoptive parents to protect the adoptive parents (Freeman and Freund, 1998); a similar process can be at work regarding the birth father. These "ghosts" serve many functions in the inner world of the adopted child; therapy can help the child resolve and integrate these fantasies (Freeman and Freund, 1998, p. 28). Such fantasies may be present even if information is available, and fantasies about having parents other than one's actual parents are not uncommon in nonadopted children.

It is not uncommon for adoptees to seek out their birthparents as they reach adulthood; this can be a developmentally constructive experience, and should be encouraged by agencies providing information, while protecting confidentiality unless children and birthparents choose to meet (Huse, 1989). In 1971, adoptees began protesting the practice of withholding information about their birth parentage and organized the Adoptees' Liberty Movement Association (Caplan, 1990); through legal and other advocacy efforts by adult adoptees, a precedent has been established favoring open records and disclosure of parental identity.

Perhaps the most complex adoption issues involve those children who have been removed from families they have known and who have been adopted when older, many by court order; these children often experienced neglect and physical and/or sexual abuse, and frequently had transitioned through several placements. Many waited for years to be adopted because of "special needs," such as emotional and behavioral problems, retardation, autism, physical handicaps, and AIDS.

Children who have been sexually abused often develop serious behavioral disturbances (including sexual acting out) that adoptive parents may not be able to deal with, resulting in termination of the adoption process *(adoption disruption)* or the finalized adoption *(adoption dissolution)*. "Among special-needs adoption placements, the proportion of children who are victims of sexual abuse has been reported to be as high as 86 percent" (Smith and Howard, 1994, p. 491). A sexual abuse history is not always known prior to the adoption process; "a number of children kept their sexual abuse secret for years" (p. 496); some children had intensified loyalties, fears, and other feelings stemming from unresolved sexual abuse experiences with their parents.

Today, increasing numbers of children in the child welfare system have serious emotional problems, greatly taxing this system (Dore, 1999); many are "recycled" through foster and adoptive homes. Critical comprehensive and integrated social and mental health services for these children are often lacking (Dore, 1999; Shonkoff, Lippitt, and Cavanaugh, 2000). Recommendations were made by the Pew Commission on Children in Foster Care in 2004, for "collaboration between mental health and child welfare services" (Benoit, 2006, p. 279).

The Adoptive Parents

Birth parents are often referred to as the adopted child's natural parents. How does this, then, define adoptive parents, who strive to become comfortable with their child who by implication is not their child? If present, the common fertility crisis (i.e., the adoptive parents' feelings of loss, grief, and disappointment about not being able to conceive their own birth children) must be resolved before they can accept someone else's child. "The problem for the adoptive parents is that of really feeling the child 'belongs' to them" (Kadushin, 1974, p. 544).

Any sign that their children are having developmental problems or have curiosity about their birth parents can engender great insecurity in some adoptive parents. DiGiulio (1987) found that adoptive parents who felt secure in their roles were more comfortable in helping children talk about and obtain information about their birth parents.

Parents in nontraditional adoptions can face additional problems in the adoption process. Although gay and lesbian applicants for adoptive parenthood have been accorded greater acceptance, many are denied children on the basis of their sexuality, at the discretion of child welfare personnel and judges (Ryan, Pearlmutter, and Groza, 2004); generally, single gay and lesbian adults have been having greater success in being accepted as adoptive parents; "for same-sex couples, however, it is another matter entirely" (Crawford, 1999, p. 272). In Boston, in 2006, Catholic Charities announced that they would stop their adoption program because of their objections to Massachusetts law mandating that gays and lesbians be included as applicants for adoptive parenthood (Pace, 2006a). In Arkansas, where gays and lesbians are able to adopt, the Circuit Court ruled that they were also entitled to be considered as foster parents; this "remove[d] a clause drafted by the state's child welfare agency that prohibits foster parenting if there is an adult homosexual living in the household" (Pace, 2006a, p. 5). This decision was appealed by the Department of Human Services, but was upheld by the Arkansas Supreme Court on June 29, 2006.

Open Adoption: Pros and Cons

Open adoption eliminates secrecy and highlights some degree of communication (even when anonymity is retained) with all three parties of the adoption triangle; a continuum of options exists, from the birth parents having input into the selection of adoptive parents for their child, to exchanging letters and pictures with the adoptive family (through the agency), to face-to-face meetings of birth and adoptive parents, and to their ongoing interactions over the years, which may include involvement with the child. There are disagreements among professionals about this practice, not only because there is no agreement about what open adoption is but also because there is uncertainty about the impact of this practice (McRoy, Grotevant, and White, 1988).

Chapman and colleagues (1986), who advocate open adoption, see it as benefiting birth mothers, who are greatly reassured when they have taken part in planning for the adoption knowing that they will have continuing access to information; openness can also be extended to the birth father and extended birth family. Confidentiality can be maintained and negotiated. Barth (1994) argues that many adolescent mothers might relinquish their babies more readily if open adoption were available to them.

William Pierce (Caplan, 1990) strongly opposes open adoption, contending that it is "'very dangerous, tragic, and disastrous'" for birth mothers (p. 86), who may seek

> a new set of parents in the adoptive parents. Often she expects to have a role in the family, like an Aunt, a baby-sitter, a sister, or a godmother, and doesn't face the fact that she has given up the child.

You can give up your child without needing to separate from him, and "have it both ways". . . . Birth mothers don't view their child as lost, don't mourn the loss, and however positive the recognition they enjoy for their instrumental role in the adoption, they fail to move on with their lives. (Caplan, 1990, p. 89)

It has been argued that open adoptions can help the child feel more secure and enhance a well-integrated sense of identity; the child may feel less rejected by the birth parents (Pannor and Baran, 1984). However, "contact with his birth mother can backfire, inflating his sense of rejection by her and raising anxieties about her taking him back or about his adoptive parents abandoning him, too" (Caplan, 1990, p. 89). There are also "risks of 'serious interference' [with the adopted child] at every stage of development. An open adoption is likely to leave him feeling more like a foster child" (pp. 89-90).

Many adoptive parents are fearful that birth parents may reappear, and that their adoptive children might rejoin them. "This albatross is carried [by adoptive parents] well into the child's adulthood and is demonstrated through insecure possessiveness and ongoing anxiety. In sharp contrast, we witness comfort in the adoptive parents who experience openness with continued contact with the birthmother" (Chapman et al., 1987, p. 10). Disagreeing, Pierce values the "sense of entitlement" that the adoptive parents feel in closed adoption, as opposed to "inevitable sharing of that responsibility with the birth mother" (Caplan, 1990, p. 93).

Decisions about open adoption are further complicated when older children who have ties to their birth and/or former foster families are adopted. Should all past ties be severed? Today, there is generally more openness about adoption than in the past, although people accept this to varying degrees. Siegel (2003) studied a group of families (early in adoption and seven years later) who had agreed to adoptions with different degrees of openness. She reports that the adoptive parents were very positive about this process, although she cautions that openness needs to be negotiated on an individual basis with each family, and noted that relationships and needs change over time. Open adoption is a complex subject, with many potential advantages as well as possible serious pitfalls, which needs further study.

International Adoption

Impelled by the fertility crisis and the scarcity of adoptable infants, as well as fears about open adoption or birth families reclaiming their children, people in the United States, in increasing numbers over the past ten years, have been turning to international adoptions; from "1990 through 2005," there have been "226,546" international adoptions in the United States (Clemetson and Nixon, 2006, p. A18). During 2004-2005, there were "22,739 orphans" adopted from other countries (Pace, 2006b, p. 4), primarily: "Mainland China . . . Russia . . . Guatemala . . . South Korea . . . and Ukraine" (Roby and Shaw, 2006, p. 204).

China had developed more flexible adoption laws in 1991, in response to the many children found abandoned (resulting from their national policy of allowing families only one child); this has led to over "55,000 Chinese children," mostly girls, being adopted by U.S. families (Clemetson, 2006, p. A1). The great demand for Chinese babies was exceeding the supply; as a result, quite suddenly in 2006, as reported by adoption agencies in this country, these laws were about to lose their flexibility, to take effect in May 2007 (Belluck and Yardley, 2006). The new rules would exclude "people who are single, obese, older than 50 or who fail to meet certain benchmarks in financial, physical or psychological health" (p. A1). This is causing distress among applicants who would now be excluded; Chinese babies have been popular because they "are generally well cared for and have a good chance of being healthy when adopted" (p. A24).

Guatemala, "where nearly one in every 100 children is adopted by an American family," is being investigated for questionable adoption practices (Lacey, 2006, p. 1). In contrast to China and other countries, where abandoned children are the sources for adoption, in Guatemala most children are sold to baby brokers by their mothers (usually impoverished women living in rural areas), who receive (under the table) several hundred dollars, up to as much as $2,000 for each child. There is no governmental regulation of adoption practices, and adoption has become a powerful business interest, controlled by lawyers and notaries, and involving baby brokers, doctors, and foster parents. Opponents of this practice, that is "privately run and uniquely streamlined—say it has turned this country of 12 million people into a virtual baby farm that supplies infants as if they were a commodity" (Lacey, 2006, p. 1). The government of Guatemala, after much political hassle, has agreed to accept the Hague Convention on Intercountry Adoptions, which provides for safeguarding the adoption process and protecting children. If these regulations are enforced, it is anticipated that there might be drastic cuts in the number of Guatemalan babies adopted in the United States (Lacey, 2006).

The region of the world facing the most catastrophic problem with orphans is sub-Saharan Africa, where 12.3 million children have lost one or both parents who have died from AIDS; a 2003 UNICEF report observed that "nearly 80 percent of the world's AIDS orphans come form this area"

(Roby and Shaw, 2006, p. 199). There is strong resistance in African countries to international adoptions of these children for many reasons, including cultural convictions that they should remain in their home countries and retain their community and family identities; it is also customary for extended families to raise orphaned children. "In some African cultures the adoption of a child is believed to introduce alien spirits into the family" (p. 202). There is also concern that these children might be exploited and sold as slaves for farms, homes, and the sex industry—an ongoing practice reported by the International Organization for Migration in 2003 (Roby and Shaw, 2006).

Generally, the goal in most African countries is to provide help for these children within the countries through kinship care, to aid communities to assist in both kinship and group care, and through institutionalization. Because of the overwhelming magnitude of this crisis, the lack of adequate resources, and the overburdening of the kinship system with multiple family orphans, it has been recommended that international adoptions might serve the needs of some of these children; "it must be considered as a last resort for children whose needs cannot be met otherwise" (Roby and Shaw, 2006, p. 100).

There is also resistance in the United States toward adopting African children, relating to opposition to interracial adoptions and to the belief that many American children (mostly black and Hispanic), who already are on long waiting lists for adoption, should be given preference. Roby and Shaw (2006) recommend that the United States become involved in aiding people in adopting some of these African children, in a protected, regulated, culturally sensitive manner, as a partial solution to this overwhelming human catastrophe.

The Hague Convention, which the United States ratified in 2000, will be implemented in 2007; this will "make the majority of international adoptions in the U.S. a federally regulated process" (Pace, 2006b, p. 4); this would require uniform standards for licensing and practice from all agencies dealing with international adoptions, in addition to protecting children from "abduction, exploitation, sale or trafficking" (p. 4). It will also afford adoptive families a more reliable and competent service. Clinical services will be required of adoption agencies, including home assessments and pre- and postadoption counseling (Pace, 2006b).

Studies of intercountry adoptions have indicated that the majority of these children have adapted well to their new lives and new families; according to Tizard (1991), "75-80 percent [of the adoptees] . . . function . . . with no more behavioral and educational problems . . . than other children" (Vonk, Simms, and Nackerud, 1999, p. 501). Studies of adoptive parents reveal a high degree of satisfaction with their adoptive children and their adjustment (Vonk, Simms, and Nackerud, 1999). Little is known about the effects of intercountry adoptions on the birth parents, especially in countries such as the People's Republic of China, where the birth parents are often unknown.

A large study of 25,000 adopted children conducted in the Netherlands reports that "most international adoptees turn out quite well—in fact, better than children adopted within their own countries" ("The Resilience of," 2005, p. 5). Although many were referred for mental health services, this was attributed to their parents' concern about the traumas these children had lived through. In speculating about their resilience, the researchers suggested that this may have been due to the intelligence or social abilities of the children who were chosen for adoption, the motivation and qualities of the adoptive parents, and genetics. "Domestic adoptees were more likely to have parents with problems—drug abuse, alcoholism, mood disorders, or psychosis—to which they inherited a vulnerability" (p. 6).

International adoptions remain a controversial issue both in the United States and abroad. Critics have argued that adopted children are coming from countries that are in effect being despoiled of their homeless children and thus deprived of the possibility of providing indigenous resources for them; they are "exploited, victimized through colonialism, and perhaps prevented from finding internal alternative solutions for homeless children" (Vonk, Simms, and Nackerud, 1999, p. 502).

Children placed in a different culture may also be exposed to discrimination and have difficulty integrating a racial and cultural identity (Vonk, Simms, and Nackerud, 1999). European-American adoptive parents, who have never themselves experienced racism, may encounter it in relation to their adopted children; they "find themselves for the first time at the receiving end of racism or bigotry vis a vis their children" (p. 504).

Vonk, Simms, and Nackerud (1999) emphasize the lack of research on the well-being of children who were not adopted, but remained in institutions; they are not convinced that children would have done better if left in institutions: "It is difficult to argue that long-term institutionalized care produces a better outcome for an individual child than adoption" (p. 501). In addition, nonadopted orphaned children are not immune to other forms of prejudicial discrimination in their native countries (Vonk, Simms, and Nackerud, 1999).

Many adoptive parents attempt to foster cultural pride in their children, and some have taken specific steps to promote their children's cultural identities, including joining support groups of other transracial adoptive families. Chinese children adopted by American families have found "an organized subculture has developed around them, complete with play groups, tours of China and online support groups" (Clemetson, 2006, p. A1). A wide range of services providing support, Korean culture, and even trips to Korea, are available to Korean adoptees (Lewin, 1998b). Camps and day programs have also been established for adopted children from Korea, Romania, Russia, and China (Lewin, 1998b).

Interracial Adoptions

Interracial adoptions are increasing through international adoptions and as more white couples adopt black children; in 2004, approximately 4,200 black foster children were adopted by white families, almost twice the number as in 1998 (Clemetson and Nixon, 2006). This highly controversial practice is becoming more accepted by agencies, the legal system, and the general public; the large number of international adoptions has made people more accepting of multicultural adoptions, as well as aware of the many black children languishing in foster care in this country, who are in need of a permanent home; the high costs of international adoption are also prohibitive to many (Clemetson and Nixon, 2006).

Many people of black African descent have been opposed to interracial adoptions; in 1972, for example, the National Association of Black Social Workers asserted that "placing black children in white homes was a form of racial and cultural genocide" (Lewin, 1998b, p. A18); this statement was deleted from its policy papers in 1994, although the group still prefers black children being placed in black homes (Clemetson and Nixon, 2006). Opponents of interracial adoptions assert that they add to identity conflicts for children and increase the risk of social rejection, and that insufficient attempts have been made to recruit potential black adoptive parents (Hollingsworth, 1998).

Adoption practices had supported placements in which adopted children and adoptive parents were of the same race until Congress became aware that

> approximately 500,000 children were in foster care in the United States and that tens of thousands of these children were waiting for adoptive homes. Children wait a median of two years and eight months to be adopted, and studies indicated that African American children wait longer than other children. (Brooks et al., 1999, p. 169)

The Multiethnic Placement Act of 1994 was passed by Congress, stating that it is now illegal to use "race categorically or presumptively to delay or deny adoptive or foster placements" (Brooks et al., 1999, p. 167); the law also stressed the importance of recruiting more minority families to adopt children.

In 1996, this law was replaced by a new law, Removal of Barriers to Interethnic Adoption; this altered aspects of the first law (Brooks et al., 1999, p. 170) and also imposed sanctions on violators. The requirement for recruitment of minority adoptive families remained. Although placement cannot be delayed on the basis of race, culture, or ethnicity, a provision appeared mandating that these factors might be considered "based on concerns arising from the circumstances of the individual case" (p. 171). Difficult to interpret, these laws give insufficient guidance for implementation. Racial matching, per se, might not be the principal stumbling block to rapid adoption placement, as other factors also intervene "searches for missing parents, crowded court dockets . . . lengthy appeals, lack of resources, high caseloads . . . and the limitations of adoption assistance and other post-adoption support" (p. 172).

Educating adoptive interracial families to deal openly with the issue of racial differences and to help their children feel comfortable with their racial identities is emphasized currently; The Cradle, a Chicago agency, "gives transracial adoptive parents extensive counseling as well as a course on 'conspicuous families'" (Clemetson and Nixon, 2006, p. A18).

Although any adoption presents complex dilemmas, the world of foster care involves even greater complexities and uncertainties for its participants.

Foster Care

Foster children live in limbo, removed from their families and residing with foster parents who are "temporary" (but may become permanent) custodians, varying in their motivations, abilities to nurture, and commitments to providing a "holding environment" for their wards. Some forge warm, sustaining bonds with their foster children; others, unable to understand and/or cope with the children's insecurities and difficult behaviors, may terminate the placement, and "rejected" once more, the children are recycled through the system.

Losing birth families, homes, and neighborhoods can be devastating to foster children who

> struggle with the need to make sense of placement in the least hurtful way possible. These losses . . . must be explained and fully mourned before the foster child can begin to plan for the future . . . . A primary question posed by placement is: "How come you can't stay with your own family?" (Levine, 1990, p. 53)

Both foster and adoptive children wonder, "'Why was I given away'" (Chapman et al., 1987, p. 81). H. J. Sants (Caplan, 1990) termed their suffering from identity confusion "'genealogical bewilderment'" (p. 82).

Children need to mourn their losses and process what is happening to them with caring professionals. To feel alone and unable to connect with protecting adults can be devastating. Rudyard Kipling (discussed in Chapter 4) was a foster child for almost six years (starting at age six, along with his sister, Trix, three), living in England, distant from their parents in India, whom they did not see during this time. Feeling abandoned, they were also traumatized by an abusive foster mother and experienced a "conspiracy of silence"; they had no one to turn to, other than each other.

Once a year, for a month, Rudyard stayed with his aunt and her family in England, experiencing "a paradise which I verily believe saved me" (Kipling, 1937, p. 13). In later years, learning what Rudyard endured at the foster home, his aunt would "often . . . ask me why I had never told anyone how I was being treated" (p. 17); he explains:

> Children tell little more than animals, for what comes to them they accept as eternally established. Also, badly-treated children have a clear notion of what they are likely to get if they betray the secrets of a prison-house before they are clear of it. (Kipling, 1937, p. 17)

Today, children in foster homes are theoretically "supervised" by child welfare workers who may have high caseloads and inadequate training; their visits can be irregular, and of questionable quality. However, clinically trained child welfare workers, with reasonable caseloads, can make important contributions to foster children. D. W. Winnicott's wife, Clare, herself a psychoanalyst and child welfare social worker, emphasized the *special relationship* the child welfare worker develops with the child, and it is this "unique relationship" that "offers . . . therapeutic possibilities" (Kanter, 1990, p. 36); they have shared important life events, including removal of the child from his/her home, and subsequent placements; thus significant memories can be meaningfully recalled. She described how children in her care would "go over the same ground again and again" (pp. 36-37).

> It might begin with: "Do you remember the day you brought me here in your car?" And we would retrace our steps, going over the events and the explanations once more. This was no mere reminiscing, but a desperate effort to add life up, to overcome fears and anxieties, and to achieve a personal integration. In my experience, feelings about home and other important places cluster round the caseworker, so that when

the children see her they are not only reminded of home but can be in touch with that part of themselves which has roots in the past and the (outside) world. (Kanter, 1990, p. 37)

Social workers should become aware of complex emotions evoked in them as they work with foster children, which "can range from pleasure and satisfaction, to feeling they must save the child, or anger at the child's biological parents" (Coleman and Clark, 2003, p. 85). Many children in the child welfare system have serious emotional problems (Maluccio, 2006), often accompanied by trauma histories (Webb, 2006), and are "more disturbed than in times past" (Dore, 1999, p. 8); these wounded children can be fearful of developing attachments. Sensitivity, insight, and skill are needed by social workers to reach through their indifferent and rejecting facades, to offer the beginnings of a caring relationship.

Clinical skill is also needed in working with foster parents who need training, supervision, and support in their difficult roles, as they cope with children who have serious emotional and behavioral problems, and attachment disorders (Pasztor et al., 2006). "Studies of placement breakdown have repeatedly identified foster parents' inability to manage difficult child behavior as a key factor contributing to placement disruption" (Dore, 1999, p. 22).

The mental health needs of children in care are compelling. Children begin "acting out" with their foster families hours, days, weeks, or months after placement. Behavioral and emotional problems that are not understood by foster parents can result in multiple disruptions and a revolving door of multiple placements before children are referred for mental health assessments and interventions. (Pasztor et al., 2006, p. 51)

Clinical skill is also necessary in work with birth parents, who can be demanding and draining, as they experience feelings of personal loss and anger as their children are removed from them; ambivalence about placing children can be acted out against the child welfare worker. Birth parents need help in working through their losses, in addressing their psychological and relationship problems, and finding constructive outlets in their lives; they may need help in working toward family reunification or, if necessary, termination of parental rights.

Ackerson (2003) has argued that often mentally ill parents have been stigmatized because of their mental illness and may, unnecessarily, lose their children to the child welfare system; many workers are inadequately prepared to assess mental health issues or to provide help to mentally ill parents; workers should be able to assess, for example, whether a mother is mildly depressed or has a serious bipolar disorder, as well as whether her capacity for relationships and ability to parent are impaired. Those developmental processes that affect parent-child interactions, such as problems in attachment, are vital in parent assessments (Ackerson, 2003). "Policymakers and practitioners may fail to recognize or evaluate thoroughly the potential risks of problematic patterns of attachment. . . . Of particular concern are children who display disorganized and disoriented patterns of behavior" (Haights, Kagle, and Black, 2003, pp. 204-205); these patterns "are associated with a history of parent psychopathology"; they are also associated with parental abuse and neglect (p. 203).

The objective for the majority of foster children is a return to their birth families, and therefore family visits are a prerequisite, and considered so important that the Adoption Assistance and Child Welfare Act of 1980 (P.L. 96-272) "requires inclusion of regular visits in family preservation efforts"; however, "existing research suggests that, too often, visits fall short of meeting their goals" (Haights, Kagle, and Black, 2003, p. 195).

Visits can be problematic, owing to the nature of the parent-child attachment, possible mental health problems of the child and parents, and "negative messages" from the foster parents about the birth family, all of which require skilled psychodynamically aware intervention by the child welfare worker.

> Child welfare policy and practice should support parents and children before, during, and after visits. . . . *Visits may cause the parent and child to repeatedly re-experience difficult emotions associated with reunion and separation.* . . . They [caseworkers] also should make special efforts to support parents and children during transitions to and from visits. (Haights, Kagle, and Black, 2003, p. 198; italics added)

Kinship Foster Families

Kinship foster care, in which a child is placed with relatives, enables the child to remain in familiar surroundings with extended family members, and potentially provides better continuity of care; the Adoption and Safe Families Act of 1977 mandates that children should be placed with their relatives as a first choice, if this is possible (Cole, 2006). Grandparenting is one of the most prevalent forms of kinship care, especially in African-American (Beaucar, 1999c; Hollingsworth, 1998) and Latino communities (Burnette, 1999); about 4 million children are currently being raised by grandparents (Llana, 2006). Research studies have reported favorable outcomes for children in kinship care, and various services have been developed to help this population: support groups (Beaucar, 1999c; Landers,

1992); community-based interdisciplinary interventions (Whitley et al., 1999); and special housing projects for GrandFamilies (Dowdy, 1998; Llana, 2006).

Maluccio (2006) acknowledges the "obvious advantages to keeping children within the context of their families of origin," but adds that "achieving successful outcomes for children in kinship care requires . . . policy changes, and practice efforts that support kin caregivers and children" (Lorkovitch et al., 2004) (p. 6). Services are not always adequate, and many unsolved problems remain. The burden of caring for young and often disturbed grandchildren have placed many grandparents under considerable stress, especially given their advanced age; some have developed stress-related health problems (Beaucar, 1999c; Whitley et al., 1999; Worrall, 2006), and many have reported financial problems. Although kinship fostering saves money for many child welfare departments, it places relatives at a financial disadvantage, as many are poor and receive less money, oversight, and fewer services than nonrelated foster families (Cole, 2006). Grandparents in some states are unable to secure legal custody or foster care status, depriving them of "health care, food stamps and cash assistance to raise their grandchildren, and [they can be] . . . targeted for the child support payments their own children have failed to make" (Beaucar, 1999c, p. 12).

Worrall (2006), studying kinship care in New Zealand and reviewing international studies, reports a number of problems with this approach, including those discussed above, and in addition: the suspicion of maltreatment in some families; less work done with the biological parents toward reunification; and complex legal and relationship problems between the caregivers and the birth parents (p. 547).

O'Donnell (1999) raises concern about the lack of attention to the role the father plays in kinship care and finds in general that "child welfare literature has been conspicuously silent about fathers of color" (p. 429); even when children were placed with paternal relatives, "African American fathers in two kinship foster care programs seldom participated in interventions on behalf of their children and . . . caseworkers rarely engaged fathers in discussions that might lead to participation" (p. 436); the child welfare system can "maximize support" to children "by reaching out to fathers . . . along a continuum of involvement" (p. 439).

SYSTEMIC ISSUES IN CHILD WELFARE

The child welfare field is faced by multiple pressures, including an increased demand for services for children with serious emotional problems

(Dore, 1999). "Today the provision of mental health services represents one of the largest health problems facing foster children . . . ." (Fontana and Gonzales, 2006, p. 267). Although model child welfare projects operate, this is not the prevailing picture. The child welfare field is in a state of crisis, with children missing from their foster homes and "lost" by the system (Canedy, 2003), and children abused or even killed by biological or foster parents (Brick, 2006; Jones, 2003; L. Z. Jones, 2006). The Casey Foundation and the Brookings Institute have found that human services are in a state of crisis "with conditions so dysfunctional that reform is essential" (O'Neill, 2003, p. 9). Funding and bureaucratic problems, long endemic in child welfare, persist, including high caseloads, low salaries for social workers, and high staff turnover (Beaucar, 1999b). Child welfare workers generally receive inadequate supervision and support; for many, "issues of support, respect, training and respite are critical factors in job satisfaction" (O'Neill, 2003, p. 9). Though "the need for professionally prepared child welfare workers is indisputable," it is frequently unmet (Chavkin and Brown, 2003, p. 54).

Child welfare workers often experience burnout, due to clinical and organizational stressors, including the need to make difficult placement decisions; feeling ineffectual; overidentifying with fragile and traumatized clients; and working with violent, threatening people (Dane, 2000). Child welfare workers are subject to *vicarious traumatization*, a syndrome endured by many clinicians working with trauma victims (Dane, 2000), as though they themselves are directly traumatized through exposure to the client's reported experiences. The symptoms of vicarious traumatization include "decreased sense of energy . . . social withdrawal . . . increased sensitivity to violence, fear . . . and hopelessness" (p. 29).

When the child welfare system becomes active in a case, the legal system also becomes involved. "The state's custody of a child is a legal issue, and ultimately a judge must rule on whether or not parents can regain custody of their children" (Smyke, Wajda-Johnston, and Zeanah, 2004, p. 270); courts make determinations of serious child abuse or neglect and mandate protective services, and are often a nexus of serious systemic problems, including such high volumes of abuse and neglect cases that a "caseload crisis" has developed (Liederman, 1995, p. 431). Children are assigned lawyers to represent their interests in court proceedings. A recent study found that "not only do lawyers have too many cases, but they also do not have adequate support in their offices to handle their work" (Davidson and Pitchal, 2006).

Managed care, with its cutbacks on mental health and substance abuse services, has had a serious impact on parents and children in need of long-term intensive services.

Case Illustration

The reported case of Matthew illustrates how one child's life and psychological development were affected by his traumatic experiences with his birth mother, the uncertainty about the permanency of his foster placement, and the systemic problems he encountered with the child welfare system (Paret and Shapiro, 1998). The fact that Matthew's birth family is "Hispanic and poor, his foster mother Caucasian and middle class" (p. 302), at times influenced custody decisions.

When Matthew was six weeks old, the police, who "suspected that his [single] mother was selling drugs," (Paret and Shapiro, 1998, p. 304) removed him and his brother from their home because the house was "'filthy'" and "'unsafe'" Matthew's mother, Ms. Rivers, was no longer involved with Matthew's father "and could not even provide his [the father's] name" (p. 306). She promised to attend a drug rehabilitation program; the next day Matthew was returned to her. When Matthew was thirteen months old, Ms. River, feeling stressed, requested inpatient drug treatment.

> Matthew was placed with a foster mother, Ms. Smith, for the first time. At the time of placement the caseworker described Matthew as "ill, dirty, frightened, and developmentally lagging." The foster mother noted that, although it was February, Matthew was dressed in a light-weight summer jacket and wore no socks. When Ms. Smith put him in the high chair and started to prepare food, tears poured down his face, but he did not make a sound. The silent crying continued on and off for a few days. Matthew gradually responded to her care and allowed her to feed, bathe, rock, and comfort him. This fragile homeostasis often broke down; he would suddenly become angry, yell, and repeatedly hit a doll on the head with his fist. Ms. Smith thought he might be re-enacting something he had seen or experienced. (Paret and Shapiro, 1998, p. 304)

During the two months Matthew stayed with Ms. Smith, he began to develop language, was emotionally responsive, and seemed happy. He was then returned to his birth mother, who had finished her drug program. However, the situation remained unstable: She was resistant to services, and "the severity of Ms. Rivers' psychological impairment and vulnerability became more evident" (Paret and Shapiro, 1998, p. 305). Ms. Rivers' own childhood had been traumatic; her mother had been schizophrenic and Ms. Rivers was a foster child with one family for ten years, when she then began a life of shifting back and forth among groups, homes, shelters, and hospitals. As an older adolescent, she became addicted to drugs.

Matthew was returned to Ms. Smith when he was eighteen months old, and his unstable situation persisted, as he moved back and forth between his birth mother and his foster mother. "Whenever Matthew left his foster mother for visits with his birth mother he regressed and was frightened, angry, and clinging upon his return. The psychological intensity of these transitions did not diminish over time" (Paret and Shapiro, 1998, p. 305). Matthew lived mostly with his foster mother for the next three years; a consulting psychologist then recommended that Matthew be returned to his birth mother.

> This consultant, Dr. Morris, described her plan as a "high-risk reunification." *Her decision was influenced by the dominant case law in the state, which was biased in favor of returning children to their biological parents.* She believed that the case law superseded the issues presented by other psychologists in the past, who had stressed the quality and valence of Matthew's attachment to his foster mother.... Dr. Morris believed that Matthew had the "resiliency" (Rutter, 1990) to handle the loss of his foster mother. (Paret and Shapiro, 1998, p. 307; italics added)

In the meantime, Matthew exhibited serious symptoms after his mandated overnight visits to his birth mother.

> Matthew was having nightmares, wetting himself day and night, and was afraid to be alone in a room. In anticipation of each visit to his birth mother, he became defiant and upset, crying throughout the two-hour trip with the state social worker. (p. 307)

At this point in time, Ms. Smith requested therapy for Matthew, now four, to help him with the planned reunification. The therapist soon understood "his reactions to the actual danger and volatile realities of his life and brought these new observations to the attention of the authorities" (Paret and Shapiro, 1998, p. 309). The court then ordered the overnight visits to stop, but he continued to visit in the daytime. The case was brought for review to the psychologist, Dr. Morris, "who took account of the new information" (p. 311) but reiterated her former position. She asserted that reunification "would not be too damaging to him if his birth mother would seriously engage in treatment and create a stable home" (p. 311).

Ms. Rivers was not able to involve herself in therapy. In the meantime, Matthew's behavior deteriorated further. In addition to her inconsistent and sometimes harsh treatment of him, Ms. Rivers began making "veiled threats to abduct him, and supervised visits were ordered by the court" (Paret and Shapiro, 1998, p. 312).

Dr. Morris reversed her opinion when Matthew was five; she now approved his adoption by Ms. Smith.

> *Dr. Morris hoped that a voluntary open adoption could be arranged.* . . . Ms. Rivers could not accept the idea of limited supervised visits and rejected this adoption plan. The agency now recommended that her parental rights be severed. . . . *It took almost two more years for the court to hear the case, make the decision to terminate Ms. River's parental rights, and complete the adoption process.* Matthew remained with Ms. Smith during this period. (Paret and Shapiro, 1998, p. 312; italics added)

Prior to the trial, Matthew was evaluated by two "independent mental health professionals" (Paret and Shapiro, 1998, p. 312). Ms. Rivers' lawyer chose a psychologist *"well known for his views that children should remain with their biological mothers, especially in cross-racial situations"* (p. 312; italics added). During the evaluation, which lasted four months, Matthew was upset and again regressed. "His lack of autonomy was infuriating to him. 'I keep telling and telling, I want to stay with Ms. Smith!' he said to his evaluators" (p. 314). After the evaluations it was another six months before the judge made the decision to allow adoption by Ms. Smith; Matthew was now six-and-a-half years old. The adoption papers were signed when Matthew was nearly seven; this was initially a happy time for him, but then a resurgence of insecure feelings followed.

> Matthew was ecstatic when he learned of the judge's decision to allow his adoption by Ms. Smith. He was radiant when he told the news to the therapist, and at home he shouted out the window to the neighborhood that he was going to be adopted. He stopped wetting and soiling, and his most dangerous behavior abated. . . . But this quiescent period did not last. He remained extremely sensitive to perceived loss, danger, or narcissistic injury, and gains could be undone quickly, suggestive of Balint's (1968) idea of a basic fault. (Paret and Shapiro, 1998, p. 315)

Basic fault is defined as a deep-seated sense of insecurity resulting from an insecure attachment to the mother, which manifests itself in development of later relationships.

Matthew made progress in continuing therapy, but his early traumas and insecurities did not just "disappear," even when the permanency of his new home was established; "his psychological wounds do not heal easily" (Paret and Shapiro, 1998, p. 322). Although he was now free of his frightening visits to his birth mother, conflict, ambivalence, and guilt about her remained; "his own survival left him with feelings of guilt about Bobby [his brother] and Ms. Rivers and what he thought he might have done to them" (p. 318). He also talked about missing Bobby, who had remained at home with their mother during this time.

This case illustrates the importance of establishing permanence as soon as possible. Although Matthew had a very strong tie to his foster mother and did experience her attachment and deep commitment to him, he lived in perpetual fear that he would be removed from her and returned to his birth mother and a nightmare existence. Matthew was fortunate to have one consistent, caring foster mother; many children like Matthew experience disrupted placements, with multiple families.

Matthew was also fortunate to have long-term therapy, which is often not available to foster children. His therapist also provided support and guidance to Ms. Smith, his foster mother, who often felt overwhelmed and discouraged about his behavior. "The therapeutic relationship enabled her to endure her own grief and frustration" (Paret and Shapiro, 1998, p. 321). When foster and adoptive parents receive supportive clinical services, placements are less likely to break down.

This case also highlights the problem of overworked courts dealing with child welfare cases; Matthew's case waited for two years before a hearing could be scheduled. Blindly applied case law influenced proceedings in two instances. In the first, the law "was biased toward the inherent rights of the birth mother"; and the consulting psychologist used this as the basis of her decision to have Matthew remain with his birth mother (Paret and Shapiro, 1998, p. 321). Although family preservation programs have proliferated, many with successful results, this is not necessarily the solution of choice for all families.

The second instance of case law involved the issue of cross-cultural adoption. Matthew did have some racial identity issues, which became apparent as he grew older; these issues often seemed intertwined with his basic struggle to find his own identity in relation to his two mothers (Paret and Shapiro, 1998).

The case of Matthew depicts one child caught in the mechanisms of child welfare and legal systems unresponsive to his needs; but Matthew is only one child who has been given a face and a voice by his therapist and foster mother. Many children become "cases" to be transferred to overworked child welfare workers and go round and round through a revolving door of foster homes and shelters. Their problems are multifaceted, and comprehensive systemic programs that recognize the individuality of each child fall very short of meeting existing needs.

CONCLUSION

Families today take many shapes and forms, but within their myriad formations, people are seeking connection and attachment, propelling them into marriages or other committed relationships and into subsequent new relationships if these fail. The wish to parent a child is strong in many, but evidently not in all; to some (attached or unattached) achieving parenthood biologically is accomplished without undue difficulty (and without needing any official sanction); others, for a variety of social and/or biological reasons, turn to reproductive technologies, adoption, and fostering (usually with bureaucratic involvement). Many wish to have a child to love, and often experience deep anguish if this possibility is excluded from their lives. Children need to form secure attachments with a sense of permanency; rejected or abandoned children whose own "recruitment" abilities (Kegan, 1982) are still intact try to attach themselves, in whatever way works, to adults who may be able to give them love or at least a token of affection; others provoke their caregivers, fearful of the affection they crave.

Psychodynamic understanding and skill are needed on the part of social workers and other clinicians working with people who need help navigating the intricacies of maintaining (or severing) partner relationships, child custody arrangements, and blended families; who need genetic counseling or reproductive technologies; or who become involved in adopting or foster parenting. Psychodynamic understanding should be embedded in basic family and child welfare social work, such as: counseling blended families; assessing the potential of adoptive applicants to provide good parenting, and helping them adapt to their new child; deciding whether parental rights of birthparents should be terminated, or if the family should be engaged in preservation efforts. With the numbers of emotionally disturbed children in the child welfare system, not only are outside mental health services needed, but psychodynamically informed care ought to be applied to help foster (and adoptive) parents cope with these children on a daily basis, without personalizing their frequent rejecting behaviors.

For psychotherapy choices, "one size does not fit all"; likewise in terms of family organizations and needs, one size does not fit all. Children can find loving homes with traditional families, as well as those with alternative organizations, such as adoptive, gay families, and single parent families. In addition, "one size does not fit all" in terms of child welfare policies; family preservation policies are necessary for some children, and for other may hinder their early adoption into permanent homes. Kinship foster care and grandparenting are ideal solutions for many families; other kinship families might be rife with mental illness or substance abuse, and child maltreatment might remain undetected.

For many, the intimacy, loving, and caring of family life is a source of strength and joy; it provides meaning and direction in life. Vaillant (1993), in discussing resilience, comments that many people who had unhappy childhoods and who were riding a life trajectory of failure were able to enter into successful marriages and enjoy a secure family life; their capacity to do so enhanced both their functioning and pleasure in life.

Children are deeply affected by family life—emotionally, cognitively, socially, and developmentally. The developmental aspects of attachment and the disruption of attachments are discussed in greater detail in Chapters 9 and 10; the internal structures of family life, with their own systemic organizations, including rules, rituals, and boundary issues, are addressed in Chapter 8.

LEARNING EXERCISE

Biographies (or autobiographies) can be discussed in small groups. Group members can share their impressions of the family structure as well as the family relationships described. In what ways are the family organization and relationships affecting the persons whose lives are depicted?

SUGGESTED READING

Articles

Bassett, J. D., and J. A. Johnson. 2004. The role of clinical consultation in child protective investigations. *Smith College Studies in Social Work* 74: 489-504.
Bergner, D. 2006. The case of Marie and her sons. *The New York Times Magazine* July 23: 28-35, 48, 53-54, 56.

Brooks, D., R. P. Barth, A. Bussiere, and G. Patterson. 1999. Adoption and race: Implementing the multiethnic placement act and the interethnic adoption provisions. *Social Work* 44: 167-178.

Freeman, M., and W. Freund. 1998. Working with adopted clients. *Journal of Analytic Social Work* 5(4): 25-37.

LaSala, M. 1998. Coupled gay men, parents, and in-laws: Intergenerational disapproval and the need for a thick skin. *Families in Society* 79: 585-593.

O'Donnell, J. M. 1999. Involvement of African American fathers in kinship foster care services. *Social Work* 44: 428-441.

Parks, C. A. 1998. Lesbian parenthood: A review of the literature. *American Journal of Orthopsychiatry* 68: 376-389.

Books

Hartman, A., and J. Laird. 1983. *Family-centered social work practice.* New York: The Free Press.

Kressel, K. 1997. *The process of divorce: Helping couples negotiate settlements.* Northvale, NJ: Jason Aronson.

Chapter 8

The Family:
Internal Structures
and Special Family Problems

> . . . every complex organization must have more or less effective self-righting adjustments
>
> Walter B. Cannon, *The Wisdom of the Body,* 1932

INTRODUCTION

Within the variety of family organizational forms existing today, each family constructs its unique world, with its own rules, rituals, and internal alliances, negotiating its external boundaries with the outside world and its internal boundaries among its own members (Minuchin, 1974). The family, from a *structural* perspective, is a self-contained system; changes in one part of the system produce corresponding changes in another part. Members "dance" to patterned steps and movements, ever in synchrony, if not in harmony with the others. In this world of transactional forces, if a family has a need to have one member "psychologically ill," and the sick person gets better (perhaps through the "intrusion" of an outsider, such as a psychotherapist), then the family finds another member to be the "sick" one.

The structural perspective does not concern itself about what is taking place within the individual psyches of its members (as does the psychodynamic perspective); if one family member is depressed, the focus will not be on understanding the origins of that depression or on treating it, but on questions such as the role the depressed person plays in the family, how the depression creates problems in family communication, and the ways the depressed person might use the depression to manipulate family members.

Human Behavior in the Social Environment, Second Edition

Depression would be viewed from the structural perspective as an interpersonal response to the structural issues within the family.

It has been argued that it is not possible to integrate the systemic and psychodynamic approaches as they are too disparate (Hartman and Laird, 1983). The object relations perspective, however, is one integrative theory, focusing on both the present here-and-now relationships of family members in a transactional way, as well as each member's internal representations of self and significant others from the past; "we intervene at the microlevel of the interior of the family and its relation to the developing interiors of its individuals members" (Scharff and Scharff, 1987, p. 13). A father in a family might (through projective identification) act out past feelings related to being rejected by his parents in such a manner as to produce these rejections in the present by his provocative behaviors to his wife and the therapist. Rather than feeling and acting rejected and responding in a retaliatory manner, as the wife might (adding to the family dysfunction), the therapist would process these feelings internally, and then share them constructively within the family. In this context, the therapist would bring the past to life to illuminate the present; this would be similar to the approach of relational psychotherapy (discussed in Chapter 4), but would be utilized within a family context.

Intersubjectivity, a contribution from the object relations perspective, suggests that emotions can be transmitted from one person to another; this often occurs within a family. Happiness and a joy for life can be transmitted to children by parents, as can troubling emotions such as anxiety; parental depressive affect can be felt by a child (who may also be affected by parental withdrawal). Parents exposed to social traumas, such as the Holocaust (Rosenbloom, 1983) and the massacres of Native Americans (Brave Heart, 1998), can indirectly transmit their anxieties about these events to their children, who have never had these experiences themselves and who may have never even been told about them. Intergenerational transmission of child maltreatment is inferred when parents, maltreated in childhood, abuse or neglect their own children (Morton and Browne, 1998; Tracy and Johnson, 2006; Zeanah and Scheeringa, 1997). Maternal emotions can affect a child even before birth; complex hormonal interactions occur via the placenta. "Mothers with high anxiety levels are likely to produce babies who are hyperactive and irritable, have sleep disorders and low birth weight, and feed poorly" (Kaplan, Sadock, and Grebb, 1994, p. 39).

Social work has traditionally taken a family perspective; individuals are viewed in the context of their families and social environments. However, opinions differ, both within social work and in other mental health professions, as to how much emphasis should be given to the individual and how much to the family. At one extreme are clinicians who believe that the family should always be the unit of attention; others feel that the focus of treatment should be the individual. Some clinicians view the family and individual in a comprehensive, integrative way; Moultrup (1981) has stated that it is as risky for a family therapist to fail to deal with the individual as is the reverse for the individual therapist (p. 113). A multitude of theories and approaches also exist for working with families, even within a given theoretical approach. "Family therapy was, and still is, a wondrous Tower of Babel; people in it speak many different tongues" (Hoffman, 1981, p. 9).

Families change as the ages and developmental needs of their members change; infants' needs are different from those of teenagers, and family relationships and social lives are affected by these alterations. The developmental perspective emphasizes the importance of the family life cycle, which is "composed of a natural sequence of stages or periods" (Longres, 1995b, p. 297), encompassing such events as parents having children, children leaving home, parents aging, and so on. Emphasis is placed on the transitions the family makes from one phase to the next, and it is postulated that when families have difficulties it is because of transitioning problems (Longres, 1995b), such as having to face the felt loss of children growing up. Knowing where people are in their life cycles, what their age-specific capabilities and needs are, can help us direct our focus and expectations.

One strength of the developmental model is the emphasis it places on the "normative sources of stress" (Longres, 1995b, p. 298); that is, all families pass through these stages. Disagreement, however, exists about this model: no unanimity prevails on how many family developmental stages occur within the life cycle or on the tasks involved in successful transitions. This model is also criticized for its inability to accommodate to the diversity found in modern family life (Germain, 1991; Longres, 1995b). Some have suggested retaining the basic life development framework but adding other frequently occurring transitions, such as divorce and remarriage (Zastrow and Kirst-Ashman, 1997).

The developmental model is also criticized for leaving out the social and cultural influences affecting individuals and families; family development does not evolve in a vacuum. Germain (1991) prefers the "'life course'" model, as it highlights "life transitions, life events, and other life issues as outcomes of person(s): environment processes" (p. 149). Hutchison (2005) discusses the life-course perspective, which omits psychodynamic theory, while highlighting social and cultural concepts that emphasize the historical and social contexts in which a person is living; the relevance of trajectories, transitions and turning points, and the timing of events (i.e., how old the person is when an event is occurring—is it "on-time" or "off-time" in terms of his social group); the relevance of intergenerational transmission of social patterns; and the importance of human agency (i.e., self-direction and will).

This book incorporates a developmental framework, an ecological and a life course perspective, integrating an individual's and family's transactions with their social and cultural contexts, including their key transitions and turning points; these are incorporated as an essential piece of the psychodynamic biopsychosocial perspective.

STRUCTURAL THEORY

Minuchin (1974), a pioneer in the family therapy field, views family systems as an overarching concept: "a family is more than the individual biopsychodynamics of its members" (p. 89). He focuses on how families organize themselves and interact with their members, by means of *"transactional patterns"* (p. 51; italics added).

> A family is a system that operates through transactional patterns. Repeated transactions establish patterns of how, when, and to whom to relate, and these patterns underpin the system. When a mother tells her child to drink his juice and he obeys, this interaction defines who she is in relation to him and who he is in relation to her, in that context and at that time. Repeated operations in these terms constitute a transactional pattern. (Minuchin, 1974, p. 51)

Universal rules govern family organization (Hartman and Laird, 1983; Minuchin, 1974), and different levels of rules exist; a family may have rules about eating between meals or completing homework. At another level rules also define who is in charge and the roles and functions of family members. However, the most important rules relate to the existence of the family system itself. Some family behaviors may be incomprehensible to an outsider; it becomes important to understand the purpose of this behavior, rather than its origins (Hartman and Laird, 1983, p. 36). If, for example, a couple is in therapy because of continual tension and friction, "the question is not why they are fighting, but how the fighting helps to maintain the system"; from this perspective, the fighting "is not the problem but rather an attempt at a solution, and it leads us to the question, 'then what *is* the problem?'" (p. 299; italics in the original).

Families also have "rules about rules," called *metarules* (Hartman and Laird, 1983, p. 300), which tell family members whether they are free to discuss the rules themselves and whether the rules are subject to alteration. "In a very rigid, homeostatic family, there is a powerful metarule that rules may not be commented upon or altered" (p. 300).

Rules determine the specific organizational patterns of a family, including the family's subsystems, which help the family define and perform its functions. Every family has multiple subsystems, and each member is usually part of several subsystems "in which he has different levels of power and where he learns differentiated skills. A man can be a son, nephew, older brother, younger brother, husband, father, and so on. In different subsystems, he enters into different complementary [reciprocal] relationships" (Minuchin, 1974, p. 52). Each subsystem has its own boundaries, which are the "rules defining who participates, and how" (p. 53).

> For example, the boundary of a parental subsystem is defined when a mother (M) tells her older child, "You aren't your brother's parent. If he is riding his bike in the street, tell me, and I will stop him." If the parental subsystem includes a parental child (PC), the boundary is defined by the mother's telling the children, "Until I get back from the store, Annie is in charge." (Minuchin, 1974, p. 53)

Hartman and Laird (1983) emphasize that clarity and flexibility are major aspects of boundaries. Clarity provides family members with "clear and unambivalent messages" about boundary rules (p. 271). A child clearly understands that he or she is a child in the family, not a parent; or, conversely, the child may receive the message that he or she is a *parentified* child (i.e., he or she must act as a parent to his or her parents). Clarity raises the question of whether these roles are clearly defined. If individuals receive mixed messages (without clarity) about their roles, so that they do not know if they will be rewarded or punished at any given time for the same behaviors, they will become confused and perplexed in this inconsistent world.

Flexibility allows for changes in boundary formation "in adaptive ways as the circumstances and needs of the family change" (Hartman and Laird, 1983, p. 271). As parents age, for example, if flexible boundaries exist, they will allow their adult children to assume more responsibility for them.

In examining the boundary formation of families, two extremes have been observed: *enmeshment,* which is an extreme degree of overinvolvement and blurring of boundaries, and *disengagement,* in which boundaries are very rigid and family members have poor communication and maintain distance from each other. On this "continuum . . . most families fall within the wide normal range" (Minuchin, 1974, p. 54).

Hartman and Laird (1983) suggest questions to judge a family's degree of enmeshment:

> Do family members speak for each other, or do they respect the fact that the other, even a child, may have separate views? . . . Are the parents overinvolved in every aspect or decision to be made in the child's life? Does the family tolerate differences, or must time, interests, opinions, and activities be shared? (p. 272)

Nora, a middle-aged client, was involved in a family with a multigenerational history of enmeshment. Her background is replete with rejection and severe family dysfunction; she was a parentified child, mothering her younger siblings. In her current life, her enmeshment with her daughters and their boyfriends was compounded by reality problems with housing and money.

> Nora's two adult daughters, at different times, were living with their boyfriends in Nora's house (with Nora). No clear-cut agreements had been reached between them about household responsibilities and sharing rent with Nora. The daughters and their boyfriends expected Nora to do the housekeeping and cooking without their help or consistent financial contributions. Nora's daughter Charlotte had a boyfriend who was very disturbed; they were entangled in endless fights and chaos. Nora could not confront them nor could she ask them to leave. She complained, in her therapy, of increased headaches and depression.

Nora suffered emotional abuse from family members, including her parents, such as their coldly critical attitudes toward her and blatant favoritism toward her siblings despite her efforts to gain their approval; it was difficult for her to assert herself with them. In a rather unprecedented "generous" gesture, her father invited Nora and her children on a trip to an amusement park.

> Her family's behavior there embarrassed her, and she was especially mortified by her mother's inappropriate loud comments and bizarre behavior. The fact that Nora knew the workers at the park caused her further shame. Although her father implied he would pay the expenses, he backed out, leaving Nora to use most of her week's salary to pay the bill. This was followed by Nora's long stay in bed with depression.

When Nora was bequeathed an inheritance, she had an opportunity to invest the money, which would have been to her advantage as she had no assets; but she did not do this.

Nora inherited some money from her mother. Then, because both daughters were having a financial crisis, she lent them a substantial amount of money, which they promised to repay but subsequently showed little inclination to return. This added to her own financial crisis, and her feelings about this colored her relationship to her daughters.

In assessing whether families are *disengaged,* Hartman and Laird (1983) include the following questions:

> Do family members seem impervious to or insensitive to one another? Do they block each other's communications or avoid close contact, either emotional or physical or both? Some families, as Bowen (1985) has pointed out, are characterized by an "emotional divorce" between the parents . . . careful observation discloses that there is little or no affect or energy passing between them. (p. 272)

Clara, seventeen, was hospitalized on an inpatient psychiatric ward for a serious suicide attempt and anorexia nervosa (an eating disorder in which individuals literally "starve" themselves into a skeletal appearance based on the premise that they are too fat). Her parents were interviewed.

> Dr. G., Clara's father, looked bored and was impatient; he had surgical patients to attend to. Mrs. G. was distraught, worried about the confidentiality of this interview, and hoped her daughter's hospitalization could be kept secret; she was chagrined at the thought that her family and friends might know of this "disgrace." Dr. G. looked annoyed as Mrs. G. spoke and said that she should keep her mind on the main issue: Clara needs to be discharged from this place as soon as possible, so that she can complete her academic year and be eligible for a good college.

Triangles are discussed by structural theorists. Bowen (1985) emphasizes this organizing concept, which is important not only in understanding families but also in "understanding the microscopic functioning of all emotional systems" (p. 478). The process of *triangulation* develops when a two-person system experiences tension, so they "'triangle in' a third person" to relieve the tension in the system (p. 478). A classic example is the mother who, feeling uncomfortable in her relationship with her husband, forms a "close twosome" with her child, while "the father is the outsider" (p. 479). In couples or family therapy, people often attempt to triangulate therapists into the family system; self-awareness on the therapists' part enables them to observe and utilize this phenomenon in treatment without allowing themselves to be drawn into it.

Although triangulation is a normative concept frequently occurring in all families, it can reach extreme forms.

> In triangulation each parent demands that the child side with him against the other parent. Whenever the child sides with one, he is automatically defined as attacking the other. In this highly dysfunctional structure, the child is paralyzed. Every movement he makes is defined by one parent as an attack. (Minuchin, 1974, p. 102)

A given triangulation might become a fixed pattern, or it can shift back and forth, as different alliances develop. Observing triangles "brings to light special alliances, shifting coalitions, and scapegoats" (Hartman and Laird, 1983, p. 284). Bowen (1985) describes how during great stress "a system will triangle in more and more outsiders" (p. 479). Frequently encountered is a family

> in great stress that uses the triangle system to involve . . . a spectrum of outside people as participants in the family problem. The family thus reduces the tension within the inner family, and . . . the family tension is being fought out by outside people. (p. 479)

One major emphasis running through many family theories relates to issues of separation and individuation, or differentiation. This seems consistent with Mahler, Pine, and Bergman's (1975) theory of separation-individuation, but the systemic theorists and the object relations theorists look at differentiation through different lenses. Mahler, Pine, and Bergman (1975) are concerned about the child's psychological development, the growth of ego functions, and the development of self- and object representations. The family system thinkers, by and large, are not concerned with the inner states of individuals or the development of their ego functions; their focus is the system and how each individual is part of the whole; efforts are concentrated at systemic change, so that the family as a whole can develop and mature.

Bowen's (1985) concept of differentiation bridges the gap between psychodynamic and structural theories (Freed, 1985; Moultrup, 1981). Bowen observed that, generally, people with higher levels of differentiation cope better than those who are more fused with others and therefore have lower levels of differentiation. He sees this concept as the cornerstone of his theory.

> the degree of *fusion,* or *differentiation,* between emotional and intellectual functioning . . . can be used as a way of categorizing all people

on a single continuum. At the low extreme are those whose . . . lives are dominated by the automatic emotional system . . . who are less flexible, less adaptable, and more emotionally dependent . . . easily stressed into dysfunction. . . . They inherit a high percentage of all human problems.

At the other extreme are those who are more differentiated . . . whose intellectual functioning can retain relative autonomy in periods of stress . . . more flexible, more adaptable, and more independent of the emotionality about them. . . . They are remarkably free of human problems. (Bowen, 1985, p. 362)

Bowen, in his definition of differentiation, highlights the difference between intellectual and emotional functioning, which emphasizes the ego functions of impulse control and cognitive skills. This discussion of differentiation appears removed from the concept of *identity consolidation.* Yet Bowen (1985) approaches the concept of differentiation related to identity more closely when he adds that "another important part of the differentiation of self has to do with the levels of *solid self* and the *pseudo-self* in a person" (p. 364; italics in the original). Although Bowen still places emphasis on intellectual and emotional functioning, he observes that

the level of solid self is stable. The pseudo-self is unstable, and it responds to a variety of social pressures and stimuli. The pseudo-self was acquired at the behest of the relationship system, and it is negotiable in the relationship system. (p. 366)

People with a pseudo-self develop as "dependent appendages of their parents, following which they seek other equally *dependent relationships in which they can borrow enough strength to function*" (Bowen, 1985, p. 367; italics added). Bowen's description is similar to the utilization of selfobjects, an integral concept in self psychology (Wolf, 1988), and also resonates with Winnicott's description of a "continuum of the *false self* ranging from the healthy, polite aspect of the self to the truly split-off, compliant, false self that is mistaken for the whole person" (Giovacchini, 1993, p. 254; italics added).

Bowen's (1985) discussion of differentiation of self pertaining to family dynamics illuminates many puzzling behaviors of families. A particularly fascinating observation is that when people marry they *"pick spouses who have the same levels of differentiation"* (Bowen, 1985, p. 377; italics added). In other words, people with a solid self tend to marry others with a solid self and maintain a balance between the intimacy of a marriage and retaining an autonomous sense of self. If both partners are "wobbly," mutual collapse, rather than mutual support, may ensue. Sometimes people may be frightened by the degree of fusion they experience within the marital bond (or any intimate relationship), and may need to fight or flee to create "emotional distance from each other" (p. 377). The "amount of undifferentiation in the marriage" is expressed through "marital conflict; sickness or dysfunction in one spouse) and projection of the problems to children. . . . The various patterns . . . come from patterns in their families of origin" (p. 377).

Kressel (1997) has studied divorcing couples and has focused on the "*distinctive patterns* by which our couples reached the divorce decision" (p. 226; italics added), such as the enmeshed pattern. Poorly differentiated people are more prone to enter enmeshed relationships, where they reenact their struggles with separation and individuation.

> The hallmarks of this pattern were extremely high levels of conflict and ambivalence about the divorce decision. The parties debated . . . often bitterly; agreed to divorce and then changed their minds. . . . They maintained a common residence after the decision and may have continued . . . having sexual relations. . . . The impression was of parties psychically unprepared to let go. (Kressel, 1997, p. 227)

> The outcomes [after divorce] were as poor as the negotiations which produced them. The parties were bitter toward each other and dissatisfied with the terms of settlement. . . . In every instance there were significant adjustment problems with children. The more extreme forms of post-divorce turmoil—initiation of law suits, and (in one case) acts of physical violence necessitating police intervention—occurred only in this pattern. (Kressel, 1997, p. 228)

We can learn more about a family's structure through the "observation of repeating patterns of communication" (Hartman and Laird, 1983, p. 302).

Communication

The pioneers in family therapy, such as Virginia Satir (1967), focused on functional and dysfunctional communication patterns in family life. Questions such as whether messages to each family member were clear or mixed and whether people were allowed to talk for themselves were brought into focus.

Pragmatics of Human Communication

Watzlawick, Beavin, and Jackson (1967) elucidate the "pragmatics" of human communication, which refers to the "behavioral effects of communication" (p. 22). In marital and family relationships, as well as in other social contexts, nonverbal communication and body language as well as the "communicational clues inherent in the context in which communication occurs . . . even the communicational clues in an impersonal context— affects behavior" (p. 22). What message, for example, do the decor, seating arrangements, and responsiveness of the receptionist in a waiting room of a social agency give to its clients? In a similar vein, Gutheil (1992) described the psychological effects of physical environments, such as housing and institutions on people (discussed in Chapter 5).

A man boarding a train notices that a seat next to another man is occupied by his possessions. The initial impersonal message received by the newcomer is that there is no room for anyone. Being of brave heart, however, this passenger inquires if he might sit down. The manner of the other man's response, such as a smile, a quick removal of the possessions, and a gesture to sit, would convey a welcoming response; a glowering expression, a removal of the possessions accompanied by sighs, and an "inability" to place the possessions elsewhere would convey that the request is unwelcome and is causing trouble to the entitled possessor of the two seats. All these communications were conveyed with barely a word spoken!

Watzlawick, Beavin, and Jackson (1967) present several axioms of communicating, two of which are discussed here. The first axiom is: *"one cannot not communicate"* (p. 51; italics in the original). One might argue with this. "But every time I tell my adolescent son to do his homework he just stares at me as though he has heard nothing, and then he doesn't even say anything! How can you call that communication?" However, what the son *is* communicating to the father is that he has chosen to tune him out, especially about being ordered to do his homework.

Watzlawick, Beavin, and Jackson (1967) state that "if it is accepted that all behavior in an interactional situation has message value, i.e., is communication, it follows that no matter how one may try, one cannot *not* communicate" (pp. 48-49; italics in the original); this does not imply that all communication is effective or accurate or that "message sent equals message received" (p. 49). This axiom has particular relevance for viewing schizophrenic behavior.

It appears that the schizophrenic tries *not to communicate.* But since even nonsense, silence, withdrawal, immobility (postural silence), or any other form of denial is itself a communication, the schizophrenic is faced with the impossible task of denying that he is communicating and at the same time denying that his denial is a communication. The realization of this basic dilemma in schizophrenia is a key to a good many aspects of schizophrenic communication that would otherwise remain obscure. (Watzlawick, Beavin, and Jackson, 1967, pp. 50-51; italics in the original)

A second axiom discussed by Watzlawick, Beavin, and Jackson (1967) refers both to the content of the communication *(the report aspect)* and how the communication should be taken *(the command aspect),* which refers to the relationship between the two communicants. Watzlawick, Beavin, and Jackson (1967) call a communication about a communication a *metacommunication* and state this axiom fully: *"Every communication has a content and a relationship aspect such that the latter classifies the former and is therefore a metacommunication"* (p. 54; italics in the original).

If a teacher tells her class that she expects them to read 100 pages by next week, the content or report aspect of this message is the specific homework assignment; the relationship or command aspect is that she is the teacher who has this expectation with which the class should comply.

In the following illustration, a social work student is making a visit to James, a patient diagnosed with paranoid schizophrenia, living in a psychiatric foster home for adult patients. The student is talking to the foster mother, Mrs. McCarthy, who is indicating that she is in charge (command aspect) of these two young people (the social worker and James) although this is never the overt subject (report aspect) of discussion.

> Mrs. McCarthy then went on to relate her experiences in caring for children at the G. Center . . . and mentioned the names of a couple of Social Workers, and asked if I knew them. She then commented on my age, and said, "Why you're not much older than James." I said that I would guess in fact I wasn't. She said you probably haven't been out of school that long. I then said that I had been doing social work for five years. James kind of smiled and said, well I guess that would make you about 26. I said well actually closer to 28, and then he said that was how old he was. Mrs. McCarthy mentioned that she had two children and pointed to their pictures on the wall. . . . I then said that I would have to run along, and I told James that we would plan on getting together next Tuesday. He commented that he had enjoyed seeing me again. Mrs. McCarthy . . . told me to feel free to stop in at any time. (Urdang, 1979, p. 7)

In this illustration, we can see Mrs. McCarthy's maneuvers in asserting her authority and dominance. Her comments about the social worker's age affirms that not only is she older (and by inference more experienced) than the social worker, but in addition, she also implies that he is not very experienced (has not been out of school very long). By comparing his age with James's age, she implies that he is not much more competent than James. She ends the discussion by giving the social worker "permission" to visit again. All these represent covert relationship or command messages.

In his novel, *A Man in Full,* Tom Wolfe (1999) describes Charlie Croker, a powerful multimillionaire in Atlanta who has borrowed large sums of money from PlannersBanc and is unable to pay the interest due. The bank sets up a breakfast meeting not only to confront him with his indebted state but to humiliate and humble him so that he will comply with their suggested solutions. Watzlawick, Beavin, and Jackson's (1967) concepts of communication are illustrated in the following excerpts from Wolfe's book.

In the first example, the "communicational clues in an impersonal context" (in this case, the physical setting) (Watzlawick, Beavin, and Jackson, 1967, p. 22) play an important role. As described by Wolfe, this breakfast meeting takes place at PlannersBanc, an elegant establishment; however, an "inelegant" room, "cunningly seedy and unpleasant," exposed to the intense glare of the sun, was chosen to emphasize the "degradation" of the occasion, before a group of inquisitors who "knew exactly what the game was. The conference table itself . . . was put together in modular sections that didn't quite jibe . . . and its surface was . . . some sort of veal-gray plastic laminate . . . in front of each of the two dozen people present, was a pathetic setting of paperware . . . and a paper plate with a huge, cold, sticky, cheesy, cowpie-like cinnamon-Cheddar coffee bun" (Wolfe, 1999, pp. 36, 38).

Charlie Croker is used to exerting his power and influence and to being treated with due deference by others; a meeting room tastefully furnished and visible signs of hospitality would be expected by him. In this context, however, the deliberate set-up of uncomfortable physical conditions is covertly designed to humiliate him, to face up to his declining financial state and his large debt to the bank; Mr. Zale furthers this agenda through his condescending attitude toward Mr. Croker.

Harry Zale was in charge of this meeting, and utilizes nonverbal communication as well as the meeting's agenda to play on the relationship (command) aspects of this interaction: "Harry . . . just kept on writing. . . . He sighted Croker down his nose. . . . And then he said in a high-pitched, rasping voice, 'Why are we here, Mr. Croker? . . . What's the problem?'" (Wolfe, 1999, pp. 41-42).

Impairments in Functional Communication

Communication has a basic functional purpose: people must communicate to make their needs known, to have social contact, share ideas, and so on; some people have serious impairments in their basic communication abilities.

Schizophrenic individuals can be incoherent or illogical and may have difficulty communicating on even a simple level; their families can learn effective methods, such as through a psychoeducational approach, to communicate with them (Anderson, 1983). In one such behavioral program, "all families were trained in effective interpersonal communication such as identifying and giving praise, compliments, criticism, and requests for behavior change" (Falloon and Liberman, 1983, p. 124).

The prelingual deaf have made great strides in their ability to communicate through sign language (Sacks, 1989). The use of sign language versus other methods of communication, such as lip reading, is controversial (see discussion in Chapter 6). Early intervention programs aimed at teaching parents of deaf children alternative ways of communicating with them are often effective.

Some people become *aphasic*—that is, they have lost their ability to use speech as a result of various illnesses, including strokes. "For those who cannot produce intelligible speech there are alternate methods of communication, such as sign language, speech boards, and speech synthesizers" (Olkin, 1999, p. 197). One stroke patient seemed to understand what a social work student was saying but could not respond verbally; she was pained to realize "how he was locked into himself." When she introduced a pad and pen into their sessions, he wrote his responses to her and was happy to be able to communicate; his family learned how to communicate with him in this manner.

Emotional Issues Blocking Family Communication

Specific emotional problems the family may not be able to face—such as illness, learning that a child is gay, or that a family member is abusing substances—can block communication, as illustrated in the following example.

Madge, fifteen, and her parents came to the mental health clinic because she recently developed school phobia, experiencing anxiety and panic whenever she went to school. The clinical social worker, based on her understanding that school phobia was usually precipitated by separation-anxiety, explored this possibility with the family, but no significant losses, crises, or traumas were identified. Utilizing a behavioral component recommended in the treatment of school phobias, it was suggested that Madge make a gradual reentry into school. For several months, this went on in a halting fashion; feeling stuck, the therapist asked the family if anything had been left out. Was anything else happening?

At first the family said that nothing else was happening. Then, after a pause, the parents said, well, maybe there was something they should mention. Madge's mother was about to have a hysterectomy. Although the mother's condition was benign, the affect of extreme anxiety attached to this was experienced as though a life-threatening event were about to occur—and no one was talking about it. Madge's mother lost her father due to divorce when she was fifteen; Madge's father lost his mother due to cancer when he was fifteen. Madge, now fifteen, was at an age of great emotional risk according to the parents' unexpressed worldview. Madge did not know what a hysterectomy was, nor did she know that retaining the uterus was not vital for life.

When the subject of the hysterectomy was brought into the open, the nature of the operation was discussed with Madge, who also learned she could visit her mother in the hospital as well as talk to her on the telephone. After this session, the symptoms of school phobia quickly vanished, and Madge flourished in school and in her social life. A follow-up interview after the surgery revealed a successful medical outcome, good functioning, and an optimistic outlook for all members of the family.

The family had not been discussing their fears about the mother's medical problem but were nevertheless communicating their anxiety; the intersubjective transmission of affect was evident and became encapsulated in Madge's school phobia.

Family secrets are frequently encountered; family rules do not permit discussing them; this "enforced silence" can increase the anxiety of family members. "Deaths, alcoholism, mental illness, suicide, divorce, incest, illegitimacy, illness, adoption, business failures, deviance of any kind, battles over money are all examples of toxic issues which may become skeletons in the family closet" (Hartman and Laird, 1983, p. 248); often when family secrets are discussed, as noted in this case, "the reality is discovered to be far less devastating than were the fantasies" (p. 248).

There are some family secrets which are shared by members of the family, but with the prohibition against discussing these secrets outside of the family. "Concealing problems known to only the nuclear family members is what Karpel (1980) called 'shared family secrets'" (Xiong et al., 2006, p. 231). Little research has been done on the management of these secrets by immigrant families from Asia. Xiong and colleagues (2006) studied the

Hmong population in Minnesota out of concern for their recent high rates of domestic violence and murder-suicide, post–traumatic stress disorder, and other mental health problems, and their general reluctance to use mental health services out of a sense of shame. The Hmong tended to share their problems and secrets with members of their families, extended families, and their "lineage leaders"; "it is suggested that professionals who work with this population take time to assess the extent to which their client is tied to his or her lineage group and the degree of willingness to allow professionals to communicate with the lineage leader" (p. 238).

Family Rituals and Myths

Family rituals are organized patterns of dealing with daily life as well as with holidays, birthdays, transitions (such as graduation), and so on. The father, for example, reads to his son before bedtime, and then the mother comes in and kisses him good night. "During the child-rearing years, creating and maintaining rituals on a daily basis are an integral part of family life" (Sameroff and Fiese, 2000, p. 13). Rituals provide a sense of security and can afford pleasure to both child and parents. One ritual seems to be making a comeback: family meals (Foderaro, 2006; Gibbs, 2006); "after decades of decline in the simple ritual of family dinners, there is evidence that many families are making the effort to gather together at the dinner table" (Foderaro, 2006, p. A1). Studies have reported that children benefit from this experience, tend to have fewer problems with drugs and alcohol, and also "to get better grades, exhibit less stress and eat better" (p. A21).

In divorcing families, rituals can be disrupted; in blended families, "as familial patterns realign" (Kaplan and Pruett, 2000, p. 533), rituals from each family may compete for attention and can be a source of anxiety and dissension. Parks (1998) expresses concern about the lack of public rituals "recognizing lesbian family formation," which she feels is another "dimension of invisibility" facing these women (p. 385). Although many lesbian families develop their own private family rituals, according to Parks (1998) "it is the public component that is critical to the sense of validation and legitimacy such rituals are intended to bestow" (p. 385); this sentiment is echoed by many advocates of gay marriage (Chen, 2006; Mansnerus, 2006).

In child welfare work, rituals are sometimes used to help children deal with transitions (Hartman and Laird, 1983). The enactment of a claiming ritual is followed by some adoptive families, when adoptions are finalized; this is celebrated by "an exchange of vows, the expression of sentiments by extended family members, a party, pictures, and gifts" (p. 324).

Families construct their own interpretations of life, including the development of special beliefs and stories, defined by David Reiss as the "family paradigm," which is the family's "fundamental assumptions about the world in which it lives" (Hartman and Laird, 1983, p. 105). Rituals follow from paradigms; telling "family stories" is one avenue for expression of family beliefs. "Family stories may be examined by their thematic content, on the one hand, and by the process of storytelling itself, on the other" (Sameroff and Fiese, 2000, p. 12).

Myths, sometimes used synonymously with the term *family stories,* emphasize the family belief system. Mythical processes are often seen in family stories of "heroic or villainous figures, disruptive events, and identifications" (Germain, 1991, p. 134). Myths may or may not be based on facts; however, "their thematic content and process can play themselves out in the current situation—for good or for ill" (p. 134). A boy, for example, who did not know his father may have heard about how "perfect" he was, and so might internalize and perpetuate this myth of the father (which may or may not be accurate). Woods and Hollis (1990) state that myths can serve defensive functions in families, and "may be perpetuated to avoid or to deny painful feelings of self-blame, as they often are in families that exclusively attribute their miseries or misfortunes to one family member" (p. 322).

The Intergenerational Family

Some grandparents live with the nuclear family, where their involvement is immediate and continuous. Other grandparents have actual custodial care of their grandchildren, and their involvement is primary. However, even if grandparents are not involved with the family or are no longer living, they may still exert strong influence on the family. "Boszormenyi-Nagy and Spark (1973) speak directly to the need for an awareness of multigenerational patterns" (Moultrup, 1981, p. 122). They highlight issues of "merit and indebtedness"; children develop a sense of rules and expectations from their parents, which they then transmit to their own children. Children may subsequently feel some conflict in meeting these obligations if they conflict with the expectations of their peers.

Intergenerational transmission of child maltreatment has been observed (Morton and Browne, 1998; Tracy and Johnson, 2006; Zeanah and Scheeringa, 1997; italics added). If children receive "insensitive parenting," (Morton and Browne, 1998, p. 1098), they subsequently may be unable to develop caring, consistent relationships with their own children.

Bowen (1985), in discussing multigenerational transmissions, stresses the concept of the family projection process, in which "the parents and the child play active parts in the transmission of the parental problem to the child" (e.g., a mother denies her inner feelings of helplessness and overprotects her child, who feels and acts more helpless) (p. 127). Bowen (1985) states that this transmission continues through "multiple generations" (p. 384) and emphasizes the dominant role of differentiation in this process. The child who is targeted in the family projection process *"emerges with a lower level of differentiation than the parents and does less well in life"* (p. 384; italics added); over generations, the offspring of this child will have children "with lower and lower levels of differentiation" (p. 384). Moultrup (1981) comments that differentiation cannot be meaningfully conceptualized within the limits of a single generation: "It is rather a combination of issues involving the separation of selfs and the accounting of multigenerational obligations" (p. 124).

OBJECT RELATIONS FAMILY THERAPY

Object relations family therapy has many similarities to structural theory, with its emphasis on the internal organization of families. However, object relations diverges from structural theory in its concern with the inner object world of each family member and the interactions of these inner worlds of object and self-representations with the outer world of present family interrelationships. "Object relations family theory provides the theoretical framework for understanding, and the language for working with, the dynamics of both the individual self and the family system" (Scharff and Scharff, 1987, p. 14).

The utilization of the therapist's countertransference reactions is one of the foundations of treatment. Although Scharff and Scharff (1987) do not use the term intersubjectivity, their description of utilizing the therapeutic self appears synonymous with this concept. They note that, in a similar vein to Bowen's family projection process, the family will project feelings onto the therapists as they have done with other family members (projective identification); the therapists then process and utilize their reactions to these projections with the family and observe that:

> We are open to being used in the way family members are used, and yet we remain able to move outside of that to comment upon what is happening to us and thus to allow the family a new experience of such phenomena. (Scharff and Scharff, 1987, p. 9)

This view is compatible with the model of relational psychotherapy, described in Chapter 4.

Other features differentiate object relations from structural therapy. Object relations therapists deal with the past, rather than focus only on the here and now, as many structural therapists do. "In our view, *the past does still exist and is constantly reenacted in the present relationships*" (Scharff and Scharff, 1987, p. 10; italics added); insights are shared with the families; therapists choose not to rely on directives and homework (a frequently employed technique of structural therapists) but value the development of the family's self-awareness. They also encourage the expression of affects, whereas many systemic therapists "do not encourage emotional catharsis" (Scharff and Scharff, 1987, p. 10).

Fraiberg, Adelson, and Shapiro (1975) have talked about ghosts in the nursery; some parents cannot see their children as individual "objects" but relate to them through the veil of past memories. Object relations therapists are concerned with these ghosts who haunt present relationships; the goal is to bring the ghosts out into the light and banish them. Symptom removal is not the primary objective; personal growth and the development of enriched interpersonal relationships are the aims of object relations therapy.

WORKING WITH FAMILIES:
THE BIOPSYCHOSOCIAL PERSPECTIVE

The psychodynamic biopsychosocial perspective is an excellent vantage point from which to understand both the individual and the family; it enables clinicians to look *outward,* at clients' families within their physical and social environments and culture, as well as look *inward* at the individuals' anxieties, conflicts, and ego structure, and the interactive interrelatedness of these; object relations and structural theories contribute to this perspective. Utilizing constructivist insights, clinicians are enabled to search for the meanings their unique problems have for their clients, and to observe how clients choose to involve themselves in working in alliance with them. Woods and Hollis (1990) stress the interrelationship between individual and family work.

> Individual and family dynamics interplay. . . . Whatever affects one part of a system necessarily affects the other parts to some degree. Positive shifts in a family's structure or climate can result in profound personality modifications of individual members. Changes in an entire family can occur after one member has been in treatment and makes

changes. Because of this, we need not despair if we cannot gather the entire family together. When possible—whether we are seeing one family member, a subgroup, or an entire family—we search for the most accessible aspect of the system, the part that will be most responsive to intervention. (Woods and Hollis, 1990, p. 370)

Within the vast scope of social work, people seek assistance for many reasons; they may want to feel less anxious or depressed or to improve their family relationships. However, many seek services (or are referred and/or mandated for services) because of their problems in living, and may not wish to change themselves or their family relationships; they may be in trouble with the law; wish to adopt children; need help with living arrangements for elderly parents; or learn that a family member has cancer. The problem focus itself is a major determinant of the choice of service.

However, whatever the specific problem, people come with their unique personalities, ego structures, and family dynamics. Although the focus of intervention may not be on these dynamic issues, understanding both individual and family dynamics that are played out within the clients' social and cultural context is essential for offering appropriate assistance.

The Paul Norris case is presented to illustrate the psychodynamic biopsychosocial perspective in action in family-focused clinical work.

Case Illustration

Paul Norris, five, was referred to the mental health clinic with problems of anxiety, sleep disturbances, and bouts of vomiting for which no physical basis was found, resulting in several hospitalizations for dehydration. Mrs. Norris, thirty, his mother, had difficulty controlling his behavior. The biopsychosocial assessment illustrates the major features of this case.

> Mrs. Norris had been separated from her husband since Paul, her only child, was two-and-a-half years old; since then, there has been no contact with Mr. Norris, whose whereabouts are unknown. Mrs. Norris (herself an only child) and Paul live with Mrs. Norris's mother, sixty-one, and stepfather, forty-six, in comfortable housing and are supported by AFDC (Aid to Families with Dependent Children). Both of Mrs. Norris's parents work, and Mrs. Norris's primary role is mother and homemaker.

Mrs. Norris, although receiving public assistance through AFDC (which would place her at the poverty level), lives in comfortable middle-class circumstances. Paul has a room of his own and a backyard to play in.

Mrs. Norris's personality characteristics, physical health, relationship to Paul, social life, and how she views herself in the world, were explored:

> Mrs. Norris is intelligent, verbal, relates well, has many ego strengths, and functions well on a daily basis, although she suffers from moderate anxiety and has passive-dependent characteristics. She has affectionate feelings toward her son, but has difficulty controlling him. She has no social life, and all her activities center around the home; she plays bingo once a week, and her stepfather makes it clear that he will not babysit for her while she is "running around." On most Sundays, she and her mother go to flea markets. Mrs. Norris was emphatic with the clinician that she has no wish to change this and is very comfortable as a "homebody."

> Mrs. Norris has many physical ailments, some of which appeared to be psychosomatic, and has received secondary gains from her symptoms, both in the past and present. Secondary or *epinosic* gain refers to "secondary advantages accruing from an illness, such as gratification of dependency yearnings or attention seeking" (Campbell, 1989, p. 298). Her anxieties about her illnesses are communicated to Paul on both verbal and nonverbal levels; the fact that illness can bring secondary gains is also being transmitted to him.

Mrs. Norris is deeply embedded in her very enmeshed family, with separation being a major source of anxiety. From a life cycle perspective, Mrs. Norris is an adult who might be expected to have an intimate partner relationship, and friends, and perhaps involvement in outside employment or other activities in addition to her age-appropriate involvement with parenting. Her present lifestyle is more reminiscent of a teenager still under parental domination, although, in fact, teenagers usually have a more active social life than her presently restricted one. Mrs. Norris has difficulty asserting herself in the mothering role and in dealing with her mother about who has control of Paul.

Paul is the identified patient; how is he viewed by the clinician?

> Paul is an intelligent, responsive boy who is somewhat manipulative and slightly bossy; his mother reports temper tantrums. He is anxious, has sleep problems, and a number of fears, such as going into crowds. He appears to have mild motoric awkwardness and awkwardness in drawing spontaneously. Psychiatric evaluation raised question of primary skill deficits, and diagnostically he was thought to exhibit emotionally triggered cyclic vomiting. Medical evaluation ruled out a physical basis for his vomiting; asthma has also been diagnosed. He has no playmates and his life centers around the home.

> Paul is caught in a power struggle between his mother and grandmother and manipulates both of them. His grandmother overindulges him; when

Mrs. Norris objects, she is told: "Why not—how much longer do I have to live?" This guilt-provoking statement does not seem to have any basis in fact, as Paul's grandmother is in very good health. Mrs. Norris's stepfather has a positive relationship with Paul and seems to be a steadying force.

Paul's father, from Mrs. Norris's description, was not very involved in caring for Paul when they lived together. Although totally absent for the past two-and-a-half years, he is often "present" in Mrs. Norris's verbalizations of resentment toward him, to which Paul is often privy to. Myths relating to Paul's father are frequently narrated with a very negative attitude; Paul's paternal uncle has engaged in illegal activities, some of which were reported in the newspapers. Mrs. Norris has commented that "Paul has the Norris blood in him."

Paul is enmeshed in a family with a caring but anxious mother, continual power struggles for control of Paul, and negative myths about his father. Mrs. Norris had maintained a marriage (albeit strained) living apart from her parents for several years. How did this present situation come about?

A sketchy picture of the marital situation revealed poor communication, serious sexual problems, and an unplanned pregnancy. When Paul was two, Mr. Norris suggested that they move in with her parents "for convenience." Shortly after they did this, Mr. Norris left and was not heard from again. It can be hypothesized that when Mr. and Mrs. Norris married, they found in each other "spouses who have the same levels of differentiation" (Bowen, 1985, p. 377) and were unable to provide each other with needed emotional support. From a life course perspective, an important transition occurred when moving to Mrs. Norris's parental home, followed by the major turning point of Mr. Norris's abandonment of the family.

Did this abandonment by Mr. Norris cause his wife to regress? Did Mrs. Norris retreat into her family to protect herself from being hurt again? Or was a pattern of enmeshment and hostile-dependent relationships already present? The family history sheds more light on the present dynamics of the family.

When Mrs. Norris was a baby, her father became ill, developing many disabilities and requiring much care; he died when she was two-and-a-half (Paul's age when he and his mother were abandoned by Mr. Norris). Shortly after her father's death, Mrs. Norris's mother met her present husband (fifteen years her junior; thus they were about thirty-three and eighteen, respectively). When they married a year and a half later, Mrs. Norris was sent to a boarding school in another state, living there from the time she was four until she was seven. Although her mother maintained contact, Mrs. Norris felt abandoned, desolate, and lonely, and often cried. She developed a serious throat condition from which she "nearly died" when she was seven and then returned to her mother and stepfather's home, where she remained, going to public school and developing friendships.

In high school, when visual problems were discovered, she discontinued school, and kept house for her parents, who were employed, and Mrs. Norris subsequently worked (in the same factory as her mother), where she met Mr. Norris and then married him.

Although Mrs. Norris's desertion by her husband was an emotional crisis, her history of loss goes back much farther and is deeper. Many family therapists focus only on what is happening in the present transactions of family members; often the past "is thought of as that which no longer exists" (Moultrup, 1981, p. 120), but the past sheds light on Mrs. Norris's needs, losses, and early patterns of enmeshment with her family. Her history of somatizing psychological distress and the secondary gains of illness emerge; a serious physical illness allowed Mrs. Norris to escape from her institutional life; an eyesight problem enabled her to avoid school and start her pattern of being the family homemaker. Her somatizing tendencies as well as anxiety about her health have been transmitted to Paul.

Treatment

Individual and family therapy modalities were integrated. Mrs. Norris was responsive to the social work clinician, and she talked freely about herself and her anxieties, primarily fixated on her health. However, she was not seeking therapy for herself; her goal was to help Paul, and most of her attention was directed to this issue. The clinician observed that Mrs. Norris had many insights into how to help him; very little direction was given by the clinician; rather she supported Mrs. Norris's strengths in her role as mother and validated many of her constructive suggestions.

Prior to her first appointment, Mrs. Norris called to say that Paul was becoming more anxious, having nightmares, and feeling fearful that there were snakes and bugs in his bed. When seen for her initial interview, she told the clinician that Paul's anxiety had lessened. She had taken Paul to see a doctor for his asthma; he recommended that all his stuffed animals be removed from his room, and she had put them all in the attic. When she realized that this precipitated his major anxiety attack, she returned the animals to him, including his beloved teddy bear. The disturbance (precipitated by separation anxiety) immediately ceased.

Mrs. Norris asserted herself with her mother about her own mothering role, and that she, not her mother, "was in control of Paul." As the situation improved, she commented that Paul "has only one boss now." She also "suddenly" found a friend who had a son Paul's age, whom she and Paul would visit, an event enjoyable for both of them. A major breakthrough came when Mrs. Norris enrolled Paul in a summer Head Start program; the separation was successful for both. Paul did very well in this program and made a good transition to public school. During the seven-month period of treatment, Paul made steady progress: no vomiting episodes of significance were reported; his general anxiety diminished; he began sleeping better, eating well, and growing.

The clinician saw Paul with his mother, during which time they would talk together or do a small activity, such as walking around the clinic grounds; Paul sometimes gathered acorns to plant in his garden.

Mrs. Norris's anxiety diminished as did her reliance on tranquilizers; talking to the clinician helped her "feel free like a bird." It was the clinician's hope that Mrs. Norris might engage herself more deeply in therapy to further her own adult development, a greater sense of autonomy and gain a social life. Mrs. Norris, however, made it clear, that this was not her wish; she was content to be a homebody, did not want to live apart from her parents, and was not interested in outside employment, social activities, or dating.

Termination was initiated by Mrs. Norris, ostensibly relating to the progress Paul had made and her feelings that she could maintain the gains.

Mrs. Norris reapplied three months later, upon the referral of her physician, because Paul had another hospitalization for vomiting. The physician felt that Paul's problems in separating from his mother appeared to be a key issue. This next short period of treatment was rather tumultuous, with a focus on separation and encouraging brief separations and the use of a babysitter; both Mrs. Norris and Paul were resistant to this idea. After one session, Paul went home and vomited and told his mother that he did not want to see the clinician anymore and did not want to hear about babysitters anymore. Mrs. Norris returned to her pediatrician stating that she did not want to return to the clinic if it was going to make Paul worse. At this point, family sessions with Paul's grandparents were also being considered. Before this could happen, Mrs. Norris terminated. She had heard about a good gastroenterologist and was taking Paul there.

This case illustrates the power of separation and loss conflicts and how these past issues can be replayed in the present. It also illustrates the importance of understanding family dynamics and not viewing children independently of systemic issues. Although working with Mrs. Norris's strengths reduced her level of anxiety and encouraged her sense of competence, the progress was subverted by the needs of this enmeshed family system to prevail, which superseded the needs of a five-year-old boy to separate and for his mother to lead a more independent existence. Hartman and Laird (1983) indicate that "helping families . . . deal with separateness and connectedness is one of the most frequently faced challenges in family-centered practice" (p. 274). This challenge was not fully met in this case.

CONCLUSION

The family is a powerful system, whether existing in a stable, secure form or involved in disengaged, enmeshed, or disorganized patterns. Cultural values and beliefs permeate family life, yet family theory applies to families in any culture; every family has rituals, patterns of attachment, boundaries, and so on. It is not possible for people to be unaffected by their past and present family lives, as family members are the first attachment figures and generally interact with the child through adolescence and adulthood. The family exists outside the self and is also internalized as part of the self.

As clinicians working within a family system, we are often drawn into the maelstrom of its emotional forces with pulls and countervailing pushes. If we can maintain our balance and not be swept away by these intense pressures, we can then tune in to our reactions to and interactions with family members, the intersubjective experience, thereby gaining insight into the inner dynamics of a family's life.

Serious problems face families in our society; many modes of intervention become necessary, including comprehensive community and child welfare programs, preventive strategies, and constructive social policies. Strengthening family stability and mental health is also one critical piece of intervention; there are many approaches to family work, including structural family therapy, objects relations therapy, divorce mediation, and cognitive-behavioral and psychoeducational interventions. Some families do not seek help for problems of family conflict or dysfunction, but for other reasons, such as wishing to adopt a child, being confronted with a terminal illness, or needing help in planning for the needs of an elderly parent. Understanding and working with the family dynamics in all of these situations is crucial, even when not directing attention to intrapersonal therapeutic change.

There is ongoing focus on the family throughout this book as we talk about the life cycle, illness, transitions and crises, and mental health; within this context the individuality of each family member must be understood and appreciated; the construction of reality and the inner world remain unique for each person.

The birth and evolving development of the neonate into a distinct individual is examined in Chapter 9.

LEARNING EXERCISE

In a small group prepare to do a role-play, selecting some aspect of family communication, patterns of relationship, and/or specific family problem, such as divorce or maltreatment.

SUGGESTED READING

Article

Farley, J. 1990. Family developmental task assessment: A prerequisite to family treatment. *Clinical Social Work Journal* 18: 85-98.

Books

Beardslee, W. R., and H. L. MacMillan. 1993. Preventive intervention with the children of depressed parents: A case study. In *The psychoanalytic study of the child,* ed. A. J. Solnit, P. B. Neubauer, S. Abrams, and A. S. Dowling, Vol. 48, pp. 249-276. New Haven, CT: Yale University Press.

Cummings, E. M., P. T. Davies, and S. B. Campbell. 2000. *Developmental psychopathology and family process: Theory, research and clinical implications.* New York: The Guilford Press.

Kiselica, M. S. 1995. *Multicultural counseling with teenage fathers: A practical guide.* Thousand Oaks, CA: Sage Publications.

McCourt, F. 1996. *Angela's ashes: A memoir of childhood.* London: HarperCollins Publishers.

Minuchin, S. 1974. *Families and family therapy.* Cambridge, MA: Harvard University Press.

Satir, V. 1967. *Conjoint family therapy.* Palo Alto: Science and Behavior Books.

Scharff, D., and J. Scharff. 1987. *Object relations family therapy.* Northvale, NJ: Jason Aronson.

Smyth, N., and B. Miller. 1997. Parenting issues for substance-abusing women. In *Gender and addictions: Men and women in treatment,* ed. S. L. A. Straussner and E. Zelvin, pp. 123-150. Northvale, NJ: Jason Aronson.

SECTION II:
THE LIFE CYCLE

Chapter 9

Reproductive Issues, Infancy, and Early Childhood Development

But what am I?
An infant crying in the night:
An infant crying for the light,
And with no language but a cry.

Alfred Tennyson, "In Memoriam," *liv. Stanza 5,* 1850

INTRODUCTION

This chapter focuses on children from conception through the preschool years and emphasizes their physical, cognitive, and emotional growth and maturation, as well as their age-specific needs, behaviors, and problems. The prominent role of attachment is stressed, and children's development, within their family, social, and cultural contexts, is viewed transactionally.

REPRODUCTION

Conception

To conceive a child is not always a simple matter of birds and bees; for some it may be an arduous physical and emotional struggle involving failures, health complications, miscarriages, and the use of reproductive technologies. Just as there are many nontraditional forms of family organization, conception itself does not always follow the traditional pattern. In the majority of successful pregnancies, by means of sexual intercourse, a biological father's sperm fertilizes a biological mother's egg in her fallopian tube;

Human Behavior in the Social Environment, Second Edition

after four to seven days, the fertilized egg moves to the uterus, where it implants itself in the uterine wall and begins to grow. Sometimes, even though the mother's egg and father's sperm are contributed, the egg is not fertilized within the mother's body, but in a petri dish by means of in vitro fertilization (IVF). Some couples may not be the child's "true" biological parents, in the sense that the sperm and/or egg might be contributed by others; the resultant embryo is implanted in the mother, who then goes through the normal stages of pregnancy. There are occasions in which the mother may not be able to carry her own baby, and the embryo is implanted into another woman (a surrogate) who goes through the pregnancy, with the intention of giving the child to the couple paying for her services; gay men sometimes use the services of a surrogate mother. Sometimes the surrogate mother changes her mind, and wants to keep the baby she carried, which can lead to legal entanglements.

There are circumstances such as the presence of cancer in one partner, when an in vitro fertilization (while both parents are still in reasonably good health) prior to chemotherapy or radiation is the preferred option; embryos are then frozen for future implantation. Some lesbian couples prefer their own biological child to an adopted one and one member of the pair will become pregnant (usually through artificial insemination). Once pregnancy has been established many heterosexual and lesbian couples share the pregnancy and delivery experience, frequently attending birthing classes together. Some single (unattached) mothers may face the pregnancy experience alone, or may have emotional support from friends and family.

A pregnancy can be a planned, profoundly purposeful decision, or it may occur unplanned, although in this case it may be just as deeply welcomed; "half of all pregnancies in the United States are unplanned, experts say" (Rabin, 2006, p. D5). Many anticipate a coming child with positive feelings; *ambivalence* is common to all, as a readjustment in relationships and lifestyle is inevitable. Some people are devastated by the occurrence of a pregnancy and choose to abort the baby or to relinquish it for adoption, or fatalistically accept this "tragedy"; ambivalence is often present in these pregnancies; relinquishment can be a painful process.

The Fertility Crisis

The expectation that one can decide to be (and when to be) a parent can be tragically dashed when a couple discovers fertility problems, a situation reported to be of "epidemic" proportions in this country.

Infertility is often defined as not being able to get pregnant after trying for one year. Of the approximately 62 million women of reproductive age in 2002, about 1.2 million, or 2%, had an infertility-related
medical appointment within the previous year, and 10 percent had an
infertility-related medical visit at some point in the past. ("Infertility
Is Often," 2003)

There are many reasons for infertility, including disease, malformations
in the woman's reproductive system, and low sperm count. A major source of
infertility, currently, is the fact that many women are postponing motherhood
until they are older, choosing to make advances in their education and careers; for many it becomes too late to become pregnant and/or carry a healthy
baby to term.

According to the Centers for Disease Control, once a woman cele-
brates her 42nd birthday, the chances of her having a baby using her
own eggs, even with advanced medical help, are less than 10 percent,
At age 40, half of her eggs are chromosomally abnormal; by 42 that
figure is 90 percent. "I go through Kleenex in my office like it's going
out of style," says reproductive endocrinologist Michael Slowey in
Englewood, N. J. (Gibbs, 2002, p. 51)

Males may also experience a decline in fertility.

What this means is that buried deep in the Y chromosome, there may
be the same inexorable timepiece that has lately been the source of so
much anxiety among women—the dreaded biological clock. The male
version just ticks more slowly and with less urgency, and of course,
nobody pays attention to it anyway. (McGrath, 2002, p. 11)

Current research has found that "older men are more likely to father a
child who eventually develops schizophrenia" (p. 8), and an Israeli study in
2006, published in the *Archives of General Psychiatry,* reports "the risk of
autism rises in children with older fathers" (Miller, 2006, p. 8).

Fertility treatments are becoming more technologically advanced, and
have enabled many couples to have healthy babies; for some problems, procedures are fairly straightforward and not especially time-consuming. For
other problems, procedures are complex, costs are high, repeated disappointments are experienced, and the quality of marital (or partner) life may
be negatively affected for years, taking a high emotional toll on both partners; fertility drugs can also affect the mother's mood (Cohen and Slade,

2000); Jill Smolowe (1997), a journalist, wrote of her difficult experiences going through fertility treatments.

> I found every moment of that battle against biology a nightmare. The first salvo was Clomid. . . . I swallowed the pills. But rather than stimulating more eggs, the drug plunged me into a deep depression that left me unable to . . . think of anything but babies. (p. 46)

Smolowe's (1997) fertility treatments were not successful; turning to adoption, she traveled to China, and found that when "a tiny hand reached up and touched my cheek, I was, at last, a mother" (p. 46). The solution of international adoption, discussed in Chapter 7, is reached by many who have struggled unsuccessfully with the fertility crisis.

Reproductive Technologies

One of the most successful reproductive technologies is in vitro (literally, "in glass") fertilization (IVF). Louise Brown, conceived in a petri dish, achieved fame when, in 1978, she became the first test tube baby to be born (Lemonick, 1997); since then the number of such births has been dramatically increasing. "In 2003, 48,756 [in vitro] infants were born, which was more than double the 20,840 born in 1996" ("Is the Use," 2003). On December 21, 2006, Louise Brown herself gave birth to a baby boy in Bristol, England, reportedly conceived as babies have been since time immemorial.

Freezing embryos after IVF to be used in future pregnancies can lead to legal and ethical dilemmas; divorcing couples, for example, have fought over custody rights regarding the disposition of their frozen embryos.

> What exactly is a frozen embryo, property or person? And while case law holds a woman responsible for the fate of a fertilized egg inside her body, who should have the last word about an egg fertilized outside her body? (McKim, 1996, p. A20)

Some women, unable to use their own eggs for fertilization, use donor eggs from other women. How does one select which eggs (or rather, whose eggs) to use; is this always anonymous? Calvin Trillin (1999) underscores this dilemma in a humorous vein:

> Plowing through *The New York Times* on a recent Sunday, I read in the Metro Section that infertile couples in the market for smart-kid genes regularly place advertisements in the newspapers of their own Ivy

League alma maters offering female undergraduates $7,500 for a donated egg. Before I could get that news comfortably digested, I came across an article in the Magazine section describing SAT prep courses for which parents spend thousands in the hope of raising their child's test scores enough to make admission to an Ivy League college possible. So how can people who have found a potential egg donor at an Ivy League college tell whether the donor carries genuine smart-kid genes or just pushy-parents genes? (Trillin, 1999, p. 20)

Problems regarding artificial insemination were discussed in Chapter 7. How anonymous should the father be? Do children have the right to know him or know about him? Similar questions can be asked about the female donor of an egg.

A heterosexual couple using artificial insemination from an anonymous donor because the father is infertile may experience special psychological problems (Landau, 1998); many such fathers harbor the sense that the "donor is the 'real' father" (p. 79). In some cases, they feel inferior, assuming that the donor (not to mention the child) is "more gifted than they are (most of the donors are medical or graduate students)" (Landau, 1998, p. 79).

Genetics

We are in the midst of a "knowledge explosion" in genetics; in 2000, the human genome was deciphered, finding "the 100,000 genes encoded by 3 billion chemical pairs in our DNA" (Isaacson, 1999, p. 42; Wade, 2000). Accompanying these exciting findings were practical medical applications and a host of moral, ethical, and legal dilemmas, such as the heated debate on stem cell research.

Prior to genomic encoding, increasing genetic knowledge was already leading to the development of new reproductive technologies and interventions; tests (such as amniocentesis, to examine cells contained in the fluid surrounding the developing fetus) are being performed on the fetus to determine the presence of certain genetic disorders; congenital conditions (such as spina bifida, nonclosure of the developing spinal column) have been experimentally treated in the womb (Golden, 1999a). Pregnant women may face the difficult decision of whether to abort a defective fetus, such as one with Down's syndrome (a form of mental retardation more commonly found in pregnancies of older mothers). Genetic testing, performed prior to conception for people with genetically transmissible disorders in themselves and/or their families, can provide knowledge of probabilities of genetic transmission to a child.

In vitro fertilization, used in infertility treatment, has been combined with genetic interventions with couples who are not necessarily infertile. The *preimplantation genetic diagnosis* (PGD) procedure has been used for the past ten years; when the egg and sperm have formed into an 8-cell embryo in the petri dish, it is examined prior to its implantation into the mother to choose a healthy embryo and discard embryos which might be fatally flawed (Harmon, 2006). The purpose is to avoid having children born with serious incurable diseases and/or physical disabilities. People with a genetic history of serious cancers are using this method to choose a healthy embryo to avoid the possibility that their child might develop a severe malignancy when older; this procedure also detects the presence of a gene for Huntington's chorea, which does not manifest itself until later in life.

This procedure, which is unregulated in this country, is controversial; one concern is the potential danger to the child, in later life, of removing one of the embryonic cells in order to study it. Questions have also been raised about the validity of the decision making: "Do embryos containing some genetically flawed cells tend to heal themselves" (Weil, 2006, p. 52). There is also concern that this technology might be used as a form of genetic engineering:

> If the growing interest in screening for cancer signals an expanded tolerance for genetic selection, geneticists and fertility experts say it may well be accompanied by the greater use of preimplantation diagnosis to select for characteristics that range from less serious diseases to purely matters of preference. (Harmon, 2006. p. 1)

Some women make the decision to abort a baby when they learn that they are carrying a child who will be born with serious defects; some women, feeling that they were not sufficiently informed about possible birth defects, have filed "wrongful birth" suits against their doctors (Weil, 2006). The first successful major lawsuit *(Becker v. Schwartz)* was won in 1978 by a family with a Down syndrome child; the mother was not warned of this risk (due to her advanced age) by her doctor. The New York State Court of Appeals "found in favor of the family, declaring it had the right to seek financial damages for the added cost of raising a child with a disability" (Weil, 2006, p. 51).

Pregnancy

Major physiological alterations occur in the mother's body during pregnancy, accompanied by psychological shifts. For men or female partners, the anticipation of parenthood can produce strong, sometimes conflicting emotional states.

Pregnancy is typically divided into three trimesters (each of three months' duration); the developments during each trimester have important consequences for both the fetus and the mother.

The First Trimester

The first trimester produces rapid changes in the newly developing embryo, as previously undifferentiated cells change into specific tissues and organs. The baby is especially vulnerable, during this stage, to certain diseases (such as German measles) developing in the mother as well as her ingestion of drugs and alcohol; these can irreparably affect fetal development. By the second month, the embryo appears generally human in form.

The mother is also undergoing major physiological changes during this time; dramatic changes are occurring in her hormonal system, as her body adapts to the state of pregnancy; she may feel morning sickness and mood changes; there is a 25 percent chance that a pregnancy may result in miscarriage during this trimester (Cohen and Slade, 2000).

The Second Trimester

During the second trimester, the baby's further growth, organ differentiation, and maturation continue; eyes and hair develop, and regulation of the baby's heartbeat progresses. The mother usually becomes visibly pregnant and can begin to feel the baby moving inside her. Morning sickness of the first trimester tends to diminish, and the hormonal surges are modulated, triggering less emotional lability. The baby is often felt as more real to the mother, and this feeling is enhanced for many by the recent use of ultrasound pictures of their babies.

Psychodynamic theorists speak of the mother developing a greater emotional connection to the baby during this stage; her "emotional investment is drawn away from the outside world and refocused inward toward her baby and the transformations taking place inside her . . . not only is she becoming a mother physically, she is now evolving into one psychologically" (Cohen and Slade, 2000, p. 22).

The Third Trimester

By the third trimester, the baby's body is almost completely formed, the internal organs undergo further differentiation, and the nervous system and brain go through major development. An important achievement is the baby's weight gain; the mother also gains the most during this period, often causing her to feel more physically uncomfortable, especially during the last month. Psychologically, the mother is becoming more prepared for the baby's birth.

Reactions of Fathers and Other Partners to Pregnancy

Becoming a father, in general, is a positive experience: "Incipient father-hood is an exciting, compelling, and profoundly moving experience" (Cohen and Slade, 2000, p. 24). However, many fathers experience anxiety related to changes in the marital (partner) relationship, assuming financial and other responsibilities, worries about the wife's (partner's) pregnancy and health, and confusion about parental roles and involvement with the new child (Cohen and Slade, 2000). Becoming parents can also stir up "sleeping" conflicts about the parents' own childhood and relationships to their parents; this may present an opportunity to work through these conflicts and reach a higher level of integration (Benedek, 1970; Cohen and Slade, 2000; Elson, 1984; Zayas, 1987).

When lesbian couples choose to have children by means of one partner becoming pregnant, they may experience social stigmatization; "but if the two women have a secure relationship, they tend to bond strongly together as a family unit" (Sadock and Sadock, 2003, p. 869).

Multiple Births

Increased fertility treatment has led to a 55 percent increase in the number of twins born since 1980, according to the National Center for Health Statistics (Steinhauer, 1999a). In 2003, of "48,756 infants born through ART, 51 percent were born in multiple-birth deliveries" (Clay Wright et al., 2006). Pregnant women carrying twins are placed in a high-risk category, receive close medical attention, are prone to more medical emergencies, and may need to limit their activities; twins are more likely be born prematurely and may have medical complications (Steinhauer, 1999a). Raising twins can create stress, and many parents of twins meet together for support. "In the first year, many parents said if the house hadn't burned down it was a successful day," Dr. Junior said. "But then there is something so magical about watching these two beings share a budding relationship together" (Steinhauer, 1999a, p. A25).

Risk Factors in Pregnancy

The mother's nutrition, exposure to infections and radiation, utilization of alcohol and drugs (including prescribed drugs), and psychological distress can affect fetal development (Davies, 1999; Garbarino, 1982); depressed mothers may have poor nutrition, ignore medical care, and smoke more (Bakalar, 2006a). Maternal malnutrition can slow the rate of fetal growth, impair brain development, and give rise to neurological problems. Teenagers, women who are older, and/or those carrying multiple fetuses are at special risk for health problems for themselves and/or their babies. Obesity, a common medical problem today (which increases as women become older, and can therefore affect women postponing pregnancy), often causes high blood pressure and diabetes, both posing problems in pregnancy (Rabin, 2006). Babies born to mothers with HIV infections often become HIV positive as well (Zastrow and Kirst-Ashman, 2004).

Women should receive prenatal care to safeguard their health and that of the fetus; lack of "early and regular prenatal care has long been associated with poor reproductive outcomes, particularly low birthweight, neonatal death, and postpartum complications" (Cook et al., 1999, p. 129). Many pregnant women in this country do not receive adequate prenatal care (Cook et al., 1999), and 21 percent do not receive this care until after the first trimester (Perloff and Jaffee, 1999). "Rates of late entry into care are even higher among teenagers and members of racial and ethnic minority groups" (Perloff and Jaffee, 1999, p. 117).

Public health officials now advocate that women receive good medical care, "'preconception care,'" long before they become pregnant (Rabin, 2006, p. D5).

> The new guidelines, issued by the Centers for Disease Control and Prevention last spring, include 10 specific health care recommendations and advise prepregnancy checkups that include screening for diabetes, H.I.V. and obesity; managing chronic medical conditions; reviewing medications that may harm a fetus; and making sure vaccinations are up to date. (Rabin, 2006, p. D5)

Maternal Substance Abuse

Maternal substance abuse can have serious consequences for the developing fetus; *fetal alcohol syndrome,* for example, is present in many infants whose mothers' alcohol intake was absorbed in utero, and "is the leading cause of mental retardation in the United States" (Sadock and Sadock,

2003, p. 409); symptoms include "microcephaly, craniofacial malformations, and limb and heart defects are common" (p. 409).

Some states regard maternal substance abuse as a form of child abuse and have arrested or imposed legal penalties on offending mothers, but this is generally being modified. In Maryland, in 2005, after two women had been sentenced to prison for their use of cocaine during pregnancy, Maryland's "highest court ruled that the intentional ingestion of drugs by a pregnant woman cannot form the basis for a conviction under Maryland's reckless endangerment statute. NASW had joined a friend-of-the-court brief in the case" (Stoesen, 2006, p. 5).

Loss of Baby During Pregnancy

The loss of a baby due to miscarriage is usually a very painful event. "Women experience much greater grief following pregnancy loss than is commonly recognized" (Cohen and Slade, 2000, p. 30). Abortions can also be distressing to the mother and her partner, no matter the reason for the procedure, and may be followed by grief reactions. Abortions are chosen for many reasons: to save the life of the mother; in cases of rape and incest; to prevent the birth of a fetus with serious physical defects; and for social, economic, and psychological considerations. Aborting some fetuses in a multifetal pregnancy can be accompanied by "powerful feelings of guilt, anxiety, and sadness," even when necessary to preserve the life of the remaining fetuses, and minimize medical complications to the mother; "grief following abortions for fetal anomalies has been shown to be as intense as grief following spontaneous perinatal losses" (Cohen and Slade, 2000, p. 32).

Although the Supreme Court legalized women's right to abortion in the *Roe v. Wade* decision, bitter and strong political and religious debates continue between pro-choice and pro-life forces; abortion clinics have been bombed; harassment of abortion clinics' medical personnel has also taken place culminating in several murders.

Birth

In the past, the process of giving birth was a high-risk procedure, accompanied by a high mortality rate for both the mother and child. Today, with advances in medicine and prenatal care, mortality rates of mothers have dramatically decreased, and infant mortality has declined, although not consistently so. There has been an increase in babies being born prematurely, and born with low birth weights; the rates are greatest for these conditions in black babies, and more than twice as many black babies die as do white babies (Rabin, 2006).

The Delivery

The options that mothers choose for delivery include obstetrician-assisted childbirth in a hospital, which could be natural childbirth (with or without anesthesia), or utilization of a midwife at home or in birthing centers. In the past, fathers (and partners) were excluded from the delivery room. This is no longer the case; today many partners choose to be present, providing support and/or coaching assistance. Women frequently take prenatal classes (often with their partners) to prepare themselves for childbirth.

The surgical procedure, *Cesarean section,* has been increasingly used for obstetrical complications, such as prolonged labor, certain breech presentations, fetal distress, and Rh incompatibility. Concern has been voiced that cesareans may be overused or used for nonmedical reasons, which include the doctor's fear of malpractice suits (a frequent occurrence in obstetrical practices) and the doctor's convenience. The rate has been escalating and in 2004, it was 29 percent (Cassidy, 2006). At the same time induced births are becoming very popular; many are not for medical reasons, but at the mother's request, for personal preference and convenience. "As of last count, in 2003, one out of every five American births was induced—double the figure for 1990," in spite of the risk of possible complications (Cassidy, 2006, p. 20).

Cultural attitudes and customs can affect attitudes about childbirth practices. The Hmong, for example, attach special meaning to the placenta, which they formerly buried under their huts in their native Laos (Fadiman, 1997). The Hmong word for placenta signifies "jacket . . . one's first and finest garment." A Hmong's soul upon death,

> must travel . . . until it reaches the burial place of its placental jacket, and puts it on. Only after the soul is properly dressed . . . can it continue its dangerous journey . . . to . . . where it is reunited with its ancestors and from which it will . . . be sent to be reborn as the soul of a new baby. If the soul cannot find its jacket, it is condemned to an eternity of wandering, naked and alone. (Fadiman, 1997, p. 5)

In one California hospital, where many Hmong women received medical attention, some requested to take the placentas home; sometimes doctors agreed, "packing the placentas in plastic bags or take-out containers from the hospital cafeteria"; most, however did not comply, concerned either that "the women planned to eat the placentas" or that this could lead to the "possible spread of hepatitis B, which is carried by at least fifteen percent of the Hmong refugees in the United States" (Fadiman, 1997, p. 7).

Emotional Reactions to Birth

It is not uncommon for mothers, after the baby is born, to go through a period of postpartum depression, which may last for several days. In this "normal state of sadness," women may experience "dysphoria, frequent tearfulness, and clinging dependence" (Kaplan, Sadock, and Grebb, 1994, p. 36). This is attributed to a combination of factors, including dramatic hormonal changes in the mother's body, feeling stressed from childbirth, and anticipatory worries about coping with parental responsibilities. Sometimes the initial depression does not diminish but persists or deepens; a depression can also develop when the baby is one to three months old. These depressions can be related to an earlier history of depression, anxieties about mothering, a reawakening of conflicts from the mother's own parent-child relationships, or current stressors, such as marital problems or social isolation. In a small number of cases, the depression may reach psychotic proportions. "Hippocrates described postpartum disorders in ancient Greece, and recent studies in rural Africa have found rates of part partum depression just as high as that of the industrial West" ("Postpartum Disorders," 1989, p. 2).

The fact that adoptive parents can become depressed after receiving their child has recently been receiving attention; "unlike new mothers who suffer from postpartum depression, they cannot blame their symptoms by a drop in estrogen levels"; it is reported by psychologists, "who work with adoptive parents [that] the stress of being a new parent, sleep deprivation and a lack of support may put women a risk" (Tarkan, 2006, p. D5). Compounding these feelings may be a lack of resolution of the fertility crisis, not feeling immediately bonded to the child, lack of affection from the child (especially if older), and lack of preparation for the actuality of living with an adopted child. Some adoption agencies are offering more services to adoptive parents; and while some parents turn to support groups, others may need professional help (Tarkan, 2006).

Fathers may also undergo mood changes, both during pregnancy and after birth (Kaplan, Sadock, and Grebb, 1994); they may experience conflicts about being a father, changes in their marital relationship, and the burden of additional responsibilities. Some fathers experience physical symptoms similar to those of pregnancy and childbirth, which can include "nausea, fatigue, back pain, and even abdominal pain" (Ashford, Lecroy, and Lortie, 1997, p. 136).

In certain tribal societies, the father behaves as if he were giving birth. While his wife is delivering the infant, the father goes to bed and may even complain of labor pains. This custom symbolically establishes the man as father of the baby and gives him legal rights as the parent. (Ashford, Lecroy, and Lortie, 1997, p. 136)

Perinatal Loss

Perinatal loss, which is a baby's death upon delivery *(stillbirth)* or after a brief life, is a trauma for parents. In the past, the mother would be tranquilized, isolated, and rapidly discharged. "The less contact the mother had with the baby the better, and the less spoken about the baby the easier for her to forget and get on with her life" (Zeanah, 1991, p. 12). It is recognized now that parents need an opportunity to mourn and to become involved with their dying or dead children, such as naming them, holding them, and holding memorial services (Zeanah, 1991). *Pathological grief reactions,* manifested months or sometimes years following the baby's death, have unique features owing to the nature of this loss, and individual psychotherapy is recommended (Condon, 1986).

THE EVOLVING CHILD

A four-year-old girl commented: "I used to be a little baby. Then I closed my eyes, and when I opened them up—all of a sudden, I was a kid!" The first few years of life are awesome to watch, as a "little bundle" evolves into a thinking, talking, walking little person, deeply attached to his or her parents but busy exploring the world and becoming increasingly autonomous. In this section, children are discussed from a developmental perspective, encompassing their psychological, physical, cognitive, and social development.

The First Year of Life

Babies, even when welcomed with joy, are "newcomers" to their parents; their coming together and developing a synchronous way of relating is a major task of infancy. *"In the early weeks, therefore, parents and infants face a task of mutual adaptation initiated by the parents"* (Davies, 1999, p. 123; italics in the original). Perhaps this insight might be helpful to adoptive parents; that all parents, even biological ones, have to become "acquainted" with their "newcomers."

The neonate has many capacities and competencies soon after birth, including the ability to recognize sound and visual patterns and a capacity for social communication (Thomas, 1981). The beginnings of "state modulation" are present, which represents the capacity to "remain alert and attentive," on the one hand, but to be able to block out stimuli to prevent the interruption of sleep, on the other (Davies, 1999, p. 122). This is basic to developing *self-regulation* leading to the regulation of body rhythms involved in activities such as eating and sleeping and ultimately to the regulation of emotions. *"Emotion regulation is the keystone of social-emotional development during infancy"* (Crockenberg and Leerkes, 2000, p. 62; italics added). Children can adequately develop these innate self-regulatory capacities only within "secure attachment relationships" (p. 62).

The infant's *temperament,* including the *emotional reactivity* of the child, influence early transactions between parents and infants, which, in turn, affect patterns of self-regulation. Some children, with a greater sensitivity to stimuli, react with more intense emotion than placid children do. A child who cries frequently and loudly might elicit angry reactions causing the mother to withdraw or handle the child roughly, whereas the same mother might respond more gently to a placid child. The mother's "rough" handling may increase the child's reactivity and retard the development of self-regulation.

Children with special needs, such as those born drug addicted or those who are premature, require more time to self-regulate. Premature babies are initially "ill-equipped to deal with the sensory environment outside the womb," unless they receive special remediation (Sameroff and Fiese, 2000, p. 15). The development of the premature baby's central nervous system lags by the "number of weeks of prematurity"; this, combined with the illnesses and interventions experienced by them, make them "easily overstimulated, more reactive, and unsettled for a longer period" (Davies, 1999, p. 125).

Massage therapy, one program found to be effective with premature infants, has long been used for normal babies in many countries, notably in Africa and Asia; in India, "infant massage is a daily routine that begins in the first days of life" (Field, 2000, p. 495); it has been adapted for high-risk infants in this country. The Touch Research Institute has found that using massage therapy with high-risk infants—including those with regulatory problems, premature births, drug exposure, and exposure to HIV—showed good preliminary results in terms of measures such as weight gain, lowered irritability, improved sleep, fewer medical complications, and increased motor development. "Beneficial effects for the caregivers who provide the massage also may accrue" (Field, 2000, p. 499) with enhanced caregiver-child interactions. In an experimental program, teenage mothers from inner-city neighborhoods were learning massage methods "to build parenting skills" (Drummond, 1998, p. 54).

> For much of this century, the prevailing thought was that pre-term babies should not be touched, since the slightest shock could prove fatal. . . . Slowly, the medical establishment has been warming to the idea that massage helps sickly babies. (Drummond, 1998, p. 54)

Attachment

During the first eighteen months, the child's attachment to parents or other primary nurturing figures is essential for physical growth, ego development, and a developing sense of well-being, as well as actual survival; this is emphasized by many theorists, although their perspectives and language may differ. Erikson (1963) refers to the development of "basic trust vs. basic mistrust" (p. 247); Mahler, Pine, and Bergman (1975) term the early union of the mother and child "symbiosis"; Winnicott (Grolnick, 1990) stresses the holding environment provided by the good enough mother; and Bowlby (1988) posits deep instinctual needs for attachment as the foundation for a "secure base."

Bowlby's attachment theory has been supported by Main (1995), along with Ainsworth, whose longitudinal studies observed and assessed the degree of attachment found in the interactions between mothers and children. Mary Ainsworth, who began her studies of patterns of attachment in children in the 1960s, originally studied babies ranging from nine to twelve months by observing them for seventy-two hours in their homes. The ratings of her observers were then correlated with ratings from observers of the experimental program of the *Strange Situation* (Davies, 1999), as described by Karen (1990). At one year of age, the infant was separated from its mother in the lab and observed; a stranger was present with the infant,

> during two intervals . . . during another the baby was alone. . . . Ainsworth spotted three distinct patterns in the babies' reactions. One group . . . protested . . . on separation, but when the mother returned, they greeted her with pleasure . . . [and were] relatively easy to console. (Karen, 1990, p. 36)

Ainsworth categorized this group as securely attached.

The other two groups had either insecure-avoidant attachment or insecure-ambivalent/resistant attachment behaviors. Infants with insecure-avoidant attachments initially appeared self-reliant, did not seem to be affected by the mother's leaving, and tended to ignore their mothers when they returned. During home observations, their mothers often "ignored and actively rejected" these infants (Davies, 1999, p. 19). Parents often characterized these infants negatively and inaccurately, making comments such as "he's just crying to spite me"; the mothers were angrily "intolerant of the infant's distress and tended to reject or punish the infant for being distressed" (Davies, 1999, pp. 19-20).

> Avoidant babies develop precocious defenses against feelings of distress. Distress is split off from consciousness, and the defense mechanism of *isolation of affect* emerges. Avoidant infants tend not to show distress in situations that are distressing for most infants; rather they appear somber, expressionless, or self-contained. (Davies, 1999, pp. 19-20; italics added)

Children who developed insecure-ambivalent/resistant attachment patterns reacted with intense feelings upon separation from their mothers in the strange situation, and their behavior reflected the paradox of an intense wish for attachment but little expectation of attaining it (Davies, 1999). These babies were upset and angry and could not be comforted by their mothers. The mothers of the ambivalent infants were described as:

> *inconsistently responsive* to their infants' attachment-seeking behavior. Ainsworth notes, "The conflict of the C babies [ambivalent/resistant] is a simple one—between wanting close bodily contact and being angry because their mothers do not consistently pick them up. . . . Because their mothers are insensitive to their signals C babies lack confidence in their responsiveness" (Ainsworth, 1982, p. 18). The infants' heightened affect and ambivalent behavior reflects their anxious uncertainty about how their parent will respond. (Ainsworth, 1982, p. 18) (Davies, 1999, p. 22; italics added)

Infants seek their parents as a source of comfort, when they are frightened. However, what happens when parents are not only *not* comforting, but in addition are the *source* of the fright? Main (1995) has added disorganized attachment to the attachment classifications.

> Any parental behavior that directly alarms an infant should place that infant in an irresolvable paradox in which it can neither approach . . . shift its attention . . . or flee. . . . The great majority of parentally maltreated children (about 80 percent) in high-risk samples have been found to fit the disorganized category. (Main, 1995, p. 426)

In addition, this pattern of attachment has also appeared in children whose mothers themselves had disorganized or dissociated states.

> Battering parents are . . . directly frightening. . . . *Frightened* parental behavior may also alarm an infant and leave him without a strategy . . . especially likely if the parent withdraws from the infant as though the infant were the source of the alarm and/or appears to be in a dissociated or trancelike state. We have . . . observed dissociated, trancelike . . . and fearful behavior in some parents of disorganized infants who . . . seem to suffer from still partially dissociated experiences of loss or abuse. In these cases disorganized behavior may appear as a second-generation effect of the parent's own traumatic experiences rather than as a direct effect of physical or sexual abuse [of the child]. (Main, 1995, pp. 426-427)

Main's observations of the mother's reactions to her own trauma affecting the inner security of her child was "the first research" that demonstrated the "intergenerational transmission of secure and insecure attachment" (Karen, 1990, p. 37).

Criticisms of Ainsworth's work relate to issues of research design and lack of studying cultural differences. In the original research, repeated, detailed observations were made (many at home) of mother-child interactions over time. These observations were then correlated with the child's response in the experimental *Strange Situation* setting. Since a high degree of validity existed between the data sets, much of the recent research has utilized observations *only* from the *Strange Situation* to classify a child's attachment behaviors. Question has been raised about the reliability of these observations and whether one can draw valid conclusions from them about the quality of the child's attachment.

The *Strange Situation* applied to examine the effects of day care on the developing child may give inaccurate results, as these babies may have adapted to daily separations from their caretakers and therefore "the Strange Situation may not be sufficiently stressful to activate the attachment system" (Hungerford, Brownell, and Campbell, 2000, p. 523).

The *Strange Situation* has been demonstrated to have consistent results with samples of children from middle and lower classes, those who were black or Caucasian as well as interracial and interethnic babies. However, with infants living under high-risk conditions, the attachment classifications were inconsistent; it has been postulated that stress on the caregivers at different points in time would affect their attachment behaviors to their children (Davies, 1999).

Japanese children were often classified as having anxious-ambivalent/resistant forms of attachment because of their extreme reactions to separation from their mothers. However, Davies (1999) reports that Takahashi (1990) questions this, since Japanese infants are rarely separated from their caregivers even for sleeping and bathing; being suddenly separated in this experimental situation produced such great distress that this procedure may not be a valid measure of their attachment security.

Although attachment behaviors can vary cross-culturally, strong research evidence supports the fact that children need secure, consistent, responsive caregiving. *"The growing evidence of empirical studies points to quality of attachment as a fundamental mediator of development"* (Davies, 1999, p. 27; italics in the original).

Multiple attachments. Attention has shifted from a primary focus on mother-child interactions to include the child's early involvement with fathers, siblings, blended and stepfamilies, day care providers, and extended family. Grandparents often play a dominant role with children (sometimes as primary caretakers). Children frequently form bonds with many people "that are selective and provide comfort and security" (Frankel, 1994, p. 89); however, research supports the idea "that there is a hierarchy of attachments, with the mother most frequently at the top" (p. 89).

When children need foster placements, the principle of family preservation generally entails placing siblings together in the same home. "Siblings can provide, love and comfort to one another" (Whelan, 2003, p. 29), as when Rudyard Kipling and his younger sister Trix were placed together in the same foster home. However, sometimes "separation of family members can be in the best interests of the children" (Whelan, 2003, p. 22); some siblings may have very poor relationships with each other, including a "history of emotional, physical or sexual abuse between the siblings" (p. 29). Whelan (2003) advocates applying attachment theory to determine whether siblings will "contribute to, or detract from, a secure attachment environment" (p. 21).

Today, with the increase of multiple pregnancies, the exclusive mother-infant bond no longer is so exclusive, as a baby may have to share mother, with two, three, or more infants simultaneously. More knowledge is needed on the impact of being a twin or a child of other multiple pregnancies on the development of internalized object relations and the quality of early infant-caretaker interactions. It is known, for example, that twins often develop their own private language with each other, which is not immediately comprehensible to their parents.

Psychobiological Aspects of Development

The interrelationship between attachment and biological function and development is most apparent in the child's first year. Deprived of adequate nurturing, a child may not thrive; a premature child or one affected by maternal substance abuse may lack an adequately mature nervous system. Erikson (1963) illustrated this connection succinctly: "the first demonstration of social trust in the baby is the ease of his feeding, the depth of his sleep, the relaxation of his bowels" (p. 247). Eating and especially sucking are important reflexes that must be exercised and satisfied during early infancy; Freud named this stage the oral phase.

Debate, over the years, has focused on breast-feeding in terms of advantages and disadvantages to both mother and child. Recent medical research supports breast-feeding as advantageous to the child, in terms of increased ease of digestion and the transfer of the mother's immunity to certain diseases to the child. If a mother is comfortable with breast-feeding, psychological advantages may exist for both in the enhancement of intimacy and attachment. However, a child gains security primarily from being held, talked to, and cuddled during the feeding process, whether breast- or bottle-fed. Many mothers are not comfortable with breast-feeding or are biologically unable to do this, but often provide their children with excellent nurturing. Paradoxically, a mother who breast-feeds but remains uncomfortable with this, holding her child rigidly in an emotionally unresponsive manner, can precipitate anxiety and attachment problems in the child.

Many clinicians (including some psychoanalysts) have jettisoned Freud's concept of the oral phase as misleading or irrelevant. Although Rutter (1975) concedes that "the oral area is a particularly sensitive one in infants, and undoubtedly infants not only get pleasure from sucking but also tend to suck objects as a form of exploration and satisfaction," he stresses the importance of attachment in the first year of life, which "does not primarily depend on sucking and feeding" (p. 64).

It can be argued that strong biological urges exist for oral satisfaction, including sucking, that must be satisfied. An infant will suck its thumb not necessarily due to hunger but as a method of self-soothing. Putting substances in one's mouth (such as cigarettes or chewing gum) as well as eating and interest in food seem to be important to people throughout the life cycle. It is not unusual for people to overeat or chew their nails when they are nervous, and the present "epidemic" of obesity as well as the major eating disorders are centered on fixations on food, which go beyond mere satisfaction of hunger. People who talk incessantly have excessive oral needs, and the uncontrolled drinking of alcohol has an oral component. Although strong psychological determinants of these acts are present, the physical appetites and their underlying drives should not be relegated to insignificance. In fact, the close correspondence between physical and psychological need, one fueling the other, may make it more difficult for a person to combat this duality of forces.

The Neurobiological Aspects of Development

Neurobiology and emotional relatedness, affect, and the regulation of affect are closely interconnected (Shapiro and Applegate, 2000). Although it has long been observed that early emotional reactions to events often remain "fixed" in a person's personality and later functioning, the mechanisms had not been totally clear. Now, with the recent advances in neurobiology and neuroscience, it has been learned that feelings aroused by nurturing the infant receives "become 'hard-wired' into neuronal structure, thus explaining their persistence in later development" (Shapiro and Applegate, 2000, p. 9).

Freud, who was originally a neurologist, theorized that affect regulation "might be regulated by processes within the person," and "hypothesized neurobiological phenomena not yet discovered" (Shapiro and Applegate, 2000, p. 11). Hartmann also theorized about "biopsychological regulatory mechanisms," and Bowlby's concepts of the "neurobiology of attachment" formed the foundation for much of the research of present-day neurodevelopmental aspects of "caregiver-infant interactions" (Shapiro and Applegate, 2000, p. 11).

When born, the infant's brain is not fully developed, and the "wiring of the brain is incomplete" (Shapiro and Applegate, 2000, p. 14). Although orderly neurobiological progressions occur in brain and nervous system development, this progression in the young child is particularly dependent on the nurturing that the child receives. Therefore, while the brain is "thought to remain plastic and responsive to new experience throughout life," during the early years the "neuronal organization and structure of the brain is still in its formative stages" (Shapiro and Applegate, 2000, p. 15). The child's experience with caretakers, including attachment and stimulation, affect neuronal wiring in three major ways (Shapiro and Applegate, 2000). First, through a sequence of events starting in early childhood, in which "interconnections are constructed between brain systems," which are charged "with either positive or negative affects," depending on the quality of the child's experiences at the hands of caregivers. The abundance of the connections is "dependent, in part, on the quality of stimulation . . . the child receives." Second, because the brain as it develops is subject to a "use it or lose it" principle, the opportunity to form connections may be lost if stimulating experiences are not made available. Third, this sequence constitutes a "critical period" for "indices of . . . competence such as affect regulation" (Shapiro and Applegate, 2000, p. 15).

The emotional supplies the child receives also affect intelligence, a genetic endowment. Children with insecure and disorganized attachments tend to show "low self-confidence, deficient cognitive regulation, and an abnormal disequilibrium of thought under cognitive stress . . . [and some children are] adversely affected by an insecurity that curbs exploration" (Edelstein, 1996, p. 106). Children diagnosed with low intelligence often show remarkable intellectual gains when removed from a neglectful or abusive environment to a nurturing one.

The Development of Intelligence

Jean Piaget made major contributions to understanding the acquisition of intelligence and knowledge in children. He was neither concerned with theories of attachment nor how emotionality affected and was affected by cognition; for these reasons, he has been criticized and rejected by some present-day psychologists. Piaget was intrigued with the way in which children developed and constructed their cognition and understanding of the world in a step-by-step procedure. It was his hypothesis that children must essentially complete each stage of learning, before they could move on to master the next stage, which is also a point of dispute among psychologists, who have argued that children sometimes skip stages or go through them in a different order (Thomas, 1981).

Piaget conducted experiments with children, asking them to manipulate physical objects, solve puzzles, and answer questions related to subjects such as spatial relations, mathematics and logic, reasoning, physical causality, and moral feelings and judgments. He observed how their intelligence progressed from a concrete and self-centered understanding of the world to a more abstract understanding, in which different ways of viewing a situation were possible and attention could be focused on other people's perspectives and feelings. He frequently used his own children as subjects, for which he was further criticized; however, he applied his experiments to different cultures and to children all over the world.

An important Piagetian concept is *assimilation,* whereby children learn new information by comparing a new object to one that is familiar. A pear, newly introduced to a child, is different from a known apple, but it is like an apple in that it is a fruit, it is sweet, and it can be eaten. Assimilation continues throughout life. A new social work student expressed anxiety about not knowing what to say in an interview, but then, realizing that she had regularly conversed with people, felt more comfortable talking to a new "classification" of people (clients) by means of the familiar activity of conversing. She actively assimilated her past experiences of interacting with people to her present task of interacting with people in a professional situation.

accomodation — Piaget also introduced the concept of *accommodation,* a process by which children, encountering a strange phenomenon, adapt to the new idea or experience. This social work student, now reasonably comfortable with interviewing, is suddenly confronted with psychotic patients as clients. She protested, "They don't make sense; they can't relate! I don't know how to talk to them." The ability to adapt to this new experience, to change one's conception of the world (or psychotic clients) and integrate it into one's learning, is the process of accommodation.

equilibration — Assimilation and accommodation usually act together, and the mechanism that regulates this process is *equilibration,* which "leads to expanded forms of thought and broader levels of assimilation. It thus insures that new accommodations become integrated within existing forms of thinking" (Elkind, 1981, p. 5). As the social work student gets to know psychotic patients, it then becomes apparent that they too are people who also talk and interact but in a different way. Therefore going through the phase of assimilation as she realized that clients are people and that conversing can be applied to clinical work, she has now reached a higher level of development (accommodation) as she adapts this newly acquired skill, clinical interviewing (through the process of equilibration) to psychotic patients who communicate in a different way.

Piaget's Sensorimotor Phase

During the first two years of life, cognition evolves through infants' sensorimotor experiences, such as sucking, visual and auditory sensations, and an increasing sense of awareness of their own different physical states. "The first law of dawning psychological activity could be said to be the search for the maintenance or repetition of interesting states of consciousness" (Piaget, 1995a, p. 202). First, a lot of "hit and miss" activity occurs; then the baby begins to realize that a sequence of events takes place that leads to certain predictable outcomes (or *causalities*). In the following excerpt, Piaget describes how the baby experiences assimilation.

> With all this activity, a baby naturally hits upon lots of new elements. Not always does he successfully find the breast: his mouth sometimes finds his hand, the pillow, the covers, or something else. The assimilation of the world to the self is the phenomenon most typical of psychic

behavior in its beginnings. . . . A foreign body with which the mouth of a baby comes in contact is not interesting in itself but only from the point of view of its place in the baby's scheme of things, that is, as something suckable that activates sucking. Thus, the object is assimilated by the schema of sucking. (Piaget, 1995a, pp. 202-203)

Sensorimotor knowledge exists before language develops and is the foundation for all future cognition. Behavior, which was originally reflexive, evolves into voluntary movements as the baby begins to achieve eye-hand coordination. Babies become more interested in the world around them, responding to toys, mobiles, and people. A beginning sense of causality develops as the child makes certain predictions by observing causal events; the baby is hungry, the baby cries, and the mother comes. The baby smiles and laughs at the mother, and the mother will smile back; the toy telephone will make funny noises if the buttons are pressed, and the baby will press the buttons with delight.

Developmental Landmarks

The child's growth during the first year of life is remarkable in terms of gains in weight and height, brain and central nervous system maturation, and beginning adaptations to the external world. The child will begin its journey from relatively helpless infant to active, socially interactive, and inquisitive explorer.

During the first three months of life, the infant is "settling in" to the world, developing regulation of body rhythms and emotional states, forming reciprocal interactions with parents, and, at about six weeks of age, begins to smile, a "magic moment" for parents; laughter, another wonderful interactive highlight, follows shortly. Over the next several months, the baby is basically happy, outgoing, and experiences pleasure in itself and in the world. Parents (even unrelated others), unless deeply self-absorbed or frozen in emotional responsiveness, respond with affection and joy to the radiating happiness and the tender and trusting affection of this baby.

During the second half of the first year, the child enters the *practicing phase* (Mahler, Pine, and Bergman, 1975), in which locomotion and the joyful exploration of the world are primary occupations. Crawling and walking, while generally requiring extra parental energy and attention to "keep up" with the child and to provide damage control (for the child and household possessions), is usually a source of pleasure and pride to parents. Yet this very beginning, these very first steps, marks the beginning of the child becoming more autonomous. Mahler, Pine, and Bergman (1975) quote the philosopher Kierkegaard in this connection:

> The loving mother teaches her child to walk alone. She is far enough from him so that she cannot actually support him, but she holds out her arms to him. She imitates his movements, and if he totters, she swiftly bends as if to seize him, so that the child might believe that he is not walking alone. . . . And yet, she does more. Her face beckons like a reward, an encouragement. Thus, the child walks alone with his eyes fixed on his mother's face, *not* on the difficulties in his way. He supports himself by the arms that do not hold him and constantly strives toward the refuge in his mother's embrace, little suspecting *that in the very same moment that he is emphasizing his need of her, he is proving that he can do without her,* because he is walking alone. (Søren Kierkegaard [from *Purity of Heart* (1846)] as quoted in Mahler, Pine, and Bergman, 1975, pp. 72-73; italics in the original)

However, in an anxious and frightened mother, the situation is very different:

> There is no beckoning encouragement, no blessing at the end of the walk. There is the same wish to teach the child to walk alone, but not as a loving mother does it. For now there is fear that envelops the child. It weighs him down so that he cannot move forward. There is the same wish to lead him to the goal, *but the goal becomes suddenly terrifying.* (Mahler, Pine, and Bergman, 1975, p. 73; italics in the original)

Mahler, Pine, and Bergman (1975) also note Anthony's observation that "'the psychotic mother fills these moments with apprehension so that the child not only has nowhere to go, but he is afraid to get anywhere'" (p. 73). This statement also reflects the impact of the child's *attunement* to the emotions and moods of the mother, which can directly affect developmental progress. Mahler, Pine, and Bergman (1975) have observed that the first unassisted steps the child takes are "away from the mother or during her absence; this contradicts the popular belief . . . that the first steps are taken toward the mother" (p. 73). In general, mothers in Mahler, Pine, and Bergman (1975) study helped their children "move away, that is by giving them a gentle or perhaps less gentle push, as the mother bird would encourage the fledgling" (p. 73). However, once the child began to move further away, "it was as if suddenly the mother began to worry about whether the child would be able to 'make it' out there in the world" (p. 73).

Case Illustration

The following excerpt illustrates the development of Carl, a "normal" five-month-old boy, recorded by a social work student who made monthly observational home visits from the time Carl was seven weeks old until he was eight months old. This report highlights Carl's physical development, his emotional responsiveness, socialization, and his mother's sensitive attunement to his needs and interests (Urdang, 1964).

> Carl is now five months old. He sleeps from eight at night until eight in the morning and naps from about twelve-thirty until three in the afternoon, usually sleeping on his stomach. He uses about ten diapers a day. His mother puts two diapers on him at night. In the evening she sometimes removes the diaper for a while, and he likes that. He can get out of his infant seat and is trying to crawl although he cannot quite get up on his knees. He cannot roll over yet. He grabs things he sees. He is teething and chews on everything he can reach. He scratches things because he likes to hear the sound. He screams to hear his own voice, and his pitch has gone up. He recognizes more people now and is much more responsive. The cat fascinates him, and he likes to try to imitate the sounds it makes. I watched Mrs. S. bathe him and observed that he enjoyed it. (Urdang, 1964, p. 11)

Special Problems

Two special problems affecting some infants include maltreatment and other traumas and physical disabilities.

Maltreatment and Other Traumas

Many infants are subjected to physical and sexual abuse and neglect, often resulting in developmental, psychological, and neurological impairments. Child abuse is the major cause of infant mortality during the first year of life; "children under 1 year of age . . . comprise 44 percent of all child fatalities from abuse and neglect. . . . Children under age 6 account for 85 percent of children killed by child abuse (National Clearinghouse on Child Abuse and Neglect Information, 2002)" (Smyke, Wajda-Johnston, and Zeanah, 2004, p. 261). There is "something deeply disturbing about the juxtaposition of violence and infancy" (Zeanah and Scheeringa, 1997, p. 97).

Physical abuse can be mild and sporadic, but can also be frequent and may cause serious and irreparable injuries. Debate continues about the definition of physical abuse: Physical punishment, for example, is acceptable (and expected) in some cultures; professionals do not always agree on definitions; state laws vary. Cultural practices can be reported as abuse; child protective workers, for example, had been inclined to report bruises on the skin of Vietnamese children as abuse, until they became "more knowledgeable about the practice of coin rubbing, a healing practice that leaves bruises" (Wells, 1995, p. 349). Although many gray areas exist in assessment, nevertheless clear-cut cases of serious and often life-threatening instances of abuse clearly require intervention.

> Severely abused children are seen in hospital emergency rooms with external evidences of body trauma, bruises, abrasions, cuts, lacerations, burns, soft tissue swellings, and hematomas. . . . Inability to move certain extremities, because of dislocations and fractures associated with neurological signs of intracranial damage, can also indicate inflicted trauma. . . . Abdominal trauma may result in unexplained ruptures of the stomach, the bowel, the liver, or the pancreas, with manifestations of an injured abdomen. Those children with the most severe maltreatment injuries arrive at the hospital or physicians office in a coma or convulsions, and some arrive dead. (Kaplan, Sadock, and Grebb, 1994, p. 787)

Serious neurobiological effects of violence in infants and young children are possible; "profound and perhaps permanent brain changes can result following violent trauma in the first 3 years of life" (Zeanah and Scheeringa, 1997, p. 107). Brain injuries "from shaking an infant can range from subclinical tears in the periphery of the retina, through retinal hemorrhages and subdural bleeding, to death" (Smyke, Wajda-Johnston, and Zeanah, 2004, p. 261).

Infants can be affected by witnessing parental violence, both directly by experiencing fear and indirectly through their reactions to the mother's response to this assault; parents who are involved in partner violence also tend to abuse their children (Davies, 1999; Smyke, Wajda-Johnston, and Zeanah, 2004; Zeanah and Scheeringa, 1997). Two of the most frequently observed disorders in infants exposed to violence are attachment disorders and post–traumatic stress disorder (PTSD) (Smyke, Wajda-Johnston, and Zeanah, 2004; Zeanah and Scheeringa, 1997). In research with infants experiencing PTSD, it was discovered that "in addition to the classic triad of reexperiencing, avoidance/numbing of responsiveness, and hyperarousal, the investigators also found that new fears and new aggression were present in infants after the traumatic event that had not been present before" (Zeanah and Scheeringa, 1997, p. 111).

The role of traumas other than maltreatment, such as car accidents and hospitalizations occurring in infancy, can also affect the child's personality development (Gaensbauer, 1995). Gaensbauer's observations support the findings of Zeanah and Scheeringa (1997) that symptoms of post–traumatic stress disorder can be found in young children, "even prior to the onset of language fluency" (Gaensbauer, 1995, p. 123).

Terr, in 1988, observed that young children who might not be able to give verbal reports of trauma nevertheless could act out their trauma, and asserted that for children, even younger than twenty-eight months, "traumas create powerful and lasting visual images; the child's enactments or behavioral memories derive from these 'burned in' visual imprints rather than from verbal memory" (Gaensbauer, 1995, p. 124). When children express themselves in nonverbal ways they often "give evidence that salient sensory and somatically based elements of a preverbal traumatic experience have been encoded and retained in memory over extended periods of time" (Gaensbauer, 1995, p. 125).

Munchausen syndrome by proxy is a form of physical (and psychological) abuse that has received attention recently (Mercer and Perdue, 1993; Parrish and Perman, 2004; Sadock and Sadock, 2003). Some children, usually of preschool age (Parrish and Perman, 2004), are repeatedly brought to the hospital by "overly cooperative parents" because of unusual, "peculiar or puzzling" physical symptoms for which no clear-cut medical diagnosis can be found (Sadock and Sadock, 2003, p. 884). However, it was discovered that a parent or other involved adult injures the child or causes the child to become ill "by injecting toxins or by inducing the child to ingest drugs or toxins to cause diarrhea, dehydration, or other symptoms—and then eagerly seeks medical attention" (p. 884). The person inflicting the illness or injury denies any knowledge of how the child developed the problem; "symptoms quickly cease when the child and the perpetrator are separated" (Mercer and Perdue, 1993, p. 75). The diagnosis was made with increasing frequency by secretly videotaping the parents' actions in the hospital. "As commonly noted among other forms of child abuse, such distorted dynamics do not necessarily preclude very close, sometimes symbiotic relationships between the perpetrator and the child" (Parrish and Perman, 2004, p. 145).

Sexual abuse of infants and toddlers accounts "for approximately 10 percent of validated sexual abuse cases in the United States, while another 28 percent of victims are between 4 and 7 years of age" (Smyke, Wajda-Johnston, and Zeanah, 2004, p. 262). Children who are most vulnerable for negative outcomes are those who have been abused at very young ages; they are also likely to be exposed to more physical abuse and neglect; "their sexual abuse experiences were more likely to have been chronic and to have involved multiple perpetrators, one of whom was a parent or stepparent" (Kaufman and Henrich, 2000, p. 201).

Although child neglect is more frequent than abuse and produces a high percentage of fatalities, it has received substantially less attention than problems of blatant physical and sexual abuse (Nelson, Saunders, and Landsman, 1993; Wells, 1995). "Reports of neglect account for the majority of referrals to the child welfare system for very young children, and neglect is the single greatest reason that infants and toddlers are placed in foster care" (Smyke, Wajda-Johnston, and Zeanah, 2004, p. 262). Although a lack of unanimity exists in defining neglect (Nelson, Saunders, and Landsman, 1993), it usually implies inadequate supervision of the child, general physical neglect, including poor nutrition, inadequate hygiene and clothing, and lack of medical attention. This child frequently "has a history of failure to thrive, malnutrition, poor skin hygiene, irritability, withdrawal, and other signs of psychological and physical neglect" (Kaplan, Sadock, and Grebb, 1994, p. 790), and may have been subjected to abandonment, inadequate housing (including poor sanitation), and educational neglect (Nelson, Saunders, and Landsman, 1993).

Parental characteristics contributing to chronic neglect include being unmarried and having large families typically with insufficient resources; extreme poverty is often present (Nelson, Saunders, and Landsman, 1993).

> Because neglect is intricately tied to poverty and income, the poorest of the poor are at the highest risk. The rate of known neglect is nine times greater in families with incomes under $15,000 than in families above that level. (Thomlison, 1997, p. 52)

Neglectful mothers are often found to be depressed and lonely, to have a high rate of substance abuse, to be socially isolated, to have little interaction with their children, and to possess poor parenting skills (Nelson, Saunders, and Landsman, 1993); there are mothers, in all social classes, who may become depressed to the point of emotional unresponsiveness to their infants.

> What is the experience of an infant within a primary relationship that fails to respond appropriately to his personal and intersubjective needs? From the observation of babies in this predicament, this maternal failure appears catastrophic. The infant patient, so dangerously dependent on his mother's/caretaker's capacity to identify and understand,

expresses extreme anxiety, fragmentation and, finally, defeat. Because the anxiety is embedded in their relationship—often underpinned and driven by intergenerational patterns of relating—it is enduring. Therefore the concept of cumulative trauma (Khan, 1963), the repeated breaching of the adaptive and defensive structures available to the immature ego, is pertinent. (Baradon, 2005, p. 49)

Physical Disabilities

Some children are born with physical disabilities such as blindness, deafness, or motor handicaps. If a child cannot gaze at its mother's face and see her smile, will attachment be thwarted? If a deaf child cannot hear language, will cognitive development be impaired? The concept of the plasticity of the brain suggests that the brain has sufficient flexibility and adaptability so that other pathways will be developed to permit developmental progress (Thomas, 1981). The developmental course of disabled children might be different from children without handicaps, but nevertheless they can achieve good developmental progress, depending upon the nature of the actual deficits and given that they have the average expectable environment. Early prevention programs (discussed next) are often of valuable assistance to parents of disabled children providing support, rehabilitative services, and guidance.

PREVENTIVE PROGRAMS

The federal government provides financial aid to states (as part of the Individuals with Disabilities Education Act passed in 1987) to provide early intervention services to infants, toddlers, and their families (Gilkerson and Stott, 2000). Although optional, all fifty states provide services through this program, mostly to children with developmental delays or who have medical or psychiatric conditions that would probably lead to developmental delay. Although all programs have a multidisciplinary staff and a family-centered approach, some conflict exists about the degree to which the focus should be on parent-child relationships.

Historically, early intervention programs focused on educational and rehabilitative services directed toward "the amelioration of developmental deficits through child-focused, stimulation models using primarily developmentally prescriptive, Piagetian, or behavioral approaches to develop training programs or recommendations for families that would enable them to teach their children at home" (Gilkerson and Stott, 2000, p. 461). Emphasis was given to empowerment of the families as they collaborated with the staff. Ongoing research highlighted the importance of the child's relationships with the family and the "relational processes in promoting the development of children with disabilities" (Gilkerson and Stott, 2000, p. 463), although this is not accepted as an emphasis in all programs.

Gilkerson and Stott (2000) advocate a holistic approach, which blends a strength-based, family-centered approach with an infant mental health perspective.

> Infant mental health helps us focus on how people understand, respond to, and make meaning of their own experiences. It offers the possibility for holding the pain as well as the hope. The crux of early intervention rests on how individual practitioners respond to individual children and families. (Gilkerson and Stott, 2000, p. 469)

Specialized programs for infants who are at risk for serious psychosocial problems exist under various auspices, tend to be comprehensive, to utilize multidisciplinary staff, and to integrate different theoretical approaches. When severe maltreatment is suspected, child welfare services and the courts are involved, sometimes removing children from their families (temporarily or permanently), or making critical decisions about referrals (or mandating) parent guidance and/or mental health services; in some special programs, family courts become "natural collaborative partners with other agencies and with community-based organizations" (Van Horn and Hitchens, 2004, p. 246). The quality of foster care is variable; Pasztor and colleagues (2006) stress that "foster parents are not receiving the role clarity, training, information, and support they need to responsibly help address increasingly complex health and mental health challenges" (p. 53). There are some model programs, with excellent foster homes, including therapeutic foster care (Benoit, 2006).

Many programs offer intensive home-based treatment to families; many projects, such as Seligman's (1994), are built on the work of Selma Fraiberg, whose insights about the "ghosts in the nursery" led to the understanding of how parents' relationships to their children can be dominated by their own conflicts about being parented (Seligman, 1994). Many practitioners are "emphasizing the central place of relationships in human development," and are "pragmatic integrationists" who provide "social support to troubled children and adults" (Dowling, 2005, p. 4).

The Infant-Parent Program based at San Francisco General Hospital, works with clients who are "psychologically and socioeconomically disadvantaged"; many belong to minority groups (Seligman, 1994, p. 482); problems include "parental psychopathology that impedes parenting, disorders of attachment, inorganic failure to thrive, parental drug abuse, and infant characteristics, including developmental disabilities, that place special stress on the caregiving system" (p. 483). Some of the children were placed in foster homes owing to abuse and neglect.

Seligman incorporates home visiting and the provision of concrete services, within a psychoanalytic framework, with an emphasis on the development of a therapeutic relationship with parents, and the encouragement of parental self-reflection.

The parents in Seligman's project (1994) often had characterological problems and sometimes low-level psychoses and, combined with their serious social problems, required "extraordinary efforts" from clinicians. These families had had:

> Few, if any, positive experiences with social agencies or psychotherapy. . . . They have felt that the fragile capacity for hope . . . has been betrayed. . . . These disappointments have often repeated those suffered in their earliest relationships . . . and these new parents are now reenacting these painful relationship patterns with their infants. The infant-parent therapist is often attempting to enter a system of . . . relationships that is dominated by . . . an overall sense that . . . intervention will make no difference. (Seligman, 1994, p. 485)

Persistent efforts to reach out to families rather than giving up on those who have difficulty keeping regular appointments is an important principle of this program. Supportive and concrete services were provided to the families, such as making referrals for other needed services or actually driving clients to appointments. These efforts were often necessary before other types of psychological work could be carried out; these procedures actually "enhance such work; a number of crucial interpretations are made in irregular situations, such as while driving parents and infants to appointments or while watching television at families' homes. Interpretation is thus integrated with an array of other intervention tactics" (Seligman, 1994, p. 485), and is similar to Kanter's (1990) utilization of Winnicott's holding environment as an underlying basis for engaging in case management activities with clients (discussed in Chapter 3 of this book).

The development of the therapeutic relationship, which in itself is a "corrective attachment experience" (Lieberman, Silverman, and Pawl, 2000, p. 483), is seen as the key factor in helping the parents understand how their past relationships are alive inside them now and how they are reenacting aspects of these relationships with their therapists and with their own infants.

Utilizing "nondidactic developmental guidance" with parents encourages them to think and reflect about their children's needs and experiences. "The infant-parent psychotherapist might ask the mother what she thinks of her child's interest in the toys rather than giving direct instruction in play techniques" (Seligman, 1994, p. 489). However, in the following illustration, we can see a behavioral suggestion (not identified as such) was made to the mother, Paula, with good results. Paula had difficulty responding to her infant Naomi, showing "a kind of emotional blankness, rather than malevolence" (Seligman, 1994, p. 490). When Naomi was a year old, the therapist brought her some washable crayons and a pad, as her mother had been upset about Naomi marking up the walls.

> She [Naomi] opened them with pleasure and presented them to her mother. . . . Paula was . . . unresponsive and effectively mute. The therapist then wondered *what it would be like if she sat on the floor with Naomi, and just kind of did whatever she did.* . . . Soon, the two of them were scribbling together with glee. Paula then spontaneously said that no one had ever done this with *her* as a child. . . . She became tearful and pleased at the same time. (Seligman, 1994, p. 491; italics added)

If the interactions between mother and child begin to change, benefits can be experienced by both; the elation, joy, and welcoming of a mother *by* her child can evoke joy in a mother, if she is open to this. "Adaptive changes in behavior and intrapsychic life can be synergistic, especially when *the infant's special ability to support and reinforce parental responsiveness is at work*" (Seligman, 1994, p. 489; italics added); when this happens "the self-righting tendencies of infant-parent caregiving systems can take hold, and progressive changes may occur unusually rapidly" (p. 489).

The Toddler

The first birthday finds the child beginning the *toddler phase,* characterized by major developments in language and speech, greatly increased locomotion and motor skills, the development of play, and major advances in cognition, including the formation of mental representations. The toddler begins the *practicing subphase,* with pleasure in walking and exploring the world, then goes through the dramatic *rapprochement subphase,* with ambivalence about independence/dependence, and is on the road to object constancy, with internalized representations of mother and of self at the end of toddlerhood (Mahler, Pine, and Bergman, 1975).

Toilet training is one of the major developmental achievements. Normal struggles with parents about this, relating to autonomy, reflect similar struggles in other areas of the toddler's life, such as feeding and dressing oneself. Erikson (1963) characterizes this phase as the achievement of "autonomy vs. shame and doubt" (p. 251). The child begins to form a sense of self- identity, and "mine" as well as "I do it" are frequently used words and phrases.

Although children struggle to attain self-sufficiency during toddlerhood, the attachment to parents remains a primary need; the intensity of these two opposing wishes is at the root of many "emotional storms" and tantrums of this period. Children begin to use soft and cuddly objects, such as teddy bears, as transitional objects, which Winnicott described as an important stage in the psychological separation from their mother; they can be comforted by an object that is like their mother, but not their mother, and one which they can control (Mahler, Pine, and Bergman, 1975; see discussion in Chapter 3 of this book).

Language Development

Language, which begins during the latter half of the first year with exuberant babbling and extends to a few words toward the end of the first year, increases dramatically by eighteen months. However, language develops at different rates, and some normal children may say only a few words by the time they reach age two (Rutter, 1975). Children have actually been communicating with their parents from early infancy in nonverbal ways, and language greatly enriches the level and depth of communication. "The social-affective exchange occurring between infants and caregivers provides the foundation for the social or pragmatic aspects of communication" (Prizant, Wetherby, and Roberts, 2000).

Language has many developmental purposes including facilitating children's engagement in social communication; enabling them "to process and organize experience," by telling stories about their experiences; and providing "a way of sharing [their] inner life in an active way" (Davies, 1999, p. 178). Language aids children in understanding people and the world around them and assists toddlers with self-regulation, as they learn to use words instead of action.

Stern (1985), observing that language can be used as a "transitional phenomenon," described the "crib talk" of a two-year-old girl whose "goodnight" talking rituals with her father and her "monologues" after he left her room were recorded (pp. 172-173).

The important features of her monologues were her practice and discovery of word usage. . . . But even more striking . . . is that it was like
watching "internalization" happen right before our eyes and ears. After father left, she appeared to be constantly under the threat of feeling
alone and distressed. . . . To keep herself controlled emotionally, she
repeated in her soliloquy topics that had been part of the dialogue
with her father. Sometimes she seemed to intone in his voice or to recreate something like the previous dialogue with him, in order to reactivate his presence and carry it with her toward the abyss of sleep. This
of course, was not the only purpose that her monologue served . . . but
it certainly felt as though she were also engaged in a "transitional phenomenon," in Winnicott's sense. (Stern, 1985, p. 173)

Cognitive Development

Brain development progresses rapidly during the child's first two years;
in the toddler period, the major cognitive event is the "integration of perceptual and cognitive functions" and the beginnings of "self-awareness" (Davies,
1999, p. 171).

The child remains in the latter part of the sensorimotor phase into the
second year, moving into the *preoperational phase* during the second year,
and progressing in this phase until age seven (Piaget, 1995b). During this
time, language, symbolic play, and drawing skills are elaborated; a child's
thinking at this stage tends to be concrete, and an *egocentric view* of the
world emerges. Egocentricity refers to children's cognitive inability to see
(and understand) things from another's perspective or point of view; they
are convinced by their own "prelogic" logic; what makes sense to them *is*.

A three-year-old child insisted to her grandfather that the moon was moving, denying his assertions that the moon looked as though it were moving
because their car was moving; the moon was not moving. The grandfather
attempted to explain this in different ways, but the child insisted, No! The
moon was moving! She could see this happening, and this was her final
conclusion. Piaget (1995b) comments that the child "takes his own immediate perception as absolute," and cites his observation that:

Most of the boys in Geneva go on believing till they are 7-8 years old
that the sun or the moon follows them on their walks because they always happen to be above them. They are greatly perplexed when they
have to say which of two boys walking in different directions is being
accompanied by these heavenly bodies. (Piaget, 1995b, p. 100)

Piaget (1995b) asserts that many adults remain "egocentric in their way of thinking" (p. 95).

The toddler's sense of reality is developing, and toddlers can have diffi- ~~animism~~ culty distinguishing what is real from what is unreal. They have a sense of *animism;* that is, inanimate objects can be alive, so if an arm of a chair falls off because it is broken, the child may think this action hurts the chair; if toddlers trip on a rug, they may think the rug has tripped them. They engage in magical thinking and may believe that if something has happened, the cause was their action; if, the mother dies, it was because he or she was bad that Mommy disappeared.

Piaget introduced the concept of *object permanency,* which raises the ~~object permanency~~ profound puzzle of whether an object out of sight continues to exist for the child. He observed that infants will not look for, nor attempt to retrieve, an object (such as a ball) when it rolls away from them. When they reach the age of eighteen to twenty months, they have developed the sense of permanence and will look for and/or reach for the missing object. Is Piaget's concept of object permanence the same as Mahler's concept of object constancy, and does it take place at the same time?

Mahler, Pine, and Bergman (1975) observed that children develop an early sense of permanence of physical objects, but only later (at closer to three and a half years) do they develop a sense of mother's permanence. The later acquisition of object constancy involves more intense feelings being attached to the mother than to physical objects.

> The mother, an "object" in the psychoanalytic sense . . . is far more than an "object" in the merely physical-descriptive sense. We expect that repeated contact and high arousal make for differences in the rate of acquisition of a concept of permanence. (Mahler, Pine, and Bergman, 1975, p. 110)

Piaget's (Elkind, 1981) famous principle of *conservation* asks, does an object change in size (or volume) if its shape or container changes? Children in the preoperational stage have difficulty with this idea and tend not to understand aspects of this until they are about six or seven years old. In a classical experiment, Piaget poured equal amounts of water into containers of the same size, and children agreed that the same amount existed in each container. Then, when he poured the water from one of the containers into a taller container, the children said that the taller container had *more* water. The logical capability of understanding this was not accessible until a later age.

As children navigate their perplexing *Alice in Wonderland* world without a white rabbit as a guide, they need parental guidance to help them find a path through the maze of daily reality. Good enough parents offer this assistance; however, this passage becomes overwhelming and incomprehensible when the assistance is not only unavailable but the guides, through their own confusions, depressive withdrawal, or maltreatment, add uncertainty, unpredictability, and fear.

The Development of Play

The infant's initial exploration of objects continues on a more advanced level into the toddler phase. Toddlers generally love exploring the contents of drawers, pulling things out, and taking things apart. They love sandbox play, in which they put sand in pails, pour it out, and, with great delight, pour water into their creations.

Play becomes more social, and they enjoy playing and exploring with others. "When young children want to engage another human being . . . they ask, 'Do you want to play with me?'" (Colarusso, 1993, p. 241). Children enjoy pretend games; one three-and-a-half-year-old served pretend soup to her parents' guests, asking each guest which ingredients they would like in their soup, as she poured it into her doll dishes and watched with pleasure as they drank this soup and expressed their satisfaction with it.

Play takes on symbolic meaning as the child's imagination develops (Davies, 1999); one of the earliest types of symbolic play occurs when the toddler substitutes one object for another. Davies (1999) describes a boy, sixteen months old, who, when playing with cooking utensils, "stepped into two pots and said, 'Shoes'; about a year later, a more 'dramatic substitution' occurs when the child makes believe he is 'someone else'" (p. 183).

Play, the development of imagination, and use of symbolic representations serve many psychological functions for children, enabling them to understand how the world works, anticipate events, work out difficult experiences, and cope with emotions. One three-and-a-half-year-old girl, being prepared by her parents for upcoming back surgery, was told she would be awakened during the operation and asked to wiggle her fingers and toes. When her grandfather visited, she put a rubber tube on his arm representing an IV, told him to lie down on the bed, close his eyes, then she "operated" on his back, told him to "wiggle your fingers and toes," and when he succeeded at this, she said he could "wake up and have some presents."

Toilet Training

A major developmental event for the toddler is toilet training, in which a clash of will between parent and child often ensues; one toddler commented, "I can't want to try." Toilet training is usually not easy for parents and children; basic issues about autonomy and control are involved, based on complex physiological and psychological processes involving the child's bodily sensations and feelings, which the parents are now trying to regulate. Children are often more aggressive and angry when parents begin training too early "because they face the frustrating situation of the parent's exerting control over *an internal body function*" (Davies, 1999, p. 190; italics added).

Freud asserted that instinctual feelings about bowel movements, retention, and control, were major concerns during this period, which he called the anal phase. "Pleasurable and unpleasurable sensations are associated both with the retention of feces and with their expulsion, and these bodily processes, as well as feces themselves and fecal odors, are the objects of the child's most intense interest" (Brenner, 1974, p. 24). As with Freud's other instinctual theories, issues of anality are downplayed if not altogether ignored. Emphasis is placed on the larger contextual issues of autonomy and control that are played out between children and parents (Rutter, 1975). I would argue that physical sensations relating to bowel activities are important; since pleasurable physical sensations are associated with bowel activities. Although disturbed bowel activities occur within a psychosocial context involving attachment issues, conflict, and aggression, they also have a strong physiological component.

It is not uncommon for childhood disturbances to be accompanied by toileting problems such as bed-wetting or encopresis; some adult psychotic patients, in a regressive state, play with their feces or smear them on walls. Some adults obtain pleasure by giving themselves frequent enemas (not medically prescribed) and become quite anxious when they cannot do this. Some mothers are excessively preoccupied with their children's bowel habits; giving their children regular enemas can be a source of excitement to them. Buxbaum and Sodergren (1977) refer to cases "where the mothers or caretaking people had for different reasons a pathological and therefore pathogenic interest in the processes of elimination" (p. 211).

> Sphincter control is one of the areas in which a partial symbiotic relationship between mother and child can develop. The child remains dependent on the mother's ministrations beyond the usual time. However, the mothers promote this dependency in order to satisfy their own needs. One patient reported that his mother did not allow him to

flush the toilet until she had seen the results, and she wiped him until he was 9 years old. A woman patient reported a similar procedure, which was followed by an enema if the mother thought she had not defecated a sufficient amount. She finally locked the mother out of the bathroom when she was 16 and gave herself the enema if she needed it. She continued to do this into her adult life—it remained her form of sexual satisfaction. (Buxbaum and Sodergren, 1977, p. 210)

Relationships to Parents

Toddlers' relationships to their parents can be stormy at times: the precursor of adolescence. The tasks of toddlerhood are enormous as children become more autonomous, explore their strange world with its "illogical" logic, communicate when they understand more than they can say, and separate (to a degree) from parents for whom they feel intense attachment and fear losing. Parents generally feel great pleasure at their toddler's developing personality, loving overtures, inquisitive mind, and charming language; parents can also feel frustrated and angry at their tantrums, their refusals to let parents dress them (especially when an appointment must be kept), their messy eating, and the continual need to baby-proof possessions while constantly watching the unsteady toddler who has a poor sense of what is dangerous. One loving father, referring to the impossible places that his son climbed, remarked: "I think he is trying to kill himself."

Parents may have difficulty finding a balance between limit setting and permissiveness, and between providing closeness and allowing for appropriate autonomy. The toddler needs ongoing help in self-regulation, and, to the extent that good enough parents can provide a holding environment that is secure, structured with firm limits, and consistent, the child will thrive.

On the other hand, being confronted with insecure attachments and violence and having no adults to rely on can be especially threatening to a toddler.

> This unreliability can be particularly devastating to toddlers, whose increased ability to function autonomously rests on the parent's ability to encourage and applaud their strivings toward mastery, while remaining a constant and reassuring source of support and mirroring. Such young children may increasingly doubt their own competency, and may gradually come to avoid contact with potential sources of help, instead of seeking out trusting and helpful relationships.
>
> Conversely, young children who experience violence may evidence their distress by desperately clinging to a parent or caregiver, unable

to tolerate the peril of repeated loss. In this case, one may see behaviors that include anxiety, clinginess, inconsolability, sleep disturbances, toileting problems, and temper tantrums related to difficulties in separation. For the young child who is learning to actively master his or her own aggressive impulses . . . exposure to uncontrolled hostility on the part of others may unleash a wave of regressed, disorganized, and unchecked aggressivity. (Marans and Adelman, 1997, p. 207)

The Preschooler

From ages three to six, children make great strides in socialization, cognitive abilities (including logic and reasoning), language, locomotion and motor coordination, self-regulation and impulse control, identity and gender identity, and can say with confidence: "Now I am a kid!" Their world expands, and extended family, friends, and preschool activities (if available) are important parts of their lives. Preschoolers love to tell stories that include descriptions of their daily activities: "I went to the doctor today and he said to walk across the room, and then he looked at my back and then I put my pants on and went home."

The Development of Language

Language continues to develop rapidly, and, by age three, children have the ability to ask questions. This capacity "to ask 'why' and 'what' gives him power over his own learning," and when parents answer, this furthers the opportunity to add words to his vocabulary (Davies, 1999, p. 238). Children develop "'private speech,' talking to themselves a great deal, saying out loud what older children and adults say to themselves in silent thought" (p. 239). This often takes place when they are playing; they seem to use this speech to gain self-direction and to assist in gaining "self control, as when a child repeats parents' limit-setting words to himself: 'Don't run in the house, Amani'" (Davies, 1999, p. 240).

Bretherton (1996) stresses the importance of the dialogue between parents and children in "guiding the child's construction of internal working models through joint talk about past and future"; it can also "facilitate a child's memory productions" (p. 16). Stern (1985) asserts that "language is potent in the service of union and togetherness" (p. 172) and highlights the importance of language in developing the child's

ability to narrate one's own life story, with all the potential that holds for changing how one views oneself. . . . It involves thinking in terms of persons who act as agents with intentions and goals that unfold in some causal sequence with a beginning, middle, and end. (p. 174)

Case Illustration

Children can have difficulty developing language for many reasons, including general developmental delays or specific physical problems, such as hearing disabilities. However, psychological conflicts were at the root of Susan's speech and developmental problems when she was referred for a social work evaluation at three years and ten months of age, with a diagnosis of "delayed articulation ability," and "a poor speaking environment in the home," in the sense of speech not being sufficiently encouraged. Her mother reported that Susan's speech is not clear, and she does not speak in sentences. However, she does have "private speech," as she "jabbers as she plays . . . usually baby talk." Susan was lagging in speech development; generally, by age three, children speak distinctly and by four, they use sentences.

> Susan, a pretty girl, was attractively dressed, somewhat hyperactive, had indistinct speech, and a marked tendency to control her parents. Her mother, Mrs. B., thirty, and her father, Mr. B., thirty-two, had been married thirteen years and adopted Susan when she was five days old. Their biological son, who is one year old, is developing well, and "says several things plain." The parents function at a high level and seem comfortable financially, although Mr. B. works long hours as a store manager, six days a week. Mrs. B. is a homemaker and has no outside activities or interests, other than attending church. They report a positive marital relationship and socialize with friends, but Mrs. B. emphasized: *"We never leave Susan."* No medical or psychiatric problems were reported in the family; the only concern expressed was related to Susan's speech problem.

The Bs adopted Susan from a lawyer. The Bs know nothing about Susan's parental or genetic history. Susan's developmental landmarks were within normal parameters: She talked at nine months (which is on the early side), walked at twelve-and-a-half months ("maybe she was a little slow with coordination"), and has always been affectionate; she had an initial problem with colic, which cleared up, and she has always been a good eater. She was toilet trained at two; "it was real easy."

As the parents discussed Susan, two major factors stood out. Mrs. B. had difficulty separating from Susan and had difficulty setting limits. Susan's pediatrician wrote, "Susan never learned to mind her parents; she runs them instead of their controlling her."

> The parents commented that they talked a great deal to Susan as she grew up . . . "that's about all we did . . . we stayed with her, talked to her, devoted all our time to her . . . she was like a toy, I guess." The B.s are aware of a difference in their feelings toward Susan and the baby . . . if the baby cries, they let him. "It is easier to say no to him than to Susan . . . why, I don't know." Mrs. B. "can't stand for her to be crying . . . I feel sorry for her." For the first six months of her life, a nineteen-year-old girl took care of Susan. "She was real good with the baby." Mrs. B. continued her secretarial job. After that, Mrs. B. "never left her." Until this past summer, Susan did not play with other children. "She did not want to leave me at all."

The parents also reported that since Susan was two-and-a-half-years old, she has been sleeping in her parents' bed.

> Sometimes they try putting her in her room; but she wakes up and cries. For her to go to sleep, one of her parents would lie down with her in bed; sometimes for a half hour. She sleeps soundly if someone is with her . . . "if she feels someone's body close to her, she is o.k. She seems to think we will leave her." During the day, she naps on the couch in the living room; the mother states she usually works in the kitchen and living room while Susan naps. Sleep problems first occurred when Susan was sixteen months old while on vacation with her parents for two weeks and sleeping in the same bed with them during a visit with relatives. When returning home, Susan persisted in this; at first, her parents would let her sleep in their bed then transfer her to her room. She began objecting to the transfer: "woke up at night crying . . . it did not work."

Although preschoolers want to remain close to mother, they venture into the outside world from "a secure base" and enjoy playing with children. Sometimes the toddler needs a "gentle push" out of the nest (Mahler, Pine, and Bergman, 1975, p. 79), but Mrs. B. cannot do this. Why is there a "desperation" in her need to be with Susan and to never let her feel she has been abandoned?

> Mrs. B. and her brother, two years younger, lived with their mother and father. When Mrs. B. was about two or three, her mother's nightgown caught fire, and she died from burns and pneumonia which set in. Her father left home right after this incident, and Mrs. B. and her brother were raised by an aunt and uncle who had four children of their own. She felt "they wanted me . . . they were like parents to me." Mrs. B.'s father married about a year after his wife's death, but he had minimal contact with his children. Mrs. B. married when she was sixteen and completed high school after her marriage.

Losing one's mother at age two is a very traumatic event because of the child's intense attachment at that age as well as the child's lack of the cognitive and verbal skills to process this event. Mrs. B. also lost her father who abandoned his children at that time, which may have been motivated by his intense grief, rather than overt rejection, in the usual sense. This terrible loss was probably "encoded" in Mrs. B.'s neurophysiological system, while perhaps only a dim awareness of the actual memory remained.

Although other factors may have contributed to Susan's difficulties (including the birth of her brother and her parents' possible ambivalence about adopting a child), the issue of Mrs. B.'s abandonment seems primary. The fact that Susan was adopted facilitated Mrs. B.'s identification with her as she was also an "adopted" child (whether or not this was a legal fact). Susan's difficulties began before her brother was born; they seem to have come to a head when Susan was at the same age that Mrs. B. suffered the loss of her own mother. The intergenerational transmission of the loss of Susan's grandmother, whom she never knew, was a major family dynamic.

The Use of Play

Play remains important as the child develops symbolic thinking, engages in exploration and discovery, and copes with developmental anxieties. In the following illustration, Nathaniel Hawthorne's five-year-old daughter, Una, watches her grandmother die. Hawthorne is critical of Una's behavior relating to her grandmother's death, feeling that she is unsympathetic and callous, in fact, "fiendlike" (Herbert, 1993, p. 169). Hawthorne does not seem to realize that Una is attempting to master this difficult situation through play; he was deeply attached to his mother and looked to Una for the comfort she could not provide.

> Not only does the child speak bluntly of death, but she is also fascinated by the slow failure of his mother's body. Nathaniel is appalled by this specter of annihilation, while Una "takes a strong and strange interest in poor mother's condition, and can hardly be kept out of the chamber—endeavoring to thrust herself into the door, whenever it is opened." On the day following Nathaniel's paroxysm of sobbing, Una playacts the deathbed scene in heroic detail: "She groans, and speaks with difficulty, and moves herself feebly and wearisomely—then lies perfectly still, as if in an insensible state. Then rouses herself, and calls for wine. Then lies down on her back, with clasped hands—then puts them to her head." As Nathaniel witnesses this performance, he is startled to realize that the child appears to take pleasure in torturing him. (Herbert, 1993, pp. 169-170)

The Drifters

The previously described developmental stages of childhood occur successfully in the average expectable environment; what happens to children if they do not have a stable, caring, and consistent environment? Observations from one important study that focused on such a group of children illustrate the importance of attachment, developmental progression, and good ego functioning, and what happened when this went awry.

In *The Drifters* (Pavenstedt, 1967), we encounter children from impoverished and disorganized families with multiple risk factors, who were part of a pilot study aiming to understand their special needs and those of their families, and to offer remedial services to them through a therapeutic nursery school and outreach social work to the families. The underlying assumption was that *"only by supporting overall developmental maturation can children be helped to attain the personality and cognitive tools with which to build satisfactory lives for themselves"* (Pavenstedt, 1967, p. 5; italics in the original). The project stressed the importance of working with children in their formative years because *"the children's early experiences are the most decisive influence in the perpetuation of the maladaptions of these families over generations"* (p. 7; italics in the original).

The twenty-one children described in this study came from thirteen families and were of preschool ages (three and four); ten of the families were white and three were black. Typically, each couple had different ethnic and religious backgrounds. This classic study, done more than forty years ago, still stands fresh in its insights and compassion for this population.

Mattick (1967a) described these children, who initially appeared similar to other preschoolers by virtue of their

> friendly ingratiating manner. . . . On the whole they are responsive to people. . . . However, as . . . we . . . watched the quality of the children's interaction with people as well as their . . . play behavior, it became apparent . . . that these children were different. (p. 55)

The children displayed a poor self-image, low self-confidence, confusion about their identity, and a tendency to devalue themselves; a low level of enjoyment was evident, and they showed no discernible drive toward goals (Mattick, 1967a). In addition,

> There were many signs of confusion . . . about who they were . . . rapidly shifting . . . between infantile and adult mannerisms . . . referring to themselves as "me" or in the third person. . . . Very few . . . said *I* . . . a

nonspecific *her* was used . . . in talking about . . . anything at all. [The failure of] clear self-differentiation and self-acceptance was demonstrated when a child was confronted with a positive statement. . . . The response to . . . "What nice clean hands you have!" . . . would be a puzzled look. . . . A direct question such as "Who are you?" would be more likely to bring a reply of "Nobody". . . . [A number of children] when led to the mirror . . . would claim to see the teacher only. (pp. 59-60; italics in the original)

These children had relationships with people that were need oriented, distrustful, shallow, and nonspecific, and their approach to others was ingratiating and manipulative (Mattick, 1967a). They had not yet attained the concept of object permanence and seemed frightened by the separation and closeness issues inherent in the rapprochement crisis. The "disappearance" of objects or persons, or even parts of persons or of their own selves, appeared absolute:

Even their own hands covered with sand brought an anguished shout or frightened stare. . . . One child stared at a teacher each time she had put on tights. . . . "But where's you legs, her gone?" . . . It took several months in nursery school before the children could express . . . their preoccupation with the problem of separation, loss and abandonment. (p. 68)

Much time passed before the team appreciated the centrality of the issue of separation and its significance for relationship building with such children (Mattick, 1967a).

The children had poor language skills and had difficulties conceptualizing, symbolizing, and problem solving. Their ability to carry knowledge from one situation to another (the ego function of integration) was limited. They did not know how to play, received little encouragement from their parents to explore and play with toys, and internalized their parents' devaluations and expectations that they would not succeed. Creative work brought home from school might be responded to scornfully by a father as "junk"; a gift to one child might be appropriated by a sibling without parental protection of the recipient's property rights or emotional needs (Mattick, 1967a, p. 79).

Although appearing uninterested in many aspects of what was happening around them, the children paid a great deal of attention to self-selected outside stimuli that they felt were needed to protect themselves. "Auditory and particularly visual *hyperalertness,* with excessive focusing on the actions of adults, existed alongside their striking unresponsiveness to large segments of the external world" (Mattick, 1967a, p. 62; italics added).

The children were very responsive to a nurturing and well-structured nursery school experience. Three major teaching approaches were emphasized, as follows: The establishment of a structured, predicable environment; providing a "corrective relationship" in which the children could feel supported, learn to play, and regulate their emotions; and providing opportunities for "actively experiencing the environment" (Mattick, 1967b, p. 171).

The thirteen families in the study were seen as "disorganized" to varying degrees; the parents had unmet developmental needs which took "precedence over the needs of the children" (Bandler, 1967, p. 231). Active outreach intervention was provided to families through home visits with a focus on educating the parents through methods such as modeling and discussion. The relationship with the caseworker was a critical aspect of the work and served as a bridge that enabled the parents (often socially isolated) to move back into the community. For some, attendance at family nursery school parties was a new experience that helped further their socialization.

Overall, the children responded positively to the program, becoming "more alive and they showed pleasure in their activities"; they developed a greater capacity for learning and becoming involved in age-appropriate activities (Mattick, 1967b, p. 200).

The needs of disadvantaged preschoolers are very apparent today and "have become increasingly complex in the past decade," related to multiple environmental, economic, health, and family risk factors; integrated preventive mental health services should be offered to children and their families within the preschool setting. (Edlefsen and Baird, 1994, p. 566).

Psychosexual Development

During preschool years, awareness of gender identity (which began at age two when children learned whether they were a boy or a girl) increases but now becomes more sophisticated and complex. Children tend to engage in behaviors that are gender related; girls may be more interested in dolls or having their fingernails polished, whereas boys are often immersed in play with toy cars and fire engines. The extent to which these patterns are influenced by socialization and parental gender stereotypes has been debated; some assert that the sexes are equal in constitution and physical endowments. Recent research supports the presence of many physiological differences between the sexes in gender development, but suggests many ways that each sex can make adequate adaptations and take on opposite sex roles; women can be competent doctors, construction workers, astronauts, and engage in military combat; men can become good nurses, preschool teachers, and stay-at-home dads.

Some children are conflicted about their gender identity; feelings that they should be the opposite sex may be persistent and troublesome to them; in the past these children were often referred for psychological treatment because of nonconformity, but now there is increased acceptance of their gender preferences (Brown, 2006).

> But as advocates gain ground for what they call gender-identity rights, evidenced most recently by New York City's decision to let people alter the sex listed on their birth certificates, major change is taking place among schools and families. Children as young as 5 who display predispositions to dress like the opposite sex are being supported by a growing number of young parents, educators and mental health professionals. (Brown, 2006, p. A1)

Controversies and conflict surround permitting children to live out their gender preferences, including parental anxieties and difficulties adapting, concerns about prejudice and discrimination (and violence) against these children, and debates about giving them hormones to delay puberty (to give them more time to decide what sex to be). Some people who are transsexual may undergo sex change surgeries when they become adults (discussed in Chapter 11).

Preschool children develop sexual feelings, become interested in their genitals, and may find that masturbation is pleasurable. Many enjoy games of sexual exploration with other children or make overtures to adults (Davies, 1999). The child's developing attachment to the parent of the opposite sex, accompanied by sexual feelings, and competition with the parent of the same sex, was termed the Oedipus complex by Freud (and sometimes referred to as the Electra complex in girls) and is one of the most strongly debated topics in psychoanalytic theory.

The Oedipus complex, based on the ancient myth of Oedipus, who unknowingly married his mother and killed his father, postulates that children during the oedipal phase work through their conflictual feelings; eventually these wishes are given up and an identification is formed with the same-sex parent. During this process, the child's superego, or conscience, emerges. The boy during the oedipal stage (out of fear of retaliatory anger by the father) develops *castration anxiety;* the girl develops *penis envy* (because of alleged feelings of inferiority and jealousy related to a lack of a penis). The concept of penis envy is especially objectionable to many feminists, some of whom have rejected Freudian theory based on their belief that Freud viewed women as being inferior.

"From the time Freud (1897) first proposed [the Oedipus complex], scholars both within and outside psychoanalysis have debated its existence, questioned its importance, and refuted its universality" (Tang and Smith, 1996, p. 563). Freud initially thought that the root of neurotic conflict was sexual trauma in the patient's childhood; he then discovered that this so-called trauma never took place; the patient instead had a sexual wish or fantasy which produced so much guilt that it was repressed; the aim of analysis was to bring this unconscious material to consciousness, and help patients accept and work through their conflicts. This led to Freud's formulation of the Oedipus complex. Although some regard this theory as a major insight, others are appalled, insisting Freud was mistaken to downplay or ignore the actual trauma that might have in fact occurred—that many women who were victims of childhood sexual abuse were wrongly treated by analysts, and that the problem of sexual abuse was kept undercover much longer than necessary. Some attribute to Freud the motivation that he knew about childhood sexual abuse but was silent about it for his own political ends. The controversy regarding recovered memories of childhood sexual abuse is discussed in Chapter 2.

Many parents and nursery school teachers have reported expressions of normal sexuality in preschoolers (Berzoff, 1996b; Davies, 1999; MacFarlane et al., 1986). One mother reported the following conversation between her daughter and her husband (Berzoff, 1996b):

> Four-year-old Lilly, who had been dressed for bed, suddenly began to take off her nightgown in a kind of strip tease before her father, saying, "Bosom Dance, Bosom Dance." Her father responded, "Lilly, put your nightgown back on! What are you doing?" Lilly replied, "Daddy, you know I've been thinking that a 3-year-old couldn't marry you but I bet a 4-year-old can!" (p. 35)

In this instance, the father is helping Lilly "regulate her emotions" and is setting limits on her behavior. He is not being "seduced" by her into sexual acting out with her.

However, MacFarlane and colleagues (1986) point out, when

> a parent is very needy and has trouble with boundaries in the family, he or she could easily misinterpret the child's Oedipal/Electra behavior as sexual attraction and might act on this misinterpretation in a way that leads to sexual exploitation of the child. (p. 24)

At the same time, MacFarlane and colleagues' formulation seems to give little or no credence to the possibility that a child in the Oedipal/Electra phase may actually experience erotic feelings as a natural feature of that phase. This appears at odds with the reported manifestations of normal sexuality in preschoolers as noted above. If such feelings do exist it would be all the more important that caregivers help the child cope with them in a neutral and protective way.

One psychological dilemma for sexually abused children may be that the actual eroticization they experience can leave them feeling confused and guilty. It is not uncommon for social work students to tell a sexually abused child: "It is not your fault—what Daddy did was wrong!" However, if the child has in fact experienced erotic arousal, the clinician's failure to help the child deal with this might leave the child feeling unsupported, isolated, and complicit. If Daddy was wrong (and bad), so is the child. At the same time, the child needs to understand the inappropriateness of this sexual involvement on the part of the adult and not bear the burden of responsibility for it.

Sexual acting out of children can present problems for their therapists who may find the children's

> sexualized behavior arousing; this causes discomfort and guilt, and may lead to avoidance of the sexual material. . . . If a therapist responds to a child in a sexual manner or fails to set appropriate limits, then he or she may be viewed as similar to the child's parents. (MacFarlane et al., 1986, p. 202)

Moral Development

According to Freudian theory, as the Oedipus complex is resolved, the superego (the conscience of the child) evolves. Objections to this construct emphasize that the development of moral thinking starts at a much earlier age, and continues progressively as children learn to distinguish "right" from "wrong" in relation to the approval of parents and other important people in their lives. During the preschool years, children develop a "more internalized sense of right and wrong" (Davies, 1999, p. 259). Moral development is discussed further in Chapter 10.

CONCLUSION

This chapter has followed the child's evolution from conception through birth and infancy to becoming a preschool "kid," with a developing personality, intelligence, and social skills. Biological, psychological, and social factors in concert affect children, as they, in turn, affect their social environ-ment. Attachment to consistent, warm, and caring nurturing figures is the foundation of healthy physical and psychological development—as essen-tial to survival as is the air we breathe and food we eat.

Emphasis has been placed on looking at children through a developmen-tal lens; it is through the study of the multiphysical, cognitive, psychologi-cal, and social abilities and demands of each stage that we can evaluate children's progress and understand their given capabilities and vulnerabili-ties. Individual case studies are needed to determine whether a given child has passed through each stage successfully or whether developmental lags have occurred.

When delays do occur, many children compensate later; some children, however, develop severe maturational delays, which can be due to illness, physical disability, or developmental disabilities such as retardation or autism. In the case of the children in *The Drifters* (Pavenstedt, 1967), the disorganized families in which they were raised and inadequate parental nurturing led to serious ego deficits, including problems with separation, identity, and high levels of anxiety and hyperalertness. Intensive early inter-vention through a therapeutic nursery school and outreach work with the families enabled the children to overcome these deficiencies and gain a sense of mastery. Early intervention services have been emphasized by many writers; the sooner a child at risk receives rehabilitative services and/ or caring nurturance, the self-righting tendencies of development will assert themselves; the acquisition of resilience often needs outside help.

Resilience, discussed in Chapter 4, is related to the capacities of people to adapt to the nonexpectable environment, to survive, and to function well; in examining parent-child interactions, another perspective on resilience emerges. Some people, such as Mrs. B., Susan's mother, are resilient. She survived the death of her mother and abandonment by her father and was able to sustain a stable marriage, to hold a job, and develop friendships. However, when she became a parent, and her child became a toddler (as she was when her own mother died), holes appeared in the protective armor of her resilience; parenthood brought her in touch with early trauma that had been safely buried. Family dynamics, such as the development of enmeshed or disengaged relationships, are generally related to the parents' early at-tachment difficulties, which may not emerge until a new family is formed, and parents experience a new level of intimacy, reliving their past develop-mental vicissitudes through the mirror of their own children's experiences.

A psychodynamic developmental approach to studying children and their families provides us with insights that one can find only by going be-neath the surface of presenting symptomatology, enabling us to provide constructive and healing experiences to children and their families so that they can continue their interrupted maturational journeys. Children have an enormous capacity to love, to give, and to forgive; if parents can tune in to this, they can be well rewarded. Helping families reclaim the happiness and joy of close relationships that was undermined in their earlier lives can be a major achievement.

LEARNING EXERCISE

Observations of infants and young children within the context of their families have been receiving increasing attention in the mental health field. Select a family with an infant or young child (other than a family member or a client) and make a home visit, observing the child's development and parental-child interactions. Include an interview with either parent (or both parents) about the child's skills and activities, as well as their experience of parenting.

SUGGESTED READING

Articles

Boo, K. 2006. Swamp nurse. *The New Yorker* February 6: 54-65.

Fish, B., and B. Chapman. 2004. Mental health risks to infants and toddlers in foster care. *Clinical Social Work Journal* 32: 121-140.

Meek, H. W. 2005. Promoting self-awareness: Infant observation training as a model. *Smith College Studies in Social Work* 75: 33-58.

Shapiro, V., and M. Gisynski. 1989. Ghosts in the nursery revisited. *Child and Adolescent Social Work* 6: 18-37.

Talbot, M. 1998. Attachment theory: The ultimate experiment. *The New York Times Magazine* May 24: 24-30, 38, 46, 50, 54.

Books

Akhtar, S., and S. Kramer. (eds.) 1998. *The colors of childhood: Separation-individuation across cultural, racial, and ethnic differences.* Northvale, NJ: Jason Aronson.

Davies, D. 2004. *Child development: A practitioners guide,* 2nd ed. New York: Guilford Press.

Fraiberg, S. 1968. *The magic years: Understanding and handling the problems of early childhood.* New York: Basic Books.

Hughes, D. A. 1998. *Building the bonds of attachment: Awakening love in deeply troubled children.* Northvale, NJ: Jason Aronson.

Osofsky, J. D. (ed.). 2004. *Young children and trauma: Intervention and treatment.* New York: The Guilford Press.

Zeanah Jr., C. H. (ed.) 2000. *Handbook of infant mental health,* 2nd ed. New York: The Guilford Press.

Chapter 10

Middle Childhood and Adolescence

When the voices of children are heard on the green
And laughing is heard on the hill,
My heart is at rest within my breast
And every thing else is still.

William Blake, *Songs of Innocence*

ELEMENTARY SCHOOL YEARS

The toddler has evolved into a preschooler, and now the preschooler is an elementary school child, involved with learning, with the world outside the immediate family, and engrossed in school, social activities, and friends. In the "average expectable environment," when all goes well, the child is exuberant about life's possibilities and excitements. Talking to friends on the phone or sending e-mails, or planning for a party are great events. A ten-year-old girl shares two e-mails with us:

Tomorrow I am going on a field trip with my Girl Scout troop to Shaws (a shopping store) to learn about nutrition and health. I am so excited! Then after that, I have basketball, which I love soooo much. I am thinking of doing the Spelling Bee with my friends: Virginia, Susan and Paula.

She decided to participate in this group spelling bee and reported the results:

This is how I did. I went through five rounds, then lost. The two words we got wrong were extraterrestrial and suspiciously. I knew how to spell extraterrestrial, but my teammates were arguing with me. They thought it was *Extraterrestrail,* but I knew that was wrong.

I got to go make valentine cards for my classmates!

Human Behavior in the Social Environment, Second Edition

Middle childhood (ages six to twelve) is a time "when most of all the child develops (or fails to develop) mastery of his environment" (Rutter, 1975, p. 86). In addition to the child's increased involvement in the outside world, there is an integration of intellectual and psychological capacities. Erikson (1963) refers to this stage as "industry vs. inferiority"; the child is ready for the "'entrance into life', except that life must first be school life, whether school is field or jungle or classroom" (p. 255). The child learns to master skills, and if unable to do this, will develop a sense of inferiority. In our country, the world of the latency-aged child centers around school, which "seems to be a culture all by itself, with its own goals and limits, its achievements and disappointment[s]" (p. 256).

Children in middle childhood develop greater self-control and mastery over their impulses, replacing impulsivity with words, thought, and fantasy; their conscience and moral sense mature; and their social awareness increases. A six-year-old commented to an elderly guest at a party: "I know you are 95. But I don't think you are 95—I think you are 71!" Major gains in testing reality and in cognitive development are made, and involvement with peers becomes important (Davies, 1999). "Logical exploration tends to dominate fantasy, and the child shows an increased interest in rules and orderliness. . . . The ability to concentrate is well established by age 9 or 10" (Kaplan, Sadock, and Grebb, 1994, p. 47).

In Freudian terminology, this period is referred to as the latency stage, because this is a period of relative emotional (and drive) quiescence between the upheavals of the oedipal period and the turbulence of adolescence. Rutter (1975), however, does not agree that it is a period of sexual quiescence.

> In fact Freud was clearly wrong about sexual latency, as it is a period of *increasing* sex interests. Sex talk and games with a sexual component are frequent, but often they are concealed from adults. Some children even develop immature heterosexual love relationships, although these usually remain largely or entirely in fantasy. (Rutter, 1975, p. 86; italics in the original)

Thirty years have passed since Rutter made his statement; it has now been observed that sexual interests and dating develop during the preteen and early-teen years; it is not uncommon for fifth graders to go on dates, which is a step beyond fantasy (Jarrell, 2000); middle-school surveys and anecdotal information from mental health professionals, educators, and adolescent physicians point to this phenomenon.

Piaget (1995a) observed that ages seven to eleven are the time for the de- Concrete velopment of *concrete operations,* in which children learn how to develop Operations conceptual and representational thinking, enabling them to figure out in (Piaget). their heads what they had previously needed real actions to understand. The child can classify, order, and find alternatives. For a child who wants a toy, thinking has moved beyond: "It is mine" and "I want to play." It is a toy that does certain things because it has certain properties, and it costs five dollars, but in another store it costs four dollars, and both toys do the same thing.

> The school-age child is now capable of having a clear sense of right and wrong, of having empathy with the feelings of others, and of "playing by the rules." Optimally, the school-age child engages in aspects of daily living such as hygiene, dressing, and looking after possessions with greater autonomy. The capacity for operational thought and problem solving, along with increased frustration tolerance, increases the range of potential activities and sources of satisfaction. (Marans and Adelman, 1997, p. 212)

Many attributes of latency are illustrated in the behavior and thinking of Derek, a nine-year-old Caucasian boy, who was referred to his school's social worker by his fourth-grade teacher because of his "difficulty in focusing and following directions in class and because of his difficulties in peer relations." During one therapy session, Derek described what happened when he and his friend got lost going to school that morning. His narrative depicts his competent problem-solving skills based on his well-developed concrete operations.

> Derek missed the school bus this morning, so his mother put him and his friend on a public bus. After riding for fifteen minutes, he and his friend realized that they were going in the wrong direction and asked the bus driver what to do. He let them off at the next stop, in front of a gas station. They proceeded to look for a telephone, but neither of them had any money. Derek thought of searching for a dime in the change slot of the pay phones; after a few tries, they found a dime and called Derek's home. There was no answer, so Derek called his mother at work. She came and drove them to school. I remarked that Derek had been very resourceful and asked Derek if he knew what that meant. Derek replied with a huge grin, "Yeah, it means smart."

Derek's social worker recognized his competence, an attribute important to latency-age children and especially important to Derek, who struggled with strong feelings of incompetence. His second-grade teacher had labeled him learning disabled but had no evaluation done; she frequently called the class's attention to Derek's academic difficulties and poor social skills. Derek developed nervous habits, such as nail biting and nose picking, which further isolated him from his peers; he became anxious about school. When asked to write down some of his worries, he wrote: "getting brain damage," but then crossed this out. His social worker felt that "deep down, Derek may be truly worried that he is incompetent, learning disabled, stupid, and a 'nerd' (a name that other children sometimes call him)."

Although Derek had problems with peers, he had a friendship with a boy in his class and several playmates in his neighborhood. Harry Stack Sullivan (1953) asserted that during the preadolescent period, children develop a special close relationship with "a *particular* member of the same sex who becomes a chum or a close friend" (p. 245; italics in the original); this is an important part of psychological development, and during this time the child "begins to develop a real sensitivity to what matters to another person . . . [and thinks about] 'what should I do to contribute to the happiness or to support the prestige and feeling of worth-whileness of my chum'" (Sullivan, 1953, p. 245).

School-age children may be ashamed of being in therapy because others may think something is wrong with them; their developing conscience may add to anxieties that their behavior and thoughts are bad; they are usually not comfortable talking about feelings directly (Davies, 1999). The use of "play, structured activities, and talk is an effective approach in middle childhood" (p. 346). Derek's social worker found that her "attempts to encourage him to verbalize his feelings felt like an intrusion to him"; he is "more expressive in his artwork than he is verbally."

> Derek drew a picture of his house; he seems to have a lot of confidence about his ability to transfer what he sees into his art. He spoke about how difficult it would be to draw the stairs, but, in fact, he went right to drawing the stairs and seemed pleased with them. What is most interesting about the drawing is the anthropomorphic features on the door and on the facade of the house.
>
> The two windows in the door even have what look like eyeballs. Derek explained that they are stickers. The doorbell is the nose and the mail slot is the mouth, grimacing. Derek pointed out to me the face on the house itself. Two upstairs windows are the eyes, a center window, the nose, and the living room window is a grimaced mouth, with gritted teeth. The face on the house appears angry or frightened. When I wondered aloud what the house is feeling, Derek quickly added smile lines to its mouth.

The social worker sensed that Derek was expressing frightening and/or angry feelings through his drawing, but when she tried to explore this directly, he immediately changed an "angry or frightened" face on the house to a happy face. She reflected later that asking Derek to discuss feelings may have made him feel too vulnerable. Changing her approach, she helped him extend the playful and imaginary aspects of his activity rather than confront him directly.

> I asked Derek to take out the picture of his house. I explained that since he had shown me that face on his house, I thought we could play a pretend game and have him make other houses and buildings that could talk to one another. I asked Derek if he knew what a speech bubble was, and he drew one for me. Derek liked the idea and knew immediately which buildings he wanted to draw.

> Derek then proceeded to draw a series of houses and buildings with eyes, noses, mouths, braces, hands, missing teeth, and pockets. He developed a story about one of the buildings owing others money and the verbal conflict that ensued. Derek's story struggled through such themes as anger, injustice/fairness, disappointment, trust, deceit, and, finally, resolution. I was able to get bits and pieces of information from Derek about some of the connections to his life, but this was territory to carefully tread upon because I knew that too much direct questioning might inhibit Derek's self-expression.

School

Erikson (1963) refers to school as being a culture unto itself; every classroom has a racial and ethnic composition, an interpersonal environment, and its own values, standards, and rules. Each class is part of the school community, which can be nurturing and motivating, or restrictive, punitive, and unable to protect its charges from violence and harassment; preoccupation with violence can lead to inattentiveness, which in turn can lead to poor school performance (Marans and Adelman, 1997). The school environment itself contributes to a child's sense of well-being as well as academic achievement; the ecological concept of goodness-of-fit is particularly relevant when looking at a child's school adjustment.

For some children, like Andrea, age seven, school was a sanctuary from a difficult and chaotic family situation:

> Andrea's parents are divorced. Her mentally ill father remarried and, when his new child was born, distanced himself from Andrea. Andrea's single mother is overwhelmed caring for her and her two teen brothers, one of whom had to be hospitalized for a psychotic episode. School is a positive factor, helping Andrea develop resilience. Her first- and second-grade teachers were both very patient and supportive in helping Andrea succeed in school. The school nurse has helped Andrea's mother set limits with Andrea; she also knows that Andrea's tendency to experience psychologically triggered vomiting is part of Andrea's wish to go home; the nurse helps keep her in school.

Some schools (and many in poor inner-city areas) are overcrowded, lack resources, and may not provide adequately for children with special needs. Child maltreatment, family problems, living in unsafe environments, mental health problems, learning disabilities, and attention deficit disorders can contribute to children's school problems. A poor goodness-of-fit in classrooms, where teachers—such as Derek's second-grade teacher—can contribute to the academic and social deterioration of students through negative assessments and interaction. A child who is maltreated at home and is enduring a negative social experience at school, as well as a poor learning environment, "ultimately loses in both settings" (Anderson and Seita, 2006, p. 82).

Controversies regarding public school education are frequently debated including quality of education, adequacy of teachers, funding responsibilities, the impoverishment of inner-city schools, school vouchers, school integration, violence, and dropout rates. Nationally, school dropout rates are very high; "nearly 1 out of 3 public high school students won't graduate," and for Latino and African-American children, "the rate approaches an alarming 50 percent" (Thornburgh, 2006, p. 32). Ultimately, these children have difficulty earning an adequate income when they reach adulthood (Thornburgh, 2006); "helping to keep students in school and to promote academic success are critical steps toward promoting greater and more competent adult role performance" (Richman and Bowen, 1997, p. 95). Literacy and education have become increasingly important in our technology-based society.

President Bush's "No Child Left Behind" policy, signed into law in 2002, is controversial, with opponents arguing that it lacks sufficient funding, and that the emphasis on passing standardized testing places undue pressure on teachers to the neglect of other important aspects of the curriculum. The Center on Education Policy called this practice "narrowing the curriculum," and found that "71 percent of the nation's 15,000 school districts had reduced the hours of instructional time spent on history, music and other subjects" (Dillon, 2006b, p. 1).

Schools have not improved in closing the disparities in scores between the races; black and Hispanic children continue, by and large, to have lower scores than white children, although there are some success stories; however, "on average, African American and Hispanic students in high school can read and do arithmetic at only the average level of whites in junior high school" (Dillon, 2006c, p. A1). "Experts have suggested many possible changes, including improving the law's mechanisms for ensuring that teachers in poor schools are experienced and knowledgeable, and extending early-childhood education to more students" (pp. A1, A21).

Concern has been voiced about inadequate tutoring; some schools have provided in-house tutoring, rather than using other resources, as required, and some "private tutoring companies with suspect credentials have been allowed to bid for tutoring because of loose eligibility rules"; insufficient tutoring is troubling because "those who don't become successful readers by fourth grade are more likely to drop out and far less likely to earn a college degree" ("Tutoring Gap," 2006, p. A32).

The "No Child Left Behind" policy can also be disadvantageous to children with emotional problems who come from troubled families, as the main emphasis is on academic performance, "and neglects the social and communal aspects of public education" (Anderson and Seita, 2006, p. 81). These children often have trouble relating to teachers, act out, and then receive "exclusionary punishments," which they then view "as attack or rejection, and become even more aggressive or disengaged from school and teachers" (p. 81). There is an increasing shortage of services to these troubled children, owing to funding restrictions, as many nonteaching positions, such as social workers, have been eliminated.

Homeschooling has been growing at a rapid rate since the 1980s when it first began to develop seriously (Kilborn, 2000; Saulny, 2006a; Talbot, 2000). Initially, this method of schooling was adopted by some conservative Christian families who wanted to separate themselves and their children from mainstream culture; "now it is being adopted more broadly, by parents who are disenchanted with the regimentation of schools, public and private, and the idea that a child's age, alone, marks the threshold of learning" (Kilborn, 2000, p. A1). According to a survey done in 2003 by the United States Department of Education, "from 1999-2003, the number of children who were educated at home soared, increasing by 29 percent, to 1.1 million students nationwide"; of this group "21 percent used a tutor" (Saulny, 2006a, p. A1). Tutoring, which became more popular and available, owing to the No Child Left Behind Act, has been growing in popularity; in this format, tutors, not parents, are the educators. Detractors are concerned about children missing the socialization and community processes involved in attending school (Erickson's school culture), but parents who favor this approach argue that they provide outside socialization experiences for their children, and also are involved in homeschooling support groups.

Pilot projects, often introduced by social workers, have viewed school in an ecological perspective and education in a comprehensive way, as a link to other community programs (Dupper and Poertner, 1997; Winters and Maluccio, 1988). Social workers have an important role to play in elementary and high schools, to be involved in activities such as special education evaluations, crisis intervention, sexual and physical abuse case finding and referrals, group work, individual and family work, and suicide and violence prevention. Many school social workers, however, "struggle for recognition" within their schools, and some are threatened with losing their positions owing to budgetary concerns (Anderson and Seita, 2006; Beaucar, 1999d).

Special Education

It was determined by the federal government in 1975 that children with disabilities were entitled to receive special education: The "'Education for All Handicapped Children Act' mandated all states to provide free and appropriate educational services to all children" (Sadock and Sadock, 2003, p. 1180). This includes children with learning disabilities, which "affect at least 5 percent of school-age children"; children with learning disabilities now comprise about 50 percent of the children receiving special educational services (Sadock and Sadock, 2003). Currently approximately 7 million children are receiving special education services (Greenhouse, 2005). In some cases children are placed in special education classes (sometimes they are sent to private specialized schools or treatment programs); for others, supplementary services are provided while they remain in their regular classrooms. As part of this program "school districts work with parents to develop an individual program for each student with a disability" (p. A1).

Families and school districts do not always agree about necessary services; in one publicized case, the parents felt the school district should pay for private education for their son, as the public school plan involved him being in a class which they felt was too large to meet his needs. The legal dispute reached the United States Supreme Court, which ruled that families who dispute the school system's decisions "have the legal burden of proving that the plan will not provide the 'appropriate' education to which the federal law entitles all children with disabilities" (Greenhouse, 2005, p. A1).

Special Problems of Middle Childhood

It is not unusual for children to have a mix of problems related to violence and mental health; these are discussed in the sections that follow.

Violence

There is a "trend toward children of younger ages becoming perpetrators, victims, and witnesses of violence" (Murphy, Pynoos, and James, 1997, p. 223). Homicide is the third most common cause of death among elementary school children (Glodich, 1998; Osofsky, 1997). School-age children are developmentally ready to engage in the wider world; as they fight against normal regressive pulls, involvement with violence may be a very "disruptive" experience, "requiring various attempts to ward off the associated feelings of fear and helplessness" (Marans and Adelman, 1997, p. 212).

> As with younger children, school-age children may respond to their exposure to violence with circumscribed symptoms, involving sleeping difficulties, nightmares, worries about burglars, bodily injury, and death. In addition, regression to earlier modes of relating to parents may be prominent. For example, increased struggles over food, self-care, school-work, or household responsibilities may be some of the behavioral phenomena that accompany children's attempts to defend against and give expression to the anxiety associated with witnessing interpersonal violence. (Marans and Adelman, 1997, p. 212)

If children continue to be upset, secondary problems can develop, such as poor school performance, which can further lower their self-esteem (Marans and Adelman, 1997). Violence has also been associated with childhood depression, post–traumatic stress disorder, and attention deficit symptoms (Murphy, Pynoos, and James, 1997). Children subject to violence might respond with aggression to their friends, and their "identifying with the aggressor may become a chronic hedge against feeling vulnerable to attack as the child courts recognition and affiliation with the toughest figures on the neighborhood streets and becomes involved in antisocial and violent activities" (Marans and Adelman, 1997, p. 213).

Illustration of a Violence Remediation Program

Schools frequently offer violence prevention programs with a general emphasis on "teaching strategies to promote nonviolent conflict resolution" (Murphy, Pynoos, and James, 1997, p. 223). However, this approach, with its emphasis on teaching appropriate behaviors, does not touch upon the trauma many children have already experienced, nor does it focus on their reactions, symptoms, interferences with their development, and their relationships. Murphy, Pynoos, and James (1997) describe a comprehensive program in an elementary school that offered children touched by violence a program that included three months of individual psychotherapy, then three months of group therapy, followed by three months of involvement in a mentorship program; parents, police, and teachers were also included.

These children had also been exposed to other serious problems including death of parents, physical abuse, rape or sexual abuse, neglect, and the knowledge that seven children known to them had been murdered. The group goals included providing support and helping the children accept their experiences, increasing their ability to tolerate feelings and respond emotionally to others, and developing their social skills (Murphy, Pynoos, and James, 1997). Each group had five to eight members, and sessions were ninety minutes long.

Leaders, aware that latency children generally "fear some form of peer rejection and being overwhelmed by negative emotions," chose age-appropriate group activities, such as motoric activities, drawing, and games (Murphy, Pynoos, and James, 1997, p. 234). Once mutual trust and acceptance were established, the children began sharing their traumatic experiences; hearing the other children speak and express their fears was a validating experience for them:

> In one group, the therapist noted that two boys who were without fathers had become friends. The first boy had . . . [made] efforts to resuscitate his father after waking up to find him unresponsive in a living room chair. The second boy had addressed his witnessing of domestic violence and drug use that led his mother to ask his father to leave the family. The therapist [commented], "I have noticed you two have become friends and wonder if you have been drawn to each other because of painful feelings you share about being without your father." The first child immediately responded, "Yea, that's true, he knows what it's like. . . . Being the oldest, I have had to look after my younger brothers and sisters." The other boy, also an eldest child, nodded in agreement. The therapist then continued, "Sometimes, it feels like you don't get to be just a kid," and, the second boy responded, "I have to look after my mom, too." (Murphy, Pynoos, and James, 1997, p. 249)

The group support enabled children to discuss trauma that they had not been ready to reveal in their prior individual therapy sessions. One boy, who told his teacher " 'I want to be dead when I grow up' " (Murphy, Pynoos, and James, 1997, p. 239), told the group how, when he was seven, he had seen his best friend murdered. He had never told anyone about this event before; he was afraid that if he did, he would be in danger, too.

The group discussed plans for revenge and other retaliatory measures against perpetrators, and alternative ways of handling these feelings were explored. The boy who was afraid to talk about his best friend's murder commented that "he would want to get back at this person . . . by shooting him with a gun, too" (Murphy, Pynoos, and James, 1997, p. 240).

> The children then mutually examined their respective revenge fantasies and their struggles over human accountability. Another spoke of wanting to beat up an uncle who had so badly beaten him. Another child spoke of wanting to run over the man who had run over his best friend. The group therapist addressed these expressions of two underlying wishes by saying, "I bet you'd like him to feel as bad as you did and to make sure he can never make you feel like that again." In response, one child began to discuss whether putting people in jail might not answer the wish for retribution, punishment, and protection. (Murphy, Pynoos, and James, 1997, p. 240)

Latency-age children are concerned with rules and developing a moral code of behavior. Even in the average expectable environment this is not an easy task. How much more complicated it is when antisocial "amoral" codes control their lives, and violence is a regular occurrence.

These children were helped to express their grief, which was facilitated by using exercises such as "writing a letter to the deceased or absent parent or sibling" (Murphy, Pynoos, and James, 1997, p. 240). The latency child's concern with fairness was intensely expressed as "protests of unfairness over [their] loss" were often noted (pp. 240-241). These losses were compounded by the traumatic events that frequently surrounded the losses. "Special attention is then needed to address *the interplay of trauma and grief that complicates childhood bereavement*" (p. 241; italics added). Children often felt "shame and humiliation" over some of their losses, which was alleviated through group validation.

Parents or guardians were involved in one of the group sessions with the children; this was of "noticeable therapeutic benefit to both parents and child" (Murphy, Pynoos, and James, 1997, p. 241), especially when the traumatic loss was mutual.

Police officers attended several group sessions, giving the children an opportunity to discuss directly their grievances about the police; by doing so they lessened the distrust and poor communication that existed between them. In one instance, a child told the officer about how upset he was over the way his cousin was treated by the police when he was arrested; in another instance, a child's grievance was that the police had not found the person who ran over his best friend.

Efforts have been increased to involve police constructively in solving community problems, including a national community policing initiative

(Jenkins et al., 1997). One of the "'core components' of community policing [is] the development of community partnership and problem solving. Community policing demands a relationship with the community that is built on the positive contact between patrol officers and community members" (p. 306).

Mental Health Problems

Many children today experience mental health problems; government studies report "that at least six million children have difficulties that are diagnosed as serious mental disorders" (Carey, 2006e, p. A11). According to "Melnyk et al. (2002) . . . 70 percent of children and teens affected by mental health problems do not receive any treatment" (Fontana and Gonzales, 2006, p. 267).

Many children under treatment for psychiatric problems are caught in a bewildering tangle of diagnostic confusion; there is frequently a lack of unanimity on what is wrong with them, and they receive more than one diagnosis, which often change over time. These difficulties are attributed to several factors: the insufficient number of child psychiatrists; other disciplines with their own points of view making diagnoses; "the patchwork nature of the health care system"; the notion that children's own development can cause the picture to change; and the fact that "the field is fiercely divided over some fundamental questions, most notably about bipolar disorder. . . . Some experts say that bipolar disorder is being over diagnosed, but others say it is often missed" (Carey, 2006e, p. A11).

There is also controversy regarding the large numbers of children who are receiving psychiatric drugs, including many who are taking a combination of these drugs (Harris, 2006).

> Last year in the United States, about 1.6 million children and teenagers—280,000 of them under age 10—were given at least two psychiatric drugs in combination. . . . More than 500,000 were prescribed at least three psychiatric drugs. More than 160,000 got at least four medications together, the analysis found. (Harris, 2006, p. A1)

Concerns have been expressed about the drugs' efficacy, their side effects, and that there are insufficient studies of the effects of these drugs on children. It is also a possibility that these children are being medicated as a way of controlling their behavior in lieu of their receiving other types of therapy, of provision of services to their families, and of addressing and ameliorating adverse environmental factors if necessary.

The utilization of these medications for foster children "remains controversial and intense" (Benoit, 2006, p. 287).

> It is confounded by racial issues, because African American and Hispanic children are overrepresented minorities within the child welfare system . . . [these] children are more likely to receive medication alone and not to receive adjunctive therapies. This concern . . . has reached the level of courts in many states, where specific permission from the courts has to be received before certain medications can be used. Although the overt intent is to protect foster children . . . the result in many cases is to introduce a barrier to timely care. (Benoit, 2006, p. 287)

Frequent emotional problems of children include anxiety disorders (e.g., post–traumatic stress disorder), conduct disorders, and depression; bipolar disorder, as noted above, is increasingly diagnosed in children, but whether it occurs in children or is being overdiagnosed remains controversial. Pervasive developmental disorders, such as autism, are being diagnosed more frequently; this is discussed further in Chapter 14. Attention-deficit/hyperactivity disorder, ADHD, is one of the most often diagnosed and treated behavioral disturbance of childhood.

Attention-Deficit Hyperactivity Disorder

Attention-deficit hyperactivity disorder (ADHD) has received considerable attention professionally and in the popular press. This serious problem particularly affects school performance, as ADHD children have difficulty concentrating and listening to others and are overactive and impulsive. "Individuals often have difficulty sustaining attention in tasks or play activities and find it hard to persist with tasks until completion" (American Psychiatric Association, 1994, p. 79). Hyperactivity is characterized by

> excessive running and climbing in situations where it is not appropriate . . . by having difficulty playing or engaging quietly in leisure activities . . . by appearing to be often "on the go" or as if "driven by a motor" or by talking excessively. (pp. 78-79)

The cause of ADHD is not known and the incidence is higher in boys than girls. It has been speculated that "contributing factors for ADHD include prenatal toxic exposures, prematurity, and prenatal mechanical insult to the fetal nervous system . . . [There is also] evidence for a genetic basis"

(Saddock and Sadock, 2003, p. 1223). Although it can coexist with other serious childhood disorders, if left untreated it can also lead to problems of school failure and poor conduct. Drugs, notably Ritalin, have been found to be highly effective in treating children with this disorder (Noble, 1999; "Study Sheds," 2000).

Psychostimulants are prescribed, seemingly paradoxically, for this disorder of overactivity; however, a rationale for their use is that in such individuals psychostimulants may be stimulating *deficient inhibitory* central nervous system functions, so that the resulting increased inhibition lowers motor activity levels and reduces excessive responsiveness to environmental stimuli, that is, distractibility. Dextroamphetamine and methylphenidate (Ritalin is the best known of this group) "are the only proven treatment" for ADHD ("ADHD Update," 2006). Research that has stirred debate about the dangers of taking these drugs has recently emerged, as some patients were found to have developed blood pressure and heart problems. "The bottom line is that ADHD drugs are not likely to cause cardiovascular problems in anyone who does not already have underlying cardiac risk. . . . Careful screening and monitoring make sense" (p. 4). Questions have also been raised as to whether these drugs affect growth; research on this has been inconclusive; "researchers will have to do studies taking into account the adolescent growth spurt" (p. 4). Finally, serious concern has been expressed about the abuse of these drugs and the problem of overdosing. In most of these cases, the children adversely affected were actually not the patients for whom the medication was prescribed.

> The stimulants used to treat ADHD have some potential for abuse, because crushing pills and snorting (snuffing) them can produce a cocaine-like high. Several studies indicate that nearly 10 percent of students in grades 7-12 have used nonprescribed stimulants; that as many as a third of young ADHD patients have been asked to sell or give away their medications; and that 7 percent-15 percent have done so. ("ADHD Update," 2006, p. 4)

There are now new forms of this medication, such as "extended-release formulas" (which will not cause highs) that are being marketed ("ADHD Update," 2006, p. 5).

One criticism about Ritalin relates to the misdiagnosis (and overdiagnosis) of ADHD; children who are not adequately stimulated in school can become restless and appear to have these symptoms, as can children with an oppositional disorder, or those from disorganized or chaotic families (American Psychiatric Association, 1994). Questions have also been raised as to whether some children (including those below age six) are being inappropriately medicated for this condition as well as for other conditions, such as depression (Goode, 2000).

ADHD can be found in very young children, in adolescents, and increasingly in adults; "one estimate is that 1.5 million adults, 10 percent of them over age 50, now take stimulants for ADHD" ("ADHD Update," 2006, p. 4). It is particularly critical during latency years that diagnosis and treatment of this problem take place; untreated ADHD can lead to school failure, secondary behavioral problems, social difficulties, and the inability to attain a sense of mastery and competency.

> Children who do not learn to read and to gain social approval from peers by grade four and/or who develop social incompetence, impulsivity, and aggressive behavior during this period are at high risk of developing a mental disorder (Institute of Medicine, 1994). Additional risk factors for development of a mental disorder include poor parenting, high levels of family conflict, and a low degree of bonding between children and parents. (Dulmus and Rapp-Paglicci, 2000, p. 299)

ADOLESCENCE

Adolescence is a time for intense privacy and intense friendships—a turbulent, joyful, optimistic time, but also a time of confusion, mood changes, and feelings of wonderment, excitement, and alarm at the beginnings of sexual development. It is time to leave the world of kids, although still feeling like one, but now the stakes are higher, as adulthood, with its responsibilities and difficult choices, beckons. It is also time to develop one's identity (Erikson, 1963).

Although the universe expanded for the schoolchild, the family remained clearly at its center, and family rituals and outings were major high points. Now family events may feel boring, friends replace relatives as central figures, and the magnetic attraction of social activities, dating, and driving pull the adolescent further from home. However adolescents do not wish to sever connections with their families; they struggle to find the right distance without losing the comfort of closeness as they reenter the rapprochement crisis at a higher level (Blos, 1962).

For the family, life can be delightful and stimulating as the adolescents' mental growth and social involvement increase, but also bewildering as parents observe the adolescent "darting away" from them and then returning for "emotional refueling" (Mahler, Pine, and Bergman, 1975); parents may feel puzzled as their adolescent develops values and habits that may be different from their own. Tensions can escalate as parents struggle to decide what limits to place on their adolescent's behavior and how to enforce them. Yet, overall, in the average expectable environment, adolescents do basically get along with their parents (Rutter, 1975; Sadock and Sadock, 2003), and generally "are receptive to parental approval and disapproval, and most adolescents and their parents can bridge the generation gap successfully" (Sadock and Sadock, 2003, p. 38).

Adolescence has been divided into three periods: early adolescence (from ages eleven to fourteen); middle adolescence (from fourteen to seventeen), and late adolescence (from seventeen to twenty) (Kaplan, Sadock, and Grebb, 1994). Adolescence occurs earlier now (physically) and is considered to last longer (due to greater time needed to achieve full adulthood in our society) than it has in the past, when it had extended from ages thirteen to eighteen.

Although some adolescent turmoil is normal (Sadock and Sadock, 2003), excessive turmoil and despair are also possible, as are serious risk-taking behaviors, such as drug and substance abuse, promiscuous sexual activity (putting them at risk for pregnancy and AIDS), gambling addictions, and "accident prone behavior, such as fast driving, skydiving, and hang gliding" (Kaplan, Sadock, and Grebb, 1994, p. 55). Adolescents are prone to depression, eating disorders, and have a high rate of suicide. Many have experienced violence, have witnessed homicide, and are victims of family maltreatment; some have reacted by running away, becoming homeless, and/or turning to prostitution.

Many adolescents encounter discrimination based on race, ethnicity, or sexual orientation; those from different cultures may experience conflict between family values and peer values, and struggle with the problems of assimilation and bicultural identity.

Physical Development of Adolescents

Adolescents experience biological changes, including major increases in height and weight and hormonal activity, producing primary and secondary sexual characteristics and sexual feelings (de Anda, 1995). These biological changes do not uniformly occur; girls generally reach puberty two years before boys do, and the age differential at which individual boys and girls reach puberty can be several years. As both growth spurts and sexual development are so prominent, and as peer approval is so important, early or late achievement of puberty can affect one's social standing and social image (de Anda, 1995).

Precocious or delayed growth, acne, obesity, and enlarged mammary glands in boys and small or overabundant breasts in girls are some deviations from the expected patterns of maturation. Although these conditions may not be medically significant, they often lead to psychological sequelae. Adolescents are sensitive to the opinions of peers and are constantly comparing themselves with others. Any deviation, real or imagined, can lead to feelings of inferiority, low self-esteem, and loss of confidence. Girls are more sensitive to early physical manifestations of puberty than are boys (Kaplan, Sadock, and Grebb, 1994, p. 51).

Adolescents (as well as many adults) sometimes go to great lengths to alter their physical appearance, including undergoing cosmetic plastic surgery. Although eating disorders (discussed in Chapter 13), seen predominantly (although not exclusively) in adolescent girls, have multiple interacting psychological factors, preoccupation with appearance (especially thinness) is a key feature. Teenage boys (as well as many athletes) may take steroid drugs to improve their physical appearance and athletic prowess.

Many teens currently use tattoos, body piercing (such as lip rings, navel rings), scarification, and branding, which has special meaning from a psychodynamic perspective; "the skin and its decorations can be seen as a transitional area where inner and outer realities converge . . . they also unambiguously demarcate the bearer from others" (Rosenblum et al., 1999, p. 334).

> The prevalence of tattoos among adolescents points so the normative developmental crises in identity consolidation, for which tattoos may offer a concrete and readily available solution. Furthermore, feeling vulnerable to a rapidly evolving body over which they have no say, adolescent may find that self-made and openly visible decorations restore a sense of normalcy and control, turning a passive experience into an active entity. (Rosenblum et al., 1999, p. 334)

Adolescents often engage in impulsive and risk-taking behaviors, although intellectually they have the capacity to understand the implications and consequences of their behaviors. However:

> in real life . . . [they] find it more difficult to interrupt an action under way . . . to think before acting . . . and even to choose between safer and riskier alternatives. . . . Adolescents' judgment can be overwhelmed by the urge for new experiences, thrill seeking, and sexual and aggressive impulses. They sometimes seem driven to seek experiences that

produce strong feelings and sensations. Resisting social pressure is also more difficult for teenagers. ("The Adolescent," 2005, p. 1)

Current research highlights the significant changes that are taking place in the structure of the adolescent brain; the

> human brain circuitry is not mature until the early 20s (some would add, "if ever"). Among the last connections to be fully established are the links between the prefrontal cortex, seat of judgment and problem-solving, and the emotional centers in the limbic system, especially the amygdala. These links are critical for emotional learning and high-level self-regulation. ("The Adolescent," 2005, pp. 1-2)

There are also ongoing mutual interactions between hormones and brain development. Because of the many complex changes, "things can go wrong in many ways, and some of them involve the onset of psychiatric disorders" ("The Adolescent," 2005, p. 2). As with adolescent growth in general, there is much individual variation in the progression of brain development, and adolescent problems are "not all in their brains but have many causes" (p. 3).

Psychological Developments in Adolescence

A major psychological task of adolescence is the development of an identity (Erikson, 1963) and resolving, in greater depth, problems of separation and individuation. Blos (1962), who refers to adolescence as a "second step in individuation" (p. 12), views many adolescent rebellions and psychological storms as serving this process.

> Before the adolescent can consolidate this [identity] formation, he must pass through stages of self-consciousness and fragmented existence. The oppositional, rebellious, and restive strivings, the stages of experimentation, the testing of the self by going to excess—all these have a positive usefulness in the process of self-definition. "This is not me" represents an important step in the achievement of individuation and in the establishment of autonomy; at an earlier age, it is condensed into a single word—"No!" (Blos, 1962, p. 12)

The restive and rebellious components of the adolescent experience are related to action and acting-out behaviors in many adolescents. Dugan (1989) notes that although the term *acting out* often carries a "pejorative" connotation and is seen as "pathological," this behavior "may also be an indicator of hope and potential for success in the face of adversity" and may lead to the development of "resiliency" (p. 157). Dugan (1989) contrasts acting out to the development of "patterns of inhibition, inaction, and compliance [which] are shown to foreshadow the development of a sense of helplessness and despair" (p. 158). Frequently, acting out has "communicational aspects," and can be a "'cry for help'"; in fact, there is an "adaptive capacity of being able to act in relationship to others, even when such behavior results in provocation or annoyance" (p. 158).

Adolescents can experience troubling feelings as they move toward individuation.

> Adolescent individuation is accompanied by feelings of isolation, loneliness, and confusion. Individuation brings some of the dearest megalomaniacal dreams of childhood to an irrevocable end. They must now be relegated entirely to fantasy: their fulfillments can never again be considered seriously. The realization of the finality of the end of childhood, of the binding nature of commitments, of the definite limitation to individual existence itself—this realization creates a sense of urgency, fear, and panic. Consequently, many an adolescent tries to remain indefinitely in a transitional phase of development; this condition is called *prolonged adolescence*. (Blos, 1962, p. 12; italics in the original)

The early phase of adolescence is often accompanied by a need for privacy and creating distance from parents, "represented by closed doors in bedrooms and bathrooms, and secretiveness usually initiated by self-consciousness about body change" (Newton, 1995, p. 27). As the adolescent turns to peers, it is not uncommon for them to develop "secrets with best friends and subsequently a peer group" (p. 27).

An interesting transitional phenomenon in early- and mid-adolescence is the keeping of diaries; "diary writing is a strategy commonly used to cope with age-specific problems in adolescence, particularly by females" (Seiffge-Krenke and Kirsch, 2002, p. 401). "Daydreams, events, and emotions which cannot be shared with real people are confessed with relief to the diary" (Blos, 1962, p. 94); the diary also provides the writer with a "surrogate friend" (Seiffge-Krenke and Kirsch, 2002, p. 402). The friend is usually female, and often given a name (Blos, 1962; Dalsimer, 1982); in Anne Frank's diary, her "friend" is called Kitty. This diary friend is an "imagined 'other' whom the adolescent brings to life [in] an effort at restitution for the loss at the heart of the adolescent experience" (Dalsimer, 1982, p. 521).

Diaries give their writers an opportunity to work through and reflect on their lives, conflicts, and goals; these documents offer insights into the adolescents' inner lives, fantasies, and sequences of development (Blos, 1962; Dalsimer, 1982). Dalsimer's (1982) analysis of the diaries of Anne Frank captures Anne's depiction of her unique adolescent experience.

During World War II, Anne, from the age of thirteen to fifteen, was confined to living in a hidden attic with her own family, a second family, and a dentist, to escape the deportation of Jews from Amsterdam to concentration camps. Although living in this "abnormal" world, Dalsimer (1982) found Anne to be a "delightful girl—bright, lively, curious, mischievous, whimsical, passionate" (p. 487). She was also a good observer of other people and her own inner experiences.

> Even within the confines of the secret annexe, we see the familiar movement back and forth, during adolescence, between the world outside the family and the family itself. The extrafamilial world offers a refuge from the conflict that, with the onset of puberty, invades the bonds with parents; at the same time, the family becomes a refuge from the anxieties aroused in new relationships. It is this repeated movement back and forth that ultimately brings about what Blos (1967) has called the "second individuation process" of adolescence. (Dalsimer, 1982, p. 515)

Anne falls in love with Peter, the teenage son of the other annexed family.

> Like any teen-ager in love, Anne finds herself suddenly bursting into tears, thinking that perhaps Peter doesn't like her at all, or only thinks of her casually. The mood swings, the excitement, the restlessness, the exhilaration—all the characteristics of first love are recorded here. (Dalsimer, 1982, p. 507)

Anne is sexually attracted to Peter, and the intensity of her feelings frighten her: "'I am afraid of myself, I am afraid that in my longing I am giving myself too quickly'" (Dalsimer, 1982, p. 512); then, seeming to need some external control, she asks her father about the situation in a way that almost guarantees his response: "'Daddy, I expect you've gathered that when we're together Peter and I don't sit miles apart. Do you think it's wrong?'" (p. 512).

> As is characteristic of adolescents, Anne has found a way of externalizing the conflict which, until then, had been internal. Predictably,

her father tells her not to spend so much time alone with Peter. This allows Anne to espouse the other side of her ambivalence. In defiance of her father's request that she not go to Peter's room, she declares emphatically to Kitty [her diary], "No, I'm going!" The "war that reigns incessantly within" is no longer within; it is between Anne and her father, each expressing an aspect of Anne's own conflict. By telling her father, she has drawn the lines of battle between them. At the same time, she has succeeded in reengaging him in her intimate concerns, calling upon him to be once more the authoritative and protective father of childhood. (Dalsimer, 1982, p. 512)

Although it is generally understood that adolescents rebel from authority as they seek autonomy, it is less understood (and put into practice) that they also need external limits to help them regulate their emotional states and behaviors, recapitulating their earlier needs for parental assistance in developing self-regulation—albeit now, they need this assistance on a higher level and in more complex ways.

Sexual Development in Adolescence

The adolescent develops sexually, which is a total biopsychosocial occurrence; physical changes, including hormonal activity and sexual feelings, intermingle with psychological reactions and adaptations, and identity formation. To isolate sexuality as simply a biological phenomenon would be an inaccurate representation of its complexity. Puberty is experienced universally in all cultures—sometimes welcomed and heralded in socially sanctioned ways, sometimes ignored or hushed. Many "hunter/gatherer and herding cultures" had "rituals" which recognized the onset of puberty and the initiation into "adult status" (Newton, 1995, p. 25).

It is not uncommon for adolescents in our culture to feel uncomfortable and awkward in their new bodies and both sexually excited as well as guilty with their newly developing sexual feelings. Sexual experimentation is common, sometimes leading to pregnancy or sexually transmitted diseases; in the United States, 40,000 new cases of AIDS are reported each year, mostly in black and Hispanic young people engaging in heterosexual sex, the majority of whom are unaware of their condition (McNeil Jr., 2006). Adolescent prostitution is a common phenomenon in runaway adolescents who also use intravenous drugs (Kaplan, Sadock, and Grebb, 1994); HIV/AIDS is particularly prevalent in this population. HIV/AIDS is discussed further in Chapter 13.

The emphasis on sex-education programs in the schools, in this country, is on abstinence; in "too many school districts around the country, young people are being denied critical information about contraception that could protect their health and save their lives" (Wilgoren, 1999, p. A16).

The rate of teenage pregnancy has dramatically decreased; this has been attributed to a decrease in adolescent sexual relations as well as to an increased use of birth control (Lacey, 1999). Teenage parents are discussed in Chapter 7.

It is not uncommon for adolescents to experience homosexual feelings early in adolescence (Blos, 1962); usually, this is a stage on the way to the development of heterosexuality. However, a number of adolescents realize that their sexual orientation is gay, lesbian, or bisexual, and this realization can cause distress and confusion.

Gay, Lesbian, and Bisexual Adolescents

Joyce Hunter, a researcher at Columbia University who has been studying the gay and lesbian youth culture since the 1970s, when few adolescents came out, observed in 1997 that teenage openness about homosexuality, as well as general public acceptance of this, had undergone a dramatic change (Cloud, 1997). Since then, there has been even greater acceptance; in "1997 there were approximately 100 gay-straight alliances (GSAS)—clubs for gay and gay-friendly kids—on U.S. high school campuses. Today there are at least 3,000 GSAS. . . . In the 2004-2005 academic year, GSAS were established at U.S. schools at the rate of three per day" (Cloud, 2005, p. 44). On college campuses, "gay equality has . . . : become a '90s version of Birkenstock environmentalism for many youths. Even in certain parts of suburbia, gay is becoming more than O.K.; it's cool" (Cloud, 1997, p. 82).

Prejudice and discrimination remain, and some teens continue to struggle with their own conflicts about sexual identity; they face the possibility of rejection by their parents, peers, teachers, and social institutions; they may become socially isolated and depressed (Hunter and Schaecher, 1995; Proctor and Groze, 1994); research has indicated that they are "at higher risk for suicide than their straight peers are" (Cloud, 2005, p. 45). However, the dramatic change in social attitudes, the many support groups, and positive attention in the media and on the Web has reduced the stigma and consequent shame; they "no longer need endure the baleful combination of loneliness and longing that characterized the childhoods of so many gay adults" (p. 44).

There are also groups of people who strongly believe it is possible (and desirable) to change one's sexual orientation to heterosexuality (a belief once accepted by psychoanalysts, but since given up by most); the "Christian right" is active in promoting a "healing" that will return the individual to "'heterosexuality [which] is God's design'"; their strategy involves "inclusion, prayer, the promise of change"; often role models (people who have given up their homosexuality) discuss their transformation in the media (Cloud, 2005, p. 44).

Some adolescents struggle against their homosexual feelings, denying or suppressing them, and become involved in at-risk behaviors such as

> engaging in unprotected sex with people of the same sex or the opposite sex, even getting pregnant or fathering a child, so that no one will suspect the young person's homosexuality . . . [using] alcohol or other drugs . . . [and putting themselves] at significant risk for HIV infection. (Hunter and Schaecher, 1995, p. 1057)

Teenagers may have brief, experimental homosexual experiences; some may become anxious, and "need reassurance about the normality of an isolated homosexual experience and confirmation that it does not indicate a permanent homosexual orientation"; however, for other teenagers "a homosexual orientation is already determined by this time"; some teens may need professional help in understanding their conflicts and wishes in regard to their sexual orientation (Sadock and Sadock, 2003, p. 37). It is important that clinicians providing this assistance be sensitive to the adolescent's conflicts and his or her readiness (or lack of readiness) for resolution and commitment; and it is also vital that clinicians do not impose a political agenda—either steering the teenager away from homosexuality toward heterosexuality, on the one hand, or advocating for a committed gay orientation, on the other.

Social workers deal with many teenagers who may be gay or lesbian, but are often afraid to discuss their sexual orientation; many times they are "invisible in family services" (Proctor and Groze, 1994, p. 511); those in shelters or residential care "are treated differently from other participants" (Hunter and Schaecher, 1995, p. 1060); teens who remain closeted may not receive the understanding they need and may have special difficulty in relating to others, including their social workers (Hunter and Schaecher, 1995). Attunement to the needs of this population is an important professional challenge for clinical social workers.

Cognitive Development in Adolescence

During adolescence, considerable growth and development occurs in the brain, which results in the adolescent's "higher and more complex cognitive ability and behavioral repertoire" (Newton, 1995, p. 33), even, if, as

Formal
Operations
(Piaget)

noted earlier, they are not always able to act on their cognitive understandings. Adolescents enter Piaget's stage of *formal operations,* in which they think more abstractly and conceptually, becoming involved in the world of ideas. Piaget and Inhelder (1995) have observed that adolescents are able to analyze their own thinking and develop theories, and look at situations from multiple perspectives.

> The fact that these theories are oversimplified, awkward, and usually contain very little originality is beside the point. From the functional standpoint, [adolescents'] systems are significant in that they furnish the cognitive and evaluative bases for the assumption of adult roles. (Piaget and Inhelder, 1995, p. 437)

Discussing adolescents in foster placement, Levine (1990), emphasizes how the development of formal operations processes enables adolescents to think through their family life with different perspectives, which has the potential of leading to internal conflict resolution and growth; preadolescent children (who are in the concrete operations stage of development) have difficulty dealing with the abstract, think that "'what is, ought to be,'" and feel that they are to blame for being placed by their parents in foster care (p. 58). Adolescents, with their capacity for abstraction, "can deal with ideas and possibilities" and have the capability of comparing "their parents to other parents, and in doing so become aware of their parents' limitations. Their faith in parental infallibility erodes" (pp. 58-59).

During adolescence, creativity often flourishes, idealism develops, and the adolescent becomes interested in the "world of ideas—humanitarian issues, morals, ethics, and religion" (Kaplan, Sadock, and Grebb, 1994, p. 53). Piaget and Inhelder (1995) discuss the tendency for adolescents' "egocentrism" to manifest itself in a "sort of Messianic form such that the theories used to represent the world center on the role of reformer that the adolescent feels himself called upon to play in the future"; gradually, this egocentrism recedes in a process called "decentering" (p. 440). Many teenagers join the Peace Corps, do community volunteer work, and make constructive contributions to school newspapers, literary magazines, orchestras, dramatic societies, and student government.

Moral Development in Adolescence

Piaget observed that morality evolves along with children's cognitive thinking. In the preoperational stage, children obey the rules of the adults who care for them; during the stage of concrete operations, children follow

the rules rigidly but are not able to see subtle distinctions or allow for different interpretations; in the stage of formal operations, adolescents can think
about rules in terms of the needs of society (Kaplan, Sadock, and Grebb,
1994).

Kohlberg, utilizing Piaget's theory, developed his own conceptual framework, in which he highlighted three phases of morality. In *preconventional
morality,* the child responds to parental authority and punishment through
obedience; during the phase of *morality of conventional role conformity,*
the child is concerned with the opinions of others and seeks to feel validated
and accepted. In the final phase, *morality of self-accepted moral principles,*
the child has internalized a set of moral and ethical concepts, operates on
this basis, and is capable of thinking through conflicting situations to arrive
at a decision of how to respond (Kaplan, Sadock, and Grebb, 1994).

The development of morality in individual adolescents is dependent on a
number of circumstances: the moral code of their families and social environments; the overt and covert messages they receive from their families
about acceptable behavior; and the quality of their attachments and identifications with their parents. An important distinction is between the adolescents' ability to think morally and their capacity to act morally; as they
respond to their impulses and tendencies toward risk-taking behaviors, some
immoral behavior may be the consequence. Developing a personal moral
code is part of the struggle to form their own sense of identity.

Can adolescents whose behavior has been judged by society to be immoral and illegal have the capacity to make valid moral and legal judgments
about the illegal behaviors of their peers? In an innovative social experiment, teenagers charged with lesser, nonviolent legal misdemeanors are being judged by juries of their peers (who had previously been charged with
legal misdemeanors themselves) in about 1,035 youth courts throughout
the country; many successes have been reported, and the trend is growing
(Caplan, 2005).

> All told, these junior courts will hold more than 100,000 trials this
> year. . . . Advocates say they not only help relieve criminal-court
> backlogs but have also proved they can turn around a kid who has
> gone wrong . . . [they] are often more effective in preventing repeat
> crimes than are other methods used by cities to discipline first-time
> offenders. . . . The experience is also more attuned to teenagers' moral
> development, conveying not just that there are consequences for their
> behavior but also that society cares about them. (Caplan, 2005, p. 63)

The Bronx Youth Court, which by mid-2000 had been operating for two years under the auspices of New York City's Probation Department, differs from other youth courts as it "judges more serious offenses—drug possession with intent to sell, robbery, weapons charges" (Sengupta, 2000, p. 32).

Youth Courts raise tantalizing questions about both the effectiveness of peer group opinion on decreasing teenage delinquency behaviors, as well as the impact on the "court officers" themselves in terms of potentially enhanced self-esteem, feeling respect from authorities, and the internalization of a new moral code. The developmental processes of adolescence speak to the potential feasibility of such a plan due to the influence of peer groups at this age, the increased capacity of the adolescent to think through problems from different perspectives, and the move to higher levels of moral development.

Family Life of Adolescents

One typical struggle between teenagers and their families relates to familial direction, rules, and control; parents often walk a fine line between rigid overcontrol of their teenagers and not providing enough guidance or setting any limits. Parents may be struggling with their own unresolved adolescent issues, which have been reawakened by experiencing their children's adolescence, causing parent-child conflicts about authority. The Vietnam War ushered in social changes in this country including civil protest, the breakdown of authority, and the increased use of drugs. Parents and social institutions became more permissive, and children were given freedom they may not have been ready to handle.

At present, there seems to be a general turning away from this "permissiveness" toward a greater concern with structure and limits, and parents are evidently keeping a closer eye on their college-age children. Many colleges, for example, now provide greater in loco parentis structure, guidance, and rules, often at the request of parents, and sometimes at the request of students: "Many parents are former students who worry that their children will repeat their wild college years and who have much to say about college life. . . . Students increasingly want to talk about their varied and difficult backgrounds" (Bronner, 1999, pp. A1, A15).

Major family disruptions, such as divorce or joining a newly formed blended family, can create special stress for the adolescent who is in the midst of working out separation-individuation issues. Familial maltreatment, parental substance abuse, or mental illness can leave the adolescent conflicted and emotionally vulnerable. A strong association exists between poor relationships with parents and/or actual family.

Special Problems of Adolescents

Although adolescents' behavior at times can appear tumultuous, their mood swings difficult to understand, and their arguments with families intense, these events are considered within the range of to-be-expected, everyday occurrences; however, some adolescents are affected by serious emotional and family problems.

Family Dissolution

The dissolution of a family is painful for all its members and occurs primarily by divorce, separation, death, and abandonment.

Divorce. Although seemingly removed from the family, the adolescent still needs a secure base. Loss and its resolution are a normal part of the adolescent experience; loss accompanied by the "finality" of family breakdown makes emancipation far more painful and complex. Adolescents whose parents are divorcing may become depressed or act out. Suicide attempts by teens are not uncommon during the separation or divorce process, in part because of the message this attempt sends parents to preserve the unity of the family. Adolescents can, however, adapt to divorce, especially when parents are supportive of them and do not triangulate them into the divorce process (Isaacs, Montalvo, and Abelsohn, 2000).

Divorcing parents due to their own preoccupations, often "abdicate" their parental role (Isaacs, Montalvo, and Abelsohn, 2000, p. 182).

> We use the term abdication to describe parents' almost complete failure to carry out the usual socialization functions: taking a tender interest in the youngster's everyday triumphs, struggles, and disappointments; consistently checking curfews and actively appraising the adolescent's girlfriends and boyfriends; meeting periodically with teachers . . . and making occasional but necessary checks with the other parent. The youngster is left to make it alone. Two levels of the abdication phenomenon can be differentiated. The first is the absence per se of indispensable parental functions because of parental depression, obsessive preoccupation, or physical absence. . . . The second is more directly linked to the spousal battle. Here, abdication serves to sustain a parent-adolescent, cross-generational coalition that undermine or excludes the other spouse. (Isaacs, Montalvo, and Abelsohn, 2000, p. 182)

Abdication of parental involvement also occurs in families other than those affected by divorce. In some families there is chronic abdication, neglect, and abuse, and many homeless adolescents are "push out" and "throwaway" teens who have been physically and/or emotionally abandoned by their families (Loppnow, 1985), and many others have run away from group homes and foster homes (Bass, 1995).

Runaways and homeless teens. The numbers of runaway and homeless teens in the United States is difficult to assess, "as is the case with any transient and ill-defined population" (Kidd, 2003, p. 235); however, "the homeless youth population is estimated to be between 500,000 and 1.3 million young people each year (Center for Law and Social Policy, 2003)" ("Homeless Youth," 2006, p. 2). The lives of these young people are replete with multiple problems, including family breakdown, parental substance abuse, domestic violence, frequent moves, and physical and sexual abuse of the adolescent (Bass, 1995; Kidd, 2003).

Many homeless youth become involved in stealing, prostitution, and drugs. A high percentage of all prostitutes are teenagers; many are runaways and "were taken in by pimps and substance abusers" (Sadock and Sadock, 2003, p. 39). These teens also have many physical problems, including HIV/AIDS, and a high incidence of mental disorders, such as depression, conduct disorder, post–traumatic stress disorder, and psychotic symptoms; they also have a high rate of suicide attempts (Kidd, 2003); "strategies are needed to identify suicidal runaways" (Rotheram-Borus and Bradley, 1991, p. 122).

Karabanow (2006) argues against stereotyping street kids, and in his study of ninety-eight homeless teens in Canada, emphasized their diversity, their individuality, and their sense of self-agency.

> Street youth place much thought and reflection in how they perceive themselves and their external environments. If anything, these youth are not the commonly characterized "victims" of externalities, but rather, are willing players (albeit within a context of poverty, family violence, and problematic social structures/institutions) in carving out their positions in this world. In other words, they are much like any of us—active participants in defending and shaping their place. (Karabanow, 2006, p. 51)

Karabanow (2006) has observed that street kids go through several stages: "contemplation" (p. 55), during which they anticipate and plan for this experience; "entering" (p. 57), which is the initiation and adaptation to this new experience; "building an identity" (p. 62), evolving how they see themselves in their new lives; and "disengagement/exiting" (p. 65), as they think of leaving. For the majority "the positive aspects are street life are short-lived and most youngsters begin to experience many of the limitations to such a lifestyle" (p. 66); new meanings, sense of identity, and goals need to be developed.

Interventions with homeless teens should offer comprehensive services, such as meeting their basic needs of housing, food, health, and mental health care, including substance abuse treatment, schooling, vocational training and employment, as well as providing early intervention (if possible) and assessment of family factors (is reunification an option?). One complex problem to be assessed is the nature of their relationships with their peers, who may be a source of support and/or negative influence for ongoing at-risk behaviors (Kidd, 2003). Many of these adolescents have had difficult relationships with adults and negative experiences with social agencies, and providers need to be sensitive to their possible difficulties in relating, their vulnerabilities, resistances to changing their lifestyles, as well as recognizing their individuality, sense of self-agency, inherent strengths, and hopes, and build upon these strengths (Karabanow, 2006; Kidd, 2003).

Teenagers leaving foster placement. For some adolescents, the stability of a good foster home can be a *protective* factor in developing coping skills and resilience. There has been an increasing trend for adolescents between ages twelve and eighteen to be adopted by their foster parents; this number has risen "from 6,000 in 2000 to 10,000 in 2004" (Hamilton, 2006, p. 58). Increased financial benefits to adoptive parents have contributed to this trend; in the past, though foster parents received a stipend for care, this was stopped if they were to adopt their foster child; now payments often continue until the child is eighteen. Federal tax credits for adoption have been increased; greater effort has been made to find adoption homes for eligible teens. Not all of these adoptions are successful; approximately "a quarter of adolescent adoptions fail before they're finalized, vs. about 12% of adoptions overall" (p. 58).

There are about half a million children in this country who live in foster care; until the recent past, their placements ended abruptly at age eighteen, and they would be on their own; they would "age out' of foster care" (Georgiades, 2005, p. 503). This group of "some 24,000 a year nationwide . . . is gaining new attention, as youths speak out and research reveals the numbers who end up in homeless shelters, jail and long-term poverty" (Eckholm, 2007, p. 1).

They had been abandoned by the child welfare system, and "forced into the world with little else but bad memories, patchwork educational experiences and no money" (Beaucar, 1999a, p. 7). Their problems included homelessness, failure to graduate from high school, joblessness, and in the case of many young women, having babies "within four years" of leaving (p. 7).

In one large study, Courtney and Barth (1996) found that adolescents who were discharged from kinship foster care (discussed in Chapter 7) "seem to be most likely to either return home or make a relatively smooth transition out of foster care" (p. 82).

In addressing this problem, the John Chafee Foster Care Independence Act of 1999 "mandates states to extend provision of IL [independent living] services until youths reach 21 years of age" (Georgiades, 2005, p. 503). Under this act, services include providing assistance in daily living, education, employment, social skills, parenting, counseling, and preventive health measures; Medicaid coverage until age twenty-one is paid for. For those who qualify, there are stipends and monthly subsidies. A qualitative study was carried out in Florida (Georgiades, 2005), asking youth (both those using these services and those not participating) about their perceptions of this program and their needs. Suggestions included early intervention, the development of closer relationships between counselors and the participants, more attention to life skills and to parenting issues, individualized help, an outreach component for "runaways and inmates," and the involvement of mentors, who had been former foster children themselves, and inclusion of an ongoing evaluative component by the participants (p. 509).

In an innovative program in Michigan, mentors (former foster children) are successfully working with newly emancipated foster youth; one of their first projects was to conduct a luggage drive—so that these young people would have suitcases for their possessions, rather than the garbage bags they were using. Many of these young people are now on state youth boards where they help shape policy; "for the hundreds who have joined, the youth boards, with their weekly meetings and election of officers, have offered personal breakthroughs as much as a way to influence policy" (Eckholm, 2007, p. A11).

Ironically, by contrast with especially vulnerable foster teens facing independent living, an ostensibly high-functioning group of adolescents, namely college students, who generally have far greater resources and more stable life histories, routinely receive far more structured help with their adaptation to adult living and campus life (Bronner, 1999).

Depression

Depression for many adolescents is mild, occasional, and part of their normal mood swings. However, for some, depressed feelings are more than a *transient state* of sadness; depression can be experienced as a pervasive, underlying sense of despair, loneliness, hopelessness, and emptiness; other symptoms of adolescent depression can include weepiness, boredom, physical symptoms, sleep problems, and changes in eating habits (Mack and Hickler, 1981). Depression is associated with many other adolescent problems, such as teenage pregnancy (Wakschlag and Hans, 2000), substance abuse (Slaby and McGuire, 1989), and running away (Bass, 1995; Kidd, 2003); it "has been singled out as a major etiologic factor in suicide" (Braga, 1989, p. 7). There are "high rates of comorbid depression with chronic PTSD [post–traumatic stress disorder] among children and adolescents" (Murphy, Pynoos, and James, 1997, p. 231).

Many adolescents do not ask for help with their depressive feelings but "may more easily complain of chronic boredom, lack of interest for activities and simply lack of 'drive'. These symptoms frequently alternate with temper tantrums, restlessness, defiance, acting out and 'dare devil' type of activities" (Braga, 1989, p. 7).

Adolescent depression also exists in various disguised forms. Rossman (1982) uses the terms "masked depression" and "depressive equivalents" to describe how the adolescent uses "acting-out or disruptive behaviors . . . to translate depressive thoughts or feelings into action equivalents"; in addition, "failing grades, truancy, drug and alcohol use, social withdrawal and accidents" can be part of the symptomatology, and "depressed children may walk in front of an oncoming train or car or suffer multiple athletic injuries" (Slaby and McGuire, 1989, p. 23).

Substance Abuse

Many teenagers experiment with drugs and alcohol; for some it becomes a way of life. A University of Michigan study funded by the National Institute on Drug Abuse has found that the "percentage of U.S. adolescents who use illicit drugs or drink alcohol continued a decade-long drop in 2006," and that "the rates are now down from recent peak levels in the mid-1990s" ("Illicit Drug Use," 2006, pp. 1, 3). Marijuana remains the most popular drug, but it too has declined. However, there is now a very high use of prescription drugs including "narcotics, tranquilizers, and sedatives" (p. 14). According to Columbia University's National Center on Addiction and Substance Abuse (CASA), approximately "2.3 million kids ages 12 to 17 took legal medications illegally in 2003" (Banta, 2005, p. 35). In addition to the possibility that teens can become addicted to these drugs, they can also become seriously ill. Such drugs can become more dangerous when taken with alcohol, or with illegal drugs, which is not uncommon. "Pain medications, which are powerful nervous-system depressants, are particularly dangerous—and especially prized" (p. 35).

The "pharming party" has become a popular social event. At these parties, teens will trade drugs with each other; "'if I have something good, like Oxycontin, it might be worth two or three Xanax'" (Banta, 2005, p. 35). Teens get drugs through trading, may have some left over from their own treatment (sometimes they pretend they have medical problems in order to get prescriptions), by rifling family medicine cabinets, and from some Internet pharmacies. As mentioned earlier, some children taking pills for ADHD give them or sell them to friends; the over-the-counter decongestant Sudafed, ground up, has recently been used to induce a high.

Alcohol has continued to be frequently abused drug by adolescents, as indicated in many studies. "According to an annual survey of U.S. youth, three-fourths of 12th graders, more than two-thirds of 10th graders, and about two in every five 8th graders have consumed alcohol. . . . When youth drink they tend to drink intensively, often consuming four to five drinks at one time . . . data show that 11 percent of 8th graders, 22 percent of 10th graders, and 29 percent of 12th graders had engaged in heavy episodic, or binge, drinking within the past two weeks" ("Statistics on underage drinking," 2006).

Substance abuse exists within a broader social-cultural context (Nowinski, 1990).

> America has become a drug oriented society; in other words, our ethics with respect to the use of mood-altering chemicals are basically permissive and sympathetic. The past two generations have witnessed a proliferation in the development and use of both licit and illicit mood-altering chemicals. We use drugs—those we obtain from physicians as well as those we obtain in liquor stores and on the street—to enhance feelings of well-being and to help us cope. Adolescents are not very different from adults in this regard. The adolescent subculture, despite differences in form, has a great deal in common with its adult counterpart; this is true across the socioeconomic spectrum. (Nowinski, 1990, p. 12)

Substance abuse may contribute to adolescents' scholastic underachievement because of its neuropsychological effects (Newton, 1995); it is often an important factor in adolescent suicide (Hoberman, 1989) and is highly correlated with fatal car crashes among teens (Nowinski, 1990); intravenous drug use can lead to HIV infection (de Anda, 1995). The three major causes of death for adolescents and young adults (accidents, homicides, and suicides) are associated with drug and alcohol use (Newton, 1995).

Nowinski (1990) discusses factors contributing to adolescent substance abuse, including the adolescent personality (taking risks, living in the present, and/or rebelliousness); peer pressure (difficulty deviating from the adolescent "substance-using subculture") (p. 21); adolescent alienation (feeling "a disconnection from parental and societal values and ideals, traditions and rituals") (p. 21); internal and external stress, such as maltreatment, living with dysfunctional families, loss, as well as poor coping skills, insecurity, and low self-esteem.

Close associations are found among depression, substance abuse, and suicide; "few addicts, in fact, have not contemplated suicide, and many have acted on these thoughts in one way or another" (Nowinski, 1990, p. 50). One study reported that "as many as 40-50 percent of adolescent and college-aged suicides were abusing alcohol and/or drugs at the time of their death" (Hoberman, 1989, p. 67). Depression as expressed by adolescent substance abusers should be taken seriously, "and suicide risk must be thoroughly evaluated and treated" (Morehouse, 1989, p. 358).

Adolescents are accident-prone, and "alcohol and drug-related fatal car crashes are more common by far among youths than any other age group" (Nowinski, 1990, p. 11). Depressed adolescents "drink or take drugs and drive. Decreased reaction time and careless driving contribute to their own injury or death and that of innocent others. Forty-five to 50 percent of fatal car crashes in this group are associated with alcohol use" (Slaby and McGuire, 1989, p. 23).

Native Americans as a group have a high rate of alcohol abuse, resulting in a "disproportionate toll among American Indians" (Moran, 1999, p. 52). Alcohol abuse starts early; for many Native American youths (male and female), drinking begins in the preteen years and the pattern of alcohol abuse is established for roughly 90 percent of these youths by the twelfth grade; the "frequency and amount of drinking are greater, and the negative consequences are more common" (p. 53).

There have been many substance abuse prevention programs directed at adolescents, and their "effectiveness has been seriously questioned" (Skiba, Monroe, and Wodarski, 2004, p. 343). Research indicates that "programs based on information and attitude change alone have minimal effect on adolescent substance-using behavior and in some case contributes to experimentation" (p. 343); the programs with the best record of successes are "comprehensive, have multiple components, and are directed at individuals, families, peers, schools, communities, the media, and the workplace" (p. 346).

Many colleges are taking an assertive, proactive role in addressing the problem of heavy drinking on campuses, including alcohol education programs; one option that is attracting an increasing number of students is the choice to live in alcohol-free dormitories (Wilgoren, 2000).

It is difficult to motivate substance-abusing adolescents to seek treatment, but developing their motivation is essential. "When adolescents are unmotivated for treatment but are coerced into entering a program, they usually act out or become passive participants who drink when the opportunity arises" (Morehouse, 1989, p. 357); this requires considerable clinical skill. Nowinski (1990) discusses the "arrogance" of the adolescent addict:

> They are desperate, but all they reveal is indifference . . . they may become very controlling over others, very demanding, exceedingly defensive, and blaming. This is the point at which they most often enter treatment. The clinician needs to be prepared for it. (p. 50)

Cigarette Smoking

Smoking has been declared a major public health problem; "tobacco use is associated with approximately 400,000 premature deaths each year in the United States—25 percent of all deaths" (Sadock and Sadock, 2003, p. 444). Teenagers are at special risk, as they "become addicted to nicotine faster and at lower doses" ("The Adolescent," 2005, p. 2); in addition, "early smoking may trigger changes in DNA that put young smokers at higher risk for cancer even if they quit later" (Golden, 1999b, p. 48). Teenage nicotine use is also associated with "many other health risk behaviors, including higher risk sexual behavior and use of alcohol or other drugs" ("Youth and Tobacco," 2006).

In high schools, currently "twenty-three percent" of students smoke cigarettes; in particular about "26 percent of whites, 22 percent of Hispanics, and 13 percent of African Americans"; in middle school "eight percent" of students smoke ("Youth and Tobacco," 2006, "Cigarette Smoking"). It is estimated that, daily, "approximately 4,000 young people between the ages of 12 and 17 years initiate cigarette smoking and an estimated 1,140 young people become daily cigarette smokers"; in addition, "thirteen percent of high school students are current cigar smokers" and an "estimated 10 percent of males in high school are current smokeless tobacco users" ("Cigarette Smoking").

Suicide

Suicidality is one of the most serious mental health risks faced by adolescents; it is the third leading cause of teenage death following accidents and homicides (de Anda, 1995; Sadock and Sadock, 2003). There are about 1,100 college students who commit suicide each year, "making suicide the second leading cause of death among college students, after motor-vehicle accidents" (Rawe and Kingsbury, 2006, p. 62). The actual number of adolescent suicides are probably underestimated and completed suicides "are three times the reported rates . . . taboos, impact on relatives, and exclusionary clauses in insurance policies militate against more accurate disclosure" (Slaby and McGuire, 1989, p. 24). In addition, some accidents (such as one-car fatalities) and homicides (provoked by the victim) can be suicidal in nature. Males have a higher rate for successfully completed suicides; females have a higher rate for suicide attempts (de Anda, 1995).

The rates for white adolescents are higher than for African-American teenagers; however, "suicide among black teen-agers, once quite rare, has sharply increased over the last two decades, a troubling rise that might reflect the strain some black families feel in making the transition to middle-class life" (Belluck, 1998a, p. A1). Latina teenage girls are especially "endangered"; they have the highest rates for attempted suicide (usually nonlethal) compared to non-Hispanic black and white teenage girls ("Young Latinas," 2006, p. A22). The ethnic group with the highest suicide rate is Native Americans; within this group, "the highest rates are found among younger Native Americans (15-24 years old)" (Ivanoff and Riedel, 1995, p. 2361).

Adolescents who attempt suicide are often depressed, have a high rate of drug abuse, and usually have multiple stressors in their lives, including families with "higher rates of conflict and dysfunction, divorce, separation, and parental death, particularly at an early age" (de Anda, 1995, p. 27). Physical abuse has also been found in some of these families (de Anda, 1995; Slaby and McGuire, 1989), and it is not uncommon to find a family history of suicide (de Anda, 1995).

In the teenage population, it is not uncommon to find the *cluster effect* after a teenage suicide; that is, others engaging in *copycat* behavior—teens in the same school or community as the "successful" suicide victim will make their own suicide attempts. Some teens enter suicide pacts with a friend, committing suicide together.

Vivienne: An adolescent suicide. Vivienne (Mack and Hickler, 1981), discussed in Chapters 1 and 3, committed suicide when she was fourteen—an act precipitated by the loss of her favorite teacher (her selfobject), when he moved across the country. "Most suicide attempts occur after a 'major disruption of a personal relationship', either parental or romantic" (de Anda, 1995, p. 27).

Vivienne lived in a traditional family with three children; her father was a minister, and her mother was a homemaker with (unfulfilled) artistic interests. Vivienne excelled in her private school and was creative, writing poetry, and keeping a diary; these protective factors, however, were not strong enough to protect her.

Vivienne was depressed, which was neither recognized nor treated; in fact, what was "most impressive from the behavioral standpoint is not what Vivienne demonstrated of her depression, but, rather how well she concealed its essential features" (Mack and Hickler, 1981, p. 97). Her emotional pain was revealed in her diaries and her poetry and, toward the end, in her letters to the teacher who had been so special to her. Her suicide was

> a direct outgrowth of [her] depression, while the depression in turn derives from the structure of her personality. . . . Yet for Vivienne herself the "terrific depressions" seemed to have a kind of independent life, to come at her as if "from the middle of nowhere." (Mack and Hickler, 1981, p. 94)

Vivienne had great sensitivity and an unusual ability to identify with (as well as feel overly responsible for) others. Although warmth and caring were expressed in the family, Vivienne's mother was described by Vivienne's sister, Laurel, as "often abstracted, absorbed in her own struggles. 'My mother was always sick, always tired . . . she needed attention. . . . Sometimes she got attention by making people feel guilty'" (Mack and Hickler, 1981, p. 9). Vivienne's mother tended to see Vivienne "in terms of her own personal needs, as a treasure . . . the one to whom she turned with her burdens. . . . In the last weeks of her life Vivienne felt especially the weight of her mother's problems and needs" (p. 109). Vivienne's mother reported feelings of alienation from Vivienne as an infant.

Vivienne's suicidal thoughts were related to her low self-esteem and her "inability to experience herself or her world as having enough value to make living tolerable" (Mack and Hickler, 1981, p. 136). Vivienne's *ego ideal,* "the agency of personality carrying the principal responsibility for regulating self-esteem, became a rigid taskmaster, insisting upon the most exalted standards of human conduct and intimacy" (p. 136).

> It [the ego ideal] is built on the one hand upon the internalization of parental values and expectations, while at the same time it looks to society to provide objects and examples with which to structure more realistic aims and goals. . . . But the selection of models or examples is powerfully determined by the residual needs of childhood. . . . In Vivienne's case we have seen how deeply affected the structure of her ego ideal was by early injury to the self and by the example of parents,

especially her mother, who sought to fulfill through this child, from whom she felt estranged, her own longings for perfection. (Mack and Hickler, 1981, p. 137)

Vivienne felt a special closeness to her father, but he stated that "he never really knew Vivienne or 'where she was'. Sweet and gentle, he was, nevertheless, indecisive, had difficulty handling his son, and surrendered much of the authority in the family to his wife" (Mack and Hickler, 1981, p. 109). He also felt responsible for "'all the problems of the world,'" according to Laurel, and it was this quality with which Vivienne identified (p. 109).

Other family problems existed. Vivienne's parents had problems with Laurel and with Vivienne's brother Rob, who was sent to a private school during his first three grades and lived with his grandparents, coming home on weekends. "'I had to get him out of the house,' Paulette [Vivienne's mother] explained. 'He had problems with his father, acted out against the girls, and did nasty things behind my back'" (Mack and Hickler, 1981, p. 7). During adolescence, Laurel acted out sexually; once, there was concern that she might be pregnant.

Vivienne's early school experiences were unhappy. Laurel described how "'we were different from everyone else. . . . We wore old-fashioned dresses that Mommy smocked herself. Other girls wore smart shifts'" (Mack and Hickler, 1981, p. 8). Vivienne excelled academically, which also "set her apart as 'different'. 'She always seemed to be the butt of playground jokes,' Laurel remembers" (p. 8). Vivienne's mother observed that "'Vivienne felt awfully isolated and alone, but she didn't let you know any of that. She developed this sarcastic wit that would be devastating. I think it alienated other children even more'" (p. 8).

When Vivienne entered private school in the sixth grade, where the teacher who became her favorite taught, he "spotted Vivienne and another girl as two sixth-graders who had been outcasts in public school" (Mack and Hickler, 1981, p. 12). He reached out to these children, and Vivienne thrived and blossomed with his caring, empathic relationship. However, she was not only unable to maintain these gains without his presence but deteriorated emotionally when he left. His departure "had a greater significance than his loss as a person. It struck at the core of Vivienne's psychological vulnerability" (p. 101).

Attempted suicide by Hispanic adolescent females. In examining the high rate of suicide attempts in Hispanic females, *familial factors* and *self-image* have been found to be of key significance, shaped by cultural factors but not determined exclusively by social factors; it has been observed that "the vast majority (80 percent) of adolescent Hispanic females do not attempt suicide" (Zayas et al., 2000, p. 53). Although substance abuse is highly associated with adolescent suicide, this does not hold true for Hispanic teens.

> The suicide attempt typically occurs within the context of a progressive intensification in conflicts between the adolescent and her parents. An acute situation, usually an intense argument with parents regarding issues associated with autonomy or sexuality, embodied in the adolescent's involvement with a boyfriend, often triggers the suicide attempt. (Zayas et al., 2000, p. 56)

Differences in levels of acculturation between Hispanic female teens and their parents play an important role in suicidal behavior, as does being socioeconomically disadvantaged. "Fewer incidents of suicide attempts are reported among middle-class adolescent females than among girls of lower socioeconomic status" (Zayas et al., 2000, p. 56). Family dysfunction, including marital conflict and psychological problems in the parents, affect the parents' ability to help their adolescents. Families with a traditional Hispanic structure "emphasize restrictive, authoritarian parenting, especially with regard to girls . . . [which] may affect a family's capacity to respond flexibly to a daughter" (p. 57).

Hispanic female teen suicidal behavior tends to be viewed exclusively in relation to the mother-daughter tie; fathers have not been studied because they are often not present in the home; those adolescents who live for a longer period with fathers in the home tend to be less prone to suicide.

Mothers who are immigrants may not have the extended family support they had prior to immigrating, and therefore "mothers of those who attempt suicide may seek their daughter's companionship . . . and become overdependent on their daughters, creating a situation in which the adolescent feels she must parent her mother" (Zayas et al., 2000, p. 58). Abdication of some maternal functions, such as providing guidance and support, as well as "interruptions of mutuality" in the mother-daughter relationship, have been found in these cases (p. 58).

As is typical of Vivienne and many other adolescents who have attempted suicide, Hispanic females are often depressed and have low self-esteem; they frequently "perceive themselves as 'bad' and to blame for family problems" (Zayas et al., 2000, p. 59). Coping with anger is especially difficult, as a Hispanic adolescent "may be socialized by her own more tradition-bound parents to suppress her anger"; and this, combined with inadequate problem-solving skills, may be decisive factors leading to the suicide attempt (p. 59). The intent of the suicide attempt is generally "intended to solve an interpersonal problem or draw the attention of others who can assist the adolescent in coping" (p. 59). Although Hispanic teens may experience interpersonal stress in peer relationships, this is usually not a factor in suicide attempts; family problems play a dominant role.

Many Hispanic mothers of suicidal teen daughters had psychological problems themselves when they were adolescents, including suicide attempts or other acting-out behavior, such as pregnancies or running away. "Often the mother's conflicts in adolescence were related to her relationship with her own mother, reflecting a possible intergenerational dynamic" (Zayas et al., 2000, p. 58). Although the mother-daughter relationship is of major importance, the role of the father also needs to be evaluated because, even if absent, fathers "remain psychologically and emotionally present in their daughters' experience" (p. 60).

Homicide as suicide. Black and Hispanic men tend to view suicide as a passive response to frustration and condone a more outwardly direct approach.

> Dying is regarded as more honorable if it accompanies rage and aggression rather than passive solitude. Provoking a fight and being killed as a result may be culturally more appropriate as an expression of suicidal intent, but it will be reported as homicide. (Wyche and Rotheram-Borus, 1990, p. 327)

Teens with other ethnic backgrounds may also place themselves at risk of being killed and this risk may be related to both male and female adolescents remaining in (or seeking) situations in which they are severely abused and battered.

Toni Morrison (1977), in her novel *Song of Solomon,* describes the black teenage hero Milkman who is being pursued by his girlfriend, angry with him because he wishes to end their relationship; she has attempted to kill him six times. Milkman, who is depressed over family relationships, does not care if he dies. He also does not care if she dies. He lies passively in his friend's apartment as he hears his girlfriend breaking the window, coming to stab him with a knife:

> He lay there as still as the morning light, and sucked the world's energy up into his own will. And willed her dead. Either she will kill me or she will drop dead. Either I am to live in this world on my own terms or I will die out of it. (Morrison, 1977, p. 129)

She stabs him with a butcher knife but not fatally; she raises the knife again, but "could not get her arms down. . . . The paralyzed woman and the frozen man" (p. 130).

Suicide prevention. Clinicians, parents, and teachers can fear that talking to adolescents about suicide may *give* them this idea, but this is not so. Rather, *not* talking about suicide can give impetus to this process if the intent is present. The teacher, although supportive to Vivienne, did not understand the seriousness of her intent when she wrote to him about hanging herself, although he responded to her suffering. If he had responded to her threat, he might have alerted her family.

Whenever adolescents (or adults) refer to "ending it all" or are depressed or feel hopeless and alone, suicidal ideation should be discussed and clarified. If earlier suicide attempts have been made (as they were in Vivienne's case, but went "unnoticed"), and if adolescents also abuse substances, have poor impulse control, a history of suicide in the immediate family, or if recent suicide has been publicized in the media or in their school, then these individuals are at risk.

Teens can make suicide attempts to get attention or retaliate against someone who has hurt them, without actually intending to die. However, any attempt should also be taken seriously, as it can lead to future suicidal acts. Asking what purpose the suicide would serve can shed light on the underlying motivation and message of this act.

Some adolescents are full of "anger and hatred" and have "fantasies of future revenge"; clinicians are usually concerned about their "aggressivity, impulsivity and potential for violence, and may overlook the possibility that they may become seriously suicidal if they lose connectedness with the treatment setting, for instance, in the aftermath of a precipitous discharge" (Braga, 1989, pp. 14-15). Hoberman (1989) observed that "while older adolescents were more likely to be described as sad or despairing, younger suicides were much more likely to display anger prior to suicide" (p. 66).

A mental health assessment is important as serious conditions, such as psychosis, can underlie the suicidal wish; family evaluation is usually a critical part of assessment. The adolescent should receive immediate help; sometimes hospitalization must be considered.

Violence

Many adolescents are exposed to violence in their homes and communities; in response, they may engage in self-defeating or high-risk behaviors, which may not only cause physical harm but can also interfere with other aspects of their development (Marans and Adelman, 1997).

> Reactions [to violence] may range from staying away from school in order to avoid the potential for violence on the streets and in the classroom, to arming themselves as protection, to involvement in gang or

other criminal activities. As with disturbances of neurovegetative functions, withdrawal into fantasy, social isolation, and regressive symptomatology, these responses serve the adolescent's attempts to guard against and even reverse feelings of helplessness and overwhelming fear. (Marans and Adelman, 1997, p. 215)

Homicide rates among young people are very high; it is the second leading cause of death among fifteen- to twenty-five-year-olds (Glodich, 1998; Osofsky, 1997; Sadock and Sadock, 2003); black adolescent males have a much higher homicide rate than that of other racial or ethnic groups (Sadock and Sadock, 2003, p. 40); white adolescent males, and both black and white adolescents between ages sixteen and nineteen are "victims of violent crime more than any other age group," followed by twelve- to fifteen-year-olds (Glodich, 1998, p. 321). On an annual basis, almost "a million young people between the ages of twelve and nineteen are raped, robbed, or assaulted, often by their peers. The rate of victimization is substantially higher for Black male adolescents" (Glodich, 1998, p. 322).

Juvenile delinquency

Research based on self-reports suggests that "a majority" of young people in this country "will commit at least one delinquent act by the time they reach adulthood" (Williams, Ayers, and Arthur, 1997, p. 142); delinquency generally "represents a transient response to adolescence" (p. 143) and most will give up this "antisocial" behavior during adolescence. However, teenagers and young adults do "commit the bulk of crimes and are by far the most arrested age group in our society"; adolescents can also be arrested for committing so-called *"status offenses"* that include "running away from home, being truant from school, violating curfew, having sexual relations, being ungovernable, and being beyond the control of parents" (Zastrow and Kirst-Ashman, 2004, p. 310; italics in the original).

Conduct disorders are associated with delinquent behaviors, but not all delinquents have conduct disorders; delinquent behavior has been related to family breakdown, domestic violence, parental attitudes and behaviors relating to antisocial behaviors, abdication of the parenting role, and parental substance abuse and mental illness. Many delinquents (mostly boys) "have been found to be more likely to come from families where the parents are suffering from depression" (Williams, Ayers, and Arthur, 1997).

Adolescents, with their strong affiliations with peers, tend to have friends with similar values and backgrounds; "high levels of delinquent behavior are strongly correlated with high levels of association with delinquent friends" (Williams, Ayers, and Arthur, 1997, p. 149). Neighborhood influences contributing to juvenile delinquency include "high population density and mobility, physical deterioration, low attachment to the community, and high crime" (p. 146). School failure is often a major factor; "the level of an individual's commitment to education is considered one of the best predictors of delinquent behavior for adolescents" (p. 148). A report by the Justice Department and six major U.S. foundations

> found that minority youths are more likely than their white counterparts to be arrested, held in jail, sent to juvenile or adult court for trial, convicted and given longer prison terms, leading to a situation in which the impact is magnified with each additional step into the juvenile justice system. (Butterfield, 2000, p. A1)

Gang violence. Teenagers have belonged to gangs for many years, as an extension of their need for peer group involvement. Gangs vary in their organizations and goals; many are drug-involved and criminally oriented. There is no agreement on what constitutes a gang, and "the inadequacy of the knowledge base about delinquent gangs is a major obstacle to developing effective intervention strategies" (Zastrow and Kirst-Ashman, 2004, p. 311). Although many are composed of racial minorities, some gangs are white, and while most are male, others also have female members, and some all-female gangs do exist. Juvenile gangs have been increasing, and their drug activities and violence have been escalating (Zastrow and Kirst-Ashman, 2004).

Gangs, generally developing in industrialized urban settings, now also proliferate in small cities and suburban and rural areas (Regulus, 1995). Gang members often include young adults who remain in the gangs as leaders, using the gang as a base for illegal activities, including dealing in drugs. Recently supergangs and multigang alliances have developed, leading to gang memberships with as many as several hundred and sometimes several thousand members; smaller gangs of the past averaged from fewer than twenty to fewer than one hundred members (Regulus, 1995).

> Contemporary gangs are more violent than earlier gangs for several reasons. They have greater access to guns; intergang competition over status, turf, and criminal enterprises is more pervasive; and drug use has increased among gang youths. In addition, the more serious gang violence occurs in communities where the general youth culture has become more asocial and alienated, consequently promoting fear and emphasizing violence as a means of survival and social domination. (Regulus, 1995, p. 1046)

Adolescents who have weak attachments to their families, who lack a positive affiliation with their schools, who receive little direction and control, and who have few opportunities in their communities tend to be drawn to gangs, who socialize them into their "value orientations, codes of loyalty, and behavioral styles [which are] consistent with gang membership" (Regulus, 1995, p. 1046).

Success in stabilizing or diminishing gang activity has been related to community organization efforts and the provision of other opportunities for teens; efforts that were punitive and suppressive were not effective (Regulus, 1995). In Chapter 4, we discussed the development of comprehensive community strategies for dealing with such problems as unemployment and inadequate education. Work with gangs can be encompassed in this type of strategic planning; Regulus advocates actively involving gangs and their members interactively with those involved in this planning effort.

CONCLUSION

Peter Pan, the title character of the play (Barrie, 1904), was a wonderful latency-age child living in Never-Never Land, surrounded by his chums, ever coping with an exciting but benign environment, having fun, free from the constraints of adult supervision. Dangers abounded, but they were well known, such as Captain Hook and crocodiles, and Peter was protected by the fairy Tinkerbell. Wendy became his "child-mother," and he was not averse to her tender ministrations. Peter did not want to grow up; middle childhood was the ideal state to be in.

Peter's spirit exists in latency children who are excited about exploring their world, who enjoy their involvement in sports and computer games, and who love being with friends. However, Never-Never Land is not within reach of many children today; they do not have the luxury of fighting only fictional pirates; their world is populated by real dangers experienced through community and family violence, substance-abusing parents, broken homes, and schools that are fortresses rather than comforting and exciting places. If they run away, it is not to an enchanted forest but to cities where they are not welcome, to empty warehouses and vacated slum dwellings, and to friends who are also outcasts. No Tinkerbell offers them protection.

Some children and teens live under benign conditions, as Vivienne did. Vivienne's demons were internal, and her guilt and lack of pleasure in herself and in life culminated in her suicide; she had no happy future to dream about. She could not live Peter's carefree existence. Some teens deal with their demons through reckless actions and frantic activities; they may seem to be having fun, but often their behavior is driven by inner anxiety and despair; Peter's exuberance is not there.

How can we keep Peter's spirit alive in children or help them develop it if it has never come to life? We face a great challenge as we consider reaching out to our lost children and to their parents, many of whom were lost children themselves. And how can we infuse our schools, institutions, and neighborhoods with Peter's welcoming and sunny optimism?

Peter chooses to stay in Never-Never Land, forever a boy; our children grow and become adolescents, then adulthood beckons. Peter felt he could not live in Wendy's world; if he had and grew to manhood, we would like to think that his exuberant spirit would have remained, as a spark of love, laughter, and delight that would infuse his friendships and be shared with his children.

As we turn to explore adult development, we need to remember grown-ups are just that: grown up from kids, and their child past is part of their adult present. Perhaps every grown-up, at least sometimes, wishes for a Never-Never Land to allow them to leave their adult responsibilities behind and run free.

LEARNING EXERCISE

Interview an adolescent (who is not a client or a relative). Discuss his or her view of life, families, friends, school, interests, and plans for the future. How does the adolescent describe his or her ethnic and cultural backgrounds? Do they experience any conflict or stress in relation to this? What are his or her thoughts about problems facing adolescents today?

SUGGESTED READING

Articles

Morrow, D. 1993. Social work with gay and lesbian adolescents. *Social Work* 38: 655-660.

Palombo, J. 2001. The therapeutic process with children with learning disorders. *Psychoanalytic Social Work* 8: 143-168.

Podell, C. 1989. Adolescent mourning: The sudden death of a peer. *Clinical Social Work* 17: 64-78.

Sontag, D. 2002. Who was responsible for Elizabeth Shin? *The New York Times Magazine* April 28: 56-61, 94, 139-140.

Zayas, L. H., C. Kaplan, S. Turner, K. Romano, and G. Gonzalez-Ramos. 2000. Understanding suicide attempts by adolescent Hispanic females. *Social Work* 45: 53-63.

Books

Angelou, M. 1997. *I know why the caged bird sings.* New York: Bantam Books.

Becker, M., and B. Shallgi. 2002. A psychoanalytic approach to integrating family and individual therapy in the treatment of adolescents. In *The psychoanalytic study of the child,* ed. A. J. Solnit, P. B. Neubauer, S. Abrams, and A. S. Dowling, Vol. 48, pp. 203-217. New Haven, CT: Yale University Press.

Canino, I. A., and J. Spurlock. 2000. *Culturally diverse children and adolescents: Assessment, diagnosis and treatment,* 2nd ed. New York: The Guilford Press.

Guterson, D. 1995. *Snow falling on cedars.* New York: Vintage Books.

Miller, J., I. Rodriguez Martin, and G. Schamess (eds.) 2003. *School violence and children in crisis: Community and school interventions for social workers and counselors.* Denver: Love Pub.

Osofsky, J. (ed.) 1997. *Children in a violent society.* New York: The Guilford Press.

Chapter 11

Adult Development

When I was a boy of fourteen, my father was so ignorant I could hardly stand to have the old man around. But when I got to be twenty-one, I was astonished at how much he had learned in seven years.

Mark Twain, *Atlantic Monthly,* 1874

INTRODUCTION

Adolescence had previously been considered the final stage for the consolidation of an individual's psychological development; but today, it is recognized that developmental and psychological changes continue in the adult personality even into late adulthood. This chapter discusses the latter part of the life cycle, from the twenties through midlife into late adulthood. Although characteristics and tasks of each life stage are presented, it is with the understanding that considerable variation exists as to when and how people go through these stages.

Neugarten's (1979) concept of "off-time" and "on-time" events is relevant, as life events today can occur at unexpected times in the life cycle, differing from past patterns; many first-time parents of infants may be in middle adulthood, rather than, as traditionally, in early adulthood; grandparents may be in the role of parenting their grandchildren, and increasingly they attend college or run for political office. Sid Smith, 95 (Verbatim, 2006), a candidate for Congress, commented: "At 95, who needs term limits?" End-of-life issues are faced not only by the elderly, but by children living in neighborhoods pervaded by violence and homicide.

Many social changes have resulted from the recent cultural revolution centered on gender, including the advent of the women's movement, the

Human Behavior in the Social Environment, Second Edition

less-well-publicized men's movement, and the increasing recognition of gays, lesbians, and transgender people; gender is addressed next, to add this perspective to our understanding of the life cycle.

GENDER

Women's issues, including equal rights to education and employment, have been raised as major social concerns especially over the past forty years, resulting in political and legislative advances and effecting changes in society, family, and personal lives. Women's studies, a new field of scholarship, has affected the development of psychological theories by increasing the focus on the psychology of women; in the social work field this has led to new programs, such as services for battered women and rape crisis counseling. Many women feel emancipated from previous restrictions on their lives; some feel they remain oppressed by the stereotyping and prejudice they continue to experience. Some women feel stressed sorting out their priorities, establishing their own identities, and resolving conflicting demands between family and work.

Men have also been affected as they have adapted to changes in the lives and attitudes of women and as they face their own issues. A men's movement as well as an academic field of men's studies have also developed, although on a smaller scale.

Major shifts have also occurred in the recognition and acceptance of people who are gay, lesbian, and transgender; although prejudice and discrimination against these groups persist, the degree of their freedom to declare their identities, find support, and live openly with their declared orientations and with the increasing legal rights they have gained have indeed been dramatic in a relatively short period of time.

Women's Issues

Women's rights and opportunities were limited at the turn of the twentieth century; the lack of suffrage was one major restriction. Women's suffrage, a major achievement of the early women's movement, was codified in the nineteenth amendment to the Constitution in 1919, ending women's political disenfranchisement. Another landmark was the formation of NOW, the National Organization for Women, in 1966 (Longres, 1995b).

> The National Organization for Women adopted a statement of purpose calling for attacks on discrimination in the legal system, employment, and education that had limited women's ability to control their

own lives. In regard to women's role in the family, the statement declared: "We believe that a true partnership between the sexes demands a different concept of marriage, an equitable sharing of the responsibilities of home and children and of the economic burdens of their support." (Longres, 1995b, p. 204)

Career Issues

Dramatic changes have occurred in employment and educational opportunities for women, and although diminishing, sex discrimination persists; men tend to get paid more than women do for the same work (Lewin, 2006a), and a "glass ceiling" is present in some fields, limiting women's advancement (Zastrow and Kirst Ashman, 2004, pp. 334-335). However, large numbers of women are now employed in occupations that were considered traditionally "male" vocations, including construction workers, police officers, pilots, astronauts, doctors, lawyers, judges, and elected political offices. In 2007, Nancy Pelosi was named the first woman Speaker of the House of Representatives, and Senator Hillary Clinton became the first woman of one of the major parties to declare her candidacy for President.

Women are heavily involved in the military in Iraq, and although they are barred by Congress from being involved in actual "offensive warfare," they do assume "'supporting' combat roles" (McGirk, 2006, p. 38). However, the war in Iraq is not a conventional war, and there is no way to draw clear boundaries between combat and noncombat roles.

In response to dwindling military-recruiting numbers and demands by women's groups for more equality between the sexes, the Pentagon, in 1994 loosened the ban and allowed women to take on "supporting" combat roles. In Iraq, that can involve anything from piloting combat helicopters to accompanying infantrymen and Marines on house-to-house raids and searching Iraqi women suspects for pistols and suicide belts. As the insurgency has grown more diffuse, increasing numbers of women are finding themselves in the teeth of combat. (McGirk, 2006, p. 38)

Although some controversy persists, service women have proved themselves competent and are increasingly accepted. "In Iraq's danger zones, officers say, female MP's, medics and pilots have earned the right to be treated as equals" (McGirk, 2006, p. 38); a problem for women soldiers who are mothers is the "trauma of separation from their children. . . . It's particularly trying for new mothers" (p. 43); Internet and webcam services have facilitated communication between family members.

Many mothers outside the military also experience stress related to conflicts between work and family obligations; critics note that employers often do not make sufficient accommodations to meet the needs of working mothers, such as facilitating arrangements for caring for children and for elderly parents (an increasing concern of adult children), offering flexibility when determining the hours of work, and providing parental leaves. There is a growing trend, however, for companies to offer good day care services for children as well as day programs for elderly parents; some companies are flexible about part-time employment, or job sharing (i.e., one job is held by two people on a part-time basis). Political initiatives continue to be proposed to provide paid annual leave for employees to care for young children or relatives who are ill.

Although many mothers are single parents who raise children alone, fathers now have greater involvement in family life and child care than formerly (Crockenberg and Leerkes, 2000; Ross, 1984); there has been an increase in the number of stay-at-home fathers (Overturf Johnson, 2005). Many employed men provide care for their children during the day while their wives work; the fathers then go to work on the night shift.

Women's Developmental and Clinical Issues

Proponents of women's studies have argued that masculine traits have been valued and female traits ignored in the development of psychological theories, and that insufficient attention has been paid to the "development of interdependence, intimacy, nurturance, and contextual thought," which are women's ways of being and knowing (Belenky et al., 1986, pp. 6-7). Gilligan (1982) observed that "sensitivity to the needs of others and the assumption of responsibility for taking care lead women to attend to voices other than their own and to include in their judgment other points of view" (p. 13). Self-in-relation theorists (from the Stone Center at Wellesley College) see women as a group dominated by men and that they have adapted to their inferior position (Berzoff, 1996c).

Is this portrait of women universally true? Are we stereotyping women (as well as men) in these descriptions? During the past fifteen years, postmodern feminist psychoanalytic critiques have questioned some of these assumptions and asked whether these qualities belong to all women, to all cultures, to all ages, and so on? Citing the work of Comas-Diaz in 1994, Berzoff (1996c) asserts that one's identity is more complex than an identity that is based only on gender, just as it is more complex than an identity that is based only on race, ethnicity, or social class. Berzoff (1996c) stresses the importance of the postmodernist point of view in clinical work; although she does not refer specifically to the social work value of individualization, this seems present in her words.

> If we are truly to understand women in clinical work, then we must be able to attend to the difference, the paradox, the ambiguity between and among them. While the concept of difference sparked the very psychology of women, it will be the appreciation of a complex multiplicity of gendered possibilities that will ultimately help our clients, both women and men, achieve their full relational potentials. (Berzoff, 1996c, p. 258)

Two points should be added to Berzoff's comments. One relates to the development of intersubjective sensitivity, involving our understanding of prejudices and biases, so that they do not negatively affect our attunement to clients' feelings. In marital therapy, for example, might a feminist therapist "favor" wives because they are "oppressed" and not see their part in a relationship difficulty?

The second point is that women's generalized anger directed toward men is often accepted as a valid expression of righteous indignation rather than its own form of sexism, and remains unexamined. Although societal injustices to women must be righted, are all men guilty of oppressing women and being insensitive to their needs? Are we engaged in a battle of the sexes? Judith Herman (1997) asserts that this is so when she comments that "the subordinate condition of women is maintained and enforced by the hidden violence of men. There is war between the sexes" (p. 32).

Do women have no hidden violence? Women are known to have rages, to commit child abuse, and to act in other violent ways. Recently, violence in both gay and lesbian relationships has been acknowledged (Carlson and Maciol, 1997; Leland, 2000). "Because of gender-based stereotypes about who becomes a batterer and who becomes a victim, it is often difficult for people to perceive gay men as victims and lesbians as abusers" (Carlson and Maciol, 1997, p. 109).

A final point is the unfounded statement that male theorists have not been concerned with intimacy and attachment. Many serious male leaders in the object relations school including Fairbairn, Winnicott, and Bowlby—Bowlby (1969) devoted an entire book, *Attachment and Loss* to the subject—have focused on these issues. It was Margaret Mahler, a female analyst, who emphasized separation, individuation, and autonomy; but Mahler saw these unfolding within the context of warm, connecting relationships to others. Although criticized for emphasizing autonomy, her overarching concern with relationships has often been overlooked.

In agreeing with Bowlby, Mahler affirmed her recognition that significant interpersonal as well as intrapsychic relationships are essential from birth to death. We wish to highlight this point for there are those who have understood Mahler as valuing independence, self-reliance and autonomy to the exclusion of object need and connection. From our readings of Mahler's writings and our talks with her, we understand separation-individuation theory as acknowledging a common human need for others as well as a need for autonomy. (Edward, Ruskin, and Turrini, 1992, pp. xxii-xxiii)

If indeed a battle of the sexes is going on, how are men being affected?

Men's Issues

When men's issues are discussed, they do not center on societal oppression, as women's issues often do, but rather on society's changing constructions of manliness and the issues surrounding this (Lichtenberg, 1995); greater recognition is also being given to men in their role as fathers (discussed in Chapter 7). Attention has also focused on the fact that definitions and roles of masculinity can vary by class, race, ethnicity, and culture (Lichtenberg, 1995), and men as well as women feel stress related to their own sexual roles (Germain, 1991). Men are entering fields that have been traditionally women's fields, such as nursing; some men are successfully employed as "Super Mannies" [nannies] (Barovick, 2002, p. F12).

It has been asserted that men have been acculturated to develop a "macho" image, which includes emphasis on characteristics such as aggression, domination, and physical prowess, while sensitivity, emotionality, and asking for help are frowned on; but men also have a capacity to experience intimacy (Lichtenberg, 1995). Although it has been argued that women seek psychotherapy more often than men (often put forward in support of the idea that women have more problems because they are "oppressed" by men), men are no less likely to have psychological problems but may have more difficulty asking for help.

Attention has focused on unequal opportunities for women regarding education and career paths; however, men's increasing failure to make use of available educational opportunities is a growing problem. Although more men currently attend college and graduate than they had been twenty years ago (Lewin, 2006a), colleges, which had been "dominated by males are becoming the place where the boys are not" (Lewin, 1998a, p. 1). Currently, "what is beyond dispute is that the college landscape is changing. Women now make up 58 percent of those enrolled in two- and four-year colleges and are, over all, the majority in graduate schools and professional schools too" (Lewin, 2006a, p. 18). Generally, women are found to take college work more seriously, study more, achieve higher grades, and complete their degrees; men from low income groups, and who are black and Hispanic, often do not attend college (Lewin, 2006a). Arthur Levine, the president of Columbia University Teachers College, stated that "we need to be concerned that higher education is losing poor and minority men, that more African-American men are going to prison than to college" (Lewin, 1998a, p. 38).

Men's violence toward women, including wife battering, rape, and sexual harassment, has come under much greater scrutiny as a result of the women's movement. Actually, male violence is directed more often toward other men than toward women (Lichtenberg, 1995), but such violence is usually between physical equals. Violence has been viewed as a consequence of insecure feelings about one's masculinity (Lichtenberg, 1995). Self-help programs and group therapy for men who are violent toward women have been increasing. Issues addressed in these groups include feelings of sexual insecurity, unmet dependency needs, and feelings of isolation (Lichtenberg, 1995).

Zosky (2005) has questioned the feminist perspective that asserts that men's violence to women is primarily a societal phenomenon based on the premise that "men are acculturated into roles of power and women are urged to adopt roles of passivity" (p. 44). If this were so, she asks, why aren't all men abusive, rather than only a small minority of men? She stresses the importance, when working on a clinical level with these men, of utilizing object relations, attachment, and developmental theories, especially Mahler's theory of separation/individuation, in order to gain the greatest insight; "men who experience disruptions in nurturing during critical phases of the separation-individuation process may later manifest intrapsychic deficits that result in their engagement in domestic violence" (p. 44). While acknowledging the presence of violence and abuse in their early lives, she emphasizes the impact of early "developmental ruptures" and their inability "to achieve object constancy" (p. 56), and suggests that "treatment providers should consider the possibility that clients are acting-out patterns of behavior based on early, internalized working models" (p. 57).

Discussions of sexual abuse often refer to female abuse, perpetrated by men; the fact that many male abusers were also victims of sexual abuse themselves as children has come to light. The full scope of male sexual abuse is not known because it tends to remain underreported (Cermak and Molidor, 1996). Although sexual abuse can have serious psychological effects on girls and women, it can also have serious psychological consequences for boys and men later in life (Cermak and Molidor, 1996; Nasjleti, 1980).

In a study of male adolescent sexual abusers, it was found that many had been sexually victimized as children; "the majority of treatment programs in North America address sexual victimization of their clients" (Burton, 2003, p. 277). Although not all boys who have been abused become abusers, certain characteristics of the severity of their abuse can predict later abusive behavior (Burton, 2003).

Specifically, a youth was twenty-three times as likely to be in the sexually abusive group if the following conditions were present: the youth was abused by both men and women, the perpetrator was related to him, the perpetrator used a forceful modus operandi (MO), the youth was abused over several years, and the acts included penetration (Burton, 2003, p. 279).

Although boys are usually victimized by men, sexual abuse of boys has also been committed by women; " 'boys are more likely than girls to be abused by women (20 percent vs. 5 percent) . . . , and 40 percent of the reported cases of day care sexual abuse involve female offenders' (Berliner and Elliott, 2002, pp. 56-57)" (Zastrow and Kirst-Ashman, 2004, p. 178); professionals must be aware of this often-hidden problem of sexually abused boys (Cermak and Molidor, 1996); "feminists may have unintentionally done a disservice to the male victims" who might have been overlooked because of the primary focus on the "plight of all *female* victims . . . this oversight may have had the effect of re-victimizing these boys" (p. 398; italics in the original).

Gay, Lesbian, and Transgender Adults

Lesbian Women and Gay Men

There are approximately 5 million gay men and 5 million lesbian women in this country (Vitello, 2006); generally, men use the term *gay,* while women prefer to be called *lesbian;* male homosexuality is a term in disfavor by the gay movement, whose members have "adopted the slogan 'gay is good' and emphasized a newly found self-pride" (Berger and Kelly, 1995, p. 1064). Gay men and lesbian women can also be members of ethnic and cultural groups, whose competing value systems and discrimination may cause stress; gay men and lesbian women may find discrimination against them in both their own racial and ethnic communities as well as in the gay community (Adams Jr. and Kimmel, 1997; Alquijay, 1997; Berger and Kelly, 1995; Chan, 1997).

Lesbians and gays can be exposed to overt rejection and discrimination, but sometimes prejudices are expressed in more subtle interpersonal ways; this may lead to the development of *internalized homophobia,* that is, they have internalized the negative feelings directed toward them by people in our culture, as other minority groups who face ongoing discrimination have done (Berger and Kelly, 1995, Tully, 1995). In addition, just like everyone else gays and lesbians must cope with the general array of life issues, such as parenting problems and dealing with their own elderly parents; they may face the tendency of some therapists to reduce all of their problems to their homosexuality rather than help them with other concerns.

A major battle fought by the gay and lesbian communities has been with the psychiatric establishment, which classified homosexuality as a mental disorder until 1973; it was then accepted as one lifestyle and means of sexual expression among many, rather than a mental disorder (Kaplan, Sadock, and Grebb, 1994).

Many psychoanalysts for more than ten years after this decision continued to describe "homosexuality as a 'perversion', and analysts continued to speak of their ability to 'cure' the 'serious character disorders' of their gay patients" (in essence, to change them to heterosexuals) (Goode, 1998b, p. A19). Viewing homosexuality as an illness, the analytic societies refused to admit homosexual applicants to training institutes—a situation that has since drastically changed.

The situation of lesbian women and gay men in the United States today reveals dramatic gains in greater acceptance, more openness, and recognition of many of their legal rights, although there are still struggles and continuing conflicts. Controversies and advances related to civil unions, gay marriages, and gay adoptions are discussed in Chapter 7, reproductive issues in Chapter 9, gay and lesbian teenagers in Chapter 10, gay and lesbian elderly later in this chapter, and HIV/AIDS in Chapter 13.

Transgenderism and Transsexualism

A gay male identifies himself as a man and a lesbian identifies herself as a woman; both feel sexual attraction to members of their own sex. A *bisexual* person is sexually attracted to members of both sexes but may or may not have sexual relations with people of both sexes. However, some people feel that they have been born the wrong sex; they feel deeply (and desperately) that they should have been the opposite sex, and many take measures to correct this situation. Jan Morris (1997), a writer who was born male, is now a woman after hormonal and surgical treatment. She recalls that at about three or perhaps four years of age she "realized that I had been born into the wrong body, and should really be a girl" (Morris, 1997, p. 11). Transsexualism, in Morris's (1997) view, is not a "sexual mode or preference . . . not an act of sex at all," but a "passionate, lifelong, ineradicable conviction," of which "no true trans-sexual has ever been disabused" (p. 15). Consequently, until middle adulthood, a "sexual purpose dominated, distracted, and tormented my life: the tragic and irrational ambition, instinctively formulated but deliberately pursued, to escape . . . into womanhood" (pp. 16-17).

Transgender is the umbrella term used to encompass the spectrum of people who range from "cross-dressers (those who dress in clothes of the opposite sex) to transsexuals (those who surgically 'correct' their genitals to match their 'real' gender)" (Cloud, 1998, p. 48). The phenomenon of transgenderism is historically worldwide (Lesser, 1999). Some transgender people have partially altered their sexual appearances with hormone treatments, electrolysis, clothing, or partial surgery. George Jorgensen became Christine Jorgensen in 1952, at the beginning of this movement for men; women didn't become involved until about ten years ago, when the surgery, which is more complicated for them, became available (Vitello, 2006).

Harry Benjamin popularized the term *transsexual* in his book *The Transsexual Phenomenon,* which was published in 1966; the term subsequently received "medical-psychological status" (Lesser, 1999). Lesser cites the four criteria Benjamin ascribed to transsexuals: the first is "a lifelong gender dysphoria" (which is extreme misery with one's given gender); the second criteria involves "major disruption of identity development with resultant personal adjustment problems"; followed by seeking an actual sex change through treatment by means of hormone therapy and surgery; and, finally, engaging in cross-dressing (p. 182).

The request for sexual transformation surgery initially caused considerable controversy in the medical community, and a protocol, established by Benjamin, for medical intervention has been developed; compliance with its mandates is required before sexual surgery will be performed. These include "a psychiatric evaluation, endocrinological screening, and a two-year, real life test in the preferred gender" (Lesser, 1999, p. 183).

Transsexuals have experienced prejudice and discrimination similar to that experienced by homosexuals, including hate crimes and murders (Goldberg, 1999b); sometimes they have experienced discrimination by gays. The transsexual author and activist Riki Anne Wilchins, who considered herself lesbian, found that "gay and feminist groups long rejected her as not a 'real woman' and thus not a 'real lesbian'" (p. A27). Generally, gay men are more accepting of men becoming women than lesbian women are of women becoming men; some lesbian women see this change as a betrayal of feminism (Vitello, 2006). "In private conversations and in public forums like women's colleges, the questions about how to frame the relationship among lesbians, former lesbians and young women who call themselves 'gender queer' rather than lesbian at all, seem largely unresolved" (Vitello, 2006).

As the gay movement became mainstream, "it jettisoned transgenders as too off-putting" (Cloud, 1998, p. 48). Anger was expressed by transgenders against the Human Rights Campaign (the largest gay lobbying group in the country), which opposed including them in the Employment Nondiscrimination Act. However, greater rapport has developed between these groups, and transgenders have been building their own political power, with a lobbying group called Gender PAC (Public Advocacy Coalition), in Washington.

New laws in many states have helped transgenders, such as changing the sexual classification on their birth certificates so that documents such as driver's licenses and passports "can reflect reality" (Cloud, 1998, p. 49). Some businesses have added nondiscriminatory clauses to protect their employment rights, and a number of cities (as well as the state of Minnesota) have protections in place against housing and employment discrimination.

New York City, in 2006, had proposed and considered a plan to be adopted by the city's Board of Health to allow people to change their gender identification on their birth certificate without having had sex-change surgery or any other type of medical intervention (Cave, 2006). This proposal came after four years of deliberation.

> It is an outgrowth of the transgender community's push to recognize that some people may not have money to get a sex-change operation, while others may not feel the need to undergo the procedure and are simply defining themselves as members of the opposite sex. While it may be a radical notion elsewhere, New York City has often tolerated such blurring of the lines of gender identity. (Cave. 2006)

On December 5, 2006, the New York City Board of Health did in fact approve "the Health Department's proposal to allow transgender individuals to acquire new birth certificates reflecting their acquired sex" only for those who "had made a full gender transition—whether surgical or medical—and expected to remain permanently in the newly acquired gender," but not yet for those who for whom it was simply a matter of choice (Board of Health, 2006).

STAGES OF ADULT DEVELOPMENT

Adult development is generally classified into three stages: early (from about ages twenty-two to forty); middle (ages forty to sixty); and late adulthood (from age sixty to the end of life). Each life stage can bring its rewards and strains and presents opportunities for further psychological development.

A major controversy concerns the theory of *continuous development,* as opposed to the theory of *discontinuity.* Proponents of continuous development believe that childhood psychodynamics and behaviors remain throughout adulthood. Discontinuity advocates insist that longitudinal research studies demonstrate that discontinuity prevails during adulthood (Cohler and Galatzer-Levy, 1990); that is, people change, and personalities are not fixed in permanent patterns; life events (including unpredictable events) play a critical part in personality development (Cohler and Galatzer-Levy, 1990).

I would suggest that both continuities and discontinuities are present in a person's life that become apparent when a person's life-cycle progressions and regressions, resilience and vulnerabilities, as well as underlying patterns of attachment and relationships are examined. As we study any individual we must individualize that unique person in terms of past history, including development of self-esteem, cohesion of self, ego functioning, defenses, coping mechanisms, and adaptation, in addition to significant themes in the person's life narrative. *A major criterion of mental health is the capacity to grow and to change.* The biopsychosocial perspective is essential in examining the life course, as individuals, with their biologically given attributes and deficits and their level of psychological development, interact with their environments (physical, cultural, political, and social). From an ecological perspective (Germain, 1991), both person and environment affect and change each other. The stages of adult development are presented in this chapter within this perspective.

Levinson's Life Course

Erikson (1963) received recognition for adding the perspective of adult development to child development studies; however, while underscoring the interaction of people and their environments, Erikson "leaves the mechanisms of development, as opposed to the content, essentially unexamined" (Stevens-Long, 1990, p. 138). Levinson and colleagues (1978) and Levinson and Levinson (1996), by contrast, were interested in the processes of adult development; they did not think that development took place the way our four-year-old (in Chapter 9) described it: "I used to be a little baby. Then I closed my eyes, and when I opened them up—all of a sudden I was a kid!"

Levinson (1986) discusses the life course, which describes the characteristics of a life in its "evolution from beginning to end" (p. 3). This evolution "involves stability and change, *continuity and discontinuity,* orderly progression as well as stasis, and chaotic flux" (Levinson, 1986, p. 3; italics added). Levinson and colleagues' (1978) original landmark study involved men; the second study (Levinson and Levinson, 1996) focused on the lives of women; "both genders go through the same periods of adult life structure development just as they go through the same periods of infancy and adolescence" (Levinson and Levinson, 1996, p. 36), but there are large differences in "life circumstances, in life course, in ways of going through each developmental period" (p. 36).

Each phase of the life cycle is an "era," which "has its own bio-psycho-social character" (Levinson and Levinson, 1996, p. 17). These eras overlap; "a new era begins as the previous one approaches its end. A *cross-era transition,* which generally lasts about five years, terminates the outgoing era and initiates the next" (p. 19). Levinson and Levinson's (1996) "key concept" is the "life structure: the underlying pattern or design of a person's life at a given time" (p. 22). They explain that "the primary components of a life structure are the person's *relationships* with various others in the external world" (p. 22). The life structure is not static but changes during life-cycle successions. Their research concern was with "how various aspects of self and world influence the formation of a life structure and shape its change over time" (Levinson et al., 1978, p. 42).

> A life structure may have few or many components. The *central components* are those that have the greatest significance for the self and the life. They receive the greatest share of one's time and energy, and they strongly influence the character of the other components. Only one or two components—rarely as many as three—occupy a central place in the structure. The *peripheral components* are easier to change or detach. (Levinson and Levinson, 1996, p. 23; italics in the original)

Levinson and Levinson (1996) also include people's concerns about what *does not* happen. What Schlossberg (1981) calls a "non-event," Levinson and Levinson (1996) refer to as "important *unfilled components:* a person urgently wants but doesn't have a meaningful occupation, a marriage, or a family; and this absent component plays a major part in the life structure" (p. 23; italics in the original). Family (including extended family) and occupation are usually major components of people's lives. "Underlying and permeating all relationships with the external world is the relationship to the self" (p. 24).

In addition to changes in the life structure over time, significant events in life also occur, such as a birth or an illness, which Levinson and colleagues (1978) refer to as "marker events," and they "are usually considered in terms of the adaptation they require" (p. 55).

Levinson (1986) predicts that the study of the life course will develop into an interdisciplinary field, because of the inseparability of people from their life situations and vice versa. He expresses concern that "each discipline has claimed as its special domain one aspect of life, such as personality, social role, or biological functioning, and has neglected the others"; he has observed that "the resulting fragmentation is so great that no discipline or viewpoint conveys the sense of an individual life and its temporal course" (p. 4).

Early Adulthood

The years from seventeen to twenty-two span the early adult transition, "a developmental period in which the era of childhood draws to a close and early adulthood gets under way" (Levinson and Levinson, 1996, p. 19). The early adulthood era itself begins at twenty-two and ends in the forties, during which life changes are made, and responsibilities assumed. Erikson terms this (1963) the stage of "intimacy versus isolation" and emphasizes the young adult's readiness for "intimacy, that is, the capacity to commit himself to concrete affiliations and partnerships and to develop the ethical strength to abide by such commitments, even though they may call for significant sacrifices and compromises" (p. 263). Intimacy has another significant dimension, which is permitting another to get physically and emotionally close to one's vulnerable self; this seems relevant in understanding the fears of intimacy that are so prevalent today, both in "normal" people and in people with actual psychopathology.

Erikson has been criticized for his exclusive emphasis on the intimacy of heterosexual relationships; however, his underlying principles apply to many homosexual relationships, such as commitment and the integration of sexuality, trust, and mutuality within the relationship; the strong advocacy by many for recognition of homosexual marriages speaks to this point. Erikson's emphasis on procreation during this stage is also a priority of many gays and lesbians who become parents biologically or through adoption or fostering (discussed in Chapter 7).

Today, however, with the great diversity of lifestyles, people may not choose ongoing intimate relationships to have their needs met; many can have other types of rich relationships and lifestyles without feeling isolated. Levinson and Levinson (1996), when talking about the life structure, mention activities, books, and even locations with which people become involved. One might question whether a life that avoids intimacy lacks something essential to complete fulfillment.

Erikson (1963) cites Freud who when asked "what he thought a normal person should be able to do well . . . was reported to have said 'Lieben und arbeiten' (to love and to work)" (p. 265). Erikson (1963) feels that "we cannot improve on the professor's formula" (p. 265). Levinson and colleagues (1978) also emphasize occupation, marriage, and family, "although there are significant variations in their relative weight and in the importance of other components" (p. 44). When Levinson and Levinson (1996) speak of the family, they include the extended family and observe that "the relationship to family is also interwoven with the relationship to ethnicity, race, occupation, cultural traditions" (p. 23).

Early adulthood is the era "of greatest energy and abundance and of greatest contradiction and stress" (Levinson, 1986, p. 5).

> Biologically, the 20s and 30s are the peak years of the life cycle. In social and psychological terms, early adulthood is the season for forming and pursuing youthful aspirations, establishing a niche in society, raising a family, and as the era ends, reaching a more "senior" position in the adult world. This can be a time of rich satisfaction in terms of love, sexuality, family life, occupational advancement, creativity, and realization of major life goals. But there can also be crushing stresses. (Levinson, 1986, p. 5)

Economic pressures and the need to make difficult choices are among the stresses faced by young adults; this is also a time when "we are most buffeted by our own passions and ambitions from within and by the demands of family, community and society from without" (Levinson, 1986, p. 5).

Systemic stresses may include lack of opportunities (such as high unemployment rates), discrimination, lack of adequate housing, economic problems, and living in violent neighborhoods. Family stresses encompass marital (and partner) conflict, sexual incompatibility, infertility, parent-child conflict, and problems with extended families. Divorce, a process that can be very painful and stressful, is a common occurrence.

Young adults may struggle with unresolved identity issues and attachment and self-esteem problems; they can become depressed and/or involved with substance abuse; this is also the period when schizophrenia tends to develop. Although men and women have the same rates of schizophrenia, men usually become schizophrenic at earlier ages (sometimes starting in adolescence) than women. Over 50 percent of male schizophrenic patients were hospitalized for schizophrenia before they were twenty-five. Most men develop this disorder between ages ten and twenty-five, while women generally develop schizophrenia between ages twenty-five and thirty-five (Sadock and Sadock, 2003).

Cognitive Development

Cognitive abilities continue to develop beyond the formal operations stage achieved in adolescence, although some adults never achieve the formal operations stage; as Piaget (1995b) noted, many adults remain "egocentric in their way of thinking" (p. 95). Michael Basseches postulated that *"dialectical thinking"* is a fifth (postformal) stage of cognitive development, beyond Piaget's formal operations, which develops in adulthood; it leads to a cognitive stance that acknowledges the role of conflict or contradiction in life (Stevens-Long, 1990, p. 131). The appreciation of *contradiction* and *paradox* is essential to the development of postformal or dialectical thought.

> Contradiction and paradox hold special interest. . . . Basseches believes that dialectical thought seeks contradictions among systems as a positive source for understanding change. Contradiction or paradox is not experienced as an unfortunate problem, but as an exciting opportunity for the emergence of a new idea. Basseches claims that the dialectical thinker understands how every effort to organize or systematize knowledge omits something—something that will eventually threaten the system with contradictions and create change. (Stevens-Long, 1990, p. 131)

Levinson (1986), reflecting a similar viewpoint, commented that:

> In studying the development of the life structure, we are not yet wise enough about life to say with precision that one life structure is developmentally higher, or more advanced, than another. We still know very little about the complexities and contradictions of the human life course. (p. 10)

Play in Adult Development

Colarusso (1993) reminds us to consider the role of play in adult development; it is as important in this phase as it was in childhood; as life becomes more complex, "play becomes an indirect approach to seeking an adaptive, defensive, skill-acquiring, and creative expression. It is a mode of coping with conflicts, demands, deprivation, loss, and developmental yearnings throughout the life cycle" (pp. 225-226). A close relationship exists between play and creativity; Noam (1996) views creativity "as an expression of the inner self taking the person into ever new, often surprising directions. . . . Wherever pursued, it always implies a deepening sense of awareness and curiosity, the most important counterforces to repetition and stagnation" (p. 152). Vaillant (1993) describes creativity as the "peculiarly human capacity for putting in the world what was not there before . . . [it] seems closely interwoven with the alchemy of the ego to bring order and meaning out of chaos and distress" (p. 2).

Play also involves the capacity to have fun—to be able to return, at least for a little while, to never-never land and enjoy it. This is related to the capacity for autonomous gratification (discussed in Chapter 2): being able to relax, to take pleasure in life, in one's body, and in one's sexuality, and in a variety of relationships to others. The ability to play (in action) and to enjoy playing (in feeling) adds to one's pleasure in life; this can, for example, help a person adapt to retirement and feel entitled to enjoy it (Bakalar, 2006b); the absence of the capacity to play and experience pleasure is found in schizophrenia and depression, discussed in Chapter 14.

The ability to laugh with others and to laugh at oneself is another aspect of play. Humor, as Witkin (1999) points out, is generally missing in the social work literature, although it may be "making a comeback" (p. 101). In discussing relational psychotherapy in Chapter 4, the genuineness of the therapeutic relationship was highlighted; the careful use of humor in clinical work is one significant way to "humanize" the relationship, which may help establish for the client that he or she can contribute enjoyably to a social give-and-take.

Humor may "strengthen the immune system and act as a buffer against stress. Laughter . . . is a social lubricant" (Witkin, 1999, p. 101). Humor, with its healing functions, has been found to be effective with seriously sick children; for example, clowns are now part of some pediatric services. To a pediatrician who complained that clowns do not belong in intensive care units, one clown retorted: Neither do children!

Witkin (1999) cites Siporin, who states that laughter allows people to "'have fun, to grow, to be free and human, to celebrate one's own life with the fellow members of one's community'" (p. 101). Humor is also a defense mechanism (Chapter 2) that can help people handle stress or conflict by draining the seriousness from situations and by providing an alternative and usually safe way of discharging tension, often with some element of hostility or aggression. "We all recognize that humor makes life so much easier. . . . Freud suggested [humor] 'can be regarded as the highest of these defensive processes'" (Vaillant, 1993, p. 72).

Sexuality

That sexuality is an intrinsic part of adulthood states the obvious; sexuality is not compartmentalized within the person but is closely interrelated to the whole personality (Kaplan, Sadock, and Grebb, 1994). Although sex outside of an extended relationship is not uncommon, many young adults seek marriage or long-term partnerships in which emotional and sexual intimacy are interrelated.

Sexual problems related to psychological, biological, or relationship difficulties frequently trouble young people; these factors are often interrelated. Although sex permeates our culture through movies, magazines, and television, personal communication about a couple's own sexual relationship is often lacking between partners. Sex can be a sensitive subject, tied up with taboos as well as deep feelings involving self-esteem and shame. "Performance anxiety" is not uncommonly a causal (sometimes *the* causal) factor in some sexual problems. Masters and Johnson in 1970, in their landmark study *Human Sexual Inadequacy,* described the problem of *"spectatoring"* (Scharff and Scharff, 1991, p. 28; italics in the original).

> In [spectatoring] a man stands outside himself looking on at his erectile difficulty, anxious lest his erection fail, thus precipitating its failure because of this anxiety. The concept of spectatoring is an important contribution to understanding the way anxiety about the situation contributes, as an independent factor with a life of its own, to sexual failure. (Scharff and Scharff, 1991, p. 28)

Certainly women, too, may be preoccupied with their sexual performance.

Physical and medical factors should be evaluated by a physician as part of understanding a client's (and a couple's) sexual difficulties. Substance abuse, for example, can affect sexual functioning in many ways, and serious "sexual dysfunction occurs within a month of significant substance intoxication or withdrawal" (Kaplan, Sadock, and Grebb, 1994, p. 669).

Physiological factors that can contribute to male dysfunction include genitourinary tract surgery; "Parkinson's disease and other neurological disorders involving the lumbar or sacral sections of the spinal cord . . . [and] Prozac [is one of the drugs] implicated in retarded ejaculation" (Kaplan, Sadock, and Grebb, 1994, p. 668). Women's sexual responses can be affected by endocrine diseases such as hypothyroidism, diabetes mellitus, and endometriosis; drugs including antihypertensive medications, central nervous system (CNS) stimulants, and tricyclic drugs (Kaplan, Sadock, and Grebb, 1994). People with physical disabilities may experience a variety of sexual dysfunctions. "A key issue is the absence of discussion about sex and disability" (Olkin, 1999, p. 226).

> Texts on sexuality barely acknowledge disability. . . . Conversely, it is startling how many books on disability do not discuss sexuality, or do so only cursorily. Much is still unknown about the interaction of disability and sexuality. [When discussed], the focus usually is on adults with acquired disabilities.

> However, ignoring persons with congenital disabilities reinforces the prevailing myth that such persons are asexual, as if early onset of a disability prevents healthy psychosexual development. Furthermore, information for two partners with disabilities is virtually nonexistent and quite scant for gay or lesbian relationships with disabilities. (Olkin, 1999, pp. 226-227)

Olkin (1999) refers to the journal *Sexuality and Disability* as the major contributor of professional writing on this subject and adds that "a sizable proportion of the literature is about the mechanics of sex . . . to the neglect of psychosocial and interpersonal factors" (p. 227).

Psychological and interpersonal factors, such as attachment difficulties, can be the primary cause of sexual conflict. Writer Anton Chekhov was sexually impotent only when relationships with women became emotionally significant and veered toward permanency (Rayfield, 1997). A history of childhood abuse—especially sexual abuse—can lead to adult sexual problems (Cruz and Essen, 1994).

> Some victims tend to act out sexually, which may contribute to compulsive sexual involvement, indiscriminate, numerous sexual partners, and/or sexual preoccupations; while at the other extreme, some patients might avoid sexual contact and manifest sexual difficulties such as sexual inhibition, arousal problems, low or nonexistent sexual desire, or fear of sex. Problems with achieving orgasms or erections, flashbacks, numbing or pain during sexual intercourse, or feelings of guilt, shame, or anxiety during sex are all too common with some survivors. (Cruz and Essen, 1994, p. 141)

Sexual dysfunction can cause depression; conversely, depression itself can be the root of sexual dysfunction; depression affects both mood and body, with distressing mixed *mood-based* and *vegetative* symptoms (Kaplan, Sadock, and Grebb, 1994). At the end of Chapter 1, the case of Mrs. Billings, hospitalized for depression was discussed, highlighting the interweaving of her psychological distress, the couple's sexual problems, and their relationship difficulties. Low sexual interest or *hypoactive sexual desire,* which was one of Mrs. Billing's problems, is experienced by many (American Psychiatric Association, 1994; Kaplan, Sadock, and Grebb, 1994; Scharff and Scharff, 1991). Determining the *baseline* of this disorder is important, as it can be a chronic problem or one of recent onset related to emotional distress, marital problems, and/or a physical condition. "Decreased desire is one of the disorders that exists most frequently at the interface between sexual and marital difficulty" (Scharff and Scharff, 1991, p. 29).

Gay, lesbian, bisexual, and transgender couples also develop sexual problems in their relationships, as varied as those presented by heterosexual couples; these problems also need to be assessed within a biopsychosocial framework.

Family Development

Varieties of family organizations were discussed in Chapter 7, and internal structural organization of family life in Chapter 8. Becoming a parent, and separation-individuation issues are addressed in the following section.

Parenthood as a developmental phase. Becoming a parent can be a transforming psychological experience. Children have added richness and pleasure to many lives, evoked a special love, and provided the opportunity to participate in a child's evolution from babyhood to adulthood.

At the same time, parents often undergo more subtle internal personality changes. Benedek (1970) refers to the parents' "emotional investment in the child [which] brings about *reciprocal intrapsychic processes in the parents* which normally account for developmental changes in their personalities" (p. 124; italics added). Elson (1984) suggests that the

> factors impinging upon the parent-child relationship are reciprocal and complex. The child influences the parent to nearly the same extent that the parent influences the child. This is the unique significance of the simultaneous ongoing process of the self experience in parents and children. (p. 302)

Ross (1984) discusses the changes in a father's identity as he assumes a "parental identity" (p. 382), which can lead to progressive or regressive changes in personality. (Ross utilizes the popular Piagetian concepts of assimilation and accommodation in his description.)

> They *assimilate* images of their children and of themselves as parents with the available structures of their existing personality and in turn

accommodate to the repeated novelties occasioned by parenthood. In the face of these inner and outer demands, fathers may be thrust toward higher levels of identity organization. Or else they may capitulate, regress, or simply retreat from their newfound generational status. (Ross, 1984, p. 382; italics added)

Ross (1984) emphasizes how a father's psychological reactions can shift in relation to the changes in the child's developmental stages and their evolving interactions. The

subtle psychological changes within the adult resonate with the more visible upheavals in the child's momentous emotional growth. Thus, in order to comprehend the child's and father's relation to each other, one must glimpse at least the dialectical nature of their multifaceted, ongoing interaction. (Ross, 1984, p. 382)

Ross's observations about fathers apply equally to mothers.

Parenthood affects the marital relationship, necessitating changes in the couple's lifestyle and relationship. No longer can a couple devote their primary attention to each other; the new child becomes the focus of concern. For many, parenthood is a joyful experience and can deepen the marital relationship. However, the adaptations required and the new demands on money, time, and occupational constraints can create strain, as can the requirement for emotional giving (when one or both parents possess limited emotional resources, a rivalry with the infant may develop, sometimes with disastrous consequences). Researchers studying marital relationships longitudinally have noted a general decline in marital satisfaction during parenthood; "generally the changes involved in rearing children and the accompanying stresses have been hypothesized as the reasons for that regression" (Mackey and O'Brien, 1999, p. 587). The stresses often involved in being a single parent can affect parent-child interactions and may complicate or thwart parental developmental progression.

Separation-individuation in young adulthood. The separation-individuation process continues throughout the life cycle (Mahler, Pine, and Bergman, 1975). Blos (1962) has observed adolescents going through a second individuation process, and Akhtar (1995) described a third individuation process occurring in people during the immigration experience.

Colarusso's (1997) concept of a third individuation process relates to parenthood; there is a "continuous process of elaboration of self and differentiation from objects that occur in young adulthood, focusing in particular on involvements with children, spouse and parents" (pp. 77-78).

Separation-individuation dilemmas permeate young adulthood, whether or not one becomes a parent; a progression usually evolves toward separation from parents, the development of greater autonomy, and achievement of a more integrated sense of identity. Many young adults and their parents successfully adapt to the changes in their relationship, although separation can be both an internal and interpersonal struggle, and include parents' attempts to control, be possessive, or become preoccupied with the lives of their adult children; young adults, in turn, may cling, often turning excessively to parents for emotional and financial support and advice.

Young adults' relationships to their parents are also colored by their choice of a spouse or partner. Although parental response may be positive, it is not unusual for tensions to develop in this arena, as in-laws can object or relate negatively to the partner or spouse on the basis of race, ethnicity, social class, sexual orientation, educational achievement, earning capacity, personality, their own internal conflicts, or the way this relationship alters their involvement with their children.

Cultural values shape one's adaptation to adulthood and parenthood. In Asian families, as discussed earlier, interdependency is strongly valued within the family rather than independence (Wong and Mock, 1997). Education is often emphasized (especially for males), and parents may exert a strong influence on educational and career choices, discourage early dating, and oppose interracial relationships. However, Asian Americans "like all young adults . . . may begin to see young adulthood as a means to achieve physical and psychological distance from the family" (p. 197). Variations exist in their response to separation-individuation and family loyalties.

> Like most young adults, Asians experience a consolidation of their identity and values during this period. Some may question their own adherence to familial values. Some may stay closely allied to family values. . . . At the other extreme, some may not associate primarily with other Asians, unconsciously rejecting their family. Some Asians report having a "dual identity" defined by specific context. When they are at home, they are Asian ethnic identified . . . as per parental expectations. When they are away, this identity may be suppressed, and they may represent themselves as more Americanized. (Wong and Mock, 1997, p. 197)

Achieving parenthood may consolidate the young adult's sense of adulthood, and relationships with parents may enter a new phase, as grandparents accept the adulthood of their offspring and share in the joy of a new child; it may be a time of "fence mending," as old conflicts fade in the midst of the excitement of participating in a new life. Parenthood can also be a time of renewed conflict, when grandparents not only refuse to let go, but become more involved and controlling of their grandchildren and how they are raised (see Norris case in Chapter 8). If grandparents become primary caretakers of children, the ground becomes fertile for an intensification of parental conflict for adult children; a complicated course of continued identity development and individuation may ensue.

Development at Midlife

Midlife spans the ages from forty to sixty-five. Although physical capacities may gradually decline, most people are capable of leading an "energetic, personally satisfying and socially valuable life" (Levinson, 1986, p. 6). Erikson (1963) terms this the "generativity versus stagnation" phase; midlife is the "central" stage of development, because "generativity encompasses the evolutionary development which has made man the teaching and instituting as well as the learning animal" (p. 260). Generativity is "the concern in establishing and guiding the next generation" (pp. 260-261); without the motivation and capacity to do this, Erikson observes, there is often a "pervading sense of stagnation and personal impoverishment" (p. 261).

During midlife people often reflect on their life and progress and may, as a result, become more mature, creative, responsible, and loving (Levinson, 1986). Kaplan, Sadock, and Grebb (1994) acknowledge the pressures and depressions that may develop but believe that midlife can be a positive time. Levinson (1986), crediting Erikson, also emphasizes generativity and responsibility "for the development of the current generation of young adults" (p. 6), observing that many people "become 'senior members' in [their] own particular worlds, however grand or modest they may be" (p. 6). Levinson and colleagues (1978), however, see stagnation (which Erikson views in negative terms) as having positive attributes, commenting that "both generativity and its opposite pole, stagnation, are vital in a [person's] development" (Levinson et al., 1978, p. 30). The fight against stagnation is part of the developmental struggle that leads to the recognition of vulnerability in the self and "becomes a source of wisdom, empathy and compassion for others" (p. 30).

Levinson and colleagues (1978) also comment that "unfortunately, middle adulthood is for many persons a time of progressive decline—of growing emptiness and loss of vitality" (p. 20). People can experience internal conflict and external pressure in midlife; sometimes an interaction of both occurs. There are an increasing number of midlife men who are not working; "millions of men [about '13 percent'] . . . in the prime of their lives, between

30 and 55—have dropped out of regular work"; although jobs are available, these men cannot find work comparable to what they have done in the past, and they refuse employment that undervalues their qualifications (Uchitelle and Leonhardt, 2006, p. A1). Although most of these men had been blue-collar workers, the numbers of those who have had high level positions involving Internet and managerial experiences have increased. These men manage financially through disability insurance, severance packages, employment of other family members, and borrowing against the value of their homes. There are also about 2 million former prisoners (between ages thirty and forty) looking for work, but are largely unsuccessful because of their prison background (Uchitelle and Leonhardt, 2006).

At the same time women's employment rate is increasing, and as noted earlier, more women are receiving higher education and entering professional schools.

There is also a decline in the number of midlife men who are married, especially those who did not graduate from college (Porter and O'Donnell, 2006).

> Once, virtually all Americans had married by their mid-40s. Now, many American men without college degrees find themselves still single as they approach middle age. . . . The decline in marriage can be traced to many factors, experts say, including the greater economic independence of women and the greater acceptance of couples living together outside of marriage. (Porter and O'Donnell, 2006, p. 1)

Studies have indicated that people in midlife can experience "particular disharmony, lowered morale, increased concerns about health, and increased anxiety and depression" (Cohler and Galatzer-Levy, 1990, pp. 225-226); they suggest that these anxieties "appear to account for first appearances of psychiatric illness in mid-life" (p. 226).

A person can be a leader at work, or recently laid off, can be surrounded by friends, family, and colleagues, or have just ended a marriage (or partnership) with its multiple disrupted relationships with family, extended family, and social network; can be financially secure, or financially strapped by children starting college, paying for the care of elderly parents, or living at a poverty level; can feel overburdened by responsibilities with little time (or capacity) to play and experience pleasure. One can enjoy good health with minor ailments or face a debilitating or life-threatening illness. Unresolved inner stresses and conflicts and unresolved self-esteem issues may make a difference between a relatively benign versus a more disturbed midlife period.

Midlife traditionally is the time when children reaching adolescence leave home and parents face the empty nest syndrome; some parents would love to have an empty nest as their children, now college graduates, choose to return home to live. "There has been a recent popularization of the term 'boomerang' kids," applied to this group; "*Newsweek* magazine (2002) recently described 'adultolescents' (or the 'mini-me generation') who are supported by their parents into their late twenties in order to get a start in a difficult economy" (Shulman, 2005, p. 106).

People of midlife age traditionally became grandparents and considered retiring; couples may have turned toward each other as they contemplated enjoying their leisure years without the responsibility of children. Today, many people follow this tradition, but many others are single, and many women in their forties (and men in their forties and older) become parents of infants; grandparents may be assuming major (or full) responsibility for raising their grandchildren; people often chose to work into their seventies and beyond; and many formerly married couples are now divorced and living alone or with blended families (or are going through successive divorces).

Although generativity concerns are important, midlife adults are often preoccupied with the generation *before* them—their own parents, who are aging and living longer. Parent caring can become a major task.

Physical Changes in Midlife

Midlife brings about major bodily changes and signs of incipient aging; these can become "a major, sometimes dominant, influence on mental life" (Colarusso, 1997, p. 80). Most people in midlife have good health and vitality; however, gradual declines and changes in the body can include having less physical energy, a decreasing level of metabolism (which can result in weight gain), the development of joint pains, changes in heart and kidney functioning, and problems with the gastrointestinal tract (Zastrow and Kirst-Ashman, 1997). Vision may decline, and hearing problems can develop. There tends to be a general increase in health problems such as diabetes, heart problems, and cancer.

Many people with health problems nevertheless continue to have high levels of functioning. Others find that disabilities dramatically alter their lives, their self-image, and relationships. Some people are responsive and supportive caretakers for their ill or disabled spouse or partner; other spouses or partners may feel overwhelmed by the new responsibilities, and separations or divorces often ensue; the divorce rate is higher for couples when a partner is disabled than for nondisabled couples.

Changes in bodily appearance and functioning, including the onset of menopause in women and changes in male sexual functioning (sometimes complicated by urinary and/or prostate problems), can affect psychological well-being, but the potential exists for positive adaptations (Colarusso, 1997). People often "mourn for the lost body of youth," and when they come to terms with the reality of their physical changes, this "is experienced to a large degree as a separation-individuation phenomenon" (p. 81); if this is achieved, this can lead to attaining "new experiences and . . . developmental potentials" (p. 81).

Generally midlife adults remain sexually active; for some, sexual activity increases and/or becomes more pleasurable as child care responsibilities fade, and couples can be more attentive to each other. The onset of menopause can remove fears of pregnancy and add to the sense of greater sexual freedom. People may also experience sexual dysfunction, in part physical and sometimes psychological or relational, or an interaction of these factors. The recent advent of Viagra has made a medication available to ameliorate male erectile disorders, and the large demand for it bears witness to the numbers of men with this problem. Recent advances have occurred in promoting similar drugs for women with sexual problems related to impaired blood flow to the genitalia; this is often caused by menopausal changes, atherosclerosis, and diabetes (Mann, 1998).

Psychological Development in Midlife

Jung referred to the development of increased psychological *introversion* (a tendency to turn inward) in midlife. Neugarten has termed this "interiority" (Cohler and Galatzer-Levy, 1990, p. 225). There is "increasing preoccupation with the meaning of life" and a tendency to become aware of the passage of time and mortality. Colarusso (1997) has observed that people go through a fourth individuation phase, focusing on the dilemmas of attachment and loss, involving the "ironic awareness that one will die and be deprived of involvement with loved ones at the very time that a mature understanding of the importance of others for one's health, happiness, and security is at its peak" (p. 79). Colarusso (1997) observes that "at no other point in life is the potential for attachment—and loss—so great" (p. 79).

Grandparenthood in midlife is one factor promoting the fourth individuation phase (Colarusso, 1997). The grandparents' investment in and idealization of their grandchildren serves reparative developmental functions, including bonding and comforting, which can protect against anxieties about aging and dying. Becoming a grandparent may also raise anxiety about aging: "grandparenthood is often greeted with ambivalence, reflecting, in part, the struggle to accept a personal end" (Colarusso, 1998, p. 132).

Colarusso speaks of the grandchild granting "genetic immortality" to the grandparent; but genetic immortality cannot be a literal fact for those grandparents who have no genetic connection to their grandchildren. Regardless of genetics, continued emotional connection through their grandchildren's memories of them may promise a kind of immortality to many.

Some grandparents experience greater freedom to involve themselves with their grandchildren than they could with their own children, in part because they do not have the full responsibility for care. They may have also worked out their psychological conflicts over parenting with their own children and are free to see these new little people in their individuality, rather than as ghosts from the past.

Parent Caring

As the Baby Boomers reach their fifties, their parents are becoming older and "are moving into the ranks of what is often called 'the old-old', where disability and thus the need for care become increasingly likely" (Toner, 1999, p. A1). For some midlife adults, parent caring can produce great stress—greater than the emotional upheavals of dealing with the empty nest syndrome (Neugarten, 1979). People in midlife, known as the "sandwich generation," must deal with the needs of their parents as well as their children and grandchildren. Shulman (2005) points out, that in the past women in their forties would be involved with their adolescent children, and with parents who were in their sixties or seventies. Now "sandwich generation" refers more to

> people in their late 40s or early 50s caring for very young children, as well as for parents in their 80s. . . . I call this the "hero sandwich generation" because it is so much bigger and challenging . . . in New England parlance, a hero sandwich is also called a sub or grinder, which may describe these relationships even more accurately! (pp. 105-106)

It has been estimated by the National Alliance for Caregivers "that about 6.5 million people, nearly a fifth of the population 65 years and older, required assistance and about 22 million families—nearly 1 in 4—are providing some form of assistance to an older relative or friend" (Rimer, 1998a, p. A1). Caring for elderly relatives is costly to caregivers in actual financial expenditures for maintenance needs and services (Gross, 2006a), loss of time spent at work, and missed opportunities for advancement. Almost three-fourths of participants in one survey reported that "elder care had affected their health" (Rimer, 1999, p. A8). Caring for elderly relatives with dementia can cause particular stress and bring on depressive symptoms in caregivers. "Their caregiving burden has long been recognized as a major public health concern" (Kennedy, 2000, p. 144).

Development in Late Life

People remain as unique in their later years as they were when younger; we tend to stereotype the elderly *(ageism)* and to distance ourselves from *them.*

> Those who are young or middle-aged or who resist the label of "old" do not seem to understand . . . that we are all becoming old. As Simone de Beauvoir wrote . . . understanding ourselves as aging entities is perhaps the most difficult task we face. (Shield and Aronson, 2003, p. 33)

According to a U.S. Census Bureau report in 2006, "today's older Americans are more prosperous, better educated and healthier, and those differences [from previous generations] will only accelerate as the first boomers hit retirement age in 2011" (Lyman, 2006a, p. A1). One major finding is that both older men and women have fewer disabilities than in past years; they might develop disabilities in future years, but "it will happen later with more of the years beyond 65 free of disability—an increase in what scientists call health expectancy" (p. A1). Although, until very recently, women tended to live longer than men, this picture is now changing: according to the National Center for Health statistics, in April, 2006, "the gap between them has shrunk to five years, the narrowest since 1946. If current trends continue, in 50 years men and women will live the same length of time" (Zernike, 2006b, p. 1). Although general prosperity prevails, there are still pockets of poverty, especially affecting blacks and Hispanics, particularly older women of these groups who live alone (Lyman, 2006a).

The elderly, a rapidly growing age group in this country, can be divided into three categories: the young-old, ages sixty-five to seventy-four; the old-old, ages seventy-five and older (Sadock and Sadock, 2003); and the "oldest old" who are past age eighty-five, and are "the most rapidly growing segment of the older population" (p. 51). Today they number more than 4 million (Lyman, 2006a); many in this group are "frail elderly." More people are also living past 100, and it has been predicted that "by 2050 an unbelievable 834,000 people over age 100 will be alive" (Qualls and Abeles, 2000, p. 3).

As we search for some commonalities to help us understand this phase of adulthood, we are thwarted by extreme differences in the aging process itself. In early childhood, the differences among children in achieving developmental landmarks were slight; perhaps weeks or months. In adolescence, the range of variation was greater; a two year lag might mark the growth spurts and maturational level of peers. For older adults, the range of variation can be measured in decades, and life trajectories can differ drastically. One can be youthful at eighty-five, physically healthy and intellectually vigorous; someone else can be old at sixty, totally incapacitated by a severe stroke.

In the elderly population,

> only 5 percent require institutional care and only 10 percent require assistance in the community. Two-thirds of older adults report themselves in good to excellent health. Three-quarters report no more than minor if any limitations in activities of daily living. (Kennedy, 2000, pp. 4-5)

The frail and the sick elderly, however, need medical, psychiatric, and social services, as well as assisted-living arrangements from relatives, community caretakers, assisted-living apartments, and nursing homes. Kennedy (2000) states that "the costs of their health needs, both personal and societal, pose substantial economic and policy challenges" (p. 1) and that "dementia is the major cause of functional dependence in the elderly" (p. 5).

Mr. Hunter, eighty-seven, is at an age when some of his contemporaries are indeed "frail elderly," yet he is accomplishing the Eriksonian (1963) task of "developing integrity versus despair," being involved in living and maintaining attachments to others.

Mr. Hunter, a black man living in a small town in Staten Island, was described to the writer, Joseph Mitchell (2000), as

> one of those strong, self-contained old men you don't see much any more. He was a hard worker, and he retired only a few years ago, and he's fairly well-to-do. He's a widower, and he lives by himself and does his own cooking. (pp. 6-7)

When Mitchell phoned to arrange a meeting, Mr. Hunter told him that he was too busy that day for a visit. "An old lady I know is sick in bed, and I made her a lemon-meringue pie, and I'm going over and take it to her. Sit with her awhile. . . . You'll have to make it some other time" (Mitchell, 2000, p. 7).

When the visit takes place, Mr. Hunter discusses his cooking and church activities with Mitchell as he frosts a three-layer cake:

> The preacher at our church is a part-time preacher. . . . Most Sundays, he and his wife take Sunday dinner with me, and I always try to have something nice for them. . . . A gospel chorus from down South is . . . coming to my house for Sunday dinner. . . . Did you have your lunch? (Mitchell, 2000, pp. 8-9)

Mr. Hunter appears to be in control of his own destiny and to have found meaning in his religion, the social affiliations with his church, and involvement with caring for others. He takes pride in his accomplishments and his mastery over his daily life. Mr. Hunter would fall within the high-functioning end of the spectrum of late adulthood.

People in late adulthood face multiple losses and depletion on many levels; but, like Mr. Hunter, many are actively involved in life and make plans for the future; "maintaining the ability to continue to be valued, valuable and relevant in a present dominated by younger generations is a central developmental task of late adulthood" (Colarusso, 1998, p. 131).

Levinson and Levinson (1996) discuss *adolescing,* which connotes "'moving toward adulthood' and suggests positive growth toward a potential optimum" (p. 21); by contrast, "*senescing,* which means moving toward old age . . . suggests negative growth and dissolution" (p. 22). Viewing the life cycle from a child-development perspective will probably lead to drawing a "rather bleak picture of adult development, since they [this perspective] tend[s] to ignore the often rich potentialities and achievements of middle and late adulthood" (Levinson and Levinson, 1996, p. 21).

> In late adulthood we are mostly senescing, but some vitally important adolescing may be done toward the end of the life cycle as we seek to give fuller meaning to our lives, to life and death as ultimate stages, and to the condition of being human. The approach of death itself may be the occasion of our growing to full adulthood. (Levinson and Levinson, 1996, p. 21)

Older adults have made major strides over the years in combating ageism, the stereotypical, prejudicial way of measuring older people in terms of their limitations, with an emphasis on their decline; advances include prohibitions against discriminating against the elderly in employment, and senior citizens are now a political presence felt at state and federal levels of government.

Biopsychosocial Concerns of Older Adults

Socioeconomic Status

Although general economic well-being prevails among many of the elderly, recent economic changes especially the erosion of pension plans have cast a pall on this rosy economic picture; in addition, as noted, many elderly people already live below the poverty level. There are now many large, well-known corporations with a history of solid and stable pension funds, who are dismantling or freezing these benefits; as companies face bankruptcy or other financial distress, pension plans are jettisoned; "some are deciding that they either cannot, or will not, keep making the decades-long promises that a pension plan involves" (Walsh, 2006a, p. A1). As a result, many older workers are delaying their retirements or working at other jobs. Some companies are encouraging workers to invest in their own 401(k) accounts, but "research shows that many people fail to put money into their retirement accounts or invest it poorly once it is there" (p. A20).

Government pension plans have always been even more secure than those in the private sector; "years of supporting court interventions have enshrined the view that once a public employee has earned a pension, no one can take it away" (Walsh, 2006b, p. A1). However, some state and local governments, facing financial difficulties, are beginning to cut back on pension plans. Although this is being done on a small scale now, there is concern that this trend may spread "as local officials take stock of unexpectedly large obligations to retired public workers, . . . [and] are starting to question whether service cuts, sales of government property, and politically acceptable tax increases can ever go far enough to bring things into balance" (p. A1). Complicating this picture is the fact that insurance plans, to pay for retirees health care, are not sufficiently funded; these "local troubles also offer a sense of the challenge in store on a national scale as the obligations of Medicare and Social Security rise sharply to cover the retirement of the baby boom generation" (Walsh, 2006c, p. A10).

Paying for health care (including prescription medications) poses an additional economic burden for many elderly people (Zastrow and Kirst-Ashman, 2004).

Work and Retirement

Some older adults eagerly anticipate retirement with plans for activities including leisure pursuits, involvement with grandchildren, volunteer work, travel, or study. An increasing number of older adults continue to be employed; the Age Discrimination in Employment Act, which ended the practice of mandated retirement at seventy, was passed by the U.S. Congress in 1967. For some, continuing employment is a preferred choice; for others, because of pension cuts and other financial hardships, it becomes a necessity.

Many political figures and others prominent in their fields range from "young old" to "oldest old." In 1985, a man was killed by a New York City police car driven by an officer who was intoxicated (Lacayo, 1988).

> [His widow] sued the city for $29 million, partly for the loss of her husband's future income. Because her husband was 71 at his death, the jury might have concluded that his income-producing years were mostly behind him. No problem. Her attorney was 86. . . . Octogenarian Harry Lipsig . . . perhaps the winningest liability lawyer in America. (Lacayo, 1988, p. 56)

A new trend is the development of "bridge jobs," which are "part-time or full-time jobs typically held for less than 10 years following full-time careers"; people are finding that "as life spans lengthen, pensions tighten, and workplace rules change, hopping from full-time work to full-time leisure is appearing less realistic and, to some, less desirable" (Cullen, 2006, p. 48). Many companies welcome these employees, and make creative use of their talents.

There are many people, fifty and older, who continue their education formally, attaining college or higher education degrees, or informally, through courses and lectures. Continuing education "is a $6 billion business" (Ellin, 2006, p. B1). William A. Dravis, the president of Learning Resources Network, commented that "'thirty years ago you had two kinds of senior courses: sewing and knitting. . . . Now older adults are interested in the total spectrum of art, literature, travel, spirituality, cooking, health'" (p. B4); many also gain satisfaction through volunteer work (Jirovec, 2005).

Elderly people often become caretakers for their grandchildren (Chapter 7), and/or for their disabled spouses. With the deinstitutionalization of the mentally ill, young adults with mental illness and developmental disabilities frequently lived with their parents. "As the result of increased longevity . . . parents provide care over longer periods, fulfilling the description of them as 'perpetual parents' (Jennings, 1987)" (Botsford and Rule, 2004, p. 423). Often plans were not made for the future of these adult children, and permanency planning, as parents are aging, has become an important priority; this is discussed further in Chapter 14.

Social Involvement

For some people, losing work means losing their social networks; other older adults maintain large social networks; and some prefer (and may always have preferred) a more solitary existence. Often people outlive their social networks and experience loneliness; as disability increases and mobility decreases, simply getting to where social activity takes place can be difficult.

> One elderly man, a former physician, living in a nursing home, outlived his wife and his colleagues with whom he had been actively involved. He had no children, and physical infirmity necessitated his move to a nursing home; one cousin, his only remaining relative, visited him regularly but was now moving to another state as her husband was retiring. The nursing home's social worker enabled him to feel less depressed and alone and to think of ways, even in these limited circumstances, in which he could feel more fulfilled and less isolated.

Adult children are often an important source of emotional comfort as well as helpful to their parents in their daily coping. Relationships with adult children are varied and can be complex; role reversal is not uncommon and is a frequent cause of conflict—now it is not the parent telling the teenager that he or she cannot have the car this Saturday—it is the adult child telling the parent that he or she should not be driving at all! Shulman (2005) objects to the concept of role reversal: "it is infantilizing and presumptuous to imply that a parent becomes a child in later life," she prefers the idea of "collaborating with an aging adult to meet his/her needs" (p. 115).

> Elders' wisdom and experience, qualities often untouched by physical frailty, are often overlooked as a source of guidance for younger people. Treating older people as children only makes that wisdom less available. Unless there is a dementia or an illness that requires total care, most older people are able to move in and out of health crises and back to independent functioning. Although some social roles may have to be left behind, others (e.g., being a parent) generally endure as part of the aging individual's identity. As a parent, an elderly person still holds symbolic and actual meaning to his or her child. That meaning profoundly affects their relationship with one another. (Shulman, 2005, p. 116)

Although "collaborative" relationships with elder parents are an ideal goal, achieving this is not always easy and can be stressful, especially when parents are resistant to change and to accepting needed assistance; prior chronic family dysfunction can also complicate dealing with the parent's life changes. The new life crisis of aging, on the other hand, can present opportunities for families to work out past issues and reach a higher level of compatibility.

Relationships with grandchildren (and great-grandchildren) can be very meaningful to the elderly, providing a sense of continuity and hope that they will be remembered, enhanced by sharing family history and passing on mementos of their lives (Colarusso, 1998). The "feeling held" engendered by loving responses of the grandchild can be very soothing. However, if the grandparent is feeling depletion anxiety, grandchildren may be rejected because they "become but another painful reminder of the nearness of death" (p. 133).

When people reach late adulthood, their children and grandchildren may be so involved in their own lives that the elderly person becomes "increasingly aware of feelings of irrelevance or redundancy" (Colarusso, 1998, p. 134). Friends of the same age are very important to elderly people; if they are friends from the past, they can share memories and "confirm the importance and reality of a distant past" (p. 134). Newly made friends can also be an important source of support.

> Friends of the same age confirm and substantiate one's importance in the present. . . . They share a common position in the life cycle and similar relationships . . . serve as buffers against an increasingly short and precarious future. The end of life, in the presence of mental or physical illness, is less threatening when the developmental task is shared. (Colarusso, 1998, p. 134)

The "ethnic enclave" has been important for many elderly immigrants. In one study, a group of immigrants left their communities to move with their children and so were "uprooted again. . . . This group was unable to rejoin or locate an ethnic enclave in their new locale and within weeks to months developed depression and/or other mild organic symptoms" (Kao and Lam, 1997, p. 210).

The beneficial effects of pets on children and adults in many settings (discussed in Chapter 5) have received increasing attention in the literature (Germain, 1991; Netting, Wilson, and New, 1987; Risley-Curtis, Holley, and Wolf, 2006). When provided with pets, many older adults who had been living alone responded with improved mental states and a decrease in physical symptoms. "As companions, animals may assist in minimizing loneliness and may provide opportunities for tactile stimulation. In addition, touching a pet has been shown to affect the cardiovascular system" (Netting, Wilson, and New, 1987, p. 61).

Some elderly people have found new friends in retirement communities, assisted-living programs, foster homes for the elderly, and community programs, such as old-age centers. As noted in Chapter 7, intergenerational housing has been developing, allowing elders to live with people of all ages rather than in "segregated" settings. Hope Meadows, an innovative, multiracial community project, involves hard-to-place foster children, foster parents, and elderly residents who are active assistants in the program.

> Low-to-middle income seniors receive reduced rent in exchange for volunteering a minimum of six hours a week. The result—a near miracle in a society dominated by divorce and generational disjunction—is a place where everyone knows everyone else, a stimulating haven for seniors and permanence for some of our nation's most vulnerable kids. "Hope is really quite different," says Carol Spigner, a former Clinton Administration children's welfare official. "It is probably the first child-welfare effort that has institutionalized intergenerational relationships, which are key, as part of a community." (Barovick, 2001, p. G2)

Cognitive Development

Mental abilities do not inevitably decline in the elderly, and considerable variations exist. Dementias, which can be all encompassing, do develop in some people, while many have only minor problems with short-term memory loss. Recently, a multiplicity of programs are being developed to help people improve their minds, decrease forgetfulness, and prevent dementia. "From 'brain gyms' on the Internet to 'brain-healthy' foods and activities at assisted living centers, the programs are aimed at baby-boomers anxious about entering their golden years and at their parents trying to stave off memory loss or dementia" (Belluck, 2006, p. A1). There are no solid research findings, to either support or refute the efficacy of these programs; and although people may show improvement on test scores, there is no follow-up to assess the effects on their daily functioning. Some positive psychological benefits may result, and there are basically no harmful effects (as might occur with taking medications). Programs associated with this focus, such as good nutrition and cardiovascular exercises are beneficial; "the strongest evidence suggests that cardiovascular exercise also probably helps the brain, by improving blood circulation, experts say" (p. A20).

Conversely, some older adults can think in *more* complex ways, a continuation of the postformal mode of thinking developed in midlife.

Older adults often appreciate the complexities of a problem, including the interrelationships of motivation, logic, and irrationality. Therefore, they may no longer do well on tests of formal operations, because, finding the underlying assumptions unacceptable, they may "no longer see problems of pure logic as relevant or interesting" (Stevens-Long, 1990, p. 133).

> Edelstein and . . . Noam (1982) have described the intellectual behavior of older adults as a reunion of logic and affect . . . the search for a socially adequate solution to problems rather than acceptance of the most "logical" solution. Wisdom . . . develops from an appreciation of the long-term consequences of action, and from the attempt to mediate between the demands of logic and emotion. The experience of responsibility in adult life is prerequisite to the development of wisdom. (Stevens-Long, 1990, p. 134)

Reminiscence

Reminiscence, recalling and talking about the past, is a common and normal process in late adulthood, which serves as adaptation but can lead to emotional problems if used excessively (Colarusso, 1998). Reminiscing can protect people from a painful present; it is a way of renewing memories and internalized ties to important people in their past; it aids self-esteem by helping people remember and feel good about past experiences and accomplishments; it can help people adapt to the idea of dying. Listening to family stories from the past can bring people closer together, as memories become shared knowledge. Colarusso (1998) emphasizes

> that in no other phase of development does the focus on the past have such a positive impact on the adaptive functioning of the ego as occurs in late adulthood. With each reminiscence, the self is redefined and delineated in relationship to one's position in the life cycle. (p. 131)

Reminiscence has been used successfully in working with elderly Asian immigrants, as "it is helpful to encourage the client to talk about their birthplace or native land and skills they feel proud of" (Kao and Lam, 1997, p. 217). This creates "an emotional connection with clients [which] opens the way to engage them in treatment" (p. 217). This suggestion is applicable to elderly clients from many backgrounds.

A word of caution about the use of reminiscences: it should not be "pushed" on clients as a "helpful" therapeutic procedure, as some people may be made uncomfortable talking about the past; for some, the past is full of sadness and trauma. Although talking of painful events can be healing for some, for others this can be distressing and retraumatizing. In a Jewish Home for the Aged in Toronto, half of their patients with Alzheimer's disease lived through the Holocaust. As their short-term memory disappeared, they now live in the past and are "condemn[ed] once again, to the death camps"; according to Dr. Michael Gordon, a gerontologist at the home, "'The most dramatic are those who [had] managed to compartmentalize their experience . . . [now] the Holocaust absolutely dominates their lives'" (Wong, 2002, p. A1).

Sexuality

One of the myths about the elderly is that they become asexual in feelings and behavior. This is far from the truth; overall, older people may have some decrease in the frequency of sexual activity and may experience biological problems complicating (or slowing down) their sexual response. However, many remain both sexually interested and active. One problem for older heterosexual women is the relative absence of men, as women tend to outlive their male partners. "At age 80 there are four women for every man. Most women over age of 65 are widowed; most men are married" (Kennedy, 2000, p. 176); as noted earlier in this chapter, it is expected that in the future men will catch up to women in longevity.

Dating is of great interest to many in retirement communities; generally, men look for younger women, and although many women prefer younger men, they do not have the same choice (Rimer, 1998b). One eighty-five-year-old woman, who was rejected by many men after their first date with her because they wanted someone younger, commented: "Where do bald men with arthritic knees get off acting like this?" (p. A1). Many older men find that they are much sought after; this, however, "lasts only until they lose their driver's license . . . or lose their health" (p. A1). Many seniors have expressed anxieties about dating behavior.

Many nursing homes have restrictive rules (or unspoken patterns of regulation) regarding the expression of a patient's sexual behavior (Kennedy, 2000; Zastrow and Kirst-Ashman, 2004). Staff (and relatives of patients) sometimes must be educated "about the rights to privacy that competent, sexually consenting adults retain as residents of nursing homes" (Kennedy, 2000, p. 188); this negative attitude existed for years prior to the present concern with AIDS. Public health measures about safe sex in institutions might be easier to encourage if this were an open topic of discussion rather than a subject that is ignored. The same dilemma exists in high schools, where sex education emphasizes abstinence.

Some patients with dementia may act out sexually, which must be handled appropriately and distinguished from normative sexual interests (Kennedy, 2000). If nursing homes have a problem with heterosexual sexuality, problems become especially compounded when a question of accepting homosexual behavior arises.

Research indicates that most elderly gay and lesbian people are well-adjusted; many have a large social network, and have "exceptional ego strength and resilience as a result of the process of coming out and adapting, even in the context of a predominantly homophobic culture" (Thompson and Colón, 2004, p. 484). However, there is a range of adaptation; "Friend (1999) found less 'successful' aging when the individual internalized and conformed to homophobic images, resulting in 'living in the closet', usually with shame and self-loathing, or 'passing' in a heterosexual lifestyle or marriage" (p. 485). Gay and lesbian elders also face a range of socioeconomic and cultural problems similar to those faced by heterosexual elders.

Gay and lesbian elders tend to have specific concerns about legal matters, such as the rights of a partner to inherit, and they have institutional concerns, such as discrimination on the part of institutions or hospitals; another concern is "the expectation that homosexuality is not an aspect of life to be appropriately eulogized" (Thompson and Colón, 2004, p. 496).

An interest in having special facilities built for homosexual elders developed in response to fears of institutional discrimination (Bragg, 1999). Many of the developers, who are also gay, are building retirement communities and assisted-care facilities "marketed specifically for homosexuals, places that will allow gays to grow old surrounded by other gays, where they do not have to live, and ultimately die, amid lingering condemnation" (p. A1).

This might not be the preferred solution for everyone; some may lack funds to finance this type of private care. People from different cultural and ethnic groups might prefer other lifestyles or may feel discrimination from white gay and lesbian people based on their "other identities." African-American gay men, for example, may be uncomfortable living in institutions with white gay men; this may be related to preexisting tensions between some members of both groups (Adams Jr. and Kimmel, 1997).

AIDS and the elderly. Many people (including doctors) believed until recently that senior citizens were not at real risk for acquiring AIDS. However,

nearly 27 percent of people living with AIDS in the U. S. are 50 or older—a proportion that is expected to increase. This vanguard group must confront the ordinary ailments of age complicated by the extraordinary ferocity of the AIDS virus. (Gorman, 2006, p. 55)

This group includes some who had become infected with HIV earlier and were already receiving successful treatment; however, "between ten to fifteen percent of HIV/AIDS new cases occur in individuals fifty and older" (Levy-Dweck, 2005, p. 37); in those between forty-four- and sixty-five-years old, greater increases were seen "among blacks, Asian/Pacific Islanders, and American Indians/Alaskan Natives" (p. 38). Many gay men continue to become infected through sexual activity with men; however, "transmission through heterosexual contact . . . continues to grow at the most rapid pace," and the numbers of women being infected is dramatically rising, especially those who are older than sixty-five (Levy-Dweck, 2005); "one-third of these women acquire AIDS through sharing infected needles" (p. 39).

Many older people do not see a need to use condoms (Gorman, 2006; Levy-Dweck, 2005); in retirement communities there are "single men, dubbed 'condominium Casanovas', [who] often flit from one woman to the next, sometimes passing along AIDS. Widowers often hire prostitutes" (Drummond, 1999, p. 84H).

Problems in combating this disease include denial by older people that they are vulnerable, lack of preventive sex education for this population (as many assume they are not sexually active), the tendency for doctors not to inquire about AIDS (or test for it) in the elderly, as well as misdiagnosis, the symptoms of AIDS can be similar to other diseases affecting the elderly; for example, development of the "AIDS-related dementia complex" (which progresses more quickly in late adulthood) (Kennedy, 2000, p. 176) can be misdiagnosed as Alzheimer's disease (Levy-Dweck, 2005, p. 43).

Efforts at prevention are critical, and when a person is infected, early detection is necessary to start effective treatment (many people do not know they have this disease); there has been little research on how medications for AIDS interact with other medications taken by the elderly, and many clinical trials of AIDS drugs have not included elderly patients (Gorman, 2006).

Elder Abuse

Elder abuse has been receiving greater attention; most victims of abuse are the frail elderly; although abuse can occur in custodial institutions, and at home by paid caretakers, most of the perpetrators are family members. Abuse may be physical, psychological, sexual, and/or financial. Neglect is the most frequent form of abuse, and the perpetrator is often the adult child, motivated by financial gain. It is difficult to know the numbers of seniors who are abused, but it is estimated that 10 percent of the elderly population are subjected to abuse (Sadock and Sadock, 2003). Congress plans to consider "the Elder Justice Act of 2006, which would create the first nationwide database on elder abuse, replacing inconsistent or unavailable statistics. The legislation, which has bipartisan support, also assigns a federal official to coordinate projects and technical assistance" (Gross, 2006b, p. A1); as of February 2007, the bill was still pending.

Mental Health Problems of the Elderly

Although a close connection exists between physical health and mental health throughout the life cycle, this is especially true in the elderly population. "For both causality and course of illness, mental and physical health are inseparable in aged persons" (Kennedy, 2000, p. 2). Although physical illness, depression, and dementia increase with age, most seniors nevertheless "are neither demented nor seriously depressed. *Physically healthy seniors* have the lowest rates of anxiety, depression, and substance abuse among the adult population" (p. 3; italics added).

The effects of prescription and nonprescription drugs often mimic symptoms of emotional disorders in the older population, owing to such factors as incorrect dosage, changes in an older person's ability to absorb a drug, the patient's difficulty in following intake instructions, idiosyncratic sensitivity to the medication, and the effect of interacting medications—so-called polypharmacy—which might be prescribed by different physicians (Kaplan, Sadock, and Grebb, 1994).

The many changes experienced by the elderly, including their own sense of physical and cognitive depletion, can place them at risk for mental illness (Kaplan, Sadock, and Grebb, 1994). Another stressor can be the anticipation of their own death.

Being an immigrant can be stressful, and emotional problems have developed in both first- and second-generation elderly immigrants who have lost their network of friends and relatives on whom they have depended. "With the loss of these helpers, as a result of geographic moves or death, such individuals may experience such symptoms of emotional trouble as depression, hypochondria, insomnia, or even paranoia" (Kao and Lam, 1997, p. 208).

The emotional problems with which elderly people struggle can be exacerbations of chronic conditions, reactive difficulties in adapting to multiple losses and transitions, or a combination of these. The most common psychiatric problems in the elderly are depressive disorders, cognitive disorders, phobias, and alcohol use disorders; they "also have a high risk for suicide and drug-induced psychiatric symptoms" (Sadock and Sadock, 2003, p. 1321). The elderly also tend to suffer from sleep disorders, vertigo, somatoform disorders (physical symptoms that are psychologically based), and hypochondriasis (preoccupation with, and exaggeration of, physical complaints).

Most of the treatment for mental illness in older adults is not provided by psychiatrists but by primary care physicians; many doctors as well as other practitioners in the health field receive insufficient education in mental health problems of the elderly (Kennedy, 2000).

Depression. Approximately 30 percent of elderly patients seeing primary care physicians have depressive symptoms, and about half of this group have an actual depressive disorder (Kennedy, 2000). The elderly are organically reactive to depressive symptoms, which can worsen symptoms of their physical illness and impair their functional capacities (Kennedy, 2000). They also experience serious depression after bereavement more frequently than younger people do; however, depression in the elderly seems to be associated more with the development of physical illness and disability (Kennedy, 2000). It has been observed, for example, that more than 50 percent of elderly people who have had strokes become depressed within a period of six months.

The suicide rate in the elderly is higher than in any other group; "the suicide rate for white men over the age of 65 is five times higher than that of the general population" (Sadock and Sadock, 2003, p. 1326); although depression is usually present, physical illness and loss are major precipitating factors (Kennedy, 2000; Sadock and Sadock, 2003).

Depression in the elderly is not always easy to diagnose; it often occurs in conjunction with physical problems, and some of its symptoms, such as memory loss and inability to concentrate, can be misdiagnosed as dementia (the reverse is equally true). Some people do not appear affectively depressed; their depression "is expressed more in physical terms, like vague complaints of aches and pains or gastrointestinal distress" (Brody, 2006, p. D7).

> Depression and physical illness can be a deadly combination. Depression—or at least depressive symptoms—are common in response to serious illness of any kind. Some diseases, including multiple sclerosis, hypothyroidism, lupus, hepatitis, AIDS, vitamin deficiencies, and anemia, may produce depression in a more direct biological sense. Drugs that can cause depressive symptoms include antihistamines, anti-anxiety drugs, blood pressure medications, steroids, and antibiotics. A careful medical history and physical examination are important before diagnosing depression at any age, but especially in the elderly. ("Depression in," 2003, p. 5)

Depression can *affect* physical health in many ways: a patient may lack energy or feel too hopeless to seek medical care; may spend more unnecessary time in bed; can be more prone to die after a heart attack or stroke; and "in one study, depression raised the death rate in a nursing home by 50 percent over several years" ("Depression in," 2003, p. 6). Depression in the elderly can be treated successfully; "but most of the estimated six million elderly Americans who suffer from depression receive little more than a prescription for an antidepressant if they receive treatment at all, psychiatrists say" (Carey, 2006a, p. A15). Studies show that elderly people can benefit from a variety of talk therapies, and that often a combination of medication and psychotherapy can be beneficial (Carey, 2006a, d; "Depression in," 2003). "Whether they favor drugs, talk therapy or a combination, therapists agree that simple case management—helping connect people with community services, get treatment for physical problems and complete chores—can also help them turn the corner" (Carey, 2006d, p. D5).

Cognitive disorders. Dementia (major significantly irreversible, global, and/or partial impairments of cognitive functioning) affects 4 million people in the United States at an estimated cost of $100 billion a year in direct services for physicians, hospitals, and caretaking agencies (Kennedy, 2000). The indirect costs, which are related to the expenses and lost wages of family members, are estimated to be another $100 billion. It is projected that the number of persons developing dementia will double during the next forty years (Kennedy, 2000).

Dementia, as a classification, covers a number of disorders, including dementia produced by AIDS, syphilis, vascular impairment, strokes, brain tumors, and chronic alcoholic intoxication. Patients with dementia experience a steady downhill loss of cognitive abilities that seriously impair their overall psychosocial functioning (Kennedy, 2000). One of the most common and publicized forms of dementia is Alzheimer's disease (AD), "which develops gradually and at first almost imperceptibly, with symptoms that resemble ordinary memory lapses. Soon the lapses become more pervasive, and people with AD lose the ability to learn and remember anything new" ("Alzheimer's Disease—Part I," 1992).

> Sometimes slowly, sometimes rapidly, they descend from forgetfulness into confusion. They can no longer remember the names of friends and family members or find their way around in places that are not completely familiar. They begin to avoid social contacts, because they cannot follow the drift of a conversation. Cooking, driving, using tools, handling money, and even obeying simple instructions become overwhelmingly difficult. At this stage they can still function adequately

using simple routines in a familiar environment, but they seem apathetic and withdrawn. ("Alzheimer's Disease—Part I," 1992, p. 2)

Patients may have difficulty controlling their impulses and emotions, and in their confusion "they dimly sense that they are losing everything, so they sometimes become suspicious and develop delusions, talking to imaginary persons or accusing family members of being impostors" ("Alzheimer's Disease—Part I," 1992, p. 2). In the last stages, they become totally disoriented and may not even know who they are, lose control of their bowel and bladder functions, have serious sleep problems, and often cannot take care of themselves in the most basic ways, such as dressing themselves or eating.

Deterioration proceeds, and patients are ultimately bedridden "and apparently oblivious" ("Alzheimer's Disease—Part I," 1992, p. 2); they die of "malnutrition, dehydration, infection, or heart failure. In nearly half of cases the immediate cause of death is pneumonia" (p. 2). The time between onset of the symptoms and death ranges from two to twenty years, averaging from seven to ten years.

It is important to make an accurate differential diagnosis of this disease, and a neurological assessment is imperative, with the performance of neuropsychological and memory tests. Sometimes what appears to be Alzheimer's is not and may be drug intoxication, thyroid disorders, subdural hematoma, or other diseases that can often be treated. It is also important to differentiate Alzheimer's disease from depression; complicating this diagnosis is the fact that depression is often present in Alzheimer's disease as well as coexisting with other dementias. The "Alzheimer's Disease Neuroimaging Initiative" is a five-year study sponsored by the National Institute on Aging, which began in 2005, aimed at early detection and prevention of Alzheimer's disease; "the earlier we can detect Alzheimer's disease, the better chance we have of finding ways to treat or prevent it; and the more we learn about risk factors and potential treatments, the more important early detection will become" ("In Search of," 2006, p. 5).

Families, who differ in their capacities to cope with this illness as well as with the required caretaking responsibilities, assume care for the majority of dementia patients; the toll on them is particularly high (Kennedy, 2000). In a recent large study (Carey, 2006c), it was observed that elderly caregivers for their spouses are at risk themselves for "serious illness and at increased risk for dying prematurely" (p. A27). The greatest risk was for those caring for patients with psychiatric disorders and dementia. "It is no surprise, experts say, that the illnesses that produce the most stress are those, like dementia, that seem to leach away a loved one's intelligence and personality" (p. A27). Kennedy (2000) finds that some of the most difficult behaviors for

families to cope with are incontinence, nighttime wandering, and assaultive-
ness. "Perhaps cruelest of all is the patient's loss of capacity to recognize
the loved caregiver" (p. 74).

Many families who attempt to take care of the relative at home feel guilty
when this is no longer feasible.

> One client discussed with her student social worker her decision to place
> her husband, who had Alzheimer's disease, in a nursing home. She ex-
> plained that her husband, formerly a gentle and loving man, had beat her,
> and how he often wandered away from the house, and she had to go in
> search of him. She had feared both for her own safety and his. It took her
> two years initially to make the decision that she could not take care of him
> at home. She said that, in retrospect, she should have placed her husband
> in a nursing home a year earlier than she did. Then, as if feeling guilty for
> saying that, she became tearful, and while showing the social worker a
> photo of her husband and herself before he became sick, she said he had
> expected her to take care of him when he got old, and that she had let him
> down. She said, "It's not fair, if it were any other illness, I could have cared
> for him—but not this one." Later in the session, she discussed how lonely
> she felt without her husband. "I miss him so much. I am nothing without him."

Anxiety disorders. Anxiety disorders are found in the elderly, often (but
not necessarily) in people, who have had a history of problems with anxiety.
Although the severity of symptoms may be milder in younger people, the
actual impact on older people can be severe; the elderly may have more difficulty adapting to stress due to a weakened autonomic nervous system;
experiencing post–traumatic stress disorder also tends to produce more serious symptomatology in this population (Sadock and Sadock, 2003).

Substance Abuse

Substance abuse is a serious, often hidden problem in the elderly; it is on
the increase, as Baby Boomers age; many who experimented with drugs
when they were adolescents have continued with this habit, becoming addicted (Kluger and Ressner, 2006); one consequence of this problem has
been "a lifetime of neglect of overall health" (p. 55).

> Hard numbers are not easy to come by, but older addicts are clearly a
> growth sector in the drug-recovery industry. There are an estimated
> 1.7 million Americans over age 50 addicted to drugs, according to
> the Substance Abuse and Mental Health Services Administration
> (SAMHSA), a division of the Department of Health and Human Ser-
> vices. By 2020 SAMHSA expects the number to reach 4.4 million.
> Already an ongoing federal study has found that the number of older

Americans seeking help for heroin or cocaine abuse roughly quadrupled from 1992 to 2002. (Kluger and Ressner, 2006, pp. 54-55)

Many elderly people who are dependent on alcohol often have chronic drinking problems that have existed since they were young or midlife adults (Sadock and Sadock, 2003). They have serious medical problems (often liver disease) and tend to be unmarried, widowed, divorced, or never married; many are men in the homeless poor population. Sadock and Sadock (2003) report that 20 percent of patients in nursing home are dependent on alcohol, and alcohol and abuse of other substances are involved in 10 percent of mental health problems in the elderly; furthermore, the elderly have greater dependence on certain medications including hypnotics, anxiolytics (tranquilizers), and narcotics, as well as nonprescription drugs, and nicotine and caffeine.

Death

There is no one way to die, as there is no one way to live; nor is there just one way that people feel about this experience. Some people have deep religious beliefs, which may include strong beliefs in an afterlife. Some have made a peace with the end of life without the support of religion. Some are able to reconcile life conflicts with themselves, their close friends, and family, and face death with equanimity. Others do not.

Erikson (1963) talks about an older person facing aging and death with integrity. Colarusso (1998) reflects that if one has lived a fulfilled life, has reconciled the demands of the superego with the ego ideal, and has come to terms with "the inevitability of the death of all living things," then the person may have achieved "wisdom" (p. 136).

Older adults need an opportunity to discuss their fears, their wishes as to how they want to die, and whatever is on their mind that needs to be "settled." Some have many fears but do not want to talk about them or at least not in the orderly way we might wish them to. In working with people who are dying or fearing death, it is important to listen and to understand direct expressions of fears as well as metaphors or other indirect ways of expressing concerns.

Systemic issues do not leave us even in the process of dying. Although we may ask people about how they might want to die, this often is irrelevant to what actually happens. Cloud (2000), in reporting on this subject, asserts that "we should choose to die well. Too many of us don't" (p. 60). Citing a TIME/CNN poll, Cloud (2000) observes that although seven out of ten Americans express a wish to die at home, three-fourths actually die in medical institutions; and more than a third of terminally ill people are in intensive care units for a minimum of ten days. "Specialists say 95 percent of pain in terminally ill people can be mollified, but studies show that nearly half of Americans die in pain, surrounded and treated by strangers" (pp. 61-62). There is a need for expanded hospice care and home care services.

Although the "American health care system has long given patients a terrible choice: people told that they have a terminal illness must forgo advanced medical treatment to qualify for hospice care," such as chemotherapy or life-sustaining dialysis for patients with renal failure, leading to avoidance of more appropriate hospice care and resorting to high-cost in-patient care. Instead, it has been reported recently that a number of hospices and private healthcare insurance providers are offering a choice, giving "patients the medical comfort and social support traditionally available through hospice care, while at the same time letting them receive sophisticated medical treatments that may slow or even halt their disease" (Abelson, 2007, p. A1). It is felt that this is a rational and humane alternative that will be increasingly adopted.

Death, of course, can occur at any stage in the life cycle; death and loss are discussed further in Chapter 12.

CONCLUSION

Attaining maturity, and with it the capacity to assume responsibilities, is the ultimate achievement of adulthood—perhaps never fully attained as we struggle with residues from earlier periods. The achievement of maturity also enables us to regulate our emotions—a task central in infancy but continuing in importance as our emotions, relationships, and life situations become more complex. Maturity ideally allows us to be at peace with ourselves; to appreciate our strengths and accept our vulnerabilities; and to be able to meet our needs while being open to meeting the needs of others and putting those first when necessary, as when our children cry out to us in the middle of the night and we are tired. Maturity means the capacity to forgive ourselves for our past mistakes and to forgive others for theirs.

Gaining maturity affords us a greater perspective on life and our relationships. Life's struggles and pain can endow us with a sensitivity and compassion for others, including people who are different from us, and give a deeper appreciation of life and close relationships. As Colarusso (1997) reminds us, deeper connections to others produce feelings of poignancy as we realize the prospect of loss, especially as we move into later phases of adulthood.

Life is full of transitions and changes; the meanings we make of these, beyond the objective happenings themselves, are critical to how we react and adapt. It is important to understand "how people 'make sense' of the course of their lives, including problems in maintaining a coherent sense of self" (Cohler and Galatzer-Levy, 1990, p. 222). Levinson's concern with the life structure and its meanings to people at varying points in time carries a similar message (Levinson and Levinson, 1996).

The search for meaning, however, is a cognitive exercise (albeit with an affective connection) occurring at a conscious level; but our past history is always with us, even if not acknowledged, recognized, or remembered. If we asked Mrs. B., Susan's mother (in Chapter 9), about the meaning of her daughter to her and of her attachment to her daughter, she could answer this. However she did not seem to be aware of the meaning of the deep emotional impact on her of her own mother's early death and how this connected to her fears of being apart from Susan. In what has been described as anniversary suicides, people have committed suicide at the same age a parent was when that parent also committed suicide. Does the suicidal offspring always understand the meaning of this act?

As we turn to Chapter 12 on transitions, crises, and loss, the combined perspectives of looking at objective events, the cognitive meanings people make of these events, their affective reactions, and the conflicts and traumas these events evoke will further our deepest understanding. If indeed the wisdom of late adulthood enables people to integrate logic and emotion, let us borrow this wisdom as we continue to explore and understand human development.

LEARNING EXERCISE

Interview an elderly person (not a relative or client) and discuss his or her views of life and social world. What values does he or she hold to be important, and what are some of the main factors that contribute to his or her present satisfaction and/or dissatisfaction with life? What are his or her views about the needs of the elderly population?

SUGGESTED READING

Articles

Cain, B. 1988. Divorce among elderly women: A growing social phenomenon. *Social Casework* 69: 563-568.

Mackey, R. A., and B. A. O'Brien. 1999. Adaptation in lasting marriages. *Families in Society* 80: 587-596.

McDermott, C. J. 1990. Empowering elderly nursing home residents: The resident's campaign rights. *Social Work* 35: 155-157.
Schroffel, A. 2004. Characteristics of female perpetrators of domestic violence in group therapy. *Smith College Studies in Social Work* 74: 505-524.

Books

Akhtar, S., and S. Kramer. (eds.) 1997. *The seasons of life: Separation-individuation perspectives.* Northvale, NJ: Jason Aronson.
Kennedy, G. J. 2000. *Geriatric mental health care: A treatment guide for health professionals.* New York: The Guilford Press.
Levinson, D., and J. Levinson. 1996. *The seasons of a woman's life.* New York: Knopf.
Nemiroff, R., and C. Colarusso. 1990. *New dimensions in adult development.* New York: Basic Books.
Qualls, S. H., and N. Abeles. (eds.) 2000. *Psychology and the aging revolution.* Association.
Scharff, D., and J. Scharff. 1991. *Object relations couple therapy.* Northvale, NJ: Jason Aronson.

SECTION III:
SPECIAL ISSUES

Chapter 12

Life Transitions, Turning Points, Crises, and Loss

There is a sadness in coming to the end of anything in life. Man's instinct clings to the Life that will never end.

Stuart Dodgson Collingwood,
The Life and Letters of Lewis Carroll, 1898

INTRODUCTION

We like to think that a permanency exists in our lives, we will remain, our parents will, and our homes will stay the same. However, perhaps the only permanent aspect in our lives is the inevitability of change, beginning from the moment of conception, and advancing as the embryo becomes a fetus. Birth abruptly expels the child from the womb into its first encounter with mother, who now experiences holding a real child who for so long had been part of her body. Otto Rank saw this expulsion from the womb as the birth trauma, the root of all separation anxiety.

Change not only brings with it anticipation, excitement, anxiety, and new opportunities, but also the loss of what has been. Watching their child walk across the stage to receive a high school diploma is one of life's most poignant moments for many parents; pride and love are intermingled with sadness and the realization that the child has begun the transition from adolescence into the beginnings of early adulthood, often accompanied by leaving home. "The pain of loss and suffering that so assuredly accompanies living is ever present at all stages of the life cycle" (Kramer, 1998, p. 211).

This chapter discusses the nature of life transitions, turning points, and crises that people encounter, and how they can produce breakdown, but also have the potential of producing further growth. Losses are addressed from the perspective of those inevitable in transversing the life cycle as well as those experienced in painful life events, such as divorce. Loss can also be experienced in relation to positive life events; changes, even those most eagerly anticipated events—such as in a promotion, eagerly awaited, means saying good-bye to one's old position and perhaps to one's colleagues.

This chapter concludes with a discussion of death, the ultimate loss, including death of people close to us as well as the anticipation of our own passing. Although this subject can be frightening and extraordinarily painful, it also presents opportunities for working out conflictual relationships, renewing a sense of meaning of life, and enhancing closeness to others through feeling love and that we are valued.

TRANSITIONS

Schlossberg (1981) has developed a useful model for the analysis of transitions and how people adapt to them, and includes three sets of factors: the first relates to the characteristics of the transition itself, such as whether it represents a loss or a gain; the second relates to the characteristics of the pretransition and posttransition environments, such as the presence of support systems; and the third relates to the characteristics of the individual, such as the person's psychosocial competence.

Schlossberg (1981) asserts that a transition has occurred if the event brings about new ways in which people think about themselves and the world, which then calls for a "corresponding change in one's behavior and relationships" (p. 5). She includes nonevents (which are events that have not occurred, such as not becoming pregnant); it is what Levinson and Levinson (1996) refer to as "important *unfilled components* in the life structure" (p. 23; italics in the original). When clients seek clinical services, it is our inclination to ask: what happened? We might not think to ask: what did *not* happen?

Characteristics of the Transition

Schlossberg (1981) describes the following seven specific attributes that characterize transitions.

Role Change: Gain or Loss

Transitions often involve changes in one's role. Becoming engaged might be a *role gain*. Losing a job, by contrast, might represent a *role loss;* whether a negative or positive change occurs, "some degree of stress" is experienced by the person (Schlossberg, 1981, p. 8).

Affect: Positive or Negative

People have feelings about going through a transition, which can be primarily positive (as in getting married) or primarily negative (as in bereavement); ambivalence usually accompanies role changes; new parents, for example, typically have mixed emotions (Schlossberg, 1981).

Source: Internal or External

People often have a choice in their life decisions; at other times, a determination is made for them by life circumstances or by other people. Some people may choose to go to medical school, because that is their dream; others might feel they are left without a choice, because it is their parents' dream. The key element involved here is the perception of "control over one's own life" (Schlossberg, 1981, p. 9).

The concept of *locus of control* is important in the psychology of motivation; developing a good sense of agency, that is self-direction and will, a similar concept, addressed in Chapter 2. People who believe that they have no control over their lives are said to have an *external* locus of control. It is thought that people who have (and believe they have) an *internal* locus of control have better mental health; and this is an important indicator of resilience (Richman and Bowen, 1997). Pinderhughes (1983) has popularized the concept of *empowerment* in social work, which she sees as "the treatment goal for all clients"; it is defined as "the ability and capacity to cope constructively with the forces that undermine and hinder coping, the achievement of some reasonable control over their destiny" (p. 333).

Timing: On Time or Off Time

In the life-cycle perspective, major life events occur at relatively predictable points in time. Schlossberg (1981) refers to Neugarten's (1979) concept of on-time and off-time events, and to the fact that many people compare themselves with others with regard to where they are in terms of life-cycle events. Neugarten (1979) has claimed that timing has become less relevant because events in our diverse society today are now occurring at off times. Schlossberg (1981) contends that the timing of life events is still relevant, as people remain concerned about where they are in comparison to others of the same age.

Onset: Gradual or Sudden

Many of life's events are expected, gradual, or planned for, such as graduations, marriages, and the birth of a baby at the end of a pregnancy. Generally, it is easier to adapt to an event that one has anticipated and prepared for than to be surprised by a sudden event, such as a natural disaster, a heart attack, or, more positively, a promotion one has not anticipated (Schlossberg, 1981).

However, although life events of gradual onset enable people to prepare for them, it does not mean that they necessarily do so. People may deny an upcoming change and do nothing mentally or in reality to plan for the change. Paradoxically, some people may be better prepared for sudden changes, because they may have fantasized about them, even if they thought the event was unlikely to happen.

In Chapter 9, we discussed a four-year-old about to have back surgery who playacted the event with her grandfather, helping her to anticipate what was going to happen and to cope with it. The technique of *anticipatory guidance* can be helpful to clients facing a transition; children about to be placed in a foster home may feel less overwhelmed, if they have a chance to process this, to anticipate the steps of what might happen, and to rehearse what they might do and feel in this new situation.

Duration: Permanent, Temporary, or Uncertain

How long the transition will last affects one's adaptation to it; if the transition event is something positive, such as a promotion, one can feel good about it being permanent; if the event is undesirable, one will feel better to think that it will be over soon (Schlossberg, 1981). It should be added that the idea of "permanency," even of a desirable event, such as the thought of being married to a person forever, can add to one's anxiety.

Probably the greatest distress is connected to events that are uncertain in outcome, especially negative events, such as illness (Schlossberg, 1981). To be left with ambiguities rather than answers can be devastating.

Degree of Stress

Although all transitions involve some stress, it is important to look specifically at the magnitude of stress involved for a person in the process of transition. Schlossberg (1981) refers to the well-known Social Readjustment Rating Scale devised by Holmes and Rahe in 1967; the premise of the Holmes-Rahe scale is that all change, whether negative or positive (even vacations and holidays), produces stress, and people who have gone through multiple changes in a short time are at greater risk of becoming sick. The scale ranks different types of stress; the highest stress is associated with the death of a spouse; and the lowest stresses are events such as vacations. A person's general state of mental and physical health are also ranked. Schlossberg (1981) has some reservations about the Holmes-Rahe Scale, including the lack of attention to individual variation, since the subjective reactions people may have to a given stressor vary.

Schlossberg (1981) also places emphasis on the "balance between a person's deficits and resources at the time the event occurs" (pp. 9-10). By resources she refers to the person's general biopsychosocial state, including supportive relationships and capacity to cope. She observes that the ratio of strengths to deficits can vary over time.

Characteristics of Pretransition and Posttransition Environments

Schlossberg (1981) categorizes environmental influences affecting a person's adaptation to transitions as follows: interpersonal support systems, institutional supports, and physical setting.

Interpersonal Support System

Emphasizing that the ability to care for others as well as to receive and accept support for oneself is important, Schlossberg (1981) highlights three types of supportive systems that help people adapt to stressful transitions: intimate relationships, the family unit, and the network of friends; these concepts were discussed in Chapter 5.

Institutional Supports

Institutions refer to a wide variety of community organizations and their roles in providing services and emotional support (Schlossberg, 1981). Work organizations, for example, can be sources of stress and/or support for their employees. Societal rituals, such as weddings and graduations, provide needed support and validation to people; by contrast, supportive rituals are not available to people going to court for a divorce.

Physical Setting

The physical setting including weather, neighborhoods, and living arrangements is also relevant in coping with transitions. In discussing personal space, Schlossberg (1981) emphasizes the importance of "comfort, privacy, and aesthetics" (p. 12). (This topic was also addressed in Chapter 5.)

Characteristics of the Individual

Schlossberg (1981) discusses eight attributes of the individual contributing to adaptation to transitions, as follows:

1. psychosocial competence
2. sex (in the sense of gender and sex-role identification)
3. age (and life stages)
4. state of health
5. race-ethnicity
6. socioeconomic status
7. value orientation
8. previous experience with a transition of a similar nature.

As these psychosocial characteristics are similar to those already discussed in this book, we will not detail them here.

Not every transition has a great emotional impact on people; however some transitions are *turning points,* which are events of special meaning and significance to the individual.

TURNING POINTS

Turning points are "turns in the road, changes in the direction or the trajectory of our lives" (McAdams, Josselson, and Lieblich, 2001, p. xv). These turning points can be experienced in positive or negative ways, and "sometimes what is experienced initially as tragedy or loss is later emplotted as epiphany or insight leading to growth" (p. xvii). A person may not be cognizant that he or she is going through a turning point when it is occurring; in fact, this is considered by some to be one of its conditions; "they are only recognized to be turning points as time passes and as it becomes clear that there has been a change in direction" (Wheaton and Gotlib, 1997, p. 1).

Emphasizing the *internal nature* of turning points, Wethington, Cooper, and Holmes assert that a person experiencing this phenomenon must have "a self-reflective awareness or insight into the significance of the change" (Schultz, 2001, p. 73). Clausen emphasizes the effect of turning points on four types of self-identity and life direction: "reformulations of life role, of life perspective, of life goals, or of self, the latter including profound realizations about one's strengths and weaknesses" (p. 74). Bruner (2001) focuses on *autobiographical turning points* that are within the writer's awareness, and are a "gateway to major inner change" (p. 31).

> Turning points are steps toward narrational consciousness. Not surprising that, in most autobiographies, they are located at points where the culture in fact gives more degrees of freedom . . . for example, high school graduation is one such point. . . . "At that point I started thinking about what I was, and I decided that". . . . All such passages are marked by a mental verb. This signals an "inside" transformation, a change in intentional state. (Bruner, 2001, p. 33)

Oscar Wilde's tragic imprisonment was a major turning point in his life: He was bankrupt, divorced by his wife, forbidden contact with his sons, and forced to do hard prison labor, for which he was unsuited. "He died broke, reviled, and largely alone" (Schultz, 2001, p. 68). During this period he wrote *De Profundis,* a *conversion narrative,* in which he described imprisonment as a turning point in his life, observing his "epiphany in prison, a self-realization in which he sees, for the first time, into his true nature" (p. 68). Wilde spoke of "the curative value of suffering," reflecting on the changes in his identity from pre-prison to his post-prison existence, which was now "committed to forgiveness, love, sorrow, and humility" (p. 74).

Although turning points are not theoretically difficult to define, pinpointing them in a given life can be more difficult. For example, how does one decide on the *durability* of a turning point: if a person declares himself changed, has this change lasted? According to Schultz (2001), if durability is not present, and "if the turning point produces no lasting behavioral outcome, then it [a turning point] probably did not happen" (p. 83). However, Schultz adds, there needs to be room for relapses. "Life is complex. There will be slippage. Even when change is relatively modest or fitful, the turning point concept may apply. It seems important to acknowledge that some turns might be more momentous than others, more sustaining" (p. 87).

Some authors stress that self-reflection, encompassing awareness of changes in self- and life direction, are deemed necessary for turning points to occur. However, is it possible to reach a turning point without any current or retrospective awareness? There are many instances, such as the denial of a death or a disability, where no cognitive "meaning making" of the event occurs, but in which the emotional consequences can be profound, and life-altering.

Franz Kafka was the firstborn child in his family. A younger brother, Georg, was born when Kafka was two, and died two years later, and a second brother, Heinrich, was born that year. Heinrich died six months later, when Kafka was almost five. Pawel (1984), a Kafka biographer, asserts that these losses had a strong impact on Kafka, but observes that Kafka barely refers to these events, and when he does, his accounts are "consistently flat, factual, and devoid of affect" (p. 16).

> It seems inconceivable that the grief of his parents, barely recovering from one death only to be struck by a second, could have been lost on the five-year-old and, once again, only child. And the fact that this particular tragedy never became part of the "memory come alive" makes it not less but, on the contrary, potentially far more significant than any conscious recollections. (Pawel, 1984, p. 16)

Laub and Sampson's (2003) longitudinal study of men with criminal histories focuses on the question of why some men who committed crimes in their teenage years were able to desist from crime in later years. Building upon the classical study of delinquents by Sheldon and Eleanor Glueck, Laub and Sampson (2003) interviewed a sample of these formerly incarcerated juveniles in their old age. The men who desisted from crime generally experienced turning points highlighted by successful marriages, employment, and serving in the military. Successful marriages had the greatest leverage.

> Marriage, especially strong marital attachment, has been implicated as a predictor of desistance from crime among men. . . . This idea was illustrated most directly by a former delinquent who had been married for forty-nine years when we interviewed him at age 70; "If I hadn't met my wife at the time I did, I'd probably be dead. It just changed my whole life . . . *that's my turning point right there.*" (Laub and Sampson, 2003, p. 41; italics added)

These men did not *choose* marriage as a *pathway* to desistance, but the consequent chain of interacting events led to this. For example, "as the investment in social bonds grows, the incentive for avoiding crime increases, because more is at stake" (Laub and Sampson, 2003, p. 41). Being married can have many consequences: enhancing self-esteem and feelings of being loved; becoming a parent can present responsibilities and rewards; and married life can change daily activities, with less time available to spend with former criminal associates. In cases where the men did not marry, or had an unsatisfactory marital relationship, they continued offending. However, the authors add, being married, does not provide a simple, causal, all-encompassing explanation. "From our perspective, the influence of marriage is nonetheless complex, operating through multiple mechanisms, *not all of which necessitate cognitive transformation*" (Laub and Sampson, 2003, p. 44; italics added).

Turning points can be considered in a broad sense, meaning any event that sets in motion some disruption in the normal chain of events, and provides new opportunities and/or a new direction (which can be positive or disastrous). These events have a psychological impact (even if a person is *unaware* of this), and can be externally triggered (e.g., being drafted into the army or being laid off from work) or internally triggered (as in deciding to get married or to emigrate).

Although most definitions of turning points highlight individual agency in the process, turning points can occur, I believe, without the input or even the actual presence of the subject, but can deeply affect the subject's life course. A critical (externally induced) turning point in Rudyard Kipling's life (discussed in Chapter 4) occurred about a year *before* he was born, when his English parents decided to move to India. How different would his life course have been had he never known India, not been separated from his parents for six years, but remained with them in England, and been raised among his English cousins?

CRISIS THEORY

The concept of crisis has been used in different ways by different authors; it is most often applied to external crises, often disasters, and usually unanticipated crises, such as witnessing (or being wounded in) a school shooting or losing one's home in a fire. The destruction of the World Trade Towers on 9/11 was a crisis that rocked the country; in New York "tens of thousands of Manhattan residents suffered emotional difficulties severe enough to warrant psychiatric treatment" (Goode, 2002, p. A15). The war in Iraq has produced much serious stress and trauma in military personnel. "The life-threatening character of the daily job steadily erodes an individual's psychological immune system" (Zabriskie, 2004, p. 41).

> The military has mobilized mental-health units . . . just behind the front lines. As the fighting has intensified over the past year, their number has increased. The goal, says [Major] Rabb is "to let troops know they're not going crazy because they have some emotional and physical and psychological aftereffects of the traumatic events that they witnessed." (Zabriskie, 2004, p. 42)

Erikson (1963), among others, has discussed *developmental* or *maturational crises,* which accompany changes through the life cycle; Mahler,

Pine, and Bergman (1975) refer to the *rapprochement* crisis. Crisis, however, in a clinical sense is generally equated with overwhelming stress; people are said to be in a state of crisis if they are experiencing such extreme stress that their usual coping mechanisms are not adequate to facilitate adaptation.

A crisis state can be experienced when going through an anticipated life event in an unanticipated manner, such as the premature birth of a child, or can be triggered by internal conflicts, such as separation anxiety or sexual confusion. These can trigger states of anxiety and/or depression and might precipitate a suicidal crisis.

Many clinicians agree that a state of crisis may be produced by both external and internal conditions. The classical writings on crisis theory address both; today, however, in practice, many place emphasis only on the external systems' elements of crisis management and on cognitive-behavioral adaptations, that is, helping the person with crises affecting social functioning by utilizing problem solving, finding appropriate resources, and enhancing coping mechanisms.

In discussing such crisis intervention in the emergency room, Puryear (1984) states:

> The five main principles of emergency room crisis intervention are: setting limited goals, employing focused problem solving, expecting the individuals or family to take some action on their own behalf, providing support for that action, and building self-reliance and self-esteem. These principles are employed in six basic steps: establishing rapport, taking charge, assessing the patient or family's problems and assets, closing and follow-up. . . . Specific techniques, such as assigning tasks, active listening, positive reinforcement, reversing, and reframing are employed to help mobilize people in crisis. (p. 33)

Caplan's definition of a crisis as "an upset in a steady state" (Rapoport, 1970, p. 277) is frequently used. People generally manage to adapt to change and "maintain a state of equilibrium" (p. 276). However, through life-cycle changes, life transitions, and external and internal crises, people may experience "sudden discontinuities by which the homeostatic state is disturbed and which result in a state of disequilibrium," but they may nevertheless be able to cope with these sudden changes through "adequate adaptive or equilibrating mechanisms" (p. 276). If not, they may enter a state of crisis, as their usual ways of solving problems are inadequate

> to the task for a rapid reestablishment of equilibrium. The *hazardous events,* or stress factors that precipitate the crisis require a solution that

is novel to the individual in relation to his previous life experience and usual and normal repertoire of problem-solving mechanisms. (p. 276; italics added)

The factors (or hazardous events) precipitating the crisis may be related not only to present life stresses but to past events, and "may reactivate and trigger off unresolved or partially resolved unconscious conflicts" (Rapoport, 1970, p. 276). Although often overwhelming the person with strong emotions, the crisis can at the same time serve as a catalyst in fostering recall of old memories and feelings; this offers an opportunity not only to resolve the present crisis but to work through past conflictual material. "Thus the crisis with its mobilization of energy may operate as a 'second chance' in correcting earlier distortion and maladaptions" (p. 277).

Three basic types of events are hazardous for the homeostatic state: "a threat, a loss, or a challenge" (Rapoport, 1970, p. 277).

A threat may be directed to instinctual needs or to an individual's sense of integrity or autonomy. A loss may be that of a person or an experience of acute deprivation. A challenge may be to survival, growth, mastery, or self-expression. Each of these states has a major characteristic affect. Threat carries with it high anxiety. Loss is experienced with affect of depression or mourning. Challenge is accompanied by some anxiety but carries with it an important ingredient of hope, release of energy for problem-solving, and expectation of mastery. (Rapoport, 1970, p. 277)

Rapoport (1970) highlights the major goals and techniques of crisis intervention. As time is of the essence, clients should be seen as soon as possible; long delays on waiting lists will adversely affect this group. Crisis work does not lend itself to a lengthy diagnostic process; "diagnosis and treatment go hand in hand" (p. 288); immediate help is essential while the state of crisis is ongoing. Individuals and families may become more resistant to clinical intervention once the crisis has passed; in the midst of a crisis, they are more amenable to reorganization (psychologically) individually and as a family. "A little help, rationally directed and purposefully focused at a strategic time, is more effective than more extensive help given at a period of less emotional accessibility" (p. 287). Although time limits are set (usually not more than six weeks, and often less) a flexible use of time is recommended; that is, people might need to be seen several times a week and/or for longer periods (more than one hour) each session.

A primary task of the clinician is to lower the client's anxiety; it is helpful for clinicians to share their thoughts with the client about what the problem is and what the "operating dynamics" are, in a way that "enables the client to get a manageable cognitive grasp of the situation" (Rapoport, 1970, p. 288). This understanding is very important as cognitive confusion often exists and the person is "bewildered and literally does not know how to grasp and understand what has been happening to him, how to evaluate reality, or how to anticipate, formulate, and evaluate the possible outcome of the crisis" (p. 281).

It is important to convey a sense of hope to the client; this involves having a "quality of intensity and investment in the client" (Rapoport, 1970, p. 289). Clinicians "should communicate actively both concern and authenticity," and at the same time utilize their "authority based on expertness and competence" (p. 300). Giving direction and advice, as well as helping the client develop a sense of autonomy and mastery as soon as possible, are often very effective when clients are overwhelmed. The establishment of a contract with the client is emphasized, as this helps to establish time boundaries, structure, and goals with the client's full participation.

Some variation exists in how crisis intervention ends; time limits are considered important, and clients are helped to anticipate future stress and think about how they might cope with it. In some models of crisis intervention, the client is given the choice of continuing in more conventional therapy (usually with another clinician) or is offered the option of returning in the future, if needed.

Many writers stress the importance of knowing the precipitating problem leading to the crisis. Rapoport (1970) has observed that sometimes the cognitive mastery gained from understanding the precipitating stress can be so therapeutically helpful that the client needs no additional clinical help. Some writers have emphasized that the precipitating factor might have stirred underlying psychological pain, which in itself needs to be explored. Hoffman and Remmel (1975) are cautious about accepting the precipitating event at face value as the main focus; they talk about the *precipitant,* which is "the thought or feeling aroused by the precipitating event. . . . It is the pain connected with the earlier unresolved conflict, and it is precisely this experience that impels the client to pick up the telephone to call for help" (p. 260).

Hoffman and Remmel (1975) are referring primarily to the traditional clinical model of clients seeking help with internal psychological distress, even if precipitated by an external event, such as a wife calling for help because her husband had left her. Although this abandonment will be upsetting to most wives, the precipitant might be the pain arising from past and previously unexplored losses and/or rejections.

Crisis intervention, however, is often applied to situations in which clients do not pick up the phone and call for help but in which they are offered help, as in extreme, externally produced crises such as fires or military combat. Complex and subtle distinctions must be considered here; some crises produced by external disasters, such as Hurricane Katrina in New Orleans, are so overwhelming that most people will be in a state of shock and disequilibrium after experiencing them. However, even in these crises, people still bring with them a past history of attachment and loss that will eventuate in differentiated and individual ways of responding both to the crisis and to offers of help.

The degree to which the emotional meaning of the crisis and the conflicts underlying it are addressed also relate to the theoretical orientation of the clinician and the helping agency. Smith (1976) has observed that two divergent approaches are taken to crisis treatment: "Jacobsen, Strickler and Morley (1968) refer to them as the generic and individual approaches to crisis intervention" (p. 167). Clinicians using the *generic* model analyze specific hazardous events (such as going through the divorce process), then develop specific treatment protocols related to the stresses produced by the crisis and the tasks needed to resolve it. In the *individual* approach, no tasks are predetermined, but the focus is "on the problem-solving activities that each individual must accomplish in resolving the crisis. . . . Psychological tasks are used to resolve the crisis but these tasks differ from one client to another" (Smith, 1976, p. 167).

The following case illustrates an individual approach and is followed by a discussion of a generic approach to crisis intervention.

Case Illustration of the Individual Approach → problem solving activities
to Crisis Intervention   to resolve the crisis.

Aguilera and Messick (1974) discuss the case of Mr. Z., which illustrates an effective use of crisis intervention techniques. Mr. Z., forty-three, president of a large corporation, was married and had three children. He apparently was in a state of equilibrium until the day he collapsed at work with a heart attack and was immediately hospitalized. He had been in good health and had no history of cardiac problems. However, his father and one brother died at about his age and his only living brother was seriously incapacitated, all due to heart problems. Mr. Z. had taken good care of his health and diet, and exercised vigorously; he was "determined to avoid dying young or becoming an invalid like his brother" (p. 100).

Mr. Z. was an "exceedingly difficult patient," who was anxious, slept poorly, denied being worried about his physical problem, and demanded constant explanations of everything. His heart attack was judged to be mild with a good prognosis. His doctor felt that he was not coping well with his illness and referred him for crisis intervention.

> In the first session the therapist observed Mr. Z.'s overt and covert signs of anxiety and depression and determined, through discussion with him his *perception* of what hospitalization meant to him, his usual *patterns of coping* with stress, and available *situational supports*. (Aguilera and Messick, 1974, p. 102; italics added)

This approach is generally used in crisis work: assessing how the client perceives the problem, the client's usual ways of coping, and using available situational (or environmental) supports, which, in this case, involved talking with Mr. Z.'s wife and doctor. The crisis therapist felt that the primary problem was Mr. Z.'s fear that he would either die or become an invalid and also felt that his wife needed emotional support to support her husband. Understanding the source of Mr. Z.'s anxiety and observing his poor coping in the hospital, the crisis therapist recommended that he be removed from intensive care to a private room, and be allowed half-hour periods of phone calls three times a day so that he could continue to be involved with his business.

When this was accomplished, Mr. Z. relaxed considerably and adapted to the hospital regimen. He shared with the clinician his feelings about the past losses of his father and brother, and his anxieties about his own future. The following excerpt illustrates how an interview focused on concerns in the here and now becomes a critical tool in crisis intervention.

> Through discussion and verbal feedback, it was possible to get Mr. Z. to view his illness and the changes it would make in his life in a realistic perspective. No, he was *not* an invalid. Yes, he *would* be able to work and live a *normal* life. No, he would *not* have to give up sailing, just have someone else do most of the crewing. Yes, he *would* be able to resume his activities but would continue them at a more leisurely pace. . . . Gradually he became more accepting as he began to realize the impending myocardial infarction was a warning he should heed and that with proper care and some diminishing of his usual hectic pace he could continue to live a productive and useful life. (Aguilera and Messick, 1974, p. 104; italics in the original)

In addition to providing emotional support to his wife, the clinician discussed with her some needed changes in his lifestyle; Mrs. Z. was also helped to understand that her husband was not fragile and *could* cope, thus relieving some of the burden on Mrs. Z. "The children and Mrs. Z. were encouraged to continue in their daily activities so that Mr. Z. would not feel that his being at home was disrupting to their lives" (Aguilera and Messick, 1974, p. 105). Anticipation of future events, such as Mr. Z. returning home, were discussed; this is typical in crisis intervention. Six sessions took place, which were contracted in advance, with emphasis on his strength and autonomy—all features of crisis work.

Mr. Z. and his wife were helped to adapt, and their anxiety was greatly reduced. Mr. Z. could "intellectually understand his reasons for his denial and dependence/independence conflicts" and could accept the possibility that his illness could recur: "'At least now I've learned to relax and roll with the punches'" (Aguilera and Messick, 1974, p. 105).

Mr. Z. was in a crisis: he was overwhelmed with anxiety; his basic equilibrium was disturbed, as was his family's equilibrium. Mr. Z. was fortunate to be referred to a clinician; many people with similar problems are not afforded this opportunity. Mr. Z. received important psychological help; his losses and his fears about his own mortality and disability were surfaced as he faced his own worst nightmare and coped with it.

Analyzing Mr. Z.'s case in terms of Schlossberg's (1981) classification of transitions:

1. We observe a role change, as Mr. Z. temporarily lost his role as an executive and took on the role of patient.
2. His affect was negative, as his anxiety level was high and he was depressed.
3. The source was external, as he had no control over this event (even though it occurred internally, within his body).
4. The question of whether this was on time or off time is debatable (he was in the prime of life, and not "old enough" to be disabled this way, although it is not uncommon for people to have heart attacks at his age; it was, however, an on-time event in terms of his family history).
5. The onset was sudden (extremely so), although at some level he may have been anticipating this could happen.
6. The duration of this transition was permanent, in that it was clear that he was vulnerable to heart problems, and some damage had been done.
7. It was also temporary, as the critical point of the illness had passed, and he could resume his previous level of functioning, with some limitations.
8. It was also uncertain because the condition could recur.
9. The degree of stress he experienced was very high, although this improved with intervention.

In looking at the pretransition and posttransition environments, we observe that he was able to control his employment status and had a good interpersonal family support system. However, due to this stress, his wife was "caving in," and, without the intervention, she might not have been able to deal with his demanding and anxiety-provoking behaviors; her inability to support him appropriately might have led to further maladaption and disequilibrium in the marital situation. The couple's sexual relationship and how Mr. Z.'s heart problem might affect this, realistically and subjectively, was one factor that was not discussed in this case. Olkin (1999) has observed that there is often an "absence of discussion about sex and disability" (p. 226).

Mr. Z.'s immediate physical setting, the cardiac intensive care unit, was not advantageous for him emotionally, adding to his distress. An environmental modification was made, as the clinician recommended that he be moved to a private room; the change improved his mental state.

In terms of his individual characteristics, we can say that Mr. Z. had a high level of psychosocial competence, that he was identified with his male role, that he was in Levinson and Levinson's (1996) transition-building life stage of young adulthood going into middle adulthood, that his state of health had been good, and that he made a good recovery (with a good prognosis) from his cardiac problem. Mr. Z. had a high socioeconomic status, and his value orientation seemed dominated by work and success. He had no previous experience with a transition like this, but he faced a similar situation with his father and his two brothers, and probably with himself in fantasy. His success in mastering this event, entailing as it did his being in a temporarily dependent state, would probably enable him to cope better if he were to fall ill again, though he might benefit from additional support in that event.

Absent Mr. Z.'s high level of psychosocial competence, not every person going through this experience would have adapted so well in such a short period of time. Someone, for example, with a fragile ego, a latent psychotic fear of annihilation, or a panic disorder might have seriously decompensated during such a medical crisis and would have been in need of more extensive help; a marriage on the verge of dissolution might also have produced different consequences.

Illustration of the Generic Model of Crisis Intervention

Clinicians using the generic model analyze specific hazardous events and develop specific treatment protocols related to the stresses that these crises produce and the tasks needed to resolve them. One well-known generic model involves working with mothers who have given birth to premature babies (Kaplan and Mason, 1965). The authors have analyzed the stresses that mothers go through in such an event, including having an unanticipated delivery; experiencing anxiety about whether the baby will live and, if so, be normal; returning home without the baby (who usually needs to remain at the hospital); and adapting to the baby's return home.

Kaplan and Mason (1965) found that the mother must complete four psychological tasks which are necessary for her adaptation and for the development of a positive relationship with her child. When the baby is delivered, the mother's first task is "preparation for a possible loss of the child" (p. 124); next she must come to terms with "her [feelings of] maternal failure to deliver a normal full-term baby" (p. 124). As she grapples with these tasks, "anticipatory grief and depression" occur simultaneously (p. 124). The third step, after the baby has been in the hospital for several weeks, is "the resumption of the process of relating to the baby" (p. 124); finally, she learns in what ways a premature baby is different due to "its special needs and growth patterns" (p. 125).

As they are structured and specific, the protocols that have proliferated for specific tasks related to crisis types have often been carried out by paraprofessionals. Protocols can also sensitize clinicians to clients' possible reactions in a specific crisis; In addition, knowing that many people have similar feelings in similar situations, the clinician can validate a client's feelings about the crisis.

Analyzing hazardous events has led to the development of prevention programs, such as *primary prevention* programs, set up before an anticipated crisis might occur. Working with patients and families prior to admission to hospitals or nursing homes, for example, can help them anticipate problems and their own adaptations, and prepare them to work on these specific issues.

News reports of community disasters, often mention that crisis teams are being sent to help people deal with their feelings and changed life circumstances. This form of *secondary prevention* can help people express their feelings, gain support, and hopefully prevent emotional decompensation.

However, when generic crisis intervention deals only with tasks inherent in a specific hazardous event, the specific meaning of the crisis to the individual and the psychological conflicts that may be precipitated by this event are often left unexplored; in addition, variations in individual adaptations are not acknowledged, even though they may be highly significant. Recognition of such variations (e.g., the presence of severe psychopathology or characterological patterns) requires some effort at differential diagnosis.

Woods and Hollis (1990) discuss a case in which a supportive policewoman, using a generic model, was providing crisis intervention for a woman who had been raped. The policewoman, who had learned in her training that the expression of anger was an essential piece of the rape protocol, pressured the woman to talk about her anger; but the woman, unbeknownst to the helper, was experiencing flashbacks and was still too frightened even to feel her anger. Woods and Hollis (1990) express concern about generic models that are designed and utilized in a rigid way; in addition, they express concern about inadequacy of training for many of the people carrying out this work.

Discussion

Crisis intervention is widely practiced today. From the systems perspective, it is one of the short-term models in particular favor with managed care companies. Generally, it is time limited, focused on a primary (i.e., immediate and apparent) problem, and aims to help clients restore their previous level of functioning and equilibrium. Crisis intervention has been used very effectively in many situations, as we saw with the case of Mr. Z. However, a number of serious problems are encountered with this approach: (1) the ways in which a crisis may mask underlying psychological issues can be overlooked; (2) it may be applied blindly to people for whom crisis is a way of life; and (3) it may be seen as a cure-all substitute for needed ongoing support and psychotherapy.

Psychological Issues in Crisis Intervention

As originally envisaged, crisis intervention has the potential not only to return people to their baseline level of functioning but also to help them reach higher levels of personality organization by working on key issues while the person is open to change. However, the views of different clinicians, as to how this happens, or even, whether this should happen, reveal inconsistencies. In fact, some lack of clarity exists in this regard in Rapoport's (1970) classical article on crisis intervention. On the one hand, Rapoport asserts that crisis intervention has a strong focus on the here and now and relies heavily on problem-solving approaches. However, without describing the mechanisms involved, she also comments that crisis intervention can produce important personality changes and help resolve old conflicts, a view also expressed by Woods and Hollis (1990).

Hoffman and Remmel (1975) do not accept the premise of simply applying specific tasks to help clients solve their presenting problems; they are concerned with discovering the underlying precipitant, which is what actually motivates the call for help. Golan (1980) expresses concern that if clinicians look with a narrow focus only at the problem to be solved, they may "miss entirely the clues that other, more lasting disruptions are taking place concurrently" in the client's life (p. 547). She also discusses transitional issues in a person's life that might be "obscured by the acute aspects of the immediate situation" (p. 543).

Crisis As a Way of Life

Although crisis is generally seen as a disturbance in a steady state, for some people living in crisis is a "quasi-steady" state; crisis work has sometimes been misapplied when working with this population (Rapoport, 1970). Some of these people have borderline personalities or character disorders; Reiner and Kaufman (1959) have described people with these underlying tendencies to be impulsive and to act out, creating chaos for themselves and others in their world; their crisis orientation is a way of protecting themselves from feeling their underlying depression. "Persons with character disorders are constantly threatened by the anxiety stemming from an unresolved depression. Much of their activity is designed to ward off the anxiety" (p. 7).

> These impulse-ridden people appear to be in a perpetual state of crisis. It is not so much that they enjoy the uncertainty and chaos, as that they must have "something happening" in order to feel alive. . . . One must relate to these clients in the midst of their crises, or not at all. A further difficulty is that these acting-out persons—in spite of the intensity of their emotions—cannot enter into a discussion of their feelings and behavior. Their way of communicating is through action. (Reiner and Kaufman, 1959, p. 8)

Owing to these clients' intense feelings, their manipulativeness, and the tendency to enmesh the clinician in their chaos, it is not unusual for the latter to be drawn into this maelstrom. Beginning social work students are especially vulnerable, as they attempt to "fix" the problem and restore peace. It is also not uncommon to see this anxiety and chaos transmitted to the agency itself, as staff become involved in an atmosphere of crisis.

People with character disorders and borderline personalities need long-term, supportive treatment, and traditional crisis-oriented work is not the treatment of choice, although in certain situations emergency help is essential (Rapoport, 1970; Woods and Hollis, 1990).

Crisis Intervention As Insufficient Treatment

Time limits for crisis treatment are strictly adhered to; usually six weeks is the maximum time allowed. Some clients need more time to work out their crisis-related problems, and these time constraints can result in pressuring clients who need a slower pace and more time to integrate the traumatic events they have experienced (Woods and Hollis, 1990). Caplan (1976), the father of crisis theory, has questioned his original recommendation for six weeks of therapy following bereavement. He has observed that although people can mobilize useful resources during the initial crisis, this state is "usually followed by a *prolonged* period of adjustment during the adaptation to a radically new pattern of life . . . the issues involved . . . demanded that [he, Caplan] continue supportive contact" (Caplan, 1976, p. xv). Applegate and Bonovitz (1995) express concern about underlying developmental issues being left untouched in brief treatment; patients' "core psychosocial issues [remain] unseen and untreated. They remain frozen in failure" (p. 10).

Crisis intervention serves many useful purposes and can help restore functioning when it has been derailed; it can also be beneficial as a part of an ongoing therapy when a client becomes immobilized. It was suggested in Chapter 2 that when executive functioning and cognitive functioning falter, it is important to restore these functions, and methodologies developed through the application of crisis theory can be very helpful in this process. Crisis therapy is frequently valuable when it is the treatment of choice; it is problematic today because often no choice is given. Instead, it is mandated by managed care and its providers because it appears to be efficient, "neat," and inexpensive.

LOSS AND GRIEF

Loss, in a normative way, accompanies us throughout the life cycle, as we separate from our parents, change jobs, watch our children become adults and move away, face the death of people we know, and contemplate our own ending. Throughout this book other losses have been discussed, such as giving up a baby for adoption, being placed in a foster home, becoming an immigrant, and learning that one is infertile. During the divorce process, parents mourn the ending of a marital relationship, and children witness the end of their family as they knew it; these children may experience additional losses, such as their family home and leaving their old school, neighborhood, and friends (Davies, 1999). Disability and illness present many losses, including depletion of energy, sensory deprivation (resulting from loss of hearing and sight), loss of a sense of body integrity (as in amputations or mastectomies), and loss of ability to communicate (as in aphasia produced by strokes). These *primary* losses can lead to *secondary* losses related to an inability to take care of oneself, the dissolution of a marriage or partnership, and the loss of a social network, which can, in turn, produce lowered self-esteem, reactive depression, and anxiety states.

Parents of children with disabilities, chronic illness, and psychiatric illness also experience the loss of the child "that might have been," and some writers have discussed the perpetual mourning such parents experience. Gombosi (1998), a psychoanalyst who is also the father of an autistic child, discussed the "trauma" of this discovery when his son was two and the sense of "dislocation" that he has observed in parents of autistic children, "accompanied by intense feelings, including sadness, rage, fright, and intense attachment to the child" (p. 262). He feels that parents can adapt to having an autistic child, but "I think most successful parents of autistic children have a profound sense of the tragic in their lives" (p. 263).

FACING DEATH

It is painful to think of death coming to those we are close to; it is especially painful to think of ourselves dying; perhaps this is why most of us tend to deny that this will happen. Noam (1996) cites Woody Allen as saying "'I do not want to gain immortality through my work, I want to gain it through not dying!'" (p. 155). Dying means saying good-bye to all that we know and all whom we know. It also faces us with the existential dilemma of not being.

> I did not do badly in the almost 80 years of my life. I even learned how to live a little from the people who did not know and came to me to learn. But now I am stuck again. I am not ready to die, not ready to say good-bye to this life. I am not ready to say good-bye to myself. That seems to be the worst: to say good-bye to myself. (Grotjohn, 1985, p. 297; Colarusso, 1998, pp. 127-128)

As it is so difficult a subject for us to face we tend to assume no one wants to talk about it, least of all a person who is facing death. However, terminally ill patients usually want to talk about dying; the frequent problem is no one wants to listen. Dempsey (1971) talks about the inaccessibility of doctors and other helping professionals when it comes to listening. A patient is quoted by Dempsey as saying: "It's hard to carry on a conversation with Dr. X. when he comes in the room with a stethoscope in his ears and puts a thermometer in my mouth." It was observed, in one large hospital in Chicago, thirty years ago, that while the professional staff was certain patients were too emotionally vulnerable to talk about their impending deaths, the patients were able to find one group of staff members who would listen, the cleaning women, usually conversing with them in the middle of the night.

Today, there is more attention focused on palliative or end-of-life care; but "although some progress is being made, end-of-life care in this country is still mediocre, at best" (Berzoff and Silverman, 2004, p. 7).

One of the most distinguished pioneers in the field of death and dying is Elisabeth Kübler-Ross (1969), who stressed the importance of bringing this subject out into the open and talking freely about it with patients and their loved ones. Death has always been with us; however, changes have occurred in the way we respond to death now from the way people responded in the past. Paradoxically, as Kübler-Ross herself emphasizes, it is a fact that we generally handled this event better in the past than we seem able to do now, despite (or perhaps because of) all the advances in our modern medicine. In fact, these very advances may have complicated the whole process of dying.

People generally died at home in the past, with family and friends around them. The family physician probably knew the patient most of his or her life and was part of the social network of the family. Today, people tend to die in hospitals, attached to the best machines that modern medicine has discovered. Kübler-Ross (1969) asks: "Is this approach our own way to cope with and repress the anxieties that a terminally or critically ill patient evokes in us?" (p. 9).

Through her experience in talking to dying patients, Kübler-Ross developed a typology of five stages of coping mechanisms with which these patients deal with their terminal illness, which are denial and isolation, anger, bargaining, depression, and acceptance.

Stages of Coping with Death

First Stage: Denial and Isolation

Initially when told about the seriousness of their illness, most patients react with denial that this is happening; "'No, not me, it cannot be true'" (Kübler-Ross, 1969, p. 38). Patients will gradually give up their denial, but how and when (its timing) they do this varies considerably.

Second Stage: Anger

Once people no longer deny the problem, feelings of "anger, rage, envy, and resentment" tend to dominate their feelings; the question now is: "'Why me?'" (Kübler-Ross, 1969, p. 50); this stage can be difficult for family and staff to deal with; "this anger is displaced in all directions and projected onto the environment at times almost at random" (p. 50). Doctors and especially nurses are frequently criticized; families are "received with little cheerfulness and anticipation" (p. 51); families generally react "with grief and tears, guilt or shame, or avoid future visits, which only increases the patient's discomfort and anger" (p. 51).

Third Stage: Bargaining

In bargaining, the patient, who has gone through the first two stages, now makes some compromise or bargain to receive an extension of time, or some special privilege. Many of these bargains are made privately with God and often are kept a secret. Sometimes the patient will make special requests to the staff.

> The bargaining is really an attempt to postpone; it has to include a prize offered for "good behavior," it also sets a self-imposed "deadline" (e.g., [attending] the son's wedding), and it includes an implicit promise that the patient will not ask for more if this one postponement is granted. (Kübler-Ross, 1969, p. 84)

One woman wanted very much to leave the hospital for her son's wedding. The hospital took special measures to ensure that this could happen. "She had made all sorts of promises if she could only live long enough to attend this marriage" (Kübler-Ross, 1969, p. 83). She looked very happy when she left the hospital. "I will never forget the moment when she returned to the hospital. She looked tired and somewhat exhausted and—before I could say hello—said, 'now don't forget I have another son!'" (p. 83).

Fourth Stage: Depression

As terminally ill patients weaken or undergo more surgery or treatments, they no longer deny their illness, and their anger is usually superseded by deep feelings of loss. This loss can be on many levels, such as bodily depletion or disfigurement, finances (in part related to medical costs), employment, and ability to care for their children. Kübler-Ross (1969) distinguishes the ensuing *preparatory depression* from a *reactive depression:* a preparatory depression "does not occur as a result of a past loss, but is taking into account impending losses" (p. 86). Kübler-Ross (1969) emphasizes the point that "the patient is in the process of losing everything and everybody he loves"; he will not really be helped by reassurance but if "allowed to express his sorrow he will find a final acceptance much easier" (p. 87). It is not necessary even to talk; "It is much more a feeling that can be mutually expressed and is often done better with a touch of a hand, a stroking of the hair, or just a silent sitting together" (p. 87).

Fifth Stage: Acceptance

If the patient has successfully gone through the first four stages, he will reach the final stage of acceptance. Kübler-Ross (1969) observes that "this is not a happy stage" and in fact "is almost void of feelings" (p. 113). During this final phase, "It is as if the pain had gone, [and] the struggle is over," and the patient has gained some "peace and acceptance" (p. 113). The patient may lose interest in the outside world, and this may be an especially difficult time for the family. This is a time that "we may together listen to the song of a bird from the outside," and the presence of others may be reassuring to know "that he is not left alone when he is no longer talking" (p. 113).

Hope

Although each stage has its own tasks, Kübler-Ross (1969) talks about hope, "the one thing that usually persists through all these stages" (p. 138). She notes that "no matter what we call it, we found that all our patients maintained a little bit of it and were nourished by it especially in difficult times" (p. 139).

THE MOURNING PROCESS

Bereavement places a person in a vulnerable state; their physical and mental health can be negatively impacted (Kramer, 1998). The importance of grief and mourning have been emphasized in the literature; "loss and the incapacity to mourn appropriately is one core aspect of most types of psychopathology, not only depression" (Noam, 1996, p. 167). Although mourning is discussed most frequently in relation to death, it is also necessary to grieve other important losses in life.

Normal Grief

People are often in a state of shock when faced with the immediacy of a loss; it is an encompassing feeling that affects both the person's mind and body. People feel sad, cry frequently, and may feel that they are losing control of themselves or that they are "going crazy"; this is related to the intensity of the feelings, being flooded by emotions when they are unanticipated (or sometimes being numb and unable to feel). They become preoccupied with memories of the person lost and may have difficulty concentrating on other things. Sleep is often disturbed and frequent dreams of the one who died may trouble the bereaved. Disturbances in eating and weight loss (or weight gain) can occur; physical symptoms such as headaches may be present.

The person's preoccupation with the deceased may be expressed by wearing the deceased's clothing, touching his or her possessions, talking about him or her to others, and sometimes sensing the deceased's presence or having a visual illusion of him or her. These experiences are considered within the range of normal reactions (and sometimes people need to be reassured about their "normalcy"). In one study of widows and widowers in Wales, it was found that hallucinations of their deceased spouses were very common; most of the people interviewed felt that the presence of the hallucinations "helped" them (Rees, 1975, p. 70).

Linda Valli (a client discussed in Chapters 2 and 15) reported the following experience after her aunt died.

> At her aunt's funeral when she was a child, she saw her aunt in the coffin, which was a very upsetting experience for her. Shortly after this, she "saw" her Aunt sitting in a chair in the living room. . . . "She was sitting there— smiling!"

This "hallucination" was viewed as an "encapsulated" incident, occurring at the time of a death and its associated trauma for her.

Lindemann (1965), a pioneer in the field of bereavement (following his study of survivors of the Coconut Grove fire in Boston), has observed that if grief work is successfully accomplished, a person will achieve "emancipation from the bondage to the deceased, readjustment to the environment in which the deceased is missing, and the formation of new relationships" (pp. 10-11).

Bereavement rituals, found in all cultures, are often beneficial to mourners, though one can go through the rituals outwardly without mourning internally, and although support and the sharing of feelings with others is often very important to people, coming to terms with the loss is basically a personal process. "Beneath the surface of consciousness remains a core of deep sorrow that the bereaved person has to work through alone. Profound sorrow is silent" (Szalita, 1974, p. 673).

People vary in how and when they mourn; for many, after a loss, major life readjustments must take place, which (as noted in the previous discussion on crisis work) often take a long time; many people need support during this period as well.

Experiencing Grief

It is difficult to face loss, both in terms of the reality of the lost object itself and experiencing the intense feelings that usually accompany this loss. Erich Lindemann (1965) observed that "many patients try to avoid both the intense distress connected with the grief experience and the necessary expression of emotion" (p. 11). The intense pain of loss was expressed eloquently by George Foy (1999), who wrote about the death of his infant son in an intensive care unit when he was one month old. Foy, who is a professional writer, did not know if he would be able to write this story; he was so overcome with emotion that it seemed writing about it might prove impossible.

Foy was intensely involved with his son, Olivier, during his month of life. When Olivier died, Foy and his wife arranged a private burial; his preparations for the funeral helped sustain him, maintaining his feeling of connection with his son. The night before Olivier was to be cremated Foy was unable to sleep; he realized that after the cremation, the loss would be final, and that it would be impossible for him to do "anything more to take care of him. And then you will know, finally and absolutely, that you have lost [Olivier]" (Foy, 1999, p. 51). However, the worst part is the "beast," which is "quite simply, missing him, knowing he will not be with you ever again except in the makeshift and unworthy stories you tell" (p. 51).

Pathological Grief

The inability to mourn can produce a number of physical and psychological symptoms. People can experience pathological forms of grief, including depression, suicidal thoughts, substance abuse, and/or acting-out behaviors. People may develop somatic symptoms similar to those of the deceased person. "A woman whose late husband had suffered for years from Parkinson disease developed a Parkinson-like tremor, gait, and masklike face" (Szalita, 1974, p. 674).

People who have strongly ambivalent feelings toward the person who has died generally have more difficulty mourning that person and are more prone to pathological grief that is often accompanied by intense (and usually irrational) feelings of guilt.

Children and Loss

Children react to grief and loss in terms of their general developmental and cognitive stages, as well as their individual psychological makeup. A three-year-old boy was faced with the sudden death of his mother after a school shooting and continually asked his father where his mother was. His father tells him that his "mom's stomach was hurt," or "Mom went to sleep," or "You know where Jesus lives, don't you? Mama went to see Jesus."

> But [the boy] continues to look under the bed for his mommy. "Mom's in heaven," [father] tries to explain.
>
> "She'll fall out," [the boy] says, "When is she going to come home?"
>
> [The boy] talks to his rocking horse, whom the family named Cactus. "Cactus, my mom can't come home."
>
> And then at night, [the boy] tells his father, "I want to go to heaven too." (Labi, 1998, p. 37)

In this dialogue, we see the boy's deep distress over feelings of loss and abandonment and his age-appropriate lack of understanding permanency; he thinks concretely and attempts to master the situation by explaining it to his toy horse. However, he returns again to the wish that mother reappear; his primary concern is reconnecting to his mother.

Children suffer after parental loss and need considerable support, a chance to mourn their parents, and retain some connection and memories of them. They respond best if supportive caretakers to whom they are already attached (if possible) are available, or if not, people who have the capacity and motivation to reach out and attach to them.

Loss of Parents with AIDS

AIDS has taken the life of many adults and "left tens of thousands of children with dead or dying parents" (Aronson, 1996, p. 422). Although loss of a parent is always painful, children struggling with the trauma of parental AIDS and loss face multiple social problems and internal conflicts. For children experiencing parental loss to go through the mourning process successfully, "caring, supportive figures are crucial . . . [and] provide a 'holding environment'" (p. 423). Many of these children do *not* have a supportive, holding environment; they have had "significant gaps in their care as they are shifted to various relatives during [parental] hospitalizations" (p. 424). The ways the children and their parents "cope with such breaks in their connectedness can be critical to a more adaptive grief process" (p. 424).

One of the successful outcomes of mourning is the development of a positive identification with the lost object. Complicating this process for some children are a combination of their own ambivalent feelings toward the dead parent as well as criticisms about this parent from current caretakers.

In one case, a therapist worked with two sisters, Caitlin, twelve, and Mary, eight (Aronson, 1996). Prior to their mother's death, the girls were neglected by her and experienced abuse at the hands of her boyfriends. Caitlin and Mary were lying and stealing, and their grandmother threatened to put them in a foster home. The grandmother had a long-standing conflictual history with the girls' mother. The therapist attempted to help the sisters with their identification issues about their mother.

> During the course of treatment, the girls decided, on their own, to make two lists entitled "Ways to remember our mother" and "Ways *not* to remember our mother." Ways to remember mother included talking, crying, looking at pictures, and eliciting stories from their grandmother about the mother. Ways not to remember her included stealing, lying, cursing, playing hooky, not listening to adults, using drugs—all behaviors that they had heard attributed to their mother. Over time, the girls came to realize their pathological identification with their dead mother and began to develop identifications that were more positive, often based on stories told by their grandmother. (Incidentally, it took much work to help the grandmother understand the importance of relating stories that cast the mother in a positive light.) (Aronson, 1996, p. 426; italics in the original)

In another situation, Melissa, twelve, a Hispanic girl whose mother died of AIDS, told her therapist that she would make a point to walk by the cemetery where her mother was buried every day on her way home from school (Aronson, 1996). Melissa lived with an aunt and was "forbidden" to discuss her mother's death in her aunt's home. She spoke of her great distress at not being able to "ameliorate her mother's condition. . . . Melissa also described tearfully but helplessly pleading with her mother not to shoot up. She began to weep openly over the loss of her mother and the profound changes that had occurred in her life as a result" (p. 429). Melissa and her therapist discussed her loss and also how she missed sharing her progress with her mother. The therapist (in a variation of anticipatory work) discussed with Melissa how she might miss her mother in the future.

> We began to discuss what it would be like at the time of her prom and graduation, events that she would be unable to share with her mother. With help, Melissa acknowledged that through each stage of her life—graduation, marriage, and childbearing—she would be thinking of her mother and would need to reevaluate the loss in light of both

her own development and her mother's wishes and aspirations for her. (Aronson, 1996, p. 429)

Other specific problems tend to complicate the mourning process and subsequent adaptation for this group of children. The person who becomes the caretaker for a child following parental death plays a very important role in that child's life; "the caretaker should ideally be a substitute object already known to the child, to whom the child may transfer attachment" (Aronson, 1996, p. 429). This can be problematic for these children, many of whom have come from broken homes and have lived with various relatives and in foster homes.

It is also important that the child be allowed to express grief; this is not always permitted, "especially if the dead parent was an IV drug user or a homosexual—issues that the family . . . may not wish to have verbalized" (Aronson, 1996, p. 430).

Although these issues are characteristic of the problems surrounding AIDS, they are also relevant for many other children whose parents suffer from other protracted and disruptive illnesses in comparable circumstances. The approaches to intervention just described may also be applicable to them.

Factors Complicating the Mourning Process

Grief can be difficult for people to express for many reasons, such as having conflictual feelings about the person who died or abandoned them. People may also not be able to express grief about situations that do not receive social approval. This has been termed "'disenfranchised grief'" (MacGregor, 1994, p. 164), which is encountered when people have been disenfranchised by society from the normal grieving process because their loss is not "'openly acknowledged, publicly mourned, or socially supported'" (p. 164).

Disenfranchised grief can exist when one partner in a "secret" gay or lesbian relationship has died, and the grieving partner has no one with whom to share this pain. Parents of children with a serious mental illness may experience disenfranchised grief when the mental illness is stigmatized and they feel a lack of support in expressing their loss (MacGregor, 1994).

In some situations, bereavement ceremonies and rituals themselves have become disenfranchised. Families of psychiatric patients who have died in institutions often receive no assistance with bereavement when the patient has died, and peers in the institution as well as staff members close to the patient may not have any opportunities within the institution for memorial services or other alternative ways to share their sadness (Fauri and Grimes, 1994).

In the past, many Native Americans have been denied opportunities to formalize their burial rituals (Chapter 1). The Lakotas not only suffered massacres and other traumas of loss, but for many years were denied their ritual mourning ceremonies by the U.S. government (Brave Heart, 1998).

> For American Indians, historical unresolved grief involves the profound, unsettled bereavement that results from generations of devastating losses which have been disqualified (Doka, 1989) by prohibiting indigenous ceremonies and by the large society's denial of the magnitude of its genocidal policies. (Brave Heart, 1998, p. 288)

Mourning Past Losses

Past losses that have never been resolved are often discovered during the course of clinical work, and therapy offers a second opportunity to help clients work through these losses. Such losses can be related to an actual death or other life events, including separations relating to divorce or abandonment. Adoptive children, even those adopted from infancy, often have active fantasies about their "lost" birth parents (Chapter 7).

Sometimes clients see no value in exploring these losses. "For reasons, then, of death or remoteness, these figures seem totally unavailable, and frequently clients consider them insignificant or unimportant in their lives" (Hartman and Laird, 1983, p. 249). However, when clients are ready to look at these losses and their effects on their present life, this may be the "turning point in the client's family work, the most effective strategy for change" (p. 249).

Earlier in this chapter, we mentioned Linda Valli, who had visual hallucinations after her aunt's death. Linda's mother died when she was thirteen; she felt her mother was angry with her before she died, and Linda assumed that she herself was bad and at fault. She never fully grieved for her mother, but experienced anxiety, a poor self-image, and inner constriction instead.

> Linda's mother died of a cerebral hemorrhage when Linda was thirteen. With feelings of sadness, Linda described how, from the time she was twelve, she worried about her mother's health and had fears of her death, as her mother's health declined and her headaches increased. Father, from her description, was a distant figure who had little involvement with the family. Although there was "probably" an early positive relationship with her mother, Linda could not clearly remember this, and felt her brother was preferred. There was significant marital discord, and Linda's mother appeared to have been depressed, but it seemed as though she was not as chronically unhappy as she was during her last year. Linda cried as she talked about going to church and lighting a candle for her mother and saying a prayer for her to live.

During the course of her therapy, Linda's phobic symptoms cleared up, her self-esteem improved, and her tendency to internalize her negative and angry feelings decreased markedly. Reconnecting to her feelings and memories about her mother, and looking at their relationship, her mother's death, and her reactions to it from a different perspective were among the critical issues addressed in helping Linda integrate a stronger self-image.

Pill and Zabin (1997) offered time-limited, twelve-week group therapy sessions to women whose mothers had died when they were children, observing that they had a chronic and deep sense of isolation stemming from their early feelings of loss. The authors felt that the group method was effective in helping them process this experience, as it provided both emotional support and validation for their feelings, and a decreased sense of isolation. As they did not have mothers, they often felt they were different from other children and felt embarrassed and stigmatized. Their grief was compounded by "not being allowed to talk about their mothers," and if they had the rare opportunity of meeting someone else who had this experience, "they felt an immediate bond" (p. 187).

Difficulties in separation, transitions, endings, and feelings of inadequacy were among other common themes Pill and Zabin (1997) found, as well as difficulty acquiring social skills; as other children seldom came to visit, "social skills were not reinforced" (p. 189). Owing to their sense of unworthiness, they often were not comfortable having their needs met by others; many assumed a caretaking role in relation to others instead. Linda Valli, at age thirteen, had also assumed a caretaking role when, after her mother's death, she felt responsible for her ten-year-old sister; she "felt sorry for her." Linda "feels heartbroken now to see the unhappiness in her sister's current life."

Many of the women in the group felt fear and insecurity, "could not trust that others would remain available for them," and lived with frequent "fears of abandonment and rejection" (Pill and Zabin, 1997, p. 190). Guilt, which is frequently found in children experiencing parental bereavement, was often expressed. The group experience also helped the women mourn and share their grief; many made psychological efforts to connect with their mothers, both through internal processing and sometimes by discussing their mothers with others who knew them. Some group members also had poor preexisting relationships with their mothers, involving various forms of rejection or maltreatment; the group experience gave them an opportunity to work through these feelings.

Individual and group therapeutic experiences offer people the opportunity to work through past losses. Although loss may not be the focus of treatment, this issue may surface in the process of termination of therapy.

Termination of Therapy

Termination of therapy often brings with it ambivalent feelings for the client, including positive feelings of accomplishment and achievement (assuming the therapy was successful), fear of being "on one's own," as well as feelings of loss. Termination is usually a difficult experience for social work students to face, as they must deal with a multitude of feelings themselves, including their sadness in saying good-bye to clients, their discomfort in hearing the client's feelings of loss and anger directed at them, and to bear their feelings of guilt upon termination; this is especially so when the termination is based on the student's placement coming to an end rather than a planned ending based on the client's needs and accomplishments.

The ending of therapy, with its focus on separation, can catalyze a client's past experience with separation and loss; this can bring up past losses that were never resolved, which the client now has the opportunity to resolve or at least begin to recognize. A child who was abandoned by a parent and is now being "abandoned" by a student-clinician may share his or her conviction that the clinician is leaving him or her because the child was "bad"; this can provide much "grist for the mill" and lead to the opportunity to correct the distorted self-image as well as the irrational guilt.

Many people who have endured losses in the past did not have the opportunity to say good-bye or discuss the relationship and its meaning to them at the time. A good termination enables people to experience saying good-bye, which can leave them feeling that they will be missed, that they and the clinician have a meaningful relationship, and that they are valued. Fleeing from or avoiding saying good-bye forecloses this opportunity.

CONCLUSION

Transitions, crises, changes, and losses are inevitable parts of the life cycle; a person's experience with these events must always be examined within the biopsychosocial framework. People react differently to different crises and may also respond in different ways to the same type of crises at another point in their lives. Life events always have both an objective reality as well as a subjective meaning to people.

Major losses are deeply felt by most people, but some people with a history of past early losses may be especially vulnerable to present losses. People suffering from schizophrenia are also particularly vulnerable to loss and may seriously decompensate during such times. For some like Vivienne, a loss may also represent the loss of a selfobject, and they may be left not only bereaved but devastated, "empty," and without direction.

It is important not to isolate people who have losses or impending losses, and to engage them in discussion at a level of which they are capable and motivated for; it is critical to realize how painful feelings of loss can be and how people, including clinicians, often try to avoid them. We have to be ready to listen and to come to terms with our own pain.

A final point is that people may need help in dealing with the loss experiences that underlie many presenting problems. Applying cognitive-behavioral approaches exclusively to a couple with marital problems, each married for the second time, may overlook the fact that neither partner has resolved the ambivalent feelings toward the first spouse, which is coloring their present interactions.

A major arena in which loss is evident is in the medical field, when people are confronted with serious illnesses and disabilities that can create havoc in every aspect of their lives, discussed in Chapter 13.

LEARNING EXERCISE

The major subject in your biographical reading has traversed important transitions, losses, and turning points. Consider information brought out in the biography/autobiography that sheds light on the ways the subject was affected by these experiences and how he or she coped or failed to cope with them.

SUGGESTED READING

Articles

Omin, R. 1989. To die in treatment: An opportunity for growth, consolidation and healing. *Clinical Social Work Journal* 17: 325-336.

Siebold, C. 1991. Termination: When the therapist leaves. *Clinical Social Work Journal* 19: 191-204.

Zambelli, G., and E. Clark. 1994. Parentally bereaved children: Problems in school adjustment and implications for the school social worker. *School Social Work Journal* 19(Fall): 1-15.

Books

Albom, M. 1997. *Tuesdays with Morrie.* New York: Doubleday.

Berzoff, J., and P. R. Silverman. (eds.) 2004. *Living with dying: A handbook for end-of-life healthcare practitioners.* New York: Columbia University Press.

Davids, J. 1993. The reaction of an early latency boy to the sudden death of his baby brother. In *The psychoanalytic study of the child,* ed. A. J. Solnit, P. B. Neubauer, S. Abrams, and A. S. Dowling, Vol. 48, pp. 277-292. New Haven, CT: Yale University Press.

Kübler-Ross, E. 1969. *On death and dying.* New York: The Macmillan Company.

Vastola, J., A. Nierenberg, and E. H. Graham. 1986. The lost and found group: Group work with bereaved children. In *Mutual aid groups and the life cycle,* ed. A. Gitterman and L. Shulman, pp. 75-90. Itasca, IL: F. E. Peacock Publishers.

Worden, J. W. 1996. *Children and grief: When a parent dies.* New York: The Guilford Press.

Chapter 13

Illness and Disability

Minor surgery is that which is performed on someone else.

Aphorism

INTRODUCTION

Our physical selves are intricately intertwined with our self-image, psychological states, functional capacities, and social relationships; in this chapter, we focus on the significance of the body, and the ways in which illness and disability affect us and others around us. A mind-body interactionist approach is taken, although the centuries-old conflict of whether the mind and body are separate entities (mind-body dualism) continues, and arises from our "almost irresistible desire to see ourselves as being somehow above nature, above the body" (Sacks, 1990, p. 44). I support Sacks's observation that we need to understand "how individual persons grow and become, and their growing and becoming are correlated with their physical bodies" (p. 47). In a similar vein, Virginia Woolf (Fenton, 2003) observed:

> "Literature does its best to maintain that its concern is with the mind; that the body is a sheet of plain glass through which the soul looks straight and clear." Whereas the truth of the matter is that "all day, all night, the body intervenes; blunts or sharpens, colours or discolors, turns to wax in the warmth of June, hardens to tallow in the murk of February." (p. 45)

Ved Mehta, the Indian writer, developed meningitis at the age of three; this led to blindness that profoundly affected his personality and life course.

Human Behavior in the Social Environment, Second Edition

Chekhov (Rayfield, 1997), who died at forty-four, suffered from TB (beginning in medical school), an ordeal which shaped his life in many respects; "his efforts to ignore and to cope with disease form the weft of any biography" (p. xvii). The effects of a person's illness on significant others is also critical; Conan Doyle's wife developed TB; her thirteen-year struggle with this illness dramatically altered his life course, and had a major impact on their two children.

Our self-concepts are connected to our perceptions of our bodies; notions of beauty and attractiveness often figure into how we feel about ourselves, and have spawned the highly profitable cosmetic and physique enhancement industries, as well as the increasing utilization of cosmetic surgery. Today, many doctors go into the field of cosmetic medicine; "obstetricians, family practitioners and emergency room physicians are gravitating to the beauty business, lured by lucrative cosmetic treatments" (Singer, 2006, p. A1).

Congenital malformations, especially disfiguring ones, can damage a person's self-esteem. "Man has an instinctive loathing for these [malformations] and they tend to cause aversion in fellow-beings and an irrational sense of shame in the victim" (Sandblom, 1982, p. 56). Lord Byron, for example, was born with a clubfoot, which affected his personality as well as his writing.

> A perfect example of the profound effect of a malformation on both life and personality, thereby influencing creative work, we find in Lord Byron, whose clubfoot, in his own words, was his "curse of life." Byron was intensely sensitive to the deformity, which he tried to conceal in every way, and any allusion to it would drive him into a furious rage, especially when made by a female. His own mother did not hide her disgust with the child and had him subjected to extremely painful treatment by a quack. (Sandblom, 1982, p. 57)

Some people are preoccupied with their bodies' health and illness, even when not ill (hypochondriasis), or may have distorted views of their body (body dysmorphic disorder; anorexia nervosa). The famous twentieth-century Japanese writer, Yukio Mishima, preoccupied with his body and its beauty, was desperate over inevitable bodily decline through aging; the theme of betrayal by his body in fact figured in his later novels (Scott-Stokes, 1974). When he failed in his pursuit of samurai ideals, he ultimately committed suicide by disembowelment (seppuku), a direct if ritualized attack on the body.

The social network of a seriously ill person can be affected in major ways, including demands for care, fear of loss, and changes in routines and activities, and can even have far-reaching social and even political consequences, such as the striking example of hemophilia suffered by the son of Czar Nicholas and his wife Alexandra (Massie, 1967). The boy's distress prompted his parents to seek the help of Rasputin, a charismatic "healer," who could soothe the boy and relieve his pain. Alexandra became so dependent on him that Rasputin's influence in the political sphere far exceeded his medical interventions. As his power increased, popular resentment against him grew; which some observers attributed as a major precipitating factor in the downfall of Nicholas and Alexandra.

This chapter initially focuses on the impact of illness and disability on individuals and families at various points in the life cycle; selected case vignettes are presented discussing specific medical problems in interaction with biopsychosocial factors in the patient's life. The next section discusses the mind-body interaction, including sleep problems, eating disorders, epilepsy, and somatization. Then, three current major public health problems are presented: two are related to the body's metabolism, obesity and diabetes, while the third, the viral and immune system disease, HIV/AIDS, is a worldwide epidemic. This chapter concludes with a discussion of critical systemic issues such as the impact of economics (including lack of insurance coverage for many) on medical services, the medical, legal, systems, and ethical issues involved in organ transplants, and, finally, the role of nursing homes and home care.

We observe many medical paradoxes today; people are turning, in large numbers to technologically advanced medical programs, such as reproductive technologies and organ transplantation. At the same time we see many turning to alternative or complementary therapies, spending over $27 billion a year; "48 percent of American adults used at least one alternative or complementary therapy in 2004, up from 42 percent a decade ago, a figure that includes students and retirees, soccer moms and truckers, New Age seekers and religious conservatives" (Carey, 2006f, p. A1). It is likely that failure on the part of practitioners to listen, to communicate, and to devote sufficient time to them are among the reasons. An increased sense of agency supported by the approach of some alternative therapy practitioners may be another factor; one cancer patient "felt 'more empowered, more involved' in her treatment plan" (p. A20).

People are also living longer, and according to one researcher, Robert W. Fogel of the University of Chicago, humans in the industrialized world have undergone "'a form of evolution that is unique not only to humankind, but unique among the 7,000 or so generations of humans who have ever inhabited the earth'" (Kolata, 2006, p. 1). This change is evidently not genetic; the "biggest surprise emerging from the new studies is that many chronic ailments like heart disease, lung disease and arthritis are occurring an average of 10 to 25 years later than they used to" (p. 18). However, in juxtaposition to this fact, we are also witnessing increasing numbers of people with disabilities in our society; the ability of medicine to prolong life, often, paradoxically, increases the number of people who survive with disabilities, including premature babies; children who would have died at early ages in the past now live with illnesses such as cystic fibrosis, spina bifida, and congenital heart disease. "Chronic disease and its effect on children and families has replaced acute illness as the most serious issue in pediatric medicine" (Boice, 1998, p. 927). In addition, many who now live past age eighty-five are more subject to chronic illness and infirmities.

Enormous systemic problems face this country in the provision and delivery of adequate and comprehensive medical services. Robert L. Kane, a gerontologist at the University of Minnesota, commented that:

> we are spending megabucks to understand the genome, but . . . we still don't have a basic system of care that responds to chronic disease. . . . We can't come up with a health care system that really responds to what people need. (cited in Rimer, 1998c, p. A20)

In addition, the social worker's function itself in many settings has been reduced from active psychosocial intervention to a primary focus on discharge planning, often performed in a brief, perfunctory manner with a focus on concrete services.

On a more positive note, the tremendous advances in legal protections and services for people with disabilities are recognized; the Rehabilitation Act of 1973 and the Americans with Disabilities Act (ADA) of 1990 have been lauded as landmark legislation. "During the past 20 years the United States has experienced a public policy revolution affecting people with disabilities" (Orlin, 1995, p. 233).

THE BIOPSYCHOSOCIAL PERSPECTIVE IN CLINICAL WORK WITH PEOPLE WITH ILLNESS AND DISABILITY

The social worker was asked by the chief pediatrician to talk to Mary, twelve, recovering from unsuccessful eye surgery; the prognosis is poor, and it is expected that Mary's eyesight will deteriorate, eventuating in blindness. The family and the doctors had been optimistic about this surgery; no one had expected such a poor outcome. The doctors did not know Mary or her family personally as she had come to the hospital from an outlying rural area; they felt it would be helpful for the social worker to talk with Mary and her family and to share her impressions and recommendations with the doctors before they met the family.

Case Illustration of Impending Blindness

The social worker went to Mary's room and found her alone. She was a pretty, slightly overweight, Mexican-American girl, quiet and solemn but friendly, and related positively to the social worker. She did not complain, indicated that she felt no pain, and appeared to be stoic, but one sensed an underlying anxiety concerning her eyes and her hospitalization. Later that day, the social worker met with Mary's parents. The mother spoke Spanish with little English while the father had greater command of English; they were accompanied by their young daughter-in-law who spoke English well and acted as an interpreter. They were warm and friendly people, but were anxious and very concerned about Mary's well-being.

> Mary's father, thirty-six, and mother, thirty-seven, have been married seventeen years and have six children, Claudia, fifteen, Mary, twelve, Vincent, eleven, Joan, seven, and Jo, two and a half. The oldest child, Jim, eighteen, has been married for eight months and lives with his wife in the family home. (It was Jim's wife who participated in the interview with Mary's parents.) The family lives on a ranch with other Mexican-American families in a rural area in a southwestern state. Mr. F. is employed as a laborer, and Mrs. F. is a homemaker. The family is active in the Catholic church.

The social worker asked the family about Mary's eye condition and her feelings about this problem.

> When Mary was four, physically healthy and developing well, a younger sister poked her in the eye, and she has had trouble seeing since then. Currently, the tentative diagnosis is acute glaucoma as a result of associated iris bombe, right eye. The operation several days ago was a peripheral iridectomy on the right eye. Parents reported that Mary had anxiety about this hospitalization and was afraid she might lose both eyes. Father has no hospitalization insurance and has made arrangements to pay the bill on a monthly basis. "We want to do what is best for her . . . if she gets her eyesight back, it's OK."

An important question is the degree of functional incapacity the medical condition might cause. According to the ADA (Americans with Disabilities Act), disability refers to "a physical or mental impairment that substantially limits one or more of the major life activities of such individuals" (Orlin, 1995, pp. 234-235). Mary's major life activity at twelve would be attending school. Closely related to this would be her social life and peer relationships; the social worker also inquires how her life is affected by her eye problem; it is essential to obtain a baseline of Mary's academic and social functioning, within the context of her family, social, and cultural domains.

> The children attend school near the ranch, and the family has positive feelings about this facility. "It's a small school—you can learn more." Although Mary is twelve, she remains in the second grade, as her eye problem has led to lack of progress in reading. No facilities are available for children with visual disabilities in this school, and no referrals have been made to other resources (which are very sparse in the county). Theresa, Mary's sister-in-law, reports that Mary gets tired in school and says her head hurts. But Theresa notes that if she is not in school, she is OK. "I guess reading affects her eyes." Theresa feels that her eyes are holding her back. Sometimes in the mornings, Mary will ask her sister-in-law to write her a note to tell the teacher that "when she gets tired of reading she doesn't have to read anymore, can put her head down."
>
> Theresa describes Mary as being very quiet, shy, and "quick to cry." However, she is usually more cheerful and outgoing than she seems in the hospital. She "likes to joke around, likes to dance." But sometimes she feels sick, then she wants to go to bed and rest. When she is in bed, she does not seem to want to talk to anyone. Theresa reports that Mary has frequent headaches (sometimes as many as three a week, other times she has none); Theresa attributes this behavior to her eye problem.

Mary has a serious functional incapacity in terms of her impaired school functioning. A number of pieces to this puzzle are missing; it is not clear why Mary cannot read. Does she have a learning disability interacting with her visual problem? We do not know the cause of her headaches (pressure from the glaucoma, eye strain, a secondary physical problem, and/or depression). Signs suggest that Mary may be depressed such as crying easily, frequently needing to go to bed (stating she is in pain), and not wanting to talk to anyone at these times. It is possible that depression could be causing the headaches; it is also possible that she might feel depressed because she has so many headaches or that she just wants to be alone because she is in so much pain.

On a systems level, it is of serious concern that Mary continues to remain in the second grade (which may also be very depressing for her) and that these questions have not been explored. Ideally, an intensive, comprehensive medical/psychiatric, educational, and psychological evaluation should be done, but this was not routine in the rural area where Mary lived. A public health nurse is involved with the family, but her role is not clear.

There has been some discussion, according to the family, with the public health nurse about sending Mary to the school for the blind in a city ninety miles away. Theresa says that Mary "is little and afraid to go." Mary's parents state that she cries when this is discussed and does not want to go there; they have not decided what to do, but the whole family seems reluctant to go along with this possible change.

The nurse's "helpful suggestion" runs counter to the family's core way of life; Mary is probably terrified about being separated from her family and living in an institution. Although some discussion has taken place about "solutions," it does not seem that the family or public health nurse are "attuned" to Mary's inner anxieties; when Mary goes to bed and does not want to talk to anyone, she may be suffering in silence.

It does not seem that any interventions have been made by the school to offer special education or provide Mary with special materials and consultation so that she can read and her education can continue. Possibly prejudice toward Mexican Americans is involved; we would hypothesize that if a middle-class Caucasian child had the same presenting problems, more active intervention on her behalf would have occurred, and her educational status would have received considerable attention.

The social worker also explored Mary's family life and relationships.

Family relationships appear to be warm and supportive, and no family problems were reported. Theresa states that the parents are very understanding to the children, "never hit them, always explain." The children get along well, and all enjoy playing with the baby. The children "watch out for Mary" when they play with her because of her eye problem.

Neither psychiatric problems nor serious health problems were reported in the family. The parents came from large families and had little schooling, chopping cotton at an early age. Mother's pregnancy with Mary was uneventful, and Mary's developmental landmarks were within the normal range.

Mary's family life seems stable and supportive; the family appears sensitive to Mary's vulnerability in terms of her eye problems. The social worker inquires about Mary's social environment and social relationships.

The atmosphere on the ranch is very congenial, and the neighbors are cooperative and helpful. The children play together, and Mary has many friends, although it is not clear if she has any close friends (or chumships). Mary was described as a quiet girl who does not "like to run around much." Theresa, who grew up on the ranch and has known Mary a long time, reported that "the children make fun of her being chubby."

Mary lives in an environment in which people are friendly; she is part of this world, yet she experiences some "discrimination" as she is teased about her chubbiness. Perhaps her playmates sense her visual problems and are frightened and uncomfortable about this so that they displace it by teasing her about her weight, a "safer" subject. If she does become blind and is different in this way, how will this affect her friendships? Paradoxically, can this social group, while being of the same ethnicity and class, and being supportive on one level, also be rejecting because she is different—and will become more different as her eyesight deteriorates? And if Mary, age twelve, remains at the second-grade level (with seven-year-olds), might this not set her further apart socially?

Discussion

Mary was afraid she would lose both her eyes; therefore, she must know (and feel apprehensive) about her eye problems. Mary needed a supportive, ongoing relationship so that she could share her fears about becoming blind and about being sent away. The family was responsive to support and open to talking about their concerns as well as future plans. Theresa should be included in the family work; she would be an asset in terms of her positive relationship to the family and her sensitivity to Mary's feelings.

Developmental stage. Developmentally, Mary is entering adolescence, marked by increasing growth, the development of sexuality, emotional turbulence, working out separation from the family, and planning for a future. She is at an age in which self-consciousness about appearance is considerable (and she is already being teased about her "chubbiness"), as is the need to be accepted by peers. Adolescents often share secrets with each other and feel best understood by a close circle of friends. Will Mary find someone with whom she can share her special anxieties and physical similarities?

Blindness. Many people do adapt to blindness and can lead rich and productive lives. After receiving training (such as mobility training and the use of modern technological devices), blind people often go to school, work, have families, and enjoy leisure activities and a social life (Asch, 1995). Providing good educational resources for visual impairment for Mary is essential; however, she also needs sensitive psychosocial help as does her family; facing this great loss, they all need to make major adaptations, on multiple levels, in their lives.

Barbara Ceconi, (cited in Chapter 1), who lost her eyesight suddenly while in college, commented that "the feelings I experienced during this time were akin to those of grieving the loss of a significant friend or family member. I was mourning the loss of my eyesight" (Ceconi and Urdang, 1994, p. 181). Becoming blind is an overwhelming event for anyone at any age. Krauz (1980) worked with legally blind veterans from diverse religious, ethnic, and racial backgrounds and found that blindness was experienced by all as a major trauma; she cites the Reverend Thomas Carroll's statement that blindness is not only an injury to the eyes but also is a "destructive blow to the self image . . . a blow almost to [one's] being itself" (p. 37).

Krauz (1980), makes the strong point that many of these veterans, although having access to rehabilitation services, would not use them; some had been blind for several years without applying for assistance; the men were strongly defended against accepting their blindness, which kept them from accepting rehabilitation services, and from mourning their loss; as a result, many were lonely and depressed. Krauz cautions against confronting denial too rapidly and emphasizes the need for first developing a supportive relationship with the patient. Denial is a defense frequently found in patients with serious disabilities; "a person with a severe handicap often denies it on a conscious as well as an unconscious level" (Szalita, 1974, p. 679).

Cultural perspective. Mary and her family are Mexican American and live in a small ethnic community; socioeconomically, they are in the lower class. Cultural influences were apparent, although the family was not known long enough to assess this in depth. Family solidarity and the incorporation of the kinship family model is important in Mexican-American families; the pattern of interdependence with extended family groups has been referred to as *"familismo"* (Falicov, 2005, p. 234; italics in the original); Theresa, Mary's new sister-in-law, lives with the family, which is also a common pattern. The family is protective toward its members and expects loyalty from them; the family tends to protect Mary and is sensitive to her visual limitations.

On the basis of the family's interest and involvement with Mary, it is hypothesized that they would be amenable to ongoing supportive and educational help with her problems, including advocacy for appropriate education. "Because of their familistic orientation, family therapy usually is easily accepted by Mexican Americans" (Falicov, 2005, p. 238). Many families would be upset at the thought of institutionalization for their child; for Mary's family this would be intensified by their strong cultural pattern of connectedness rather than separation (Falicov, 2005). Mary does not need institutionalization; she needs special resources for the visually handicapped in her own school and community, or in a neighboring community. A social worker can help the family understand the need for this, and, if they concur, he or she can help them advocate for these services.

Mary will need the family's support to develop the ability to counteract the potential intrinsic dependence blindness can produce and to prepare her for appropriate employment; the combination of inadequate education, disability, and minority status can create special problems for employment and earning capacity. "Hispanics with disabilities have the highest proportion of unemployment" (Olkin, 1999, p. 21). Mary could also benefit from the family's support in coping with her impending loss, and developing a satisfying social life.

Though this section has focused on disabilities, children also experience other illnesses; Paul Norris, five, (Chapter 8) had required hospitalizations for vomiting, which was understood to represent somatization; some children have life-threatening illnesses (or accidents); they and their parents generally respond positively to supportive interventions. Children facing death often want to talk about it; with support they can feel less anxiety and more "held," and the terror of being "abandoned" can diminish.

Adolescents and Illness

Adolescence, accompanied by its own inner turbulence, can be an especially difficult time to cope with illness; if the illness is terminal or the prognosis uncertain, anxiety can be overwhelming. As peer relationships are so important, social acceptance can be critical for those who feel "different." Disabled adolescents' sexual concerns may not be addressed, and if they have a genetic disease, their concerns about transmission to their own offspring may go unheard (Boice, 1998).

Susan, seventeen, is a bright, very short, pretty adolescent who has spina bifida, a chronic congenital condition, due to an embryological failure of the two sides of the vertebral column to close; the presence and severity of the symptoms depend on the degree to which the spinal cord is involved (in many instances, it is seen as an incidental finding on X rays, the spinal cord is not involved, and the person has no symptoms). Unfortunately, Susan had serious impairments, including lack of mobility and minimal bowel and bladder control.

> Susan propelled herself in a wheelchair. She related very well to the social worker and was open in talking about herself. She had a sense of humor and appeared good natured and easygoing, but her frequent eye tics seemed one indication of an underlying tension.

> Because of her difficulties with bowel and bladder control, she wore diapers and was changed by her mother. Susan attended high school, where she excelled academically and was going to graduate in four months. In many respects, Susan functioned very well and had friends and extracurricular activities in school. But Susan's adolescent issues were greatly intensified by her physical condition and parental attitudes toward it.

> No plans had as yet been worked out for Susan after her upcoming graduation; her mother appeared to be denying this event, saying, "it is still far off." Susan and her mother disagreed regarding social activities; Susan

wanted to have some freedom—to be permitted to go places by herself. She wanted to attend her senior prom, but her parents would not permit this. Susan stated: "Some day, I will be on my own . . . my parents do not prepare me for it." In talking about her physical problems affecting her life, Susan stated: "I guess that's four-fifths of my problem."

Susan has many strengths: she is a high-functioning teenager who relates well and is actively engaged in high school life; she does not appear to be "stigmatized" nor isolated, and talks of having many friends. Susan's adolescent problems center around separation-individuation problems in relation to her parents, compounded by restrictions imposed by her illness, such as the reality of her mother changing her diapers.

A clinical social worker could offer individual supportive help to Susan and her family, by exploring the families' attitudes toward her illness and thoughts about her future; her parents may have trouble facing separation from her. The utilization of appropriate rehabilitative and higher educational resources in the community, as well as possible resistance to using them, could be explored. Susan might benefit from the services of a part-time attendant who could help with diaper changes and other bodily needs as a step in the "weaning-away" from mother, which may be a difficult process requiring insight into the dynamics and developmental issues involved.

Serious illness and disabilities with which adolescents live can have profound psychological consequences for them as well as for their families; comprehensive clinical social work services should be available to this population.

Health Problems in Middle Adulthood

During middle adulthood people are generally involved in building their careers, developing a family life, and extending their friendships; illness and disability can cause major disruptions in their basic functioning, relationships, and plans. Two cases are discussed here; one is of a fifty-year-old man who underwent a leg amputation; the second case involves a forty-one-year-old woman with multiple sclerosis.

A man with a leg amputation. Mr. J., fifty, an unmarried man, worked as a foreman in a plastics factory, lived with his father, and was in excellent health until a recent industrial accident necessitated the amputation of one leg below the knee. Mr. J. became depressed, and told the hospital social worker that he felt hopeless about his condition, although his medical prognosis was good; he would be fitted with a prosthesis, and should be able to return to work, with some modifications.

Mr. J. is a stocky man of medium height, who appeared indifferent to the social worker when she came to his hospital room. His affect was flat; he was fairly unresponsive and conveyed the impression that he could manage on his own and did not need any help. The social worker understood his discomfort with her but did not accept his statement that he did not need help at face value. She brought out into the open his reluctance to talk to her and expressed her interest in getting to know him, talking about how his accident had affected his life and how she could assist in making plans for the time when when he left the hospital. Mr. J. accepted this with reservations and gradually began to talk more about his work.

Over several meetings, he talked of his anxieties about managing, not being as much of a man anymore, and his discomfort about other people staring at him; they would just think about his leg and would not be at ease with him. He also could not stand the idea of being helpless. Mr. J. cried as he talked about how he always managed to cope and how he helps his elderly father who lives with him. "Now I am the invalid . . . the cripple."

During the course of their work together, Mr. J.'s depression lifted, and he made plans to be fitted with a prosthesis, to move ahead with his life, and to return to work. Although Mr. J.'s disability is neither life threatening nor disabling in a major way, and he can resume his major roles and responsibilities in life, nevertheless the loss of his leg was traumatic to him at a deeper level. Any major change in the body image (such as disfigurements from burns or mastectomies) can affect feelings about body integrity, self-image, and identity. It is a loss that must be grieved, as any major loss must be grieved. The feelings of loss should be validated by others who may be too quick to reassure: Oh, it's all right—you can manage without it!

A woman with multiple sclerosis. Mrs. Brown, forty-one, requested therapy because she has multiple sclerosis, which she is having trouble accepting, and is feeling depressed. Although midlife is often the time for a woman to expand her horizons, as her children are growing up, in this situation Mrs. Brown's horizons are becoming more limited. Her husband has been supportive, but her two daughters, sixteen and eighteen find it difficult to accept her condition, and family tensions have increased; she thinks that family counseling might be helpful.

Multiple sclerosis is an inexorably progressive, degenerative disease of the white matter of the central nervous system (CNS), with lesions that are characteristically scattered over time and in different parts of the CNS; it progresses by acute episodes with local symptoms that typically disappear partially but never completely. Each episode leaves residual damage, which cumulatively debilitates the individual and ultimately leads to death. Symptoms can include poor coordination, difficulty in walking, visual impairment, and speech difficulties.

Mr. and Mrs. Brown came together for the first appointment. Mrs. Brown, a neatly dressed woman, has pleasant features, which became more noticeable as her mood lifted. Her gait is uneven and unsteady, but she can walk by herself. She is a bright woman, somewhat reserved, who has a baseline of high-functioning and good family relationships. Mr. M., forty-three, presents a distinguished appearance, is intelligent, reserved, and quite concerned about his wife. He seems very stable and is well functioning.

Mrs. Brown has had symptoms of her illness for three or four years but did not know her diagnosis until one year ago. Her major symptoms are lack of coordination and dizziness; at times, her eyesight is affected; the words start to blur after she reads one or two pages. She walks erratically, and her right side has been affected. She has not been able to write for the past two years, although she can do some printing with her left hand, and she is not able to sew. She has had trouble with her bladder (another typical symptom), but this has subsided. The illness fluctuates; sometimes she is in a state of remission. Although she does not have a "real bad case," she was also told that she would never be any better. "It was like the friendly undertaker!"

Mrs. Brown, who had been a very active woman, has become functionally impaired; she continues to do some housework and some cooking, but her ability to do this is erratic, depending on the course of her symptoms. She had a "good day" yesterday, when she attended her oldest daughter's graduation from high school. She defines a "good day" as one in which she does not feel too dizzy. Mrs. Brown, who has a good work history, has also been a committed homemaker, and her inability to carry out responsibilities as in the past upsets her. In addition, she has delegated some of her responsibilities to her daughters, which has caused "some tremendous battles." The girls are also ashamed of their mother's condition.

Joan, the oldest girl who is about to enter college, is a "tremendous girl"—has friends and many activities but "goofs off at home" and will not help out. Hilda, sixteen, is "a bear for work" but is upset about Mrs. B.'s being different; "other mothers are normal." One day, Hilda was shopping with her mother when Mrs. B collapsed in the parking lot. "She was very embarrassed." Sometimes, when walking down the street, her oldest daughter will walk behind Mrs. B.

The second session was a family meeting; when they arrived, Joan stated that she did not want to be there and she did not want to talk but nevertheless became involved in the discussion. The family's baseline relationships were very warm; this was apparent beneath the tensions that were present. At one point, all three women were crying and explained: "We're a very emotional family." Mr. and Mrs. B. also expressed warm feelings for each other, and Mrs. Brown stated, "he's my best ally." Family therapy enabled the family to share their feelings about Mrs. Brown's illness and the consequent changes in their lives, and to examine their interactions, which had become dysfunctional under the changed circumstances.

> Mrs. Brown said that one of the most difficult things for her is to be in a situation in which she needs to ask for help; she spoke of feeling guilty; this then led into a discussion of how her guilt about this produces guilt in the girls. Joan stated: "She expects us to read her mind!" Mrs. Brown responded: "I do feel guilty; no question about that—I feel guilty about being sick!" She also spoke about being angry—"my life is being turned upside down." When the clinician commented that she must wonder why this was happening to her, she commented that she frequently did wonder that.

The Browns terminated treatment after seven sessions. Mrs. Brown found she was feeling much better and was less depressed. She felt that family relationships had improved and that "things were out in the open and aired." In this case, the mother was the primary patient, but her illness affected her husband as well as her children, who were going through adolescence with their own needs to separate and their self-consciousness about being different in any way. They also feared losing their mother.

Children and adolescents are affected by any major illness of their parents and need an opportunity to talk about this. In discussing the impact of breast cancer on women, Spira and Kenemore (2000) observed that teenage daughters are particularly affected by this occurrence and were often noted "to be more withdrawn, fearful, hostile, or rejecting" (p. 187). Their concerns included fear of their mother dying; and if the cancer were in remission, fear that it could recur; fear that they might get the illness; fear of their own sexuality (which might also lead to this illness); and concerns about changing roles in the family.

Spira and Kenemore (2000) emphasized the importance of open communication between mothers and their daughters about their disease; improved communication can, as was observed in the Brown case, lead to less anxiety and closer relationships. The more this openness develops, "the easier it may be for the adolescent girls to have their own reactions and thus facilitate the tasks of separation and reconnection" (p. 190).

Adolescent sons may also be quite devastated by maternal cancer and may find it more difficult to talk about than daughters; it can be assumed erroneously that they are adapting well and do not need help.

Illness in Late Adulthood

Mrs. Gibson, a black woman, lived by herself in a rural area of a small city. Although only fifty-three, she is approaching late adulthood; she seems closer to the elderly in her life problems because of her ill health and its effect on her lifestyle, and faces the social problems of elderly black women living alone in poverty. She has no children; her second husband from whom she had been divorced had remarried and died a few years ago. Mrs. Gibson was diagnosed with lupus erythematosus and pulmonary insufficiency secondary to it.

Lupus is an inflammatory disorder of the body's connective tissues, which are the structural, supportive tissues of all organs. The disorder is believed to be the body's immune reaction against its own tissues, but its cause is unknown. As connective tissue is universally present throughout the body, many organ systems are typically involved, and the symptoms therefore vary considerably. Recurrent inflammation of the outer lining of the lungs may occur.

Close interrelationships exist among the nervous, endocrine, and immune regulatory systems. The immune system is involved in healing, resistance to microorganisms, and allergy, and, when impaired, in the development of autoimmune disease, exemplified by lupus.

The social worker described meeting Mrs. Gibson.

> Mrs. Gibson has pleasant features, wears glasses, and was neatly dressed. She is intelligent and related well. She is a quiet, reserved person who is very concerned about her illness and feels pressured by her financial situation. Although generally composed, she began crying as she talked about herself; underlying depression and anxiety were present.

As the social worker talked with Mrs. Gibson about her living situation, a picture of poverty and hardship emerged.

> Mrs. Gibson receives a small social security allotment for disability. Although her mortgage payments on her home and her utilities are minimal, she is left with fifty dollars a month, after she paid for her medicine. She finds that often she does not have enough left for food. Sometimes at the store, her sisters let her add her groceries on to their bills. She would like to work, but she feels that she is "undependable" due to her health. Some days she feels well; other days, she does not. On Wednesdays, she "helps out" one sister and receives a few dollars for this. She sometimes helps another sister clean her house on Saturdays—earns another few dollars; both jobs are "difficult" for her. "I get so short of breath."

Until several months ago, Mrs. Gibson had been receiving her medicine from a local private charity; they stopped doing this without giving her a reason. She did not apply for public assistance; when she applied two years ago, she was told she would not be eligible for disability unless she was bedridden or confined to a wheelchair. She also felt that the man who spoke to her on the phone was angry with her, so she never pursued this further.

Mrs. Gibson was very worried about her health: "I try not to think about my condition." In addition to her lupus, she also needs new glasses and a new lower dental plate, as "this one is too big—it hangs out."

> For the last two months, she had been hearing a noise in her head [this is a lupus-related symptom]. "I hear it day and night—sometimes it stops, but for the most part it is continuous." Occasionally, it is extremely loud— "seems like firecrackers." She can drown out this noise with a radio or by sitting close to a loud, ticking clock. She is bothered by this noise at night and usually does not sleep well; sometimes she is "so deaf" she cannot hear anything, and sometimes one side of her face "feels dead."

> She finds she eats fairly well, but "sometimes I don't want it—I eat a lot of things I don't want—I can't always afford milk and stuff I like."

> Mrs. Gibson has had to cut back on her activities; she cannot walk very much and tends to get dizzy if she does. She has trouble making her bed and sweeping: "I get out of wind." Recently, she used parts of two days to mop her floor; it would have been a strain to do it all at once. She has had to stop her enjoyable activity of sewing on her sewing machine; it makes her head feel worse.

> Mrs. Gibson was never a "sickly person"; lupus began eight years ago. Sometimes the lupus flares up, and she has to go to the hospital; she "never knows" when this will happen. Sometimes she is hospitalized for four to five days; other times it lasts for two weeks.

Mrs. Gibson, although living alone, is socially involved with her sisters, her niece, and her church; while these involvements are sustaining in many ways, Mrs. G. could not fully enjoy them due to her lupus and her anxieties in relation to her illness.

> Although people do come by to see her, she reports that "I stay gone most of the time—I just leave—I can't bear to look at the house." She spends a lot of her time at a sister's home (who lives close by) but mostly "just sits there." Her sister has six children, and her sister's thirteen-year-old daughter comes over to Mrs. Gibson's house to sleep at night. When she does not come, Mrs. Gibson spends the night with her sister. She is afraid to sleep alone in case she gets sick.

> Mrs. Gibson is active in a Methodist church. She attends church services on Sundays and goes to the Ladies Circle every Tuesday night and a prayer meeting on Wednesday evenings. She finds she usually feels "pretty good" when she first gets there, but sometimes feels "sick" as the evening proceeds.

Mrs. Gibson openly discussed her anxiety; the social worker felt Mrs. Gibson was afraid she might die; feeling "sick" in church could be related (at least in part) to mental associations to religious subjects such as eternity, funerals, and death.

> Mrs. Gibson stated that her nerves are "real bad." She tends to worry, and is "bothered if the least little something happens—if a friend dies, it stays in my mind—makes me sick." She could not be specific as to how this affected her—"You can't hardly explain—it is just something you can't explain."
>
> She finds that now "when the phone rings, it scares me so bad." She feels that "sometimes it seems like people call me up more to tell me things." The other night, for example, she received a phone call from her niece who lives in another state. She called to tell Mrs. Gibson that she just learned she has diabetes. At first, Mrs. Gibson discussed this as though it were an indication of her niece's hostility, then she stated that she had "practically raised" her niece; "maybe she wanted me to know."

Mrs. Gibson had a "nervous attack," probably an anxiety or panic attack, seventeen years ago. "I don't know what my problem was—everything just scared me." She was instructed to stay in bed for two weeks—"not answer the phone—do nothing." Mrs. Gibson has reacted to her present illness with anxiety as well as depression.

Many questions were raised by this comprehensive biopsychosocial assessment; a consultation with Mrs. Gibson's physician was needed to understand more about the course of her illness, prognosis, and recommendations of what would be realistic for her in terms of her daily functioning. To what degree are depression and anxiety affecting her physical symptoms? Conversely, is the lupus itself (or medication) causing any biologically based emotional changes? Might Mrs. Gibson benefit from an occupational therapy evaluation, to explore activities in which she might engage within the confines of her physical limitations? A part-time homemaker services might be helpful, but this did not exist in her locale.

From a social perspective, Mrs. Gibson's desperate financial situation was a major concern. The social worker encouraged Mrs. Gibson to reapply to the welfare department, informing them that she had already been qualified as disabled under social security. Mrs. Gibson called the social worker back later to say that she had done this; when the welfare worker questioned if she was really disabled, Mrs. Gibson informed her about her social security disability; the worker then "smiled" and proceeded to fill out her application.

Mrs. Gibson was also experiencing considerable psychological distress and would probably be responsive to an ongoing supportive social work relationship. Mrs. Gibson had many social supports in her life; from a cultural perspective involvement with extended families and church, often found in the African-American culture, were present. However, her anxieties and

thrive: プロスペサ

suspiciousness of the motivations of others (in terms of their response to her illness) may keep her from fully internalizing these supports; at times, she withdraws from people who seem to be reaching out to her.

When dealing with service providers, Mrs. Gibson, who is reserved and stoic, can easily fall between the cracks and thus fail to obtain necessary services. Concrete needs are critical, but so is her emotional state. Mrs. Gibson did not seek out the social worker but responded readily when approached. The medical social worker is in a crucial position to reach out to patients in the hospital; the Mrs. Gibsons of today would likely be neglected as social workers disappear from medical settings and, when present, are often permitted to offer only brief concrete services.

THE BODY-MIND INTERACTION

Although debate continues about the interactions of the body and mind, increasing evidence points to their dynamic interaction. The cases presented in this chapter illustrate the profound psychological effects of physical illness on individuals. Research at the Mount Sinai Medical Center in New York appears to show that "some heart attack patients developed symptoms of post-traumatic stress disorder . . . severe enough to affect their chance of recovery," including avoidance of "reminders of the experience" and "intrusive reliving experiences (flashbacks and obsessive thoughts)" ("The Traumatized Heart," 2002, p. 7).

Conversely, psychological problems often cause major physical changes in patients. Research, "much of it conducted in the past 10 years, has consistently shown that depressed people are more vulnerable to coronary artery disease, . . . lowered blood supply to the heart muscle . . . congestive heart failure, . . . and deaths from heart attacks"; in a "six-year study of 5,000 people age 65 and over, those who had frequent depressive symptoms were 40 percent more likely to develop coronary artery disease and 60 percent more likely to die" ("Can a Troubled Mind—Part I," 2003, p. 1).

Infant research has led to observations of psychosomatic interrelatedness; young children react physically to emotional factors in their lives (Mrazek, 2000). Many years ago, the early work of Bowlby and Spitz (Karen, 1990) demonstrated the serious effects of maternal deprivation on young children, resulting in failure to thrive—sometimes even leading to death. The close relationship between neurobiology and emotional relatedness, affect, and the regulation of affect in children was described in Chapter 9 (Shapiro and Applegate, 2000), and the strong relationship between physical and psychological problems in the elderly was illustrated in Chapter 11 (Kennedy,

2000). Trauma in children and adults may be followed by a post–traumatic stress disorder, which often includes a "physiological reactivity" to stimuli eliciting associations to the traumatic events, as well as "difficulty falling or staying asleep" (American Psychiatric Association, 1994, p. 428). Depression is marked by both psychological and physical distress, including fatigue and lack of energy, sleep problems, significant weight loss or weight gain, physical pain such as headaches, and sexual dysfunction (American Psychiatric Association, 1994).

The new field of "psychoneuroimmunology (PNI) [which] poses a systemic model that assumes ongoing reciprocal influence among psychological and physiological processes" provides a basis for an integrated approach (Wood et al., 1989, p. 400). As early as 1949, Alexander asserted that "'every bodily process is directly or indirectly influenced by psychological stimuli because the whole organism constitutes a unit with all of its parts interconnected'" (p. 400). Wood and colleagues (1989) note that it has taken forty years for the nonpsychiatric medical community to accept this idea, and credit PNI research for this progress.

Perhaps one of the most striking examples of a unitary mind and body is that of pseudocyesis, so-called false or hysterical pregnancy. In girls or women affected by this condition, "not only do they fervently believe they are pregnant, but they also have bona fide symptoms to back up their claims, like cessation of menstruation, abdominal enlargement, nausea and vomiting, breast enlargement and food cravings," and can even, if uncommonly, have positive findings on pregnancy tests (Svoboda, 2006, p. 6). A classical example of pseudocyesis, is Queen Mary Tudor (so-called Bloody Mary), who, apparently in profound personal and political need for an heir, may well have unconsciously induced this condition in herself; in its sad dénouement, it may have contributed to her emotional and royal downfall. This condition, as it closely mimics a real pregnancy in signs and symptoms, "raises the possibility that pseudocyesis is the result of a delicate mind-body feedback loop: an initial emotional state induces abnormal hormone secretion, which in turn has its own physical and psychological effects" (p. 6).

Epilepsy

Seizure disorders are another endlessly perplexing mind-body borderland. For example, focal seizures arise in a relatively delimited region of the brain; symptoms associated with them can be mistaken ". . . for psychiatric symptoms, especially panic attacks, flashback memories, or dissociative symptoms (involving . . . altered consciousness or a feeling of unreality)"; in addition, "psychological problems . . . [including] schizophrenia . . . anxiety disorders, especially agoraphobia . . . [and] periodic depression" often co-exist with seizure disorders ("Epilepsy and Psychiatric Disorders," 2006, pp. 4-5). Personality patterns in some individuals that are often described as "stickiness" and aggressiveness can accompany seizure disorders.

Sleep Problems

Sleep problems illustrate the integrality and interaction of mind and body within the context of social and systemic factors. Sleep is a basic biological need; it "is as powerful as the drive to eat or breathe" ("Sleep Disorders—Part I," 1994, p. 1). In *Macbeth,* distraught in the aftermath of the murder of the king, to which she has vehemently urged her husband, Lady Macbeth is utterly incapable of sleep. Shakespeare describes what she has lost: "Sleep that knits up the ravell'd sleeve of care/The death of each day's life, sore labour's bath/Balm of hurt minds, great nature's second course/Chief nourisher in life's feast."

Many Americans struggle with sleep problems related to an inability to fall asleep (insomnia) as well as difficulty staying awake as a result of insomnia and/or other contributory factors. Sleep disturbances are especially prominent in the elderly population (Kennedy, 2000). The United States, a "chronically sleep-deprived" country, "long ago exchanged the effortless biological cycle of sleeping and waking for the tyranny of electric lights, job-plus-kids living, graveyard shifts and packages that absolutely, positively have to be there overnight" (Goode, 1998a, p. D1).

In extreme sleep deprivation, when people have been kept awake for a week, "they become irritable, disoriented, and uncoordinated; they have difficulty in concentrating and may develop hallucinations and delusions" ("Sleep Disorders—Part I," 1994, pp. 1-2); in less extreme situations, disturbances in sleeping can "affect physical as well as mental health" (p. 2). Psychiatric conditions themselves, such as anxiety disorders, substance abuse, and especially depression, can cause sleep disorders. Sleep deprivation often leads to accidents, which are not uncommonly fatal. In a national study presented to Congress, it was observed that people working on shifts and young men driving long distances at night "were the most vulnerable to fatigue-related automobile accidents" ("Sleep-Depriving," 1999, p. A22). Over 1,500 deaths and 40,000 injuries each year are related to driving accidents, attributed "at least in part . . . [to] fatigue" ("Sleep-Depriving," 1999, p. A22). It has also been reported that "two-thirds of workplace accidents . . . are caused by human error, many of them the result of a failure of alertness" (Goode, 1998a, p. D1).

These problems may be compounded by rising prescription and consumption of sleeping medications: "About 42 million sleeping pill prescriptions were filled last year . . . up nearly 60 percent since 2000" (Saul, 2006, p. A1); at the same time, experts "fear doctors may be ignoring other conditions, like depression, that might be the cause of sleeplessness" (p. A1).

On the potentially constructive side, "sleep experts say that more and more employers, aware of the hits they take to health, safety and productivity because of sleep deficits, are taking action"; interventions include sanctioned napping on the job and "stress-reduction and sleep-improvement training series, which includes stretching, breathing exercises and developing restful presleep routines"; yet "most businesses still reject public napping" (Russo, 2006, p. A16). In addition, more attention is being focused on early diagnosis of sleep disorders, such as sleep apnea (Russo, 2006).

Building "cultural competency" into health care delivery can be critical in understanding what may be a confusing sleep symptom presentation. At Maimonides Hospital, in Brooklyn, at a clinic especially designed to serve a large Chinese population, a Chinese physician reported that an eighty-year-old Chinese woman asked to see a doctor, "said it was urgent, but when examined she would say only that she had been unable to sleep for about a week." She "eventually revealed that her husband had died the previous week, and that she had been crying and having anxiety attacks, details that a Chinese woman her age might consider inappropriate to admit," but presumably could to an interviewer aware of her sensibilities (Confessore, 2006, p. A27).

Eating Disorders

Although eating disorders are generally classified under psychiatric disorders, because of their psychological symptoms (such as body image distortions, overvaluation of thinness, its associations with identity difficulties, and anxiety), they are included in this section due to their clear and critical relationship to the body (disrupting major physiological processes to such a degree that serious illness or death may result).

Individuals (most typically female, although this disorder has increasingly been found in men) suffering from anorexia nervosa are intensely preoccupied with being thin and usually have a distorted body image, insisting that they are overweight, even when they appear skeletal in reality. It is reminiscent in some ways of the failure-to-thrive infant problem, in which the infant does not eat (related to lack of adequate nurturing and consequent anaclitic depression), leading to growth failure and possibly death.

By contrast with the infant's situation, avoidance of eating by teens and adults, even when related to emotional difficulties, is very much under conscious control (in fact, the theme of control is one of its central and defining characteristics). Yet anorexics persist in not eating, despite the serious consequences. Paradoxically, people with anorexia may be quite preoccupied with food, often collecting recipe books and cooking for others. "They may cut food into tiny pieces, weigh it, hoard it, or pocket it and throw it away" ("Eating—Part I," 1992, p. 1). Denial is a major defense; they do not think that they have a problem and are highly resistant to intervention; hospitalization is often required. Physical symptoms in women include:

> Symptoms of starvation: dry skin, brittle nails and hair, constipation, anemia, loss of bone, swollen joints. The level of female hormones falls drastically, and sexual development may be delayed or arrested in very young women. Body temperature, heart rate, and blood pressure sometimes become dangerously low; potassium may be lost, with the resulting danger of cardiac failure. ("Eating—Part I," 1992, p. 1)

Bulimia nervosa occurs more frequently than anorexia; it involves episodes of binge eating usually followed by self-induced vomiting or use of laxatives. Referring to the DSM-IV definition, it is noted that "bulimia implies two or more episodes of binge eating (rapid consumption of a large amount of food) each week for at least three months" ("Eating—Part I," 1992, p. 1). Cases are encountered in which both anorexia and bulimia may occur simultaneously or at different times. People with this disorder may go on severe diets or eat normally between binges; they may also exercise compulsively. Although not considered as life threatening as anorexia, nevertheless serious physical consequences can occur:

> It can cause stomach aches, nausea, bloating, fatigue, weakness, sore muscles . . . erosion of dental enamel by acidic vomit, and scars on the hand from pushing fingers down the throat. Probably the most serious physical dangers are dehydration, loss of potassium, and rupture of the esophagus. ("Eating—Part I," 1992, p. 1)

Somatization

Somatization is another connecting link between psychological problems and the production of physical symptoms. This defense mechanism, discussed in Chapter 2, was described as a conversion of psychological tensions and conflict into somatic (physical) problems and complaints. Lipowski

(1988) defines somatization as a "tendency to experience and communicate somatic distress and symptoms unaccounted for by pathological findings, to attribute them to physical illness, and to seek medical help for them" (p. 1359). So it is not uncommon for people to appear in the general practitioner's office with presenting symptoms of physical distress, which are masking and at the same time reflecting and expressing psychological distress. In many cultures, such as the Chinese, asking for help with physical problems is more acceptable than reporting psychological distress (as described above regarding the woman with her sleep problem). Generally speaking, this is not untrue of our own culture.

People with post–traumatic stress disorders or dissociative disorders often initially exhibit only somatic symptoms; in the discussion of group work with traumatized Cambodian women, in Chapter 6, their anxieties frequently appeared in the guise of physical symptoms (Nicholson and Kay, 1999). Research has found that early childhood influences play a major role in the development of somatization; if children observe illness and pain in their family they may be vulnerable to developing somatizing traits (Lipowski, 1988), as seen in the Paul Norris case discussed in Chapter 8.

As people with panic disorders usually experience extreme anxiety about their physical health, some researchers "suggest that hypochondriasis is its essential feature" (Lipowski, 1988, pp. 1363-1364). Somatizing patients have been known to provoke feelings of antipathy in their doctors, who can become very frustrated when people insist that they are sick, demand medical care, often complain about their treatment, "and are inclined to doctor-shop" (p. 1361).

Although many patients present with the somatizing syndrome described by Lipowski, not all people with somatization symptoms have similar behaviors, nor are the origins necessarily similar; somatic symptoms expressed in people victimized by trauma, may be specific to the trauma experience. Somatization has occasionally been observed in adolescent girls whose mothers had breast cancer; in one case the daughter developed migraines, and in another a daughter reported breast pain (Spira and Kenemore, 2000).

It is equally important to be aware of complaints of a psychological disorder that may be masking an underlying physical disease; a person with symptoms of anxiety could be suffering from hyperthyroidism. Psychotic symptoms can be caused by acute intermittent porphyria, believed to have been the cause of the "madness" of King George III. The excessive secretion of adrenal steroids in Cushing's disease can be accompanied by depression; individuals taking steroids for medical conditions may also experience depression. Mood changes, hallucinations, and unprovoked aggressive behaviors may be manifestations of temporal lobe seizures; the inattention

seen in a person with petit mal seizures can be confused with attention deficit disorder. It is sound practice to ask patients seeking clinical intervention
to have a medical evaluation as part of the assessment process.

OBESITY AND DIABETES

The prevalence of obesity in American society has been receiving much
media attention; obesity is associated with the risk of developing many
health problems, including diabetes, which has become epidemic among all
age groups.

Obesity

According to a recent report from the Centers for Disease Control and
Prevention, the incidence of obesity has been greatly increasing over the
past twenty years; The National Center for Health Statistics reports that "30
percent of U.S. adults 20 years of age and older—over 60 million people—
are obese" (Terry, 2006, para. 2)). Children have also been significantly affected; "the percentage of young people who are overweight has more than
tripled since 1980. Among children and teens aged 6–19 years, 16 percent
(over 9 million young people) are considered overweight" (para. 2).

Many health problems are associated with being overweight or obese;
"hypertension, dyslipidemia (for example, high total cholesterol or high
levels of triglycerides), type 2 diabetes, coronary heart disease, stroke, gall-
bladder disease, osteoarthritis, sleep apnea and respiratory problems, and
some cancers (endometrial, breast, and colon)" (Terry, 2006, para. 2).

There have been many speculations about its cause as well as proposed
solutions including avoiding fast foods, labeling the fat content and ingredients of all packaged foods, removing soda and candy vending machines from
schools, improving the nutritional and fat-free content of school lunches,
and encouraging participation in physical activities for all age groups. In
studying the relationship of mental health and weight, no clear-cut evidence
has emerged from studies; however some people "may console themselves
with 'comfort food' because they are anxious, lonely, angry, or suffering
from low self-esteem"; there is "a characteristic type of depression with
symptoms that include lethargy and overeating" ("Is Obesity," 2004, p. 3).
Obesity may be a common pathway for a multiplicity of factors, and needs
to be addressed in a comprehensive way; each individual with obesity must
be approached from the perspective of multidisciplinary, individualized
case study.

Diabetes

Diabetes has become a major national health problem in this country. There are two major types of diabetes: "Type 1, a malfunction of the immune system that affects one million people in the United States" starts at an early age and has devastating effects on many organ systems, frequently leading to blindness and cardiovascular and kidney disease, and "Type 2, which most often affected the old and overweight, now afflicts some 20 million Americans and is the nation's fastest growing health problem" (Pérez-Peña, 2006, p. A1); it is associated with overweight and lack of exercise, and is now affecting more and more children and adolescents.

In New York City alone, an "estimated 800,000 adult New Yorkers—more than one in every eight—now have diabetes, and city health officials describe the problem as a bona fide epidemic" (Kleinfield, 2006a, p. A1); furthermore,

> within a generation or so, doctors fear, a huge wave of new cases could overwhelm the public health system and engulf growing numbers of the young, creating a city where hospitals are swamped by the disease's handiwork, schools scramble for resources as they accommodate diabetic children, and the work force abounds with the blind and the halt. (p. A1)

It also appears that there is a relationship between diabetes and Alzheimer's disease:

> several large studies have found that compared with healthy people of the same age and sex, those with Type 2 diabetes are twice as likely to develop Alzheimer's . . . even people who had borderline diabetes were 70 percent more likely than those with normal blood sugar to develop Alzheimer's. (Grady, 2006b, p. A15)

Another troubling issue is the unexpected finding that "among the mentally ill, roughly one in every five appear to develop diabetes—about double the rate of the general population"; in particular,

> psychiatrists must confront the fact that diabetes, marked by dangerously high blood sugar, is often aggravated, if not precipitated, by some of the very medicines they prescribe: antipsychotic pills that have been linked to swift weight gain and the illness itself. (Kleinfield, 2006b, p. A1)

and the antibodies created to lie in wait for further invaders can be detected within six weeks to a year. But some infected T cells survive, and the virus continues to deplete the immune system, causing the symptoms formerly known as AIDS-related complex (ARC), which include fatigue, night sweats, and weight loss. ("AIDS—Part I," 1994, p. 2)

Ultimately, the body is no longer able to fight against these continued infections, and other diseases invade the body; "the most common infectious disease among people with HIV is pneumocystis carinii pneumonia, which is caused by a microorganism that normally inhabits the lungs" ("AIDS—Part 1," 1994, p. 2). In the past, once AIDS developed, death would occur in about eighteen months. Recent medical breakthroughs, although not curative, have been able to prolong the lifespan of AIDS patients and decrease their suffering. It is important that these new medications be started as early as possible; therefore early detection of AIDS is considered imperative. It is even more critical that HIV infection be prevented; many public health education measures, such as emphasis on safe sex and clean needles for intravenous drug use, have been promoted, although not with uniform success.

Prevention

The achievement of vital AIDS prevention objectives stands at the intersection of national and international politics, moral and religious values, and ingrained custom and preferences. Many countries, because of alarming rates of AIDS, and in spite of the secrecy and stigma surrounding this disease, have taken successful measures to combat it. "Cambodia has become one of the world's few success stories in the struggle against AIDS, and it has achieved that success partly by vigorously promoting condoms" (Kristof, 2006, p. A31). In Saudi Arabia, where, government statistics "on the disease were sealed in envelopes and guarded like national secrets," significantly greater openness was being reported (Fattah, 2006, p. A3). In southern India, noted for male resistance to the use of condoms, the journal Lancet attributed a "favorable trend to an increasing use of condoms by men and an insistence by prostitutes that their partners use them. That decline, in turn, reduced the transmission of H.I.V. to spouses" (Altman, 2006b, p. A5).

Paradoxically, while promotion of needle exchange to prevent intravenous transmission has also been vigorously opposed by social conservatives in the United States, a religiously conservative group in China has taken a different tack in the face of devastating AIDS and drug addiction problems (counter to the central government's playing down of the problem). The predominantly Muslim region of Xinjiang, with "a population of about 20 million and an officially estimated 60,000 infections . . . and the highest H.I.V. infection rate in the country" has overcome cultural and political resistance. (French, 2006, p. 4). Beginning in 2005, "the authorities in Xinjiang have been trying everything from needle exchanges and drug substitution programs—to community outreach programs, often giving briefings to imams and mullahs" (p. 4).

In Kenya, the United States has been funding "Population Services International, a nonprofit group, [which] is organizing abstinence clubs for 10- to 15-year-olds" (Dugger, 2006b, p. A3); researchers "found that classroom debates and essay-writing contests on whether students should be taught about condoms to prevent the spread of H.I.V. increased the use of condoms without increasing sexual activity" (Dugger, 2006a, p. 13); In South Africa, where, despite the fact that its

> health minister has long touted salad, vitamins and assorted quack cures over antiretroviral drugs, which she has called toxic, Treatment Action Campaign, probably the world's most effective AIDS group . . . became famous for distributing its "H.I.V. Positive" T-shirts—Nelson Mandela wore one—and organizing mass protests like its 2003 civil disobedience campaign, which pushed the government into the antiretroviral rollout. (Rosenberg, 2006, p. A22)

The United Nations as well as the U.S. government have been actively promoting treatment and prevention of AIDS throughout the world. Yet, although markedly increased spending on AIDS by the U.S. government is expected to prevent 9 million deaths in coming years, the "administration has taken information about condoms off government web sites, and its AIDS prevention efforts abroad, when aimed at young people, have emphasized abstinence to the exclusion of condoms" (Kristof, 2006, p. A31). In the United States, the emphasis on abstinence and teens taking abstinence pledges also characterizes sex education programs, which many critics feel is to the detriment of preventing AIDS in adolescents. "The evidence indicates that a balanced approach—encouraging abstinence but also promoting condoms—is far more effective at protecting young people in America or abroad from sexually transmitted infections, including H. I. V." (p. A31).

In one innovative program in New York City, teenagers provided AIDS prevention education to their peers ("Teen-Agers Learn," 1999). Dante Notice, seventeen, was involved in an AIDS committee at his high school in the Bronx, and observed that many of his peers were sexually active but were indifferent to learning about AIDS. He advocates the advantages of peer-to-peer communication in educating teens about AIDS. "'I can put it in words they can understand in a way that adults can't do,' he said. 'I can break it down for them in a street kind of way'" (p. 29).

In the United States, debates continue about legal protections and sanctions related to the transmission of HIV. On one side, civil libertarians are concerned with protecting the privacy of individuals with the disease; others want laws that permit notification of partners of AIDS patients, and some demand exists for legal sanctions against those who knowingly transmit this disease to others. It is a criminal offense in a number of states to "transmit or expose others knowingly to H.I.V.," (Richardson, 1998, p. A1). A law in California "makes it a felony—punishable by up to eight years in prison—to knowingly expose or infect an unaware person to HIV" ("*Los Angeles Times* Looks," 2003, para. 1). It is the inclusion of

> the specific-intent clause [which] has caused an ongoing debate between HIV advocates, who say that the law's language protects HIV-positive people from unfounded accusations, and law enforcement officials, who say that the measure limits their ability to prosecute such cases. Since the law was enacted in 1998, only one person has been convicted under the measure. ("*Los Angeles Times* Looks," 2003, para. 1)

In "a sharp break from the early days of the AIDS epidemic, when the stigma of the disease and the fear of social ostracism caused many people to avoid being tested," and in a "major shift of policy, the federal government" (represented by the Centers for Disease Control and Prevention) has recommended "that all teenagers and most adults have H.I.V. tests as part of routine medical care because too many Americans infected with the AIDS virus don't know it" (McNeil, Jr., 2006, p. A1). Controversy exists between proponents favoring prevention and early intervention, and those concerned about violation of civil liberties, including issues relating to informed consent and pretest counseling.

The stigma associated with homosexuality in the black and Hispanic communities is very strong, making it harder for gay people to identify themselves as such; this (in addition to the stigma against drugs) keeps many people in these groups from seeking medical services for AIDS, even if they are not gay. Serious outreach efforts to these communities and to the vulnerable young people at risk are needed.

outrun: dejar atrás

SYSTEMS ISSUES

Medical care in the United States is a paradoxical picture of heroic and technologically advanced life-saving and life-prolonging measures, model rehabilitative programs, and state-of-the-art research, which coexist alongside often overcrowded hospitals, inadequate nursing homes, and millions of people without medical insurance, unable to pay the escalating costs of care.

Our technical advances frequently outrun our ethical and legal judgments as we debate issues such as when life starts, affecting the utilizing of reproduction technologies, pregnancy termination, and stem cell research, and the dilemma of how or when life should end, and whether patients should be kept alive often against their will, in questionable states of health, pain, and severe disability.

Economic Problems

Many medical advances, including open heart surgery, organ transplants, and reproductive technologies require huge expenditures of money; prescription medications are increasingly more expensive and not affordable by many. The prescription drug plan under Medicare, in effect since 2005, has been criticized as inadequate and difficult to decipher. Chronic conditions affecting many, including children, often require prolonged intensive care and/or long-term hospitalizations that can bankrupt the average family. Costs for health care have increased "more than 60 percent in the past five years" (Kingsbury, 2006, p. 53). Insurance coverage is not available to many; in 2005, 46.6 million people were without health insurance coverage; there are 8.3 million children without coverage ("Income Climbs," 2006). Premiums and deductibles are expected to rise in 2007 for the 177 million employees who do carry medical insurance (Kingsbury, 2006).

HMOs and the overriding concept of managed care have been one of the "solutions" to this crisis of providing affordable medical care. Managed care emphasizes health preventive measures and reducing unnecessary medical procedures; many doctors and patients have expressed dissatisfaction with this system because of its concerns with cost effectiveness rather than the quality of medical care. Doctors who in the past were free to make independent medical judgments based on their clinical experience now must have them seconded by bureaucrats. They often see more patients in less time, leaving little if any time to get to know them and to establish the vital doctor-patient relationship with them. Many doctors have left the profession or have found alternative ways to practice (Gorman, 1999). Doctors are also leaving the profession due to exorbitant malpractice insurance premiums (often double what they had been) (Eisenberg and Sieger, 2003).

> Even in states where malpractice insurance remains relatively affordable, doctors are increasingly practicing more "defensive medicine," trying to gird themselves against possible lawsuits by ordering unnecessary tests and thereby driving up health-care costs. (p. 50)

Organ Transplants

Organ transplantation, initially a rare experimental procedure, has become commonplace today, raising medical, legal, systemic, and ethical issues. One major concern is the relative scarcity of available organs in relation to the thousands of people on waiting lists for organs including heart, lung, liver, or pancreas. In May 2005, in an attempt to ameliorate this problem,

> new rules nationwide put patients who needed transplants most at the top of the list—people who would soon die without a transplant, but who had a good chance of surviving after one. . . . Previously, lungs went to whoever had been waiting longest, even if another patient needed them more. (Grady, 2006c, p. 1, p. 20)

In what had been considered a "revolutionary" procedure, and seen as a possible solution to the shortage problem live donors (often relatives of patients) have donated a portion of their liver (other live donors have provided kidney and bone marrow grafts) (Grady, 1999). It had been determined that the liver's "right lobe could be removed safely for adults"; nevertheless, doctors have expressed concern about donors who may feel pressured to agree and "may be taking too much of a risk" (p. A12).

This anxiety was borne out in 2002, when a brother made "the ultimate sacrifice," dying as a result of his donating half of his liver. The roughly "1-in-100 risk of dying may not seem like bad odds, but there's more to this ethical dilemma than a simple ratio. The first and most sacred rule of medicine is to do no harm" (Gorman, 2002, p. 41). On the other hand, in relation to the shortage of available organs, a survey had shown "that most people will accept a mortality rate for living organ donors as high as 20 percent"; yet, if "you feel you can't say no, is your decision truly voluntary?" (p. 41).

In one well-publicized case, a seventeen-year-old girl with leukemia was expected to die unless she had a bone marrow transplant; when no donors were found after an extensive search, the parents decided to have another child, in the hope that the baby's bone marrow would be compatible with that of the ailing sister (Morrow, 1991). The mother, forty-three, became pregnant and delivered a healthy baby girl who was judged to be a compatible donor.

When the baby was fourteen months old, the procedure (which is considered harmless for donors) took place, and the older daughter received the transplant. Although this family was seen as a warm, nurturing family who welcomed the baby in her own right, many ethical dilemmas were stirred up. "Is it morally acceptable for parents to conceive a child in order to obtain an organ or tissue to save the life of another one of their children?" (Morrow, 1991, p. 54).

Nursing Home Care

Nursing home services are needed by people who require 24-hour supervision and care; many are elderly, although younger people may also need these services. For some patients the care is temporary, until they recover sufficiently to return home; others may remain indefinitely, either due to medical need, or lack of a home to return to. Nursing homes vary in the level of care and comfort they provide to patients; some are excellent, others "adequate," and some appalling. Nursing homes have come under increasing scrutiny, as many provide inadequate services to their residents, who are often helpless to protest; periodic scandals erupt and are reported in the media. In California, where an intensive investigation was undertaken, it was alleged that "in 1993 alone, more than 3,000 people died as a result of unacceptable care" ("Toward Nursing," 1999, p. A26).

The lack of psychiatric care in nursing homes for those in need has been challenged; it has been estimated that "less than 1 percent of elderly nursing home residents who might benefit from psychiatric intervention receive it" (Kennedy, 2000, p. 262). In addition to patients with emotional problems complicating aging, such as those with depression or anxiety, many nursing homes now care for psychiatric patients who have been deinstitutionalized from state hospitals (Borson et al., 1987). "Considerable evidence indicates that psychiatric problems are frequently undiagnosed or misdiagnosed and that opportunities for effective intervention may be obscured by diagnostic bias toward 'incurable' conditions" (p. 1413).

Sometimes patients with difficult-to-manage psychiatric problems were being managed with "physical and chemical restraints [which] were inappropriately being used," while the underlying disorders were generally not being treated (Sadock and Sadock, 2003, p. 1335). These devices were in frequent use despite research reports "that they do not safely control agitated behavior and suggestions from cross-cultural studies that similar patient populations can be managed without their use" (p. 1335). Sadock and Sadock (2003) stress the need for psychiatric consultation in nursing homes as an integral part of coordinated patient care; "nursing homes are in fact neuropsychiatric institutions, and input from mental health professionals is necessary if the homes are to fulfill their missions" (p. 1336).

Patients in nursing homes are extremely diverse in culture, ethnicity, education, lifestyle, and personality; often their individuality is ignored, they are infantilized, and priority is placed on their adaptation to institutional needs (Levenson, 1998). "It is not surprising that people who live in nursing homes sometimes refer to themselves as inmates" (Meyers, 2006, p. 273). Meyers (2006) emphasizes the importance of the nursing home social worker developing relationships with patients, appreciating their individuality, helping them develop their strengths and creativity and finding new meaning in life; patients should be empowered to make their own decisions and choices, and to become part of the community of patients, "where people feel they matter to each other" (p. 277). Nursing home practices "can exacerbate loneliness, boredom and depression rooted in an environment where residents have lost control over basic physical and social aspects of their lives" (Levenson, 1998, p. 3).

Home Health Care

Although many alternatives exist for older people, such as assisted living residences, the most popular choice is to remain at home. Conover (1997) noted that many Americans are receiving a variety of home-care services which keep them from being institutionalized. One level of home care is provided by homemakers who help with cooking and housework but provide no medical or physical care, such as bathing. Many people can manage with assistance of this nature. Others, needing more care, require the services of a licensed home health aide.

Many home health aides provide excellent services but problems exist, such as selection and ongoing supervision of workers; neglect and abuse have been observed in some situations. Older adults with paid caretakers can be "vulnerable in the same way as babies left with nannies"; now, however, "there is a new kind of nanny—and a caretaking relationship fraught with guilt, resentment and love that we are very likely to be wrestling with for years to come" (Conover, 1997, pp. 126-127).

CONCLUSION

Illness and disability are normative parts of the life course; however, as advances in medicine have been made and life has been prolonged, we see more people living with disabilities across the life cycle. Paradoxically and sadly, as medicine has made magnificent scientific and technological advances, the humanistic qualities that were present in the family doctor of the past are often lacking; patients, viewed as organ systems, are shunted from specialist to specialist.

The present crisis in managed care has only intensified this trend away from humanistic medicine. Efficiency, productivity, and enormous amounts of paperwork take precedence over sitting and talking with, and getting to know, patients. Medical social work, with its expertise and experience, is vanishing in many sectors, replaced by solution-oriented and task-focused discharge planning and referral.

From the systemic perspective, problems relating to health care (and paying for it) are tremendous and complex, a subject of national discourse. Almost every medical advance brings in its wake new economic as well as moral and ethical dilemmas.

One major advance has been that the voices of the ill and disabled are now being heard, legislation is being passed on their behalf, and employment practices are changing in their favor. We read of Special Olympics and wheelchair entrants in marathon races. The front page of the *New York Times* reported that Brooke Ellison was the first quadriplegic to graduate from Harvard; it quoted her as saying: "'I've always felt that whatever circumstances I confront, it's just a question of continuing to live and not letting what I can't do define what I can'" (Steinberg, 2000, p. A1). Brooke and her mother, Jean Ellison, have written a book, *Miracles Happen: One Mother, One Daughter, One Journey,* recounting their experiences, which was released in 2002.

In working with people who are physically ill and with their families, the support and caring that we as clinical social workers can offer are part of the healing process. The body and mind are a unit, each affecting the other.

LEARNING EXERCISE

Case Presentation: Ask for student volunteers to present cases in which issues of illness and disability exist. Discussion can include: type of illness, effect on functioning, attitudes toward illness and receiving care, available supports, adaptation and strengths, and special problems.

SUGGESTED READING

Articles

Donner, S., and B. Batliwalla. 2005. Two social workers' experience with late onset blindness: An intersubjective perspective. *Smith College Studies in Social Work* 75: 49-64.

Lawrence, S. A., and K. M. Zittel. 2000. Heart transplantation: A behavioral perspective. *Journal of Human Behavior in the Social Environment* 3(2): 61-79.

Spira, M., and E. Kenemore. 2000. Adolescent daughters of mothers with breast cancer: Impact and implications. *Clinical Social Work Journal* 28: 183-195.

Books

Bloch, J., and J. Margolis. 1986. Feelings of shame: Siblings of handicapped children. In *Mutual aid groups and the life cycle,* ed. A. Gitterman and L. Shulman, pp. 91-108. Itasca, IL: F. E. Peacock Publishers.

Fadiman, J. 1997. *The spirit catches you and you fall down: A Hmong child, her American doctors and the collision of two cultures.* New York: Farrar, Straus and Giroux.

Friedman, E. 1997. The impact of AIDS on the lives of women. In *Gender and addictions: Men and women in treatment,* ed. S. L. A. Straussner and E. Zelvin, pp. 197-221. Northvale, NJ: Jason Aronson.

Olkin, R. 1999. *What psychotherapists should know about disability.* New York: The Guilford Press.

Roos, S. 2002. *Chronic sorrow: A living loss.* New York: Brunner-Routledge.

Zarem, S. 2003. Signs of connection: Working with deaf parents and hearing children in a nursery setting. In *The psychoanalytic study of the child,* ed. R. A. King, P. B. Neubauer, S. Abrams, and A. S. Dowling, Vol. 58, pp. 228-245. New Haven, CT: Yale University Press.

Chapter 14

Mental Health Problems

... Mrs. Tickit, finding no balsam for a wounded mind ... suffered greatly from low spirits. ...

Charles Dickens, *Little Dorritt*

INTRODUCTION

Most people have experienced emotional distress, ranging from minor bouts of anxiety, depression, and psychosomatic symptoms to more severe problems, such as major depressions or panic disorders. In this chapter, we turn our attention to some of the major mental health problems affecting people, and use the *Diagnostic and Statistical Manual of Mental Disorders* as the basis for categorization; this is a generally accepted standardized format for deciding on and assigning a diagnosis. However, it has been found lacking as a tool to provide a comprehensive assessment of the person's inner and outer realities; it is "comprehensive but shallow, ultimately too superficial to capture the complexity of human motivation, the depth of emotional pain" (Carey, 2006b, p. D5). A new manual was issued by the American Psychoanalytic Society in January 2006, called *The Psychodynamic Diagnostic Manual,* which focuses on "individual personality patterns," that is seen as a supplement the DSM, rather than a replacement. Dr. McWilliams, a psychologist, commented that people cannot be looked at only as symptom pictures; "most of the people who come in for therapy do so for a kind of sickness of the soul, or for some interpersonal disaster" (p. D5).

This addition is clearly compatible with this book's orientation. But to be fully comprehensive, the biopsychosocial framework will be applied in the presentation in this chapter; mental health problems are intertwined with social problems, often in a vicious circle. Depressed mothers, living in socially adverse conditions, are often unable to respond to their babies, who then fail to thrive or are otherwise neglected, and a spiral of state intervention, and increased depression may then ensue; it can be difficult to tell where social adversity begins and individual illness leaves off, or vice versa.

This chapter, while leaving aside other important mental health problems, focuses on several major problems significant in social work practice, including schizophrenia, depression and suicide, borderline personalities, anxiety disorders (such as post–traumatic stress disorders), the addictions, and developmental disabilities. The combination of deinstitutionalization and managed care has led to a seriously inadequate mental health services. On the positive side, advances in educational services and supports have been provided to patients and to families, and there has been greater recognition of patients' civil, political, and employment rights; these topics are also addressed in this chapter.

SCHIZOPHRENIA

Schizophrenia, throughout recorded history, has been viewed through different perspectives and cultural lenses; those suffering from it have been treated in varying ways, ranging "from kindness, and soothing medications, to restraints, cruelty, and even putting the unfortunate sufferer to death" (Karon and VandenBos, 1996, p. 7). Schizophrenia remains a mystery to us; although we know more about the brain chemistry involved and how to reduce its severe symptomatology, no cure exists as such. For many, it is a lifelong, chronic disease with remissions and decompensations. Although a number of people with this illness make good recoveries and attain a high level of functioning, many others face a tragic life of missed opportunities.

Schizophrenia is viewed as "not one disorder, but several, with genetic roots and brain malfunctions that may be entirely different or overlapping" ("The Negative Symptoms," 2006, p. 3). Considerable variability is found in its symptoms and course; "one patient may present with extreme social withdrawal, retreating to bed for weeks at a time, another with episodes of depersonalization and feelings of being controlled by external forces, and still a third has marked anorexia with severe weight loss" (MacKinnon and Michels, 1971, p. 230).

Schizophrenia touches every aspect of a person's life, most frequently occurring in late adolescence or early adulthood. People with schizophrenia often lack the insight that they suffer from a serious disorder, which may further impede their full participation in life. Mr. S., who is thirty-five, had his first schizophrenic breakdown as an adolescent; he felt he had been a "loser," and was "weird" and "different from everyone." . . . He was always "afraid of everyone and everything." He missed the "on-time events" of adult development; when first becoming ill, he "wanted to come to the hospital," hoping people could make him well; he "wanted to go to college, have a job, and have a girlfriend." Now in adulthood, none of his hopes has been fulfilled.

Schizophrenia is a "disorder that affects the total personality in all aspects of its functioning: emotion, volition, outward behavior, and most particularly, the thinking process. While not all patients show the same range or magnitude of disturbances . . . the hallmark of this disorder is that it permeates every aspect of the individual's functioning" (Bemporad and Pinsker, 1974, p. 524).

Arieti (1974) observed that meaning and logic lie beneath schizophrenic thought processes which, on the surface, can appear totally meaningless and illogical (Chapter 2). Karon and VanderBos (1996) described a patient who was considered " 'confused' because he drank from his own urinal"; another patient, who was paranoid, shed light on this action by commenting: " 'If you only drink your own urine and only eat your own feces, you will never die' " (p. 54). Since fear of annihilation and death is so common in schizophrenia, this "defense against death" becomes understandable.

In Mark Vonnegut's (1975) autobiography he discussed his own severe schizophrenic break that occurred after college graduation (Chapter 2). He once picked up a quantity of tobacco tins in a store and walked out with them without even thinking of paying. His friend Simon questioned his need for this large quantity of tobacco. Mark's act had its own logic; it was very important to have a continual supply of cigarettes, although not for the usual reasons most people have for smoking.

> Smoking was an important reminder of who I was. It was my clock. Cigarettes seemed to keep time. They had a continuity with the real world that I seemed to be losing. As long as I smoked cigarettes I was alive. As far as I knew, dead people didn't smoke cigarettes. (Vonnegut, 1975, p. 102)

Karon and VanderBos (1996) cite Lidz (1973), who described schizophrenic thought as having an " 'egocentric overinclusiveness,' " meaning that a person has "the feeling that things which logically are not related to the self *are* related to the self, or that things which realistically one cannot influence are being influenced by one's actions" (p. 54). In addition, sometimes "the patient regresses under stress and uses modes of thought that were more typical of an earlier period in life, or were dreamlike" (p. 55); they note Rudolf Ekstein's (1971) observation that "while there is no general schizophrenic language, each patient has a meaningful personal language which the therapist must learn" (p. 55).

It is ironic that the DSM-IV (American Psychiatric Association, 1994) does not include thought disorders at all, which most clinicians (past and present, including Sadock and Sadock, 2003) view as the core characteristic of schizophrenia. Current research has focused attention on the "thinking deficiencies" of schizophrenic patients; "studies suggest that these cognitive limitations affect real-world functioning and the outcome of the illness . . ." ("The Negative Symptoms," 2006, p. 1). Rather than list thought disorders, the American Psychiatric Association's (1994) preference was to list disordered speech, as this was observable; "inferences about thought are based primarily on the individuals' speech," whereas there was an "inherent difficulty in developing an objective definition of 'thought disorder' " (p. 276).

Thought disorders are a composite of the actual content of the thoughts as well as the thought processes themselves; a person, for example, may lack coherence, logic, be unable to abstract, have loose associations, and sometimes use frequent puns (Sadock and Sadock, 2003). The listener often cannot "make heads or tails" of what the person has just said.

The following letter was addressed by a patient to one of the male physicians in her hospital (Noyes, 1953). The content itself is bizarre; it is also difficult to understand what the patient is trying to communicate; illogic and incoherence predominate, and puns and clang associations such as "plant" and "tant" are present. This communication serves to distance the reader from the letter writer, rather than enhancing a rapport between them. Only the first paragraph of this letter is presented here.

> Dear Dr. _____ ,
>
> "My Plan," or as my mother used to call you, "the Little Plant," or else one little Plant for I was the other Plant, called "Tant." Will you please see that I am taken out of this hospital and returned to the equity court so I can prove to the court who I am and thereby help establish my identity to the world. Possibly you do not remember or care to remember that you married me May 21, 1882, while you were in England and that I made you by that marriage the Prince of Wales, as I was born Albert Edward, Prince of Wales, I am feminine absolutely, not a double person nor a hermaphrodite, so please know I am England's feminine king—the king who is a king.

[Two paragraphs follow, and then the letter is signed.]

Sincerely,

"Tant"

Queen of Scotland, Empress of the World, Empress of China, Empress of Russia, Queen of Denmark, Empress of India, Maharajahess of Durban, "Papal authority" as a Protestant (Noyes, 1953, pp. 374-375).

This degree of thought disturbance is not present in all people with schizophrenia; some—especially patients with paranoid schizophrenia—may have thought processes that are more intact, and their thought disturbances may be limited to specific areas of dysfunction. The ego functions (Chapter 2) of a schizophrenic person are extensively impaired to one degree or another; but it is important to assess them on an individual basis and track their variation over time. The most obvious symptoms of schizophrenia are delusions and hallucinations; however, more insidious problems (and much less responsive to medications than the more florid symptoms of delusions and hallucinations) are the "negative symptoms" of schizophrenia.

These "negative" symptoms are so called because they are an absence as much as a presence: inexpressive faces, blank looks, monotone and monosyllabic speech . . . seeming lack of interest in the world and other people . . . anhedonia . . . and avolition (lack of will, spontaneity, and initiative). About 25 percent of patients with schizophrenia have a condition called the deficit syndrome defined by severe and persistent negative symptoms. ("The Negative Symptoms," 2006, p. 1)

A major disturbance exists in the patient's expression of emotions or affect: "the patient's subjective emotional experience may be diminished, flattened, or blunted. . . . He has difficulty expressing and communicating the emotional responses of which he is aware. This affective deficit not only leads to estrangement from others, but also to an inability to enjoy the solitude that results" (MacKinnon and Michels, 1971, p. 231). The capacity to relate is markedly impaired;

he has few friends and does not trust people. . . . He learns to protect himself by maintaining emotional distance, preferring his own autistic world to shared experiences in the world of others. . . . The mistrust, fear of closeness, ambivalence, and clinging dependency of the schizophrenic patient influence all of his human contacts. (pp. 237-238)

Executive functioning is typically markedly impaired; patients usually have "difficulty in managing money and remembering to take their drugs. . . . Providing for their daily needs, holding a steady job, or maintaining even casual social relationships is often too much for them"; they frequently cannot manage without the "auxiliary ego" of others; hence the need for living with families, foster families, or in group homes (and sometimes hospitals) ("Families in the Treatment—Part I," 1989, p. 1).

Their perceptions of outer reality are usually disturbed; the actions and activities of others are often misinterpreted. Inner perception, that is, self-awareness and attunement to inner feelings, is markedly impaired, while at the same time a preoccupation with inner states exists; this is often a fragmented rather than an integrated process.

The person with schizophrenia has a weakened sense of identity, ranging from a poor self-image to fragmented ego states, with fears of bodily disintegration and annihilation. Boundaries are often diffuse; in Chapter 2, we noted how Mark Vonnegut begged his friend to hypnotize him so that he could control Vonnegut; being under his friend's control, Vonnegut would know that he himself existed.

Many chronically mentally ill patients also have serious problems with alcohol abuse, which can cause serious treatment complications, including regression and the possible need for hospitalization; "Acute intoxication can exacerbate psychotic symptoms. Alcohol abuse undermines psychosocial interventions and interferes with compliance with medication" (Mulinski, 1989, p. 339).

To schizophrenic patients, the world is often puzzling and very frightening; it loses its solidity as patients lose their sense of cohesiveness and identity. The person with a sense of total dissolution and fear of annihilation, living in a world that is also felt to be crumbling, needs to feel safe; structure and caring relationships that are warm but not intrusive are of primary importance. Herein lies much of the complexity involved in working with schizophrenic people; they need closeness but fear it, and relating to others is usually a major problem. They need structure and limit setting but often fight this, not wanting to be controlled by others. The hospitalization they may desperately need, because it provides a safe haven, may nevertheless terrify them, at least initially.

General agreement (although not unanimous) prevails on the benefits of medication; medication advances provided the first breakthrough in psychiatric treatment of schizophrenia and enabled the deinstitutionalization movement to begin. For the first time, a way was found to decrease psychotic thought processes and help people maintain better contact with reality as well as control their behavior.

Concerns have been expressed about the many physical side effects of the continual use of antipsychotic medication; in addition, current research has implicated antipsychotic medications in the marked increased of diabetes among mentally ill patients (Kleinfield, 2006b, p. A1). Many patients are resistant to taking these medications and often do not take them if they are without supervision; this problem is compounded by the lack of care and supervision that exists for many people with mental illness. Ethical and civil rights issues have also been involved in this problem; some people feel it is a violation of a patient's rights to mandate either medication or hospitalization; this is discussed further at the end of this section.

In the following illustration, Mr. S., discussed earlier, who was in a state psychiatric hospital, had been taken off all medications for two weeks as he was being prepared to take part in trials of a new antipsychotic drug. In the following session, he was seeing a social work intern, who was hopeful that they could continue their previous discussions about activities for Mr. S.

> Instead of talking about activities, he talked about death, decay, and the maggots that were eating his brain and body. He told me about people who were chasing him with clubs, who wanted to beat his brains out, and spoke about eating cats, and rotting in hell. I did not know how to handle this psychotic process, so I just allowed him to continue talking, as I listened anxiously.

Some guidelines are generally followed in working with schizophrenic patients. These are based on the nature of the illness. They include providing structure and limits, reality testing, development of skills in daily living, enhancing relationships, and enhancing self-esteem. Some theorists are primarily behaviorally oriented; others incorporate psychotherapy as part of the overall treatment.

Although about one-third of schizophrenic patients live with their families (while many are homeless), some advances have been made in the provision of group homes for the mentally ill. Work with families, using such services as psychoeducational therapy for the families, as well as family therapy has also been emphasized.

Work with Schizophrenic Patients

Clinicians can help patients anchor their anxieties and navigate the complexities of life, providing a model for thinking, solving problems, and interacting with others. If patients can internalize these functions, they will achieve a higher level of integration. From a self psychology perspective, the therapist becomes an important selfobject for the patient; Semrad emphasized providing support through effective, empathic human responsiveness, which permits a withdrawn or confused schizophrenic person to make effective contact with another person (Adler, 1979). Winnicott's concept of the holding environment has been applied to case management with schizophrenic clients (Kanter, 1990), and was discussed in Chapter 3.

The Clinical Relationship

Because schizophrenic patients are generally uncomfortable with people, a clinician can find it difficult to establish relationships with them. "Sessions may be characterized by frequent silences which the worker must fill, monosyllabic answers to questions, awkwardness, apparent disinterest in proceeding with treatment, or highly inappropriate discussion" (Nelsen, 1983, pp. 337-338). Shifts can occur within one session from fairly rational discussion into psychotic deterioration. Mr. S., for example, after talking about some of his earlier experiences in a realistic way, changed the subject.

> Mr. S. began to complain about how bad he felt, and how it was because people at the hospital were taking gallons and gallons of his blood. He said that "blood is brain and brain is blood," and people are taking away his brain and making him crazy. He said that it was an "atomic insanity" that caused him to have to suffer for all of his life. He began to rock back and forth rather violently in his chair and shake his legs rapidly.

The student realized that Mr. S. was having trouble tolerating this long period of talking; when she suggested they discontinue now and talk more the following week, Mr. S. seemed very relieved "and his rocking and shaking" decreased.

Although many schizophrenic patients have the ability to relate to the therapist, they can also become frightened by the closeness, and it is not uncommon to see some oscillation between closeness and retreat from it; the following dialogue occurred at the end of a session, which reflects Mr. S.'s confusion about what caring means.

> He looked at me and smiled, asking, "Are you a member of my family or something?" I said that I wasn't a member of his family and wondered what made him ask me that question. He said that usually only family members would talk to him for this long. I again told him that I was not a family member, but his therapist. He thanked me and then left the room.

After several sessions in which Mr. S. was positive and cooperative in talking with the student, a session occurred in which he was avoidant and resistant.

He turned his head away from me and wouldn't look at me during the session; he responded with one-word answers. I said that it seemed like he didn't want to talk; I wondered if he had something on his mind that he wasn't saying. He said in an angry tone that he didn't have anything on his mind but that he didn't feel like talking to me.

I wondered if he were angry or disappointed with me, which he denied. I told him that it would be okay if he were mad at me, and that I'd like to talk about it if he were. He said that talking to me didn't do any good and that he was sick of it. When I suggested that he was disappointed about our work together, he said it didn't matter, that no one in the hospital helped him anyway; we all just made him worse. After a few minutes, he got up and said he didn't want to talk anymore, and he left. I told him that I would be in my office for the rest of this half hour, which was the time reserved for him, if he changed his mind and wanted to come back; but he didn't.

Later in the day, the student saw Mr. S. on the ward; he approached and asked: "You're coming back next week, aren't you?" She assured him that she was, and their work continued positively after this incident; however, at a later date, further deterioration occurred, which the student attributed to his fear of his own progress and anxiety about possibly leaving the hospital. However, this decompensation also occurred when the social work student returned from a vacation, a point that was not openly discussed; the loss (even temporary) of a therapist can produce decompensation in a patient.

Another important point is the clinician's response; the intensity of the patient's feelings can arouse intense feelings in the clinician, and the "inevitable hopelessness, helplessness, and despair that these patients experience in therapy will inevitably be felt by the therapist" (Adler, 1979, p. 135). The use of intersubjectivity is very relevant in this work; tuning in to one's subjective reactions to the patient can often alert a clinician to the patient's unverbalized feeling state (Adler, 1979). A clinician can also feel frustrated, disappointed, and unsuccessful, because of the slow rate of progress and frequent regressions.

The social work student is especially vulnerable to these feelings; one's success as a clinician is often measured by the improvement of the patient. Paradoxically, it has often been observed that student therapists are very successful with chronic schizophrenic patients because of their genuineness, the intensity of their involvement, and their expectations for the patients' improvement, which may be novel to each patient's experience. In this excerpt, the student shares her self-doubts after one of Mr. S.'s regressive episodes.

It was not until this session that I was able to admit how intensely I was being affected by Mr. S. and his psychosis and hopelessness. I thought it was "unprofessional" and even unkind to feel so miserable, frustrated, or hopeless during our sessions. It was difficult to acknowledge insecurities about my own competence and ability as a social worker. I felt like I had no idea what I was doing! I was sure that a "better social worker" would be able to help Mr. S. more than I. I was equating Mr. S.'s lack of progress with my failure as a social worker.

The Focus on Reality

A reality orientation is extremely important with schizophrenic patients; the patient's preoccupations with the inner world needs to be directed outward, with an emphasis on enhancing coping capacities. The following discussion took place after Mr. S. complained about having a stomachache and feeling depressed and bored.

I suggested that if we thought about why his stomach was bothering him or why he was so depressed and bored, maybe we could come up with ways to help him feel better. I asked if he would like to try, and he said "OK." I thought we could start by thinking about what kinds of things he had been doing lately and how he was spending his time. He said that today he drank seven cups of coffee (by 11:00!) and skipped breakfast. I asked him about other things he did with his time. Sometimes he smoked cigarettes or watched TV but usually he sat around. When asked about groups, he mentioned that he liked music and art. I inquired if he had had a chance to think about his "mental torture" while playing an instrument or drawing; he said "only sometimes." He hadn't been going to groups lately, because he "didn't feel well." When asked if he thought going back to the groups might help him feel better, he said he would go—especially to his music group, which he liked.

I also asked if he had seen the nurse about his stomach, and he told me that she wouldn't think anything was wrong. I wondered if there was anything that he could do to help make his stomach feel better. He thought and said that maybe he could eat breakfast and he might not be hungry. I agreed and said that I when I don't eat breakfast, sometimes my stomach hurts, too.

Mr. S. began attending more activities, and through a behavior modification design earned rewards, such as going to the canteen through his increased activities; following these advances, they discussed his feelings and disappointments related to "emotional issues and relationships." Schizophrenic patients are often responsive to this type of discussion, and as they learn to connect with their feelings and express them, they can experience relief, and their anxiety often decreases. Although some clinicians work with schizophrenic people only with a concrete, task-centered orientation, many patients have the capacity to develop self-awareness and to make some connections between their inner states and their behaviors.

Team collaboration is an important as part of the therapeutic plan; working with families is also important; Mr. S.'s positive relationship with his parents "served as a motivating factor for him to work on his programs."

Community Care

When state psychiatric hospitals began closing, community care, in the form of assisted-living arrangements such as group homes for the mentally ill, was seen as the ideal alternative. Many of these facilities have been very effective, providing structure, support, and guidance for their residents and encouraging their involvement in the community. Different levels of care and supervision exist depending upon the needs of the patients. Some patients are involved in community day care programs or are enrolled in other rehabilitative projects. Support and self-help groups are also available in the community, utilizing case management, to coordinate services.

One model of care that has proven successful, and has been adopted in many locations, is Assertive Community Treatment, developed in Wisconsin in the 1970s; although it is expensive, it saves money in the long run, aiding in rehabilitation and reducing hospitalizations; a multidisciplinary team provides coordinated comprehensive services to patients, including home visits and work with families ("Assertive Community," 2006; Sadock and Sadock, 2003).

There is a range in the quality of care people receive; some obtain excellent, comprehensive services; many receive none and may wind up homeless/ and or in prisons (see Chapter 5), a reflection of the serious inadequacies in the mental health system in this country.

> After adjusting for inflation, states now spend 30 percent less on mental health care than they did in 1955. Medicaid funding for psychiatric treatment is so low that private practitioners are refusing to accept insurance payments, clinics are closing, hospitals are reducing the number of beds reserved for psychiatric patients, and psychiatric emergency rooms visits are on the rise. ("The Homeless," 2005, p. 7)

Work with Families

About forty years ago, schizophrenia was generally thought to be have developed as the result of family factors, such as faulty communication; the term schizophrenogenic mother was often used to characterize mothers of these patients. This perspective on schizophrenia influenced mental health approaches and at times kept clinicians from looking outside this framework ("Families in the Treatment—Part I," 1989).

Major breakthroughs in our understanding of schizophrenia have led to understanding its strong genetic and biochemical basis, and parents are no longer held to be the causative agents (although relationship factors can certainly contribute to exacerbations or precipitation of decompensations). At the same time that attitudes toward families were changing, many patients were returning home after deinstitutionalization. Now, families were becoming paramount in the treatment of their schizophrenic children, and professionals began to find ways of working with them. Rather than viewing the family primarily as the root of the problem, they were now viewed as reacting to and being affected by the chaotic world of their schizophrenic offspring. Families needed support; psychoeducational approaches were one way to help them with their schizophrenic children (Anderson, 1983). One major component of these programs related to understanding how schizophrenic people are vulnerable to stress, and finding ways to eliminate stress in their lives (Kopeikin, Marshall, and Goldstein, 1983).

The following is an example of this psychoeducational approach with families.

> People with schizophrenia must be approached calmly and patiently. They often prefer to be alone, and their privacy should be respected. . . . Both nagging criticism and overenthusiasm are bad. Requests and criticism should be expressed pleasantly, clearly, concisely, and specifically; for example, "you should help out more around the house" is bad, but "Please take out the garbage today" is good. Families are told that a patient's own requests, when they make simple sense, should be respected and not interpreted; if she prefers to eat alone in her room, she should be allowed to do so and her motives should not be questioned.
>
> Families are also taught to watch for signs of relapse: agitation, insomnia, loss of appetite, physical symptoms, a patient's growing conviction that people are laughing at her and talking about her. Parents are also given specific suggestions for coping with the patient's irrational fears and any threats of violence. ("Families in the Treatment—Part II," 1989, p. 2)

Another approach that many families find helpful is multiple family group meetings, or multiple family therapy ("Families in the Treatment—

Part II," 1989; McFarlane, 1983). In this model, several families who have schizophrenic members meet together with several therapists (with or without the schizophrenic member, depending both on circumstances and the model used). It is often an excellent source of support for the families and tends to break down the isolation and guilt experienced by many of these families. It has been observed that "families often speak more candidly to one another than to therapists . . . and they begin to recognize in themselves what they have first seen in others" ("Families in the Treatment—Part II," 1989, pp. 2-3). Some parents of schizophrenic adult children need supportive services, which they often do not receive, such as respite care to provide temporary relief to take care of their own needs. Many parents becoming elderly themselves and, no longer able to meet the needs of their children, are concerned about their children's lack of preparation for the future; some efforts are now being made to help them with "permanency planning" for their adult children (Botsford and Rule, 2004, p. 423).

Even when family life is proceeding comfortably, does that mean that the patient is receiving optimal care, or that efforts are being directed toward community residences and employment?

The majority of families favor "group homes, foster homes, and halfway houses that provide a decent physical environment along with some counseling and supervision; the schizophrenic patients themselves often agree"; while now acknowledging "that the family is not the main problem in schizophrenia, we must not act as though it is the main solution" ("Families in the Treatment—Part II," 1989, p. 3).

One of the most active self-help groups parents have developed is the National Alliance for the Mentally Ill (Winerip, 1999). This group is supportive, educational, and political, producing publications about schizophrenia and lobbying for legislation. It has been observed that participants are generally from the middle class; "ways must be found to include the poor as well" ("Families in the Treatment—Part I," 1989).

Community Groups for the Mentally Ill

One approach offering support to people with mental health problems is the clubhouse model; Fountain House, established with funding from the National Institute of Mental Health in 1976, was the model for this program (Jackson et al., 1996). This model is viewed as being different from the traditional day-treatment program (medical) model, held to be infantilizing and demeaning by its detractors. Dorothy Purnell, a former clubhouse member, working to earn an associate degree in human services, commented that when she was in day-treatment programs she "learned to be dependent. . . . I created ashtrays and clay animals that were stored on a shelf and eventually discarded. . . . I felt that I, too, deserved to be thrown away" (p. 176).

The clubhouse model is a competency-based program offering its members a sense of community; egalitarian relationships exist between staff and members, who manage the clubhouses together. The major focus is on the clients' "participation . . . [and] empowerment, building on . . . strengths, and maximizing client self-determination" (Jackson et al., 1996, p. 177). Although members are helped to secure clinical treatment elsewhere, and most take medication, they are viewed positively, their contributions are encouraged and appreciated, and they are helped to develop their potentialities and abilities.

Conflicts Between Empowerment and Beneficence

Many advances today promote the rights of the mentally ill, including legislation prohibiting employment discrimination against this group. Kruger (2000) emphasizes the importance of empowerment for the psychiatrically disabled and discusses his agency, the Mental Patients' Association (MPA), which works with present and former psychiatric patients; it began as a self-help group about thirty years ago. Their guiding principle is being "antipsychiatric, antisocial-control, and prohuman rights and mutual self-help" (p. 430). It was important not only to "destigmatize mental illness," but also to help others see it "as an integral part of the continuum of human life"; to improve the public image of psychiatric patients to enhance their own self-worth; and to engender the respect of others (p. 430). Self-determination and "having a voice" about one's life are important components of empowerment for patients (Kruger, 2000).

The empowerment of oppressed patients model stands in opposition to the model advocating the need for protective intervention when necessary (Murdach, 1996). Some clinicians in the empowerment camp, while acknowledging the value of medication (when appropriate and "not used to punish patients"), nevertheless oppose forcing people to take medication if they refuse (Bentley, 1993, p. 102). Bentley (1993) asserts that "social workers must stand with the right of patients to refuse medication" (p. 104). In several well-publicized cases, involuntary commitment has been opposed by some civil rights groups. However, in opposition to this viewpoint, Satel (1999), a psychiatrist, asserts that "critics refuse to acknowledge . . . that about half of all schizophrenics have no insight into their own condition and no understanding of why they need medication. As for free will, the freedom to be psychotic is no freedom at all" (p. A31).

Murdach (1996) acknowledges the dilemma social workers confront when faced with curtailing client autonomy, because of the value they place on client self-determination. However, she is concerned about protecting clients when necessary, such as from their suicidal or other self-destructive impulses. She advocates a differential use of beneficence or "benevolent intervention," which depends "on the degree of rational impairment or decisional incapacity demonstrated by the client and the amount of risk or danger present in the situation if the client is left unprotected" (p. 27). In essence, she argues, it is important to protect the client's decision making as much as possible, but some protection, ranging from mild to extreme, may be indicated depending on the degree of endangerment to the client.

DEPRESSION

Depressed or sad moods visit us through the life cycle, especially during periods of loss or other crises. However, such depressed feelings are generally temporary and do not develop into full-blown clinical depression. When a depressive disorder develops, "every facet of life—emotional, cognitive, physiological, behavioral, and social—may be affected" (MacKinnon and Michels, 1971, p. 174).

Generally, a person with clinical depression has a lowered mood, little energy and fatigues easily, lacks motivation, does not experience joy or pleasure, and cannot look forward to future events; in fact, the depressed person often feels that no future exists, and suicidal thoughts and/or intentions may be present. Self-esteem is low, and hopelessness, helplessness, and feelings of guilt are usually present. Although thought processes are not distorted as they are in schizophrenia (unless a psychotic depression is present), thinking tends to be slowed down, and people may have difficulty concentrating and are often preoccupied with themselves and their troubles. There develops a "sense of isolation from people and things, the sense of a dull, dead world" (Nemiah, 1961, p. 149). Anger (not always obvious) is intermingled with depression; in extreme situations, homicidal wishes and acts may coexist with depression. Most of the time, the anger is not felt as such by the person (as this might be too threatening) but may be internalized and directed against the self.

Physical symptoms include disturbances in appetite, which can be diminished (accompanied by weight loss) or considerably increased, leading to overeating and weight gain (which in turn can add to depressive feelings). Headaches can occur; abdominal distress, especially relating to constipation, is common. There may be a preoccupation with being or becoming ill, which can eventuate in hypochondriasis. Many depressed patients may appear at the doctor's office with physical complaints that often are treated as such, while the underlying depression goes undiagnosed.

> Mrs. Billings, who was discussed in Chapters 1 and 11, was admitted to an inpatient psychiatric facility for treatment of depression. She was tired, felt tearful, and stated that her symptoms were increasing. She complained of dizziness and shortness of breath and had gained forty pounds in the past three years, adding greatly to her self-consciousness. She had one previous psychiatric hospitalization for a suicide attempt and depression. She has very low self-esteem, strong feelings of guilt, and is very self-conscious. "It is hard for me to make friends. . . . I am uncomfortable with people."

Depression refers "both to a symptom and to a group of illnesses that have certain features in common" (MacKinnon and Michels, 1971, p. 174). Depression can range from a mild depression reactive to a life crisis (in which the person remains functional) to experiencing such an encompassing, immobilized state that hospitalization becomes essential. When depression become so severe that the patient appears almost catatonic, says little, and is preoccupied with very morbid and distorted thoughts, a *psychotic depression* may be present. Some people, on the other hand, can have a psychotic depression with agitated features; such a patient is usually restless and gives an "overall impression of intense anxiety" (p. 180).

Some people have mood swings, from depression to elated moods, accompanied by extreme hyperactivity; they are said to be *cyclothymic*. In more extreme cases, bipolar disorder is present, in which manic phases may produce erratic, irrational behaviors, including impulsive acting-out, such as excessive buying sprees (which the patient usually cannot afford), hypersexuality, and aggression. While the severe forms are readily recognized as abnormal, milder states (hypomania) are often ignored, because the individual's behavior is [mis]perceived as infectiously amusing or upbeat.

> Bipolar disorder may take years to diagnose. Alcoholism and drug abuse can disguise the symptoms and make them worse. Mixed mood states can be mistaken for many other conditions, including personality disorders. Mania often is mistaken for schizophrenia. . . . Many children diagnosed with attention deficit disorder eventually develop manic and depressive symptoms. ("Drug Treatment," 2006, p. 1).

Mania in adolescents is often overlooked. Their symptoms can be attributed to an antisocial personality disorder or schizophrenia; they may present with psychosis or substance abuse (Sadock and Sadock, 2003).

Antidepressants have been used to treat many types of depression, often with good results. Debate continues about whether medication is effective or necessary for all depressive states, and whether psychotherapy (of various schools) is just as effective or more effective with more lasting results; comprehensive treatments are increasingly advocated.

Seasonal affective disorder (SAD), recognized since the 1980s, is "a major (serious) depression that recurs each year at the same time, starting in fall or winter and ending in spring" ("Winter Depression," 2004). Treatment usually involves either antidepressant medication and/or the use of bright lights for several hours a day.

Depression often coexists with at least one other disorder, and is frequently found with borderline states, substance abuse, schizophrenia, anxiety disorders, including post–traumatic stress disorders, and somatization disorders. Depression is often not diagnosed in schizophrenia as the client's flat affect is attributed to schizophrenia rather than depression (Sadock and Sadock, 2003). Some people attempt to medicate their depression with alcohol; this can also have negative consequences as alcohol can aggravate depressive states.

Earlier, it was thought that depressive disorders could not exist in children because their superegos were not sufficiently mature to experience the guilt and conflict associated with depressive guilt. Now it is recognized that a depressive state, with its listlessness, anhedonia, unresponsiveness, and failure to thrive, can occur even in infants; depressive symptomatology is also seen in young children who have been abandoned, maltreated, or have attachment disorders; the mothers of these children are often depressed.

Reiner and Kaufman's (1959) hypothesis, in reference to people in crisis (discussed in Chapter 12), suggested that a depressive nucleus related to early deficits in nurturing underlies the acting-out behavior of the character disorder; acting-out behaviors may blunt the pain of depressive feelings. In the early editions of the *Diagnostic and Statistical Manual of Mental Disorders,* such as the DSM-I and DSM-II, depressions were apparently "classified among the personality disorders and neuroses." In a major change in 1980, the DSM-III "designated chronic depression as 'dysthymic disorder' and classified it as an affective or mood disorder, along with major depression and bipolar disorder" (Koscis, 1991, p. 8). Debate continues, and the "diagnosis of depressive personality disorder . . . has been reintroduced as a possible topic of investigation" ("Dysthymia," 2005, p. 2).

Normal Grief and Depression

Normal grief and depression share some features; sadness, loss of pleasure, and withdrawal from usual activities can occur in both. The bereaved person tends to be preoccupied with the loss, and it may take some time, ranging from weeks to months, before the person resumes former activities and develops new relationships (MacKinnon and Michels, 1971). Clear distinctions, however, are present; "the grief stricken individual does not suffer from a diminution of self-esteem. He is not irrationally guilty, and it is easy for the interviewer to empathize with his feelings" (p. 181). Although the bereaved person may "feel that his world has come to an end . . . he knows that he will recover and cope" (p. 181). As many as "50 percent of widows and widowers have symptoms typical of major depression in the first few months" ("Complicated Grief," 2006, p. 1).

If symptoms of grief remain or worsen, "the condition turns into what is now being called unresolved, protracted, traumatic, or complicated grief. It has features of both depression and post–traumatic stress disorder (PTSD)" ("Complicated Grief," 2006, p. 1).

Suicide

It can be difficult to determine the actual number of suicides in this country, as frequently deaths may not be reported as suicides, and sometimes they can be difficult to distinguish from other causes, such as accidents. Nevertheless, suicide is considered an extremely serious problem; it is estimated that more than 30,000 people commit suicide every year, and that there are approximately 650,000 people who attempt suicide (Sadock and Sadock, 2003, p. 913). More than 60 percent of suicides have been committed with handguns (Armstrong, 1998; "Confronting Suicide," 2003).

About 80 percent of those committing suicide are men, and most of these are Caucasian men who are fifty or older; it is the third leading cause of death in adolescents ("Confronting Suicide," 2003).

> Ninety percent of people who commit suicide have a psychiatric disorder. Mood disorders are the most common; up to 60 percent . . . have major depression or bipolar disorder. . . . Other psychiatric disorders associated with suicide are alcoholism and other addictions (40 percent of suicides), schizophrenia (6 percent), and anxiety disorders (10 percent). Nearly 50 percent of people . . . also have a personality disorder. In borderline personality disorder, suicidal thoughts, threats,

and attempts are among the defining symptoms. ("Confronting Suicide," 2003, pp. 2-3)

The number of people committing suicide is highest in rural areas, especially in the Rocky Mountain States (Butterfield, 2005). As in urban areas, depression, money worries, and drinking are involved, but in addition, according to Dr. Alex Crosby, these "are heightened in rural areas by social isolation, lack of mental health care and the easy availability of guns. . . . 'We have a culture of suicide'" (p. 16).

Cultural and societal attitudes toward suicide play a role in suicidal behavior. In Ireland, the dramatic increase of suicides in young men, while related to changing social factors, is also related to the Catholic Church's changing attitude toward suicide, which has become more "benign," so that suicide is "no longer vehemently condemned from the pulpit" (Clarity, 1999, p. 9). In Japan, by contrast, suicide "has little of the stigma it carries in Western societies; in literature, history and even today, suicides are often portrayed as noble, a matter of conscience or an honorable form of protest" (Strom, 1999, p. A8). In Japan, which in the past had very low suicide rates, the rate of suicide among men is reaching a record high (a rate higher than found in the United States).

In Japan, the serious economic recession, with its lower wages and accompanying numbers of layoffs, has led both to unemployment and job insecurities. It is considered very humiliating to be without work in Japan, and the shame and fear of condemnation by others for this disgraceful act is very strong (Strom, 1999). Chapter 5 discussed *karojisatsu,* which is the phenomenon of suicide being precipitated by extreme overwork, also a frequent phenomenon today in Japan, related to measures taken by employers to deal with the recession ("Japan," 1999).

In working with people who are depressed, it is important to be alert to suicidal thoughts; one needs to listen for signs of hopelessness, and despair, as well as understand serious at-risk behaviors in which the person might be engaged. Oblique communications such as references to giving away possessions cannot be overlooked. When concerned about this possibility, it is critical to ask directly about suicide. Important issues to clarify are the intent, the means, and the purpose the suicide act will serve. Underlying mental health problems need to be clarified, and the person's judgment and impulse control are important factors to consider. If the person seems to be at serious risk, it is important to seek immediate psychiatric consultation and to consider the possibility of hospitalization.

Internalized anger is usually a significant component of depressive states and is often a motivator of suicidal behavior. It is not uncommon for the suicidal person to wish to punish the survivors: "they'll be sorry when I'm gone." Homicidal acts are sometimes carried out by depressed people; people have murdered their spouses, family, co-workers, and sometimes people they do not know, and then killed themselves.

Suicide Survivors

People who are survivors of those who have committed suicide often suffer a great deal related to the actual loss, the stigma associated with this, and guilt. "Survivor-victims of a suicide are often emotionally and psychologically disrupted to such an extent that immediate supportive intervention should be initiated" (Welu, 1975, p. 144). Clinicians whose clients commit suicide can also be deeply affected by this trauma. Professional groups are becoming more aware of this problem, which needs further study; therapists affected by their client's suicide may also benefit from professional peer support groups (Ting et al., 2006).

BORDERLINE PERSONALITIES

People with borderline personalities tend to live in a world of inner chaos, deep insecurity, and unstable moods; they have deep fears of being abandoned and an unstable sense of identity. Their inner world is often displaced (and acted out) onto the external world, arousing turmoil, confusion, and anxiety in others.

The term borderline personality was officially adopted as a diagnosis by the American Psychiatric Association in 1980; until then, people with this diagnosis were classified with various other disorders ("Borderline," 1994). The mental health field has taken a great deal of interest in these patients; writings appeared and workshops were given; many focused on transference and countertransference difficulties in with this population. Clinicians continue to struggle with the turbulence created in the wake of encounters with people with borderline personalities; the question of whether this is a discrete diagnosis or an overused diagnosis overlapping other categories remains unanswered ("Borderline personality," 2006).

> The symptoms of the . . . borderline personality . . . [are] instability in mood, thinking, behavior, personal relations, and self-image. Although people . . . with this disorder cannot bear to be alone and constantly demand attention, they are often difficult to work and live with. They plague friends, family, and lovers with unreasonable demands, provoc-

ative behavior, tantrums, hypochondriacal complaints, and suicide threats. They are chronically angry, quick to take offense, and easily depressed. They are susceptible to drug and alcohol abuse and other self-destructive impulsive behavior. They repeatedly follow idealization of another person with contemptuous rejection, and their intense attachments alternate with equally sudden breakups. ("Borderline," 1994, p. 1)

In the past, people with these symptoms tended to be classified as pseudo-neurotic, narcissistic, infantile, paranoid, impulse-ridden, sociopathic, and "as-if" personalities, among others (Freed, 1980). People with depressive, cyclothymic personalities and bipolar disorders continue to present problems for the diagnostician attempting to differentiate these syndromes from the borderline personality disorder. More than half of borderline patients have had periods of depression and have a relatively high rate of depressive illness in their families. However, differences exist between them and people with mood disorders. "Their moods are much more susceptible to change in response to external events, and their depressions are often qualitatively different, with less guilt, appetite loss, and lethargy, but more loneliness, emptiness, and boredom" ("Borderline," 1994, p. 2).

Although borderline patients have mood instability and often display impulsive acting-out behaviors, their mood instability does not reach the heights of frenzied, uncontrolled behavior often displayed by the person with a bipolar disorder. The borderline personality is prone to psychotic decompensation when under stress, but these episodes are seen as brief and sporadic and tend to disappear when the stress dissipates.

Two of the major defense mechanisms of the borderline personality are projective identification and splitting. Projective identification (described in Chapter 2) is related to the defense of projection but extended to the point in which not only does the individual disavow a feeling by projecting it onto someone else, but this is done in such a way that the other person reacts with the same kind of behavior or attitudes being disavowed by the person utilizing this defense. A patient, for example, who is feeling angry will project this anger onto another person then through a psychological maneuver will say something to antagonize this other person, who will react in an angry way, which reinforces the borderline person's belief that, indeed, this person was angry.

Clinicians are frequently subject to client's projective identifications and this adds to the complexity of treatment. Many borderline patients have the capacity to "tune in" to the unconscious feelings of others, and it is not uncommon for them to pick up on a therapist's vulnerability. If, the therapist has doubts about being an adequate therapist, the patient will probably aim the provocation in this direction, so that the therapist will react in a personally defensive rather than in a clinically objective manner. Using an inter-subjective approach, if clinicians tunes into the feelings stirred up in them by these clients, they can use them as a tool in therapy, rather than being controlled by them.

Splitting is frequently utilized as a defense by borderline clients; this occurs because they are not able to tolerate ambivalent feelings or mixed emotions. They may engage in splitting in relation to their self-concepts; "extreme repetitive oscillation between contradictory self concepts" is another manifestation of the mechanism of splitting (Kernberg, 1984, p. 16). In Chapter 3, an example was given of splitting occurring in an institutional setting, in which a young male patient managed to pit the "good" staff (those he favored) against the "bad" staff (those whom he appeared to disfavor) causing institutional havoc and dissension.

Theoretical approaches to treating the borderline personality vary; a spectrum of function and dysfunction exists in people within this category, as well as varying degrees of motivation for treatment. Many of the writings address patients in outpatient or inpatient treatment settings, in which their symptomatology (whether acknowledged or denied) is the basis for their care. However, many social workers encounter people with borderline personalities in settings in which their mental health is not the focus of their concern, such as medical or child welfare settings. It is important for clinicians to find intervention strategies that can maximize support for the client and minimize the likelihood of the clinician being "swept away" by the client's overwhelming personality and manipulations.

People with borderline personalities frequently lack the capacity to self-soothe and often find themselves in turbulent emotional states that they cannot control. Adler (1985) sees helping the patient develop the capacity to self-soothe as a major goal of psychotherapy. Kernberg (1984) makes the point that in supportive psychotherapy with a borderline client, a major difference exists "between giving a patient advice on how to handle his life and helping him understand how certain 'automatic' ways of functioning are detrimental to his interests" (p. 156).

A social work student was working with G., a woman with a borderline personality structure; she was aware of G. using the defenses of splitting and projective identification and brought this pattern and its negative social consequences to her attention. G. had been at a new job for two weeks and reported to that she had alienated almost all her co-workers because she had stood up for one woman whom she thought was being mistreated.

G. seems to experience authority figures as all bad, while she projects her feeling of being abused onto, and then identifies with, those whom she perceives as being mistreated. These people to her are all good. She devalues all the others who are not assisting the victim, thus preserving the goodness of herself and the victim. We discussed this situation in terms of G. looking at people and things in general as either all good or all bad, and black or white with nothing in between, and of her being oversensitive to some people because her feelings have been hurt. G. associated this with her expecting too much and of wanting the world to be perfect—wanting everyone to meet each other's needs. She then said that she was looking for the impossible and needed to work on being able to accept people's shortcomings.

People with borderline personalities often have intense needs for relationships but are unable to maintain them because they fear engulfment (a primitive sense of danger of merging with the other person, possibly based on an equally primitive wish for this); they lack skills in forming relationships and in understanding the relationship binds in which they frequently find themselves.

A young male patient . . . had allowed a friend who was "down and out" to share his apartment until he was able to "get it together again." After a few days the "friend" had taken money from his wallet, had damaged furniture with burning cigarette butts, and had seduced the patient's girlfriend. The patient was hurt and angry, but had no awareness of the type of interpersonal information he would need to process to make more accurate predictions about others' behaviors. Rather, he was driven by the need to hold on to the relationship. (Marziali and Munroe-Blum, 1994, p. 55)

People with borderline personalities are often helped by learning how to cope with the here and now, to develop a more cohesive sense of self and better self-image, to learn how to exercise good judgment, to "size up situations" appropriately, and to establish more stable relationships. Group treatment is often effective; it can be used as the sole treatment, or as an adjunct to individual therapy. It has the potential advantage of diluting the relationship to the therapist (which can become very intense and tumultuous in individual treatment), fostering improved interpersonal skills, helping find constructive solutions to difficult reality situations, and learning to recognize emotions and their connection to behaviors. Marziali and Munroe-Blum (1994) were positive about the results of their group intervention with this population; in particular, they felt that group members learned to get in touch with their angry feelings and how to handle anger and confrontations with one another in a constructive manner. Dialectical Behavior Therapy (DBT), combining support with cognitive-behavioral techniques, has been found to be effective with this population; it is used both in groups and individual treatment (Sadock and Sadock, 2003).

Working with borderline patients is difficult for students; they are frequently caught in an emotional maelstrom and can feel confused and inept; Briggs (1979) addresses problems posed by borderline personalities. "Trainees customarily personalize responses from borderlines; since these responses are often hostile, the therapist may take them as affronts" (p. 138). Setting limits with a borderline person is also an important key to successful work; this is "one of the hardest tasks for trainees" (p. 144). Briggs (1979) notes that with experience trainees "will appreciate the fact that early limit-setting, especially with homicidal or suicidal borderlines, will help to reduce their own anxieties" (p. 136).

ANXIETY DISORDERS

Anxiety is experienced universally; it is an unpleasant feeling state, characterized by uneasiness, fear, worry, and physical and emotional distress. Sometimes it is relatively mild or temporary, however, for some, the anxiety can be overwhelming. Universal situations probably exist in which anxiety escalates into panic for most people, such as sitting on an airplane that suddenly develops serious mechanical problems midair. The rule of thumb is that anxiety does not have a cause in reality but that fear does, although a mixture can certainly be seen in emergency situations. Kafka's novels vividly portray a state of constant anxiety and dread, with the potential of terror striking from anywhere.

One characteristic of an anxiety state is "an apprehensive self-absorption which interferes with an effective and advantageous solution of reality problems" (Campbell, 1989, p. 48). Some people live in a constant state of anxiety and apprehension (a generalized anxiety disorder); for others, anxiety at times escalates into intense, overwhelming attacks of panic (panic disorders); for some, anxiety is displaced onto various external objects, such as a fear of dogs or elevators (phobic reactions); some people's anxiety is channeled into symptoms such as obsessions (continual preoccupation with certain subjects or thoughts), or into the development of routinized habits, the completion of which must be obeyed or the person will experience extreme discomfort, as in constant hand washing (compulsions). People who have experienced traumas in early life (such as sexual abuse) or in later life (such as being a refugee fleeing the horrors or war and torture) can develop serious symptoms of anxiety (post–traumatic stress disorder).

Sometimes anxiety is felt directly and/or channeled in bodily symptoms, as in various somatization disorders. It is not uncommon for anxiety and depression to coexist; anxiety and panic attacks are often part of the symptom picture of the borderline personality. Some people with severe anxiety may try to relieve it through excessive smoking or through the use of substances such as alcohol. One of the most common anxiety disorders, and often one of the most disabling, is the panic disorder.

Panic Disorders

Panic disorder usually begins before a person is thirty and frequently begins before the age of twenty; it is unusual for panic disorders to begin past the age of sixty-five ("Panic Disorder—Part I," 1990, p. 1).

> For five minutes to a half hour, the victim feels unbearable dread, a sense of unreality, and intense physical symptoms—choking sensations, labored breathing, a leaping, pounding heart, chest pain, dizziness, nausea, sweating, hot and cold flashes, numbness or tingling in the hands and feet, blurred vision. Victims fear that they will faint, lose control of themselves, go mad, or die. *Panic attacks* constitute *panic disorder* when many of these symptoms occur together repeatedly in a short period of time—say, once a week or more for a month—or when they create a persistent disabling fear of the next attack. ("Panic Disorder—Part I," 1990, pp. 1-2; italics added).

Panic attacks tend to continue to develop once the initial disorder starts; one difficult effect is the anticipation of future attacks or "anticipatory anxiety," which can be "more serious than the panic attacks themselves" ("Panic Disorder—Part I," p. 2). People then become more avoidant of situations that they fear might produce another panic attack. Agoraphobia is a subset of the panic disorders but also can occur by itself, without being accompanied by a panic disorder. Agoraphobia involves the avoidance of situations that trigger anxiety, usually public places. Its root is *agora,* which is the Greek word for marketplace. Marks (1987) noted that "this avoidance leads many agoraphobic people to become completely housebound" (p. 1161).

One client expressed her fear of driving; sometimes she is afraid to go to the mall (the modern "marketplace"). This client, who somatizes, discussed her symptoms in a somatic context; she is "afraid that I might faint in the car on the way," rather than "I am afraid of crowds," but the end result is avoidance. Somatization in anxiety disorders involves "enhanced awareness and selective attention to bodily sensations and danger-related information generally, increased sympathetic nervous system arousal, and a negative bias in appraising one's health" (Lipowski, 1988, p. 1364). People with panic disorders usually have such considerable anxiety about their physical health that some researchers "suggest that hypochondriasis is its essential feature" (pp. 1363-1364).

Opinions on treatment differ; medications (especially antidepressant drugs) are frequently used effectively (although they often do not prevent relapses); behavioral and cognitive interventions are popular ("Panic Disorder—Part II," 1990). Cognitive therapy aims to help people deal with those faulty patterns or habits of thought that are felt to exacerbate anxiety, such as the tendency to "catastrophize," which Beck (1976) describes as "a common characteristic of anxious patients, [that] illustrates anticipation of extreme adverse outcomes" (p. 93). Bandura (1976) discusses a treatment model for agoraphobic patients—who are phobic about the world outside of their home—in which the therapist participates in activities with the patient (discussed in Chapter 3).

Learning to tolerate and contain anxious feelings is an important part of most therapeutic approaches to panic disorders; however, the familiar dilemma of whether merely to eradicate symptoms or to understand underlying psychosocial problems presents itself. A woman might be experiencing panic attacks because she is unable to tolerate the impending death of her mother; events in one's current life can reactivate past traumatic events producing panic.

Post-Traumatic Stress Disorder

Post-traumatic stress disorder (PTSD) was officially recognized in the 1980s, when it was discovered in large numbers of veterans from the Vietnam War; for many years it had gone undiagnosed and untreated; an estimated 30 percent of Vietnam vets have experienced this syndrome (Kaplan, Sadock, and Grebb, 1994). Following is a description of a veteran who was seen ten years after his war experiences in Vietnam ("Post-Traumatic Stress—Part I," 1991):

> During his year in the army his platoon was repeatedly ambushed, and in one of those ambushes his closest friend was killed while he stood a few feet away. He himself hit a boy Vietcong fighter with a rifle butt and killed him. He admits that his mind keeps returning to these events, and he still has nightmares about them, but he insists that he

does not want to talk about any of that. He is constantly anxious and agitated, and he jumps at the sound of . . . [a] backfiring automobile. He becomes enraged at anything he regards as a mistake . . . by a person in authority, . . . he feels constantly bored and depressed and is "only going through the motions" at work and at home. He hardly talks to his family and has alienated most of his friends. He often carries a gun, and in moments of sudden anger he strikes his wife or starts fights with strangers over trivial annoyances. ("Post-Traumatic Stress—Part I," 1991, p. 1)

Additional study and research on PTSD have been carried out, and other previously undiagnosed conditions have become better understood, including the sequelae of severe trauma experienced by children (through maltreatment and witnessing violence); women, through rape and battering; adults who were abused as children; survivors of concentration camps and other war and torture situations; as well as the effects of catastrophic environmental events, such as hurricanes, tornadoes, and fires.

The onset of symptoms such as nightmares, flashbacks, and intrusive memories of the trauma can be almost immediate or delayed by years. It is not uncommon for events or people to trigger memories or associations. The veteran, discussed above, became agitated when a car backfired because it sounds like gunfire. Greg, discussed next, who was being seen by a clinical social worker, experienced an "unprovoked" attack of anxiety.

Greg, a teenager with developmental disabilities who exhibited some bizarre behaviors and often lived in a world of fantasy, was taken to an amusement park and allowed to drive one of the automated cars. However, after an enthusiastic start, he panicked and said that he never wanted to go back to this park again. Greg, who lived in a foster home, had a traumatic childhood; his father was murdered in a car, and although the teenager was not present at the murder, he believes he was, and that the father's body was hurled into the backseat where he was sitting. Although this boy was not capable of verbalizing this connection, it is quite probable that this is precipitated his panic attack. Although he had been a passenger in cars many times without this reaction, it is possible that driving a car for the first time may have elicited association to (and identification with) his father, who was a taxi driver.

If Greg indeed does avoid this park and other amusement rides in the future, this might be considered "a conditioned response that resembles a phobia"; it is very common for people to "over-react to anything associated with the traumatic event" ("Post-Traumatic Stress—Part I," 1991, p. 3); people also "often succumb to a kind of emotional anesthesia. Under its influence, most of their feelings seem not quite real to them, everyone is a stranger, and activities that were formerly important no longer matter" (p. 2). It is not uncommon for people with PTSD to experience dissociation (discussed in Chapter 2); in dissociation the person's sense of identity or consciousness is disrupted.

A third set of symptoms relates to the development of *hypersensitivity;* "they are edgy, irritable . . . sleep poorly and find it difficult to concentrate. Some are tense with barely stifled rage and occasionally lose control in violent outbursts" ("Post-Traumatic Stress—Part I," 1991, p. 2). Children tend to present a different symptom picture and do not have "flashbacks, emotional numbing, and amnesia." Rather, they present with "separation anxiety, school phobias, a fear of strangers, and recurrent nightmares. They also have headaches, stomach aches, and other physical symptoms" ("Post-Traumatic Stress—Part II," 1991, p. 1).

Generally, therapy aims to help the patient remember and confront the traumatic event and see its connection to his or her feelings and symptoms. This can present many difficulties, including the patient's resistance to looking at this as well as the danger of retraumatization as the patient gets in touch with the trauma. Some behavior therapists use systematic desensitization (and implosive therapy, or purposeful massive flooding with images of the trauma under controlled and protected conditions) ("Post-Traumatic Stress—Part II," 1991). Group therapy is often effective with PTSD patients as they can share experiences with others, learn how others have managed their feelings, develop new relationships, and lessen the burden of stigma (Berzoff, 1996a).

Kaplan, Sadock, and Grebb (1994) question whether adequate supports were present for the person after the trauma. Herman (1997) observed that during World War II soldiers were protected against feeling terror by the support they felt from their units and leaders; this is in sharp contrast to the loss of cohesion often experienced in combat by soldiers in Vietnam, intensified by the negative feelings they experienced when they returned home because they had fought an unpopular war. The adulation experienced by the returning World War II hero was lacking.

Clinicians may have difficulty in working with PTSD because they may experience anxiety and other disturbances by being immersed in the client's world; this is termed *vicarious traumatization.* Child welfare workers have also experienced vicarious traumatization in their work with victims of various forms of trauma and maltreatment (see Chapter 7). Supportive supervision and staff support groups are often helpful to clinicians working with trauma victims.

THE ADDICTIONS

Problems related to substance abuse have been discussed throughout this book, including its negative effect on family relationships, parenting, and its relationship to child abuse (Chapter 7); its harmful effect on the developing fetuses of pregnant women (Chapter 9); its relationship to suicide, depression, and acting-out behaviors in adolescents (Chapter 10); and its prevalence in the homeless population (Chapter 5). Its relationship to mental health problems will be discussed in detail in this section. Pathological gambling is included in this discussion; though not a physical addiction, it does produce a physical "high" and has a powerful hold over the individual.

Alcohol Abuse

The roots of alcoholism are multicausal; they may include cultural factors (such as the attitude toward alcohol), familial, and psychological factors. Whether a biological predisposition toward alcoholism exists remains an unsettled question. Many people in our culture drink and usually can keep their alcohol consumption under control; those who may occasionally drink too much at a party are not necessarily dependent on regular drinking; alcohol dependence is "characterized by lack of control" (Mulinski, 1989, p. 334). As drinking increases, so do problems in the client's general functioning and social relationships. In addition, people who abuse alcohol typically utilize "rationalization and denial to hide their loss of control from themselves and from those around them" (p. 334).

A major problem in working with persons dependent on alcohol is their resistance to treatment; often their physical and psychological dependence is so great that they will deny the need for help and minimize their amount of drinking as well as its ensuing complications. Therefore, motivating substance abusers to become involved in treatment is difficult. Sometimes this can be accomplished through caring confrontations on the part of family members; sometimes it takes leverage from external sources of control to accomplish this, such as court-mandated alcohol treatment. In some successful employee assistance programs, the aim of reaching workers while they are still capable of employment and using the leverage of dismissal from work if they do not comply with treatment has often been effective.

Alcohol has serious effects on the body and on brain chemistry, and withdrawal from serious alcohol usage must be medically monitored. It is important that treatment be focused on the drinking itself, in terms of the patient's need to drink, ways to control this, and finding alternate lifestyles and/or other interests when drinking stops. Some people have centered their life around drinking companions and have nothing with which to fill up their time and space when they attain sobriety.

For some patients, in need of structure and support, halfway houses can be helpful. Alcoholics Anonymous has been found very beneficial, and is often used an adjunct to other forms of treatment. Work with patients who abuse alcohol also needs to be culturally sensitive. Owing to the multiple stresses faced by Southeast Asian people, the abuse of alcohol as well as other substances has been a critical problem (Amodeo et al., 1996). Gay men tend to have a high rate of drinking problems, often associated with internalized homophobia, which also must be addressed in treatment (Warn, 1997).

Alcoholism is considered a chronic disease; people usually need ongoing help even after drinking initially stops. Opinions differ as to whether to focus exclusively on alcohol-related issues or to involve the person in psychotherapy related to other life issues as well. One criticism of the work with substance-abusing mothers is that it is often focused only on treating the substance abuse without offering comprehensive services dealing with poverty, lack of education, past maltreatment, and difficult interpersonal relationships as well as mothering capacities and skills (Dore, 1999).

The problem of dual diagnosis (i.e., substance abuse coexisting with other psychiatric disorders) in clients who abuse alcohol has been addressed with increasing frequency (Mulinski, 1989; O'Hare, 1995). Associations have been found with disorders including schizophrenia, depression, antisocial personality, borderline personality disorder, and anxiety. In the past, programs existed only for substance abusers or only for people with psychiatric disorders; today some progress has been made in the development of integrated programs, although, as in all substance abuse treatment programs, the need for services is far greater than the supply.

Drug Abuse

Drug abuse is a major problem in this country; in addition to the primary problems caused by this disorder, such as its serious psychological and physical effects on the user, secondary effects include its impact on employment and family relationships; drugs are illegal and most are very expensive. Many people have turned to crime and various illegal activities, including prostitution, to support their habits. In addition, a number of people who abuse drugs have been sent to prison (in alarming numbers, leading to the escalation of the prison population) where they generally receive punishment rather than treatment (Chapter 5).

Drug abuse has been difficult to treat, in part because of the variation of symptoms in individuals, even those taking the same drug. It has also been found that most people who abuse drugs usually do not abuse only one substance but several, in addition to frequent use of cigarettes. "Most heroin addicts have been, are, or will be alcoholic, and most people who start to smoke marijuana do not stop drinking alcohol" ("Drug Abuse—Part II," 1989, p. 3). Some people continually change drugs, and some will use drugs in combination with other drugs to "control each other's side effects" (the combination of a stimulant with a sedative or opioid is especially popular).

Unfortunately, space does not allow a description of the side effects of the many specific drugs on its users; following is a brief synopsis of some of the deleterious effects of drugs.

> Some acute physical effects are the impairment of reaction time and motor coordination by alcohol, diazepam, or marijuana; death from respiratory depression after an overdose of heroin or a combination of sedatives; cerebrovascular strokes caused by high doses of amphetamine or cocaine in people with high blood pressure or damaged arteries. Acute psychological dangers include . . . anxiety or paranoid reactions to marijuana; "bad trips" from hallucinogenic drug use; irritability, agitated paranoia, and unpredictable rage under the influence of stimulants; alcohol and cocaine hangovers; drowsiness caused by benzodiazepine or opiates. ("Drug Abuse—Part I," 1989, p. 1)

The use of prescription drugs has been on the increase; "the number of people who had used oxycodone, the main ingredient in OxyContin, for nonmedical reasons jumped from 11.6 million in 2002 to 13.7 in 2003" (Bowman, 2005, p. 50). Methamphetamine has been produced from cold medications, often in home labs, but as states restricted this practice, and the supply declined, the slack was taken up in Mexico, where a large quantity of crystal methamphetamine has been produced. "Sometimes called ice, crystal is far purer, and therefore even more highly addictive, than powdered home-cooked methamphetamine, a change that health officials say has led to greater risk of overdose" (Zernike, 2006a, p. A1). Crime has increased as people try to support this habit; meth users are inclined toward identity theft (Leland, 2006).

Although treatment of substance abusers has to take the complex physical reactions of a given person to a specific drug into account, the general principles of working with people with alcohol dependence, previously discussed, are similar ("Drug Abuse—Part II," 1989). People with drug abuse problems also frequently have coexisting psychiatric disorders that also need to be diagnosed and treated.

Compulsive Gambling

Gambling is an activity that many people engage in for enjoyment; church-sponsored bingo games, for example, are a popular social activity; occasional visits to a gambling casino or participating in gambling activities on a cruise ship are common. However, gambling becomes a way of life for some people, and then something that controls their lives; at that point, it can be said to become an addiction. Today, the increased availability of gambling opportunities, including state-run lotteries, gaming on Indian reservations, and real gambling on the Internet, has increased the gambling activities of many people; in some cases, this has led to serious personal crises. According to the National Council on Problem Gambling, "48 states have some form of legal gambling . . . [which] generated $80 billion in 2005" (Pace, 2007, p. 4). In the past, almost all gambling was attributed to men; now "nearly a third are women and a growing number are teen-agers" (Brody, 1999, p. D7).

Blume (1992) has described compulsive gambling as an addiction without drugs and provides the following succinct observations.

> Pathological gamblers make excuses for their losses or even deny them. A large loss of the kind any gambler should expect is an intolerable injury to their self-esteem, and they stake more and more to recoup. Losses increase erratically; the gambler's mood follows his luck, with ups and downs that can be compared to the alternating depression and hypomania of bipolar disorder. The gambler's family life and work situation deteriorate as debt grows and personal possessions, savings, and legitimate loan sources are exhausted. Lying, embezzlement, and forgery are rationalized. Eventually the gambler may ask for a "bailout," a large loan or gift to pay off debts, usually in return for a promise to give up gambling. Like detoxification without rehabilitation for a heroin addict, the bailout merely enables the addiction to renew itself and continue. (Blume, 1992, p. 4)

Gamblers often fall prey to loan sharks as well.

A number of similarities have been found between pathological gambling and substance abuse; in fact, both are often found to coexist. Other diagnoses found in compulsive gamblers include depression, bipolar disorder, schizoaffective disorder, and panic disorders (Robinson, 1997). Few treatment facilities exist for people with this problem; some private practitioners work with this group, and Gamblers Anonymous, similar to Alcoholics Anonymous, has often been effective (Robinson, 1997); federal legislation has been proposed to aid problem gamblers, but this bill did not pass; lack of federal funding remains a problem, but there are active organizations such as the Center for Gambling Studies involved in program and advocacy efforts (Pace, 2007).

DEVELOPMENTAL DISABILITIES

In a biography of novelist Jane Austen, Nokes (1997) describes the large Austen household as always struggling economically but vibrant, lively, and warmly involved with each other. However, one member of this household, George (born in 1766), the second oldest son, did not seem to be developing normally. As a baby, George was "often subject to alarming fits," but the family was reassured that this often happened to young children (Nokes, 1997, p. 38). However, George "did not thrive. Already four years old, he struggled to form a syllable and was still subject to strange fits" (p. 39); but when he reached the age of six, "the malady could no longer be disguised, nor the resolution longer delayed" (p. 43).

> Madness, or mental infirmity . . . was a sickness which afflicted not only the sufferer but also those . . . compelled to be the daily witnesses of its melancholy effects. For the sake of the other children it was agreed that little George should be sent away . . . . The Cullums [a family who provided this type of care] . . . had proved themselves quite equal to such a task. Cassandra [George's mother] made no protest . . . and the boy [was] removed into safe-keeping with . . . [this family]. There were to be no visits, no letters, . . . or family records beyond what was necessary for the maintenance of the poor child's life. It would be almost as if the boy had never existed. (Nokes, 1997, p. 43)

When George was sent to his new home, the family resolution of no contact was maintained. The Austens paid for George's care, and, later on, George's older brother visited to pay the fees "but did not linger for conversation" (Nokes, 1997, p. 522). As an adult, when Jane Austen tried to converse by the use of sign language with a man who was deaf and mute, she remembered conversing this way with George when he was a child. It was strange for her to "think of poor George," who was now past forty, and with whom she had not had contact during all this time. "But where nothing could be amended it was useless to repine, and she quickly dismissed all conscious thoughts of her idiot brother from her mind, as they had all been taught to do as children" (p. 347). When George died, he was buried about twenty miles away from Jane Austen's tomb.

> George was laid to rest in an unnamed grave in the churchyard. . . . In
> death, as in life, he was to be forgotten, his remains unmarked by any
> stone. Only George Cullum [his caretaker] was in attendance at George
> Austen's death. It was he who noted for the death certificate that
> George Austen was "a gentleman." (Nokes, 1997, p. 526)

More than 200 years later, in an editorial in *Social Work,* Witkin (1998)
expressed concern that today many people with mental retardation are also
forgotten, and he referred to them as the "invisible" population. He observes
that they do not usually "participate in the mainstream of community life,"
and that "when they do appear in public, we avoid them or develop 'special'
programs for them, rendering them invisible once again" (p. 293); it is also
his impression that social workers "have shown little interest in this group"
(p. 293). A stigma is often attached to the classification of retardation, and
those with this diagnosis are often sensitive to this, have low self-esteem,
and have internalized negative images of themselves.

Although George Austen was unfortunate in being isolated from his family (probably in part because of their shame about his condition), he nevertheless did receive good care (especially for the times he lived in); certainly
he received far more humane treatment and respect than many mentally retarded people who came later. George Austen lived in what we would today
call a specialized foster home for the retarded. During the past century and
until the 1960s, many people with retardation lived in large state institutions, often with poor physical conditions and dehumanizing (at its worst)
or infantilizing (at its best) treatment. Since retardation is a chronic disorder, little in the way of education or rehabilitation was provided; people had
no preparation for living outside the institutions. Sometimes people who
were not retarded were "dumped" into these settings because their behavior
might have been difficult or serious family problems existed, or they were
deaf (which was not diagnosed) or had other medical disorders, and no in-
depth or ongoing evaluations were done.

Today, many people with retardation have been deinstitutionalized; federal legislation, including the Americans with Disabilities Act, is in force;
special educational services are federally mandated; special residences and
group homes exist; vocational services and day programs are available.
However, many programs do not have sufficient resources to adequately
meet this population's needs.

Assessment of Mental Retardation

A person is considered mentally retarded only if this condition has started before the age of eighteen. Mental retardation can range from mild to moderate, severe, and profound. Functional assessment is an important part of the diagnosis, and the capacities of people to take care of their own hygiene, their daily living needs, work, or maintain themselves in the community are factors that are evaluated.

The specific cause of mental retardation in many people is not known. However, clear-cut causes of retardation can be determined in a number of patients; these include genetic disorders (such as Down's syndrome), illness of the mother during pregnancy (such as German measles and AIDS), prematurity, substance abuse of the mother (fetal alcohol syndrome), complications of pregnancy (toxemia), and complications during delivery that can deprive the baby's brain of oxygen (anoxia) (Kaplan, Sadock, and Grebb, 1994).

A child can acquire retardation after birth through illness (such as viral encephalitis), accidents, or child abuse, which cause traumatic brain injuries. Poor environmental conditions and various types of maternal deprivation and child maltreatment can cause what appears to be retardation; however, good early intervention programs often can reverse these conditions. Sometimes children who are not retarded have been diagnosed as such because of undiagnosed deafness and/or blindness. Mental retardation can coexist with psychopathology such as schizophrenia or mood disorders. Children with *pervasive developmental disorders* (such as autism) tend to have a high rate of serious cognitive impairments.

Clinical Issues

People who are cognitively limited also have the same human problems other people do, progress through the life cycle, are subject to a variety of psychosocial stressors, and have family relationships that cover the spectrum from warm and supportive to abusive. Their psychosocial difficulties must be evaluated from a life-cycle perspective, in terms of the developmental changes, progressions and normal regressions, expectations, and stresses of their age.

Early diagnosis facilitates early intervention efforts; this is critical in promoting optimal development for disabled children, as well as providing needed support and educational guidance for their caretakers.

Children with developmental disabilities are at greater risk for being abused than "normal" children (Olkin, 1999). A special therapeutic problem exists for children who have been abused and need therapeutic intervention but may not have the verbal skills to engage in conventional therapy; special techniques have been evolving to work with this problem, although services in this area are scarce.

School-age children need special educational services; advances in special education programs have made a major difference in educating these children. As relationships with peers are so important at this age, cognitively impaired children are vulnerable to the hurtful insults, prejudices, and discrimination from other children. One of the most pejorative terms is calling someone a "retard!" Many retarded children and adults have problems with self-esteem, can feel different from others, and, as Witkin (1998) reminds us, remain outside the mainstream.

A variety of approaches, including support from school-based programs and families, can help counter these responses. Some children may benefit from individual clinical work; some respond well to group support.

Teenagers in general go through a turbulent time; self-esteem issues of normal adolescence are intensified for retarded teens by their awareness of being different. Struggles between dependence and independence surge; it can be difficult to find the right balance between granting the autonomy teens want and maintaining the protective controls they may need; settings that foster independence and autonomy in as many spheres as is reasonable should be encouraged.

Separation-individuation issues must be worked out on many levels; some may move away from home into group homes, and this can also be a conflictual issue for them as well as their parents. Some, like George Austen, were sent away for varying periods of time in their childhood and may have reactive separation and loss issues resulting from these experiences.

Teenagers often welcome help with sex education and their conflicting feelings about sexual activity; this focus is often lacking with the cognitively impaired population. Some older teenagers and young adults may benefit from support and guidance regarding committed relationships, career opportunities, and choosing a lifestyle that, depending on their needs and inclinations, might range from living with parents, independent living, to group (or foster) homes. Options for group homes are seriously limited; while living with parents can be a benign experience, it can also be conflictual and may thwart independent strivings.

People in middle adulthood may have families of their own; those who have always lived with their families might be facing separation for the first time, as their parents age and can no longer care for them.

Older retarded adults have a similar diversity of health and lifestyle problems as do many nondisabled elderly. Some continue in independent living;

many find themselves in nursing homes. Generally, retarded people (especially those with severe or profound retardation) tend to die at an earlier age due to other physical problems (Kaplan, Sadock, and Grebb, 1994).

Many clinicians believe that people with cognitive limitations are not amenable to psychotherapy; if help is provided to them, it follows a behavioral model (which usually permeates most of the settings in which they live and work). However, some clinicians have experienced successful therapeutic encounters with retarded people, who often respond positively to supportive relationships and want to talk and think about their lives, their fears, and getting along with others. Their low self-esteem can be improved, and they can experience (for some, it may be a unique experience) not being outside of the mainstream of human discourse and finding that someone is interested in what they think and what they feel.

Mikkelsen (1994) believes that people who are mentally retarded "experience the full range of human emotions, and in some situations their cognitive limitations may actually heighten the intensity of their feelings" (p. 8).

> Many mentally retarded people who are not living with their families will have experienced repeated losses. Institutional staff members and counselors to whom they have felt close will have gone away. They will have left friends behind on moving to new residences. A previous psychotherapist may have broken off treatment before it was completed. This accumulation of losses and the fear of further losses can make retarded people hesitant to begin a new therapeutic relationship. A therapist who is not aware of these issues may wrongly regard the resulting reticence as an effect of limited cognitive capacity. (Mikkelsen, 1994, p. 8)

Work with Families

It is an unanswered question as to why George Austen was socially isolated from his family throughout his lifetime. Was it a combination of the family's shame, anger, and overt rejection? Nokes (1997) refers to an episode in Jane Austen's novel, *Persuasion.* The Musgrove family had a very difficult son who was both "stupid" and "unmanageable," and who was "sent to sea," as he "deserved" this. The family rarely heard about him, and he was "scarcely at all regretted" (p. 524). The implication here is that the motivation was overt rejection based on utter frustration and anger with this impossible son; by inference, this may be what the Austen family felt toward George.

However, Jane Austen's recollection as an adult of using sign language with George when he was a child is quite striking. Sign language is not easy to acquire; it takes some motivation and time to learn. This suggests the possibility that some involvement and investment was made in communicating with George. The brief, early descriptions of the parents' reactions to George and his medical problems sound caring. Therefore, another hypothesis is that the parents may have experienced deep grief and sadness at losing their second-born son; these feelings may have been "sealed off," so that they could deal with this act of exclusion, which was against their basic nature; if George could remain "sealed off," so could their feelings.

Having a developmentally disabled child produces many complex, conflictual feelings in parents; grief (followed by "chronic sorrow") (Chapter 12) combined frequently with guilt, anger, and resentment; many feel dazed and overwhelmed when hearing this news; some may seal off their feelings and choose to remain emotionally distant from the child rather than experience their devastating disappointment and sense of personal failure.

Families frequently overcome their distress, become supportive and involved in rehabilitative efforts on their children's behalf; many join support groups, take political action, and become active in organizations such as the National Association for Retarded Citizens. Advances have been made in the field of developmental disabilities; and with good educational and rehabilitative efforts, children often advance functionally, even if the disability itself cannot be reversed. Social workers can "instill in parents realistically positive expectations toward their children"; in addition, they can help parents learn "more effective skills" for both coping with their children's special problems and aiding in their growth (Proctor, 1983, p. 515); parents are generally seen as collaborators with the helping professionals. *Respite care* is often very helpful, depending on the degree of disability, the realistic demands placed on the family, and the capacity of the family to cope; this can also be critical even for many well-functioning families.

Every family's subjective reactions, while having certain common features, are different, and every family is unique. The baseline biopsychosocial functioning of a family must be understood in the context of their social world and culture, and their strengths and vulnerabilities must be evaluated in terms of their attitudes, relationship (and attachment behaviors) to the child, and potential to respond (and to act as collaborators) for rehabilitative services for their disabled child. Families can have concurrent problems, including family dissolution, alcoholism, mental illness, and child maltreatment; adding the extra difficulty of a disabled child may be overwhelming.

Poverty and minority status can place families under stress, and their children are generally at greater risk for developmental problems; For families already stressed for these reasons, having a disabled child can aggravate dysfunction, and both the child and siblings can be affected by the additional tension (Phillips, 1999).

Pervasive Developmental Disorders

Pervasive developmental disorders, which seriously affect language, socialization, and behavior, include several specific syndromes; autism and Asperger's syndrome, will be discussed next.

Autism

The etiology of autism, with its pervasive, disabling effects on a child's developmental processes, is still not known, although all evidence points to prominent biological factors. From a phenomenological point of view, the child's lack of emotional connectedness and attachment to other people is its defining characteristic. The term *autism* comes from the Greek word *autos,* which means self; in this context, it means the evident extreme paucity or absence of interest in others, as well as seeming self-absorption; the more extreme the autism, the less the awareness of and the greater the indifference to other people.

Autism can develop during different stages of infancy and early childhood, but it is classified as autism only if it arises by the age of three (American Psychiatric Association, 1994). Variations occur in its severity and symptomatology, as well as the presence of other disabilities, such as retardation (very frequent), epilepsy, blindness, deafness, and various physical illnesses. Serious deficits in communication include no verbal language, or few words; and "restricted repetitive and stereotyped patterns of behavior, interests, and activities" (p. 71).

In some ways, autism is a "wastebasket" classification, as many developmental abnormalities that share some of these features have been labeled autism. Although it is clear that an organic basis underlies this disorder (in the past it was thought to be caused by parental coldness and rejection), the existence of different etiologies may explain the inconsistent symptoms and the fact that autism appears at different points during the first three years of development. German measles in the mother, for example, may produce autism in a child, with deficits that are present at birth. Some abnormalities do not appear until the child is a year and a half or two years old, possibly related to factors such as a viral illness or metabolic disturbance.

A distinctive feature of autism is the child's difficulty in processing and integrating thoughts and feelings; although they maybe capable of learning, they tend to remain at a concrete level of thinking. Often considerable rigidity characterizes both their thinking and behaviors. Some children have serious behavior problems, such as tantrums (often in the context of poorly-tolerated unexpected, even minimal change), and appear to be out of control; this can at times also be related to (or intensified by) parental confusion and inconsistency in dealing with the child.

One mother described her seven-year-old son, Christopher, diagnosed as autistic. One concern was his speech: "He just doesn't talk unless he wants something." Another mother was pleased about the decreased echolalia in her son's speech, which is described as the "pathological repetition by imitation of the speech of another" (Campbell, 1989, p. 232). Some children have no speech at all; sign language is frequently used to compensate for this.

Christopher was recently toilet trained, and his mother was pleased about this and the fact that now "he makes only occasional mistakes." Toilet training is often a major problem and a frequent focus of intervention.

Christopher does not have any friends; "he is a loner," although he does respond to his older sister. (It is not uncommon to see this variation; children may show varying amounts of affection, such as wanting hugs or kissing parents or seeming to have a favorite person, although basically the interpersonal world does not seem to be a major interest.) Peter Gombosi, a psychoanalyst, has written about his own autistic son, Andrew (Chapter 12). In discussing the lack of attachment behaviors attributed to autistic children, he notes:

> But all is not as it seems. Any parent or teacher of an autistic child, or anyone who does not diagnose and "understand" from a distance, will tell you of moments of intense interchange that are never spoken of in descriptions of autism. The capacity for some kind of object relationship is not missing, but in most autistic children it is distorted and severely restricted and takes other shapes. (Gombosi, 1998, p. 256)

Christopher enjoys the rides in amusement parks; "the wilder it is the more he loves it." He also enjoys the swings at home (swinging and other self-stimulating behaviors are often favorite pastimes of autistic children). Gombosi (1998) observed that

> most develop a repetitive, circular behavior called "stimming" [self-stimulation], which seems to occupy their senses, while ignoring the world. . . . My son's roommate likes to spend his free time squishing mud between his fingers . . . [another] boy will put his hand in front of his face and wave it to and fro rapidly. (p. 256)

Christopher's mother reports that "his only interest is in eating; he is constantly eating—cereal, soup, a popsicle; he will have supper and then want something else." (Eating habits are often a major concern; some children will eat only a limited diet of three or four foods and are insistent about this; one ten-year-old girl would eat only oatmeal.) When Christopher eats in the yard, "he has a bad habit of throwing dishes into the neighbor's yard after he's finished eating"; the neighbor is "accepting of this and returns the dishes." Christopher is not destructive, and his mother can keep fragile things in the house (many parents, on the other hand, find that their children are destructive, damage things, and are difficult to control). The only thing Christopher destroys is colored newspapers.

Christopher is very active and very nervous; his fingernails are "bitten down." It is not unusual to find some autistic children engaged in self-abusive behaviors. One mother described her five-and-a-half-year old son as self-abusive at home, where he pinches himself, claws at his face, and sometimes scratches at his brother's face. Recently, he has been scratching his own scrotum.

Another mother, with a fourteen-year-old son, felt that his demands on her were high. "His demands are always directed toward me"; he will tell her, for example, "You make the chicken!" He is also concerned with sameness and rituals (another common trait): he does not like anyone to be missing and often asks the whereabouts of family members who are not at home.

Treatment Considerations

Early intervention is critical in working with autistic children and their families. It is generally accepted that behavior modification including positive reinforcement, and social skills training is a treatment of choice (Groden and Baron, 1988). Many of these children respond well and can progress to higher levels of functioning and communication within the basic parameters of this chronic disorder. Aversive approaches are generally very strictly limited, and must be reviewed and monitored. Gombosi (1998) recognizes the importance of a behavioral approach; he has commented that "for those of us raised in the psychodynamic tradition, it is both inspiring and humbling to see the improvements some autistic children can make within a strictly behavioral, intensive program, sometimes to the point where they attend school without an aide in a regular classroom" (p. 272). He also credits the "experts in the trenches," the teachers who work with these children; "how they continue so loyally, enthusiastically, and with such good cheer, with children who are not their own, in the face of the difficulties relating to these children, is a wonder to me" (p. 274).

Working with families of autistic children and coordinating efforts at home with educational approaches at school are very important; a biopsychosocial perspective discussed in relation to working with families of retarded children applies to this population.

Asperger's Disorder

Asperger's disorder has many similarities to autism; however, "there are no significant delays in language, cognitive development, or appropriate self help skills" (Sadock and Sadock, 2003, p. 1218).

> Asperger's Syndrome (AS) is an autism-spectrum disorder that is characterized by highly impaired social skills, difficulty relating to others, a lack of flexible imaginative play, and often a preoccupation with a finite and highly specific topic. AS, which typically presents less severe symptoms than classic autism, has seen a dramatic increase in its prevalence within the last 10 years. (VanBergeijk, 2005, p. 24)

A comprehensive team approach (including teachers) is necessary, and long-term intervention is needed with a focus on daily life and social skills behavioral and cognitive techniques are beneficial. Many people with AS are very intelligent, often go to college; early interventions can help them develop their high potentials. Parent support groups are recommended, and siblings can also benefit from support (VanBergeijk, 2005).

CONCLUSION

Experiencing disturbing emotional states is intrinsic to human existence; when these states become extreme, overpowering, and persist, they can be said to be pathological, although it can be difficult at times to distinguish between normal emotional states and pathological conditions. It is important to remember that we are not "pathologizing" people who have distressing psychological symptoms; we are attempting to understand what is wrong, to enable them to live more comfortably and securely, and not be "captive" to psychological states beyond their control. Practitioners advocating an exclusive strengths perspective would abolish psychopathology from their lexicon and clinical approaches; unfortunately, banishing it from treatment does not banish its insidious effects on those who experience it.

As we have attempted to show throughout this book, psychopathology in individuals is interwoven with many of their social problems, including violence, sexual abuse, suicide, the breakdown of the family, substance abuse, and homelessness; it can also coexist in people with physical illness, disability, and those receiving end-of-life care. The psychodynamic biopsychosocial approach is especially relevant in working with people who have mental health problems and their families; it enables us to provide a range of services, from the Winnicottian holding environment, with its provision of ego-supportive environmental services, to the utilization of intersubjectivity in working effectively with complicated individual and relationship disturbances.

LEARNING EXERCISE

Present clinical assessments of two cases of schizophrenic patients, including symptomatology, onset, course, mental status, ego functions, family history, and so forth; then discuss the similarities and differences in the two cases in terms of these assessments, biopsychosocial features, treatment goals, and responses to treatment.

SUGGESTED READING

Articles

Briggs, D. 1979. The trainee and the borderline client: Countertransference pitfalls. *Clinical Social Work Journal* 7: 133-145.

Carroll, E., and K. Tyson. 2004. Therapeutic management of violence in residential care for severely mentally ill clients: An application of intrapsychic humanism. *Smith College Studies in Social Work* 74: 539-561.

Solomon, A. 1992. Clinical diagnosis among diverse populations: A multicultural perspective. *Families in Society: The Journal of Contemporary Human Services* 73: 371-377.

Books

Gee, K. K., and M. M. Ishii. 1997. Assessment and treatment of schizophrenia among Asian Americans. In *Working with Asian Americans: A guide for clinicians,* ed. E. Lee, pp. 227-251. New York: The Guilford Press.

Gombosi, P. G. 1998. Parents of autistic children: Some thoughts about trauma, dislocation, and tragedy. In *The Psychoanalytic Study of the Child,* ed. A. J. Solnit, P. B. Neubauer, S. Abrams, and A. S. Dowling, Vol. 53, pp. 254-275. New Haven, CT: Yale University Press.

Jamison, K. 1996. *An unquiet mind: A memoir of moods and madness.* New York: Vintage Books.

Rohrer, G. 2005. *Mental health in literature: Literary lunacy and lucidity.* Chicago: Lyceum Books.

Straussner, S. L. A., and E. Zelvin. (eds.) 1997. *Gender and addictions: Men and women in treatment.* Northvale, NJ: Jason Aronson.

Styron, W. 1990. *Darkness visible: A memoir of madness.* New York: Random House.

van der Kolk, B. A., A. C. McFarlane, and L. Weisaeth. (eds.) 1996. *Traumatic stress: The effects of overwhelming experience on mind, body, and society.* New York Guilford Press.

Winchester, S. 1998. *The professor and the madman: A tale of murder, insanity, and the making of the Oxford English Dictionary.* New York: Harper Collins Publishers.

SECTION IV: INTEGRATION

Chapter 15

Conclusion

Perplexity is the beginning of knowledge.

Kahlil Gibran, *The Voice of the Master,* Trans.
Anthony G. Ferris, 1958

INTRODUCTION

We have explored together many aspects of life, from its beginning at conception through child development, adulthood, aging, to its ending in death. It is striking how there is nothing in life which is simple or straightforward; we have encountered complexities at all levels. Conception itself can occur in many ways today; as reproductive technologies proliferate, they bring in their wake emotional, relational, ethical, and political problems. Should children who were conceived with sperm from anonymous donors have the right to learn the identity of their biological fathers? If a couple divorces, who has the custody rights over their frozen embryos? To what extent are we moving in the direction of producing "designer" babies?

We have seen how the power of nature can control our lives, as those who live in New Orleans know; and how illness and disability can affect our emotional states and relationships, as well as how our emotional states can affect our physical well-being. We live in precarious times with anxieties about terrorism and alarm at fighting a war in Iraq, which produces incredible destruction and death. Our individual lives are intertwined with the world in which we live; Donne has reflected, "No man is an island, entire of itself."

We have observed how socioeconomic factors such as unemployment, poverty, pension cutbacks, inadequate housing (and the proliferation of homelessness), and community and family violence affect both children

Human Behavior in the Social Environment, Second Edition

and adults. Needed medical and mental health services have been seriously impacted by inadequate funding, and managed care practices have often determined what treatments are prescribed.

We have also looked at individuals and how they have developed, and discussed a number of psychological theories explicating human behavior; and although many practitioners retain strict adherence to their own school of thought, there has been movement toward integration. The "Dodo bird hypothesis" has been formulated: "i.e., all treatment approaches are equally effective"; in *Alice's Adventure in Wonderland,* the Dodo bird concluded after a race: "'Everyone has won and all must have prizes'" (Granvold, 1999, p. 72). Although I would agree that divergent schools of thought make their own unique contributions, I reaffirm the premise of this book: psychodynamic understanding within a developmental biopsychosocial framework is the foundation for sound clinical assessment and intervention, as it offers the deepest understanding of both inner and outer worlds, and their interactions. For many, a psychodynamic approach means exclusively utilizing a psychoanalytic framework with an overfocus on instinct theory. The current revisions within the psychoanalytic world itself, including the additions of constructivism, object relations theory, and self psychology, are incorporated in this book.

The assessment of ego functions, defenses, and psychopathology is essential to this multifaceted approach, which is not a "one style fits all" model, but is highly individualized, incorporating diverse approaches as needed. People have an inner world (whatever you choose to call it) that is alive, dynamic, often does not seem to make sense, contradicts itself, fuels our emotional lives, and affects the way we relate to others and feel about ourselves. Constructivist concepts, such as understanding the client's values, attributions, and experiential world, contribute to this understanding.

The importance of human attachments, throughout life, has been emphasized; without developing adequate attachment to others, our development and maturation will be stunted and go awry. We have seen, for example, in the children in *The Drifters* (Chapter 9) how their inadequate nurturing affected not only their relationship capacities, but all their ego functions, and their achievement of self-esteem and a solid self-identity.

Child welfare problems have received special attention in this book, because so many children are adrift today with no place they can call home and no family that they can say is "my forever family." Many troubled families also struggle not only with vital external problems, such as poverty, poor housing, and lack of services, but also with their own unresolved attachment problems and other emotional conflicts. These families need services on multiple levels; to be most effective, a solid psychodynamic orientation can provide the clinician with a knowledge-based as well as empathic understanding of their many needs, their frequent distrust of others, how to develop relationships with them, and how to listen to them.

Winnicott (Grolnick, 1990) has spoken of the paradoxes and riddles involved in working with patients, forging a partnership with the client, and working toward a path of mutual discovery. Sitting with their clients, students must have a solid foundation to achieve this. One such base is the understanding of a client's ego functioning. It is important always to address a client's ego functioning, how this changes over time, and how to adapt our treatment accordingly. Bandler (1963) comments that "all psychological forms of therapy are 'ego-supportive'. None of them aims to weaken or to overthrow the ego" (p. 27). The analysis of ego functions is one very important determining factor in deciding which theory to follow and which techniques to use. In Chapter 14, for example, we discussed schizophrenic patients and the impairments in their ego functions. Supportive reality-based work was deemed necessary to help them repair and rebuild these functions.

Recent attention has been focused on resilience; on how children and adults can overcome adversity; in Chapter 4, we suggested that resilience needs to be seen along with vulnerabilities, as both are often present in an individual. Dr. Minor presents a fascinating example of how intellectual brilliance and a high level of intellectual contributions can coexist with a vulnerable psychological state.

Physician William Chester Minor (Winchester, 1998) was one of the major contributors to the making of the *Oxford English Dictionary* in the 1880s. Minor was a prolific and meticulous collector and annotator of words; his scholarship was outstanding. He was also a psychiatric patient at Broadmoor Hospital for the "criminally insane." Minor, who had murdered a man while in a delusional state, would do his careful dictionary work during the day; at night he was tormented by psychotic manifestations. He believed that "small boys . . . were put up in the rafters above his bed; they came down when he was fast asleep, chloroformed him, and then forced him to perform indecent acts" (pp. 123-124).

Minor's success with the dictionary unfortunately did *not* ameliorate his condition; his condition actually deteriorated over the years. Minor had excellent cognitive and integrative capacities as well as good judgment with respect to his work. However, owing to his mental illness (for which there was no treatment then) he was not capable of responding to developmental opportunities afforded by the life cycle, other than in an encapsulated intellectual realm. His early functioning was good; he had graduated from medical school and served as a doctor in the Civil War. However, his paranoid schizophrenia, which developed in early adulthood, now controlled his life.

In concluding, the case of Linda Valli is presented to illustrate how ego functions were assessed in one client and the value derived from that analysis; in deciding which theory or theories to follow and which techniques to use, the analysis of ego functions is one very important determining factor; there are variations present in this ego analysis; some functions were strong and others needed strengthening. The case that follows illustrates how a psychodynamic orientation promoted a depth of understanding in the client, which helped facilitate her emotional growth.

CASE ILLUSTRATION OF EGO FUNCTIONS

As we discuss this case, each ego function is examined separately, and the strengths and vulnerabilities of each function are assessed. The reader may recall that Linda Valli has been discussed several times in this book—in Chapter 2, related to the development of her strengths (including her determination or will), and in Chapter 12, in terms of her mother's death when she was thirteen, and her visual hallucination of her aunt after the aunt's death. Linda was seen in weekly psychotherapy for seven months.

> Linda Valli, twenty-seven, a woman of Italian ancestry, was four months pregnant when she applied to a mental health clinic because her fears and anxieties, a chronic problem for her, had increased in intensity over the past eight months. She was afraid to drive, afraid to be by herself, and afraid to travel too far from the immediate vicinity of her home. Not only had these fears produced restrictions in living, but she also became preoccupied with them, spending time sitting and obsessing about overcoming them, and then feeling self-punitive when she gave in to the fears. She reported a positive relationship with her husband and her two-year-old daughter; no problems in her life were causing distress—"Only what is going on inside of me." Linda is a very attractive woman who is intelligent, and although "shy" and inhibited, she related positively to the clinician.

Linda's capacity for outer perception was basically sound though not optimal; despite good reality testing, she did have occasional difficulties with outer perception under stress. The "hallucination" she reported (seeing her aunt after she had died) was not viewed as a serious sign of mental disorder; this "encapsulated" symptom occurred at a time of death and trauma for her. It is not uncommon for bereaved people to have visual and auditory hallucinations of deceased persons, especially shortly after their death.

Linda's mother died when she was a teenager and sometimes she has a sensation of the presence of her mother's ghost (which is frightening to her), when she is at home. She does not hear her voice or see her: "It's just a frightening thought—it doesn't go beyond that." This was also seen as an "encapsulated" occurrence, related to her conflictual feelings toward her mother.

During therapy, Linda experienced growth in her ego functions. She could see her relationship problems with her husband more clearly, and we can see an increase in the capacity for outer perception.

> She describes her husband as sometimes having a "glass barrier" around him. She also stated that this is not new, but before coming to the clinic, it was like being in darkness . . . she said she became more aware of her husband as a person when she started becoming more aware of herself as a person.

Linda had some difficulty with her ability for inner perception, but her capacity for this was excellent; she developed this capacity further during treatment. Linda did not initially recognize many of her feelings, nor did she see a connection between her anxiety attacks and underlying conflict. Linda further developed a very good *observing ego*. Initially, she tended to suppress her feelings and to internalize emotions, particularly anger, taking it out on herself. In the following incident, we can see that Linda started her narrative with no understanding of what precipitated her upset, but was quick to make a connection, indicating that the potential for observing an issue was present but needed development.

> Linda had had an upsetting episode during the week but could not see any reason for being upset. As she began describing some of the events leading up to this distress, the significance of the events, some of which were rather humorous, became apparent. By the end of the interview, Linda could look back and laugh over it.
>
> She had been waiting for an aunt to come to her home so that she could give her a permanent wave. The aunt (to be driven by an "undependable" sister-in-law) was scheduled to arrive in the morning but did not come until the afternoon. In addition to having to wait all morning, the afternoon is not the best time for Linda. She did not really want to do it in the first place but did not want to hurt her aunt. On top of this, Linda does not like giving permanents at home because they are messy, etc. While she was giving the permanent, she was worried throughout that she would mess up the aunt's hair.

At the end of treatment, Linda described the development of her observing ego, but in her own terms. "It's like being outside myself and looking at myself—not keeping all my thoughts and feelings in—after twenty years of keeping everything in!"

Her cognitive functions were minimally impaired. She was intelligent, used good judgment, had the capacity to integrate and reflect, spoke coherently and logically, and had no thought disorder. At times, her cognitive abilities were clouded by her anxiety; as the anxiety diminished and she became more self-aware, her cognitive ability gained in strength. When she terminated, she spoke of not being "nutsy" anymore.

She engaged somewhat in magical thinking, especially in regard to her husband:

> She says that she expects her husband "will be able to read my mind." If she wants his help, she will not tell him but expects that he will know and then resents it if he does not. She realizes, she stated, that it would be better to tell him first so that he will know.

There were major problems in Linda's management of needs and feelings. She had difficulty not only expressing angry feelings but also acknowledging to herself that she had them, as was apparent in the incident of giving her aunt a permanent without being aware of her own feelings of resentment. Impulse control was not a problem; in fact, the opposite, the strong inhibition of impulses, was an issue for her. She had problems with autonomous gratification and became aware that it was difficult for her to give herself pleasure.

> Linda described baking a cake and feeling that she had to rush whenever she did this, even if she had two hours. She enjoys preparing supper, too, but when it is on the table, she finds she rushes through it. "I am at my worst after supper." I raised the issue of whether she allowed herself pleasure. Does she feel she is entitled to enjoy herself?

Linda acknowledged that allowing herself enjoyment was indeed problematic; however, her observing ego enabled her to see other examples of this, and her integrative capacity helped her put her insights into action and to change.

Linda's management of object relationships was not seriously impaired, although aspects of her relationships were problematic. Linda's strength in relationship capacity was evident in her development of the therapeutic relationship. Initially shy and presenting in a somewhat superficial manner, she soon became more relaxed and open, sharing more about herself in a progressive manner and was emotionally responsive to the therapist. She showed no fear of the therapeutic relationship, did not pull away from its developing closeness, or attempt to use it inappropriately, which indicated the absence of boundary formation problems. Although shy, she nevertheless did have the capacity to relate and had had friendships throughout her life. She was preoccupied with her present anxieties, which diminished her social relationships, but nevertheless bonds were retained. She was emotionally responsive to her two-year-old daughter. The relationship with her husband was basically stable, although some communication problems existed. As Linda's sense of self-identity was enhanced and her outer perceptive capacities increased, she saw the potential for building a closer relationship with her husband.

During the intake process, Linda's therapist had some concern about the extent of Linda's anxieties and the degree to which she might be incapacitated in her daily executive functioning. Of particular concern to the therapist was Linda's two-year-old daughter: Was she receiving adequate care from her mother at the present time? She therefore asked Linda about an average day at home.

> Linda gets up in the morning, gets breakfast, does some housework . . . if she starts to think of going somewhere, she becomes preoccupied with this and might "waste a lot of time" just sitting and worrying about it. Sometimes she is okay, and if she goes out, for example, to visit her sister, she will develop a "big fear" about having to drive home. Although Linda is not doing "the million things she can be doing," she feels she is responsive to her daughter's needs; she feeds her, comes if she calls, and so on. She referred to her daughter with positive feeling as "a little angel—a peach." During the day, her daughter is in the house playing. "She is pretty independent."

Linda's executive functioning seemed adequate: she was able to care for her daughter, and fulfill her basic responsibilities. However, it was not optimal; she spent time unproductively preoccupied with her anxieties. During the course of therapy, as she became more comfortable with herself and as her anxiety level diminished, her executive functioning improved.

As work with Linda progressed, it became apparent that she had an excellent capacity for integration. Her therapist felt that this factor contributed greatly to her making so much progress in treatment in the relatively short time of seven months. Often the capacity for integration can be difficult to assess at the beginning of therapy. The therapist "cannot usually evaluate the capacity of the client to learn and to change except as a result of helping efforts that offer the opportunity for new learning and that motivate and support the individual in his efforts to learn" (Upham, 1973, p. 147).

> During the fourth session, Linda brought out the feeling that she tends to put herself down. She realized this during the week in regard to placemats. If there are four mats, and one is the odd one, she will always give herself the odd one. This week she went out and bought something she wanted, just for herself. She stated that it is always more natural for her to go out and shop for other people. In the sixth session, she commented: "Maybe I

do take things out on myself . . . like anger—I am starting to think." She also talked about reading an article in a magazine about how people see you . . . that there are good things about you, too. She has also been thinking about this in relation to herself.

In this excerpt, we can see that Linda is actively involved in the treatment process and is integrating what is happening on many levels. Linda's reading an article, for example, on self-image and then applying it to herself, is an excellent example of integration at work. She commented: "I think of what we talk about during the week and I work things through in my own mind." Furthermore, her insight about giving to others and not to herself is immediately followed by a behavioral change, which is at a high level of integrative capacity. It is noteworthy that this behavioral change was not suggested by the clinician but was derived internally from her own insight and emotional growth.

Finally, in examining her sense of ego identity, we note a number of problems related to her sense of self and self-esteem. Early in treatment, she stated that she usually feels uncomfortable with other people: "I don't know who I am." During the early part of her marriage, she had difficulty being comfortable with the sexual relationship. "I didn't want it—I wished it weren't part of marriage and part of me." During treatment, she grew to feel considerably more positive about herself and having a firmer sense of who she was. "I'm as good as anyone else—I don't put myself down or make apologies and excuses for other people." As noted earlier, when talking about outer perception, Linda had commented that she became more aware of her husband as a person when she started becoming more aware of herself as a person.

In summation, in assessing Linda's ego functioning, we see an uneven, skewed picture in terms of strengths and weaknesses among the various ego functions. We observe a basically well-functioning person who is able to carry out her major roles (although at a reduced capacity), whose cognitive processes were essentially intact, whose outer perception was reality oriented, and who, although socially inhibited (and presently preoccupied), had a basic capacity to relate. Her integrative capacities were potentially very strong, as was her capacity to learn and grow, as evidenced by her rapid progress in therapy. She manifested more serious problems with inner perception, management of needs and feelings, and identity formation, which were a major focus of therapy. Therapy afforded Linda the opportunity for continued personality growth. Not only did her symptoms of anxiety disappear, but all her ego functions improved dramatically. It was anticipated that this freeing of her ego functions from a growth-inhibiting, "frozen" state will enable this maturational process to continue.

In examining the treatment, several factors contributed to its success. First, important strengths resided in Linda herself, including her motivation, her will to get better, her ability to involve herself in treatment and in a therapeutic relationship, her capacity to develop further an "observing ego," and her capacity to integrate. A good deal of hidden health emerged beneath the presenting picture of pathology.

The treatment, based on a psychodynamic perspective, was founded on the development of a therapeutic relationship, which enabled the work of therapy to proceed, as Linda's development of trust enabled her to reveal painful aspects of herself and her past life. Furthermore, from an object relations perspective, the relationship itself was a key factor in treatment, providing a holding environment in which Linda could feel sustained and her feelings contained. She internalized aspects of the therapeutic relationship, including the therapist's positive regard for her, which helped build a stronger sense of identity and esteem. As Bandler (1963) comments, the therapeutic relationship "is not merely the medium in which restitution and growth take place; we, as the objects to whom the patient relates (like parents and educators, via identification), take our place in his personality and contribute to its consolidation and modification" (p. 44). In addition, from a self psychology perspective, the therapeutic relationship and the utilization of empathy helped develop a more cohesive sense of self.

From a psychodynamic perspective, Linda was able to see how her past life and relationships (e.g., the physical decline and subsequent death of her mother when she was a young teenager; her mother's preference for her brother; and her father's emotional removal from the family) affected her present feelings about herself. The major focus of work was in the here and now; however, in looking at some of her patterns of behavior, it was helpful to relate these to her past. In addition, on an affective level, Linda grieved for her parents and became aware of and accepting of her angry feelings, which she stopped internalizing. She was able to discuss her superego conflict about finding it difficult to give herself pleasure.

From an ego psychological perspective, attention was directed to Linda's ego functions, which matured during treatment. Her coping skills were also addressed and were enhanced. Linda, for example, was concerned that she "might go crazy" while in the hospital giving birth to her child. "The doctor won't know . . . he won't do anything—it will be so bad, I'll be off the wall!" Her therapist asked why she felt she had to wait until it gets very bad if she becomes upset—why can't she tell someone? Linda could feel more empowered when she realized that she could have some control over this situation. Also, in terms of coping, Linda was assisted by anticipatory guidance, in thinking ahead to what plans she might make when she went to the hospital, and so on. Vaillant (1993) cites Heinz Hartmannn's comments on anticipation. "'The familiar function of anticipating the future, orienting our actions according to it and correctly relating means and ends to each other . . . is an ego function and, surely, an adaptation process of the highest significance'" (p. 71).

THE LIFE COURSE

In looking at the life cycle, it has been stressed that the life course is full of both continuities and discontinuities; that core feelings about the self and central experiences remain with us. I have suggested that good mental health involves the capacity to change and to adapt. Linda Valli had this capacity, which she was able to fulfill with therapeutic help. Some people seem frozen in their development and unable to change but may be responsive to supportive and environmental help to facilitate their social functioning.

The ecological concept of goodness-of-fit is very relevant to understanding the adaptation of people along the life course. Although Linda Valli had some problems in her relationship with her husband, it was basically a strong relationship, as was her relationship with her daughter. She also had a small circle of friends. Her internal changes enhanced all her relationships; it did not upset a precarious interpersonal balance.

Edgar Allan Poe (Silverman, 1991) experienced painful losses in his life; his later adaptations provide interesting insights into the concept of goodness-of-fit and the continuities and discontinuities in his life course.

Poe was born in 1809, in Boston, to a mother who was a beautiful and very talented actress, and who had achieved a great deal of acclaim. His father had theatrical aspirations, but was unsuccessful at this vocation, and deserted his family.

Poe had one brother and one sister, and he and his mother apparently had a very warm relationship. His mother suddenly died when he was about three. His sister became a foster child (whom he saw occasionally), while his brother went to live with his father's family and was absent from Poe's life. Poe was taken in, but less than fully accepted as their child, by a wealthy, childless family in Baltimore, and was never adopted. He had an ongoing difficult relationship with his foster father. He assumed the foster father's last name, Allan, as his own middle name, perhaps in lieu of it being his last name, as it would have been had he been adopted (Silverman, 1991).

Poe experienced early maternal loss at an age when it would have been cognitively difficult to understand and process it; he also lost his siblings and was taken in, but never officially adopted. Silverman (1991) suggests that the recurring theme in his fiction about people who are dead, but not dead, reflects his wish for his mother to regain life and for reunion with her. One can only speculate about what might have happened if Poe had been in a family with a better goodness-of-fit, if he had been helped to mourn his loss, if he had not also lost his siblings, and if his biological father had reappeared in his life.

One of the most interesting aspects concerning his adaptation occurred in his later life. When he was twenty-seven, he married his thirteen-year-old cousin Virginia and lived with her and her mother (his aunt). Apparently, this was a very congenial arrangement for all; Virginia's mother also "mothered" him (Silverman, 1991). Although we might question this nontraditional arrangement, it provided a positive goodness-of-fit for Poe.

However, tragically, Virginia developed tuberculosis and died when she was only twenty-four. At this point, Poe was overwhelmed, did not resolve his grief constructively, and soon his life descended into chaos. He became involved in unstable relationships with several women at the same time, and his drinking increased; he died when he was forty. During his marriage, he had a relatively stable life; but he was not able tolerate the loss of his young wife and the breakdown of his living arrangements (Silverman, 1991). We can speculate that the loss of his young wife precipitated inner distress related to his unresolved past grief.

Poe worked many years as a writer and critic for newspapers and magazines, gaining fame only later in his life. He was always concerned about his finances (and never received any inheritance from his foster family, because he was not an adopted heir). He would sometimes drink to excess; his drinking seems to have increased when he had employment problems (newspapers were an unstable source of employment) (Silverman, 1991). Again, we can only speculate what might have happened if he had a secure economic and employment base and had received recognition at an earlier period in his life for his tremendous talent. We also wonder how much his losses and other life vicissitudes, as well as how he experienced these, fueled his style, his subject matter, and his creative genius in general.

CONCLUSION

There has been a historic struggle in the social work profession to prove that it is "unique," and various theories, such as the currently popular strengths perspective, have been proposed as defining and proclaiming this uniqueness. The strengths perspective contributes to increasing our sensitivity to clients' resilience and capacities; however, if used as the *exclusive* intervention with clients, it is seriously limiting. We need to be concerned with our *competency,* rather than our *uniqueness.*

We should also consider how insights and theories become *integrated* into the *self* of the clinician. A piano teacher, in a master class at the Aspen Music Festival, said to his pupil: "Do not play the notes—Play the music!" However, much painstaking work needs to be done first, including learning music theory and keyboard technique, not to mention developing in-depth sensitivity to the spirit of each piece. At an unpredictable moment in time, this comes together for the student who emerges as the artist, now able to play the music, not merely the notes.

In like manner, the social work student needs to assimilate many theories and concepts concerning strengths and pathologies, as well as social problems and psychological conflicts. The student must also master a range of techniques, such as interviewing, assessment, the application of intersubjective insights, and utilization of community resources, and must also develop sensitivity to the spirit of each client. And at an unpredictable moment in time, integration occurs, and the professional self, prepared for the ambiguous and the unexpected, matures. A psychodynamic foundation nurtures and informs this professional self, enabling students to emerge as creative, competent, and compassionate clinicians.

It can be frustrating to work in a profession with so many ambiguities and uncertainties; on the other hand this work presents an exciting opportunity, as challenges confront us and new discoveries are waiting to be made. One can develop optimally if one is not lulled into accepting formulas and neat solutions, but searches for a deeper understanding of the human condition.

References

Abelson, R. 2007. A chance to choose hospice, and hope for a cure. *The New York Times,* February 10, pp. A1, B4.

Abrams, S. 2001. Summation, unrealized possibilities: Comments on Anna Freud's normality and pathology in childhood. In *The psychoanalytic study of the child,* ed. A. J. Solnit, P. B. Neubauer, S. Abrams, and A. S. Dowling, vol. 56, pp. 105-119. New Haven, CT: Yale University Press.

Abudabbeh, N. 2005. Arab families: An overview. In *Ethnicity and family therapy,* ed. M. McGoldrick, J. Giordano, and N. Garcia-Preto, 3rd ed., pp. 423-436. New York: The Guilford Press.

Ackerson, B. J. 2003. Parents with serious and persistent mental illness: Issues in assessment and services. *Social Work* 48: 187-194.

Adams Jr., C. L., and D. C Kimmel. 1997. Exploring the lives of older African American gay men. In *Ethnic and cultural diversity among lesbians and gay men: Vol. 3. Psychological perspectives on lesbian and gay issues,* ed. B. Greene, pp. 132-151. Thousand Oaks, CA: Sage Publications.

ADHD update: New data on the risks of medication. 2006. *Harvard Mental Health Letter* 23, April, pp. 3-5.

Adler, G. 1979. The psychotherapy of schizophrenia: Semrad's contributions to current psychoanalytic concepts. *Schizophrenia Bulletin* 5 (1): 130-137.

Adler, G. 1985. *Borderline psychopathology and its treatment.* New York: Jason Aronson.

Adnopoz, J. 1996. Complicating the theory: The application of psychoanalytic concepts and understanding to family preservation. In *The psychoanalytic study of the child,* ed. A. J. Solnit, P. B. Neubauer, S. Abrams, and A. S. Dowling, vol. 51, pp. 411-421. New Haven, CT: Yale University Press.

Aguilera, D., and J. M. Messick. 1974. *Crisis intervention theory and methodology.* St. Louis: The C. V. Mosby Company.

AIDS and mental health—Part 1. 1994. *The Harvard Mental Health Letter* 10, January, pp. 1-4.

Ainslie, R., and K. Brabeck. 2003. Race murder and community trauma: Psychoanalysis and ethnography in exploring the impact of the killing of James Byrd in Jasper, Texas. *JPSC: Journal for the Psychoanalysis of Culture and Society* 8: 42-50.

Akhtar, S. 1995. A third individuation: Immigration, identity and the psychoanalytic process. *Journal of the American Psychoanalytic Association* 43: 1051-1084.

Akhtar, S., and S. Kramer, eds. 1998. *The colors of childhood: Separation-individuation across cultural, racial, and ethnic differences.* Northvale, NJ: Jason Aronson.

Al-Krenawi, A. 1999. Social workers practicing in their non-western home communities: Overcoming conflict between professional and cultural values. *Families in Society: The Journal of Contemporary Human Services* 80: 488-495.

Alperin, R. M. 2004. Toward an integrated understanding of dreams. *Clinical Social Work Journal* 32: 451-469.

Alpert, J. L. 1995. Introduction. In *Sexual abuse recalled: Treating trauma in the era of the recovered memory debate,* ed. J. L. Alpert, pp. xix-xxiv. Northvale, NJ: Jason Aronson.

Alquijay, M. A. 1997. The relationships among self-esteem, acculturation, and lesbian identity formation in Latina lesbians. In *Ethnic and cultural diversity among lesbians and gay men: Vol. 3. Psychological perspectives on lesbian and gay issues,* ed. B. Greene, pp. 249-265. Thousand Oaks: Sage Publications.

Altman, L. K. 2006a. AIDS is on the rise worldwide, U.N. finds. *The New York Times,* November 22, p. A14.

Altman, L. K. 2006b. New H.I.V. cases reported to drop in southern India. *New York Times,* March 31, p. A5.

Alvarez, L. K. 2006. For troops in Iraq and loved ones at home, an internet lifeline. *The New York Times,* July 8, pp. A1, A11.

Alzheimer's disease—Part I. 1992. *The Harvard Mental Health Letter* 9, August, pp. 1-4.

American Psychiatric Association. 1994. *Diagnostic and statistical manual of mental disorders,* 4th ed. Washington, DC: American Psychiatric Association.

Amodeo, M., N. Robb, S. Peou, and H. Tran. 1996. Adapting mainstream substance-abuse interventions for Southeast Asian clients. *Families in Society: The Journal of Contemporary Human Services* 70: 403-412.

Anderson, C. M. 1983. A psychoeducational program for families of patients with schizophrenia. In *Family therapy in schizophrenia,* ed. W. R. McFarlane, pp. 99-116. New York: The Guilford Press.

Anderson, G. R., and J. Seita. 2006. Family and social factors affecting youth in the child welfare system. In *Working with traumatized youth in child welfare,* ed. N. B. Webb, pp. 67-90. New York: The Guilford Press.

Angelou, M. 1997. *I know why the caged bird sings.* New York: Bantam Books.

Applegate, J. S. 2004. Full circle: Returning psychoanalytic theory to social work education. *Psychoanalytic Social Work* 11 (1): 23-36.

Applegate, J. S., and J. M. Bonovitz. 1995. *The facilitating partnership: A Winnicottian approach for social workers and other helping professionals.* Northvale, NJ: Jason Aronson.

Arditti, J. A. 2005. Families and incarceration: An ecological approach. *Families in Society: The Journal of Contemporary Social Services* 86: 251-260.

Arieti, S. 1974. Schizophrenia: The psychodynamic mechanisms and the psycho-structural forms. In *American handbook of psychiatry,* ed. S. Arieti, 4th ed., vol. 3, pp. 551-587. New York: Basic Books.

Arieti, S., and J. Bemporad. 1978. *Severe and mild depression: The psychotherapeutic approach.* New York: Basic Books.

Armstrong, D. 1998. Police suicides rely on tools of guns, alcohol. *The Boston Globe,* August 24, pp. A1, A8.

Aronson, S. 1996. The bereavement process in children of parents with AIDS. In *The psychoanalytic study of the child,* ed. A. J. Solnit, P. B. Neubauer, S. Abrams, and A. S. Dowling, vol. 51, pp. 422-435. New Haven, CT: Yale University Press.

Asch, A. 1995. Visual impairment and blindness. In *Social work encyclopedia,* ed. R. L. Edwards and J. G. Hopps, 19th ed., vol. 3, pp. 2461-2468. Washington, DC: NASW Press.

Ashford, J. B., C. W. Lecroy, and K. L. Lortie. 1997. *Human behavior in the social environment: A multidimensional perspective.* Pacific Grove: Brooks/Cole Publishing Company.

Assertive community treatment. 2006. *Harvard Mental Health Letter* 23, November, pp. 4-5.

Attneave, C. 1982. American Indians and Alaska native families: Emigrants in their own homeland. In *Ethnicity and family therapy,* ed. M. McGoldrick, J. K. Pearce, and J. Giordano, pp. 55-83. New York: The Guilford Press.

Austin, D. 1997. The institutional development of social work education: The first 100 years—And beyond. *Journal of Social Work Education* 33: 599-612.

Babies born to singles are at record: Nearly 4 in 10. 2006. *The New York Times,* November 22, p. A19.

Bakalar, N. 2006a. Depression in pregnancy poses treatment challenge. *The New York Times,* February 7, p. D7.

Bakalar, N. 2006b. Retirement contentment in reach for unhappy men. *The New York Times,* April 4, p. D7.

Balter, L. 1999. Constant mental change and unknowability in psychoanalysis. In *The psychoanalytic study of the child,* ed. A. J. Solnit, P. B. Neubauer, S. Abrams, and A. S. Dowling, vol. 54, pp. 93-129. New Haven, CT: Yale University Press.

Bandler, B. 1963. The concept of ego-supportive psychotherapy. In *Ego-oriented casework: Problems and perspectives. Papers from the Smith College School for Social Work,* ed. H. J. Parad and R. R. Miller, pp. 27-44. New York: Family Service Association of America.

Bandler, L. S. 1967. Family functioning: A psychosocial perspective. In *The drifters: Children of disorganized lower-class families,* ed. E. Pavenstedt, pp. 225-253. Boston: Little, Brown and Company.

Bandura, A. 1976. Social learning perspective on behavior change. In *What makes behavior change possible?* ed. A. Burton, pp. 34-57. New York: Bruner/Mazel, Publishers.

Banerjee, N. 2006. Intimate confessions pour out on church's web site. *The New York Times,* September 1, p. A11.

Banta, C. 2005. Trading for a high. *Time* 166, August 1, p. 35.

Baradon, T. 2005. "What is genuine maternal love?": Clinical considerations and technique in psychoanalytic parent-infant psychotherapy. In *The psychoanalytic study of the child,* ed. R. A. King, P. B. Neubauer, S. Abrams, and A. S. Dowling, vol. 60, pp. 47-73. New Haven, CT: Yale University Press.

Barbour, J. D. 1992. *The conscience of the autobiographer: Ethical and religious dimensions of autobiography.* London: Macmillan.

Barnes, A., and P. H. Ephross. 1994. The impact of hate violence on victims: Emotional and behavioral responses to attacks. *Social Work* 39: 247-251.

Barovick, H. 2001. Hope in the heartland. *Time* 158, July (Bonus Section), pp. G1-G3.

Barovick, H. 2002. Super Mannies. *Time* 159, March, p. F12.

Barrie, J. M. 1904. *Peter Pan.*

Barth, D. 1991. When the patient abuses food. In *Using self psychology in psychotherapy,* ed. H. Jackson, pp. 223-242. Northvale, NJ: Jason Aronson.

Barth, R. P. 1994. Shared family care: Child protection and family preservation. *Social Work* 39: 515-524.

Barton, B. R., and A. S. Marshall. 1986. Pivotal partings: Forced termination with a sexually abused boy. *Clinical Social Work Journal* 14: 139-149.

Basch, M. F. 1988. *Understanding psychotherapy: The science behind the art.* New York: Basic Books.

Basham, K. 1999. A synthesis of theory in couple therapy: No longer an unlikely coupling. In *Enhancing psychodynamic therapy with cognitive-behavioral techniques,* ed. T. B. Northcut and N. R. Heller, pp. 135-155. Northvale, NJ: Jason Aronson.

Bass, D. 1995. Runaways and homeless youths. In *Social work encyclopedia,* ed. R. L. Edwards and J. G. Hopps, 19 ed., vol. 3, pp. 2060-2067. Washington, DC: NASW Press.

Bassett, J. D., and J. A. Johnson. 2004. The role of clinical consultation in child protective investigations. *Smith College Studies in Social Work* 74: 489-504.

Bastien, M. 1995. Haitian Americans. In *Social work encyclopedia,* ed. R. L. Edwards and J. G. Hopps, 19th ed., vol. 2, pp. 1145-1155. Washington, DC: NASW Press.

Bearak, B. 1998. Caste hate, and murder, outlast Indian reforms. *The New York Times,* September 19, p. A3.

Beardslee, W. R., and H. L MacMillan. 1993. Preventive intervention with the children of depressed parents: A case study. In *The psychoanalytic study of the child,* ed. A. J. Solnit, P. B. Neubauer, S. Abrams, and A. S. Dowling, vol. 48, pp. 249-276. New Haven, CT: Yale University Press.

Beaucar, K. O. 1999a. Bills seek to extend safety net for foster teens. *NASW News* 44 (7), p. 7.

Beaucar, K. O. 1999b. Case overload compounds children's peril. *NASW News* 44 (5), p. 3.

Beaucar, K. O. 1999c. Grandparent caregivers face hurdles. *NASW News* 44 (10), p. 12.

Beaucar, K. O. 1999d. The violence has come home to roost. *NASW News* 44 (6), p. 3.

Beck, A. T. 1976. *Cognitive therapy and the emotional disorders.* New York: New American Library.

Becker, M., and B. Shallgi. 2002. A psychoanalytic approach to integrating family and individual therapy in the treatment of adolescents. In *The psychoanalytic study of the child,* ed. A. J. Solnit, P. B. Neubauer, S. Abrams, and A. S. Dowling, vol. 48, pp. 203-217. New Haven, CT: Yale University Press.

Begun, A. L. 1993. Human behavior and the social environment: The vulnerability, risk, and resilience model. *Journal of Social Work Education* 29: 26-35.

Beinert, P. 1998. How the California G.O.P. got a Spanish lesson. *Time* 151, May 18, p. 58.

Belenky, M. F., B. M. Clinchy, N. R. Goldberger, and J. M. Tarule. 1986. *Women's ways of knowing: The development of self, voice, and mind.* New York: Basic Books.

Bell, C. [Brontë]. 1853. *Villette.* New York: Harper and Brothers, Publishers.

Belluck, P. 1998a. Black youths' rate of suicide rising sharply. *The New York Times,* March 20, pp. A1, A16.

Belluck, P. 1998b. Razing the slums to rescue the residents. *The New York Times,* September 6, pp. 1, 26, 27.

Belluck, P. 2006. As minds age, what's next? Brain calisthenics surge. *The New York Times,* December 27, pp. A1, A20.

Belluck, P., and J. Yardley. 2006. China tightens adoption rules for foreigners. *The New York Times,* December 20, pp. A1, A24.

Bemporad, J. R., and H. Pinsker. 1974. Schizophrenia: The manifest symptomatology. In *American handbook of psychiatry. Vol. 3—Adult Clinical Psychiatry,* ed. S. Arieti and E. B. Brody, 2nd ed., pp. 524-550. New York: Basic Books.

Benedek, T. 1970. The family as a psychological field. In *Parenthood: Its psychology and psychopathology,* ed. E. J. Anthony and T. Benedek, pp. 109-136. Boston: Little, Brown and Company.

Benoit, M. B. 2006. The view from the mental health system. In *Working with traumatized youth in child welfare,* ed. N. B. Webb, pp. 279-291. New York: The Guilford Press.

Benson, M. J. 2004. After the adolescent pregnancy: Parents, teens, and families. *Child and Adolescent Social Work Journal* 21: 435-455.

Bentley, K. J. 1993. The right of psychiatric patients to refuse medication: Where should social workers stand? *Social Work* 38: 101-106.

Berger, R. M., and J. J. Kelly. 1995. Gay men overview. In *Social work encyclopedia,* ed. R. L. Edwards and J. G. Hopps, 19th ed., vol. 2, pp. 1064-1075. Washington, DC: NASW Press.

Berlin, R., and R. B. Davis. 1989. Children from alcoholic families: Vulnerability and resilience. In *The child in our times: Studies in the development of resiliency,* ed. T. F. Dugan and R. Coles, pp. 81-105. New York: Brunner/Mazel.

Bernstein, N. 2006. Recourse grows slim for immigrants who fall ill. *The New York Times,* March 3, pp. A1, A16.

Berzoff, J. 1996a. Anxiety and its manifestations. In *Inside out and outside in: Psychodynamic clinical theory and practice in contemporary multicultural contexts,* ed. J. Berzoff, L. M. Flanagan, and P. Hertz, pp. 397-427. Northvale, NJ: Jason Aronson.

Berzoff, J. 1996b. Drive theory. In *Inside out and outside in: Psychodynamic clinical theory and practice in contemporary multicultural contexts,* ed. J. Berzoff, L. M. Flanagan, and P. Hertz, pp. 17-47. Northvale, NJ: Jason Aronson.

Berzoff, J. 1996c. Psychodynamic theory and the psychology of women. In *Inside out and outside in: Psychodynamic clinical theory and practice in contemporary multicultural contexts,* ed. J. Berzoff, L. M. Flanagan, and P. Hertz, pp. 247-266. Northvale, NJ: Jason Aronson.

Berzoff, J. 2004. Psychodynamic theories in grief and bereavement. In *Living with dying: A handbook for end-of-life healthcare practitioners,* ed. J. Berzoff and P. R. Silverman, pp. 242-262. New York: Columbia University Press.

Berzoff, J., and P. R. Silverman. 2004. Introduction. In *Living with dying: A handbook for end-of-life healthcare practitioners,* ed. J. Berzoff and P. R. Silverman, pp. 1-17. New York: Columbia University Press.

Berzoff, J., L. M. Flanagan, and P. Hertz. 1996. Inside out and outside in. In *Inside out and outside in: Psychodynamic clinical theory and practice in contemporary multicultural contexts,* ed. J. Berzoff, L. M. Flanagan, and P. Hertz, pp. 1-16. Northvale, NJ: Jason Aronson.

Bloch, J., and J. Margolis. 1986. Feelings of shame: Siblings of handicapped children. In *Mutual aid groups and the life cycle,* ed. A. Gitterman and L. Shulman, pp. 91-108. Itasca, IL: F. E. Peacock Publishers.

Bloche, M. G., and C. Eisenberg. 1993. The psychological effects of state-sanctioned terror. *The Harvard Mental Health Letter* 10, November, pp. 4-6.

Blos, P. 1962. *On adolescence: A psychoanalytic interpretation.* New York: The Free Press.

Blume, S. B. 1992. Compulsive gambling: Addiction without drugs. *The Harvard Mental Health Letter* 8, February, pp. 4-5.

Blumner, R. 2006. *The economist who died this month understood decades ago that drug prohibition was bad for public policy, the economy and society.* Minneapolis/St. Paul, MN: Minneapolis Star-Tribune. Available online at http://www.mapinc.org/drugnews/v06/n1605/a04.html.

Board of Health. 2006. Press releases, the city of New York, NY. Available online at http://www.nyc.gov/html/doh/html/pr2006/pr115-06.shtml.

Boice, M. M. 1998. Chronic illness in adolescence. *Adolescence* 33: 927-939.

Boo, K. 2006. Swamp nurse. *The New Yorker,* February 6, pp. 54-65.

Borderline personality disorder: Origins and symptoms. 2006. *Harvard Mental Health Letter* 22, June, pp. 1-3.

Borderline personality—Part I. 1994. *The Harvard Mental Health Letter* 10, May, pp. 1-4.

Borenstein, L. 2003. The clinician as a dreamcatcher: Holding the dream. *Clinical Social Work Journal* 31: 249-262.

Borson, S., B. Liptzin, J. Nininger, and P. Rabins. 1987. Psychiatry and the nursing home. *American Journal of Psychiatry* 144: 1412-1418.

Boszormenyi-Nagy, I., and G. Spark. 1973. *Invisible loyalties.* New York: Harper and Row.

Botsford, A. L., and D. Rule. 2004. Evaluation of a group intervention to assist aging parents with permanency planning for an adult offspring with special needs. *Social Work* 49, 423-431.

Bowen, M. 1985. *Family therapy in clinical practice.* New York: Jason Aronson.

Bowlby, J. 1969. *Attachment and loss,* vol. 1. New York: Basic Books.

Bowlby, J. 1988. Developmental psychiatry comes of age. *American Journal of Psychiatry* 145: 28-37.

Bowman, R. 2005. Prescription for crime. *Time* 165, March 28, pp. 50-51.

Braga, W. 1989. Youth suicide risk assessment: Process and model. In *Adolescent suicide: Recognition, treatment and prevention,* ed. B. Garfinkel and G. Northrup, pp. 1-21. Binghamton, New York: The Haworth Press.

Bragg, R. 1999. Fearing isolation in old age, gay generation seeks haven. *The New York Times,* October 21, pp. A1, A16.

Brandell, J. R. 2004. *Psychodynamic social work.* New York: Columbia University Press.

Brave Heart, M. H. 1998. The return to the sacred path: Healing the historical trauma and historical unresolved grief response among the Lakota through a psychoeducational group intervention. *Smith College Studies in Social Work* 68: 287-305.

Brave Heart, M. Y. H. 1999. *Oyate Ptayela:* Rebuilding the Lakota Nation through addressing historical trauma among Lakota parents. *Journal of Human Behavior in the Social Environment* 2 (2): 109-126.

Brenner, C. 1974. *An elementary textbook of psychoanalysis,* rev. ed. Garden City: Anchor Press/Doubleday.

Bretheron, I. 1996. Internal working models of attachment relationships as related to resilient coping. In *Development and vulnerability in close relationships,* G. G. Noam and K. W. Fischer, pp. 3-23. Mahwah, NJ: Lawrence Erlbaum Associates.

Brick, M. 2006. As time stands still in court, justice for a broken girl waits. *The New York Times,* September 23, pp. A1, A12.

Brickel, C. M. 1986. Pet-facilitated therapies: A review of the literature and clinical implementation considerations. *Clinical Gerontologist* 5: 309-332.

Briggs, D. 1979. The trainee and the borderline client: Countertransference pitfalls. *Clinical Social Work Journal* 7: 133-145.

Brightman, B. 1984-1985. Narcissistic issues in the training experience of the psychotherapist. *International Journal of Psychoanalytic Psychotherapy* 10: 293-317.

Brockmeier, J. 2001. From the end to the beginning. Retrospective teleology in autobiography. In *Narrative and identity. Studies in autobiography, self and culture,* ed. J. Brockmeier and D. Carbaugh, pp. 247-280. Amsterdam: John Benjamins Publishing Company.

Brockmeier, J., and D. Carbaugh. 2001. Introduction. In *Narrative and identity: Studies in autobiography, self and culture,* ed. J. Brockmeier and D. Carbaugh, pp. 1-22. Amsterdam/Philadelphia: John Benjamins Publishing Company.

Brockmeier, J., and R. Harré. 2001. Narrative: Problems and promises of an alternative paradigm. In *Narrative and identity. Studies in autobiography, self and culture,* ed. J. Brockmeier and D. Carbaugh, pp. 39-58. Amsterdam: John Benjamins Publishing Company.

Brody, J. E. 1998. Children of depressed parents at risk. *The New York Times,* March 3, p. C7.

Brody, J. E. 1999. Compulsive gambling: The overlooked addiction. *The New York Times,* May 4, p. D7.

Brody, J. E. 2006. Age is no barrier to lifting depression's heavy veil. *The New York Times,* May 30, p. D7.

Bronner, E. 1999. In a revolution of rules, campuses go full circle. *The New York Times,* March 3, pp. A1, A15.

Brooke, J. 1999. Diary of a high school gunman reveals a plan to kill hundreds. *The New York Times,* April 27, pp. A1, A20.

Brooks, D., R. P. Barth, A. Bussiere, and G. Patterson. 1999. Adoption and race: Implementing the multiethnic placement act and the interethnic adoption provisions. *Social Work* 44: 167-178.

Brooks, P. 1984. *Reading for the plot: Design and intention in narrative.* Cambridge, MA: Harvard University Press.

Brown, D. 1972. *Bury my heart at Wounded Knee.* New York: Bantam Books.

Brown, E. M. 1998. The transmission of trauma through caretaking patterns of behavior in holocaust families: Re-enactments in a facilitated long-term second-generation group. *Smith College Studies in Social Work* 68: 267-285.

Brown, M. 1986. Maintenance and generalization issues in skills training with chronic schizophrenics. In *Social skills training: A practical handbook for assessment and treatment,* ed. J. P. Curran and P. M. Monti, pp. 90-116. Washington Square, NY: New York University Press.

Brown, P. L. 2006. Supporting boys or girls when the line isn't clear. *The New York Times,* December 2, pp. A1, A11.

Bruner, J. 2001. Self-making and world-making. In *Narrative and identity: Studies in autobiography, self and culture,* ed. J. Brockmeier, and D. Carbaugh, pp. 25-37. Amsterdam/Philadelphia: John Benjamins Publishing Company.

Bruni, F. 1997. A cult's 2-decade odyssey of regimentation. *The New York Times,* March 29, pp. 1, 8, 9.

Burnette, D. 1999. Custodial grandparents in Latino families: Patterns of service use and predictors of unmet needs. *Social Work* 44: 22-34.

Burton, D. L. 2003. Male adolescents: Sexual victimization and subsequent sexual abuse. *Child and Adolescent Social Work Journal* 20: 277-296.

Butterfield, F. 1998. Prisons replace hospitals for the nation's mentally ill. *The New York Times,* March 5, pp. A1, A26.

Butterfield, F. 1999a. As inmate population grows, so does a focus on children. *The New York Times,* April 7, pp. A1, A18.

Butterfield, F. 1999b. Prisons brim with mentally ill, study finds. *The New York Times,* July 12, p. A10.

Butterfield, F. 2000. Racial disparities seen as pervasive in juvenile justice. *The New York Times,* April 26, pp. A1, A18.

Butterfield, F. 2005. Social isolation, guns and a "culture of suicide." *The New York Times,* February 13, p. 16.

Buxbaum, E., and S. S. Sodergren. 1977. A disturbance of elimination and motor development. In *The psychoanalytic study of the child,* ed. R. S. Eissler, A. Freud, M. Kris, P. B. Neubauer, and A. J. Solnit, vol. 32, pp. 195-214. New Haven, CT: Yale University Press.

Cain, B. 1988. Divorce among elderly women: A growing social phenomenon. *Social Casework* 69: 563-568.

Campbell, R. J. 1989. *Psychiatric dictionary,* 6th ed. New York: Oxford University Press.

Can a troubled mind spell trouble for the heart?—Part I. 2003. *Harvard Mental Health Letter* 19, April, p. 1.

Canedy, D. 2003. Two years after girl disappeared, little has changed in Florida agency. *The New York Times,* January 19, p. 18.

Canino, I. A., and J. Spurlock. 2000. *Culturally diverse children and adolescents: Assessment, diagnosis and treatment,* 2nd ed. New York: The Guilford Press.

Caplan, G. 1976. Foreword. In *Emergency and disaster management,* ed. H. J. Parad, pp. xxiii-xxv. Bowie: The Charles Press Publishers.

Caplan, J. 2005. A jury of their peers. *Time* 166, July 18, p. 63.

Caplan, L. 1990. *An open adoption.* New York: Farrar, Straus, and Giroux.

Carbaugh, D. 2001. "The people will come to you": Blackfeet narrative as a resource for contemporary living. In *Narrative and identity: Studies in autobiography, self and culture,* ed. J. Brockmeier and D. Carbaugh, pp. 103-127. Amsterdam/ Philadelphia: John Benjamins Publishing Company.

Carey, B. 2006a. For elderly, antidepressants may trump therapy. *The New York Times,* March 16, p. A15.

Carey, B. 2006b. For therapy, a new guide with a touch of personality. *The New York Times,* January 24, p. D5.

Carey, B. 2006c. Study details risk of caring for elderly spouses. *The New York Times,* February 16, p. A27.

Carey, B. 2006d. Talk therapists cite major strides in fending off depression among the elderly. *The New York Times,* March 31, p. D5.

Carey, B. 2006e. What's wrong with a child? Psychiatrists often disagree. *The New York Times,* November 11, pp. A1, A11.

Carey, B. 2006f. When trust in doctors erodes, other treatments fill the void. *The New York Times,* February 3, pp. A1, A20.

Carlson, B., and K. Maciol. 1997. Domestic violence: Gay men and lesbians. In *Social work encyclopedia supplement,* ed. R. L. Edwards, 19th ed., pp. 101-111. Washington, DC: NASW Press.

Carlson, M. 1997. Home alone. *Time* 150, November 10, p. 30.

Caro, R. 1983. *The years of Lyndon Johnson: The path to power.* New York: Vintage Books.

Carrington, C. E. 1956. *The life of Rudyard Kipling.* Garden City, NY: Doubleday & Company.

Carroll, E., and K. Tyson. 2004. Therapeutic management of violence in residential care for severely mentally ill clients: An application of intrapsychic humanism. *Smith College Studies in Social Work* 74: 539-561.

Carvajal, D. 1999. Slavery's truths (and tales) come flocking home. *The New York Times,* March 28 (Section 4), p. 5.

Cassidy, T. 2006. Birth, controlled. *The New York Times Magazine,* March 26, p. 20.

Catalano, S. 1990. *Children's dreams in clinical practice.* New York: Plenum Press.

Cave, D. 2006. New York plans to make gender choice personal. *The New York Times,* November 7, pp. A1, A21.

Ceconi, B., and E. Urdang. 1994. Sight or insight? Child therapy with a blind clinician. *Clinical Social Work Journal* 22: 179-192.

Cermak, P., and C. Molidor. 1996. Male victims of child sexual abuse. *Child and Adolescent Social Work Journal* 5: 385-400.

Chan, C. S. 1997. Don't ask, don't tell, don't know: The formation of a homosexual identity and sexual expression among Asian American lesbians. In *Ethnic and cultural diversity among lesbians and gay men: Vol. 3. Psychological perspectives on lesbian and gay issues,* ed. B. Greene, pp. 240-248. Thousand Oaks: Sage Publications.

Chapman, C., P. Dorner, K. Silber, and T. S. Winterberg. 1986. Meeting the needs of the adoption triangle through open adoption: The birthmother. *Child and Adolescent Social Work* 3: 203-213.

Chapman, C., P. Dorner, K. Silber, and T. S. Winterberg. 1987. Meeting the needs of the adoption triangle through open adoption: The adoptive parent. *Child and Adolescent Social Work* 4 (1): 3-13.

Chast, R. 1998. Theories of everything [cartoon]. *The New Yorker* 74, p. 42.

Chen, D. W. 2006. New Jersey Court backs full rights for gay couples. *The New York Times,* October 26, pp. A1, A24.

Chenot, D. 1998. Mutual values: Self psychology, intersubjectivity, and social work. *Clinical Social Work Journal* 26: 297-311.

Chess, S. 1989. Defying the voice of doom. In *The child in our times: Studies in the development of resiliency,* ed. T. F. Dugan and R. Coles, pp. 179-199. New York: Bruner Mazel.

Choi, N. G., and L. Snyder. 1999. Voices of homeless parents: The pain of homelessness and shelter life. *Journal of Human Behavior in the Social Environment* 2 (3): 55-77.

Clarity, J. F. 1999. Lost youth in Ireland: Suicide rate is climbing. *The New York Times,* March 14, p. 9.

Clay Wright, V., J. Chang, G. Jeng, and M. Macaluso. (2006). Assisted Reproductive Technology Surveillance—United States, 2003. Surveillance Summaries. Centers for Disease Control and Prevention, Atlanta, GA. Available online at http://www.cdc.gov/mmwr/preview/mmwrhtml/ss5504a1.htm.

Clemetson, L. 2006. Adopted in China, seeking identity in America. *The New York Times,* March 23, pp. A1, A18.

Clemetson, L., and R. Nixon. 2006. Breaking through adoption's racial barriers. *The New York Times,* August 17, pp. A1, A18.

Clines, F. X. 1999. Smithsonian making room for Indian museum. *The New York Times,* September 29, pp. A1, A18.

Cloud, J. 1997. Out, proud and very young. *Time* 150, December 8, pp. 82-83.

Cloud, J. 1998. Trans across America. *Time* 151, July 20, pp. 48-49.

Cloud, J. 2000. A kinder, gentler death. *Time* 156, September 18, pp. 60-67.

Cloud, J. 2005. The battle over gay teens. *Time* 166, October 10, pp. 42-48, 51.

Cloud, J. 2006. When silence isn't golden. *Time* 168, p. 64.

Cofesí, N. I. 2002. The influence of Marianismo on psychoanalytic work with Latinas: Transference and countertransference implications. In *The psychoanalytic study of the child,* ed. A. J. Solnit, P. B. Neubauer, S. Abrams, and A. S. Dowling, vol. 57, pp. 435-451. New Haven, CT: Yale University Press.

Cohen, C. S., and M. H. Phillips. 1997. Building community: Principles for social work practice in housing settings. *Social Work* 42: 471-481.

Cohen, J. 2006. Protect or disinhibit? *The New York Time Magazine,* January 22, p. 30.

Cohen, L. J., and A. Slade. 2000. The psychology and psychopathology of pregnancy: Reorganization and transformation. In *Handbook of infant mental health,* ed. C. H. Zeanah Jr., 2nd ed., pp. 20-36. New York: The Guilford Press.

Cohen, M. N. 1996. *Lewis Carroll: A biography.* New York: Vintage Books.

Cohler, B. J. 1987. Adversity, resilience, and the study of lives. In *The invulnerable child,* ed. E. J. Anthony and B. J. Cohler, pp. 363-424. New York: The Guilford Press.

Cohler, B. J., and R. M. Galatzer-Levy. 1990. Self, meaning, and morale across the second half of life. In *New dimensions in adult development,* ed. R. Nemiroff and C. Calarusso, pp. 214-263. New York: Basic Books.

Colarusso, C. A. 1993. Play in adulthood: A developmental consideration. In *The psychoanalytic study of the child,* ed. A. J. Solnit, P. B. Neubauer, S. Abrams, and A. S. Dowling, vol. 48, pp. 225-245. New Haven, CT: Yale University Press.

Colarusso, C. A. 1997. Separation-individuation processes in middle adulthood: The fourth individuation. In *The seasons of life: Separation-individuation perspectives,* ed. S. Akhtar and S. Kramer, pp. 73-94. Northvale, NJ: Jason Aronson.

Colarusso, C. A. 1998. A developmental line of time sense: In late adulthood and throughout the life cycle. In *The psychoanalytic study of the child,* ed. A. J. Solnit, P. B. Neubauer, S. Abrams, and A. S. Dowling, vol. 53, pp. 113-140. New Haven, CT: Yale University Press.

Cole, S. A. 2006. Building secure relationships: Attachment in kin and unrelated foster caregiver-infant relationships. *Families in Society: The Journal of Contemporary Social Services* 87: 497-508.

Coleman, D. 1996. Transference: A key to psychoanalytic social work. In *Fostering healing and growth: A psychoanalytic social work approach,* ed. J. Edwards and J. Sanville, pp. 46-58. Northvale, NJ: Jason Aronson.

Coleman, D., and S. Clark. 2003. Preparing for child welfare practice: Themes, a cognitive-affective model, and implications from a qualitative study. *Journal of Human Behavior in the Social Environment* 7 (1/2): 83-96.

Coleman, D. J. 1999. Narrative performance mode (NPM) of discourse. In *The psychoanalytic study of the child,* ed. A. J. Solnit, P. B. Neubauer, S. Abrams, and A. S. Dowling, vol. 54, pp. 233-258. New Haven, CT: Yale University Press.

Colonna, A. B. 2001. Opening of discussion. In *The psychoanalytic study of the child,* ed. A. J. Solnit, P. B. Neubauer, S. Abrams, and A. S. Dowling, vol. 56, pp. 9-15. New Haven, CT: Yale University Press.

Comas-Diaz, L., and F. M. Jacobsen. 1991. Ethnocultural transference and counter-transference in the therapeutic dyad. *American Journal of Orthopsychiatry* 61: 392-402.

Comparing race/ethnicity between the 2000 census and earlier censuses. 2001. Texas State Data Center, Department of Rural Sociology, Texas A&M University. Available online at http://census.tamu.edu/Data/Redistrict/PL94-171/re-report.php.

Complicated grief. 2006. *Harvard Mental Health Letter* 23, October, pp. 1-3.

Condon, J. T. 1986. Management of established pathological grief reaction after stillbirth. *American Journal of Psychiatry* 143: 987-992.

Confessore, N. 2006. A spoonful of foreign culture helps western medicine go down. *The New York Times,* June 4, p. A27.

Confronting suicide—Part I. 2003. *Harvard Mental Health Letter* 19: May, pp. 1-4.

Conover, T. 1997. The last best friends money can buy. *New York Times Magazine,* November 30, pp. 124-130, 132.

Conway, J. K. 1998. *When memory speaks: Reflections on autobiography.* New York: Alfred A. Knopf.

Cook, C. A. L., K. L. Selig, B. J. Wedge, and E. A. Gohn-Baube. 1999. Access barriers and the use of prenatal care by low-income, inner-city women. *Social Work* 44: 129-139.

Couch, A. S. 1999. Therapeutic functions of the real relationship in psychoanalysis. In *The psychoanalytic study of the child,* A. J. Solnit, P. B. Neubauer, S. Abrams, and A. S. Dowling, vol. 54, pp. 130-168. New Haven, CT: Yale University Press.

Courtney, M. E., and R. P. Barth. 1996. Pathways of older adolescents out of foster care: Implications for independent living services. *Social Work* 41: 75-83.

Crawford, J. M. 1999. Co-parent adoptions by same-sex couples: From loophole to law. *Families in Society: The Journal of Contemporary Human Services* 80 (3): 271-278.

Crockenberg, S., and E. Leerkes. 2000. Infant social and emotional development in family context. In *Handbook of infant mental health,* ed. C. H. Zeanah Jr., 2nd ed., pp. 60-90. New York: The Guilford Press.

Crohn, J. 1997. Asian intermarriage: Love versus tradition. In *Working with Asian Americans: A guide for clinicians,* ed. E. Lee, pp. 428-438. New York: The Guilford Press.

Cruz, F. G., and L. Essen. 1994. *Adult survivors of childhood emotional, physical, and sexual abuse: Dynamics and treatment.* Northvale, NJ: Jason Aronson.

Cullen, L. T. 2006. Not quite ready to retire. *Time* 167, February 27, pp. 48-49.

Cummings, E. M., P. T. Davies, and S. B. Campbell. 2000. *Developmental psychopathology and family process: Theory, research and clinical implications.* New York: The Guilford Press.

Curran, J. P., and P. M. Monti. 1986. Social skills training with schizophrenics. In *Social skills training: A practical handbook for assessment and treatment,* ed. J. P. Curran and P. M. Monti, pp. 1-4. Washington Square, NY: New York University Press.

Cushman, L. F., D. Kalmuss, and P. B. Namerow. 1993. Placing an infant for adoption: The experiences of young birthmothers. *Social Work* 38: 264-272.

Dalsimer, K. 1982. Female adolescent development: A study of The Diary of Anne Frank. In *The psychoanalytic study of the child,* ed. A. J. Solnit, R. S. Eissler, A. Freud, and P. B. Neubauer, vol. 37, pp. 487-522. New Haven, CT: Yale University Press.

Dane, B. 2000. Child welfare workers: An innovative approach for interacting with secondary trauma. *Journal of Social Work Education* 36: 27-38.

Dao, J. 2006. In New Orleans, smaller may mean whiter. *The New York Times,* January 22, pp. WK1, WK3.

Davenport, J. A., and J. Davenport III. 1995. Rural social work overview. In *Social work encyclopedia,* ed. R. L. Edwards and J. G. Hopps, 19th ed., vol. 3, pp. 2076-2085. Washington, DC: NASW Press.

Davey, M. 2005. As town for deaf takes shape, debate on isolation re-emerges. *The New York Times,* March, pp. A1, A12.

Davey, M. 2006. As tribal leaders, women still fight old views. *The New York Times,* February 4, pp. A1, A9.

Davids, J. 1993. The reaction of an early latency boy to the sudden death of his baby brother. In *The psychoanalytic study of the child,* ed. A. J. Solnit, P. B. Neubauer, S. Abrams, and A. S. Dowling, vol. 48, pp. 277-292. New Haven, CT: Yale University Press.

Davidson, H., and Pitchal, E. S. 2006, October. *Caseloads must be controlled so all child clients may receive competent lawyering.* New York: Social Science Research Network. Available online at http://papers.ssrn.com/sol3/papers.cfm?abstract_id=943059.

Davies, D. 1999. *Child development: A practitioner's guide.* New York: The Guilford Press.

Dean, R. G. 2002. Teaching contemporary psychodynamic theory for contemporary social work practice. *Smith College Studies in Social Work* 73: 11-27.

de Anda, D. 1995. Adolescence overview. In *Social work encyclopedia,* ed. R. L. Edwards and J. G. Hopps, 19th ed., vol. 1, pp. 16-33. Washington, DC: NASW Press.

Dedman, B. 1999. Clinton faults Senate over Hispanic judicial nominees. *The New York Times,* October 10, p. 22.

Deitz, J. 1991. When the patient is depressed. In *Using self psychology in psychotherapy,* ed. H. Jackson, pp. 193-202. Northvale, NJ: Jason Aronson.

DeLaCour, E. 1996. The interpersonal school and its influence on current relational theories. In *Inside out and outside in: Psychodynamic clinical theory and practice in contemporary multicultural contexts,* ed. J. Berzoff, L. M. Flanagan, and P. Hertz, pp. 199-219. Northvale, NJ: Jason Aronson.

Delgado, M. 1997. Role of Latina-owned beauty parlors in a Latino Community. *Social Work* 42: 445-453.

Dempsey, D. 1971. Learning how to die. *New York Times Magazine,* November 14, pp. 58-60, 64-74, 81.

DeParle, J. 2006. Orphaned: An essay. *The New York Times Magazine,* August 27, pp. 26-27, 48.

Depression in old age. 2003. *Harvard Mental Health Letter* 20, September, pp. 5-7.

DeRosa, R. R., and D. Pelcovitz. 2006. Treating traumatized adolescent mothers: A structured approach. In *Working with traumatized youth in child welfare,* ed. N. B. Webb, pp. 219-245. New York: The Guilford Press.

Diamond, J. 2002. *Narrative means to sober ends: Treating addiction and its aftermath.* New York: Guilford Publications.

Diedrich, M. 1999. *Love across color lines: Ottilie Assing and Frederick Douglass.* New York: Hill and Wang.

DiGiulio, J. F. 1987. Assuming the adoptive parent role. *Social Casework: The Journal of Contemporary Social Work* 68: 561-566.

Dillon, S. 2006a. In schools across U.S., the melting pot overflows. *The New York Times,* August 27, pp. 1, 16.

Dillon, S. 2006b. Schools cut back subjects to push reading and math. *The New York Times,* March 26, pp. 1, 16.

Dillon, S. 2006c. Schools slow in closing gaps between races. *The New York Times,* November 20, pp. A1, A21.

Dissociation and dissociative disorders—Part I. 1992. *The Harvard Mental Health Letter* 8, March, pp. 1-4.

Dissociation and dissociative disorders—Part II. 1992. *The Harvard Mental Health Letter* 8, April, pp. 1-4.

Dobson, J. C. 2006. Two mommies is one too many. *Time Magazine* 168, p. 123.

Dolnick, E. 1993. Deafness as culture. *The Atlantic Monthly* 272, September 3, pp. 37-53.

Dominus, S. 2005. The fathers' crusade. *The New York Times Magazine,* May 8, pp. 26-33, 50, 56, 58.

Donner, S. 1991. The treatment process. In *Using self psychology in psychotherapy,* ed. H. Jackson. Northvale, NJ: Jason Aronson.

Donner, S., and B. Batliwalla. 2005. Two social workers' experience with late onset blindness: An intersubjective perspective. *Smith College Studies in Social Work* 75: 49-64.

Dore, M. M. 1999. Emotionally and behaviorally disturbed children in the child welfare system: Points of preventive intervention. *Children and Youth Services Review* 21: 7-29.

Dowdy, A. 1998. Housing for old, young to debut in Dorchester. *The Boston Globe,* September 10, pp. B1, B8.

Dowling, A. S. 2001. Discussion of "Early object relations into new objects." In *The psychoanalytic study of the child,* ed. A. J. Solnit, P. B. Neubauer, S. Abrams, and A. S. Dowling, vol. 56, pp. 68-75. New Haven, CT: Yale University Press.

Dowling, A. S. 2005. Introduction. In *The psychoanalytic study of the child,* ed. R. A. King, P. B. Neubauer, S. Abrams, and A. S. Dowling, vol. 60, pp. 3-6. New Haven, CT: Yale University Press.

Downey, T. W. 2001. Early object relations into new objects. In *The psychoanalytic study of the child,* ed. A. J. Solnit, P. B. Neubauer, S. Abrams, and A. S. Dowling, vol. 56, pp. 39-67. New Haven, CT: Yale University Press.

Doyle, C. A. 1924. *Memories and adventures.* Boston: Little, Brown, and Company.

Drachman, D. 1995. Immigration statuses and their influence on service provision, access, and use. *Social Work* 40: 188-197.

Drisko, J. W. 1999. Clinical work with mistrusting, aggressive, latency-age children. In *Enhancing psychodynamic therapy with cognitive-behavioral techniques,* ed. T. B. Northcut and N. R. Heller, pp. 157-181. Northvale, NJ: Jason Aronson.

Drug abuse and dependence—Part I. 1989. *The Harvard Medical School Mental Health Letter* 6, October, pp. 1-4.

Drug abuse and dependence—Part II. 1989. *The Harvard Medical School Mental Health Letter* 6, November, pp. 1-4.

Drug treatment of bipolar disorder. 2006. *Harvard Mental Health Letter* 22, May, pp. 1-4.

Drummond, T. 1998. Touch early and often. *Time* 152, July 27, p. 54.

Drummond, T. 1999. Never too old. *Time* 153, June 7, p. 84H.

Dugan, T. F. 1989. Action and acting out: Variables in the development of resiliency in adolescence. In *The child in our times: Studies in the development of resiliency,* ed. T. F. Dugan and R. Coles, pp. 157-176. New York: Brunner/Mazel.

Dugger, C. W. 2006a. Cheap solutions cut AIDS toll for poor Kenyan youths. *The New York Times,* August 6, p. 13.

Dugger, C. W. 2006b. Where AIDS galloped, lessons in applying the reins. *The New York Times,* May 18, p. A3.

Dulmus, C. N., and L. A. Rapp-Paglicci. 2000. The prevention of mental disorders in children and adolescents: Future research and public-policy recommendations. *Families in Society: The Journal of Contemporary Human Services* 81: 294-303.

Dulmus, C. N., L. A. Rapp-Paglicci, D. J. Sarafin, J. S. Wodarski, and M. D. Feit. 2000. Workfare programs: Issues and recommendations for self-sufficiency. *Journal of Human Behavior in the Social Environment* 3 (2): 1-12.

Dupper, D. R., and J. Poertner. 1997. Public schools and the revitalization of impoverished communities: School-linked, family resource centers. *Social Work* 42: 415-422.

Dysthymia. 2005. *Harvard Mental Health Letter* 21, February, pp. 1-2.

Eagle, M. N. 1987. The psychoanalytic and the cognitive unconscious. In *Theories of the unconscious and the self,* ed. R. Stern, pp. 155-188. Hillsdale: The Analytic Press.

Eating disorders—Part I. 1992. *The Harvard Mental Health Letter* 9, December, pp. 1-4.

Eaton, L. 2006. In Louisiana, graft inquiries are increasing. *The New York Times,* March 18, p. A1.

Eckholm, E. 2006a. New campaign shows progress for homeless. *The New York Times,* June 7, pp. A1, A19.

Eckholm, E. 2006b. Plight deepens for black men, studies warn. *The New York Times,* March 20, pp. A1, A18.

Eckholm, E. 2007. For former foster care youths, help to make it on their own. *The New York Times,* January 27, pp. A1, A11.

Edelson, M. 1993. Telling and enacting stories in psychoanalysis and psychotherapy. In *The psychoanalytic study of the child,* ed. A. J. Solnit, P. B. Neubauer, S. Abrams, and A. S. Dowling, vol. 48, pp. 293-325. New Haven, CT: Yale University Press.

Edelstein, W. 1996. The social construction of cognitive development. In *Development and vulnerability in close relationships,* ed. G. G. Noam and K. W. Fischer, pp. 91-112. Mahwah, NJ: Lawrence Erlbaum Associates.

Edlefsen, M., and M. Baird. 1994. Making it work: Preventive mental health care for disadvantaged preschoolers. *Social Work* 39, pp. 566-573.

Edmundson, M. 1998. Book review of: *Open minded: Working out the logic of the soul* by Jonathan Lear. *The New York Times Book Review,* August 16, p. 10.

Edward, J. 1996. Listening, hearing, and understanding in psychoanalytically oriented treatment. In *Fostering healing and growth: A psychoanalytic social work approach,* ed. J. Edward and J. Sanville, pp. 23-45. Northvale, NJ: Jason Aronson.

Edward, J., N. Ruskin, and P. Turrini. 1992. *Separation/individuation: Theory and application,* 2nd ed. New York: Bruner/Mazel Publishers.

Egan, J. 2006. Wanted: A few good sperm. *The New York Times Magazine,* March 19, pp. 44-51, 66, 81, 98, 100.

Egan, T. 1999. Hard time: Less crime, more criminals. *The New York Times,* March 7 (Section 4), p. 1.

Egan, T. 2006. Youthful binge drinking fueled by boredom of the open west. *The New York Times,* September 2, pp. A1, A10.

Eichenwald, K. 2006a. Effort to combat child pornography on internet would close sites. *The New York Times,* September 21, p. A22.

Eichenwald, K. 2006b. From their own online world, pedophiles extend their reach. *The New York Times,* August 21, pp. A1, A14.

Eisenberg, D., and M. Sieger. 2003. The doctor won't see you now. *Time,* 161, June 9, pp. 46-52, 55, 57-58, 60.

Elkind, D. 1981. *Children and adolescents: Interpretive essays on Jean Piaget,* 3rd ed. New York: Oxford University Press.

Ellin, A. 2006. No more knitting. Older students want enlightenment. *The New York Times,* November 11, pp. B1, B4.

Elliott, L., and S. Bourette. 1999. A father's stunning anger. *Toronto Globe and Mail,* August 24, pp. A1, A5.

Ellison, R. 1980. *Invisible man.* New York: Vintage Books.

Elson, M. 1984. Parenthood and the transformation of narcissism. In *Parenthood: A psychodynamic perspective,* ed. R. Cohen, B. Cohler, and S. Weissman, pp. 297-314. New York: The Guilford Press.

Epilepsy and psychiatric disorders. 2006. *Harvard Mental Health Letter* 22, May, pp. 4-5.

Erera, P. I., and K. Fredriksen. 1999. Lesbian stepfamilies: A unique family structure. *Families in Society: The Journal of Contemporary Human Services* 80: 263-270.

Erikson, E. 1963. *Childhood and society.* New York: W. W. Norton and Company.

Ewalt, P. L., and N. Mokuau. 1995. Self-determination from a Pacific perspective. *Social Work* 40: 168-175.

Fadiman, A. 1997. *The spirit catches you and you fall down: A Hmong child, her American doctors and the collision of two cultures.* New York: Farrar, Straus and Giroux.

Falicov, C. J. 2005. Mexican families. In *Ethnicity & family therapy,* ed. M. McGoldrick, J. Giordano, and N. Garcia-Preto, 3rd ed., pp. 229-241. New York: The Guilford Press.

Falloon, R. H., and R. P. Liberman. 1983. Behavioral family interventions in the management of chronic schizophrenia. In *Family therapy in schizophrenia,* ed. W. R. McFarlane, pp. 117-137. New York: The Guilford Press.

Families in the treatment of schizophrenia—Part I. 1989. *The Harvard Medical School Mental Health Letter* 5, June, pp. 1-4.

Families in the treatment of schizophrenia—Part II. 1989. *The Harvard Medical School Mental Health Letter* 6, July, pp. 1-3.

Farley, J. 1990. Family developmental task assessment: A prerequisite to family treatment. *Clinical Social Work Journal* 18: 85-98.

Fattah, H. M. 2006. Saudi Arabia begins to face hidden AIDS problem. *The New York Times,* August 8, p. A3.

Fauri, D. P., and D. R. Grimes. 1994. Bereavement services for families and peers of deceased residents of psychiatric institutions. *Social Work* 39: 185-190.

Fein, E. 1998. Secrecy and stigma no longer clouding adoptions. *The New York Times,* October 25, pp. 1, 30-31.

Felsman, J. K. 1989. Risk and resiliency in childhood: The lives of street children. In *The child in our times: Studies in the development of resiliency,* ed. T. F. Dugan and R. Coles, pp. 56-80. New York: Bruner/Mazel.

Fenton, J. 2003. Turgenev's banana. *The New York Review of Books* L, February 13, pp. 45-48.

Field, T. 2000. Infant massage therapy. In *Handbook of infant mental health,* ed. C. H. Zeanah Jr., 2nd ed., pp. 494-500. New York: The Guilford Press.

Files, J. 2006. Appeals panel removes judge presiding over Indian lawsuit. *The New York Times,* July 12, p. A16.

Firestone, D. 1999. Murder reveals double life of being gay in rural south. *The New York Times,* March 6, pp. A1, A9.

First, R. J., J. C. Rife, and B. G. Toomey. 1995. Homeless families. In *Social work encyclopedia,* ed. R. L. Edwards and J. G. Hopps, 19th ed., vol. 2, pp. 1330-1337. Washington, DC: NASW Press.

Flanagan, L. M. 1996. Object relations theory. In *Inside out and outside in: Psychodynamic clinical theory and practice in contemporary multicultural contexts,* ed.

J. Berzoff, L. M. Flanagan, and P. Hertz, pp. 127-171. Northvale, NJ: Jason Aronson.

Flanders, J. 2001. *Circle of sisters: Alice Kipling, Georgiana Burne-Jones, Agnes Poynter, and Louisa Baldwin.* New York: W. W. Norton & Company.

Fleming, A. M. 1939. Some childhood memories of Rudyard Kipling. *Chambers's Journal* Part 91, (March): 168-173. Courtesy Cushing Memorial Library and Archives at Texas A&M University.

Fleming, A. M. 1947. My brother Rudyard Kipling (Transcript, as recorded on April 17, 1947 of broadcast on April 19, 1947). Courtesy Cushing Memorial Library and Archives at Texas A&M University.

Floersch, J. 2000. Reading the case record: The oral and written narratives of social workers. *Social Service Review* 74: 169-192.

Foderaro, L. W. 2006. Families with full plates, sitting down to dinner. *The New York Times,* April 5, pp. A1, A21.

Fonagy, P., and M. Target. 2002. The history and current status of outcome research at the Anna Freud Centre. In *The psychoanalytic study of the child,* ed. A. J. Solnit, P. B. Neubauer, S. Abrams, and A. S. Dowling, vol. 57, pp. 27-60. New Haven, CT: Yale University Press.

Fontana, V. J., and M. P. B. Gonzales. 2006. The view from the child welfare system. In *Working with traumatized youth in child welfare,* ed. N. B. Webb, pp. 267-278. New York: The Guilford Press.

Foy, G. M. 1999. Burning Olivier: The brief life and private burial of an infant son. *Harper's Magazine* 299 (1790): 39-54.

Fraiberg, S. 1968. *The magic years: Understanding and handling the problems of early childhood.* New York: Basic Books.

Fraiberg, S., E. Adelson, and V. Shapiro. 1975. Ghosts in the nursery: A psychoanalytic approach to the problem of impaired infant-mother relationships. *Journal of the American Academy of Child Psychiatry* 14: 387-422.

Frank, M. G. 1996. A clinical view of the use of psychoanalytic theory in front-line practice. In *Fostering healing and growth: A psychoanalytic social work approach,* ed. J. Edward and J. Sanville, pp. 59-76. Northvale, NJ: Jason Aronson.

Frankel, S. A. 1994. The exclusivity of the mother-child bond: Contributions from psychoanalytic and attachment theories and day-care research. In *The psychoanalytic study of the child,* ed. A. J. Solnit, P. B. Neubauer, S. Abrams, and A. S. Dowling, vol. 49, pp. 86-106. New Haven, CT: Yale University Press.

Fraser, M. W. 1997. The ecology of childhood: A multisystems perspective. In *Risk and resilience in childhood: An ecological perspective,* ed. M. W. Fraser, pp. 1-9. Washington, DC: NASW Press.

Fraser, R. 1988. *The Brontës: Charlotte Brontë and her family.* New York: Fawcett Columbine.

Freed, A. O. 1980. The borderline personality. *Social Casework: The Journal of Contemporary Social Work* 61: 548-558.

Freed, A. O. 1985. Linking developmental, family, and life cycle theories. *Smith College Studies in Social Work* 55: 169-182.

Freeman, D. M. A. 1998. Emotional refueling in development, mythology, and cosmology: The Japanese separation-individuation experience. In *The colors of childhood: Separation-individuation across cultural, racial, and ethnic differences,* ed. S. Akhtar and S. Kramer, pp. 17-60. Northvale, NJ: Jason Aronson.

Freeman, M. 2001. From substance to story: Narrative, identity, and the reconstruction of the self. In *Narrative and identity: Studies in autobiography, self and culture,* ed. J. Brockmeier and D. Carbaugh, pp. 283-298. Amsterdam/Philadelphia: John Benjamins Publishing Company.

Freeman, M., and J. Brockmeier. 2001. Narrative integrity: Autobiographical identity and the meaning of the "good life". In *Narrative and identity: Studies in autobiography, self and culture,* ed. J. Brockmeier and D. Carbaugh, pp. 75-99. Amsterdam/Philadelphia: John Benjamins Publishing Company.

Freeman, M., and W. Freund. 1998. Working with adopted clients. *Journal of Analytic Social Work* 5 (4): 25-37.

French, D. C., and T. F. Tyne. 1986. The identification and treatment of children with peer-relationship difficulties. In *Social skills training: A practical handbook for assessment and treatment,* ed. J. P. Curran and P. M. Monti, pp. 280-308. Washington Square, NY: New York University Press.

French, H. W. 2006. China's Muslims awake to nexus of needles and AIDS. *The New York Times,* November 12, p. 4.

Freud, A. 1946. *The ego and mechanisms of defense.* New York: International Universities Press.

Freud, Sigmund. 1959. A note on the unconscious in psychoanalysis (1912). In *Sigmund Freud: Collected papers,* ed. E. Jones, vol. 4, pp. 22-29. New York: Basic Books.

Freud, Sophie. 1999. The social construction of normality. *Families in Society* 80: 333-339.

Friedman, E. G. 1997. The impact of AIDS on the lives of women. In *Gender and addictions: Men and women in treatment,* ed. S. L. A. Straussner and E. Zelvin, pp. 197-221. Northvale, NJ: Jason Aronson.

Gaensbauer, T. J. 1995. Trauma in the preverbal period: Symptoms, memories, and developmental impact. In *The psychoanalytic study of the child,* ed. A. J. Solnit, P. B. Neubauer, S. Abrams, and A. S. Dowling, vol. 49, pp. 122-149. New Haven, CT: Yale University Press.

Galanter, M. 1982. Charismatic religious sects and psychiatry: An overview. *American Journal of Psychiatry* 139: 1539-1548.

Garbarino, J. 1982. *Children and families in the social environment.* New York: Aldine Publishing Company.

Garbarino, J., and K. Kostelny. 1997. What children can tell us about living in a war zone. In *Children in a violent society,* ed. J. Osofsky, pp. 32-41. New York: The Guilford Press.

Garcia-Preto, N. 2005. Latino Families: An overview. In *Ethnicity & family therapy,* ed. M. McGoldrick, J. Giordano, and N. Garcia-Preto, 3rd ed., pp. 153-165. New York: The Guilford Press.

Gay, P. 1988. *Freud: A life for our time.* New York: W. W. Norton and Company.

Gediman, H. K., and J. S. Lieberman. 1996. The many faces of deceit: Omissions, lies, and disguise in psychotherapy. Northvale, NJ: Jason Aronson.

Gee, K. K., and M. M. Ishii. 1997. Assessment and treatment of schizophrenia among Asian Americans. In *Working with Asian Americans: A guide for clinicians,* ed. E. Lee, pp. 227-251. New York: The Guilford Press.

Geller, J. 1996. Mental health services of the future: Managed care, unmanaged care, mismanaged care. *Smith College Studies in Social Work* 66: 223-239.

Gelman, C. R. 2003. Psychodynamic treatment of Latinos: A critical review of the theoretical literature and practice outcome research. *Psychoanalytic Social Work* 10: 79-102.

Georgiades, S. D. 2005. Emancipated young adults' perspectives on independent living programs. *Families in Society: The Journal of Contemporary Social Services* 86: 503-510.

Germain, C. 1991. *Human behavior in the social environment.* New York: Columbia University Press.

Germain, C., and A. Gitterman. 1980. *The life model of social work practice.* New York: Columbia University Press.

Gibbs, N. 2002. Making time for a baby. *Time* 159, pp. 48-54.

Gibbs, N. 2006. The magic of the family meal. *Time* 167, pp. 50-52, 55-56.

Gilkerson, L., and F. Stott. 2000. Parent-child relationships in early intervention with infants and toddlers with disabilities and their families. In *Handbook of infant mental health,* ed. C. H. Zeanah Jr, 2nd ed., pp. 457-471. New York: The Guilford Press.

Gilligan, C. 1982. *In a different voice.* Cambridge, MA: Harvard University Press.

Giovacchini, P. 1993. Absolute and not quite absolute dependence. In *In one's bones: The clinical genius of Winnicott,* ed. D. Goldman, pp. 241-256. Northvale, NJ: Jason Aronson.

Giovannoni, J. M. 1995. Childhood. In *Social work encyclopedia,* ed. R. L. Edwards and J. G. Hopps, 19th ed., vol. 1, pp. 433-441. Washington, DC: NASW Press.

Gitterman, A., and I. Miller. 1989. The influence of organization on clinical practice. *Clinical Social Work Journal* 17: 151-164.

Gleick, E. 1997. The marker we've been waiting for. *Time* 150, April 7, pp. 31-36.

Glendinning, V. 1999. *Jonathan Swift.* London: Pimlico.

Glodich, A. 1998. Traumatic exposure to violence: A comprehensive review of the child and adolescent literature. *Smith College Studies in Social Work* 68: 321-345.

Goelitz, A. 2001. Nurturing life with dreams: Therapeutic dream work with cancer patients. *Clinical Social Work Journal* 29: 375-385.

Goguen, C. 2006. *The effects of community violence on children and adolescents.* Washington, DC: National Center for PTSD Fact Sheet, National Center for PTSD, United States Department of Veterans Affairs, July 20. Available online at http://www.ncptsd.va.gov/facts/specific/fs_child_com_viol.html.

Golan, N. 1980. Using situational crises to ease transitions in the life cycle. *American Journal of Orthopsychiatry* 50: 542-549.

Goldberg, C. 1999a. Harvard is returning bones, and a Pueblo awaits its past. *The New York Times,* May 20, pp. A1, A18.

Goldberg, C. 1999b. Spotlighting issues of gender, from pronouns to murder. *The New York Times,* June 11, p. A27.

Goldberg, J. E. 1999. A short-term approach to intervention with homeless mothers: A role for social work clinicians in homeless shelters. *Families in Society: The Journal of Contemporary Human Services* 80: 161-168.

Goldberg, S. 1995. Introduction. In *Attachment theory: Social, developmental, and clinical perspectives,* ed. S. Goldberg, R. Muir, and J. Kerr, pp. 1-15. Hillsdale: The Analytic Press.

Golden, F. 1999a. Good eggs, bad eggs. *Time* 153: January 11, pp. 56-59.

Golden, F. 1999b. Smoking gun for the young. *Time* 153: April 19, p. 48.

Goldstein, E. G. 2002. Psychoanalysis and social work: Historical perspectives. *Psychoanalytic Social Work* 9 (2): 33-40.

Goldstein, H. 1990. The knowledge base of social work practice: Theory, wisdom, analogue, or art? *Families in Society: The Journal of Contemporary Human Services* 71: 32-43.

Goldstein, H. 1999. Editorial notes: "Different" families. *Families in Society: The Journal of Contemporary Human Services* 80: 107-109.

Goldstein, J., and S. Goldstein. 1996. "Put yourself in the skin of the child," she said. In *The psychoanalytic study of the child,* ed. A. J. Solnit, P. B. Neubauer, S. Abrams, and A. S. Dowling, vol. 51, pp. 46-55. New Haven, CT: Yale University Press.

Gombosi, P. G. 1998. Parents of autistic children: Some thoughts about trauma, dislocation, and tragedy. In *The psychoanalytic study of the child,* ed. A. J. Solnit, P. B. Neubauer, S. Abrams, and A. S. Dowling, vol. 53, pp. 254-275. New Haven, CT: Yale University Press.

Goode, E. 1998a. New hope for the losers in the battle to stay awake. *The New York Times,* November 3, pp. D1, D8.

Goode, E. 1998b. On gay issue, psychoanalysis treats itself. *The New York Times,* December 12, pp. A19, A29.

Goode, E. 1999a. Deeper truths sought in violence by youths. *The New York Times,* May 5, p. A24.

Goode, E. 1999b. Return to the couch: A revival for analysis. *The New York Times,* January 12, pp. D1, D6.

Goode, E. 2000. Sharp rise found in psychiatric drugs for the very young. *The New York Times,* February 23, pp. A1, A13.

Goode, E. 2002. Thousands in Manhattan needed therapy after attack, study finds. *The New York Times,* March 26, p. A15.

Goolishian, H. A., and L. Winderman. 1988. Constructivism, autopoiesis and problem determined systems. *The Irish Journal of Psychology* 9: 130-143.

Gorman, C. 1999. Bleak days for doctors. *Time* 153, February 8, p. 53.

Gorman, C. 2002. The Ultimate Sacrifice. *Time* 159, January 28, p. 41.

Gorman, C. 2006. The graying of AIDS. *Time, 168,* August 14, pp. 54-56.

Grady, D. 1999. Live donors revolutionize liver care. *The New York Times,* August 2, pp. A1, A12.

Grady, D. 2006a. As the use of donor sperm increases, secrecy can be a health hazard. *The New York Times,* June 6, pp. D5, D8.

Grady, D. 2006b. Link between diabetes and Alzheimer's deepens. *The New York Times,* July 17, p. A15.

Grady, D. 2006c. Lung patients see a new era of transplants. *The New York Times,* September 24, pp. 1, 20.

Granvold, D. K. 1999. Cognitive and constructive psychotherapies. In *Enhancing psychodynamic therapy with cognitive-behavioral techniques,* ed. T. B. Northcut and N. R. Heller, pp. 53-93. Northvale, NJ: Jason Aronson.

Gratz, R. B. 2006. From hell to high water. *The New York Times,* February 22, p. A23.

Greenhouse, L. 2005. Burden of proof now on parents in school cases. *The New York Times,* November 15, pp. A1, A21.

Groden, G., and Baron, M. G. 1988. *Autism: Strategies for change.* New York: Gardner Press.

Grolnick, S. 1990. *The work and play of Winnicott.* Northvale, NJ: Jason Aronson.

Gross, E. R. 1995. Deconstructing politically correct practice literature: The American Indian case. *Social Work* 40: 207-213.

Gross, J. 2006a. Elder-care costs deplete savings of a generation. *The New York Times,* December 30, pp. A1, A16.

Gross, J. 2006b. Forensic skills seek to uncover hidden patterns of elder abuse. *The New York Times,* September 27, pp. A1, A23.

Grossman, L. 2006. The trouble with memoirs. *Time* 167, January 23, pp. 58-62.

Grotjohn, M. 1985. Being sick and facing eighty. In *The race against time: Psychoanalysis and psychotherapy in the second half of life,* ed. R. A. Nemiroff and C. A. Colarusso, pp. 293-302. New York: Plenum.

Groves, B. M., and M. Augustyn. 2004. Identification, assessment, and intervention for young traumatized children within a pediatric setting. In *Young children and trauma: Intervention and treatment,* ed. J. D. Osofsky, pp. 173-193. New York: The Guilford Press.

Guterson, D. 1995. *Snow falling on cedars.* New York: Vintage Books.

Gutheil, I. A. 1992. Considering the physical environment: An essential component of good practice. *Social Work* 37: 391-396.

Haights, W. L., J. D. Kagle, and J. E. Black. 2003. Understanding and supporting parent-child relationships during foster care visits: Attachment theory and research. *Social Work* 48: 195-207.

Hamilton, A. 2006. When foster teens find a home. *Time* 167, June 5, pp. 58-60, 63.

Hamilton, N. G. 1990. *Self and others: Object relations theory in practice.* Northvale, NJ: Jason Aronson.

Hanna, E. 1992. The demise of the field advising role in social work education. *The Clinical Supervisor* 10: 149-164.

Harmon, A. 2005. Hello, I'm you sister. Our father is donor 150. *The New York Times,* November 20, pp. 1, 20.

Harmon, A. 2006. Couples cull embryos to halt heritage of cancer. *The New York Times,* September 3, pp. 1, 16.

Harré, R. 2001. Metaphysics and narrative: Singularities and multiplicities of self. In *Narrative and identity: Studies in autobiography, self and culture,* ed. J. Brockmeier and D. Carbaugh, pp. 59-73. Amsterdam/Philadelphia: John Benjamins Publishing Company.

Harris, G. 2006. On psychiatric drug mix for young, proof is scant. *The New York Times,* November 23, pp. A1, A26.

Harrison, K. 2006. The girls who went away: The hidden history of women who surrendered Children for adoption in the decades before Roe v. Wade by Ann Fessler. *The New York Times Book Review,* June 11, p. 16.

Hartman, A., and J. Laird. 1983. *Family-centered social work practice.* New York: The Free Press.

Hartmann, H. 1958. *Ego psychology and the problem of adaptation.* New York: International Universities Press.

Harvey, A. R. 1995. The issue of skin color in psychotherapy with African Americans. *Families in Society: The Journal of Contemporary Human Services* 76: 3-10.

Hegeman, E. 1995. Transferential issues in the psychoanalytic treatment of incest survivors. In *Sexual abuse recalled: Treating trauma in the era of the recovered memory debate,* ed. J. L. Alpert, pp. 185-213. Northvale, NJ: Jason Aronson.

Heller, N. R., and T. B. Northcut. 1999. Clinical assessment. In *Enhancing psychodynamic therapy with cognitive-behavioral techniques,* ed. T. B. Northcut and N. R. Heller, pp. 95-132. Northvale, NJ: Jason Aronson.

Henry, J. 1999. Permanency outcomes in legal guardianships of abused/neglected children. *Families in Society: The Journal of Contemporary Human Services* 80: 561-568.

Herbert, T. 1993. *Dearest beloved: The Hawthornes and the making of the middle-class family.* Berkeley: University of California Press, Ltd.

Herman, J. L. 1997. *Trauma and recovery.* New York: Basic Books.

Hinchman, L. P., and S. K. Hinchman. 1997. *Memory, identity and community: The idea of narrative in the human sciences.* Albany: State University of New York Press.

Hoberman, H. 1989. Completed suicide in children and adolescents: A review. In *Adolescent suicide: Recognition, treatment and prevention,* ed. B. Garfinkel and G. Northrup, pp. 61-88. Binghamton, NY: The Haworth Press.

Hoffman, D. L., and M. L. Remmel. 1975. Uncovering the precipitant in crisis intervention. *Social Casework* 56: 259-267.

Hoffman, L. 1981. *Foundations of family therapy: A conceptual framework for systems change.* New York: Basic Books.

Hogan, L. 1990. *Mean spirit.* New York: Ivy Books.

Hollingsworth, L. D. 1998. Promoting same-race adoption for children of color. *Social Work* 43: 104-116.

Holloway, L. 1999. Seeing a link between depression and homelessness. *The New York Times,* February 7, p. 3.

Holmes, J. 1995. "Something there is that doesn't love a wall": John Bowlby, attachment theory, and psychoanalysis. In *Attachment theory: Social, developmental, and clinical perspectives,* ed. S. Goldberg, R. Muir, and J. Kerr, pp. 19-43. Hillsdale: The Analytic Press.

Holroyd, M. 2002. *Works on paper: The craft of biography and autobiography.* Washington, DC: Counterpoint.

Homeless families with children. 2006. *The National Coalition for the Homeless Fact Sheet #12.* Washington, DC: National Coalition for the Homeless, June. Available online athttp://www.nationalhomeless.org/publications/facts/families .pdf.

Homeless youth. 2006. *The National Coalition for the Homeless Fact Sheet #13.* Washington, DC: National Coalition for the Homeless, June. Available online at http://www.nationalhomeless.org/publications/facts/youth.pdf.

Honig, R., M. Grace, J. Lindy, C. Newman, and J. Titchener. 1993. Portraits of survival: A twenty-year follow-up of the children of Buffalo Creek. In *The psychoanalytic study of the child,* ed. A. Solnit, P. Neubauer, S. Abrams, and A. Dowling, vol. 52, pp. 327-355. New Haven, CT: Yale University Press.

Hopps, J. G., E. Pinderhughes, and R. Shankar. 1995. *The power to care: Clinical practice effectiveness with overwhelmed clients.* New York: The Free Press.

Horwitz, T. 1999. Untrue confessions: Is most of what we know about the rebel slave Nat Turner wrong? *The New Yorker,* December 13, pp. 80-89.

Howard, M. O., J. Bricout, T. Edmond, D. Elze, and J. M. Jensen. 2003. Evidence-based practice guidelines. In *Encyclopedia of social work,* ed. R. A. English, 19th ed., suppl., pp. 48-59. Washington, DC: NASW Press.

Hughes, D. A. 1998. *Building the bonds of attachment: Awakening love in deeply troubled children.* Northvale, NJ: Jason Aronson.

Hulse, C., and R. L. Swarns. 2006. Conservatives stand firm on immigration. *The New York Times,* March 31, p. A12.

Hungerford, A., C. A. Brownell, and S. B. Campbell. 2000. Child care in infancy: A transactional perspective. In *Handbook of infant mental health,* ed. C. H. Zeanah Jr., 2nd ed. pp. 519-532. New York: The Guilford Press.

Hunter, J., and R. Schaecher. 1995. Gay and lesbian adolescents. In *Social work encyclopedia,* ed. R. L. Edwards and J. G. Hopps, 19th ed., vol. 2, pp. 1055-1063. Washington, DC: NASW Press.

Huse, M. 1989. *A study of adult adoptees who request background information.* Unpublished doctoral diss., Simmons College School of Social Work, Boston, MA.

Hutchison, E. D. 2005. The life course perspective: A promising approach for bridging the micro and macro worlds for social workers. *Families in Society: The Journal of Contemporary Social Services* 86: 143-152.

Illicit drug use down among teens, prescription drug use remains high. 2006. *University of Michigan News Service,* University of Michigan, Ann Arbor, MI. Available online at http://www.ns.umich.edu/htdocs/releases/story.php?id=3065.

Income climbs, poverty stabilizes, uninsured rate increases. 2006. *U.S. Census Bureau News,* U.S. Department of Commerce, Washington, DC. Available online at http://www.census.gov/Press-Release/www/releases/archives/income_ wealth/007419.html.

Infertility is often defined. . . . (2003). Assisted reproductive technology: Home (2003). Centers for Disease Control and Prevention, Atlanta, GA. Available online at http://www.cdc.gov/ART/index.htm.

Infoplease. 2006. Encyclopedia at http://www.infoplease.com/ce6/society/A0830166 .html.

Ingram, R. E., and J. M. Price. 2001. The role of vulnerability in understanding psychopathology. In *Vulnerability to psychopathology: Risk across the lifespan,* ed. R. E. Ingram, and J. M. Price, pp. 3-19. New York: The Guilford Press.

Ingram, R. E., and M. Fortier. 2001. The nature of adult vulnerability: History and definitions. In *Vulnerability to psychopathology: Risk across the lifespan,* ed. R. E. Ingram and J. M. Price, pp. 39-54. New York: The Guilford Press.

In search of Alzheimer's disease. 2006. *Harvard Mental Health Letter* 22, October, pp. 3-5.

Isaacs, M. B., B. Montalvo, and D. Abelsohn. 2000. *Therapy of the difficult divorce: Managing crises, reorienting warring couples, working with the children, and expediting court processes.* Northvale, NJ: Jason Aronson.

Isaacson, W. 1999. The biotech century. *Time* 152, January 11, pp. 42-43.

Is obesity a mental health issue? 2004. *Harvard Mental Health Letter,* 21 (4), pp. 1-2.

Is the use of ART increasing? 2003. *Assisted Reproductive Technology (ART) Report (2003).* Centers for Disease Control and Prevention, Atlanta, GA. Available online at http://www.cdc.gov/ART/ART2003/section5.htm.

Ivanoff, A., and M. Riedel. 1995. Suicide. In *Social work encyclopedia,* ed. R. L. Edwards and J. G. Hopps, 19th ed., vol. 3, pp. 2358-2372. Washington, DC: NASW Press.

Jackson, A. 1999. The effects of nonresident father involvement on single black mothers and their young children. *Social Work* 44: 156-166.

Jackson, H. 1991. Introduction: Putting self psychology to work. In *Using self psychology in psychotherapy,* ed. H. Jackson, pp. 1-12. Northvale, NJ: Jason Aronson.

Jackson, L. C., and B. Greene. 2000. *Psychotherapy with African American women: Innovations in psychodynamic perspectives and practice.* New York: The Guilford Press.

Jackson, R. L., D. Purnell, S. B. Anderson, and B. W. Sheafor. 1996. The clubhouse model of community support for adults with mental illness: An emerging opportunity for social work education. *Journal of Social Work Education* 32: 173-180.

Jacobson, N. S. 1986. Communication skills training for married couples. In *Social skills training: A practical handbook for assessment and treatment,* ed. J. P. Curran and P. M. Monti, pp. 224-252. Washington Square, NY: New York University Press.

Jamison, K. 1996. *An unquiet mind: A memoir of moods and madness.* New York: Vintage Books.

Japan ordered to pay for worker's suicide. 1999. *Providence Sunday Journal,* March 14, p. A5.

Jarmon-Rohde, L., J. McFall, P. Kolar, and G. Strom. 1997. The changing context of social work practice: Implications and recommendations for social work educators. *Journal of Social Work Education* 33: 29-46.

Jarrell, A. 2000. The face of teenage sex grows younger. *The New York Times,* April 2 (Section 9), pp. 1, 8.

Javier, R. A. 1996. Psychodynamic treatment with the urban poor. In *Reaching across boundaries of culture and class: Widening the scope of psychotherapy,* ed. R. Pérez Foster, M. Moskowitz, and R. A. Javier, pp. 93-113. Northvale, NJ: Jason Aronson.

Jenkins, P., R. Seydlitz, J. G. Osofsky, and A. C. Fick. 1997. Cops and kids: Issues for community policing. In *Children in a violent society,* ed. J. Osofsky, pp. 300-322. New York: The Guilford Press.

Jiménez-Vázquez, R. 1995. Hispanics: Cubans. In *Social work encyclopedia,* ed. R. L. Edwards and J. G. Hopps, 19th ed., vol. 2, pp. 1223-1232. Washington, DC: NASW Press.

Jirovec, R. L. 2005. Differences in family functioning and health between older adult volunteers and non-volunteers. *Journal of Gerontological Social Work* 46: 23-35.

Johnson, G. 1997. Comets breed fear, fascination and web sites. *The New York Times,* March 28, p. A9.

Johnson, K. 2006. TV screen, not couch, is required for this session. *The New York Times,* June 8, pp. A1, A21.

Jones, L. Z. 2006. 95 pounds heavier, angry son faces mother who starved him. *The New York Times,* February 11, pp. A1, A14.

Jones, M. 2006. Shutting themselves in. *The New York Times Magazine,* January 15, pp. 46-51.

Jones, M. J. 1986. Speaking the unspoken: Parents of sexually victimized children. In *Mutual aid groups and the life cycle,* ed. A. Gitterman and L. Shulman, pp. 211-227. Itasca, IL: F. E. Peacock Publishers.

Jones, R. L. 2003. Beneath the foster care failures, New Jersey's heavy burden. *The New York Times,* August 12, p. A18.

Josselson, R. 1995. Narrative and psychological understanding. *Psychiatry* 580: 330-343.

Kadushin, A. 1974. *Child welfare services,* 2nd ed. New York: Macmillan Publishing Co.

Kahn, E. M. 1979. The parallel process in social work treatment and supervision. *Social Casework* 60: 520-528.

Kanter, J. 1990. Community-based management of psychotic clients: The contributions of D. W. and Clare Winnicott. *Clinical Social Work Journal* 18: 23-41.

Kao, R. S.-K., and M. L. Lam. 1997. Asian American elderly. In *Working with Asian Americans: A guide for clinicians,* ed. E. Lee, pp. 208-223. New York: The Guilford Press.

Kaplan, D. M., and E. A. Mason. 1965. Maternal reactions to premature birth viewed as an acute emotional disorder. In *Crisis intervention: Selected readings,* ed. H. Parad, pp. 118-128. New York: Family Service Association of America.

Kaplan, H. S. 1974. *The new sex therapy: Active treatment of sexual dysfunctions.* New York: Brunner/Mazel.

Kaplan, H., B. Sadock, and J. Grebb. 1994. *Synopsis of psychiatry: Behavioral sciences/clinical psychiatry.* Baltimore: Williams and Wilkins.

Kaplan, M. D., and K. D. Pruett. 2000. Divorce and custody: Developmental implications. In *Handbook of infant mental health,* ed. C. H. Zeanah Jr., 2nd ed., pp. 533-547. New York: The Guilford Press.

Karabanow, J. 2006. Becoming a street kid: Exploring the stages of street life. *Journal of Human Behavior in the Social Environment* 13 (2): 49-72.

Karen, R. 1990. Becoming attached. *The Atlantic Monthly* 265, February, pp. 35-70.

Karon, B. P., and G. R. VandenBos. 1996. *Psychotherapy of schizophrenia: The treatment of choice.* Northvale, NJ: Jason Aronson.

Karoshi and Karojisatsu in Japan. 2004. *Asian Labor Update,* no. 52, July-September. Asia Monitor Resource Centre, Hong Kong. Available online at http://www.amrc.org.hk/5206.htm.

Kaufman, J., and C. Henrich. 2000. Exposure to violence and early childhood trauma. In *Handbook of infant mental health,* ed. C. H. Zeanah Jr., 2nd ed., pp. 195-207. New York: The Guilford Press.

Kegan, R. 1982. *The evolving self.* Cambridge, MA: Harvard University Press.

Kelley, T. 1998. To surf, perchance to dream. *The New York Times,* October 1, p. E1.

Kennedy, G. J. 2000. *Geriatric mental health care: A treatment guide for health professionals.* New York: The Guilford Press.

Kent, M. M., M. K. Pollard, J. Haaga, and M. Mather. 2001. First glimpses from the 2000 U.S. census. *Population Bulletin* 56 (2): 19.

Kernberg, O. 1965. Notes on counter-transference. *Journal of American Psychoanalytic Association* 13: 38-56.

Kernberg, O. F. 1984. *Severe personality disorders: Psychotherapeutic strategies.* New Haven, CT: Yale University Press.

Kershaw, S. 2006. Through Indian lands, drugs' shadowy trail. *The New York Times,* February 19, pp. 1, 20-21.

Kidd, S. A. 2003. Street youth: Coping and interventions. *Child and Adolescent Social Work Journal* 20: 235-261.

Kilborn, P. T. 1999. Third of Hispanic Americans do without health coverage. *The New York Times,* April 9, pp. A1, A18.

Kilborn, P. T. 2000. Learning at home, students take the lead. *The New York Times,* May 24, p. A1.

Kilgore, C. 1988. Effect of early childhood sexual abuse on self and ego development. *Social Casework* 69: 224-230.

Killer was "angry at life." 2006. CNN.com, October 3. Available online at http://www.cnn.com/2006/US/10/03/penn.shooter/.

Killing in Texas spotlights attacks on social workers. 2006. *The New York Times,* March 20, p. A19.

Kim, R. 2001. Chinese lead Asian tally. *San Francisco Chronicle,* May 16. Available online at http://www.sfgate.com/cgibin/article.cgi?file=/chronicle/archive/2001/05/16/MN101414.DTL.

Kingsbury, K. 2006. Pressure on your health benefits. *Time* 168, pp. 53-54.

Kinzie, J. D., P. K. Leung, and J. K. Boehnlein. 1996. Treatment of depressive disorders in refugees. In *Working with Asian Americans: A guide for clinicians,* ed. E. Lee, pp. 265-274. New York: The Guilford Press.

Kipling, R. 1937. *Something of myself: For my friends known and unknown.* New York: Doubleday, Doran & Company.

Kipling, R. 1982. *How the whale got his throat. From: Just so stories for little children Rudyard Kipling: Illustrated,* pp. 209-212. New York: Avenel Books.

Kirby, L. D., and M. W. Fraser. 1997. Risk and resilience in childhood. In *Risk and resilience in childhood: An ecological perspective,* ed. M. W. Fraser, pp. 10-33. Washington: NASW Press.

Kiselica, M. S. 1995. *Multicultural counseling with teenage fathers: A practical guide.* Thousand Oaks, CA: Sage Publications.

Kleinfield, N. R. 2006a. Diabetes and Its Awful Toll Quietly Emerge as a Crisis. *The New York Times,* January 9, pp. A1, A18.

Kleinfield, N. R. 2006b. In Diabetes, One More Burden for the Mentally Ill. *The New York Times,* June 12, pp. A1, A17.

Kluger, J., and J. Ressner. 2006. Balding, wrinkled and stoned. *Time* 167, January 23, pp. 54-56.

Kohut, H. 1971. *The analysis of the self: A systematic approach to the psychoanalytic treatment of narcissistic personality disorders. The psychoanalytic study of the child: Monograph no. 4.* New York: International Universities Press.

Kolata, G. 2006. So big and healthy grandpa wouldn't even know you. *New York Times,* July 30, p. 1.

Kopeikin, H. S., V. Marshall, and M. J. Goldstein. 1983. Stages and impact of crisis-oriented family therapy in the aftercare of acute schizophrenia. In *Family therapy in schizophrenia,* ed. W. R. McFarlane, pp. 69-97. New York: The Guilford Press.

Koscis, J. H. 1991. Is lifelong depression a personality or mood disorder? *The Harvard Mental Health Letter* 8, August, p. 8.

Kotler, J. 1999. Tribe fights planned adoption of twins. *Toronto Globe and Mail,* August 20, p. A11.

Kramer, B. 1998. Preparing social workers for the inevitable: A preliminary investigation of a course on grief, death, and loss. *Journal of Social Work Education* 34: 211-227.

Krauz, S. L. 1980. Group psychotherapy with legally blind patients. *Clinical Social Work Journal* 8: 37-49.

Kressel, K. 1997. *The process of divorce: Helping couples negotiate settlements.* Northvale, NJ: Jason Aronson.

Kristof, N. D. 2006. When Prudishness Costs Lives. *The New York Times,* December 18, p. A31.

Kruger, A. 2000. Empowerment in social work practice with the psychiatrically disabled: Model and method. *Smith College Studies in Social Work* 70: 427-439.

Kübler-Ross, E. 1969. *On death and dying.* New York: The Macmillan Company.

Labi, N. 1998. The hunter and the choirboy. *Time* 151, April 6, pp. 28-37.

Lacayo, R. 1988. The case of the little big man. *Time* 132, July 18, p. 56.

Lacayo, R. 1997. The lure of the cult. *Time* 150, April 7, pp. 45-46.

Lacayo, R. 1998. The new gay struggle. *Time* 152, October 26, pp. 32-36.

Lacey, M. 1999. Teen-age birth rate in U.S. falls again. *The New York Times,* October 27, p. A14.

Lacey, M. 2006. Guatemala system is scrutinized as Americans rush in to adopt. *The New York Times,* November 5, pp. 1, 6.

Landau, R. 1998. Secrecy, anonymity, and deception in donor insemination: A genetic, psycho-social and ethical critique. *Social Work in Health Care* 28: 75-89.

Landers, S. 1992. Grandparents trying to raise kids' kids. Second-time-around families find aid. *NASW News,* March, p. 5.

LaSala, M. 1998. Coupled gay men, parents, and in-laws: Intergenerational disapproval and the need for a thick skin. *Families in Society* 79: 585-593.

Laub, J. H., and R. J. Sampson. 2003. *Shared beginnings, divergent lives: Delinquent boys to age 70.* Cambridge, MA: Harvard University Press.

Lawrence, S. A., and K. M. Zittel. 2000. Heart transplantation: A behavioral perspective. *Journal of Human Behavior in the Social Environment* 3 (2): 61-79.

Lee, E. ed. 1997. *Working with Asian Americans: A guide for clinicians.* New York: The Guilford Press.

Lee, H. 2005. *Virginia Woolf's nose: Essays on biography.* Princeton, NJ: Princeton University Press.

Lee, J. A. B., and C. R. Swenson. 1986. The concept of mutual aid. In *Mutual aid groups and the life cycle,* ed. A. Gitterman and L. Shulman, pp. 361-377. Itasca, IL: F. E. Peacock Publishers.

Lee, L., and P. Fleming. 2003. Estimated number of children left motherless by AIDS in the United States, 1978-1998. *Journal of Acquired Immune Deficiency Syndromes* 34, no. 2: 231-236. Available online at http://www.ncbi.nlm.nih.gov/entrez/query.fcgi?cmd=Retrieve&db=PubMed&list_uids=14526213&dopt=Abstract.

Lee, M., and G. J. Greene. 1999. A social constructivist framework for integrating cross-cultural issues in teaching clinical social work. *Journal of Social Work Education* 35: 21-37.

Lee-St. John, J. 2006. A place for the kids of war. *Time* 168, July 17, p. 15.

Leland, J. 2000. Silence ending about abuse in gay relationships. *The New York Times,* November 6, p. A14.

Leland, J. 2006. Meth users, attuned to detail, add another habit: ID theft. *The New York Times,* July 11, pp. A1, A17.

Lemonick, M. D. 1995. Can the Galapagos survive? *Time* 149, October 30, pp. 80-82.

Lemonick, M. D. 1997. It's a Miracle. *Time* 151, December 1, pp. 34-46.

Lemonick, M. D. 2006. Has the meltdown begun? *Time* 167, February 27, pp. 58-59.

Lesser, J. G. 1999. When your son becomes your daughter: A mother's adjustment to a transgender child. *Families in Society: The Journal of Contemporary Human Services* 80: 182-189.

Levenson, D. 1998. Nursing homes: More than just medical. *NASW News* 43 (2), p. 3.

Levin, J. D. 1991. *Treatment of alcoholism and other addictions: A self-psychology approach.* Northvale, NJ: Jason Aronson.

Levine, K. G. 1990. Time to mourn again. In *Preparing adolescents for life after foster care: The central role of foster parents,* ed. A. N. Maluccio, R. Krieger, and B. A. Pine, pp. 53-72. Washington, DC: Child Welfare League of America.

Levinson, D. 1986. A conception of adult development. *American Psychologist* 41 (1): 3-13.

Levinson, D., C. Darrow, E. Klein, M. Levinson, and B. McKee. 1978. *The season's of a man's life.* New York: Knopf.

Levinson, D., and J. Levinson. 1996. *The seasons of a woman's life.* New York: Knopf.

Levy-Dweck, S. 2005. HIV/AIDS fifty and older A hidden and growing population. *Journal of Gerontological Social Work* 46: 37-50.

Lewin, T. 1998a. American colleges begin to ask, where have all the men gone? *The New York Times,* December 6, pp. 1, 38.

Lewin, T. 1998b. New families redraw racial boundaries. *The New York Times,* October 27, pp. A1, A18-A19.

Lewin, T. 2006a. At colleges, women are leaving men in the dust. *The New York Times,* July 9, pp. 1, 18-19.

Lewin, T. 2006b. Unwed fathers fight for babies placed for adoption by mothers. *The New York Times,* March 19, pp. 1, 23.

Lewis, M. L., and C. G. Ipen. 2004. Rainbows of tears, souls full of hope: Cultural issues related to young children and trauma. In *Young children and trauma: Intervention and treatment,* ed. J. D. Osofsky, pp. 11-46. New York: The Guilford Press.

Lichtenberg, P. 1995. Men overview. In *Social work encyclopedia,* ed. R. L. Edwards and J. G. Hopps, 19th ed., vol. 2, pp. 1691-1697. Washington, DC: NASW Press.

Lieberman, A. F., R. Silverman, and J. H. Pawl. 2000. Infant-parent psychotherapy: Core concepts and current approaches. In *Handbook of infant mental health,* ed. C. H. Zeanah Jr., 2nd ed., pp. 472-484. New York: The Guilford Press.

Lieberman, F. 1984. Singular and plural objects: Thoughts on object relations theory. *Child and Adolescent Social Work* 1: 153-157.

Liederman, D. S. 1995. Child welfare overview. In *Social work encyclopedia,* ed. R. L. Edwards and J. G. Hopps, 19th ed., vol. 1, pp. 424-433. Washington, DC: NASW Press.

Life-giving support. 2004. *Harvard Mental Health Letter* 20: January, p. 7.

Lindemann, E. 1965. Symptomatology and management of acute grief. In *Crisis intervention: Selected readings,* ed. H. Parad, pp. 7-21. New York: Family Service Association of America.

Lipowski, Z. 1988. Somatization: The concept and its clinical application. *American Journal of Psychiatry* 145: 1358-1368.

Lipton, E. 2006. FEMA will try to recoup millions distributed for hurricane relief. *The New York Times,* March 18, p. A11.

Llana, S. M. 2006. Seniors raising their grandkids get a new boost. *The Christian Science Monitor,* February 8. Available online at http://www.csmonitor.com/2006/0208/p01s02-ussc.html.

Longres, J. F. 1995a. Hispanics overview. In *Social work encyclopedia,* ed. R. L. Edwards and J. G. Hopps, 19th ed., vol. 2, pp. 1214-1222. Washington, DC: NASW Press.

Longres, J. F. 1995b. *Human behavior in the social environment.* Itasca, IL: F. E. Peacock Publishers.

Lopez, S. 1998. Hide and seek. *Time* 151: May 11, p. 60.

Loppnow, D. 1985. Adolescents on their own. In *A handbook of child welfare context, knowledge, and practice,* ed. J. Laird and A. Hartman, pp. 514-531. New York: The Free Press.

Los Angeles Times Looks at Debate Over Law Criminalizing Knowing HIV Transmission (2003). *California Healthline.* California HealthCare Foundation, Oakland, CA. Available online at http://www.californiahealthline.org/articles/2003/9/11/Los-Angeles-Times-Looks-at-Debate-Over-Law-Criminalizing-Knowing-HIV-Transmission.aspx?archive=1.

Lott-Whitehead, L., and C. T. Tully. 1993. The family lives of lesbian mothers. *Smith College Studies in Social Work* 63: 265-280.

Luey, H. S., L. Glass, and H. Elliott. 1995. Hard-of-hearing or deaf: Issues of ears, language, culture, and identity. *Social Work* 40: 177-182.

Lyman, R. 2006a. Census report foresees no crisis over aging generation's health. *The New York Times,* March 10, pp. A1, A17.

Lyman, R. 2006b. Census reports slight increase in '05 incomes. *The New York Times,* August 30, pp. A1, A12.

Lynch, V. J. 1991. Basic concepts. In *Using self psychology in psychotherapy,* H. Jackson, pp. 15-25. Northvale, NJ: Jason Aronson.

MacFarlane, K., and J. Waterman, S. Conerly, L. Damon, M. Durfee, and S. Long. 1986. *Sexual abuse of young children.* New York: The Guilford Press.

MacGregor, P. 1994. Grief: The unrecognized parental response to mental illness in a child. *Social Work* 39: 160-166.

Mack, J. E., and H. Hickler. 1981. *Vivienne: The life and suicide of an adolescent girl.* New York: A Mentor Book, New American Library.

Mackey, R. A., and B. A. O'Brien. 1999. Adaptation in lasting marriages. *Families in Society* 80: 587-596.

MacKinnon, R. A., and R. Michels. 1971. *The psychiatric interview in clinical practice.* Philadelphia: W. B. Saunders Company.

Mahler, M., F. Pine, and A. Bergman. 1975. *The psychological birth of the human infant.* New York: Basic Books.

Mahoney, M. J. 2003. *Constructive psychotherapy: A practical guide.* New York: The Guilford Press.

Main, M. 1995. Recent studies in attachment: Overview, with selected implications for clinical work. In *Attachment theory: Social, developmental, and clinical perspectives,* ed. S. Goldberg, R. Muir, and J. Kerr, pp. 407-474. Hillsdale: The Analytic Press.

Maluccio, A. N. 1980. Promoting competence through life experiences. In *The life model of social work practice,* ed. C. B. Germain and A. Gitterman, pp. 282-302. New York: Columbia University Press.

Maluccio, A. N. 2006. The nature and scope of the problem. In *Working with trau-matized youth in child welfare,* ed. N. B. Webb, pp. 3-12. New York: The Guilford Press.

Maluccio, A. N., B. A. Pine, and R. Warsh. 1996. Incorporating content on family reunification into the social work curriculum. *Journal of Social Work Education* 32: 363-373.

Mann, A. 1998. Cross-gender sex pill. *Time* 151, April 6, p. 62.

Mansnerus, L. 2006. Legislators vote for gay unions in New Jersey. *The New York Times,* December 15, pp. A1, C15.

Marans, S., and A. Adelman. 1997. Experiencing violence in a developmental context. In *Children in a violent society,* ed. J. Osofsky, pp. 202-222. New York: The Guilford Press.

Marin, R. 2000. At-home fathers step out to find they are not alone. *The New York Times,* January 2, pp. 1, 18.

Marks, I. 1987. Behavioral aspects of panic disorder. *American Journal of Psychiatry* 144: 1160-1165.

Marmor, J. 1971. Dynamic psychotherapy and behavior therapy: Are they irreconcilable? *Archives of General Psychiatry,* 24: 22-28.

Marriott, M. 2006. Blacks turn to internet highway, and digital divide starts to close. *The New York Times,* March 31, pp. A1, A15.

Marziali, E., and H. Munroe-Blum. 1994. *Interpersonal group psychotherapy for borderline personality disorder.* New York: Basic Books.

Masaki, B., and L. Wong. 1997. Domestic violence in the Asian community. In *Working with Asian Americans: A guide for clinicians,* ed. E. Lee, pp. 439-451. New York: The Guilford Press.

Mason, P. 1975. *Kipling: The glass, the shadow and the fire.* New York: Harper & Row, Publishers.

Massie, R. K. 1967. *Nicholas and Alexandra.* New York: Atheneum.

Mattei, L. 1996. Race and culture in psychodynamic theories. In *Inside out and outside in: Psychodynamic clinical theory and practice in contemporary multicultural contexts,* ed. J. Berzoff, L. M. Flanagan, and P. Hertz, pp. 221-245. Northvale, NJ: Jason Aronson.

Mattei, M. de L. 1999. A Latina space: Ethnicity as an intersubjective third. *Smith College Studies in Social Work* 69: 255-267.

Mattick, I. 1967a. Description of the children. In *The drifters: Children of disorganized lower-class families,* ed. E. Pavenstedt, pp. 53-84. Boston: Little, Brown and Company.

Mattick, I. 1967b. Nursery school adaptations and techniques. In *The drifters: Children of disorganized lower-class families,* ed. E. Pavenstedt, pp. 163-204. Boston: Little, Brown and Company.

Mayes, L. C. 1999. Clocks, engines, and Quarks—Love, dreams, and genes: What makes development happen ? In *The psychoanalytic study of the child,* ed. A. J. Solnit, P. B. Neubauer, S. Abrams, and A. S. Dowling, vol. 54, pp. 169-192. New Haven, CT: Yale University Press.

McAdams, D. P., R. Josselson, and A. Lieblich. 2001. The narrative study of lives: Introduction to the series. In *Turns in the Road: Narrative studies of lives in transition,* ed. D. P. McAdams, R. Josselson, and A. Lieblich, pp. xi-xiii. Washington, DC: American Psychological Association.

McCarthy. M. 1957. *Memories of a Catholic Girlhood.* New York: Harcourt, Brace and Company.

McCarthy T. 2005. Stalking the day laborers. *Time* 166, December 5, pp. 36, 39.

McCourt, F. 1996. *Angela's ashes: A memoir of childhood.* London: HarperCollins Publishers.

McDermott, C. J. 1990. Empowering elderly nursing home residents. The resident's rights campaign. *Social Work* 35: 155-157.

McFarlane, W. R. 1983. Multiple family therapy in schizophrenia. In *Family therapy in schizophrenia,* ed. W. R. McFarlane, pp. 141-172. New York: The Guilford Press.

McFeely, W. S. 1991. *Frederick Douglass.* New York: W. W. Norton and Co.

McGirk, T. 2006. Crossing the lines. *Time* 167, February 27, pp. 36-40, 43.

McGoldrick, M., J. Giordano, and N. Garcia-Preto. 2005. Overview: Ethnicity and family therapy. In *Ethnicity & family therapy,* ed. M. McGoldrick, J. Giordano, and N. Garcia-Preto, 3rd ed., pp. 1-40. New York: The Guilford Press.

McGrath, C. 2002. Father time. *Time* 159, June 16, pp. 11-12.

McKim, J. 1996. Marital split creates embryo custody case. *The Boston Globe,* December 4, pp. A1, A20.

McLuckie, A. 2005. *Narrative family therapy for paediatric obsessive compulsive disorder. Family therapy and mental health* 16 (4): 83-106.

McNeil Jr., D. 2006. U. S. urges HIV tests for adults and teenagers. *The New York Times,* September 22, pp. A1, A18.

McRoy, R. G., H. D. Grotevant, and K. L. White. 1988. *Openness in adoption: New practices, new issues.* New York: Praeger.

Meek, H. W. 2005. Promoting self-awareness: Infant observation training as a model. *Smith College Studies in Social Work* 75, 33-58.

Mehta, P. 1998. The emergence, conflicts, and integration of the bicultural self: Psychoanalysis of an adolescent daughter of South-Asian immigrant parents. In *The colors of childhood: Separation-individuation across cultural, racial, and ethnic differences,* ed. S. Akhtar and S. Kramer, pp. 129-168. Northvale, NJ: Jason Aronson.

Mehta, V. 1979. *Daddyji.* Oxford: Oxford University Press.

Mehta, V. 1984. *The ledge between the streams. [Continents of Exile].* New York: W.W. Norton & Company.

Mehta, V. 1987a. *Sound-shadows of the new world. [Continents of Exile].* New York: W.W. Norton & Company.

Mehta, V. 1987b. *Vedi.* New York: W.W. Norton & Company.

Mehta, V. 1988. *Mamaji.* New York: W.W. Norton & Company.

Mehta, V. 2001. *All for Love [Continents of Exile].* New York: Thunder's Mouth Press/Nation Books.

Mehta, V. 2003. *Dark Harbor: Building house and home on an enchanted Island.* New York: Thunder's Mouth Press/Nation Books.

Melvill, H. 1855/1856. Penny Pulpit Sermons No. 2,365, p. 454. In *Golden lectures for 1855.* London: James Paul.

Mercer, S. O., and J. D. Perdue. 1993. Munchausen syndrome by proxy: Social work's role. *Social Work* 38: 74-81.

Meyer, W. S. 2005. The "mother" returns to psychoanalysis: Sándor Ferenczi, welcome home. *Smith College Studies in Social Work* 75: 15-31.

Meyers, S. 2006. Role of the social worker in old versus new culture in nursing homes. *Social Work* 51: 273-277.

Midgley, N., and M. Target. 2005. Recollections of being in child psychoanalysis: A qualitative study of a long-term follow-up project. In *The psychoanalytic study of the child,* ed. R. A. King, P. B. Neubauer, S. Abrams, and A. S. Dowling, vol. 60, pp. 157-177. New Haven, CT: Yale University Press.

Mikkelsen, E. 1994. Is psychotherapy useful for the mentally retarded? *The Harvard Mental Health Letter* 11, August, p. 8.

Miles, C. 1998. Mothers and others: Bonding, separation-individuation, and resultant ego development in different African-American cultures. In *The colors of childhood: Separation-individuation across cultural, racial, and ethnic differences,* ed. S. Akhtar and S. Kramer, pp. 79-112. Northvale, NJ: Jason Aronson.

Miller, J., I. Rodriguez Martin, and G. Schamess, eds. 2003. *School violence and children in crisis: Community and school interventions for social workers and counselors.* Denver: Love Publishing.

Miller, L. 2001. *The Brontë myth.* New York: Alfred A. Knopf.

Miller, M. C. 2006. Commentary. *Harvard Mental Health Letter* 23, December, p. 8.

Minuchin, S. 1974. *Families and family therapy.* Cambridge, MA: Harvard University Press.

Mishne, J. M. 1982. The missing system in social work's application of systems theory. *Social Casework* 63: 547-553.

Mitchell, J. 2000. Mr. Hunter's grave. In *Life Stories: Profiles from The New Yorker,* ed. D. Remnick, pp. 3-26. New York: Random House.

Mitchell, S. 1988. *Relational concepts in psychoanalysis: An integration.* Cambridge, MA: Harvard University Press.

Mittler, P. 1992. Educating children with severe learning difficulties: Challenging vulnerability. In *Vulnerability and resilience in human development: A festschrift for Ann and Alan Clarke,* ed. B. Tizard and V. Varma, pp. 163-181. London: Jessica Kingsley Publishers.

Montgomery, A. 2002. Converging perspectives of dynamic theory and evolving neurobiological knowledge. *Smith College Studies in Social Work* 72: 177-196.

Morales, J. 1995. Gay men: Parenting. In *Social work encyclopedia,* ed. R. L. Edwards and J. G. Hopps, 19th ed., vol. 2, pp. 1085-1095. Washington, DC: NASW Press.

Moran, J. R. 1999. Preventing alcohol use among urban American Indian youth: The seventh generation program. *Journal of Human Behavior in the Social Environment* 2: 51-67.

Morehouse, E. 1989. Treating adolescent alcohol abusers. *Social Casework: The Journal of Contemporary Social Work* 70: 355-363.

Morris, J. 1997. *Conundrum.* London: Penguin Books.

Morrison, T. 1977. *Song of Solomon.* New York: The Signet Press.

Morrison, T. 1999. *Paradise.* New York: Plume.

Morrow, D. F. 1993. Social work with gay and lesbian adolescents. *Social Work* 38: 655-660.

Morrow, L. 1991. When one body can save another. *Time* 137, June 17, pp. 54-58.

Morton, N., and K. D. Browne. 1998. Theory and observation of attachment and its relation to child maltreatment: A review. *Child Abuse and Neglect* 22: 1093-1104.

Mother-to-child transmission of HIV. 2006. *HIV/AIDS.* Geneva, Switzerland: World Health Organization. Available online at http://www.who.int/hiv/mtct/en/.

Moultrup, D. 1981. Toward an integrated model of family therapy. *Clinical Social Work Journal* 9: 111-125.

Mrazek, D. A. 2000. Somatic expression of disease. In *Handbook of infant mental health,* ed. C. H. Zeanah Jr., 2nd ed., pp. 425-436. New York: The Guilford Press.

Mulinski, P. 1989. Dual diagnosis in alcoholic clients: Clinical implications. *Social Casework: The Journal of Contemporary Social Work* 70: 333-339.

Murdach, A. D. 1996. Beneficence re-examined: Protective intervention in mental health. *Social Work* 41: 26-32.

Murphy, L., R. S. Pynoos, and C. B. James. 1997. The trauma/grief-focused group psychotherapy module of an elementary school-based violence prevention/intervention program. In *Children in a violent society,* ed. J. Osofsky, pp. 223-255. New York: The Guilford Press.

Murphy, S. B., C. Risley-Curtiss, and K. Gerdes. 2003. American Indian women and domestic violence: The lived experience. In *Women and girls in the social environment: Behavioral perspectives,* ed. N. J. Smyth, pp. 159-181. New York: The Haworth Press.

Nasjleti, M. 1980. Suffering in silence: The male incest victim. *Child Welfare* 49: 269-275.

Nelsen, J. C. 1983. Treatment issues in schizophrenia (1975). In *Differential diagnosis and treatment in social work,* ed. F. J. Turner, 3rd ed., pp. 337-346. New York: The Free Press.

Nelson, J. C. 1974. Teaching content of early fieldwork conferences. *Social Casework* 55: 147-153.

Nelson, K. E., E. J. Saunders, and M. J. Landsman. 1993. Chronic child neglect in perspective. *Social Work* 38: 661-671.

Nemiah, J. C. 1961. *Foundations of psychopathology.* New York: Oxford University Press.

Nemiroff, R. A., and Colarusso, C. A. 1990. *New dimensions in adult development.* New York: Basic Books.

Netting, F. E., C. C. Wilson, and J. C. New. 1987. The human-animal bond: Implications for practice. *Social Work* 32: 60-64.

Neubauer, P. B. 2001. Emerging issues: Some observations about changes in technique in child analysis. In *The psychoanalytic study of the child,* ed. A. J. Solnit,

P. B. Neubauer, S. Abrams, and A. S. Dowling, vol. 56, pp. 16-26. New Haven, CT: Yale University Press.

Neugarten, B. L. 1979. Time, age, and the life cycle. *American Journal of Psychiatry* 136: 887-894.

Newhill, C. 1995. Client violence toward social workers: A practice and policy concern for the 1990's. *Social Work* 40: 631-636.

Newton, M. 1995. *Adolescence: Guiding youth through the perilous ordeal.* New York: W. W. Norton and Company.

Nicholson, B. L., and D. M. Kay. 1999. Group treatment of traumatized Cambodian women: A culture-specific approach. *Social Work* 44: 470-479.

Noam, G. G. 1996. Reconceptualizing maturity: The search for deeper meaning. In *Development and vulnerability in close relationships,* ed. G. G. Noam and K. W. Fischer, pp. 135-172. Mahwah, NJ: Lawrence Erlbaum Associates.

Noam, G. G., and K. W. Fischer. 1996. Introduction: The foundational role of relationships in human development. In *Development and vulnerability in close relationships,* ed. G. G. Noam and K. W. Fischer, pp. ix-xx. Mahwah, NJ: Lawrence Erlbaum Associates.

Noble, H. B. 1999. Study backs a drug for hyperactive children. *The New York Times,* December 15, p. A16.

Nokes, D. 1997. *Jane Austen: A life.* Berkeley: University of California Press.

Norcross, J. C., and B. G. Knight. 2002. Psychotherapy and aging in the 21st century: Integrative themes. In *Psychology and the aging revolution: How we adapt to longer life,* ed. S. H. Qualls and N. Abeles, pp. 259-286. Washington, DC: American Psychological Association.

Northcut, T. B. 1999. Integrating psychodynamic and cognitive-behavioral theory: A psychodynamic perspective. In *Enhancing psychodynamic therapy with cognitive-behavioral techniques,* ed. T. B. Northcut and N. R. Heller, pp. 15-51. Northvale, NJ: Jason Aronson.

Northcut, T. B., and N. R. Heller. 2002. The slippery slope of constructivism. *Smith College Studies in Social Work* 72: 217-229.

Nowinski, J. 1990. *Substance abuse in adolescents and young adults.* New York: W. W. Norton and Company.

Noyes, A. 1953. *Modern clinical psychiatry,* 4th ed. Philadelphia: W. B. Saunders Company.

Nuland, S. B. 2003. *Lost in America: A journey with my father.* New York: Alfred A. Knopf.

O'Brien, P., and D. S. Young. 2006. Challenges for formerly incarcerated women: A holistic approach to assessment. *Families in Society: The Journal of Contemporary Social Services* 87: 359-366.

O'Donnell, J. M. 1999. Involvement of African American fathers in kinship foster care services. *Social Work* 44: 428-441.

Ogden, T. H. 1982. *Projective identification and psychotherapeutic technique.* New York: Jason Aronson.

O'Hare, T. 1995. Mental health problems and alcohol abuse: Co-occurrence and gender differences. *Health and Social Work* 20: 207-214.

Ojito, M. 1999. To talk like a New Yorker, sign up for Spanish lessons. *The New York Times,* October 18, pp. A1, B4.

Olkin, R. 1999. *What psychotherapists should know about disability.* New York: The Guilford Press.

Olney, J. 1998. *Memory & narrative: The weave of life-writing.* Chicago: University of Chicago Press.

Omin, R. 1989. To die in treatment: An opportunity for growth, consolidation and healing. *Clinical Social Work Journal* 17: 325-336.

O'Neill, J. V. 2003. Child welfare reform is called essential. *NASW News,* 48 (6), p. 9.

Oppenheimer, A. 2006. Hispanics said "adiós" to Republican Party. *Miami Herald,* November 9. Available online at http://www.latinamericanstudies.org/immigra tion/hispanic-vote-06.htm .

Orlin, M. 1995. The Americans with disabilities act: Implications for social services. *Social Work* 40: 233-239.

Ornstein, E. D., and C. Ganzer. 2005. Relational social work: A model for the future. *Families in Society: The Journal of Contemporary Social Services* 86: 565-572.

Osofsky, J. D. 1997. Children and youth violence: An overview of the issues. In *Children in a violent society,* ed. J. D. Osofsky, pp. 3-8. New York: The Guilford Press.

Osofsky, J. D. 2004. Different ways of understanding young children and trauma. In *Young children and trauma: Intervention and treatment,* ed. J. D. Osofsky, pp. 3-9. New York: The Guilford Press.

Osofsky, J. D., and C. Lederman. 2004. Healing the child in juvenile court. In *Young children and trauma: Intervention and treatment,* ed. J. D. Osofsky, pp. 221-232. New York: The Guilford Press.

Overturf, J. J. 2005. Who's minding the kids? Child care arrangements: Winter 2002. *Current Population Reports.* U.S. Census Bureau, Washington, DC. Available online at www.census.gov/prod/2005pubs/p70-101.pdf.

Pace, P. R. 2006a. Court upholds gay foster parents. *NASW News* 51 (2), p. 5.

Pace, P. R. 2006b. International adoptions undergo change. *NASW News* 51 (9), p. 4.

Pace, P. R. 2006c. NASW groups back gay adoption rights. *NASW News* 51 (4), p. 4.

Pace, P. 2007. Support for problem gamblers increases. *NASW News* 52 (1), January 7, p. 4.

Panic disorder—Part I. 1990. *The Harvard Mental Health Letter* 7, September, pp. 1-4.

Panic disorder—Part II. 1990. *The Harvard Mental Health Letter* 7, October, pp. 1-3.

Pannor, R., and A. Baran. 1984. Open adoption as standard practice. *Child Welfare* 43: 245-250.

Paret, I. H., and V. B. Shapiro. 1998. The splintered holding environment and the vulnerable ego: A case study. In *The psychoanalytic study of the child,* ed. A. J. Solnit, P. B. Neubauer, S. Abrams, and A. S. Dowling, vol. 53, pp. 300-324. New Haven, CT: Yale University Press.

Parks, C. A. 1998. Lesbian parenthood: A review of the literature. *American Journal of Orthopsychiatry* 68: 376-389.

Parrish, M., and J. Perman. 2004. Munchausen syndrome by proxy: Some practice implications for social workers. *Child and Adolescent Social Work Journal* 21 (2): 137-154.

Partida, J. 1996. The effects of immigration on children in the Mexican-American community. *Child and Adolescent Social Work Journal* 13: 241-254.

Pasztor, E. M., D. S. Hollinger, M. Inkelas, and N. Halfon. 2006. Health and mental health services for children in foster care: The central role of foster parents. *Child Welfare* 85 (1), pp. 33-57.

Patterson, S. L., C. B. Germain, E. M. Brennan, and J. Memmott. 1988. Effectiveness of rural natural helpers. *Social Casework* 5: 272-279.

Pavenstedt, E. ed. 1967. *The drifters: Children of disorganized lower-class families.* Boston: Little, Brown and Company.

Pawel, E. 1984. *The nightmare of reason: A life of Franz Kafka.* London: Collins Harvill.

Pérez-Foster, R. 1998. *The power of language in the clinical process: Assessing and treating the bilingual person.* Northvale, NJ: Jason Aronson.

Pérez-Foster, R. 1999. An intersubjective approach to cross-cultural clinical work. *Smith College Studies in Social Work* 69: 269-291.

Pérez-Foster, R., M. Moskowitz, and R. A. Javier. 1996. Introduction. In *Reaching across boundaries of culture and class: Widening the scope of psychotherapy,* ed. R. Pérez Foster, M. Moskowitz, and R. A. Javier, pp. xiii-xvii. Northvale, NJ: Jason Aronson.

Pérez-Peña, R. 2006. Beyond "I'm a Diabetic," Little Common Ground. *The New York Times,* May 17, pp. A1, A25.

Perloff, J. D., and Jaffee, K. D. 1999. Late entry into prenatal care: The neighborhood context. *Social Work* 44: 116-128.

Perry, A. 2006. Bombay's boom. *Time* 167, June 26, pp. 40-44.

Phillips, R. S. C. 1999. Intervention with siblings of children with developmental disabilities from economically disadvantaged families. *Families in Society: The Journal of Contemporary Human Services* 80: 569-577.

Piaget, J. 1995a. The first year of life of the child. In *The essential Piaget: An interpretive reference and guide,* ed. H. E. Gruber and J. J. Vonèche, pp. 198-214. New York: Basic Books.

Piaget, J. 1995b. Judgment and reasoning in the child. In *The essential Piaget: An interpretive reference and guide,* ed. E. H. Gruber and J. J. Vonèche, pp. 89-117. New York: Basic Books.

Piaget, J., and B. Inhelder. 1995. The growth of logical thinking from childhood to adolescence. In *The essential Piaget: An interpretive reference and guide,* ed. H. E. Gruber and J. J. Vonèche, pp. 405-444. New York: Basic Books.

Pies, R., and E. K. Keast. 1995. Cultural factors in psychiatric syndromes. *Psychiatric Times* 12, January, 14-17.

Pill, C. J., and J. L. Zabin. 1997. Lifelong legacy of early maternal loss: A women's group. *Clinical Social Work Journal* 25: 179-196.

Pinderhughes, E. B. 1983. Empowerment for our clients and for ourselves. *Social Casework* 64: 331-338.

Podell, C. 1989. Adolescent mourning: The sudden death of a peer. *Clinical Social Work* 17: 64-78.

Porter, E. 2006. Stretched to limit, women stall march to work. *The New York Times,* March 2, pp. A1, C2.

Porter, E., and M. O'Donnell. 2006. Facing middle age with no degree, and no wife. *The New York Times,* August 6, pp. 1, 18.

Postpartum disorders. 1989. *The Harvard Medical School Mental Health Letter* 5, May, pp. 1-3.

Post–traumatic stress—Part I. 1991. *The Harvard Mental Health Letter* 7, February, pp. 1-4.

Post–traumatic stress—Part II. 1991. *The Harvard Mental Health Letter* 7, March, pp. 1-4.

Poynter-Berg, D. 1986. Getting connected: Institutionalized schizophrenic women. In *Mutual aid groups and the life cycle,* ed. A. Gitterman and L. Shulman, pp. 263-281. Itasca, IL: F. E. Peacock Publishers.

Pray, J. E. 1991. Respecting the uniqueness of the individual: Social work practice with a reflective model. *Social Work* 36: 80-85.

Prisoners of mental illness. 2003. *Harvard Mental Health Letter* 20, July, pp. 5-7.

Prizant, B. M., A. M. Wetherby, and J. E. Roberts. 2000. Communication problems. In *Handbook of infant mental health,* ed. C. H. Zeanah Jr., 2nd ed., pp. 282-297. New York: The Guilford Press.

Proctor, C. D., and V. K. Groze. 1994. Risk factors for suicide among gay, lesbian, and bisexual youths. *Social Work* 39, 504-513.

Proctor, E. K. 1983. New directions for work with parents of retarded children. In *Differential diagnosis and treatment in social work,* ed. F. J. Turner, 3rd ed., pp. 511-519. New York: The Free Press.

Protecting New Jersey's children (editorial). 2006. *The New York Times,* February 15, p. A22.

Psychodynamic therapy passes a test. 2006. *Harvard Mental Health Letter* 22, April, p. 5.

Puryear, D. A. 1984. Crisis intervention. In *Manual of psychiatric consultation and emergency care,* ed. F. G. Guggenheim and M. F. Weiner, pp. 33-41. New York: Jason Aronson.

Putnam, F. W. 1997. *Dissociation in children and adolescents: A developmental perspective.* New York: The Guilford Press.

Qualls, S. H., and N. Abeles. 2000. Psychology and the aging revolution. In *Psychology and the aging revolution: How we adapt to longer life,* ed. S. H. Qualls and N. Abeles, pp. 3-9. Washington, DC: American Psychological Association.

Queralt, M. 1996. *The social environment and human behavior: A diversity perspective.* Boston: Allyn & Bacon.

Rabin, R. 2006. That prenatal visit may be months too late. *The New York Times,* November 28, pp. D5, D8.

Race, culture, and ethnicity in the consulting room. 2006. *The Psychoanalytic Quarterly,* LXXV: 1. (The entire issue.

Ramirez III, M. 1998. *Multicultural/multiracial psychology: Mestizo perspectives in personality and mental health.* Northvale, NJ: Jason Aronson.

Rapoport, L. 1970. Crisis intervention as a mode of treatment. In *Theories of social casework,* ed. R. W. Roberts and R. H. Nee, pp. 265-311. Chicago: The University of Chicago Press.

Ratnesar, R. 1998. A place at the table. *Time* 152, October 12, p. 38.

Ratnesar, R., and A. Baker. 2006. Lonely power. *Time* 168, September 18, pp. 38-41.

Rawe, J., and K. Kingsbury. 2006. When colleges go on suicide watch. *Time* 167, May 22, pp. 62-63.

Rayfield, D. 1997. *Anton Chekhov: A life.* New York: Henry Holt and Company.

Rees, W. D. 1975. The bereaved and their hallucinations. In *Bereavement: Its psychosocial aspects,* ed. B. Schoenberg, I. Gerber, A. Wiener, A. H. Kutscher, D. Peretz, and A. C. Carr, pp. 66-71. New York: Columbia University Press.

Regulus, T. A. 1995. Gang Violence. In *Social work encyclopedia,* ed. R. L. Edwards and J. G. Hopps, 19th ed., vol. 2, pp. 1045-1054. Washington, DC: NASW Press.

Reiner, B. S., and I. Kaufman. 1959. *Character disorders in parents of delinquents.* New York: Family Service Association of America.

Remnick, D. 1998. Bad seeds. *The New Yorker,* July 20, pp. 28-33.

Ressner, J. 2006. Rousing the zealots. *Time* 167, June 5, p. 36.

Richardson, L. 1998. Wave of laws aimed at people with HIV. *The New York Times,* September 25, pp. A1, A25.

Richman, J. M., and G. L. Bowen. 1997. School failure: An ecological-interactional-developmental perspective. In *Risk and resilience in childhood: An ecological perspective,* ed. M. W. Fraser, pp. 95-116. Washington, DC: NASW Press.

Richman, J. M., L. B. Rosenfeld, and G. L. Bowen. 1998. Social support for adolescents at risk of school failure. *Social Work* 43: 309-323.

Ricketts, H. 1999. *Rudyard Kipling: A life.* New York: Carroll & Graf Publishers.

Rimer, S. 1998a. Families bear a bigger share of caring for the frail elderly. *The New York Times,* June 8, pp. A1, A18.

Rimer, S. 1998b. For aged, dating game is numbers game. *The New York Times,* December 28, pp. A1, A18.

Rimer, S. 1998c. Paradoxes are a recurring theme at an annual conference on gerontology. *The New York Times,* November 27, p. A20.

Rimer, S. 1999. Caring for elderly kin is costly, study finds. *The New York Times,* November 27, p. A8.

Ringel, S. 2003. Book Review of: *Multiculturalism and the therapeutic process* by Judith M. Mishne. *Clinical Social Work Journal* 31: 212-213.

Risk Factors and Barriers to Prevention. 2004. *Mother-to-child (perinatal) HIV transmission and prevention.* Centers for Disease Control. Washington, DC. Available online at http://www.cdc.gov/hiv/resources/factsheets/perinatl.htm.

Risley-Curtis, C., L. C. Holley, and S. Wolf. 2006. The animal-human bond and ethnic diversity. *Social Work* 51: 257-268.

Robbins, S. P. 1995. Cults. In *Social work encyclopedia,* ed. R. L. Edwards and J. G. Hopps, 19th ed., vol. 1, pp. 667-677. Washington, DC: NASW Press.

Roberts, S. 2006a. Gay marriage ruling shows that New York isn't as liberal as it (and the U.S.) thinks. *The New York Times,* July 10, p. A17.

Roberts, S. 2006b. Upstate New York suffers a "bright flight" of young adults, Census shows. *The New York Times,* June 13, p. A20.

Robin, R. W., J. K. Rasmussen, and E. Gonzalez-Santin. 1999. Impact of childhood out-of-home placement on a southwestern American Indian tribe. *Journal of Human Behavior in the Social Environment* 2 (1/2): 69-89.

Robinson, R. L. 1997. Men and gambling. In *Gender and addictions: Men and women in treatment,* ed. S. L. A. Straussner and E. Zelvin, pp. 469-492. Northvale, NJ: Jason Aronson.

Roby, J. L., and S. A. Shaw. 2006a. The African orphan crisis and international adoption. *Social Work* 51: 199-210.

Roby, J. L., and S. A. Shaw. 2006b. The African orphan crisis and international adoption. *Social Work* 51: 199-210.

Rodin, A. E., and J. D. Key. 1984. *Medical casebook of Doctor Arthur Conan Doyle: From practitioner to Sherlock Holmes and beyond.* Florida: Robert E. Krieger Publishing Company.

Rohrer, G. 2005. *Mental Health in literature: Literary lunacy and lucidity.* Chicago: Lyceum Books.

Romney pushes vote on same-sex marriage. 2006. *The New York Times,* November 20, p. A20.

Roosevelt, M. 2001. Father makes two. *Time* 158, November 19, pp. F1-F3.

Rose, E. 1996. Introduction from the founding chair of the National Study Group on Social Work and Psychoanalysis. In *Fostering healing and growth: A psychoanalytic social work approach,* ed. J. Edward and J. Sanville, pp. xvix-xx. Northvale, NJ: Jason Aronson.

Rosenbaum, D. E. 1999. Health benefits bill shows power of the disabled. *The New York Times,* June 7, pp. A1, A18.

Rosenbaum, M., and M. Muroff. 1984. *Anna O.: Fourteen contemporary reinterpretations.* New York: The Free Press.

Rosenberg, T. 2006. For people with AIDS, a government with two faces. *The New York Times,* August 30, p. A22.

Rosenbloom, M. 1983. Implications of the Holocaust for social work. *Social Casework: The Journal of Contemporary Social Work* 64: 205-213.

Rosenblum, D. S., P. Daniolos, N. Kass, and A. Martin. 1999. Adolescents and popular culture: A psychodynamic overview. In *The psychoanalytic study of the child,* ed. A. J. Solnit, P. B. Neubauer, S. Abrams, and A. S. Dowling, vol. 54, pp. 319-338. New Haven, CT: Yale University Press.

Ross, J. M. 1984. Fathers in development: An overview of recent contributions. In *Parenthood: A psychodynamic perspective,* ed. R. Cohen, B. Cohler, and S. Weissman, pp. 373-390. New York: The Guilford Press.

Rossman, P. 1982. Psychotherapeutic approaches with depressed, acting out adolescents: Interpretive tactics and their rationale. In *Adolescent psychiatry: Developmental and clinical studies,* ed. S. Feinstein, J. Looney, A. Schwartzberg, and A. Sorosky, vol. X, pp. 455-468. Chicago: The University of Chicago Press.

Rotheram-Borus, M., and Bradley, J. 1991. Triage model for suicidal runaways. *American Journal of Orthopsychiatry* 61: 122-127.

Russo, F. 2006. A place for the power nap. *Time,* July 10, p. A16.

Rutenberg J. 2006. Cheney pregnancy stirs debate on gay rights. *The New York Times,* December 7, p. A30.

Rutter, M. 1975. *Helping troubled children.* London: Penguin Books.

Ryan, S. D., S. Pearlmutter, and V. Groza. 2004. Coming out of the closet: Opening agencies to gay and lesbian adoptive parents. *Social Work* 49: 85-95.

Saari, C. 1999. Intersubjectivity, language, and culture: Bridging the person/environment gap? *Smith College Studies in Social Work* 69: 221-237.

Saari, C. 2005. The contribution of relational theory to social work practice. *Smith College Studies in Social Work* 75: 3-14.

Sack, K. 1999. HIV peril and rising drug use. *The New York Times,* January 29, p. A8.

Sackheim, G. 1974. Dream analysis and casework technique. *Clinical Social Work Journal* 2: 29-35.

Sacks, O. 1989. *Seeing voices: A journey into the world of the deaf.* Berkeley: University of California Press.

Sacks, O. 1990. Neurology and the soul. *The New York Review of Books* 37, November 22, pp. 44-50.

Sadock, B. J., and V. A. Sadock. 2003. *Kaplan & Sadock's Synopsis of psychiatry: Behavioral sciences/Clinical psychiatry,* 9th ed. Philadelphia, Lippincott Williams & Wilkins.

Saleebey, D. 2001. *Human behavior and social environments: A biopsychosocial approach.* New York: Columbia University Press.

Saleebey, D. 2003. Strengths-based practice. In *Encyclopedia of social work,* ed. R. A. English, 19th ed., suppl., pp. 150-162. Washington, DC: NASW Press.

Sameroff, A. J., and B. H. Fiese. 2000. Models of development and developmental risk. In *Handbook of infant mental health,* ed. C. H. Zeanah Jr., 2nd ed., pp. 3-19. New York: The Guilford Press.

Sandblom, P. 1982. *Creativity and disease: How illness affects literature, art and music.* Philadelphia: George F. Stickley Company.

Sanville, J. 1994. Editorial. *Clinical Social Work Journal* 22: 131-136.

Satel, S. L. 1999. Real help for the mentally ill. *The New York Times,* January 7, p. A31.

Satir, V. 1967. *Conjoint family therapy.* Palo Alto: Science and Behavior Books.

Saul, S. 2006. Record sales of sleeping pills are causing worries. *The New York Times,* February 7, p. A1.

Saulny, S. 2006a. In a gilded age of home-schooling, students have private teachers. *The New York Times,* June 25, pp. A1, A17.

Saulny, S. 2006b. A legacy of the storm: Depression and suicide. *The New York Times,* June 21, pp. A1, A15.

Schaffer, H. R. 1994. Early experience and the parent-child relationship: Genetic and environmental interactions as developmental determinants. In *Vulnerability and resilience in human development: A festschrift for Ann and Alan Clarke,* ed. B. Tizard and V. Varma, pp. 39-53. London: Jessica Kingsley Publishers.

Schamess, G. 1996. Ego psychology. In *Inside out and outside in: Psychodynamic clinical theory and practice in contemporary multicultural contexts,* ed. J. Berzoff, L. M. Flanagan, and P. Hertz, pp. 67-101. Northvale, NJ: Jason Aronson.

Schamess, G. 1999. Reflections on intersubjectivity. *Smith College Studies in Social Work* 69: 188-200.

Scharff, D., and J. Scharff. 1987. *Object relations family therapy.* Northvale, NJ: Jason Aronson.

Scharff, D., and J. Scharff. 1991. *Object relations couple therapy.* Northvale, NJ: Jason Aronson.

Schemo, D. J. 2006. At Gallaudet, Trustees relent on leadership. *The New York Times,* October 30, pp. A1, A19.

Schlossberg, N. K. 1981. A model for analyzing human adaptation to transition. *The Counseling Psychologist* 9: 2-18.

Schmitz, C. L., J. D. Wagner, and E. M. Menke. 2001. The interconnection of childhood poverty and homelessness: Negative impact/points of access. *Families in Society: The Journal of Contemporary Social Services* 82: 69-77.

Schroffel, A. 2004. Characteristics of female perpetrators of domestic violence in group therapy. *Smith College Studies in Social Work* 74: 505-524.

Schultz, W. T. 2001. De Profundis: Prison as a turning point in Oscar Wilde's Life story. In *Turns in the road: Narrative studies of lives in transition,* ed. D. P. McAdams, R. Josselson, and A. Lieblich, pp. 67-89. Washington, DC: American Psychological Association.

Scott, J. 1998. Star professors, as a team, fail chemistry. *The New York Times,* November 21, pp. A1, A17.

Scott-Stokes, H. 1974. *The life and death of Yukio Mishima.* New York, Farrar, Straus and Giroux.

Seelye, K. Q. 1999. Citing "primitive" hatreds, Clinton asks Congress to expand hate-crime law. *The New York Times,* April 7, p. A18.

Segal, U. A. 1991. Cultural variables in Asian Indian families. *Family in Society: The Journal of Contemporary Human Services* 72: 233-241.

Seiffge-Krenke, I., and H. S. Kirsch. 2002. The body in adolescent diaries: The case of Karen Horney. In *The psychoanalytic study of the child,* ed. A. J. Solnit, P. B. Neubauer, S. Abrams, and A. S. Dowling, vol. 56, pp. 105-119. New Haven, CT: Yale University Press.

Self-Help groups—Part I. 1993. *The Harvard Mental Health Letter* 9: March, pp. 1-3.

Self-Help groups—Part II. 1993. *The Harvard Mental Health Letter* 9: April, pp. 1-4.

Seligman, S. 1994. Applying psychoanalysis in an unconventional context: Adapting infant-parent psychotherapy to a changing population. In *The psychoanalytic study of the child,* ed. A. J. Solnit, P. B. Neubauer, S. Abrams, and A. S. Dowling, vol. 49, pp. 481-500. New Haven, CT: Yale University Press.

Sengupta, S. 2000. Youth court of true peers judges firmly. *The New York Times,* June 4, pp. 1, 32.

Sengupta, S. 2006. Quota's to aid India's poor vs. push for meritocracy. *The New York Times,* May 23, p. A3.

Seymour-Smith, M. 1989. *Rudyard Kipling: A biography.* New York: St. Martin's Press.

Shannon, K. 2001. Perry signs hate-crimes bill into law. *Amarillo Globe-News,* May 12. Available online at http://www.amarillonet.com/stores/051201/tex_perry .shtml.

Shapiro, E. 1978. The psychodynamics and developmental psychology of the borderline patient: A review of the literature. *The American Journal of Psychiatry* 135: 1305-1315.

Shapiro, J. R., and J. S. Applegate. 2000. Cognitive neuroscience, neurobiology and affect regulation: Implications for clinical social work. *Clinical Social Work Journal* 28: 9-21.

Shapiro, V., and M. Gisynski. 1989. Ghosts in the nursery revisited. *Child and Adolescent Social Work* 6: 18-37.

Shengold, L. 1981. An attempt at soul murder: Rudyard Kipling's early life and work. In *Lives, events, and others players: Directions in psychobiography.* ed. J. T. Coltera, vol. IV, pp. 203-251. Downstate Psychoanalytic Institute Twenty-Fifth Anniversary Series. New York: Jason Aronson.

Shield, R. R., and S. M. Aronson. 2003. *Aging in today's world: Conversations between an anthropologist and a physician.* New York: Berghahn Books.

Shonkoff, J. P., J. A. Lippitt, and D. A. Cavanaugh. 2000. Early childhood policy: Implications for infant mental health. In *Handbook of infant mental health,* ed. C. H. Zeanah Jr., 2nd ed., pp. 503-518. New York: The Guilford Press.

Shorto, R. 2005. What's their real problem with gay marriage?: It's the gay part. *The New York Times Magazine,* June 19, 23, pp. 34-41, 64, 66-67.

Shulman, L., and Gitterman, A. 1986. The life model, mutual aid, and the mediating function. In *Mutual aid groups and the life cycle,* ed. A. Gitterman and L. Shulman, pp. 3-22. Itasca, IL: F. E. Peacock Publishers.

Shulman, S. C. 2005. The changing nature of family relationships in middle and later life: Parent-caring and the mid-life developmental opportunity. *Smith College Studies in Social Work* 75: 103-120.

Siebold, C. 1991. Termination: When the therapist leaves. *Clinical Social Work Journal* 19: 191-204.

Siegel, D. H. 2003. Open adoption of infants: Adoptive parents' feelings seven years later. *Social Work* 48: 409-419.

Silverman, K. 1991. *Edgar A. Poe: Mournful and never-ending remembrance.* New York: HarperCollins Publishers.

Singer, N. 2006. More doctors turning to the business of beauty. *The New York Times,* November 30, pp. A1, A26.

Skiba, D., J. Monroe, J. S. Wodarski. 2004. Adolescent substance use: Reviewing the effectiveness of prevention strategies. *Social Work* 49: 343-353.

Slaby, A., and P. McGuire. 1989. Residential management of suicidal adolescents. In *Adolescent suicide: Recognition, treatment and prevention,* ed. B. Garfinkel and G. Northrup, pp. 23-43. Binghamton, NY: The Haworth Press.

Sleep-depriving jobs linked to accidents. 1999. *The New York Times,* June 4, p. A22.

Sleep disorders—Part I. 1994. *The Harvard Mental Health Letter* 11, August, pp. 1-4.

Smith, L. L. 1976. A general model of crisis intervention. *Clinical Social Work Journal* 4: 162-171.

Smith, S. L., and J. A. Howard. 1994. The impact of previous sexual abuse on children's adjustment in adoptive placement. *Social Work* 39: 491-501.

Smolowe, J. 1997. A battle against biology; a victory in adoption. *Time* 143, December 1, p. 46.

Smyke, A. T., V. Wajda-Johnston, and C. H. Zeanah Jr. 2004. Working with traumatized infants and toddlers in the child welfare system. In *Young children and trauma: Intervention and treatment,* ed. J. D. Osofsky, pp. 260-284. New York: The Guilford Press.

Smyth, N., and B. Miller. 1997. Parenting issues for substance-abusing women. In *Gender and addictions: Men and women in treatment,* ed. S. L. A. Straussner and E. Zelvin, pp. 123-150. Northvale, NJ: Jason Aronson.

Sollors, W. 1986. *Beyond ethnicity: Consent and descent in American culture.* New York: Oxford University Press.

Solomon, A. 1992. Clinical diagnosis among diverse populations: A multicultural perspective. *Families in Society: The Journal of Contemporary Human Services* 73: 371-377.

Solomon, P., and J. Draine. 1995. Issues in serving the forensic client. *Social Work* 40: 25-33.

Sontag, D. 1999. For a world apart, a lesson in social work. *The New York Times,* July 3, pp. A1, A5.

Sontag, D. 2002. Who was responsible for Elizabeth Shin? *The New York Times Magazine,* April 28, pp. 56-61, 94, 139-140.

Spence, D. P. 1986. Narrative smoothing and clinical wisdom. In *Narrative psychology: The storied nature of human conduct,* ed. T. R. Sarbin, pp. 211-232. Westport, CT: Praeger.

Spengemann, W. C. 1980. *The forms of autobiography: Episodes in the history of a literary genre.* New Haven, CT: Yale University Press.

Spickard, P. R., R. Fong, and P. L. Ewalt. 1995. Undermining the very basis of racism—Its categories. *Social Work* 40: 581-584.

Spiegel, D. 1990. Breast cancer study shows psychotherapy improved survival. *The Psychiatric Times,* January, pp. 1, 17.

Spira, M. 2006. Book Review of: The past in the present: Using reminiscence in health and social care by Gibson, F. *Clinical Social Work Journal* 34 (1): 125-127.

Spira, M., and E. Kenemore. 2000. Adolescent daughters of mothers with breast cancer: Impact and implications. *Clinical Social Work Journal* 28: 183-195.

Springer, C. 1999. "No way!" "You know?" "Whatever": Clinical work with adolescents. In *Enhancing psychodynamic therapy with cognitive-behavioral techniques,* ed. T. B. Northcut and N. R. Heller, pp. 183-214. Northvale, NJ: Jason Aronson.

Stainbrook, K. A., and J. Hornik. 2006. Similarities in the characteristics and needs of women with children in homeless family and domestic violence shelters. *Families in Society: The Journal of Contemporary Social Services* 87: 53-62.

Stashower, D. 1999. *Teller of tales: The life of Arthur Conan Doyle.* New York: Henry Holt and Company.

Statements that Heaven's Gate released over the years. 1997. *The New York Times,* March 28, p. A12.

Statistics on underage drinking. 2006. *Initiative on underage drinking.* Bethesda, MD: National Institute on Alcohol Abuse and Alcoholism. Available online at http://www.niaaa.nih.gov/niaaa.nih.gov/.

St. Clair, M. 1986. *Object relations and self psychology: An introduction.* Monterey: Brooks/Cole Publishing Company.

Steinberg, J. 2000. An unrelenting drive, and a Harvard degree. *The New York Times,* May 17, pp. A1, A20.

Steinhauer, J. 1999a.When babies come in twos. *The New York Times,* November 29, p. A25.

Steinhauer, J. 1999b. Young, nonwhite, female and complacent about AIDS. *The New York Times,* September 1, p. A14.

Steinhauer, J., and E. Lipton. 2006. Storm victims facing delay to get trailers. *The New York Times,* February 9, pp. A1, A22.

Stern, D. N. 1985. *The interpersonal world of the infant: A view from psychoanalysis and developmental psychology.* New York: Basic Books.

Stevens, W. K. 1998. Harmful heat is more frequent, especially at night, study finds. *The New York Times,* December 10, pp. A1, A18.

Stevens-Long, J. 1990. Adult development: Theories past and future. In *New dimensions in adult development,* ed. R. Nemiroff and C. Colarusso, pp. 125-169. New York: Basic Books.

Stoesen, L. 2006. Prisoner reentry: Reclaiming the challenge. *NASW News* 51 (6), p. 4.

Stolorow, R. D., G. E. Atwood, and B. Brandchaft. 1994. *The intersubjective perspective.* Northvale, NJ: Jason Aronson.

Storr, A. 1988. *Solitude: A return to the self.* New York: The Free Press.

Strand, V. C. 1995. Single parents. In *Social work encyclopedia,* ed. R. L. Edwards and J. G. Hopps, 19th ed., vol. 3, pp. 2157-2163. Washington, DC: NASW Press.

Straussner, S. L. A., and E. Zelvin, eds. 1997. *Gender and addictions: Men and women in treatment.* Northvale, NJ: Jason Aronson.

Strom, S. 1999. In Japan, mired in recession, suicides soar. *The New York Times,* July 15, pp. A1, A8.

Strom, S. 2006. Trained by inmates, new best friends for disabled veterans. *The New York Times,* October 31, p. A16.

Strom-Gottfried, K. 1997. The implications of managed care for social work education. *Journal of Social Work Education* 33: 7-18.

Study sheds light on best treatments for ADHD. 2000. *Psychiatric News,* January 21, p. 20.

Styron, W. 1990. *Darkness visible: A memoir of madness.* New York: Random House.

Styron, W. 1993. *The confessions of Nat Turner.* New York: Vintage Books.

Sullivan, H. S. 1953. Preadolescence. In *The psychiatric interview: Vol. 1. The collected works of Harry Stack Sullivan,* ed. S. Perry and M. L. Gawel, pp. 245-262. New York: W. W. Norton.

Sutherland, S. 1989. *The international dictionary of psychology.* New York: Continuum.

Sutton, C. T., and M. A. Nose. 2005. American Indian families: An overview. In *Ethnicity & family therapy,* ed. M. McGoldrick, J. Giordano, and N. Garcia-Preto, 3rd ed., pp. 43-54. New York: The Guilford Press.

Svoboda, E. 2006. All the signs of pregnancy except one: A baby. *New York Times, Science Times,* December 5, p. 6.

Swarns, R. L. 1998. Hispanic mothers lagging as others escape welfare. *The New York Times,* September 15, pp. A1, A29.

Swarns, R. L. 2006. Bill to broaden immigration law gains in senate. *The New York Times,* March 28, pp. A1, A12.

Sweezy, M. 2005. Not confidential: Therapist considerations in self-disclosure. *Smith College Studies in Social Work* 75: 81-91.

Swenson, C. J. 1994. Freud's "Anna O.": Social work's Bertha Pappenheim. *Clinical Social Work Journal* 22: 149-163.

Szalita, A. B. 1974. Grief and bereavement. In *American handbook of psychiatry,* ed. S. Arieti, 4th ed., vol. 1, pp. 673-684. New York: Basic Books.

Takahashi, K. 1990. Are the key assumptions of the "Strange Situation" universal? *Human Development* 33: 23-30.

Talbot, M. 1998. Attachment theory: The ultimate experiment. *The New York Times Magazine,* May 24, pp. 24-30, 38, 46, 50, 54.

Talbot, M. 2000. A mighty fortress. *New York Times Magazine,* February 27, pp. 34-41, 68-69, 84-85.

Tamura, T., and A. Lau. 1992. Connectedness versus separateness: Applicability of family therapy to Japanese families. *Family Process* 31: 319-340.

Tang, N. M. 1997. Psychoanalytic psychotherapy with Chinese Americans. In *Working with Asian Americans: A guide for clinicians,* ed. E. Lee, pp. 323-341. New York: The Guilford Press.

Tarkan, L. 2006. After the adoption, a new child and the blues. *The New York Times,* April 25, pp. D5, D8.

Tashjian, L. D. 1979. Failure in treatment of a borderline patient. *Psychiatric Opinion* 16 (7): 43-47.

Teen-agers learn AIDS counseling. 1999. *The New York Times,* May 9, p. 29.

Terry, R. 2006. Diabetes and obesity prevention by promoting healthy behaviors. *National Women's Health Information Center.* Washington, DC. Office on Women's Health, U.S. Department of Health and Human Services. Available online at http://www.4women.gov/owh/ichp/diabetes.cfm.

The adolescent brain: Beyond raging hormones. 2005. *Harvard Mental Health Letter* 22, July, pp. 1-3.

The homeless mentally ill. 2005. *Harvard Mental Health Letter* 21, May, pp. 4-7.

The negative symptoms of schizophrenia. 2006. *Harvard Mental Health Letter* 23, July, pp. 1-3.

The resilience of international adoptees. 2005. *Harvard Mental Health Letter* 22, September, pp. 5-6.

The traumatized heart. 2002. *The Harvard Mental Health Letter* 18, February, p. 7.

Thomas, A. 1981. Current trends in developmental theory. *American Journal of Orthopsychiatry* 51: 580-609.

Thomlison, B. 1997. Risk and protective factors in child maltreatment. In *Risk and resilience in childhood: An ecological perspective,* ed. M. W. Fraser, pp. 50-72. Washington, DC: NASW Press.

Thompson, B., and Y. Colón. 2004. Lesbians and gay men at the end of their lives: Psychosocial concerns. In *Living with dying: A handbook for end-of-life health-care practitioners,* ed. J. Berzoff and P. R. Silverman, pp. 482-498. New York: Columbia University Press.

Thompson, C. L. 1996. The African-American patient in psychodynamic treatment. In *Reaching across boundaries of culture and class: Widening the scope of psychotherapy,* ed. R. Pérez Foster, M. Moskowitz, and R. A. Javier, pp. 115-142. Northvale, NJ: Jason Aronson.

Thornburgh, N. 2006. Dropout nation. *Time* 167, April 17, pp. 30-35, 37-38, 40.

Thyer, B. A. 1988. Radical behaviorism and clinical social work. In *Paradigms of clinical social work,* ed. R. A. Dorfman, pp. 123-148. New York: Brunner/Mazel Publishers.

Thyer, B. A. 2003. Empirically based interventions. In *Encyclopedia of social work,* ed. R. A. English, 19th ed., suppl., pp. 21-29. Washington, DC: NASW Press.

Ting, L., S. Sanders, J. M. Jacobson, and J. R. Power. 2006. Dealing with the aftermath: A qualitative analysis of mental health social workers' reactions after a client suicide. *Social Work* 51: 329-341.

Tizard, B. 1991. Intercountry adoption: A review of the evidence. *Journal of Child Psychology, Psychiatry, and Allied Disciplines* 32: 743-756.

Tomalin, C. 2002. *Samuel Pepys: The unequalled self.* New York: Alfred A. Knopf.

Toner, R. 1999. Long-term care merges political with personal. *The New York Times,* July 26, pp. A1, A11.

Tosone, C. 2004. Relational social work: Honoring the tradition. *Smith College Studies in Social Work* 74: 475-485.

Toward nursing home reform (editorial). 1999. *The New York Times,* May 29, p. A26.

Tracy, E. M., and P. J. Johnson. 2006. The intergenerational transmission of family violence. In *Working with traumatized youth in child welfare,* ed. N. B. Webb, pp. 113-134. New York: The Guilford Press.

Trillin, C. 1999. Wanted: One egg (Ph.D. pref.). *Time* 153, January 25, p. 20.

Tully, C. T. 1995. Lesbians overview. In *Social work encyclopedia,* ed. R. L. Edwards and J. G. Hopps, 19th ed., vol. 2, pp. 1591-1596. Washington, DC: NASW Press.

Tumulty, K. 2006. Should they stay or should they go? *Time* 167, April 10, pp. 30-36, 39-40.

Turrini, P. 1996. Glossary. In *Fostering healing and growth: A psychoanalytic social work approach,* ed. J. Edward and J. Sanville, pp. 443-467. Northvale, NJ: Jason Aronson.

Tutoring gap (editorial). 2006. *The New York Times,* February 16, p. A32.

Twin babies spared death as tribe forgoes ritual. 1999. *Providence Sunday Journal,* October 10, p. A14.

Uchitelle, L., and D. Leonhardt. 2006. Men not working, and not wanting just any job. *The New York Times,* July 31, pp. A1, A14.

Upham, F. 1973. *Ego analysis in the helping professions.* New York: Family Service Association of America.

Urbina, I. 2006. Rising diabetes threat meets a falling budget. *The New York Times,* May 16, pp. A1, A25.

Urdang, E. 1964. An educational project for first-year students in a field placement. *Social Casework* 45: 10-15.

Urdang, E. 1974. *Becoming a social worker: The first year.* Unpublished manuscript. Boston College Graduate School of Social Work.

Urdang, E. 1979. In defense of process recording. *Smith College Studies in Social Work* 50: 1-15.

Urdang, E. 1994. *Self-perceptions of the beginning field instructor: The experience of supervising a social work intern.* Unpublished doctoral dissertation. Simmons College School of Social Work, Boston, MA.

Urdang, E. 1999. The influence of managed care on the MSW social work student's development of the professional self. *Smith College Studies in Social Work* 70: 3-25.

Urdang, E. (work in progress).

Vaillant, G. E. 1993. *The wisdom of the ego.* Cambridge: Harvard University Press.

VanBergeijk, E. O., and O. Shtayermman. 2005. Asperger's syndrome: An enigma for social work. *Journal of Human Behavior in the Social Environment* 12 (1): 23-37.

van der Kolk, B. A., A. C. McFarlane, and L. Weisaeth, eds. 1996. *Traumatic stress: The effects of overwhelming experience on mind, body, and society.* New York Guilford Press.

Van Horn, P., and D. J. Hitchens. 2004. Partnerships for young children in court: How judges shape collaborations serving traumatized children. In *Young children and trauma: Intervention and treatment,* ed. J. D. Osofsky, pp. 242-259. New York: The Guilford Press.

Vastola, J., A. Nierenberg, and E. H. Graham. 1986. The lost and found group: Group work with bereaved children. In *Mutual aid groups and the life cycle,* ed. A. Gitterman and L. Shulman, pp. 75-90. Itasca, IL: F. E. Peacock Publishers.

Verbatim. 2006. *Time* 167, March 13, p. 13.

Verhovek, S. H. 1999. Gun control laws gaining support in many states. *The New York Times,* May 31, pp. A1, A9.

Vitello, P. 2006. The trouble when Jane becomes Jack. *The New York Times,* August 20 (Section 9), pp. 1, 6.

Voisin, D. R., R. J. DiClemente, L. F. Salazar, R. A. Crosby, and W. L. Yarber. 2006. Ecological factors associated with STD risk behaviors among detained female adolescents. *Social Work* 51: 71.

Vonèche, J. 2001. Identity and narrative in PIaget's autobiographies. In *Narrative and identity: Studies in autobiography, self and culture,* ed. J. Brockmeier and

D. Carbaugh, pp. 187-217. Amsterdam/Philadelphia: John Benjamins Publishing Company.

Vonk, M. E., Simms, P. J., and Nackerud, L. 1999. Political and personal aspects of intercountry adoption of Chinese children in the United States. *Families in Society: The Journal of Contemporary Human Services* 80: 496-505.

Vonnegut, M. 1975. *The Eden Express: A personal account of schizophrenia.* New York: Praeger Publishers.

Wachtel, P. L. 1977. *Psychoanalysis and behavior therapy: Toward an integration.* New York: Basic Books.

Wade, N. 2000. Genetic code of human life is cracked by scientists: A shared success. *The New York Times,* June 27, pp. A1, A21.

Wagner, G. 1991. When a parent is abusive. In *Using self psychology in psychotherapy,* ed. H. Jackson, pp. 243-259. Northvale, NJ: Jason Aronson.

Wakschlag, L. S., and S. L. Hans. 2000. Early parenthood in context: Implications for development and intervention. In *Handbook of infant mental health,* ed. C. H. Zeanah Jr., 2nd ed., pp. 129-144. New York: The Guilford Press.

Walsh, M. W. 2006a. Many companies ending promises for retirement. *The New York Times,* January 9, pp. A1, A20.

Walsh, M. W. 2006b. Once safe, public pensions are now facing cuts. *The New York Times,* November 6, pp. A1, A15.

Walsh, M. W. 2006c. Paying health care from pensions proves costly. *The New York Times,* December 19, pp. A1, C4.

Walsh-Burke, K. 2004. Assessing mental health risk in end-of-life care. In *Living with dying: A handbook for end-of-life healthcare practitioners,* ed. J. Berzoff and P. R. Silverman, pp. 360-379. New York: Columbia University Press.

Walters, K. L. 1999. Urban American Indian identity attitudes and acculturation styles. *Journal of Human Behavior in the Social Environment* 2 (1/2): 163-178.

Warn, D. J. 1997. Recovery issues of substance-abusing gay men. In *Gender and addictions: Men and women in treatment,* ed. S. L. A. Straussner and E. Zelvin, pp. 385-410. Northvale: Jason Aronson.

Watts-Jones, D. 1992. Cultural and integrative therapy issues in the treatment of a Jamaican woman with panic disorder. *Family Process* 31: 105-113.

Watzlawick, P., J. H. Beavin, and D. D. Jackson. 1967. *Pragmatics of human communication: A study of interactional patterns, pathologies, and paradoxes.* New York: W. W. Norton and Company.

Weaver, H. N. 1999. Health concerns for Native American youth: A culturally grounded approach to health promotion. *Journal of Human Behavior in the Social Environment* 2 (1/2): 127-143.

Webb, N. B. 2006. The impact of trauma on youth and families in the child welfare system. In *Working with traumatized youth in child welfare,* ed. N. B. Webb, pp. 13-26. New York: The Guilford Press.

Weil, E. 2006. A wrongful birth. *The New York Times Magazine,* March 12, pp. 48-53.

Weinreb, L., and P. H. Rossi. 1995. The American homeless family shelter "system." *Social Service Review* 69: 86-107.

Weinstein, L., and L. Saul. 2005. Psychoanalysis as cognitive remediation: Dynamic and Vygotskian perspective in the analysis of an early adolescent dyslexic girl. In *The psychoanalytic study of the child,* ed. R. A. King, P. B. Neubauer, S. Abrams, and A. S. Dowling, vol. 60, pp. 239-262. New Haven, CT: Yale University Press.

Wells, S. J. 1995. Child abuse and neglect overview. In *Social work encyclopedia,* ed. R. L. Edwards and J. G. Hopps, 19th ed., vol. 1, pp. 346-353. Washington, DC: NASW Press.

Welu, T. C. 1975. Pathological bereavement: A plan for its prevention. In *Bereavement: Its psychosocial aspects,* ed. B. Schoenberg, I. Gerber, A. Wiener, A. H. Kutscher, D. Peretz, and A. C. Carr, pp. 139-149. New York: Columbia University Press.

Westerfelt, A., and M. Yellow Bird. 1999. Homeless and indigenous in Minneapolis. *Journal of Human Behavior in the Social Environment* 2 (1/2): 145-162.

Westermeyer, J. 1985. Psychiatric diagnosis across cultural boundaries. *American Journal of Psychiatry* 142: 798-805.

Wheaton, B., and I. H. Gotlib. 1997. Trajectories and turning points over the life course: Concepts and themes. In *Stress and adversity over the life course: Trajectories and turning points,* ed. I. H. Gotlib and B. Wheaton. Cambridge, UK: Cambridge University Press.

Whelan, D. J. 2003. Using attachment theory when placing siblings in foster care. *Child and Adolescent Social Work Journal* 20: 21-36.

White, J. 1997. I'm just who I am. *Time* 151, May 5, pp. 32-36.

Whitley, D. M., K. R. White, S. J. Kelley, and B. Yorke. 1999. Strengths-based case management: The application to grandparents raising grandchildren. *Families in Society: The Journal of Contemporary Human Services* 80: 110-119.

Wilgoren, J. 1999. Abstinence is focus of U.S. sex education. *The New York Times,* December 15, p. A16.

Wilgoren, J. 2000. Effort to curb binge drinking in college falls short. *The New York Times,* March 15, p. A 16.

Williams, A. L. 1997. Skin color in psychotherapy. In *Reaching across boundaries of culture and class: Widening the scope of psychotherapy,* ed. R. Pérez Foster, M. Moskowitz, and R. A. Javier, pp. 115-142. Northvale, NJ: Jason Aronson.

Williams, J. H., C. D. Ayers, and M. W. Arthur. 1997. Risk and protective factors in the development of delinquency and conduct disorder. In *Risk and resilience in childhood: An ecological perspective,* ed. M. W. Fraser, pp. 140-170. Washington, DC: NASW.

Williams, M. 1999. Flak in the great hair war. *The New York Times,* October 13, p. A20.

Williams-Mbengue, N. 2004. States' mandatory child abuse reporting laws: States that require clergy to report child abuse and states that allow clergy penitent privilege. *State & Federal Issues,* National Conference of State Legislatures, 2004. Available online at http://www.ncsl.org/programs/cyf/clergy.htm.

Winchester, S. 1998. *The professor and the madman: A tale of murder, insanity, and the making of the Oxford English Dictionary.* New York: HarperCollins Publishers.

Winerip, M. 1999. Bedlam on the streets: Increasingly, the mentally ill have nowhere to go. That's their problem—and ours. *New York Times Magazine,* pp. 42-49, 56, 65-66, 70.

Winnicott, D. 1965. *The maturational processes and the facilitating environment: Studies in the theory of emotional development.* Madison: International Universities Press.

Winter depression. 2004. *Harvard Mental Health Letter* 21, November, pp. 4-5.

Winters, W., and A. Maluccio. 1988. School, family, and community: Working together to promote social competence. *Social Work in Education* 10: 207-217.

Witkin, S. 1998. Chronicity and invisibility. *Social Work* 43: 293-295.

Witkin, S. 1999. Taking humor seriously. *Social Work* 44: 101-104.

Wolf, E. S. 1988. *Treating the self: Elements of clinical self psychology.* New York: The Guilford Press.

Wolf, E. S. 1994. Selfobject experiences: Development, psychopathology, treatment, therapeutic process, and technique. In *Mahler and Kohut: Perspectives on development, psychopathology, and technique,* ed. S. Kramer and S. Akhtar, pp. 67-96. Northvale, NJ: Jason Aronson.

Wolfe, T. 1999. *A man in full.* New York: Bantam Books.

Wolman, B. B. ed. 1973. *Dictionary of behavioral science.* New York: Van Nostrand Reinhold Company.

Wolpe, J. 1976. Conditioning is the basis of all psychotherapeutic change. In *What makes behavior change possible?* ed. A. Burton, pp. 58-72. New York: Bruner/ Mazel.

Wong, J. 2002. The return of the Auschwitz nightmare. *The Toronto Globe and Mail,* September 21, pp. A1, A8.

Wong, L., and M. R. Mock. 1997. Asian American young adults. In *Working with Asian Americans: A guide for clinicians,* ed. E. Lee, pp. 196-207. New York: The Guilford Press.

Wood, B., J. B. Watkins, J. T. Boyle, J. Nogueira, E. Zimands, and L. Carroll. 1989. The "psychosomatic family" model: An empirical and theoretical analysis. *Family Process* 28: 399-417.

Woods, F., and F. Hollis. 1990. *Casework: A psychosocial therapy,* 4th ed. New York: McGraw-Hill Publishing Company.

Worrall, J. 2006. Challenges of grandparent custody of children at risk in New Zealand. *Families in Society: The Journal of Contemporary Social Services* 87: 546-544.

Wren, C. S. 1999. Arizona finds cost savings in treating drug offenders. *The New York Times,* April 21, p. A16.

Wright Edelman, M. 2006. *Protect children, not guns. Child watch(tm) column.* Washington, DC: Children's Defense Fund. Available online at http://www .childrensdefense.org/site/News2?page=NewsArticle&id=7013.

Wright, V. C., J. Chang, G. Jeng, and M. Macaluso. 2006. *Assisted reproductive technology surveillance—United States, 2003.* Surveillance Summaries. Atlanta, GA: Centers for Disease Control and Prevention. Available online at http://www .cdc.gov/mmwr/preview/mmwrhtml/ss5504a1.htm.

Wyatt, E. 2006. Live on "Oprah," a memoirist is kicked out of the book club. *The New York Times,* January 27, pp. A1, A13.

Wyatt, F. 1986. The narrative in psychoanalysis: Psychoanalytic notes on storytelling, listening, and interpreting. In *Narrative psychology: The storied nature of human conduct,* ed. T. R. Sarbin, pp. 193-210. Westport, CT: Praeger.

Wyche, K., and M. Rotheram-Borus. 1990. Suicidal behavior among minority youth in the United States. In *Ethnic issues in adolescent mental health,* ed. A. Stiffman and L. Davis, pp. 323-338. Newbury Park: Sage Publications.

Xiong, Z. B., A. Tuicomepee, L. LaBlanc, and J. Rainey. 2006. Hmong immigrants' perceptions of family secrets and recipients of disclosure. *Families in Society: The Journal of Contemporary Social Services* 87: 231-239.

Young-Bruehl, E. 1988. *Anna Freud: A biography.* New York: Summit Books.

Young-Bruehl, E. 2006. Coming of age in New York City: Two homeless boys. *Psychoanalytic Quarterly, LXXV,* pp. 323-343.

Young Latinas and a cry for help (editorial) 2006. *The New York Times,* July 21.

Youth and tobacco Use: Current estimates. 2006. *Tobacco Information and Prevention Source (TIPS).* Washington, DC: Office on Smoking and Health, National Center for Chronic Disease Prevention and Health Promotion, Centers for Disease Control and Prevention. Available online at http://www.cdc.gov/tobacco/research _data/youth/Youth_Factsheet.htm.

Zabriskie, P. 2004. Wounds that don't bleed. *Time* 164, November 29, pp. 40-42.

Zambelli, G., and E. Clark. 1994. Parentally bereaved children: Problems in school adjustment and implications for the school social worker. *School Social Work Journal* 19 (Fall): 1-15.

Zastrow, C., and K. K. Kirst-Ashman. 1997. *Understanding human behavior and the social environment,* 4th ed. Chicago: Nelson-Hall Publishers.

Zastrow, C. H., and K. K. Kirst-Ashman. 2004. *Understanding human behavior and the social environment.* 6th ed. Belmont, CA: Thomson-Brooks/Cole.

Zayas, L. H. 1987. Psychodynamic and developmental aspects of expectant and new fatherhood: Clinical derivatives from the literature. *Clinical Social Work Journal* 15: 8-21.

Zayas, L. H., C. Kaplan, S. Turner, K. Romano, and G. Gonzalez-Ramos. 2000. Understanding suicide attempts by adolescent Hispanic females. *Social Work* 45: 53-63.

Zeanah, C. H. 1991. Guidelines suggested for assisting parents following perinatal loss. *The Psychiatric Times Medicine and Behavior,* July, pp. 1, 12.

Zeanah, C. H., and M. S. Scheeringa. 1997. The experience and effects of violence in infancy. In *Children in a violent society,* ed. J. Osofsky, pp. 97-123. New York: The Guilford Press.

Zeanah Jr., C. H. ed. 2000. *Handbook of infant mental health,* 2nd ed. New York: The Guilford Press.

Zernike, K. 2006a. As states curb homemade meth, a more potent variety emerges. *The New York Times,* January 23, pp. A1, A18.

Zernike, K. 2006b. The bell tolls for the future merry widow. *The New York Times,* April 30 (Section 4), WK, pp. 1, 5.

Zosky, D. L. 2005. Disruptions in the separation-individuation process of domestically violent men: An empirical examination of Mahler's theory. *Journal of Human Behavior in the Social Environment* 12 (4): 43-60.

Index

Human Behavior in the Social Environment, Second Edition